UNIVERSITY COLLEGE BIRMINGHAM
COLLEGE LIBRARY, SUMMER ROW
BIRMINGHAM. B3 1JB
Tel: (0121) 243 0055

DATE OF RETURN

Please remember to return on time or pay the fine

Adventure Programming

Adventure Programming

Edited by

John C. Miles

Western Washington University

and

Simon Priest

eXperientia

Venture Publishing, Inc.

State College, Pennsylvania

Production Manager: Richard Yocum
Manuscript Editing, Design, Layout, and Graphics: Diane K. Bierly
Additional Editing: Deborah L. McRann and Richard Yocum
Cover Design and Illustration: © 1999 Sandra Sikorski Design
Cover Photos: Ammonite © Richard Price/FPG International LLC, Bigeye Jacks © VCG/FPG International LLC, Cumulus Clouds © VCG/FPG International LLC, Dandelion © VCG/FPG International LLC, Fan Palm Trees © VCG/FPG International LLC.

Library of Congress Catalogue Card Number 99-66066
ISBN 1-892132-09-5

Contents

Introduction

Simon Priest
eXperientia

In this second edition, John Miles and I changed the name of the book from *Adventure Education* to *Adventure Programming*, because this new title more accurately reflects the terminology of the profession as it has evolved over the past decade. *Adventure programming is the deliberate use of adventurous experiences to create learning in individuals or groups, that results in change for society and communities.*

Adventurous experiences are activities with uncertain outcomes (due to the presence of situational risks) which necessitate people applying their personal competence to meet the challenge and resolve the uncertainty. Examples include outdoor pursuits (like backpacking, climbing, caving, skiing, and paddling), initiative activities (like Spider's Web, Nuclear Reactor, Nitro Crossing, and the Wall), and ropes or challenge courses (like high ones built among the tree tops and belayed for safety or low ones built at ground level and spotted for safety). As you read through this text, you will become more familiar with these activities and their use within adventure programs.

Change for society and communities is the altruistic end point sought by adventure programs. While the immediate goals and primary focus for learning may well be to change people, the ultimate impact is to make the world a better place to live in some small way. Play for Peace is an example of adventure programming that uses experiential games and exercises to teach concepts of peace and bring peace to children of conflict-torn nations like Northern Ireland, Bosnia, Israel, and the United States.

Learning is a shift in the way people feel, think, or behave. When one is aware of the shift, and when the shift is intended and maintained over time, then learning has been conscious, deliberate and lasting. Unfortunately, and all too often, attempts to learn or change are prevented by a lack of reflection (defeating awareness), the presence of resistance (defeating intent), and barriers to transfer (defeating maintenance). These are the principal challenges to adventure programming: how to create change that is sentient, purposeful and sustainable.

Four categories of adventure programming exist based on whether they change the way people feel, think, or behave: recreational, educational, developmental, and therapeutic. These are named for where their primary focus for learning is placed: on emotions, cognition, or action. Four examples will help to illustrate the difference using the common adventure activity of group initiative games and tasks.

Recreational adventure programs change the way people feel: their primary purpose is to entertain, energize or teach skills. If I conduct group initiatives to allow people to feel good, be revitalized, or learn to play, then my adventure program is recreational.

Educational adventure programs change the way people think: their primary purpose is to bring awareness and understanding. If I conduct group initiatives to help people learn the value of teamwork or to see the impact of miscommunication, then my adventure program is educational.

Developmental adventure programs change the way people behave: their primary purpose is to improve functional actions. If I conduct group initiatives to help people become a high-performing team or to communicate better, then my adventure program is developmental.

Therapeutic adventure programs change the way people malbehave: their primary purpose is to reduce dysfunctional actions. If I conduct group initiatives to diffuse team conflict due to arguing and sabotage, or to decrease errors due to withheld communication, mistrust and fear, then my adventure program is therapeutic.

The first section of this book examines these four categories of programming from the perspectives of different authors. As you read these introductory chapters, please realize that one adventure program can deliver all four types of programming. So if you observe overlap and duplication among these descriptions, please understand that this is simply the diversity of adventure as also exemplified by the final chapter on international adventure programs.

Subsequent sections examine history and philosophy of the field, because we should all understand the roots of what we do. Sections on social psychology and learning trace the theories behind human behavior and change. Sections on leadership and administration consider the tasks of working with people and managing adventure programs. Sections on settings and clients show the depth of adventure programming locations and the breadth of its influence with people. A final section examines the world, environmental, and spiritual perspectives of adventure programming.

Section 1

Introduction to Adventure Programming

This first section is intended to serve as an introduction to the breadth of goals addressed by adventure programming. The origins of adventure as a formal educational process have been traced back to Kurt Hahn and the Outward Bound Movement that he began, but the educational value of the outdoors and of wild places had been recognized many decades before Hahn. People began venturing into the Alps for sport as early as the late eighteenth century. A camping movement began in the United States soon after the Civil War, and outdoor recreation began to grow in importance late in the nineteenth century. People realized that natural settings and their activities there gave them joy, satisfaction, and respite from the stresses of life in the ever-growing cities. In the twentieth century they began more and more to formalize programs that used the outdoors for learning and personal growth, and eventually adventure programming appeared and what has been called the adventure education movement was initiated.

Webb opens this section by describing organized outdoor programming in colleges and universities. This is programming aimed primarily at recreational goals, but from the beginning the leaders of these programs have recognized the educational values of their activities. Webb describes the various programming models that have evolved in this realm and summarizes the activities that have been featured in these programs.

Horwood spent a long career exploring the potentials of experiential learning in formal educational settings and at all levels of schooling. His essay is a reflection, based on many decades of on-the-ground experience, on the nature and value of adventure in schooling. Horwood believes that all schooling should be an adventure, an experience that involves risk, uncertainty of outcome, coping with inescapable consequences, and action. The "teacher" is, of course, critical in this process, and he describes the factors that make schooling an adventure and what teachers must do to encourage these factors. Horwood is convinced that teachers can make learning an adventure, and suggests that much more consideration should be given to doing so. Adventure programming, in Horwood's vision, is a process that should occur in standard school settings.

Another application of adventure is the "development" of persons and organizations. Hirsch distinguishes between recreation, education, development and therapy. Development in this context involves processes of personal growth like self-esteem and self-concept, and enhancement of group and team effectiveness. The past two decades have seen applications of adventure programming in various settings in which such development was the goal. Hirsh examines examples of this such as a consulting company, Project Adventure, a YMCA camp, a university student orientation program, a foundation, and Outward Bound. She finds generic features of developmental applications of adventure programming in these examples which should be of use in program design.

Therapy is yet another realm to which adventure programming has been fruitfully applied. Gillis and Ringer provide a brief overview of what has been happening in this dimension of the field. After distinguishing adventure therapy from other adventure programs and defining it with a couple of examples, they summarize the challenges and opportunities in this arena. A major problem in this application of adventure, as in others, is lack of credible research into the effectiveness of adventure-based approaches to therapy. They suggest research questions that must be addressed.

The final selection in this section makes the simple point that adventure education has gone global, and in doing so has encountered many new challenges. The approach evolved in the West and its core cultural assumptions are derived from the Western heritage. What happens, and should happen, when adventure education models are introduced to indigenous people? What needs to be done to adapt adventure programming concepts and models to new cultural settings? Can adventure programs contribute to different cultural goals in other parts of the world, rather than only in the West where most of the programming to date has occurred? Bailey raises these and other intriguing questions.

Chapter 1

Recreational Outdoor Adventure Programs

David J Webb
Brigham Young University

Introduction

Long before the organization of Outward Bound, Association for Experiential Education, National Outdoor Leadership School, Wilderness Education Association, and Project Adventure, organized outdoor adventure programs were being sponsored by universities and colleges in the United States. Student unions, or associations of students at colleges and universities, had been providing social, educational, and recreational programs for students. These student union programs included debate clubs, social clubs, and outing clubs, to name a few. The student union became responsible for providing opportunities for students to participate in the production and attendance of theatrical plays, to put on social dances, debate societies, and to sponsor student government organizations. The "unions," their associations and clubs, provided opportunities for trekking, skiing, camping, fishing, climbing, and snowshoeing. The Dartmouth Outing Club (1911) at Dartmouth College, Williams Outing Club (1915) at Williams College, Allegheny Outing Club (1930) at Allegheny College, and The Wisconsin Hoofers (1931) at the University of Wisconsin–Madison have been providing adventure opportunity, outdoor education, and student development programs for the last 60–80 years. As colleges and universities developed extracurricular outdoor adventure programs that contributed to the welfare of the students, local communities wanted to provide similar outdoor recreation opportunities and began developing their outdoor adventure programs. The U.S. military organizations in their "moral, welfare, and recreation" branches of the Army, Air Force, and Navy have also recognized the values and benefits of outdoor adventure programs and have developed a wide range of outdoor programs on military bases throughout the world. Private businesses operate outdoor adventure programs in the form of outfitting (e.g., Western Llama Treks), climbing schools (e.g., Exum Guide School), raft trips (e.g., Sobek), and ecoadventuring (e.g., Baja whale watching tours) today. Both not-for-profit (e.g., Outward Bound) and for-profit businesses (e.g., Western Rivers Expeditions) operate outdoor adventure programs. Although there is a great diversity of organization, evolution, services, products, and delivery of outdoor adventure by these sponsoring agencies and organizations, there are definable organizational groups, four primary services, and specific values that can be recognized.

Program Goals, Benefits, Services, and Models

The outdoor adventure programs described are usually not degree granting programs. They are typically extracurricular in nature. Some universities and colleges have curricular departments that grant bachelor's, master's, or doctorate degrees in recreation related to outdoor education, outdoor recreation, or outdoor pursuits. These degree granting educational academic departments may, or may not, associate or collaborate with the extracurricular outdoor adventure program being sponsored by the student union, intermurals, campus recreation, or other departments.

Goals

Experiential in nature, these programs, services, and instructional sessions occur within a wide variety of extracurricular experiences. These experiences are aimed at providing recreational enjoyment, education and skill development, and development of moral growth. They also enhance curricular education and assist in the balanced development of the total person and his or her quality of life in the community, school, or branch of the armed forces. Outdoor adventure programs also produce income that provides or supplements the programs' funding and provides a profit motive for for-profit businesses.

The focus of one program may be primarily recreational enjoyment, with education and skill development and development of moral growth as secondary focuses, and income generation the third focus. Another program may have income generation and recreational enjoyment as the primary focus, education and skill development as secondary focuses, and development of moral growth the third focus. Yet another program may have the development of moral growth as the primary focus, education and skill development and recreational enjoyment as the secondary focus, and income generation as the third focus.

Each institution, agency, or business chooses how it wants to serve its public, and the public chooses if it will participate or not.

The financial goal may be one of generating income to cover all expenses, or to "break even." Another financial goal may be one of producing profit, with the profit being used to offset inflation, provide funds for program expansion, and/or return income to an owner. Many outdoor programs are subsidized and are given funds (a budget) that covers the cost of many expenses. This subsidy, and income generated by the outdoor program by its fees and charges, provides funding to operate the outdoor program on a *break even* status. Table 1.1 suggests that through income, recreation is offered; that through recreation, skill and education is offered; and that through skill and education, character development is offered.

Program Services

Program services are usually one or more of the following: equipment rental, equipment repair (usually bike and ski), retail sales of equipment, outdoor programs, events, and activities. The user may be charged for the services, or the services may be free. They may be available only to students of the school, only to those in the armed forces, or they may be available to all who desire to participate. Table 1.2 provides an overview of some of the rental, repair, retail, and program services provided in six activity areas, as well as indicating some of the schools providing those services.

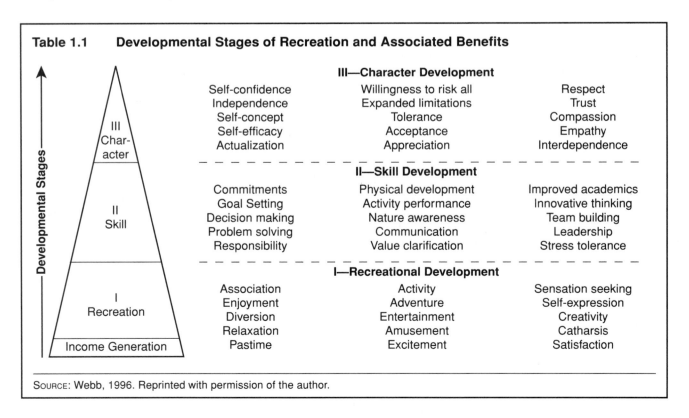

Table 1.1   Developmental Stages of Recreation and Associated Benefits

III—Character Development

Self-confidence	Willingness to risk all	Respect
Independence	Expanded limitations	Trust
Self-concept	Tolerance	Compassion
Self-efficacy	Acceptance	Empathy
Actualization	Appreciation	Interdependence

II—Skill Development

Commitments	Physical development	Improved academics
Goal Setting	Activity performance	Innovative thinking
Decision making	Nature awareness	Team building
Problem solving	Communication	Leadership
Responsibility	Value clarification	Stress tolerance

I—Recreational Development

Association	Activity	Sensation seeking
Enjoyment	Adventure	Self-expression
Diversion	Entertainment	Creativity
Relaxation	Amusement	Catharsis
Pastime	Excitement	Satisfaction

Pyramid: III Character, II Skill, I Recreation, Income Generation. Vertical axis: Developmental Stages.

SOURCE: Webb, 1996. Reprinted with permission of the author.

Table 1.2   A Listing of Four Program Services of Six Recreational Activities Found Within the College Outdoor Program Setting

ACTIVITIES	SERVICES			
	RENTAL	**REPAIR**	**RETAIL**	**PROGRAM**
Rafting	Many programs provide this service	Few programs provide this service	Some programs provide this service; used equipment	Many programs provide this service
Successful Programs	Brigham Young Idaho State Utah	Brigham Young	Brigham Young	California–Berkeley California–Davis Humboldt State
Backpacking Camping Picnicking	Most programs provide this service	Few programs provide this service	Few programs provide this service; some accessories	Most programs provide this service
Successful Programs	Brigham Young California–Irvine Miami		Brigham Young Cal. St.–Sacramento Ricks College	California–Berkeley Calgary Cornell
Rock Climbing	Many programs provide this service (usually *not* ropes)	No	Few programs provide this service	Many programs provide this service
Successful Programs	Colorado–Boulder Calgary California-Berkeley		Brigham Young	California–Davis Cal. St.–Chico North Carolina State
Winter Climbing	Few programs provide this service	No	Few programs provide this service	Some programs provide this service
Successful Programs	Western Washington California–Davis Col. St.–Ft. Collins		Cal. St.–Sacramento Brigham Young	Washington Western Washington Cornell
Alpine Skiing	Few programs provide this service	Few programs provide this service	Some programs provide this service; new/used equipment	Some programs provide this service
Successful Programs	California–Berkeley Brigham Young San Diego State	Brigham Young San Diego State California–Irvine	Brigham Young California–Irvine Cal. St.–Sacramento	Wisconsin–Madison San Diego State California–Berkeley
Canoeing Kayaking	Many programs provide this service	No	Some programs provide this service; used equipment	Many programs provide this service
Successful Programs	California–Berkeley Wisconsin–Madison Washington		Western Washington Brigham Young	San Diego Aquatics Cal. St.–Sacramento Miami

SOURCE: Webb, 1996. Reprinted with permission of the author.

Organizational Models and Influencing Factors

Organizational models used for the delivery of services would be the following: club, S/S/T (structure/safety/training), common adventure, and PE/guided (contracted). Some institutions may have two or more of these models available for their publics, each model serving people with different needs in various ways.

Club organized outdoor programs operate according to a club charter with club members making the decisions. The amount of institutional support and direction varies. Some clubs receive significant funds, building space, and other types of institutional support, with other clubs receiving no support. Outdoor programs using the club model constitute 12 percent of the total outdoor programs at colleges and universities and include the Dartmouth Outing Club at Dartmouth College (Hanover, New Hampshire) and The Hoofers at the University of Wisconsin–Madison.

S/S/T outdoor programs are supported and directed by an institution. The support may be significant or minimal. Some organizational structure and support guided by an institutional employee provides a framework for operation. This structure may have a high or low degree of control by the program participants. Some safety factors are instituted in the program. The safety factors instituted may be minimal or extensive. Training of some type is provided through the program. This training may have significant breadth and depth, or it may be minimal. A type of S/S/T program, borrowing some features from the common adventure model, is a "cooperative adventure trip," where participants make many of the trip decisions. A cooperative adventure trip is an S/S/T program because the institution has provided or made arrangements for one or more of the following: training, leadership, safety guidelines, transportation, lodging, food or similar services. The same trip, with the trip leaders making most of the decisions would also be an S/S/T style trip. Outdoor programs, at colleges and universities, using the S/S/T model constitute 66 percent of the total outdoor programs at colleges and universities and include Appalachian State University (Boone, North Carolina), University of California (Berkeley, California), Georgia Tech (Atlanta, Georgia) and the University of Calgary (Calgary, Alberta, Canada).

Common adventure outdoor programs have trips that have no institutional control or direction. Institutions provide planning resources, meeting areas, and "trip boards" where individuals plan and announce trips. (If the institution provides leadership, training, group equipment, transportation, safety or other standards, or other similar supports, the activity is not a common adventure, but an S/S/T trip). Common adventure trips are trips untouched by organizations and institutions and are completely operated and supported by the trip participants. The institutional support might be a coordinator who provides information, provides speakers or slide shows of adventures to stimulate trips, equipment rentals, equipment repairs, meeting space for pretrip and posttrip meetings. Outdoor programs, at colleges and universities, using the common adventure model are 12 percent of the total outdoor programs at colleges and universities and include the University of Oregon at Eugene, Oregon; Idaho State University at Pocatello, Idaho; and the University of California at San Francisco, California.

PE/guided (contracted) outdoor programs usually place total control of organization, service, safety, and training within a controlled and comparatively inflexible setting. Programs are courses or classes, with employed guides or instructors, who are following a specific curriculum of places to go, things to do and teach, institutional safety, and financial and organizational standards to maintain. Businesses (for-profit and not-for-profit) and degree-granting and credit-awarding educational departments primarily use this model. Equipment rentals, equipment repairs, and retail sales supplement and compliment the trip or outfitting program. Outdoor programs, at colleges and universities, using the PE/Guided (contracted) model constitute 7 percent of the total outdoor programs at colleges and universities and include Prescott College (Prescott, Arizona), Cornell University (Ithaca, New York), and Colgate University (Hamilton, New York).

Factors influencing an outdoor program include:

1. users of the program services;
2. politics: internal and external of the organization, institution, or business;
3. personality, abilities and/or interests of the program sponsor;
4. traditions of the program and sponsor;
5. financial source and size; and
6. local and regional geography.

As a result of these factors, each outdoor program will be different from the others. These factors will influence which organizational model is used, and which values and goals will be primary, secondary, and tertiary. As these factors change, the outdoor program will need to adapt and change to be able to continue to serve its public.

One outdoor program model is not better than another. Each outdoor program model delivery system provides different and specific benefits and opportunities. Table 1.3 compares these four models.

Summary

The *Outdoor Recreation Program Directory & Data/Resource Guide* (Webb, 1996) contains the data collected from surveys sent to outdoor programs at colleges and universities in North America. The data collected includes demographic information (e.g., names of outdoor programs and

Table 1.3   Comparison of Four Different Models of Outdoor Recreation Programming

ASPECT OF MODEL	Club	SST	Common Adventure	PE/Guided
Primary source of funding	Club sport & individual participant	Sponsoring organization, individual participant	Individual participant	School/college
Nature of funding	Dues & shared trip costs	Sponsoring organization funds & shared trip costs	Shared trip costs	School funds & shared trip costs
Philosophical foundations	Teaching/learning of outdoor skills; competition; enjoyment of outdoor environment	Enhancement of outdoor skills; enjoyment of outdoor environment; safety; enhanced self-confidence/concept	Individual freedom; personal growth through interpersonal interaction; enjoyment of outdoor recreation; enhancement of outdoor skills	Teaching or learning of outdoor skills
Administrative support — Type	"Standard"	"Standard"	"Standard" (trip bulletin board, meeting facilities, equipment source, advertising source, printing source; audiovisual equipment, etc.)	Teaching facilities; equipment
Administrative support — Source	College; student union	Sponsoring organization	College; student union	PE department
Organization	Specified in club constitution; officers with specific duties	Student committee as specified in a charter/constitution & procedure documents	Centers on *facilities* that make outdoor recreation actually happen (bulletin board, meeting rooms, audiovisual equipment, printing facilities, equipment rental, etc.)	Teacher/student/classroom
Source of instruction	Skilled individuals within group	Skilled individuals within group	Individual participants; commercial sources	Professional staff within school
Source of equipment	Club; individual participant; or rented commercially	Sponsoring organization or rented commercially	Individual participants; rented from commercial sources	School or rented commercially
Source of outings	Scheduled/decided by club	Scheduled/decided by club	Volunteered	Scheduled by instruction
Leadership source	Club members elected/appointed by membership	Developed within group by training & selection process	Volunteers from among participants	School/college personnel
How safety standards maintained	Club members decide standard; club leadership carries them out	Sponsoring organization & group leadership work up standard; student leadership carries them out	Participant imposed	School/college sets standards & enforces them
Main advantages — For College	Minimized supervisory & administrative time	Easy to give direction to programming	Low liability risk	Expanded courses
Main advantages — For Student	Easier access to a particular outdoor recreation; social	Safe	Maximum flexibility to meet individual needs	Course credit
Schools using these models in their outdoor recreation programs	Dartmouth College Wisconsin–Madison California–San Luis Obispo	California–Berkeley Oregon State Brigham Young Calgary	Oregon Western Washington Idaho Idaho State	Cornell Prescott College Colgate

Source: Templeton and Webb, 1972. Reprinted with permission of the authors.

administrators, phone numbers, addresses, and organizational type), financial information (e.g., incomes from rentals, repairs, retail sales, trips, and activities and expenses), and programmatic data (e.g., types and numbers of trips and participants). This information is ranked and sorted in various ways. Information about outdoor recreation industry associations and a complete chapter of information about the Association of Outdoor Recreation and Education (AORE) is also contained in this book. By reviewing this data, a better understanding of the college and university outdoor programs, and all outdoor programs can be gained.

There is a significant diversity of goals, benefits, delivery models, services, activities, financial structures, and sizes of outdoor programs. The general public, college and university communities, and associates of the armed forces have a wide range of choices, opportunities and benefits of outdoor adventure, recreation, and education. Outdoor programs will continue to expand, develop, grow, diversify, and increase the range of choices, opportunities, and benefits in both quality and quantity, to those they serve.

References

Templeton, W. M., and Webb, D. J. (1972). *Outdoor recreation at Georgia Tech*. Unpublished manuscript.

Webb, D. J. (1996). *Outdoor Recreation Program Directory & Date/Resource Guide* (2nd ed.). Boulder, CO: Outdoor Network.

Chapter 2

Educational Adventure and Schooling

Bert Horwood
Queens University

Adventure in schooling may seem a contradiction. For some, the routines and tedium of school are simply not compatible with the excitement and energy of adventure pursuits in the outdoors. My claim is that while school can be unadventurous, the same spirit of adventure found in outdoor pursuits is well-established in school practice. To support this, I'll examine commonly agreed upon characteristics of adventure and describe the means by which these same characteristics are brought into schooling. The base for this description is a distillation of my personal and professional school participation as student, teacher, supervisor, and researcher. The form of the description is essentially narrative.

First, I will present an argument to demonstrate that our working grasp of adventure is perfectly compatible with school practice and goals. There will be an account of critical schooling methods that enhance adventure. Finally, I will attend to this troubling question: given the argument and methods in use, why isn't all schooling perceived to be an adventure? In all of this I take the position that the key element in making school adventurous is the teacher, and I use the term *teacher* to mean the same kinds of roles that are commonly understood in the adventure education field by titles such as *leader, facilitator, instructor,* and the like.

There are five central characteristics of adventure that can be used as criteria to determine whether or not a given activity is adventurous. They are uncertain outcome, risk,

inescapable consequences, energetic action, and willing participation. Uncertain outcome means that there is no absolute guarantee how the activity will work out, even though there may be strong probabilities based on past experience. Uncertainty is a commonly recognized feature of outdoor adventure, but its presence in the school context may be less appreciated and, in some settings, less practiced. Yet in schools, whether there is a test, a seminar presentation, a science experiment, or a volleyball game, there can always be doubt about the outcome.

Risk is commonly understood to refer to the possibility of physical injury or death, but there are also social, psychological, and spiritual risks. It is sometimes helpful to distinguish among a novice's perception of risk, a teacher's perceptions of risk, and the actuarial risk based on statistical records. Life in most schools may be thought to be safer than life on a mountain or at sea, yet there are daily risks that must be run. These are primarily social and psychological. The risk of ridicule, of appearing to be a fool, and the danger of being shunned, are powerful hazards in the minds of students. There is also a risk of physical harm from beatings for students who deviate from peer norms where violence is found in schools.

Participants in adventure activities have some degree of control over the uncertainties and risks they face. By acting in one way or another, people can increase or decrease their exposure. In the short term, the kinds of decisions they make in the thick of the activity will shift the risks. In the longer term, experience and training can increase skills to provide even more control. With increased skills, people will frequently choose even greater exposure to uncertainty and risk.

Regardless of skill and experience, there are inescapable consequences within an adventurous activity which is the third characteristic. One reason that risky activities outdoors are quintessentially adventurous is because it is impossible to escape the consequences of wind, water, and weather. Inescapable consequences ensure that an adventure is not totally amenable to skilled control. Inescapable consequences are harder to develop in a school context. (This difficulty will be discussed more fully later.) But where school events have consequences that cannot be evaded, they have this feature of adventure.

The fourth characteristic of adventure is energetic action. Participants are called on to make extraordinary effort, to stretch themselves, to dig deeply into their resources of strength and will. The best teachers construct contexts and experiences which make similar demands on each student's determination and staying power. Such teachers regularly have challenging, difficult work for students to do. I used to quote the dictum that a poor teacher makes it easy but seem hard, and a good teacher makes it hard but seem easy.

The fifth characteristic is the willingness of the participant to be engaged. Participants must have selected the activity in some way or, at least, have given consent to it. Beyond mere consent, there is frequently an element of enthusiastic pleasure in an adventurous activity. Participants paradoxically find it exciting and fun, even as they find it threatening and uncomfortable.

To look for these characteristics in a given activity will enable an observer to decide whether or not adventure is present. For example, there was a young man on a high ropes course element who was so frightened that despite skilled intervention he was paralyzed, and ultimately experienced the indignity of involuntary urination in front of his peers. In this situation, the outcome could not be known to him; he was certainly at risk of humiliation, if not of physical harm; the consequences of his failure were inescapable and he was in a situation calling for energetic action. But four out of five characteristics does not make an adventure. The youth was unwilling to be there. There was no joy or enthusiasm for him. The flow he experienced was not exactly what Csikszentmihalyi had in mind. My point is that even recognized adventure settings may not qualify as providing adventure if the context fails to meet the criteria.

There are five critical factors which contribute to making a school event meet the criteria of adventure. They are the sequence of instruction, diversity in locale and method, the distribution of decision making between teacher and student, the degree of public exposure, and the modes of evaluation.

While a beginning science teacher I was lucky to have a skilled and experienced senior as a mentor. He summed up the whole of his teaching experience in three words, "Do. See. Reflect." He always went on to add that the doing, seeing and reflecting meant student activity within a context organized by the teacher. These words convey the critical sequence which contributes to adventure in schooling. Sometimes, instruction is reversed and students are told the fruits of someone else's reflection first—reflect, do, see. After the intended lesson or outcome has been revealed and reinforced, there may be a follow-up activity. But this violates the adventure criterion of uncertain outcome. Adventure in school lessons is always enhanced when the students' active experience comes before figuring out what it means. The standard textbook sequence of telling all in the body of the chapter and giving activities at the end is contrary to this canon of adventure. If a student already knows what a particular activity is supposed to teach, the activity becomes dull repetition, a mere "I told you so."

Diversity contributes to adventure by adding uncertainty and risk. Using a variety of locales and methods reduces predictability and, if not overdone, a pleasant "edge." As a teacher, I always found it best when students were just ever-so-slightly off balance. When classes meet in new places, or work outdoors from time to time, the advantages of what Keith King calls "invigorating environments" are available. In my experience, adventure is found in schools where teachers and students pay attention to the ambience of their classroom base, and leave it frequently. That may be as simple as doing physics experiments on acceleration with wagons on the paved hill outside the school or taking small strolling theatre groups into local malls. It might be as elaborate as internship placements or exchange visits with distant communities.

Diversity in teaching methods also contributes to uncertainty and risk. When teaching high school, I had decided that announcing tests or quizzes a day or two in advance gave neither myself nor my students a good reading on what they had learned, but gave instead a good reading of what they could cram and forget. So I began the (at first) unpopular custom of proclaiming all tests and quizzes on the first day of term. "This is the announcement of all your tests and quizzes," I would say. "From this day forward you can expect a test or quiz at any time. You should be in a continual state of readiness. There will be no further announcements." This practice generated some outrage at first. But it died away as younger students rather docilely accepted this bit of tyranny and clever seniors began to share guesses as to when the work had progressed far enough to warrant a test. The same is true for varying teaching methods among books, field work, lectures, student seminars, independent projects and so on.

During educational episodes, there are many decisions which must be taken. It is conceivable to create a setting in which almost all of the decisions are made by the teacher.

If the context is a calisthenics drill, then the students may be physically very active, but they are in a highly passive state in every other way. As decisions are shifted from teacher to student, the fuller engagement of the student becomes possible. Full engagement is needed to meet the adventure criteria that the student is willing to participate energetically, and find space for some level of enjoyment. The question of who makes which decisions is central to addressing issues of locus of control, safety levels, readiness to attempt the difficult and to run risks. My experience leads me to formulate the general principle that, the more decisions made by students, the more adventurous is the schooling.

All the adventure criteria are enhanced when school activities are made public. At a very simple level, the math problem solutions which a student writes in the privacy of his or her workbook are much safer than if he or she is asked to work a solution on the blackboard in full view of his or her peers. This effect becomes more pronounced when schoolwork is displayed or performed in public. Science fairs and drama festivals are examples of exposed schoolwork which meet the criteria of adventure. A basketball game gains an extra edge when there are several hundred cheering and jeering spectators. Every student who stands in front of the class to deliver a project report, a book review, or debating point is in an adventure mode related to the degree of public exposure. An adventurous teacher colleague of mine who has a strong community orientation in his practice, encourages students to go door-to-door in the town for various purposes, give talks and slide shows to local service clubs, and contribute regular writing and photos to the local newspaper.

There is a well-known adage that the evaluation tail wags the curriculum dog. And it is a common experience among teachers to teach for the external test which may be used to assess both students and themselves. Similarly, students (quite naturally) will bias their learning towards what they believe will be "on the test." Externally imposed evaluation standards and practices can dampen the spirit of adventure in schooling. But viewed in another way, evaluation can be used to enhance adventure. Evaluation is itself risky and uncertain of outcome. Most students are willing to make extra efforts and be tested because they want to have some concrete measure of their success.

The content and tone of the testing process varies in terms of pleasure. There is a wide variety of evaluation tools which are compatible with adventurous schooling. Portfolios that students present to a committee of peers, teachers and parents is an example. Asking students to summarize their learning in a videotaped statement is another. A teacher discovered that students produce incredible things when they are asked to review a book they've read both in writing and by making some object to represent their reaction to the book. One year, when I was tired of grading huge piles of papers, I determined to teach the

students how to grade. They received a detailed marking scheme and an example. Each student marked three other students' papers (not their own) and the scores were averaged. I checked random papers and discovered that students graded peers more rigorously and more consistently than I did. There was an unexpected bonus. Previously, I was the only person to have benefited from reading the diversity of ideas in the papers. Now, students had access to the thoughts of others. All of these devices have the ability to make evaluation part of the adventurous school.

Here I want to take Kurt Hahn as an example partly because of his status as a founding spirit in the Outward Bound Movement, a quintessentially adventure education process. In adventure circles it is often forgotten that Kurt Hahn was a schoolmaster both before and after Outward Bound was instituted. The value of adventure in character development which he brought to Outward Bound was the same that drove much of the content and methods he used in his schools at Salem and Gordonstoun. For Hahn, there was no room in schooling for passiveness, indifference, and boredom. Hahn provides a shining example of adventure in schooling, and that is dramatically revealed by the "report card" which he used.

For this report, Hahn asked teachers to say how each student displayed a number of qualities. These included esprit de corps (we might say participation in the community); sense of justice; ability to follow what he or she regards to be the right course in the face of obstacles such as discomfort, skepticism, hardship, risks, teasing, impulses of the moment, and peer pressure; ability to plan; power of imagination; ability to organize work; ability to help younger students; concentration when a task is interesting and when it is not; manners; ability to state facts precisely; standards reached in school subjects; practical work; manual dexterity; and arts, physical vigor, and lively spirit.

It is plain that Hahn expected much more of his staff and students than academic prowess. And it is this broad context of growth and development of the human potential that puts schooling at its best into the realm of adventure.

The spirit of adventure in schooling applies to the teachers as well as to the students. When a teacher uses methods like the ones outlined, the characteristics of adventure emerge and the benefits flow to the students. There are also benefits for the teacher because most of these approaches to teaching are very challenging to implement. Putting action before reflection, using diverse locales and methods, assigning (and enforcing) responsibility to students, making schoolwork public and using matching modes of evaluation all generate uncertainties and loss of direct control which require the utmost determination and discipline. Teachers on this path are being as adventurous as their students.

But despite these glowing accounts that place schooling in the realm of adventure, there is a common experience and perception that schools are more often dull and tedious, the antithesis of adventure. The central causes for this failure are unmotivated students, and the ease with which consequences of actions or nonactions can be evaded. An attitude of willingness, even if it gradually emerges from an initial doubt, is central to carry students into the full risks of learning. But risks vanish as soon as unpleasant consequences disappear. Therefore it is worthwhile to consider how adventurous teachers deal with issues of motivation and consequences.

Hahn's well-known statement about impelling students into experience invites speculation on the practical differences between *impelling* and *compelling*. The degree of choice in "challenge-by-choice" is open to debate. There are times when a distinct push is needed to move a student into adventurous action in a school context. More subtly, this is done by creating climates of high expectation, offering role model teachers who themselves lead adventurous lives, and by using various motivation devices, sometimes called *hookers*. The well-known California science educator Harry K. Wong is a master at catching the interest and constructive engagement of middle-school students. For one series of lessons, he asks the toughest character in the class to blow away a three-by-five card resting between two books on a desk. It can't be done. After other students try, and fail, they're all hooked. "What's going on here?" This creates a need to know which becomes the basis for future learning.

The term *hookers* originated with the Institute for Earth Education whose programs are exemplary in pulling students into an enthusiastic frame of mind to explore the natural world in adventurous ways with new eyes. The Earthkeepers program, normally offered by outdoor education centers to cooperating schools, touches the emotions of willingness by creating a mysterious character, EM, whose secrets will yield the understandings and feelings needed to care for the earth. Before students actually leave their school to begin the program, they receive a letter from EM inviting them to learn his secrets. This imaginary, but very real, character creates the emotional climate which equals motivation and sets the stage for full-fledged participation and enjoyment.

One of the great advantages of the outdoors as the site for adventure education is that the consequences of decisions cannot be evaded. Nature is implacable and quite indifferent to the human condition. Tides and nightfall, wind and avalanche do not pause because a person mislaid gear or failed to check the weather forecast. "No excuses" is the way that water and mountains deal with all those who venture on them. In artificial settings, like schools, it is more difficult to develop the same implacability. It is hard and sometimes unreasonable for human teachers to be unforgiving. Yet the more easily that students can miss deadlines, choose the safer paths, and evade responsibility, the less schooling can achieve adventure status. This is where discipline in its best sense becomes critical to teaching. The discipline of teachers to stick to expectations and challenging demands, especially when they have been agreed to by willing students, is essential.

Finally, there is a kind of joy, a simple pleasure, or just plain fun when school is an adventure. This is most readily apparent in the early grades. But unless teachers make deliberate efforts to the contrary, something happens as students age. Luckily there are enough teachers in whom the spirit of adventure lives, so that students may have a reasonable chance to experience the joy and satisfaction of learning throughout their lives.

Adventure in schooling exists. It resides within classrooms and accessible out-of-school venues. It may use outdoor adventure pursuits like challenge courses or canoe trips as adjuncts, but these are not essential. What is essential is the wholehearted, wide-eyed spirit of adventure in both teachers and students who, together, seek to do their utmost with hands, heads and hearts.

Chapter 3

Developmental Adventure Programs

Jude Hirsch
Georgia College and State University

Somewhere between *re-creation* and *therapy* lies *development*. That is to say, that where adventure programs are not intentionally limited to the aims of recreation, or do not seek therapeutic objectives, they will likely be classified as developmental adventure programs. As a type of adventure education, developmental programs seek to attain certain developmental goals through the use of risk and challenge. It is mainly the goals of developmental adventure programs that distinguish them from recreation and therapeutic adventure programs. This distinction, and how it affects delivery, is the focus of this chapter.

I begin by offering a brief account of the evolution of the concept of outdoor education, because understanding the historical relationship between outdoor education and adventure education is like understanding the relationship between your personal history and who you are today. In the same fashion that outdoor education has grown to include adventure education, adventure education has grown to include the set of program distinctions that are discussed in this book. Following a brief discussion of the context in which developmental adventure occurs, several actual programs are briefly described. Some examples are of longstanding programs, like Outward Bound and Project Adventure, and others are selected to reflect a unique approach or specific client groups. Taken together, they represent a fairly comprehensive set of standard cases for developmental adventure. Finally, a set of distinguishing features for developmental adventure are gleaned from the examples to capture the essence of this category of adventure education.

Fifty or so years ago the term *outdoor education* was used to refer to almost anything people did in the out-of-doors. Residential camping, school gardening, and canoeing were all referred to as outdoor education (Donaldson and Donaldson, 1958). As our profession matured, there came a need to distinguish types of outdoor education, partly to clarify what agencies and institutions would be responsible to fund and regulate delivery (Kelly, 1972), and partly because people became aware that they were doing very different things under the umbrella of outdoor education and felt a need to explain differences and similarities more clearly within the profession and to our clients. Early attempts at conceptual clarity resulted in the simple distinction between outdoor recreation and outdoor education.

Outdoor recreation took place during free time, primarily for enjoyment and re-creation, and most often involved doing something in relationship with natural landscapes. Leisure service and recreation agencies were the primary deliverers of these activities, and took responsibility for leadership development and creating standards for peer practice. Outdoor education referred mainly to experiences that sought to enhance a wide range of interdisciplinary educational objectives. While these experiences often took place in natural landscapes, other more constructed settings, like schoolyards, were acceptable.

Outdoor education was most often delivered through educational institutions, although other settings such as residential camps began to offer both outdoor education and outdoor recreation programs. These distinctions helped for a short time and laid a foundation for more complex ways of thinking about the field.

As we progressed into the 1980s, our questions became more focused on the relationships between sets of related terms that included outdoor education, experiential education, environmental education, and adventure education (Jensen and Briggs-Young, 1981; March, 1982; Miles, 1982; Raffin, 1986). Historically, we see a continuous refinement in our understanding of our field as we think and talk about what we do, why we do it, and how we do it. Some people think of outdoor education as the umbrella term, and of the other terms as subcomponents or types of outdoor education. This, of course, depends on primary perspective of the speaker. I remember a discussion I had with Milton McClaren in 1986 at Simon Fraser University in British Columbia, where he proposed that outdoor educators had it all wrong. He passionately and eloquently suggests that *environmental education* is the umbrella term from which all other terms take their primary purpose because without "place" there would be no outdoor education at all. Regardless of one's perspective on the broader field of outdoor education, our understanding of adventure education changed to include the three types of adventure programs discussed in this book.

What today is referred to as adventure education has generally been considered a subcategory of outdoor education (Cantrell, 1990; Cousineau, 1982; Ford, 1981; Grenier, 1983; Hirsch, 1992; Priest, 1986). The number and variety of names for adventure education is a reflection of its complex conceptual history. Among these names are high-adventure leisure pursuits (Meier, 1978), high-risk activities (White, Schreyer, and Downing, 1980), high-adventure outdoor pursuits (Meier, Morash, and Welton, 1987), outdoor adventure pursuits (Ewert, 1989), and risk recreation (Ewert and Schreyer, 1990). Sometime in the mid 1980s adventure education became the widely accepted name for activities that employ risk and challenge, in a variety of settings, to attain a variety of educational goals.

In an earlier attempt to clarify the meaning of adventure education, Cousineau (1978), suggested that adventure is a fundamental human need, and that there are four basic modes of adventure expression—some more socially acceptable than others. Cousineau's model was an important step in our understanding of adventure education. It was also one of the first times that an outdoor educator argued that adventure is a necessary condition for human growth and development. There followed a myriad of studies supporting the contribution of adventure to aspects of personal growth like self-concept, self-esteem, and effectance. Personal growth and group development are now thought to be central and pervasive outcomes of ad-

venture education programs (Priest, 1986; Hirsch, 1992). Developmental adventure is a type of adventure education where these outcomes are central, and where their centrality dictates the knowledge, procedural, and value base from which leaders in these programs operate. In other words, when I design and deliver a program that fits into this category, I am applying different understandings, using different procedures, and conveying different values than when my colleagues design and deliver recreation or therapeutic adventure programs. Now having said that, I need to stress the idea that we are all doing adventure education; therefore, there will be universals, and a good deal of overlap, because there isn't anything that we do in our field on which we can impose definitive boundaries. After all, we are human, and adventure education is a human endeavor. Dynamic conceptual boundaries provide structure for our thinking and help us to be clear about what we are doing, so that we can do it safely and effectively.

In 1995 Ringer and Gillis suggested four categories for adventure activities. Developmental adventure activities were described as those associated with the desire to improve behavior in important relationships. The authors suggest that learning in these programs is associated with generic themes such as cooperation, communication, and trust. At the time of their writing, a distinction is made between development and education and/or training activities, the latter being described as those activities most often used with work teams to address a change in self-concept or sense of identity (Table 3.1). In a note at the conclusion of the article, Ringer and Gillis indicate that at the November 1994 International Conference of the Association for Experiential Education, Michael Gass, Simon Priest, Martin Ringer, and Lee Gillis decided that the development category should be expanded to incorporate both training and enrichment. In other words, any activity that has as its primary goal the development of individuals or groups for the purpose of training or education, as defined in their model, would be placed in the developmental adventure category (Table 3.2).

The landscape of developmental adventure programs is varied. Clients include youth, families, employees, and anyone else who desires to be a "better person" or wishes to be part of a "highly functioning group."[1] Developmental activities take place in a wide variety of settings such as camps, schools and universities, outdoor education centers, and corporate training sites. Developmental activities employ a range of adventure programming options such as wilderness expeditions, initiative tasks, challenge courses, residential camping, base camping, and outdoor pursuits. They adhere to the tenets and procedures of experiential

---

[1]I recognize that defining a *better person* or a *highly functioning group* is in relation to participant and organizational goals. The terms are used to indicate sets of common developmental goals like communication, self-confidence, or problem solving.

Table 3.1	Goals for Adventure Experiences			
	Recreation	**Education/ Training**	**Development**	**Psychotherapy**
Primary goal	Fun, laughter, challenge, excitement, initiative, etc.	Change in sense of identify or self-concept.	Learning associated with a *generic* theme such as cooperation, communication, trust.	Learning about interpersonal processes that will be applied with participants' *significant others.*
Distinguished features	May be therapeutic, but focus in on enjoyment.	Often associated with learning for an occupation, vocation of course of study; often used with work teams.	Often (but not always) applied to remedy personal dysfunction. Usually preceded by assessment of clients.	Learning about interpersonal processes that will be applied with participants' significant others

education to engage participants in thought-provoking reflection that is assumed will result in the growth and development of individuals and/or groups. An examination of several examples of developmental adventure programs will add depth and breadth to our understanding of developmental adventure.

Inclusivity Consulting Group, Inc.

Founded in 1989 by Bill Proudman, president and senior facilitator, Inclusivity is a consulting group specializing in organizational and human resource development. The company's promotional brochure claims "a whole different spin." They teach the value of conflict to companies and organizations who want people to work together to be creative and productive. Their literature suggests that traditionally individuals have been expected to fit in or change themselves to meet the larger needs of a group, at the expense of fresh ideas and approaches. Inclusivity facilitates

---

Table 3.2   Primary Goals and Distinguishing Features for Developmental Programs

Primary Goals: Change in sense of identity or self-concept at a intrapersonal level and/or change in group/team effectiveness at the interpersonal level.

Distinguishing Features: Generic themes such as cooperation, communication, and problem solving are addressed at both levels to improve behavior in important relationships in vocational or avocational settings.

---

the development of new systems in which individuals are central to the needs of the larger organization. In these systems, differences are valued and even sought after. Conflict is deemed helpful and necessary.

At Inclusivity it is believed that the basis for building self-respect and contributing to positive group behavior is speaking for oneself. This is the foundation for learning to appreciate each other more, a necessary condition for creating and committing to a common shared vision. Creating an inclusive organization can only be accomplished when all of its members are honored for their individuality. This is the glue that binds people—and organizations—together.

Inclusivity interacts with business, education, government and the human services professions to customize programs and consulting services that recognize and cultivate people as the most valuable resource in an organization. Participants can expect to participate in a program that combines traditional organizational development strategies with adventure activities. The program's approach is process-centered and experiential, often involving interactive exercises and simulations, small group problem solving, real-life strategizing, discussion and reflection, challenge-course experiences and, occasionally, outdoor-based adventure activities. Facilitators do not tell people what to do and they do not prescribe recipes to solve complex problems. They create trusting and safe learning environments in which to redevelop skills for creating productive, inclusive, and enriching organizations.

Client comments provided in the company's promotional brochure indicate a number of important program features. Decision makers at a power company stated that Inclusivity did not deliver a packaged program. Instead they engaged in active discussion with the company to evaluate their needs and put it all together into a custom program that met the goal of changing, not people, but working relationships between people. The program was relevant to the job context, even though part of the training took clients 50 feet off the ground on a high ropes course.

The executive director of a leadership program suggested that, for that organization, the wilderness experience was crucial, and that the "taking stock" session was powerful and effective. It is noted that Inclusivity facilitators are good coaches, there to help with learning, to observe, and to be in the right place at the right time. Creating a safe atmosphere and letting people have experiences that they can't have anywhere else is a main ingredient for the work Inclusivity did with this organization.

The diversity director at a school interested in defining diversity and inclusivity, and determining how to become more of both, describes the challenge as making a quilt by bringing everyone in and trying to patch them together while retaining individual qualities that are indispensable to the strength of the whole. Inclusivity's role was to work with faculty and/or administration, trustees, and students to help everyone clarify their vision for becoming inclusive and more diverse.

In a conversation I had with Bill Proudman at the 1997 International Conference of the Association for Experiential Education in Asheville, North Carolina, I asked him to tell me what he thinks is unique about Inclusivity. He said that one challenge for him and the company is not to start from an activity place, but to start from a client-centered place where the facilitator and the client cocreate a process for changing the culture within an organization. He talked about the idea of process facilitation, where program models do not define process and the trainer is a catalyst for interpreting, with the client, what comes up. Core assumptions that guide the work people do at Inclusivity are that people already have the answers to their problems, and that connected, healthy relationships are created and sustained through unconditional understanding and love.

This example of developmental adventure offered by Inclusivity suggests that custom program design, based on an in-depth assessment of organizational issues and goals, creates an opportunity for the client to challenge assumptions and create new and more effective organizational cultures that are inclusive and value diversity.

Strasser & Partners

In 1972 B. Strasser and M. Kölblinger began to experiment with bringing management and clients together to work on aspects of intrapersonal and interpersonal relations by integrating traditional strategies with outdoor education approaches. In 1975 Strasser formed a consulting company specializing in personnel training and development and Kölblinger joined him with the specific mandate to develop their services in the area of "outdoor management development." They consider themselves pioneers in this specific area of organizational development, and in a recent conversation with Mario Kölblinger, he commented that most of his colleagues were laughing at him in the beginning.

One training option that the company is well-known for is called *outdoor project management.* In the corporate world, projects are tasks that involve considerable work load, complexity, and budget. The goal is to best meet the needs of the customer through generating interlocking processes and applying cross-functional operations to the task. In a recent conversation with Kölblinger, he suggested that modern science, technology and economy are too complicated, complex, and extensive for one brain to comprehend and for only one approach to represent sufficient perspective. Complex tasks and problems demand the integration of many points of view, many disciplines, many skills, and many individuals. Therefore, they involve different specialists who simultaneously work cross functionally. For example, a project team may be assigned the task of increasing its market share in luxury vehicles by 17 percent in one year. To this end, employees from customer service, maintenance, sales, marketing, design, production and management may form a project team.

In response to the need for more effective project management, Strasser & Partners developed an approach to training where an intact project team completes a wilderness project. Kölblinger contends that a wilderness project develops coordination and leadership within the group. As well, it addresses skills such as planning and scheduling tasks, decision making and problem solving, team motivation, determining priorities, setting targets, communicating clearly, assigning roles and responsibilities, executing crisis management, allocating resources, working cross-functional interfaces, and applying technical skills to networking, engineering, and break down structures. Table 3.3 highlights participant and facilitator roles in a sequence of activities for developing an effective project team.

Kölblinger describes several principles for designing a wilderness project (Figure 3.1). Refer to them as you read this brief account of a wilderness project that he described to a graduate class at Georgia College and State University.

A well-known automobile manufacturer was in the process of carrying out some secret tests for a new project when a severe, life-threatening snow storm hit the region. Unfortunately, they were forced to leave all of their supplies, including parts of the new product, scattered in the wilderness as they withdrew from the area. Several months later, they had been unable to retrieve anything, due to continued severe winter conditions. Recently, company sources confirmed that a major competitor had succeeded in purchasing the land on which the secret tests were being conducted, no doubt because their sources revealed the market share importance of the abandoned supplies and product parts. Title to the land, including many square miles of mountainous terrain, a large lake, and several islands, is to be given to the new owners at 5 P.M., two days hence on the

Table 3.3	Steps of Integration for Becoming a Project Team
Starting a Wilderness Project	
Facilitators	1. Setting the scenario
Participants	2. Facing the big picture
Participants	3. Struggling with chaos
Prearrangements are possible	4. Identifying work structures • needs/targets • tasks • resources • procedures • links/interdependencies • interfaces • risks
Participants	5. Assigning people • work teams • steering committees • coordinators/leaders • task forces
Prearrangements are possible	6. Establishing work rules
Participants	7. Buzzing/drawing up project plan • gaining further input • completing work tasks • negotiating for resources • identifying customer relations • coordinating procedures
Participants with facilitator input where appropriate	8. Presenting project plan in plenary assembly
Participants with facilitator input and responsibility for the safety audit	9. Discussing issues and procedures • making refinements • undergoing safety audit • establishing overall commitment
Facilitators	10. Introducing general safety rules
Facilitators	11. Releasing for realization
Participants with facilitators	12. Starting the wilderness project

Figure 3.1	Design Principles for Corporate Adventure-Based Learning Environments

1. Adventure-based anchors are used to create risk and challenge that is comparable to the work setting task.
2. Authentic problems are solved to create learning opportunities.
3. The situation is initially perceived to be significantly complex.
4. Learning is generative and accumulative.
5. Information is embedded in the task.
6. Multiple perspectives are possible.
7. Corporate subject matters (critical incidents, metaphors, methods, instruments) are integrated into the project.
8. Opportunities for reflection are available.
9. Learning is a function of social interaction.
10. Transfer of learning links are developed (action plans, follow-up, transfer management).

first day of spring. A special team of employees has been assigned the task of retrieving all of the supplies and taking them to a large island in the middle of the lake, where a helicopter will be able to lift them out of the area.

During the days that lead up to the wilderness project, the team participates in several team effectiveness and technical skill-building activities. Most of these take place in the relative comfort of a training center. Activities include group initiatives, low- and high-challenge courses, technical lessons in technical skills such as knots, lashing and traversing, and technical skills related to the requirements of the particular wilderness project. All of this preactivity is designed to prepare the group for the task by developing commitment, competency and cognition. Then the project begins. Project completion is predesigned to take one day or days, depending on client needs and wishes. After the group celebrates their success, careful and considerable plans are developed to transfer what is learned about highly functioning project teams to the corporate setting.

Kölblinger stressed that there is evidence that the wilderness project provides an experience that is transferable to the workplace. He suggested two articles in particular as important background. Chan Kim and Mauborgne (1997) suggest that fair processes profoundly influence attitudes and behaviors critical to high performance. People do care about outcomes, but no more than the fairness of the processes that produces them. The authors contend that controlling and motivating employees' behavior, incentive systems and an organizational structure that is informed by values associated with production-based ways of thinking about organizations is counterproductive to today's knowledge-based economy. More appropriate approaches to achieving organizational goals are based on valuing ideas and innovation. Fair process addresses issues like trust, commitment and cooperation among organizational members. It values people as human beings and not as "personnel" or "human assets," and outlines three basic principles, or bedrock elements, associated with a process-centered approach. The same three mutually reinforcing principles consistently emerged when Chan Kim and Mauborgne talked to people in diverse management contexts: engagement, explanation, and expectation clarity. In other words, people in highly functioning organizations want to be involved in decision making to the extent that they are asked for input and are able to refute the merits of one another's ideas and assumptions. They want to understand why final decisions are made as they are, and they want to know the rules of the game once decisions are made.

Wileman and Baker (1996) investigated research regarding the human element in project management. The findings, used by practitioners to formulate strategies to improve project management, suggest that a problem-solving approach to project management is more successful than a smoothing or forcing mode of conflict resolution. Participative decision-making styles are generally more successful than other styles, and that commitment, teamwork and a sense of mission are important areas of attention in project management. The authors describe the project management as a complex interpersonal network. In order to attain high levels of perceived success in technical performance, as well as client and project team satisfaction, effective coordination, relations patterns, and consensus building are important.

A wilderness project builds competencies in areas that will permit individuals to contribute to group success by creating a living metaphor that will enable the group to transfer learning to the workplace.

Project Adventure Inc.

According to Dick Prouty (1990), in 1971 Jerry Pieh, the principal of Hamilton-Wenham Junior-Senior High School in Hamilton, Massachusetts, received funding for a new program he called *Project Adventure*. The goal of the program was to mainstream the Outward Bound process into a secondary public school setting. He hired staff with Outward Bound backgrounds, and together with teachers and administrators began to introduce curriculum that was focused on physical education. Bob Lentz, the first director of Project Adventure (PA), was joined by several project staff and teachers in the creation and delivery of a program that had as its central goals that students would learn how to solve problems in a group more creatively and efficiently and come to understand that preconceived barriers to what was possible often held both the group and the individual from achievement. Curricular units in English, history, science, theater arts and counseling were written by teachers to reinforce these same goals while pursuing traditional academic course objectives.

Substantial program evaluation established that strong positive results were achieved in a number of areas, and in 1974 the program was awarded a National Demonstration Site Award. From 1974 to 1981, the Hamilton-Wenham School District received a dissemination grant each year to subsidize the adoption of the PA model by other schools nationally. By 1980 over 400 schools in most of the states of the country had adopted at least one component (academic or physical education) of the original PA program. Prouty (1990) offers a summary of key elements in an adventure curriculum that highlights many aspects of the program philosophy (Figure 3.2) for which Project Adventure is so well-known today.

Many seasoned adventure educators have books on their shelves dating from the mid 1970s, which were written by the early Project Adventure staff. Jim Schoell, Karl Rohnke, Steve Webster, Paul Radcliff, Dick Prouty, and

---

Figure 3.2   Key Elements of an Adventure Curriculum

1. A sense of adventure, unpredictability, drama and suspense.
2. A consistently high (but accomplishable) level of expectation demanded and created by both the intrinsic and external forces.
3. A success orientation in which growth is supported and encouraged and in which the positive is emphasized.
4. An atmosphere of mutual support in which cooperation, encouragement, and interpersonal concerns are consistently present.
5. A sense of enjoyment, fun, and the opportunity to laugh at a situation, each other, and oneself.
6. An approach to learning which makes use of group problem solving, which allows for a variety of personal contributions and which presents problems that can't ordinarily be solved individually.
7. The use of a learning laboratory that is more complex, more engaging, less predictable and less familiar than a classroom.
8. The merging of intellectual, social, physical and emotional learning and development.
9. A significant amount of cognitive work related directly to abstractions and questions previously developed, or subsequently to be developed.
10. The combining of moments of active involvement with moments of personal and group reflection and evaluation.
11. A definite organization and structure which define the limits of the experience and state expectations, but within which the participants have freedom to make decisions, choices, and even mistakes.
12. An economic and structural reasonableness which allows the curriculum to effectively compete for dollars and other resources within an educational economy which is limited in its resources.

Cindy Simpson are among a few of the names that come to mind as pioneers of "the PA way." Today, all of these people continue to be active contributors to the field through writing about and seeking new ways to expand applications of the original program concept.

Project Adventure's mission statement captures its commitment to developing people, organizations, communities, and the profession. The company wishes to be the leading organization helping others use adventure education as a catalyst for personal and professional change and growth. Its services are worldwide and include exemplary training which inspires clients to develop creative new applications in their own environments, high-quality publications, challenge course design and construction, and a wide slate of products for adventure-based programs. Perhaps their "train the trainer" workshops best exemplify their contribution to developmental adventure programs.

Picking up a Project Adventure workshop catalog is, in and of itself, an educational experience. The answer to the question "What does adventure mean?" provides an initial framework for everything PA offers. Taking the risk of self-motivated learning, developing trust and confidence in oneself, learning how to navigate and achieve as part of a group, and discovering the potential for lifelong learning adventure are the corner stones of the "PA way." Clients are challenged to bring adventure to their work and to discover a learning experience that is significant, supportive, provocative, satisfying, and fun. Project Adventure categorizes its workshops into five strands. Excluding therapeutic and recreation strands from this discussion, several workshops are examples of developmental adventure because they seek to help potential facilitators acquire the skills and understandings needed to work in their own contexts with populations to achieve the central goals outlined by Ringer and Gillis (1995) as individual growth and group effectiveness.

Prouty (1990) writes that all of the Project Adventure models would not work if there was not an effective arsenal of activities that could be used to accomplish program aims. It is the "effective" arsenal "used to accomplish program aims" that distinguishes this developmental program example. A PA program generally begins with icebreakers. These are activities that will help people to "do" together, by getting to know a little (or a little more) about each other. Some groups may need to learn names, while other groups learn new things about colleagues, classmates, or friends. Then, constantly assessing and reassessing the group and its goals, the facilitator offers the group an opportunity to participate in a spiraling sequence of warmups, games, initiative tasks, and low-rope elements. These activities are selected and framed according to the particular development needs of the group and the individuals who comprise the group. Finally, a peak experience is offered. Most often the peak experience is a high ropes course; however, alternatives such as group service projects or expeditions are also used by Project Adventure.

The PA way is characterized primarily by the use of nonwilderness training using games, initiatives, and ropes course elements to meet the particular goals for training in corporate, therapeutic, educational, and social service settings. There are a number of important components in a Project Adventure program that result in a sequence of activities. One is the need to clarify individual goals or expectations so that the individual, with the help of the group, can work toward accomplishing these goals. Another component of a PA experience is the establishment of a contract or agreement about how the group will behave collectively and how its members will interact with each other. Project Adventure's Full Value Contract is a symbolic representation of this agreement. Participants experience a variety of ways to create a Full Value Contract in a PA train-the-trainer workshop so that they can select the method that is most appropriate for their group. Even the group that meets for a couple of hours, once a week for months, will benefit from having a clear and functional behavior contract.

Project Adventure is a pioneer of debriefing. Called processing, reflecting, reviewing or debriefing, it means a deliberate process for drawing learning from the experience. It is not unusual for a person who participates in a Project Adventure developmental program to participate in a debriefing at several points throughout a program as the facilitator builds understandings and awareness to ready the group for the peak experience.

I have often referred to the Project Adventure model as "canned or simulated adventure." In 1988 I had the opportunity to get involved with the organization when, at Acadia University in Nova Scotia, I was given the opportunity to host an Adventure-Based Counseling catalog workshop and applied to become a PA trainer. I learned that my assumption that it was necessary to use a wilderness model for achieving developmental objectives was narrowly conceived. Both avenues offer valuable and different opportunities and are equally powerful mechanisms for use in our field. The PA model permits a facilitator to construct experiences that may be more pointedly tailored to the developmental goals of the client.

The carefully sequenced set of activities, that includes icebreakers, warmups, games, initiatives, and low-rope and high-rope elements, challenges participants to clarify and work toward achieving appropriate individual and group goals. In a Project Adventure program, groups live by a contract that is established through group consensus about important group norms and values, and is used by the facilitator and the group to assess individual and group progress.

YMCA Camp Pinecrest

Owned and operated by the Toronto, Canada, YMCA, Camp Pinecrest is one of the oldest youth camps in North America. Established in the early 1900s, its reputation for innovative youth programming continues to be a model for camps worldwide. In addition to its summer residential program, the camp offers custom programs for schools and organizations that foster personal growth, group interdependence, and an appreciation for the natural world. The camp's guiding principles (Figure 3.3) are testimony to a commitment to personal growth and group effectiveness. Of particular interest to this discussion of developmental adventure programs are two components of the summer youth program, the out-trip program and the in-camp adventure program.

Camp Pinecrest has a longstanding reputation as an out-trip camp. The camp offers 2- to 15-day canoe trips as an integral part of its regular summer camp program. The length and location of the trip varies according to camper age, and is supported by an extensive in-camp instructional program. Wandering through the "out-trip shacks" located next to one of the lakes that boarder the 650 acre property, one would find a broad range of expedition equipment, meeting spaces for group planning and instruction, walls covered with topographical maps highlighting trip routes, and a food area for planning and preparing out-trip menus. Racks upon racks of canoes used only in the out-trip program are located adjacent to the buildings, as is a small challenge course, designed specifically for out-trip group development.

In addition to the regular camp out-trip program, Camp Pinecrest offers a program exclusively for 15- to 19-year-olds called "Adventure Trips: Testing the Limits of Experience." Participants may select from a menu of hiking or trekking, canoeing, kayaking, mountain biking, and sailing trips that last from two to four weeks, and take place in diverse travel destinations. Adventure Trips are promoted as "values-based" travel opportunities that develop positive self-concepts, improve confidence and instill a feeling of trust in personal and group abilities. In addition to outdoor living skills, environmental education and cultural diversity, a key component of these trips is leadership development. Trips are led by experienced and well-trained staff, who work with "trippers" to develop decision-making skills and sound judgment. By exploring and ultimately meeting new challenges, trippers learn the importance of commitment, the value of cooperation within the group, and will thrill at the excitement of group accomplishment. The experience begins at the time of registration when participants are given an assignment that pertains to the mode of travel and the location of the trip. Topics such as extended expedition menus, natural history, cultural history, fitness and conditioning, and safety and emergency procedures provide a framework for participants to communicate with camp staff and each other long before they actually meet.

At Camp Pinecrest the adventure trip group prepares for departure by participating in a series of group-building activities, finalizing menus, discussing safety and emergency procedures, inspecting equipment, sharing personal

---

Figure 3.3   YMCA Camp Pinecrest Guiding Principles

Wellness: Health is the overriding theme as we work to deliver our Mission. We believe that all programs should develop the whole person, their spirit, mind and body. All programs are developed and carried out with this holistic approach. Safety and growth are paramount in all of our activities.

Small Group Experience: We focus on each individual's developmental process. The small group experience supports the individual's growth by providing opportunities for social development, group interdependence, problem solving, leadership development, and sharing. This experience is part of developing life skills and supports the YMCA's value of community.

Democratic Living: While living and learning in a small group, people are guided through an experience in democratic living. People will learn to make choices, build friendships, and cooperate with peers through shared accountability for goals and success.

Developmental Focus: Fundamentally, our experiences provide feelings of success. All programs ensure a greater understanding of self, others and the natural world through a healthy synergy between means and outcomes.

Enjoyable Program: The principle of fun addresses not only the obvious need to enjoy the experience, but also to provide a sense of spirit and a healthy attitude toward self and others.

Environmental Focus: Our focus is a holistic approach to environmental education and stewardship. People learn about the importance of recycling, reducing, and reusing resources. Environmental education is built upon the opportunities a rustic environment provides to learn about connection to and dependence on the natural world.

---

goals, and learning some basic, necessary technical skills. This part of the adventure normally takes from one to three days. Throughout the trip, personal and group goals are a central theme. At the conclusion of the trip, the group returns to Camp Pinecrest to "debrief" the entire experience, prepare for the transition back to the home setting, and discuss how learnings transfer into everyday life. In keeping with the mission of the YMCA of Greater Toronto, Adventure Trips offer opportunities for personal growth and service to others.

In addition to the Adventure Trips program, Camp Pinecrest has four challenge course areas that are dispersed around the camp property. They are designed to be used separately or as one large course. The out-trip challenge course described previously is an example of how each course area can stand alone to enhance a specific program. The in-camp adventure program uses the remaining three areas in two ways. One area, used for "adventure-based cabin counseling," is developed to be lead by cabin counselors who are trained in precamp to facilitate basic group-building activities. This area is used to focus on interpersonal competencies such as communication, problem solving, trust, and the establishment of group norms. The area consists of a large number of props for conducting cabin group initiatives and several low-ropes elements and one of several creatively shaped Fall from Height platforms.

The remaining two areas offer an alternative to more traditional skill development opportunities like canoeing, swimming, camp craft, sailing and kayaking. One is a child-centered low- and high-challenge course, designed for use by younger campers. This area contains initiative tasks and low-ropes elements that are not only sized for smaller children, but are also selected for their suitability for addressing the individual and group development issues of younger campers. This area also offers opportunities to develop technical and group competencies that are a prerequisite for progressing to the main adventure course.

The most visible of all the challenge course areas at Camp Pinecrest is the main challenge course. This course is a combination pole and tree course, comprising initiative tasks, low- and high-ropes-course elements, and a climbing tower. Together with the other challenge course areas, more than 30 ropes course elements are available to challenge campers of every age and ability to succeed in a caring and supportive environment.

I was a consultant to the camp from 1990–1994, responsible for aspects of program evaluation, staff training and recommendations for a five-year strategic plan, that resulted in an environmental learning center, broadening and strengthening out-trip offerings, and focusing on developmental adventure objectives. The entire camp program is framed by a commitment to the growth and development of individuals and groups. The out-trip and challenge course programs described here are examples of some of the tools a carefully selected and well-trained staff use to place children at the center of the camp experience.

Georgia College and State University Quest Program

Michael Gass (1990) suggests that adventure activities began to be adapted to meet the specific needs of certain populations in the early 1970s. One of the first applications was for programs in higher education. He states that the intent and perspective of adventure programs in higher education are often extremely varied. Today adventure programs in higher education encompass a wide variety of opportunities including preparing high-school students for the rigors of university, offering professional studies in outdoor education at the undergraduate and graduate levels, enhancing content in a wide variety of arts and science courses, and training residential life staff. Gass indicates that one of the greatest developments and applications of adventure programs in higher education is with incoming student orientation.

Student orientation programs are aimed at reducing the attrition rate of the undergraduate student and ensuring a more positive transition to college life (Gass, 1990). Figure 3.4 indicates areas crucial to the development of incoming students. Gass suggests that the success of orientation programs using adventure experiences lies in their ability to effectively reach these areas that will lead to student development.

The Georgia College and State University (GC&SU) Quest program is a relatively young student orientation program that was initiated in 1996 by then assistant professor in outdoor education (and later Outdoor Center Director) Jim Wall. The Quest mission states that incoming students are provided with a fun and memorable way to make the transition from high school to university. It claims to provide a powerful avenue for personal growth and the opportunity to develop the basis for lifelong enjoyment of outdoor pursuits. Students can expect to develop leadership and communication skills and a sense of community. The program offers a vehicle to meet new friends before entering university and challenges participants to challenge themselves.

Comments made by students reflect many of the areas suggested in Figure 3.4. One student stated that faculty and staff were open and understanding, and continued to be supportive after the program was over. Another student suggested after the fact, that the transition to college was easier when someone in a first university class was familiar from the Quest program. Comments about seeing familiar faces around campus and acquiring new friends to hang out with, as well as learning a lot about oneself and how to cooperate with others, support the claims made by Gass (1990) about student orientation programs. Georgia College and State University is tracking student academic progress and retention rates in order to validate their assumptions about the long-term benefits of the program.

In 1996, 22 incoming students participated in a five-day Sea Quest, and 24 students participated in two, three-day on-site programs. The on-site programs were conceived

---

Figure 3.4   Areas Crucial to the Development of Incoming Students

1. Attachment to/isolation from peers,
2. Faculty-student interaction/isolation,
3. Focus on career development and major course of study,
4. Academic interest/boredom,
5. Inadequate preparation for college academics, and
6. Dissonance/compatibility with college environment and student expectations.

by Harriett Whipple, professor in biology and adjunct to the outdoor education program. Her vision was to familiarize incoming students with the areas around the Milledgeville, Georgia, campus and to introduce service learning to the program. In 1997 Wall and Whipple combined visions to offer two, six-day programs called Sea Quest and Mountain Quest to 40 students. With the exception of different outdoor pursuits the programs followed the same format. Beginning with a day on the challenge course at GC&SU, followed by a day of travel to the mountains and the sea and low-organized recreation activities, students participated in sea kayaking or caving and rafting, completed a service project and then returned to campus for a last exciting activity on the challenge course and a cookout. Activities were interspersed with 15 hours of class time that included the Meyers-Briggs Personality Inventory, communication skills training and team building. All programs were followed by several meetings and activities during the first quarter of classes. Three credit hours were awarded to incoming students for participating in the Quest program.

The student orientation program at GC&SU expanded again in 1998. In addition to the six-day off-site programs, several two-day programs were be piloted. The vision is to host 20 incoming students on-site, each group participating in a two-day program that is facilitated by a team of faculty, staff and student leaders trained in the outdoor education degree programs. Follow-up to all versions of the Quest program is an important commitment. The Quest program is cosponsored by Student Affairs; the Advising and Career Exploration Center; the Department of Health, Physical Education and Recreation Outdoor Education Programs; and Continuing Education and Public Services.

Audubon Expedition Institute: An Extraordinary Educational Journey

At first glance, the catalog of the Audubon Expedition Institute (AEI) is about alternative education. However, I was struck by the catalog's powerful opening remarks (Figure 3.5), which define the mission of the institute. In this opening statement AEI claims to value fundamental respect for one another, professional and personal growth, and compassion, openness, fairness, equality, and flexibility. The ingredients for including the work of the Institute as developmental programming are evident in descriptions of the program and its graduates. My intuition told me that *adventure* is also implicit throughout the 33-page catalog, even though the word is not used. So I decided to speak to members of the organization at the International Conference of the Association for Experiential Education in Asheville, North Carolina, in November 1997 to see if they think what they do is adventure.

In preparation for the encounter, I reviewed the catalog to identify words and phrases that are normally associated with adventure. I found few. Yet my intuition persisted. Risk, challenge, mastery, confrontation, personal growth, newness, flow, commitment, danger, personal test, uncertainty, competence—all words that describe adventure—ring present for me in descriptions of curriculum. At the AEE conference, I asked people associated with the organization to describe experiences that they would consider representative of these words—and they did.

One person, explaining several semester journey options, said that exploring the fjords of Newfoundland, hiking the Smoky Mountain's Wilderness, and dipping into Yellowstone's thermal waters in November present new experiences that are full of opportunities for risk and challenge. Another person talked about his experience as transformational. He said that for the first time he understood how an education that integrates traditional academic subjects like ecology, English, and physical education within a learning community that includes intimate connections to all species within natural systems, helped him discover his own voice, the voices of other species, and the voice of the land. The group spoke about how each person is responsible for personal, community, and environmental health, and how they, individually and collectively, are challenged to master facilitation, group decision making, and cooperative living skills. Then, when asked to respond to the list of words representing features associated with adventure, without exception, every word I offered was considered a living component in their experience of the Audubon Expedition Institute.

Tim Hortons Children's Foundation

The Tim Hortons Children's Foundation (THCF) was created in Tim Horton's memory, his belief in the value of

---

Figure 3.5   The Audubon Expedition Institute Mission

The Audubon Expedition Institute program is carefully crafted to ensure that a student's experience will include ecological literacy, multidisciplinary learning, and conflict resolution, as well as basic elements that enable one to use the knowledge gained in personal and professional settings.

As students create their expedition community, they learn to understand and manage fear and resistance—within themselves and others, to move through difficult issues, and to effect positive change. Students learn to listen to and honor people from different walks of life while, at the same time, strengthening their own ethical base.

our children and his commitment to giving something back to communities. When Tim Horton, a well-known hockey player, died in 1974, his partner Ron Joyce established the children's foundation in his memory. In 1975 the first camp in Parry Sound, Ontario was established serving 200 children from Ontario, Nova Scotia, and New Brunswick. Today, 2,200 children attend the four camps in Alberta, Ontario, Quebec, and Nova Scotia, and an additional 3,300 children attend summer day camps and winter residential camps. In 1995 Tim Hortons merged with American hamburger giant Wendy's, though the foundation continues to operate as a separate entity. Future plans include opening a fifth camp in the year 2000, located somewhere in the United States.

Campers, boys and girls ages 9 to 12, are from monetarily underprivileged families and, were it not for the THCF, would not have the opportunity to experience camp. They come from rural and urban communities across Canada and parts of the United States, and from diverse cultural and ethnic backgrounds. Selected for this camping adventure by local store owners who work with community schools, churches, clubs, agencies like Big Brothers and Big Sisters, and the Dave Thomas Foundation for Adoption, campers are generally sent to a camp outside of their home province or state.

In the previous example, the Audubon Expedition Institute, I was clear that development is a central part of the experience and intuitive that it is an adventure program. Here I am clear that adventure is a central part of the experience and intuitive that it is a developmental program. The camps, situated in the foothills of the Rocky Mountains, on an Ontario Canadian Shield lake, on the Northumberland Strait off the coast of Nova Scotia, and on the Ottawa River south of the nation's capital, offer a wide variety of opportunities for adventure. Campers may sleep in real teepees, dig for clams, go whitewater rafting, rock climbing, sailing, hiking, canoeing or camping in the wilderness. At first glance, this example might fit more clearly into recreation adventure programming; however, the goals (Figure 3.6) as stated in their literature prompted me to investigate further.

The foundation's basic philosophical premise tips the scale toward development. These camps are built on the premise that it is possible to foster new hopes and dreams in the minds of the children who attend camp, and that the experience will show them that the future can be bright for everyone. One parent said the camp gave her children the trip of a lifetime and the ability to see life as a wonderful adventure where good things happen. Together with a commitment to developing future leaders who respect and value diversity, and community involvement, this program surpasses the goals of recreation programming because there is a conscious effort to contribute to building positive self-concept and creating an environment in which individuals and groups learn to live with respect for self, others, and the natural world.

Outward Bound

Greene and Thompson (1990) state that the program known as Outward Bound grew out of the need to instill a spiritual tenacity and the will to survive in young British seamen whose ships were torpedoed by German U-boats during World War II. Its beginnings as a school for survival has evolved into an action-oriented program for personal growth, service to others, and physical preparedness. In keeping with the metaphor of heading out to sea on an adventure that requires participants to leave the safety of home and daily routine to cope with the unfamiliar, the uncomfortable, the difficult, and the adventurous, in search of an opportunity to understand, test, and demonstrate their own resources, participants are challenged to learn about themselves and the world and discover endless possibilities for personal growth. Outward Bound participants come to realize that the limits to their own potential for personal growth are mostly imagined and self-imposed.

Outward Bound claims to have not only launched the outdoor education movement in North America, but it also is recognized as a major contributor to industry standards in safety, program design, and leadership. Any search for evidence of program adventure, program success, or descriptions will produce literature spanning several decades about Outward Bound and may contributions by Outward Bound staff. Its contribution to adventure education continues to be well-documented and a forceful claim for the use of adventure to achieve personal and group developmental goals.

Figure 3.6 The Tim Hortons Children's Foundation Goals

The Tim Hortons Children's Foundation helps campers to:

1. Develop self-confidence, self-respect, and an appreciation of their own worth as individuals.
2. Create an environment for living together in which there are opportunities for understanding people with various backgrounds and experiences.
3. Achieve and maintain physical fitness and mental well-being.
4. Develop a climate that encourages creativity, imagination, and a sense of adventure.
5. Develop an appreciation of our natural resources and an understanding of their importance.
6. Develop their capacities for initiative and leadership, and for using them responsibly and effectively in their own groups, camp, family, and community life.
7. Develop an understanding of the cultural and geographic characteristics of Canada.
8. Above all, to make the camp experience one of *joy* and *fun* for each camper.

The information in Figure 3.7 is included in course catalogs and provides an indication of the organization's mission, as well as some insight into how its mission is achieved. Offering courses that employ a wide range of outdoor pursuits like canoeing, sailing, climbing, kayaking, dogsledding, desert canyoneering, whitewater rafting, and backpacking in many of North America's premier wilderness areas, Outward Bound is a total workout in body, mind and spirit.

The organization has expanded over the years to include many adaptations of the original standard course. At the center of all courses is a balance of fun, challenge, and learning that required full participation in order to achieve success. In preparation for writing this chapter, I reviewed a number of Outward Bound documents and spoke with several staff members. I was not surprised to learn that the "standard" course has not changed much since my affiliation with one of the Canadian schools in the late 1970s. I have used Outward Bound's recipe for success on many occasions in a variety of recreation, education and corporate settings, and believe it is worth describing here.

Essentially a standard course includes some version of six components that unfold within the context of a small group experience. The first phase comprises several days of training in outdoor, backcountry travel and working together as a group. Participants engage in challenge course activities and learn technical skills to prepare for the next phase of the course. In the second phase, the expedition phase, participants undertake a series of progressively more challenging experiences, as instructors begin to relinquish planning and decision making to the group. Participants are encouraged to realize the success of their decisions and plans, and learn from mistakes. Following the major expedition, a one- to three-day solo provides an opportunity to reflect, relax and recharge after a flurry of challenging activities and group experiences. Solos take place at an isolated campsite and participants are provided with water, food, and other essentials, and monitored by instructors. The final expedition is planned and undertaken by the patrol group to apply newly developed wilderness, teamwork, judgment and decision-making skills. Instructors periodically check on the expedition group or participate as silent members, intervening only to ensure individual and group safety. Most courses include a service project to extend the ethic of service that is cultivated in the base group to the outside world. Projects may include trail construction or maintenance, assisting the elderly with chores, planting trees, duty in a soup kitchen, or teaching handicapped children how to camp. The course ends with a personal challenge event like a run, ski, row, or paddle of sufficient length to test endurance. A celebration that recognizes individual and team achievements brings closure to the course. The entire course is framed by a goal to help participants make environmentally responsible choices in daily life through learning leave-no-trace camping and travel skills, natural history and ecosystem preservation concepts.

Outward Bound offers courses that vary in activity and length. Catalog and custom courses are offered for specific client groups such as young adults, adults, women, university students, professional groups, teachers, couples, parents and children, and managers. The minimum age of clients is 16. All courses seek to help individuals and groups grow and learn within the context of a small group and a wilderness setting.

Figure 3.7   Outward Bound Outdoor Education Program

Outward Bound is the leading outdoor education program that:

1. Is founded on quality and safety—Our instructors, carefully selected, trained and reviewed are the most respected wilderness educators in the world. Though widely imitated, our courses stand without peer. Our safety record is the envy of the industry, thanks to expert, small groups, the most advanced risk management available and commitment to student safety as our number one priority.

2. Is dedicated to true adventure—Outward Bound offers true backcountry expeditions that require each individual's active involvement. Our instructors inform, inspire, then step back. With increasing skill, you lead, follow, set up camp, use technical equipment and operate safety systems.

3. Makes a difference in people's lives—Quite simply, Outward Bound works. Our courses compel you to dig deep. Amidst encouragement and support, you transcend perceived limits, and find within yourself new strengths—gain trust, compassion, resolve, respect for the environment, and the energy to put it all to work for yourself and your community.

Essential Features of Developmental Adventure Programs

Soltis (1978) offers three simple ways to establish an understanding of complex concepts. He calls one of these procedures "generic type" concept analysis. The question asked is: "What features must a developmental adventure program have to be called developmental adventure education?" He suggests that a set of potentially necessary features for developmental adventure may be drawn from clear standard cases, and then tested, in this case, against the counter that recreation and therapeutic adventure programs provide. While the clear standard cases outlined previously do not represent a definitive set of examples, I believe they do provide enough insight into developmental adventure programs to foster understanding. The features offered here, may then be tested against the other categories of adventure programs described in this book and redefined as we gain a better understanding of developmental adventure.

Developmental Goals

As review, Figure 3.8 states the central goal and themes identified by Ringer and Gillis (1995) and discussed earlier. It is clear that developmental adventure consciously seeks to effect change at the intrapersonal or interpersonal level. The arena for change is that which is considered basic for the general population. In other words, if we were to develop profiles of the basic characteristics for personal or group success, they would include the themes outlined by Ringer and Gillis. Our standard cases confirm these themes and offer additional ones for developmental adventure educators to consider.

Developmental adventure educators seek to develop in groups and individuals an appreciation of diversity. This implies actively valuing the contributions each person brings to a group, as well as nurturing a belief in oneself, and the willingness and ability to negotiate a position or solution that is based on consensus. Shared vision that honors individuality is a central theme in developmental adventure that is explicit in all of the cases discussed. The shared vision may be for an inclusive organization or a cohesive cabin group. This commitment necessitates that facilitators engage individuals and groups in a process to address diversity issues and build related competencies in areas like cooperation, communication, respect, problem solving, and safety.

There appears, as well, to be a commitment to cultivating a service ethic in participants. Service ultimately may be to one's home community or place of employment. It may evolve from an understanding of the cabin group or the management team as a community and the in-the-moment experience that the whole is greater than the sum of its parts, if we choose to make it so. Promoting environmental stewardship may be viewed as service to the global community, inspired by a reverence for and belief in the truth that we are all connected to and dependent on the natural world. Valuing social justice often defines the nature of the service project and all projects are considered as service learning. The assumption that service involves learning to serve, as well as serving to learn is a fundamental tenet of experiential education.

Self-reliance and self-effectance are goals that developmental programs hold in common. In some cases these goals are described as a healthy synergy between means and outcomes. In other cases, they are described in terms of an understanding that preconceived barriers to what is possible often hold both the group and the individual from experiencing success. Managing fear and resistance, within self and others, and believing that each individual has the capacity to make the world a better place, starting with and based on a strong and healthy self-concept, are central goals in developmental adventure programs.

Organizations and staff engaged in developmental adventure programs place intrapersonal and interpersonal growth overtly and consciously at the center of programs and services. They employ strategies to address these goals, and evaluate themselves according to how well they achieve these goals. This is not to say that these programs do not produce outcomes normally associated with recreation adventure programs. Most of the programs described in this chapter indicate that lifelong learning and enjoying outdoor recreation are products of the experience they offer; however, there is deliberate intention to go beyond the goals normally associated with recreation and leisure education. Also, it is not uncommon for developmental adventure programs to form partnerships with therapeutic programs and collaborate on aspects of program delivery, or refer participants to specific therapeutic agencies and services.

Deliberate and Sequential Process

Program activities are sequenced to build individual and group mastery by carefully bringing individuals and groups to a place where the envelope, often referred to as perceived limits, is pushed. Once mastery is accomplished, and the experience is reflected upon, another line is drawn. Group intradependence is increasingly necessary, as individuals engage risk and challenge and push themselves, and their groups, to ever-increasing levels of growth. A well-sequenced program, informed by participant goals and group commitment, led by skillful facilitators able to assess individual and group on the fly and adjust program accordingly, are the building blocks of developmental adventure.

The Use of Risk and Challenge

Risk, and consequently challenge, may be emotional, social, or physical. Both are idiosyncratic; that is, they exist in the eye of the beholder, having meaning that is personally constructed. One person may perceive the need to speak out and ask for what is needed primarily as social

---

Figure 3.8	Central Goal and Themes for Developmental Adventure

1. Change in sense of identity or self-concept at a intrapersonal level and/or change in group/team effectiveness at the interpersonal level.
2. Generic themes such as cooperation, communication, and problem solving are addressed at both levels to improve behavior in important relationships in vocational or avocational settings.

risk. Another person may perceive paddling a canoe down a wild river primarily as a physical risk and secondly as a social risk because of the possibility for negative peer judgment associated with competency. Some may perceive that being lowered to the ground by another group member who has been instructed in proper belaying technique as the ultimate challenge in risk taking. Project Adventure uses the term *challenge-by-choice* to indicate to people that each person is free to determine for himself or herself the nature and degree of challenge to participate in. A commitment to the principle of challenge-by-choice, regardless of the context of an adventure program, ensures that challenge is defined and accepted by the learner. Facilitators of developmental programs use individual and group response to risk and challenge to create nurture opportunities for growth. Therefore, within an environment of fun, learning and excitement, risk and challenge provide fertile ground.

Group Context

The interaction between a group and the individuals in the group is the most salient and powerful feature of developmental adventure. In any context, wilderness or challenge course, and regardless of the specific characteristics of the client group, it is in group activity that a major source of "grist for the mill" is created and processed. Resultant developmental opportunities may arise for an individual or for the group. Developmental adventure facilitators use a variety of techniques to encourage individuals to clarify and share goals, and seek group support for achieving them. Groups are provided with opportunities to link success criteria to group effectiveness in a continual process of assessment. Both the individual and group are challenged to change to meet personal and group goals.

Experiential Cycle

Key to the delivery of adventure education is experiential education. The origins of what is now called "the" experiential cycle is discussed by Coleman (1977) when he compares the information assimilation process to experiential learning. It is important to understand that experiential education is not just "learning by doing." We learn about crossing a busy road through experience; however, as an educational enterprise, experiential education is a deliberate process that is informed by a body of knowledge, a set of procedures, and specific values about learning and teaching. It is more than just experience. It is from this informed and deliberate process that developmental adventure educators hone their craft.

Each experience is selected to maximize opportunity for personal or group growth. The deliberate sequence of experiences discussed earlier is the experiential cycle repeated, with each new activity selected on the basis of the facilitator's assessment of individual and group progress toward developmental goals and other factors such as learning style and readiness. Sometimes the facilitator will "front-load" or "frame" an activity to mirror developmental goals. Sometimes the experience unfolds and the facilitator assists individuals or groups to address goals through "processing," "reviewing," or "debriefing." Risk and challenge is increased as mastery and understanding is reached. This does not mean that experiences are not fun or enjoyable; it means that the developmental adventure educator is more deliberate and conscious about learning from experience. Learnings are focused on developmental goals and ultimately applied to real-life situations to maximize "transfer of learning." Appropriately conceived, framed and processed, experiences provide "natural consequences" that are like reality.

All of the features offered as essential for developmental adventure imply that the facilitator possesses a particular set of competencies. Understanding the language of experiential education, the ability to design appropriate developmental programs that focus on individual and group goals, and skill in facilitating change using a range of techniques, are all important aspects of the developmental adventure program. These and other topics are addressed in subsequent parts of this book.

References

Cantrell, D. (1990, November). *Alternative paradigms in environmental education: The interpretive perspective.* Paper presented at the meeting of the North American Association for Environmental Education, San Antonio, Texas.

Chan Kim, W., and Mauborgne, R. (1997). Fair process: Managing in the knowledge economy. *Harvard Business Review,* July-August, 65–75.

Coleman, J. A. (1977). Differences between experiential and classroom learning. In M. T. Keeton (Ed.), *Experiential learning: Rationale, characteristics, and assessment.* San Francisco, CA: Jossey-Bass Publishers.

Cousineau, C. (1978). The nature of adventure education. *ANEE* (ERIC Document Reproduction Service No. Ed 171 474).

Cousineau, C. (1982). A call for simplicity in outdoor recreation. *Recreation Canada,* April, 48–50.

Donaldson, G. W., and Donaldson, L. E. (1958). Outdoor education: a definition. *The Journal of Health, Physical Education and Recreation, 29*(17), 63–64.

Ewert, A. W. (1989). *Outdoor adventure pursuits: Foundations, models, and theories.* Columbus, OH: Publishing Horizons.

Ewert, A., and Schreyer, R. (1990, March 29–31). *Risk recreation: Social trends and implications for the 1990s.* Paper presented at the Outdoor Recreation TRENDS Symposium III, Indianapolis, Indiana.

Ford, P. (1981). *Principles and practices of outdoor and environmental education.* New York, NY: Wiley & Sons.

Gass, M. (1990). Adventure programs in higher education. In J. C. Miles and S. Priest (Eds.), *Adventure education* (pp. 385–401). State College, PA: Venture Publishing, Inc.

Greene, J. H., and Thompson, D. (1990). Outward Bound USA. In J. C. Miles and S. Priest (Eds.), *Adventure education* (pp. 5–9). State College, PA: Venture Publishing, Inc.

Grenier, J. (1983). Outdoor education programs in Canadian universities. *Journal of Health, Physical Education and Recreation, 5*(49), 7–9.

Hirsch, J. (1992). *Conceptions of outdoor education that underlie outdoor education programs at English-speaking Canadian universities.* (Doctoral dissertation, University of British Columbia.) Dissertation Abstracts International, NN79700.

Jensen, M., and Briggs-Young, A. (1981). Alternatives for outdoor education programming. *Journal of Health, Physical Education, Recreation and Dance,* October, 64–67.

Kelly, E. C. (1972). Reasons for outdoor education. In G. W. Donaldson and O. Goering (Eds.), *Perspectives on outdoor education.* Dubuque, IA: W. C. Brown.

March, B. (1982). A rationale for outdoor pursuits. *Connections Journal, 1*(2), 3–4.

Meier, J. (Ed.). (1978, April). High-adventure leisure pursuits and risk recreation. *Journal of Physical Education and Recreation,* pp. 13–17.

Meier, J., Morash, T., and Welton, G. (1987). *High-adventure outdoor pursuits: Organization and leadership* (2nd ed.). Columbus, OH: Publishing Horizons, Inc.

Miles, J. C. (1982). Environmental education: Broadening the concept. *Journal of Experiential Education, 14*(1), 4–13.

Priest, S. (1986). Redefining outdoor education: A matter of many relationships. *Journal of Environmental Education, 17*(3), 13–15.

Prouty, D. (1990). Project adventure: A brief history. In J. C. Miles and S. Priest (Eds.), *Adventure education* (pp. 97–109). State College, PA: Venture Publishing, Inc.

Raffin, J. (1986). Dilemma in outdoor education. *Outdoor Recreation Research Journal, 1,* 31–40.

Ringer, M., and Gillis, H. L. (1995, May). Managing psychological depth in adventure programming. *The Journal of Experiential Education, 18*(1).

Soltis, J. F. (1978). *An introduction to the analysis of education concepts.* Reading, MA: Addison-Wesley Publishing Company.

Slopek, D. (1997, October). Giving kids a camping adventure of a lifetime. *Wendy's Magazine,* pp. 11–13.

White, R. G., Schreyer, R., and Downing, K. (1980, April). Trends in emerging and high-risk activities. *National Outdoor Recreation Trends Symposium,* Durham, NH, pp. 20–23.

Wileman, D. L., and Baker, B. N. (1996). Some major research findings regarding the human element in project management. In D. I. Cleland and W. R. King (Eds.), *Project management handbook* (pp. 847–866). New York, NY: Van Nostrand Reinhold.

Chapter 4

Adventure as Therapy

H. L. "Lee" Gillis, Jr.
Georgia College and State University

T. Martin Ringer
Martin Ringer Consulting

Introduction

Just as psychotherapy differs from casual conversation, adventure therapy differs from recreational, educational, or developmental adventure in the way in which activities are used to bring about change. In this chapter, the basic tenets of adventure therapy are described and the broad types of therapeutic programming commonly practiced throughout the world are outlined. While little is known through research as to how program types differ, some speculation is offered from the writers' experience and from other writings that can help characterize clients who participate in these therapeutic experiences. Principles that distinguish the therapeutic use of adventure from other forms of adventure are then followed by a discussion of some of the problems and benefits that arise from conducting therapy outside the clinician's office. Finally opportunities for research into the effectiveness of adventure programming in therapeutic contexts are examined.

An Overview of Adventure Therapy

Adventure therapy is the deliberate, strategic combination of adventure activities with therapeutic change processes with the goal of making lasting changes in the lives of participants. Adventure provides the concrete, action-based, experiential medium for therapy. The specific activity used is (ideally) chosen to achieve a particular therapeutic goal. For example, having two persons who have difficulties in their relationship, such as a father and son or husband and wife, paddle a canoe will require them to cooperate in order to be successful. A 14-day backpacking trip for a group of adjudicated youth provides a self-contained purposeful therapeutic community where tasks such as erecting tents, reading a compass, or cooking a meal provide challenges in communication and discipline which can be utilized for therapeutic outcomes. These are just small examples of how adventure can be programmed for therapeutic ends.

Adventure activity approaches have much of their documented history in the philosophies of experiential learning inherent in Outward Bound, a wilderness-based program teaching self-discipline and teamwork through adventure activities (Bacon, 1983). Some might even say that Kurt Hahn, who helped shaped the foundations of the Outward Bound movement might be one of the first adventure therapists, due to the work he did in molding young soldiers to develop a "will to live" (Thomas, 1980). Indeed, the use of outdoor, adventure experiences for therapeutic purposes is documented with such clinical populations as substance abusers (Gass and McPhee, 1990; Gillis and Simpson, 1991), adjudicated youth (Bacon and Kimball, 1989; Kelly and Baer, 1968; Kimball, 1983; O'Brien, 1990), clients served in private practices (Berman and Davis-Berman, 1989) and psychiatric hospitals (Schoel, Prouty, and Radcliffe, 1988; Stich and Senior, 1984; Stich and Sussman, 1981).

While we use the term *adventure therapy* (e.g., Gass, 1991; Stich and Senior, 1984) in this chapter, do note that many terms have been used historically to describe the therapeutic use of adventure programming. These terms include *adventure-based counseling* (Maizell, 1988; Schoel et al, 1988), *outdoor-adventure pursuits* (Ewert, 1989), *therapeutic adventure programs* (Wichmann, 1991), *therapeutic camping* (Rice, 1988; Walton, 1985), *wilderness therapy* (e.g., Bacon and Kimball, 1989; Berman and Davis-Berman, 1993; Levitt, 1982), and *wilderness-adventure therapy* (e.g., Bandoroff, 1990). While there may be subtle differences in how authors describe these various approaches goals appear to be the same to most people who read the literature or listen to therapists describe what they do.

Types of Adventure Therapy Programs

Gass (1993) observed, and Crisp (1997) confirmed, that at least three areas of adventure therapy exist. They include adventure-based therapy, wilderness therapy and long-term residential camping. These types of programming are characterized by where adventure therapy is taking place, for what length of time, and the type of programming being utilized.

The activity-based group work, or what Gass calls "adventure-based therapy" centers on team games, problem-solving initiatives, and sometimes with the addition of low- and high-challenge ropes course activities. This approach takes place near a facility and rarely in "remote" settings. Adventure-based therapy programs appear to be most popular in the United States. In other areas such as Europe, Australia, and New Zealand more reliance is placed on using natural settings and journey-based adventure activities (Crisp, 1997).

Wilderness therapy appears to come in both short- and long-term expedition formats. The short-term formats are often associated with Outward Bound's model (Bacon, 1983). Programs derived from the Outward Bound model utilize an expedition format that has elements of teaching and practicing wilderness skills. Expeditions range from 7 to 31 days and are mainly conducted in remote settings as the word *wilderness* implies.

Longer wilderness expeditions (60 days or longer) appear to differ from the Outward Bound model but have not been studied with as much clarity to be able to clearly highlight their differences here. From observation, it would appear that many of these programs focus on survival skills.

The long-term residential camping programs appear to be flourishing in the southeast and mid-Atlantic regions of the United States through programs designed by Eckerd Family Wilderness and Three Springs, Inc. It would appear from available literature that published efficacy studies have not been as abundant as the reported growth of these programs. There do not appear to be any long-term residential adventure therapy programs outside the United States.

Research results indicate that outcomes of adventure therapy programming are still mixed. It remains difficult to tell just what is taking place in these various settings that falls under the label of adventure therapy. It is difficult to definitively categorize studies exclusively into the three areas described here. Indeed, many programs are a mixture of an activity base that highlights ropes course activities and some form of an expedition.

There is little literature to date that describes the rationale for choosing one particular approach over another. For example, why does one program use 10-day expeditions with adjudicated youth while another uses mainly adventure-based therapy for what appears to be the same client group? There remains much research work to do in finding answers to this question.

Common Characteristics of Adventure Therapy Activities and Programs

Adventure therapy activities are most often group-based, and interventions are derived from principles underpinning psychology, sociology, education, and other disciplines that inform the process of human change. The goals of adventure therapy interventions are developed in response to client needs; sometimes those needs are from individual clients within the group, and other times the needs are those of the entire group. Common goals of adventure therapy include resocialization, reducing criminal offending, treating substance abuse, providing remedy for dysfunctional interaction with others, and improving clients' management of their own emotional and social lives. Adventure therapy targets participants' cognition, affect, behavior, and personality. The purpose of many adventure therapy programs is to remedy dysfunction in the client. Although adventure therapy is primarily a group-based process, some one-on-one therapeutic techniques and family therapy techniques are used in most programs.

Some clients are referred to programs on a voluntary basis, but others are offered placement on programs as a trade-off for reduced prison sentences or a reduction in other sanctions. Examples of such client groups are young offenders (Gillis and McLeod, 1992). Successful indoor adventure activities have been used for treating substance abuse with adjudicated adolescents and incarcerated adults (Gillis and McLeod, 1992), victims and perpetrators of abuse (Simpson and Gillis, 1997), clients with eating disorders (Maguire and Priest, 1994) and difficult populations in school settings (Handley, 1993).

Adventure therapy involves both the use of traditional therapeutic interventions and the strategic use of an activity perceived as being very risky by the client as a therapeutic milieu. The additional factor in adventure therapy as compared to conventional therapy programs is the potential to harness the physical environment and the adventure activities themselves for therapeutic outcomes. The adventure therapist needs to be a strategist who is constantly asking, "How will this next activity and its associated physical conditions create opportunities to create therapeutic movement in this group of clients?"

For the sake of keeping it simple, this chapter will use *adventure therapy* as a generic term to denote an active, strategic approach to working with people with a variety of abilities utilizing adventure activities, which involve some form of perceived risk, as the primary therapeutic medium. The "depth" to which programs work with clients determines whether or not an adventure program is adventure therapy or some other form of adventure such as recreation (Ringer and Gillis, 1996). This difference is explored next.

The Difference Between Recreational Adventure Programs and Adventure Therapy Programs

General-purpose adventure programs seek to entertain or educate their participants although they may provide opportunities for personal growth. Adventure therapy programs however focus *specifically* on creating circumstances likely to engender change in participants. Adventure activities are used because of their powerful therapeutic leverage. Both recreational adventure programs and adventure therapy programs need to be physically safe, responsive to participants' needs, and purposeful. Effective adventure therapy programs have the following *additional* features:

1. Potential clients are assessed and screened prior to their being accepted into a program. Such assessment is intended to screen out persons who have a strong tendency towards behaviors that make them unmanageable in wilderness and remote settings and settings with high levels of potential physical danger. Examples of such behaviors included current substance abuse, sexual (abusing) aggression, physical violence, and psychosis. Programs with restricted admission, specially designed activities and highly skilled staff

may still be able to target clients with these "unsuitable" behaviors, but general-purpose adventure therapy programs are not equipped to do so (Cline, 1993; Tippett, 1993).

2. Persons of psychological significance to the clients, such as relatives, friends and mentors are often involved in the program. Since most adventure therapy programs are relatively short term, the persons who comprise the client's social system are involved so that the changes in the clients persist after the adventure therapy program has ended (Barrett, 1994; Stainton and Balston, 1995).

3. Programs incorporate "treatment" plans for each client as well as plans to suit the development of each *group* of clients (Bacon and Kimball, 1989; Berman, 1995; Gray and Yerkes, 1995).

4. Multidisciplined staff teams are usually deployed because the combination of outdoor activity of skills and therapeutic skills required is usually beyond the capacity of any one leader. Leader teams are made up of persons who have a proven capacity to work together and who can communicate clearly with each other about their own areas of expertise (Berman, 1995; Ringer, 1997; Ringer and Berman, 1995).

5. Interventions are constantly "fine tuned" because the complexity of human systems suggests that progress is not predictable for any part of the system (Gass and Gillis, 1995). Regular reviews are conducted on program effectiveness from the point of view of each client, the group as a whole, and each leader or therapist.

6. Program design and implementation includes follow-up, clear termination with each client, closure of each group, and referral of clients to other agencies where applicable (Gerstein, 1994).

Those six "quality" criteria could well apply to community-based psychotherapy programs, but they still do not answer the question, "On what therapeutic principles or principles of human change do you base your interventions?" In our research into adventure therapy programs we have found that the nature of the intervention depends heavily on the client-presenting problem, the goal of treatment and the type of diagnostic issues on which programs focus.

In broad terms it is possible to view adventure therapy programs as applying principles from four different psychological orientations. These are, existential or humanistic, psychodynamic, systemic and behaviorist. The behaviorist forms of intervention are generally applied to impulsive and nonreflective clients. Programs of a more humanistic, psychodynamic, or systemic nature tend to cater to developmentally mature client groups (Ringer and Gillis, 1996). Two examples will be used here—one that illustrates the application of psychodynamic principles in adventure therapy and the other that integrates behaviorist principles with an adventure activity.

An Example of a Psychodynamic Approach in an Adventure Setting

Larry was referred to an adventure therapy program because he was "beating up" his wife. He was placed in a group that met for one day's activities each week. The therapist's assessment was that Larry exhibited aspects of narcissistic personality (Cline, 1993; Meares, 1992; Tippet, 1993), and so required long-term treatment where attention was paid to enabling him to repair deficits in his early development and construction of his self-structure. This goal was achieved by careful sequencing of fun activities so that group members slowly built up trust in each other while the challenge level and risk level was still low. Close attention was paid to the quality of the relationship between the therapist and the participant(s), and outbursts of anger and frustration were dealt with firmly but without isolating or rejecting the participant.

Larry was a strong, fit young man who took pride in his body. For instance, he would strip off his shirt and dive into cold water if it would help the group achieve a goal. He made a show of helping the less physical members of the group—in particular the women. Larry soon began to challenge the expertise of the group leader and talked at length about how he (Larry) had been an instructor for the helicopter evacuation team, and hence had excellent skills in rappelling and climbing.

Core elements of psychodynamic interventions are the use of transference, countertransference and projection amongst group members as sources of information that can lead the participants to useful insights. Susan, the group leader, often felt herself withdrawing from Larry and becoming angry with his dismissive behavior. She used this information by reflecting to Larry how, despite the fact that she saw him being "helpful" at a factual level, often when he spoke she struggled to find a place for herself in the group. She also wondered aloud what it was like for other group members to have just one person (Larry) who took on the role of helper, organizer and instructor. At one point Larry had an angry outburst and accused Susan of mocking him and not appreciating what he had to offer. Susan mused aloud that this seemed like a familiar feeling to him. She maintained this "neutral" reflective theme in the group and later followed up in one-on-one therapy sessions with Larry.

Following a psychodynamic-based adventure approach to adventure therapy involves using the relationship with the therapist and the activity itself to unearth previously repressed or out-of-awareness patterns of thinking and behavior in participants. Adventure therapy has a group component where clients habitual pattern of interaction become visible. The addition of stress arising from risk cuts quickly though some clients' defenses. Intense focus on learning and applying new physical skills can also distract clients from erecting their usual "false selves." Once these patterns are visible, psychodynamic therapeutic processes gradually enable clients to identify the origins of these dysfunctional patterns in their early life. The clients' internal representation of themselves as worthwhile people is gradually restored by repeated occasions where they find the therapist and other group members attentive and affirming. However, psychodynamic approaches are not suitable for all client groups. For example, male adolescents who have been referred because of repeated criminal offending often exhibit such extreme impulsive behavior that they need to be placed in programs that create strong containers. On entry to programs these clients are more suited to behaviorist-oriented interventions.

An Example of a Behaviorist Approach in an Adventure Setting

> *It is late afternoon, cold, and a sudden downpour accompanied by strong wind catches our group on an exposed hillside. Packs are thrown to the ground and we all pull our raincoats from the top of our packs. Soon we are on our way again. But Jason is not with us. He is back where we stopped. He has pulled everything out of his pack to reach his raincoat at the very bottom. His sleeping bag lies in a stream of water and he now angrily rams equipment back into his pack. His tears mix with the rain on his cheeks and his face is locked into a grimace of rage and shame. Here, Jason is learning that his choice to ignore this morning's instructions on packing a pack has unpleasant consequences. Maybe he will generalize this learning to his home life.*

Behaviorist-oriented interventions use both the natural environment and the human interaction to provide concrete "natural consequences" and "logical consequences" for participants' maladaptive behavior. The hope is that participants will internalize new behaviors and continue to behave in new ways that are likely to be appropriate for the environment to which they will return after the therapy program has ended. Sometimes behaviorist interventions are used to establish a stable climate in the group for more humanistic and psychodynamic styles to be introduced later.

The application of behaviorist principles to adventure interventions is most suitable when clients' internalized sense of responsibility is diminished, when they are constantly "acting out," and when they have a limited capacity for self-reflection. Because of the suitability of these "black box" therapies to lawbreaking clients, many programs for criminal offenders use behaviorist-oriented strategies.

Difficulties in Working With Adventure for Therapeutic Purposes

Introducing adventure activities to therapeutic settings can raise challenges that are not experienced in traditional office-based therapeutic programs. In the office setting, therapists tend to have a single role—that of therapist—whereas in adventure settings therapists often also take the roles of instructor and of safety supervisor. These multiple roles lead to the therapist being quite visible to clients as a whole person and hence change the therapeutic dynamic.

Multiple Roles: No More Blank Screen

For the psychodynamic therapist working one-on-one in an office-based setting the therapist's stance approaches that of a "blank screen" (Maxwell, 1996) onto which the client projects his or her internal world. In adventure settings the therapist has multiple roles and so may be simultaneously the therapist, the setter of limits on physical safety, and the outdoor skills instructor. The screen is far from blank (Larned, 1996). This necessitates a different mode of working and adventure therapists are still grappling with this issue. There may be equally powerful therapeutic opportunities in the therapist being more visible to the client but this has, as yet, been poorly explored.

Power Relationships Are Changed

Power relationships can be reversed in adventure settings. The person at the rear of a canoe controls the direction of the boat. Shooting the rapids with the client in control or climbing a cliff while the client provides the belay may result in new things happening in the therapeutic relationship. The significance of this change in power has yet to be researched in the context of adventure therapy. Further power issues arise when physical activities are conducted that require high skill levels. In these cases the psychotherapist seldom has the technical outdoor skills or the safety skills to take charge of the activity. So the less therapeutically minded practitioner may be "in charge" and setting limits on clients' behavior. Sometimes the adventure therapist may see therapeutic potential lost through the outdoor pursuit instructor's lack of awareness of psycho-

logical issues. This problem can be partly overcome through adequate preplanning when therapist and instructor share information and perspectives on their tasks and develop role clarity before starting with the group.

Opportunities for Psychotherapists

Although some psychologists are enthusiastic adventure therapists (Crisp, 1996), there is a scarcity of clinically trained psychotherapists who currently practice adventure therapy (Ringer, 1997). Adventure therapy is becoming better organized and more popular throughout the world. Many adventure practitioners have shared their vision for developing adventure therapy programs; some realize their lack of clinical skills to turn this vision to reality. For those therapists who do take to the woods to try adventure therapy there are some spectacular rewards. Wonderful things happen when you spend 10 days in the wilderness with dysfunctional adolescents. The experience of working in radically new structures of time and space is illuminating. For example, on a 10-day expedition the therapist is "on call" for 240 hours on end and therapeutic sessions seldom begin and end as they do in an office setting. Outdoor adventure activities also create opportunities for exploration of therapeutic techniques. Have you ever wondered how the therapeutic dynamic would shift if you were walking alongside your client on a long hike? The communication in the dyad becomes very rich as variations in pace and space create a new therapeutic context. The campfire is another powerful therapeutic milieu, as is the mountain top as you contemplate the clouds catching on fire when the sun sinks to the west.

While the attraction to practicing therapy using adventure appears to continue to grow, the evidence that what is happening in the field is indeed working remains mostly anecdotal. Therapists who wish to introduce adventure into a traditional setting are hindered by a lack of credible research that confirms the effectiveness of adventure-based approaches. Formal research is most often the concern of aspiring students and much of what is done never reaches professional journals. Thus the credibility of adventure therapy suffers and will continue to do so until the field produces an improved base of published research.

Research Opportunities in Adventure Therapy

Available reviews of the literature (Bandoroff, 1990; Burton, 1981; Ewert, 1987, 1989; Levitt, 1982; Shore, 1977) appear to agree with the later findings of Hattie, Marsh, Neill, and Richards (1997) and Cason and Gillis (1995) that globally measured self-esteem has been found to increase following participation in adventure programming, though the longevity of such change and its transfer to other settings has not been empirically validated. These mentioned reviews along with writings of Bacon (1983, 1987, 1988; Bacon and Kimball, 1989), Chase (1981), Gass (1991), Kimball (1983, 1991), Haussman (1984), Roland (Roland, Summers, Friedman, Barton, and McCarthy, 1987), Schoel et al. (1988), Stich (Stich, 1983; Stich and Gaylor, 1983), and Witman (1989) support the fact that primarily adolescents have been positively impacted by adventure activities in therapeutic settings. Additional dependent variables have been studied including self-reported changes in locus of control and problem solving, staff observations of behavioral change, and other measures such as grade point average and attendance. Results of changes on these measures have been less conclusive.

Authors of available literature do not clearly indicate the population that the writer is working with, or the presenting problem(s) of that population. In many cases they do not even clearly state the outcome of the research. Trying to determine the difference between the use of therapeutic challenge activities, wilderness activities, and expeditions is difficult at best. Clearer and "cleaner" standardization of nomenclature will allow us to more clearly refine our ability to discuss benefits of different approaches to therapeutic adventure programming.

There is still no *one clearly defined and researched* method of conducting therapy with adventure activities. An increasing problem is how programs that are primarily based on challenge ropes courses or using only group initiatives are combined in the literature with programs that are primarily wilderness- (outdoor pursuit-) based. What is more troublesome is that the majority of research studies are not specific enough in their methodology so that the reader can determine if one program's findings can be compared with another's. Even practitioners from different programs, in conversations with one another at a conference, will use terms like adventure therapy or wilderness therapy interchangeably often assuming they know what each other means. The need for specificity regarding method used, as well as an accurate description of the techniques employed or protocol being followed, is long overdue in the field of adventure therapy.

The field of adventure therapy has everything to gain from putting together results of our work into a *collective document* that addresses accomplishments and effectiveness. Secondly, by *examining clinically significant events* in adventure therapy programs that are or were deemed to be of importance *by the consumer* and by communicating in language that is understandable to mental health, adventure therapy can achieve greater credibility with the more traditional field of mental health and those who hold the purse strings and benefit our potential consumers who may then be able to access adventure therapy as a viable approach to treatment.

A comprehensive analysis is needed that can address the efficacy of adventure therapy across populations, problems, and settings. We know very little of how our work stacks up collectively.

A survey is needed to highlight similarities and differences in activity-based, expedition, and residential camping that falls under the rubric of adventure therapy. As a field of practitioners, adventure therapists wait around as if someone else will do the research that will keep them in the field. Adventure therapists are their own worst enemy in that they do not value evaluation of their work or spend the time necessary to share what they do collect.

To answer the question of which approach works best with which population, researchers must make better attempts to clearly describe activities they are assessing, for how long, and with what population. A common set of information needs to be specified in writing about adventure therapy programs. Such information should include specifics about the type of programming (activity-based, expedition-based, camping-based), demographics of the population (including age, gender, and problem or diagnosis), the measurement instruments employed, and the goals of the program. A good place to start such definitions is within the titles and abstracts that are available to researchers over accessible databases.

Numerous questions also exist about competence of leaders in adventure therapy and what competencies are needed to call oneself an adventure therapist (Ringer, 1994). Once adventure therapists have gained more clarity about what works with which client groups, there will be an urgent need for the field to clarify the nature of skills and knowledge required by practitioners in order to provide quality leadership.

These are but a few of the opportunities that the field of adventure therapy must grasp in order to gain credibility and have more to say to colleagues in mental health than "we know it works, we see the impact of adventure activities on our clients, that's all we need to know."

Conclusion

Adventure therapy is a generic term that encompasses a myriad of approaches to the integration of adventure and therapy. There is great potential for group-based outdoor adventure to provide an innovative context for therapeutic interventions. Adventure offers an active experiential orientation. The natural setting offers concrete and consequential environment and the potential for meaningful practical tasks that can be harnessed for therapeutic outcomes. There are significant challenges in the application of adventure for therapeutic outcomes. First, therapists are forced into multiple roles with clients, some of which may be countertherapeutic. Second, therapists must be multiskilled. Third, the blocks of client contact are usually much longer than in conventional clinic-based therapy.

Fourth, there is much work to be done in order to demonstrate the effectiveness of adventure therapy to the larger world of mental health.

Effective programs are carefully designed, integrated with other interventions, and run by highly skilled practitioners who have an understanding of the psychology of human change as well as a practical ability to use adventure for personal change. Furthermore, professional-quality programs are constantly evaluated as to how they are working and how they can be improved. Good quality practice arises from practitioners paying close attention to the link between client group needs, activities carried out, program goals, and the model of human change implicit in the intervention. The relative youth of the field of adventure therapy offers a rich opportunity for psychotherapists who are attracted to the use of adventure for personal change and to adventure practitioners who wish to develop their expertise in human change processes.

References

Bacon, S. (1983). *The conscious use of metaphor in Outward Bound* (ERIC Document Reproduction Service No. ED296848). Denver, CO: Outward Bound.

Bacon, S. (1987). *The evolution of the Outward Bound process* (ERIC Document Reproduction Service No. ED295780). Greenwich, CT: Outward Bound.

Bacon, S. (1988). *Paradox and double binds in adventure education*. Greenwich, CT: Outward Bound.

Bacon, S. B., and Kimball, R. (1989). The wilderness challenge model. In R. D. Lyman, S. Prentice-Dunn, and S. Gabel (Eds.), *Residential and inpatient treatment of children and adolescents* (pp. 115–144). New York, NY: Plenum Press.

Bandoroff, S. (1990). *Wilderness-adventure therapy for delinquent and predelinquent youth: A review of the literature*. Unpublished manuscript, University of South Carolina, Columbia, South Carolina.

Barrett, J. (1994). Introduction. In J. Barrett (Ed.), *Enabling troubled youth: Conference and study weekend* (pp. 1–5). Ambleside, UK: Basecamp, Mabie Forest, Scotland.

Berman, D. (1995). Adventure therapy: Current status and future directions. *Journal of Experiential Education, 18*(2), 61–62.

Berman, D. S., and Davis-Berman, J. L. (1989). Wilderness therapy: A therapeutic adventure for adolescents. *Journal of Independent Social Work 3*(3), 65–77.

Berman, D. S., and Davis-Berman, J. L. (1993). *Wilderness therapy*. Dubuque, IA: Kendall/Hunt Publishing Co.

Burton, L. M. (1981). *A critical analysis and review of the research on Outward Bound and related programs*. (Doctoral dissertation, The State University of New Jersey, Rutgers, New Jersey). Dissertation Abstracts International, 42, 1581B.

Cason, D. R., and Gillis, H. L. (1993). A meta-analysis of adventure programming with adolescents. *Journal of Experiential Education, 17*(1), 40–47.

Chase, N. K. (1981). *Outward Bound as an adjunct to therapy*. (ERIC Document Reproduction Service No. ED241204).

Cline, F. (1993). Apples and onions. In M. A. Gass (Ed.), *Adventure therapy: Therapeutic applications of adventure programming in mental health settings*. Dubuque, IA: Kendall/Hunt Publishing Co.

Crisp, S. (1996). When does wilderness adventure become therapeutic? *Australian Journal of Outdoor Education, 2*(1), 9–18.

Crisp, S. (1997). *International models of best practice in wilderness and adventure therapy: Implications for Australia*. 1996 Winston Churchill Fellowship Final Report.

Ewert, A. (1989). *Outdoor adventure pursuits: Foundations, models, and theories*. Worthington, OH: Publishing Horizons, Inc.

Ewert, A. (1987). Research in outdoor adventure: Overview and analysis. *Bradford Papers Annual, 2*, 15–28.

Gass, M. A., and McPhee, P. J. (1990). Emerging for recovery: A descriptive analysis of adventure therapy for substance abusers. *Journal of Experiential Education, 13*(2), 29–35.

Gass, M. A. (1991). Enhancing metaphor development in adventure therapy programs. *Journal of Experiential Education, 14*(2), 8–13.

Gass, M. A. (1993). *Adventure therapy: Therapeutic applications of adventure programming*. Boulder, CO: Association for Experiential Education.

Gass, M.A., and Gillis, H. L. (1995) CHANGES: An assessment model using adventure experiences. *Journal of Experiential Education 18*(1), 34–40.

Gerstein, J. S. (1994). *Experiential family counseling*. Dubuque, IA: Kendall/Hunt Publishing Co.

Gillis, H. L., and McLeod, J. (October, 1992) Successful indoor adventure activities for treating substance abuse with adjudicated adolescents and incarcerated adults. *Proceedings of the 20th International Conference of the Association for Experiential Education*.

Gillis, H. L., and Simpson, C. (1991). Project choices: Adventure-based residential drug treatment for court-referred youth. *Journal of Addictions and Offender Counseling, 12*, 12–27.

Gillis, H. L. (1995). If I conduct outdoor pursuits with clinical populations, am I an adventure therapist? *Leisurability, 22*(2), pp. 5–15

Gray, S., and Yerkes, R. (1995). Documenting clinical events in adventure therapy. *Journal of Experiential Education, 18*(2), 95–101.

Handley, R. (1993). *Mirrors & mountaintops: Cauldrons of tension: Enhancement skills for wilderness programs.* In Fifth National Conference on Children With Emotional and Behavioral Problems, Western Australia: South Coast Wilderness Enhanced Program.

Hattie, J., Marsh, H. W., Neill, J. T., and Richards, G. E. (1997) Adventure education and Outward Bound: Out-of-class experiences that make a lasting difference. *Review of Educational Research, 67*(1), 43–87.

Haussmann, S. E. (1984). *A qualitative study of year-round outdoor therapeutic camping programs.* Dissertation Abstracts International, 45/09-A, 2835. (University Microfilms No. AAD84-27540.

Kelly, F., and Baer, D. (1968). *An alternative to institutionalization for adolescent delinquent boys.* Boston, MA: Fandel Press.

Kimball, R. O. (1983). The wilderness as therapy. *Journal of Experiential Education, 5*(3), 6–9.

Kimball, R. O. (1991). Empowerment: How and why they work: Special report: Challenging teens in treatment. *Adolescent Counselor, 4*(2), 24–29.

Larned, A. (1996) *The client/clinician relationship: What is important? Comparing the therapeutic relationship in adventure-based therapy and traditional psychotherapy.* Unpublished master's thesis, Smith College, Northampton, Massachusetts.

Levitt, L. (1982). How effective is wilderness therapy: A critical review. In F. E. Bolteler (Ed.), *Proceedings: Wilderness Psychology Group Third Annual Conference* (pp. 81–89).

Maguire, R., and Priest, S. (1994). The treatment of bulimia nervosa through adventure therapy. *Journal of Experiential Education, 17*(2), 44–48.

Maizell, R. S. (1988) *Adventure-based counseling as a therapeutic intervention with court-involved adolescents.* Dissertation Abstracts International, 50/06-B, 2628. (University Microfilms No. AAD89-21901).

Maxwell, P. (1996). Psychoanalytic psychotherapy: A blank screen? *Psychotherapy in Australia, 2*(4), 42–46.

Meares, R. (1992). *The metaphor of play: On self, the secret and the borderline experience.* Maryborough, Australia: Hill of Content.

O'Brien, M. (1990). *Northland wilderness experience: An experiential program for the youth of Taitokerau* (ERIC Document Reproduction Service ED 372886). Auckland, New Zealand: The University of Auckland Psychology Department.

Rice, S. (1988). *A study of the impact of long-term therapeutic camping on self-concept development among troubled youth.* Dissertation Abstracts International, 49/07-A, 1706. (University Microfilms No. AAD88-19365).

Ringer, T. M. (1994). Leadership competencies for outdoor adventure: From recreation to therapy. In *Adventure-based interventions with young people in trouble and at risk: Proceedings of a national one-day conference adventure-based interventions and a study weekend enabling troubled youth.* Ambleside, UK: Basecamp, Mabie Forest, Scotland.

Ringer, T. M. (1997). *A preliminary exploration of the requisite nature of university courses in adventure therapy for Australian practitioners.* Unpublished master's thesis. Faculty of Education, Edith Cowan University, Perth, Australia.

Ringer, T. M., and Berman, D. (1995, Fall). Training models for adventure therapists: Important issues. *Newsletter of the Therapeutic Adventure Professional Group of the Association for Experiential Education, 3*(2), 1–3.

Ringer, T. M., and Gillis, H. L. (1996). *From practice to theory: Uncovering the theories of human change that are implicit in your work as an adventure practitioner.* Spawning new ideas: A cycle of discovery: 24th annual international conference, Spokane, Washington, Association for Experiential Education.

Roland, C., Summers, S., Freidman, M., Barton, G., and McCarthy, K. (1987). Creation of an experiential challenge program. *Therapeutic Recreation Journal, 21*(2), 54–63.

Schoel, J., Prouty, D., and Radcliffe, P. (1988). *Islands of healing: A guide to adventure-based counseling.* Hamilton, MA: Project Adventure, Inc.

Shore, A. (1977). *Outward Bound: A reference volume.* Greenwich, CT: Outward Bound, Inc.

Simpson, C., and Gillis, H. L. (1997). *Working with those who hurt others: Adventure therapy with juvenile sexual perpetrators.* Paper presented at First International Adventure Therapy Conference: Exploring the Boundaries, Perth, Australia, July 3, 1997.

Stainton, R., and Balston, L. (1995). Adventure therapy: A synopsis of key elements of program design. *Adventure Therapy Newsletter,* p. 2–4.

Stich, T. F., and Gaylor, M. S. (1983). *Outward Bound: An innovative patient education program.* (ERIC Document Reproduction Service No. ED247047).

Stich, T. F., and Sussman, L. R. (1981). *Outward Bound an adjunctive psychiatric therapy: Preliminary research findings.* (ERIC Document Reproduction Service No. ED239791).

Stich, T. F. (1983). Experiential therapy. *Journal of Experiential Education, 5*(3), 23–30.

Stich, T. F., and Senior, N. (1984). Adventure therapy: An innovative treatment for psychiatric patients. In B. Pepper and H. Ryglewicz (Eds.), *Advances in training the young adult chronic patient, New directions in mental health services* (No. 21, pp. 103–108). (ERIC Document Reproduction Service No. ED292928). San Francisco, CA: Jossey-Bass.

Thomas, J. (1980). Sketch of a moving spirit: Kurt Hahn. *Journal of Experiential Education, 3*(1), 17–22.

Tippet, S. (1993). Therapeutic wilderness programming for borderline adolescents. In trust with adolescents in treatment. *Therapeutic Recreation Journal* (3), 22–28.

Walton, R. A. (1985). *Therapeutic camping with inpatient adolescents: A modality for training in interpersonal cognitive problem-solving skills (self-esteem residential treatment)*. Dissertation Abstracts International, 47/08-B, 3549. (University Microfilms No. AAD86-28822).

Wichmann, T. F. (1991). Of wilderness and circles: Evaluating a therapeutic model for wilderness adventure programs. *Journal of Experiential Education, 14*(2), 43–48.

Witman, J. P. (1989). *Outcomes of adventure program participation by adolescents involved in psychiatric treatment*. Dissertation Abstracts International, 50/01-B, 121. (University Microfilms No. AAD89-07355).

Chapter 5

A World of Adventure Education

Joseph Bailey
Linn-Benton Community College

Introduction

The global community is becoming more connected with each new technological breakthrough. Cultures are interacting in business and in multitudes of other ways. Intercultural exchanges are occurring at a frequency and depth that is unique to our time, and this situation requires a willingness to listen and understand and accept cultural perspectives. This is the situation of adventure education as it spreads across the world. Adventure education historically was an expression of colonialism. The Outward Bound model, for instance, was transplanted from Great Britain to Malaysia. It incorporated British ideas about education, philosophy of education, and instruction. These were offered to the Malaysian people, and there was little effort to incorporate Malay culture. Times have changed, and today those who would take an adventure education model into another culture are becoming aware that they must do so in a multicultural way, blending elements of the traditional model with elements derived from the particular culture of the participants.

This chapter is intended to be part of the continuing dialogue between cultures trying to understand each other. It is written in English, which has been the main language for discussion of adventure education in the world so far, yet this language carries embedded in it cultural assumptions, and this must be admitted. Unfortunately the work of many who do not write in English are relatively unknown. There is limited appreciation in the English-speaking world of the thinking and practice of people outside of it. This must somehow be changed.

A Definition of Adventure Education

Adventure education involves a particular set of activities, often set in the outdoors. It uses kinesthetic learning through active physical experience. It involves structured learning experiences that create the opportunity for increased human performance and capacity. There is a conscious reflection on the experience, and application that carries it beyond the present moment. In this chapter, the definition of adventure education is based on the description of the experiential learning cycle of Kolb (1984), though admittedly this model is founded on cultural assumptions of the West. Also, a clear distinction must be made between adventure recreation and adventure education, with the emphasis in the former being on the enjoyment and satisfaction derived from an activity, while in the latter the social and personal learning is the key value. Priest and Gass (1997) provide a more detailed review of the definitions of importance here.

Adventure and Education

The very idea of incorporating adventure into education is puzzling from some cultural perspectives. In some countries, adventure may even seem contradictory to their educational goals. The culture of the United States supports and even mythologizes adventure, with the rugged and individualistic adventurer regarded in a heroic light. In Singapore, on the other hand, with its very structured and deliberate social system, one central goal of the educational system is to have all citizens working toward a common purpose, and the ideal is conformity to social norms. Stepping beyond the bounds of what is acceptable is not a desirable trait (Chew, 1996).

Adventure in the United States often carries with it the connotation of individual risk and divergence. In Asian countries there is a focus on the group and on convergence. Many adventure education practitioners have observed that U.S. participants have trouble with teamwork. Russians, on the other hand, work very well together, but have difficulty with personal initiative. Bill Proudman (1997, personal communication) was part of a program that brought members of the Association for Experiential Education from the United States to introduce adventure education to Russia. He observed that Russians could easily participate in a successful group jump rope exercise far beyond the level possible for most U.S. groups. Problems occurred when the Russians were asked to perform anything that was contrary to the norm, leadership, or group interest. At one point he asked the students to define experiential education, and they said, "Experiential education is what Bill Proudman wrote in the *Journal of Experiential Education.*"

Dan Garvey's experience with a woman in India offers another illustration of these different cultural perspectives on the adventure education idea (1996, p. 27), and may help explain why the idea has not caught on in pre-industrial societies:

> After I carefully explained how solos were often conducted within the Outward Bound framework, the wide-eyed woman slowly repeated to me, "You mean you take people into a remote setting, you take away their food and their shelter and ask them to survive for three days, and at the end of the three days, you collect the people, bring them back and talk about what it was like for them to be without food and shelter?" Then there was a long pause, and with the utmost respect, but with the most profound questioning, she simply said, "This is what you call education?" Having been to India on several occasions, I tried to imagine a woman who worked with the untouchable community in Madras, a community in which members spend a significant amount of their time every day simply obtaining food and shelter. How difficult it was for her to imagine deprivation of these basic needs as being an educational experience that one would pay money to take part in.

The point here is that even the most basic assumptions that are taken for granted in one culture, may be inconceivable to people in another. The adventure programmer in India will need to find some other approach if he or she is to contribute to the growth of someone with such a different life experience than that of the programmer.

The Adventure Experience

Another challenge is to identify the activities which will be appropriate for a cultural setting other than the one in which conventional activities have worked well. The list of activities used in adventure programming is long: backpacking, canoeing, caving, climbing gyms, community service, desert trekking, kayaking, mountaineering, orienteering, rafting, raft sailing, rappelling, rock climbing, ropes courses, running, solos and others. The selection of activity may involve several factors including physical geography, native experience and expertise, and historical experience. The physical environment will obviously determine what can and cannot be done. If there is no snow, skiing is out. No mountains means no mountaineering, and so on. More subtly, the very approach to teaching may be influenced by the geography. For instance, the rugged terrain and consistently bad weather of the North Cascades in Washington leads to a style of leadership that may be called directive or even controlling. The risk is such that students must learn many skills before they can be trusted with their own safety. Some Europeans have observed that such a teaching approach doesn't change when the American instructor is working on terrain involving much less hazard. The tendency to be directive is still there. So, the geography is one factor that affects the selection of activity and programmatic structure.

A second factor is native experience and expertise. What do the people who live here do that might provide an appropriate cultural analogue to conventional adventure education activities? Karl Rohnke (1996, p. 7–8), for instance, discovered that games are highly prized by the Inuit people of Baffin Island. Most of the games occur in a small indoor space because of the climate. Maintaining a high level of expertise at the competitive games required putting up with considerable pain, as in cheek pulling. People stand side-by-side and pull each other's cheeks and the one who can stand the pain the longest is the winner. This may seem like an odd example, but the point is that cultures have their ways of learning and enjoying themselves, and such activities might provide a starting point for initiating adventure education.

Sometimes people may not wish to play the games conventionally used in adventure programs because they make them appear silly or threaten loss of face. Most games used in the United States would not work for the Germans, Italians or Turks for these reasons (Emiroglu, 1997, personal communication). Also, gender roles vary in different cultures. Kunz and Putnam (1996, p. 6) offer a good example from Russia:

> The staff was excited about the activities . . . but in working with them over a period of time, a different issue emerged—that of leadership and control. Particularly among men and women . . . the core group, the men who had been taking the greatest roles, were unconvinced that women had anything to offer in this arena. It became clear that what was needed was some experiential learning! We asked if they would like to do an activity the following day in which the women took the leading roles and the roles that required the most strength. "Yes" from the women; cautious exchanged glances from the muscle-flexors. The next day, we brought the group together and asked them to do a Trust Fall activity in which the women would catch the men. Silence and dropped jaws. There were many, both men and women, who were hesitant, but the women who had spoken up the day before stepped forward and began organizing themselves as catchers. It was clear from their faces that this was a traumatic moment. Several of the women were tight-lipped, the men more so. No one stepped forward to be the faller. "You go first, Brian!" We had gone through a few introductory trust activities leading to this point, but it was clear that few minds had been altered. Lifetimes of thought patterns, the social constructs of previous generations, preassigned roles dictating leadership and the order of the sexes were all being challenged.

The people in the Russian example were not ready for such a challenge to the norms of their social order. The activity chosen is one of proven usefulness in many contexts, but this time it was not the best choice. Or, it came at the wrong moment in a sequence of experiences. The program goal was not served. The citing of examples of this sort could go on, but the point seems clear—choice of the activities that comprise the adventure experience must be appropriate culturally. Much study of the cultural assumptions and conventions is a necessity when moving a program into a new cultural context.

Other differences between nations and cultures of interest to adventure educators include:

1. Conceptions of teamwork, individual initiative, and leadership vary. In some cultures the individual is subjugated to the group, while in others individual initiative is highly prized. In Australian aboriginal communities, for instance, there is great emphasis on community and interdependence and there is sensitivity to the effects of one's actions on others (Campbell et al, 1995, p. 143). Teamwork is more highly prized in some places than others. Americans are taught from their early schooling to act individually and be competitive; working together is more the norm in Malaysia (Cheong, 1996, p. 50).

2. Responses to the stresses of adventure activities may reflect cultural values:

> Participants in experiential programs express their discomfort in "strange" ways. Some participants might laugh out of context at the "misfortune" of other team members in order to hide their own feelings of embarrassment and nervousness. Most Asians are not fond of touching each other, and would find any training activity involving close body contact to be very difficult. In addition, few Asian participants are able to "open up" and share their feelings in a deep personal way. (Campbell et al, 1995, p. 144)

3. A common discussion heard among instructors around the world focuses on the wish for administration, risk management and social constraints to go away so that they can "just teach." Each country, though, has its own unique set of organizational and social challenges and solutions that support or hinder the delivery of adventure education.

4. Risk management is more of a concern in some places than others. Adventure educators in the United States must deal with the most severe threat of litigation, thus they must focus most carefully on risk management. Risk management is less of a concern in Russia, Germany, and Australia.

Conclusion

Years ago I sat on the banks of the Selway River in Idaho with a small group of visiting Japanese students. They stared up at the stars in complete awe. Every one of them had a deep appreciation of nature, yet none had before experienced the celestial light of a clear night sky. They stayed up most of the night just looking skyward—one of those unplanned moments in a learning experience that are so common around the world. Adventure education will continue to spread around the earth, in part because it helps people find moments in their lives like this. The Maori of New Zealand will continue to develop their formalized adventure education based on their multigenerational knowledge. The social workers of Belgium will use their knowledge to sculpt a unique version of adventure education, as will the Outward Bound instructor leading a course through the Florida Everglades. Native wisdom across the world will offer new sights to adventure programmers. The challenge for all of us will be to listen, to understand and appreciate the diversity that exists behind different languages and borders.

Luca Santini's words (1996, p. 36) apply to most of the adventure programs around the world:

> Adventure is still a new and pioneering field in Italy. I do think that regardless of cultural attitudes or initial resistance to adventure, the fundamental mechanisms—getting people involved, creating a supportive environment and cohesive group—work for everyone and in every culture.

References

Campbell, J., Wagner, R. J., Brown, H., Kolblinger, M., Lim, T. K., and Main, M. (1995). International and cultural perspectives. In C. C. Roland, R. J. Wagner, and R. Weigand (Eds.), *Do it and understand: The bottom line on corporate experiential learning.* Dubuque, IA: Kendall/Hunt Publishing.

Cheong, T. Y. (1996). Bing, bong, bang. *Zip Lines, the Project Adventure Newsletter, 30,* 50–51.

Chew, E. (1996). Of spiders and longkang fish. *Zip Lines, the Project Adventure Newsletter, 30,* 38–40.

Garvey, D. (1996). From Moscow to Moscow. *Zip Lines, the Project Adventure Newsletter, 30,* 26–31.

Kolb, D. A. (1984). *Experiential learning.* Englewood Cliffs, NJ: Prentice-Hall.

Kunz, B., and Putnam, L. (1996). Experiential education in the new Russia. *Zip Lines, the Project Adventure Newsletter, 30,* 44–47.

Priest, S., and Gass, M. (1997). *Effective leadership in adventure programming.* Champaign, IL: Human Kinetics.

Rohnke, K. (1996). Karl's corner. *Zip Lines, 30,* 6–7.

Santini, L. (1996). Il mundo d'avventura in Italia, *Zip Lines, 30,* 36–37.

Section 2

Historical Perspectives on Adventure Programming

How did adventure programming evolve into the important educational enterprise it is in the final decade of the twentieth century? What individuals and organizations led the development of this field? These are the central questions of this section. A comprehensive and analytical history of adventure programming remains to be written, but the essays here are a step toward such a history.

Raiola and O'Keefe open this section with an overview. They show how many strands of thought and practice eventually coalesced into what came to be called *adventure education*. Kurt Hahn and Outward Bound are treated in the next two essays. Any history of the field pivots on Hahn, and Miner writes as a disciple of Hahn and as a "founder" of Outward Bound, at least in the United States. He shares a "present at the creation" perspective on the birth of this adventure education prototype. Richards complements Miner with his more scholarly and comprehensive treatment of Kurt Hahn.

The history of adventure education is one of leaders such as Hahn, Miner, Paul Petzoldt and others. It is also a history of organizations. Since adventure education has been outside the educational mainstream, the strength of numbers, or organized and focused group effort, has been necessary for progress and development of the field. As Garvey reveals, the Association for Experiential Education (AEE) has played a key role in linking the diverse elements of the field. Practitioners of adventure education are often rugged individuals, risktakers and adventurers who are iconoclasts and have little tolerance for bureaucracy and organization. This history of AEE is one of attempting to meld this motley crew into a group to promote their common interests and coordinate their diverse activities—to encourage sharing and cooperation to achieve a measure of efficiency in developing programs and meeting challenges.

The Wilderness Education Association (WEA) has been more narrowly focused than AEE. Its aim has been to teach responsible outdoor leadership, and especially use of that basic adventure education resource—wilderness. This association has, since its inception, been a player in one of the more important issues facing the field—certification of outdoor leaders. The origins and history of the WEA are important to an understanding of this issue.

Two of the most important programs in the history of the field are unquestionably the National Outdoor Leadership School (NOLS) and Project Adventure. Bachert describes how NOLS appeared and evolved. You will learn how NOLS came from Outward Bound through the medium of Paul Petzoldt and how WEA, with Petzoldt again, emerged from NOLS. All of this is a history of emerging priorities and goals for adventure education.

Project Adventure has, as Prouty's history recalls, been a vehicle to extend adventure education into conventional educational settings. While WEA has reached into higher education, Project Adventure has influenced common schools and continues to grow and extend its influence in that arena.

As other sections of this collection reveal, adventure education has spread and developed all over the world. The focus here is upon its evolution in the United States, but any comprehensive and thorough historical treatment will need to look globally. Chris Loynes describes how adventure programming has developed in the United Kingdom, which brings the story back to Hahn and highlights the importance of looking beyond the boundaries of the United States for developments in the field.

What emerges from a reading of the selections in this section is a picture of programmatic evolution and extension. This extension has been in fits and starts, influenced by strong personalities and marked by disagreement and often outright conflict. Yet the field has grown and matured and, as these essays attest, increased in its breadth and depth.

Chapter 6

Philosophy in Practice: A History of Adventure Programming

Edward Raiola and Marty O'Keefe
Warren Wilson College

Introduction

Many researchers trace the origin of adventure education to Kurt Hahn, founder of Outward Bound. We believe its roots are much more far-reaching, rich, and broad than this. We agree that Kurt Hahn and Outward Bound have had a huge impact on adventure education. We also know that prior events and people made it a ripe time in history for Outward Bound to come to the United States in the early 1960s and create such a huge wave of momentum that is still building today.

The layers of history teach us more when we explore them in depth. Each person who investigates the past can piece together a story that gives today's events perspective

1592–1670	1712–1778	1746–1827	Early 1800s	1823	1854	1861	1864
John Amos Comenius Advocate—sensory learning; explore actual object before reading about it	Jean-Jacques Rousseau Émile—educated according to principles found in nature	Pestalozzi Direct experience; taught practical skills; learner formulate principles and generalizations on own	First camps organized John Dewey First campus school—University of Chicago; school = mini-community Progressive Education Movement	Round Hill School: George Bancroft and Joseph Cogswell	YMCA established	Frederick Gunn: Gunnery Camp	Congress grants Yosemite Valley to California to be operated as a state park; later became Yosemite National Park

and meaning. The beauty of looking at past events and people who "made history" is that each of us can pick out unique events and people that we feel really had an impact on what adventure education is for us today. And, each perspective adds merit to the whole. We challenge each of you reading this chapter to explore beyond this text and add to the history we have outlined. You will continue to add to the richness and value we can gain from understanding the history of adventure education. We will be better at creating the history of tomorrow, today!

Adventure Education— Toward a Definition

What do you think of when you hear the term *adventure education?* Whenever we have asked that question individuals conjure up varying images of what the phrase means. Images have ranged from the Mountain Dew advertisement "been there, done that" rappel off a thousand-foot cliff to group activities that include teamwork and have a challenge course as part of the experience.

Adventure itself is a human need. More than a word, adventure is an atmosphere, an attitude, a climate of the mind. Adventure is the curiosity of people to see the other side of the mountain, the impulse in us that makes us break our bonds with the familiar and seek greater possibilities. Although there is not yet consensus on a precise definition of what adventure education is, many researchers and practitioners (Bunting, 1990; Hollenhorst, 1986; Ewert, 1989; Priest, 1990) agree that it contains elements of excitement, uncertainty, real or perceived risk, effort, and interaction with the natural environment.

Phipps (1985) suggests that the adventure experience is essentially a psychological happening attained through physical activities. Bunting sees outdoor adventure education as "environmental communication because, as in interpersonal communication, there is interdependency between . . . participants, as well as between the environment and participants" (Bunting, 1990, p. 453). She views adventure education as a vehicle for learning about ourselves and about interrelationships.

According to Cinnamon and Raiola (1991):

> One of the most important themes in outdoor adventure education is that the participants should be provided with the necessary skills, both mental and physical, to enable them to experience success in using and preserving the outdoors. The emphasis is not on winning or losing, but rather on facing the challenges of the activity. Some of the generally accepted goals are personal growth, skill development, excitement and stimulation, challenge, group participation and cooperation and understanding of one's relationship to the natural environment. (p. 130)

Historical Development

In order to understand adventure education, it is necessary to review its historical roots. The pioneers were men and women with a vision of the impact that group-focused outdoor learning and living could have on the lives of participants. When we explore the development of adventure education we must go back to the beginnings of experiential education, the organized camping movement, conservation

1872	1876	1885	1892	1901–1908	1902	1905	1906
Yellowstone— first National Park established	Appalachian Mountain Club established	Adirondack State Park established	Camp Avery: national science camp for boys; reserved a month for girls; by 1902 served girls exclusively Sierra Club established by John Muir Hull House: first Settlement House: Jane Adams and Ellen Gates Starr founders	Theodore Roosevelt in office	Congress passes Reclamation Act— Roosevelt's idea Laura Mattoon: Summer expedition to New Hampshire with group of girls; establishment of her camp	Forest Service established National Audubon Society founded	Gulick and Curtis: founded Parks and Recreation Association of America YWCA established Boy's Club of America established

education, nature study, outdoor education, and environmental education. They each have influenced and shaped what we now call *adventure education*.

It is important to understand that adventure education is a form of experiential education. Experiential education emphasizes direct experience as a resource that can increase the quality of learning through combining direct experience that is meaningful to the learner with guided reflection and analysis. It is a teaching and learning approach that allows numerous opportunities for the learner to connect cognitive (head), kinesthetic (body), and affective (spirit or emotional) aspects. It is a conscious mixing of concrete experience, reflective observation, abstract conceptualization and active experimentation.

Some of the earliest roots of adventure education can be traced to the basic philosophical teachings of experiential educators such as Comenius, Rousseau, and Pestalozzi (Hammerman, 1980). Comenius (1592–1670) emphasized the use of the senses in learning: seeing, touching, tasting, hearing—"a child should experience the actual object before reading about it" (Hammerman, 1980, p. xv). Rousseau (1712–1778) became famous for his teaching of the boy Émile through the principles found in nature—again, teaching through the use of the senses. Pestalozzi (1746–1827) emphasized the use of practical skills in learning—believing the child would later form generalizations and principles based on the practical skills (Hammerman, 1980). The reader is referred to other chapters in this volume for a detailed philosophical perspective.

During the nineteenth century attempts at using adventure and the outdoors as educational tools can be found in the organized camping movement. Organized camping is defined as:

a sustained experience which provides a creative, recreational, and educational opportunity in group living in the out-of-doors. It utilizes trained leadership and the resources of natural surroundings to contribute to each camper's mental, physical, social, and spiritual growth. (American Camping Association, 1980, p. 8)

Many of these same observations are used to describe adventure education. Educators began teaching through expeditions, camping and challenge activities in the United States as early as 1861 in the organized camping movement.

Mr. and Mrs. Gunn, who ran the Gunnery School in Connecticut for young boys (1861–1881), developed one of the first programs using camping as part of an educational program. The whole school went on a two-week, 40-mile journey at the end of the school year in August, 1861. Everyone hiked and then set up a camp to "live simply, doing their cooking and chores, swimming, fishing and participating in games, songs and stories by the camp fire" (Eells, 1986, p. 6).

Laura Mattoon was one of many activists and innovators in the early twentieth century concerned with the instruction and personal growth of young women. After having hiked and camped with her family in Canada, she became an educator who taught at private girls' schools in Massachusetts and New York. She decide to lead an expedition in the summer of 1902 to the New Hampshire wilderness with eight older students from her school. This expedition required that they establish and set up their camp in the forest, chop wood, haul water and cook for themselves. They hiked mountain trails, swam, participated in

1908	1910	1911	1912	1914	1916	1917	1918
Theodore Roosevelt called first White House Conference on Conservation American Nature Study Society: Lyberty Hyde Bailey, president	Boy Scouts of America established Gulicks: Camp Fire Girls established in Vermont and Maine	Camp Directors Association of America established (later became ACA) Anna Bostford Comstock: *The Handbook of Nature Study*	First Girl Scout Troop and Camp, Savanna, GA —five-day camping trip; Girls Scouts of America established	WWI begins in Europe	National Park Service established National Association of Directors of Girls' Camps (NADGC) established from efforts of Charlotte Gulick, Luther Gulick, Florence Marshall, and Charlotte Farnsworth; Charlotte Gulick first president	United States enters WWI	Armistice ends WWI

geological field studies and made crafts. Eleanor Eells (1986) states that this experiment was so successful that it led to the establishment of a permanent camp and education program. Each succeeding year saw a larger group of female campers. Mattoon's main goal was:

> to challenge old boundaries set for girls. For reasons different from the men, she stressed the rigors of the "primitive camp." While the men were trying to recapture the ideals of the past for boys, Mattoon aimed to overcome them for girls. (Miranda and Yerkes, 1996, p. 68)

Laura Mattoon later became a major player in the development of the American Camping Association as we know it today. She was also influential in the development of the National Association of Directors of Girls' Camps, which was founded in 1910 in response to the fact that women were not allowed to join the Camp Directors Association of America. Yet, there were over 200 women directing camps at the time. Mattoon and others were instrumental in building a strong organization, and the National Association of Directors of Girls' Camps merged in 1924 with the Camp Directors Association of America to become what is known today as the American Camping Association. Mattoon was considered the "Godmother of Camping." (For a more extensive reading on organized camping see Eells, 1986, and Miranda and Yerkes, 1996.)

John Dewey (1938) applied many of the ideas of earlier philosophers of education: Plato, Aristotle, and William James, among others. His writings, work, and teaching influenced many of the school and camping programs from the turn of the century to the present day. He believed that education should be concerned with living and learning through direct experience and should be directed toward the whole person—physically, mentally and emotionally. According to Knapp (1994):

> In the early years, the development of outdoor and experiential education accompanied the spread of the Progressive Education Movement. . . . The field of outdoor and experiential education and the Progressive Education Movement evolved from a common philosophical base and shared common roots in the early 1900s. Our profession was truly a catalyst for social change in the early years and still may be today. (p. 8)

In the late 1920s and early 1930s a number of public school programs developed using the environment and overnight camping. One of the many pioneers in this field was L. B. Sharp who began experimenting with education in camp settings. It is interesting to note that he received his doctoral degree in 1929 from Columbia University, the first person to receive a doctorate in camping education. While at Columbia he studied with some of the pioneering practitioners of experiential education: John Dewey, William Kilpatrick, Boyd Bode and Elbert K. Fretwell. These mentors strongly influenced his thinking on how youth should learn.

Sharp became director of Life Camps, a camp for underprivileged city children, in 1927. He totally revamped the camp to work with children in small groups in the outdoors. He took principles about teaching methodology and learning environments from the school setting and transferred these to the camp setting. Life Camps were very

1920	1924	1925	1926	1929	1930s	1930	1932
19th Amendment ratified: gives women the right to vote in federal elections	Camp Directors Association of America and National Association of Directors of Girls Camps merge to become Camp Directors Association (later named ACA)

White House Conference on Outdoor Recreation held | L. B. Sharp: Life Fresh Air Fund of New York City: Life Summer Camps | Elliot Joslin: Camp for Diabetics established near Boston | Stock Market crashed in October; Great Depression begins

L. B. Sharp: dissertation: "Extending Education Through Camping" | Depression

Camps viewed as adjunct to school program. Few attempts to correlate outdoor learning activities to regular curriculum | White House Conference on Child Health and Protection —dealt with recreation services of kids with disabilities | Camp Directors Association renamed American Camping Association (ACA)

American Youth Hostels established |

successful during his tenure. In 1940 he developed a center for advanced leadership training called *National Camp*. Through National Camp and its programs, Sharp influenced many professional outdoor educators. In 1944 and 1946 he began to use the term *outdoor education* synonymously with public school camping.

Toward the mid 1900s, more sophisticated school and organized camping programs emerged which were strongly influenced by the work of John Dewey and other educators. The Nature Study Movement arose from growing discontent with rote learning and isolation of learning from world phenomena and experiences. Nature study emphasized participants' direct experience in understanding and appreciating the natural world. William Gould Vinal, one of the leaders in the Nature Study Movement, coined the term *nature recreation* and emphasized enjoyment and appreciation as important ingredients of nature study. In 1911 Anna Bostford Comstock published *The Handbook of Nature Study,* which served as a guide for teachers and naturalists. It is still considered a valuable reference today. Another important figure in the Nature Study Movement, Liberty Hyde Bailey, a horticulturist and great lover of nature, was the founding president of the American Nature Study Society in the late 1920s. The purpose of the organization was to develop an understanding and appreciation of the beauty and mystery of nature.

Another movement, which paralleled the development of nature study, was conservation education. Interest in conservation education grew out of concerns about misuse of soil, range, forest and wildlife resources. One of its principal efforts was to integrate conservation education into school curricula. Important figures throughout history in the Conservation Education Movement include George Perkins Marsh, author of *Man and Nature* (1864), who emphasized that people are an integral part of the natural world; Gifford Pinchot, who popularized the need for conservation and the concept of multiple use (1890s to 1910); and President Theodore Roosevelt, who dramatically increased the public ownership of lands and established the National Conservation Commission to oversee and supervise these natural areas (in office from 1901–1908).

Both the Nature Study and Conservation Education Movements stressed hands-on learning and interaction with the outdoors. Out of the rich history and background of conservation and nature study education developed outdoor education: education *in, about* and *for* the outdoors.

The 1950s and early 1960s saw a rapid development of school camping and the term *outdoor education* began to be applied more generally. The concept was broadened to include experiences not only in residential camps but on school grounds and in the community. Curricula were developed for kindergarten through high school, and colleges and universities began special programs for educating teachers in the outdoors. These programs included elements of challenge, risk, group participation and cooperation, excitement, and skill development. All of these early programs used direct and purposeful experiences, they were real and meaningful in that they had natural consequences and required the participants to become actively involved in the activities.

During the 1960s national environmental trends encouraged people to develop an understanding of and responsibility toward our natural resources. Stuart Udall's *The Quiet Crisis,* Aldo Leopold's *Sand County Almanac* and Rachel Carson's *Silent Spring* were widely read and debated:

1933	1933–1938	1935	1936	1937	1938	1939	1940
Civilian Conservation Corps established; built many trails still in use today	New Deal—Franklin Roosevelt	Wilderness Society established	First graduate/undergraduate course offered in recreation, New York University	Students attending State Teachers College at Cortland (NY) could register for an outdoor leadership training course; women majoring in physical education were required to attend a two-week training camp in June	American Alliance of Health, Physical Education, Recreation, and Dance established	WWII begins in Europe	W. K. Kellogg Foundation and Julian Smith: The Battle Creek Outdoor Education Program L. B. Sharp: National Camp—leadership training for staff of school

The word "ecology" was on everyone's lips—even those who knew little of its meaning. The outdoor education field became a change agent for attitudes and values. During this attitude-formation stage, the term "environmental education" developed as an extension of conservation education and outdoor education to be all-encompassing. (Ford, 1981, p. 46)

John Kirk, in his paper "The Quantum Theory of Environmental Education" (1977), explored the development of environmental education from the roots of the Conservation, Nature Study, School Camping, and Outdoor Education Movements. In the 1960s, key events and people in all these arenas, along with powerful national events, caused a "quantum jump" toward philosophies and passions of these fields. Environmental education has taken its own course over the last 30 years. However, the fields of environmental education and adventure education have turned back toward each other in more recent history as professionals in both fields have come to recognize that the other has something to offer their "cause."

Emergence of Adventure Education

From the 1960s to the present, a resurgent interest has grown in experiential learning and outdoor programs here in the United States. Kurt Hahn, the founder of Outward Bound, and Paul Petzoldt, founder of the National Outdoor Leadership School and the Wilderness Education Association, have shaped the growth of adventure educa-

tion as we now understand it. (See the appropriate chapters in this book to get a more in-depth account of each of these organizations.)

In 1962 Hahn's Outward Bound (OB) concept, which began in England, was introduced to America with the establishment of the Colorado Outward Bound School:

> What began as a wartime school for survival has evolved into an action-oriented program for personal growth, service to others and physical preparedness. In short OB is learning about oneself and the world through adventure and service to others. Outward Bound has created a sophisticated adventure-based education program to stimulate personal growth. (Green and Thompson, 1990, pp. 5–6)

With a descriptive motto of "to serve, to strive and not to yield," Outward Bound in the United States has become the largest and most widespread adventure-based education institution with five U.S. schools: Colorado, Hurricane Island, North Carolina, Pacific Crest and Voyageur. Outward Bound USA has also established nine urban programs specifically designed to address the needs of inner city youth and the social, cultural and educational problems existing in larger cities. It is interesting to note that some of the same philosophers that influenced Hahn are in the fabric of these earlier movements as well: Plato, Aristotle, Alfred North Whitehead, John Dewey, Thoreau, and William James among others.

The National Outdoor Leadership School (NOLS) was founded in 1965 by Paul Petzoldt. Petzoldt had been chief instructor for the Colorado Outward Bound School and he realized the need for better prepared leaders for all outdoor

1941	1943	1945	1949	1950	1953	1958	1960
United States enters WWII Kurt Hahn: Outward Bound established in Aberdovy, Wales	Eleanor Eells: chair of committee on specialized camping services; focus was on standards and programs for children with physical handicaps, emphasizing what the child can do safely, rather than on limitations	WWII ends	New Jersey School of Conservation established Aldo Leopold: *Sand County Almanac* published	Northern Illinois University established the Lorado Taft Field Campus	Conservation Education Association established Outdoor Education Association, Inc., established; L. B. Sharp, executive director	Outdoor Recreation Resources Review Commission established	Multiple Use Act passed

schools and programs (Petzoldt, 1974). The National Outdoor Leadership School is recognized as a leader in the field of wilderness education and outdoor leadership. NOLS currently has branch schools in Wyoming, Alaska, Washington, Arizona, Africa, Mexico, Chile, and Canada. Since 1965 NOLS has taught wilderness skills, conservation and leadership to more than 30,000 students.

In 1977 Paul Petzoldt and other leaders from the academic community concerned with the development of outdoor leadership, the role of education and the preservation of wildlands, founded the Wilderness Use Education Association (later to be called the Wilderness Education Association [WEA]). WEA seeks to train outdoor leaders, promote and develop a sense of stewardship toward the environment and promote skills and knowledge necessary to lead and teach in the outdoors. It places a strong emphasis on developing leadership, judgment and decision-making skills. WEA currently offers courses through an affiliate system of 38 colleges, universities and outdoor organizations across the United States.

The Outward Bound Movement inspired many educators to use experiential methods. In 1971 Jerry Pieh, then a principal of Hamilton-Wenham Junior-Senior High School, wrote a three-year grant proposal to develop a comprehensive, experiential curriculum, applying the Outward Bound concepts to the classroom. This new program was called *Project Adventure*. The original curriculum focused on the tenth grade in the areas of physical education, English, history, science theater, arts, and counseling, integrating the concepts of experiential education and adventure. "No other innovative education proposal spinning off from Outward Bound has enjoyed a greater success with the education establishment than Project Adventure" (Miner and Boldt, 1981, p. 336).

Today Project Adventure is an international organization with offices in Massachusetts, Georgia, Oregon, and Vermont and international sites in Australia, New Zealand and Singapore. It presently offers training and workshops in five different "strands:" physical education/recreation, academic, therapeutic, professional development and community development. Since 1974 it has published books for the field of adventure education covering topics from games, to challenge ropes courses, to theory and practice. It has been the leader in designing and installing challenge ropes courses since 1971.

Recent History

The 1980s and 1990s have seen exponential growth in the adventure education field. The executive challenge programming, now called *experience-based training and development* emerged in the early 1980s. Within these programs the methodologies and philosophy of adventure education are used with managers and executives across the country and around the world. Wilderness therapy, now called *adventure therapy,* began with some of the early camping movement programs, such as the Life Camps, and became more refined with Outward Bound in the 1970s and 1980s. Working with a variety of clients in a therapeutic setting, adventure therapists have taken the base of adventure education's philosophy and methodologies, and applied them to diverse groups of clientele. Through the passage of the Americans With Disabilities Act (1990), accessible programming has increased. This area needs to be addressed in the future to make sure programming is accessible to all who desire it. The emergence of The Association of Challenge Course Technology (1993), with its development of challenge course building standards,

1962	1963	1964	1965	1966	1968	1970	1971
Rachel Carson: *Silent Spring* published	Udall: *The Quiet Crisis* published	The Wilderness Act passed	NOLS established	Elliot: FoxFire Program established	National Trails System Act passed	Environmental Education Act passed	Project Adventure began from Tittle III grant
Colorado Outward Bound School established, first OB in United States		Civil Rights Act passed	National Recreation and Parks Association established	Stewart Brand: World War IV—precursor to New Games Tournaments	Wild and Scenic Rivers Act passed	First Earth Day, May 1	
			Vietnam War —United States involvement escalates	Endangered Species Act passed			

and the Accreditation Standards (first begun in 1993) by the Association for Experiential Education, the risk management aspect of adventure education continues to be an important topic. Programming for women and girls has its own rich history and renewed interest has developed in the later part of the 1990s as an important contribution of adventure education programming. (See related chapters in this book.) Outward Bound has sparked a new initiative called *expeditionary learning* (1993), once again taking adventure education into the schools. It is interesting to realize how the rich beginnings of adventure education come back around to be paramount even as the needs of the times change!

Future Challenges and Opportunities

We see growth for adventure education in the coming decades. In the school systems we see it providing students with opportunities to develop intrinsic motivation, learn lessons about risk taking, responsibility, and commitment. It also can add elements of excitement to the learning journey and provide lessons in collaboration, cooperation, and trust.

A second important area for growth will be in helping participants to face critical social issues such as community building in neighborhoods or conflict resolution in war-torn countries. Organizations such as Project Adventure and Play for Peace are leading the way. Project Adventure's community development strand provides an avenue for communities to work together on pressing diversity issues through adventure and play. Play for Peace, an initiative of the Association for Experiential Education,

began its work in 1996 with the purpose of "bringing children of conflicting cultures together through play. It promotes positive relationships among people who have a history of intercultural tension" (Play for Peace, 1996):

> Our field is uniquely positioned to play a key role in facing social issues, and in moving all parts of the whole toward solutions. The holistic nature of our activities, with their ability to access the personal, and even spiritual parts of ourselves, gives us an opportunity to act, and an obligation to act, once we know the opportunity. (Prouty, 1994, p. 21)

Adventure education has been, and continues to be, an evolving field, shaped by the needs of both participants and the specific environment in which it occurs. As we move into the next century, these basic concepts and values will continually respond to global, social, and environmental changes.

References

American Camping Association. (1980). *Camp standards with interpretations.* Martinsville, IN: Author.

Bunting, C. J. (1990). Interdependency: A key in environmental and adventure education. In J. C. Miles and S. Priest (Eds.), *Adventure education* (pp. 453–458). State College, PA: Venture Publishing Inc.

Cinnamon, J., and Raiola, E. (1991). Adventure skill and travel modes. In David Cockrell (Ed.), *The wilderness educator: The Wilderness Education Association curriculum guide* (pp. 129–130). Merrillville, IN: ICS books.

1972	1973	1974	1976	1977	1979	1980	1981
Steve Van Matre: *Acclimatization* published	Stewart Brand: first New Games Tournament	Association for Experiential Education established	Andrew Fluegelman (editor): *The New Games Book* published	Camp Allen, NH: The Tree Perch Program —for kids with disabilities	Joseph Cornell: *Sharing Nature With Children* published	Vinland National Center, MN: the first accessible challenge course	Boston University's Executive Challenge Program established
Title IX Education Act passed	Federal Rehabilitation Act: mandated public property be accessible	First North American Conference on Outdoor Pursuits in Higher Education	Anne LaBastille: *Woodswoman* published	Wilderness Use Education Association established (renamed Wilderness Education Association in 1978)	Steve Van Matre: *Sunship Earth* published	Camp Riverwood, MA: a ropes course experience for campers with moderate to severe mental retardation	Roland and Havens: *An Introduction to Adventure: A Sequential Approach to Challenging Activities With Persons Who Are Disabled* published
		Public Law 92-144 passed: requires education in the least restrictive environment and cites need for recreation for people with disabilities				China Galland: *Women in Wilderness* published	
						Women Outdoors established	

Dewey, J. (1938). *Experience and education.* New York, NY: Collier Books.

Ells, E. (1986). *History of organized camping: The first 100 years.* Martinsville, IN: American Camping Association.

Ewert, A. W. (1989). *Outdoor adventure pursuits: Foundations, models and theories.* Columbus, OH: Publishing Horizons, Inc.

Ford, P. (1981). *Principles and practices of outdoor/environmental education.* New York, NY: John Wiley & Sons.

Green, J., and Thompson, D. (1990). Outward Bound USA. In J. C. Miles and S. Priest (Eds.), *Adventure education* (pp. 5–6). State College, PA: Venture Publishing Inc.

Hammerman, W. M. (1980). *Fifty years of resident outdoor education: 1930–1980 It's impact on American education.* Martinsville, IN: American Camping Association.

Hollenhorst, S. (1986). *Toward an understanding of adventure and adventure education.* Unpublished manuscript.

Kirk, J. (1977). *The quantum theory of environmental education.* In National Association for Environmental Education Sixth Annual Conference, YMCA of the Rockies, Estes Park, Colorado.

Knapp, C. (1994). Progressivism never died—It just moved outside: What can experiential educators learn from the past? *Journal of Experiential Education, 17*(2), 8–12.

Miner, J. L., and Boldt, J. (1981). *Outward Bound USA: Learning through experience in adventure-based education.* New York, NY: William Morrow and Company.

Miranda, W., and Yerkes, R. (1996). The history of camping women in the professionalization of experiential education. In K. Warren (Ed), *Women's voices in experiential education* (p. 63–77). Dubuque, IA: Kendall/Hunt Publishing Co.

Petzoldt, P. K. (1974). *The wilderness handbook.* New York, NY: W. W. Norton and Co., Inc.

Phipps, M. L. (1985). Adventure—An inner journey to the self: The psychology of adventure expressed in Jungian terms. *Adventure Education Journal, 2*(4/5).

Play for Peace. (1996). [Brochure].

Priest, S. (1990). Semantics of adventure education. In J. C. Miles and S. Priest (Eds.), *Adventure education* (pp. 113–117). State College PA: Venture Publishing.

Prouty, D. (1994, Spring/Summer). Change and the adventure field. *ZIP Lines, the Project Adventure Newsletter,* No. 25, 21.

1984	1985	1988	1990	1993	1994	1996	1997
AEE: *Common Practices in Adventure Programming* published	President's Commission on Americans Outdoors	Schoel, Prouty, and Radcliffe: *Islands of Healing* published Mike Fischesser: first Challenge Course Symposium held for builders and installers (later to become Association for Challenge Course Technology)	Passage of the Americans With Disabilities Act	Association for Challenge Course Technology incorporated	ACCT Challenge Course Installation Standards completed	Play for Peace established	ACCT Technical Standards for Challenge Course Operation completed

Chapter 7

The Creation of Outward Bound

Joshua L. Miner
Outward Bound, Inc.

Adventure-based education has its roots in many sources. It has no one "father." But if for some reason we wanted to single out an individual for that honor, Kurt Hahn would most certainly be a likely candidate. This great twentieth-century educator of German birth and British citizenship, a gentleman of the old school who has been proclaimed "a citizen of global mankind," was an inventor of institutions.

Hahn's Salem Schule in Germany, created in the throes of that nation's ordeal of defeat following the First World War, was one of the fine innovative schools of the Western world. Imprisoned by the Nazis and rescued at the behest of the British government, Hahn re-created the essence and esprit of Salem in a new school in northern Scotland. This unique version of a British public school, where the future Prince Consort of England and the future Prince of Wales would be educated, was Gordonstoun. That school—or more explicitly, the Hahnian principles that identified Gordonstoun—has in turn inspired an international consortium of schools whose headmasters gather annually in what they call their Round Square Conference (named after the distinctive building of that name at Gordonstoun; the conference meets annually to share the member schools' successes and problems and to help keep alive the educational-humanitarian spirit of Gordonstoun's founder).

Out of Gordonstoun, and Hahn's genius for working with people and events, came the first Outward Bound school, and in time the global Outward Bound movement, with its schools in England, Germany, Africa, Australia, New Zealand, Canada, and the United States—and notably in the American case came also the extraordinary array of Outward Bound spin-offs and adaptive programs that have taken root in and deeply influenced U.S. education and other special action. It was through our long association with Outward Bound that I came to know and treasure the friendship of Kurt Hahn.

Out of Gordonstoun, too, along with 18 years of patient, persistent effort, came the British County Badge Scheme. Personally launched by an ultimately convinced Prince Philip as the Duke of Edinburgh's Award Scheme, this was Hahn's plan for making a comprehensive form of adventure education and service opportunity available to all British youth. Out of that scheme have come counterpart programs in 29 countries, not least being the Congressional Award plan in the United States.

Even with that remarkable bundle of achievement as a social inventor, Hahn was not through. In 1955 Air Marshal Sir Lawrence Darvall, Commandant of the NATO Defense College, said to him:

> The conservative, nationalistic officers attending our school are achieving a remarkable degree of international understanding in a mere six-month course. Think how much more could be accomplished by a nonmilitarist school for young people with an international student body!

Fired by Darvall's concept, Hahn joined forces with him in the seven-year campaign that brought forth Atlantic College (now United World College of the Atlantic) in Llantwit Major, Wales, a two-year precollege school enrolling students from many nations. Recognizing that international understanding cannot be inculcated in the classroom alone, the skills program included a distinctively Hahnian component, referred to as its "humanitarian curriculum"—rescue and community services to those "in danger and in need." This was the start of the United World College movement.

Rowing bareheaded on a blazing hot day in his nineteenth year, Kurt Hahn suffered a severe sunstroke. The injury, centering at the cerebellum, where the spine joins the base of the brain, threatened to cripple him. To ease his suffering, he spent a year in a darkened room. Periodically thereafter—"despair stalking him like a sinister shadow," as Henry Brereton has written—the affliction returned in full force, casting him back into the dark. Even after a great London neurosurgeon performed a series of brain-decompressing operations that helped him greatly, light and heat remained his lifelong torment.

In those lonely ordeals of his young manhood he was working out a life principle that years later a remarkable physical educator would articulate and Hahn would make his leitmotiv: "Your disability is your opportunity." To make his confinement productive, he devised regimens of physical activity and disciplined thought. He practiced the standing high jump—scarcely to the delight of the Oxford students living beneath him—and the legend is that he broke records in that event. With the study of Plato's *Republic* fresh in his mind he conceived a new kind of school, where the worlds of thought and action would no longer be divided into hostile camps. Later he wrote out the concept and put it away for future reference.

Hahn was born into a cultured Jewish family in Berlin in 1886. His father was a successful industrialist. His mother was a beautiful woman of artistic temperament and powerful faith in the innate goodness of man. One of her forebears was Jecheskiel Landau, Chief Rabbi of Prague in the eighteenth century, whose writings on the Talmud are still taught at academies of Jewish studies. His grandmother on his mother's side was his adored "Anschulka," whose wise and droll sayings he noted down in a book. ("Anschulka, which of your eight children is the best?" "A mother is like a shopkeeper—she has various kinds of goods.") The home in which he grew up, radiating human warmth, was a gathering place for the city's intelligentsia and artists.

His father, enamored of England, built the family summer residence Wannsee in English country-house style. Kurt, the eldest of three sons, was a born teacher. In the summers at Wannsee he would gather the young people in the pavilion and read them tales of heroic adventure. Often he led them on long hikes over rough terrain. At

Gottingen, one of several German universities he attended, his Greek professor told him, "If you are interested in the old in order to help the new, it is not the German universities that can help you, but Oxford." He studied at Oxford from 1910 to 1914. On August 1, 1914, he took leave of his English friends to return home. Two days later Great Britain declared war on Germany.

In the war Hahn held a succession of minor Foreign Office posts from which he nevertheless emerged as a person of influence. He worked with the moderates—against unrestricted submarine warfare, for a negotiated peace—and became one of their spokesmen. Although his counsel did not prevail, the quality of his work won the attention of persons in high places. He was made adviser to Colonel von Haeften, who was in turn political adviser to General von Ludendorff.

At the war's end, Hahn was assistant to Prince Max of Baden, Germany's last imperial chancellor. The prince was a scholarly, humane man who in a speech in 1917 dared to say, "To love your enemy is the sign of those who remain loyal to the Lord even in time of war." The two men shared an enthusiasm for Plato's educational ideas, and in 1920 Prince Max founded a coeducational boarding school with Hahn as headmaster. This was the Salem (*shalom, salaam,* peace) Schule; it was the school Hahn had conceived seven years before.

The times were, quite literally, fearful. Defeated Germany was on the edge of anarchy. The school thwarted two plots, one by Communists to kidnap Prince Max, another by nationalists to murder Hahn. Typically, Hahn was more concerned over his would-be assassins' despair for the nation's plight than he was to see them punished. Guerrilla bands were setting fire to farms. Salem boys joined the night patrols guarding the lonely countryside. It was in that time that William Butler Yeats wrote the lines, so prophetic of the coming European tragedy, that Hahn would come to quote often, a statement of his lifelong concern:

> The best lack all conviction, while the worst
> are full of passionate intensity.

Yeats was defining the very condition that Prince Max and Hahn had set out to deal with. Through Salem, and by spreading the Salem gospel to other educators, they sought to nurture a German youth with convictions rooted in personal responsibility, kindness, and justice. The intent, in Hahn's words, was to equip young people "to effect what they have recognized to be right, despite hardships, despite dangers, despite inner skepticism, despite boredom, despite mockery from the world, despite emotion of the moment." The school's report to parents, developed at Salem and later used at Gordonstoun, evaluated the degree to which the students displayed these traits.

Hahn was at once a champion and hard taskmaster of youth in its conflicts with the elder generation. If young people were to play an influential role in society, he insisted, they must earn the right. Even as he welcomed the German youth movement of that time, he took sharp issue with indulgent adult attitudes. Long after I first knew him, in the time of the youth revolt in the England and United States of the 1960s, it was uncanny to discover that in Germany of 1928 he had said:

> With phrases such as "Youth Culture" these people besmear the souls of the young with the ointment of flattery—as though the young no longer had to become anything, but were everything already. They rob them of their joy of development and do violence to the natural process of spiritual growth.

Inevitably, the ideals of Salem clashed with the spirit of Nazism. Apprehensive of the growing strength of Hitler's movement, Hahn stepped up his efforts to win the German educational community over to Salem principles. But the Nazi tide continued to rise. In 1932 five storm troopers trampled a young Communist to death in front of his mother. They were arrested, tried, and condemned to death. In his notorious "Beuthen telegram," Hitler hailed them as comrades and demanded their release. "Your freedom," he said, "is our honor." For Hahn this was in fact the hour when men of honor must declare themselves. He sent a letter to all Salem alumni:

> Hitler's telegram has brought on a crisis that goes beyond politics. Germany is at stake, her Christian civilization, her good name, her soldiers' honor. Salem cannot remain neutral. I ask the members of the Salem Union who are active in a SA or SS to break with Salem or with Hitler.

It was, said a Briton who was teaching at Salem at the time, "the bravest deed in cold blood that I have witnessed."

Sir Roger Birley, who was Hahn's contemporary as headmaster of Eton, has given us a record of his courage in the German crisis. Discussing the education provided under Hahn at Salem, Birley wrote:

> But there was a second element quite as important. It was impressively expressed in an address Kurt Hahn gave in Hamburg on 16 February 1933. (The significance of the date, 17 days after the Nazis gained power, will be obvious.) It began with a study of the Fascist state and educational ideals, and an account of Fascism which seems to make inevitable the uncomfortable statement which is to be found in the address, that, if one looked at the educational principles of the Italian youth organizations, "you find that you might be quoting the whole Salem Certificate of Maturity with its capacity to endure hardships, to face dangers, a talent for organization, prudence, a fighting spirit, presence of mind, success in dealing with unexpected difficulties"—and then come the words, "Only one item is and must be missing: The power of carrying out what is recognized to be just." And a little later, "*Sacro egoismo,* sacred egoism. There is also sacred lying, sacred killing, sacred perjury, sacred breaking of promises." To speak in this way of Fascist principles at that moment was indeed courageous, but Kurt Hahn went on to turn to his own country, and it was with continual references to the state of things in Germany that he gave his reasons why Salem rejected Fascist education. Among these was to be found this one: "We need to be able to feel that as a people we are just and kindly. On this consciousness depends our inner strength."

Hahn became a marked man. In the mass arrests following the Reichstag fire in February 1933, he was jailed. The shock waves swiftly reached Britain, where his friends—some from the Oxford days, others gained as Salem's fame had spread—took up his cause. When Prime Minister Ramsay MacDonald made official representations, Hahn was let go. In July he left for England.

In those first months of exile he was profoundly depressed. At 47 he had lost his homeland, his school, the battle for German youth. A man of means, overnight he had become a nearly penniless refugee. Worse, his spiritual resources were depleted. When he was asked to found a new school along Salem lines, he lacked the will. When he was offered an established school to work with, he said, "I do not have time to overcome the inertia of tradition." Then he returned to Moray, the north of Scotland country where he had spent the convalescent summers of his Oxford years. He met old friends among the fishermen and crofters of the district. On the wharf in Hopeman Harbor, he listened to Captain Danny Main tell tales of men of simple courage against the forces of the sea. With another friend, Lord Malcolm Douglas-Hamilton, he inspected the empty castle at Gordonstoun, badly in need of repair, as a possible site for a school. Its vistas seized his spirit, and he knew again the truth that he would summon so often in guiding others: "Your disability is your opportunity."

Gordonstoun opened as a school for boys in April 1934; by September there were 21 students (among them a Greek prince of Danish blood named Philip, who one day would marry the future queen of England). The board of governors included the Archbishop of York, later of Canterbury;

the headmaster of Eton; the master of Trinity College at Cambridge; a distinguished British historian; and the future governor-general of Canada. The school's enrollment grew steadily.

In 1938 Hahn became a naturalized British subject. It was in character that even as he struggled to cope with the acute money problems of an expanding, unendowed school, he poured part of his energies into national concerns—alerting the British people to the dimensions of the Hitlerian threat, calling on them to hear the muffled cries from the concentration camps, campaigning at the War Office for a system of training that in months, he declared, could make British infantrymen the equal in stamina, hardihood, and self-confidence of German soldiers whose training had started years before in the Hitler Youth.

War broke out. The British Army commandeered Gordonstoun, and the school had to trek to wartime headquarters in Wales. The move was a major disability. In it Hahn found a new opportunity—and brought forth Outward Bound.

Opportunity's name was Lawrence Holt. Hahn had been trying to launch a "county badge scheme," an ambitious national plan for fostering physical fitness, enterprise, tenacity, and compassion among British youth. But in the wartime climate his prestigious County Badge Experimental Committee—scientist Julian Huxley, historian George Trevelyan, and others—had made small headway. At that same time, Holt, a Gordonstoun father and Hahn admirer who was partner in Alfred Holt & Company, a large merchant-shipping enterprise, was gravely concerned about the human toll in the Battle of the Atlantic. He was convinced that due to faulty training, many seamen on torpedoed merchant ships were dying unnecessarily. Unlike sail-trained old-timers, he maintained, the younger men and youths had not acquired a sense of wind and weather, a reliance on their own resources, and a selfless bond with their fellows. "I would rather," he told Hahn, "entrust the lowering of a lifeboat in mid Atlantic to a sail-trained octogenarian than to a young sea technician who is competently trained in the modern way but has never been sprayed by the salt water."

Hahn proposed they join forces to start a new kind of school offering young people one-month courses that would use Hahn's county badge scheme to implement Holt's quest for training to turn attitudes around. Holt agreed, his company providing funds and the maritime staff members. The school, called Outward Bound at Holt's insistence, opened at Aberdovey, Wales, in 1941. It was not, as the mythologized version has it, a school for young merchant seamen. While many of the students were youngsters sponsored by Holt's Blue Funnel Line and other shipping companies and from the government training ship HMS *Conway,* others were apprentices sent by industry, or police, fire, and other cadets, or boys on leave from their regular schools or about to go into the armed ser-

vices. It was Holt himself who articulated a Hahnian concept in words Hahn never forgot. "The training at Aberdovey," Holt said, "must be less a training *for* the sea than *through* the sea, and so benefit all walks of life." The month-long course was, in fact, a mix of small-boat training, athletic endeavor to reach standards of competence, cross-country route finding by map and compass, rescue training, an expedition at sea, a land expedition across three mountain ranges, and service to the local people. The school was fortunate from the outset in two key staff members. Jim Hogan, a resourceful young schoolmaster whom Hahn had recruited from the national educational system to be secretary of his County Badge Experimental Committee, was warden. His assistant in charge of athletic activity was Captain B. Zimmerman, who had been a great innovative physical educator in Germany until he fled his country to avoid Nazi imprisonment. Hahn had brought him from Switzerland to Gordonstoun. It was "Zim" who first exhorted his charges that their liability was their opportunity, who—seizing on Holt's phrase—talked of "training through the body, not of the body," and worked on each student until he could proclaim, "The bug has bit!"

Although beset by a prodigious series of start-up difficulties, Outward Bound worked from the first. The youths who came were the products of Britain's dozen years of depression and dole. Invariably, when they were told what they were expected to achieve in 30 days, murmurs of incredulity and derision ran through the group. But they were soon caught up by "the magic of the puzzle," Hahn's odd phrase for the phenomenon he knew so well—that when a young person "defeats his defeatism" to meet a challenge, it primes him to try for still more difficult achievement. There was a half-concealed pride of accomplishment in the assertion of the Cockney boy, exhausted and footsore after his first cross-country effort: "Cor blimey, if this had been Larndon, they'd shift them bleedin' hills." A moving human story underlay the statement of the half-caste lad from Liverpool, warmed by his watch-mates' acclaim for his self-improvement: "This is the first time in my life I have seemed to matter." Wise old Alec Fraser, the former missionary who served as the school chaplain, saw what was happening: "They come for the wrong reasons, and they leave sorry for the right ones that it's over."

Holt's prepositional distinction—training through rather than for—was always to be the essence of the Outward Bound dynamic. Life-enhancing experience is obtained through the sea, the mountains, the wild lake country, the desert. Outward Bound has evolved since those early Aberdovey days. But it has not departed from Hahn and Holt's essential concept of an intense experience surmounting challenges in a natural setting, through which the individual builds his sense of self-worth, the group comes to a heightened awareness of human interdependence, and all grow in concern for those in danger and in need.

In my year and a half as a member of Hahn's staff at Gordonstoun I came to know his philosophy as an educator in day-to-day practice. The core of his educational purpose was to conserve and strengthen the attributes of childhood into manhood. "What happens in adolescence," he asked, "to your children who in the nursery are so self-confident and happy?" Too often youngsters who were joyous, zestful, and enterprisingly curious, with the gift of wonder and an inborn compassion, grew "dimmed and diluted." Adolescence became "the loutish years," a shallow prematuring while strengths remained undiscovered and untrained. Hahn pledged himself "to unseat the dogma that puberty need deform." To this end he sought to create an educational environment where "healthy passions"—craving for adventure, joy of exploration, zest for building, devotion to a skill demanding patience and care, love of music, painting, or writing—would flourish as "guardian angels of adolescence."

One of my early responsibilities was The Break. It was essential, in Hahn's thinking, that a healthy youngster "have his powers of resilience, coordination, acceleration, and endurance purposefully developed." The Break was his unique contribution to physical education. He had invented it in the early Salem days, and from the beginning had made it an imperative part of the Gordonstoun scheme. Four mornings a week, during a 50-minute break in what Hahn called "the sedentary hours," each boy took part in two of a half-dozen events—sprinting or distance running, long or high jumping, discus or javelin throwing. He competed only against himself, trying to better his previous best performance. The frail youngster who broke 10 feet in the long jump for the first time in his life got as big a cheer as the track team star beating his previous mark at close to 20. Every boy had to do every event. That same star jumper might be a dud at throwing the discus. It was as important to overcome a weakness as to develop a strength.

When I was put in charge of The Break, I became a fascinated witness to its remarkable results. It was not just that the average performance would have put the average American schoolboy to shame. The great satisfaction lay in seeing the physical duffer discover that through trying from day-to-day he could do much better than he would have dared to dream. He had learned, in Hahn's phrase, to "defeat his defeatism." You could see him shed—Hahn again—"the misery of his unimportance." His new-found confidence would carry over into his peer relationships, his classroom performance, the quality of work on his project. It was not unusual for a timid or sensitive boy with an undeveloped physique to emerge from the chrysalis of his underconfidence a competent athlete, surprised to find himself confirming what the headmaster had so often told the school: "Your disability is your opportunity."

Hahn was then 65. He was running the school, making frequent trips to London to raise money for it and advance other projects, and shuttling across the Channel in his campaigns to influence the postwar education of German youth. "I am," he told me, "an old man in a hurry." I wondered how many obstacles he had hurdled with that trumpet cry of determination. The hurry part was literally true. He climbed stairs two at a time, took an entire down flight in a single r-r-r-p-p! His day marched. Frequently it began with three separate breakfast meetings. In theory they were staggered, but usually he wound up circulating from one to the other.

But however tight the day's schedule, he found time to reconnoiter about the school. "A headmaster's job," he said, "is to walk around." His antennae were always out, fine-tuned and waving, probing for each lad's potential strengths that they might be developed, for his innate weaknesses that they might be overcome. Repeatedly he homed in on some shielded aspect of a boy's ego that others had missed and that cast a sudden light on deviant behavior. He was his own psychologist, drawing on a vast bank of observations.

The day's end was signaled at that hour of the evening when Hunter brought the London taxicab around to Gordonstoun House. Hunter would drive him across the moors to the sea cliffs. Then Hahn would get out and jog along the line of the cliffs, his way illuminated by the headlights of the cab following behind.

But the days did not always end so routinely. Periodically, roused from slumber by his call, four or five of us—housemaster, teachers, activity leader—would make our way through the night to his study. The call would have but one meaning—some boy was in trouble. Perhaps a student had been caught stealing. Hahn would have spent a long evening getting the report, talking with the boy and with the student leaders who knew him best. Conscious of the contrast between our disheveled aspects and his neat daytime attire, we would wait for him to stop pacing the floor and tell us why we were there. Finally, when he had given us the facts, came the inevitable dreaded question, the blue eyes boring in: "Josh! When did you first notice this boy was in difficulty, and what did you do about it?"—dreaded because one had sensed and done nothing. When a boy was in danger of expulsion at Gordonstoun, it was not he but the adult community who was on trial. A boy steals because he has some deeper trouble. If one is sensitive enough, if one cares enough, one can detect symptoms of the trouble early, when there may still be time for remedy.

On the morrow Hahn would decide the penalty, posting the facts on the bulletin board to prevent the rumor-mongering he detested: "Put it on my tombstone, 'Here lies Kurt Hahn. He scotched a rumor every day.'"

He ran the school in tensile fashion. It began with his hiring strong people who would stand up to him. Offering Henry Brereton the post of director of studies in 1935, he said, "You must defend your department. If I want to send a boy into the hills for his health just before examinations, you must resist me." He staffed the school's nautical department with a Royal Navy officer and a Merchant Navy officer, in the belief that the inevitable conflict of two traditions would be a creative force—as it proved to be. When I became director of activities, I found that Brereton and I were duty bound to maintain a rival stance, lest either poach on the other's share of school time. If Hahn thought we were not being wary enough, he took some subtle action, created some threat of encroachment, to put us on guard.

The same tensilizing principle infused his way with the young. His core tenet, stated a thousand times as though it were cut in bronze, was: "It is the sin of the soul to force young people into opinions—indoctrination is of the devil—but it is culpable neglect not to impel them into health-giving experiences." The indoor type was to be chased outdoors, the introvert turned inside out, the extrovert outside in. The tough were to be gentled, the timid emboldened. Above all, the complacent were to be disturbed: "It is my mission in life to molest the contentedly unfit."

He was an intrepid traveler; a journey with him was exhilarating. To see him cope with the usual frustrations of getting from one place to the next was to observe in microcosm ways in which he advanced his grand designs. Policemen, taxi drivers, ticket agents were his instant confidants. No matter how negative an agent's initial response, the ensuing friendship almost surely produced the needed overnight train accommodation or pair of plane tickets. Henry Brereton, who accompanied him on trips to Germany in the difficult travel years right after the war, has provided a lovely reminiscence:

> Timetables seem to adjust to his whim, engine-drivers are in league with him and hold up the start of the express whilst he conducts an excited invalid infinitely slowly to her reserved compartment, saying with irritating assurance as guards blow whistles and porters shout and safely seated travelers stare from the windows, "We have plenty of time, my dear. Don't hurry. There's plenty of time."

Brereton's vignette catches Hahn in a moment that, in its small but touching way, reflects the very heart of his personal philosophy. This was his profound commitment to the Samaritan ethic. He had one hero above all: the compassionate traveler on the road to Jericho. Again and again he called for the Parable of the Good Samaritan to be read to the school. In the years to come I was to witness the growing power of his ultimate conviction—that through help to those in danger and in need youth can strike the deepest chords of the human spirit. It would become a creed: "He who drills and labors, accepts hardship, boredom, and dangers, all for the sake of helping his brother in peril and distress, discovers God's purpose in his inner life."

In the 1960s Kurt Hahn made periodic trips to this country. His visits to Andover were great occasions—for renewing our friendship, hearing his views about the state of the world, telling him about developments in U.S. Outward Bound, getting his counsel. He took a keen interest in my Outward Bound briefings. In the beginning it pleased him greatly that we had been drafted to set up the final training for the Peace Corps. He was enthusiastic about the American innovation of the solo; in his philosophy, periods of solitude were an essential human need. "You cannot harvest the lessons of your life except in aloneness," he said, "and I go to the length of saying that neither the love of man nor the love of God can take deep root except in aloneness." Sometimes he had concerns. Were the schools giving first aid in place of honor in the timetable? Did this or that school operate so far into the wilderness as to get away from other people and hence from opportunities to give aid or effect rescues? Only once, however, in my time as Outward Bound's president, did he give me a directive: "You will not let the word *Christianity* creep into Outward Bound. You will simply practice it." He was captivated by the adaptive program phenomena, so different from what had happened in Britain.

Invariably his counsel enriched us. Usually the advice I sought was on some question of strategy or tactic, and he had a way of elevating the discussion to one of principle. I remember once asking him whom at Phillips Academy he thought I should go to for help in weaving Outward Bound philosophy into the fabric of the school. He said:

> There are two people—your doctor and your leading historian. If the doctor is worth his salt, he is concerned about the physical well-being of young people, and their future well-being as adults. If the historian is worth his salt, he will have detected the symptoms of a decaying culture, and will be sympathetic to what you're trying to do.

For all of Hahn's intense interest in what we were doing in Outward Bound, I was aware that his main concerns were elsewhere. It is a remarkable fact that in his long, intimate association with the Outward Bound movement, he never held an official position. As an inventor of institutions, it was a part of his genius that he was content to leave their administering to others.

On most of those visits his primary interest was in advancing the Atlantic College project in Wales and its subsequent United World College movement. Atlantic College—later United World College of the Atlantic—with its concept of bringing together students from many nations in a precollege program, was an immediate success. Today there are also the Lester Pearson United World College of the Pacific in British Columbia, the United World

College of Southeast Asia in Singapore, the United World College of the Adriatic in Italy, the Waterford Kamhlaba United World College of Southern Africa in Swaziland, the Simon Bolivar United World College of Agriculture in Venezuela, and the Armand Hammer United World College of the American West in Montezuma, New Mexico.

Rescue and community services to those in danger and in need. The late Earl Mountbatten of Burma, long the movement's international leader, confirmed a heartfelt Hahn thesis: "It's hard to hate someone when you're both helping to save a life."

That is a variation of Hahn's "Whoever saves a life will never take a life." No other human being, perhaps, responded as avidly as Hahn to William James's call to seek "the moral equivalent of war." He recognized that Tennyson's "peace of the broken wing"—peace that softens rather than tests moral fiber—was itself a menace to peace. The answer, Hahn was convinced, lay in "the passion of rescue." His moral equivalent of war was to "enthrall and hold the young through active and willing Samaritan service, demanding care and skill, courage and endurance, discipline and initiative." With each new visit I observed the conviction grow more resolute.

While U.S. Outward Bound evolved in many ways that Hahn had never contemplated, there was no aspect of that evolution that he failed to approve. On the contrary, he was an enthusiastic, though always thoughtful, receptor to each new development. In the beginning much of the change related to a broadening of the student constituency for our schools. The initial constituency was simply that defined for us by the British precedent: boys and young men from ages $16^{1}/_{2}$ to 23. From very early on we ensured that that constituency would be as broad as possible by requiring that half of each school's enrollment should be scholarship students. This was a deliberate decision to prevent Outward Bound from developing a "preppie" stigma. Knowing that it would be fatal to our purposes if the organization came to be thought of as available just to the affluent, we wanted a broad socioeconomic mix. One important consequence of this policy was that a share of the scholarships went to disadvantaged youngsters in the inner cities, many of them entangled in difficulties with society, some of them already adjudicated. This was one of the factors that led to Outward Bound's pioneering of large-scale projects successfully employing adventure-based education as a rehabilitation vehicle in working with delinquent youth.

The first major break with our constituency precedent was the introduction and astonishing success of courses for young women, along with the equally "astonishing" discovery that girls could handle—at times even with a superior blitheness—the same courses, of the same degree of difficulty, that had been designed for boys. Then came highly popular adult coed courses. These were followed, inevitably, by courses for adult women, likewise highly

successful—to the discomfort of whatever remnants there were of a once rather pure macho esprit. By then all adult age limits were off, and some of the schools also introduced junior courses.

Another way in which the Outward Bound program has evolved is in the increasing importance accorded the service project that is a component of every course. At the same time, often responding to needs not unrelated to those revealed in service activity, schools have introduced into their programs a growing variety of courses for particular student constituencies. These range from courses especially designed for business executives and other enterprise managers to those for individuals whose special needs entail some form of handicap. Heartening results are being achieved with students who have, for example, physical handicaps or hearing impairments, or who, again for example, are seeking release from drug or alcohol dependency or are emotionally disturbed. In one such undertaking a prominent New England treatment hospital and an Outward Bound school have joined forces in an adolescent chemical dependency rehabilitation program. In another that has attracted national attention, Outward Bound is conducting a therapeutic program for Vietnam veterans afflicted with post traumatic stress disorder, or PTSD, a mental condition marked by combat-induced flashbacks, feelings of isolation and depression, violent outbursts, and low self-esteem.

The city as an Outward Bound environment has long intrigued the schools, and several are embarking on urban-based programs. The current outstanding instance is New York City Outward Bound. Adults—often young business executives—are paired with inner city teenagers in three-day courses that manage to incorporate urban versions of the various wilderness challenges—including rock climbing and a Tyrolean traverse—encountered in a regular Outward Bound course. The service project may be providing recreation to children crowded with their families into one of the city's hotels for the homeless, or taking a group of Black women living in a Brooklyn home for battered women on an ice-skating expedition.

Most of the foregoing is illustrative of the fact that in the last decade Outward Bound has become increasingly concerned for the well-being of persons who have been visited with misfortunes that the more fortunate among us have escaped. This appears to confirm something that Kurt Hahn seems always to have known: that there is a force inherent in the Outward Bound dynamic that generates compassion.

In 1968 Hahn made what proved to be his final journey to the United States. Deeply concerned about the worldwide violence generated by youthful rebellion and racial conflict, he was looking for guidance from the American experience. Long before, he had given to Sir Robert Birley, headmaster of Eton, counsel that Birley never forgot: "Whenever you have to deal with a boy who is a rebel, remember that you must get him to face the question: Are you going to be a fighter or a quarreler?" Now he was looking for ways to harness productively the fighting spirit of young people in revolt.

For two months he crossed the continent and back, from Harvard to West Coast campuses, from Harlem to Watts, seeking new knowledge about student and racial tensions, new leads to healing forces. Fred Glimp, who was Dean of Harvard during the student riots there that year, still marvels at Hahn's keen comprehension of the issues and events on the Cambridge campus. Five years after his 1968 visit to the headquarters of the National Urban League's street workers in Harlem, they had vivid recall of the 82-year-old gentleman from England who came up the stairs two at a time. On Hahn's visit there, a boy who had recently returned from a course at Hurricane Island told him, "It gives you a feeling of great power if you breathe life into a dead person." This was one more affirmation of the message he was carrying on his cross-country safari: "The passion of rescue releases the highest dynamic of the human soul." As he made that safari, his sun-induced affliction was heavy upon him. At such places as New York's Horace Mann School, Wayzata, Minnesota, and the Athenian School in Danville, California, people still remember the dim, imposing figure at the front of a darkened, crowded room, tirelessly answering—and asking—questions, offering his ideas ("I am anxious to carry conviction on this") in response to theirs.

He was intent on inventing a new institution. His dauntless mind worked toward a grand plan under which a "Service by Youth Commission" would coordinate forces enabling young people to contribute productive energies that otherwise would be spilled in confrontation or drained by frustration. Central to the plan was the removal by aid-and-rescue agencies of age restrictions preventing service by adolescent volunteers, and an international call to young men and women to help in the fight against unnecessary death and suffering. "Lifesaving," Hahn kept telling his American audiences, "is the job of the layman. The less serious things we can leave to the doctors."

In the Watts section of Los Angeles, he listened eagerly for two and a half hours as Ted Watkins, chairman of the Watts Labor Community Action Committee, talked about his work with ghetto youth. Ted told him about the Watts young people painting telephone poles to spruce up the streets, starting a chicken and pet farm, converting derelict lots into "vest-pocket parks." Ted said, "Every youngster should be called on to make a sweat investment. He needs something he can protect." Hahn liked that. He made it a theme of his Service by Youth plan.

As his grueling safari ended, his affliction worsened. I drove him to the Boston airport with blankets blacking out the car windows. He wore the homburg hat with the broad, turned-down brim, an arrangement of green felt lined with lead foil shielding the back of his neck, and two pairs of dark glasses. At the plane's door his hand came up in the familiar farewell gesture. I was wrenchingly aware of that aircraft carrying off one whose comprehending concern for our sick world was irreplaceable.

Back in London and Scotland he worked on the Service by Youth plan. For all the grandiose scale of his thinking, the ideas he set down were cogent, down-to-earth, feasible. In a very real sense, I believe, he foresaw the coming tragedies of student shootings at Kent State and Jackson State and was working to prevent them. But he was not able, as he always before had been, to exert the force of his personal drive in support of that project. Struck by a car on a country road near Gordonstoun, he never fully recovered from the accident; yet he turned even that misfortune to opportunity. The mishap gave him a new idea. He wrote Prince Philip, urging his support for a plan to reduce road deaths by including first aid in the driving test. The prince did take up that cause, giving it his earnest backing.

In retirement at last in Hermannsburg, Germany, living in an apartment at one of Salem's satellite schools, Kurt Hahn died on December 15, 1974. He was 88.

There was one "unfinished business" aspect of Outward Bound's evolution that always concerned Hahn, as it has long concerned Outward Bounders everywhere, that I must mention. This is the perennial question of the "follow-up."

U.S. Outward Bounders sometimes do an unconscious disservice by quoting out of context the closing line of Hahn's address at the 1965 Outward Bound Conference at Harrogate, England, where follow-up had been one of the important debated subjects. His concluding words were, "Outward Bound can ignite—that is all—it is for others to keep the flame alive." The line is usually quoted under the impression that Hahn in a sense was negating the follow-up question by relegating the responsibility to a vague, undefined "others." The error of the impression lies, I think, in failure to appreciate (perhaps not even to have seen) what the context was. For in his preceding paragraph Hahn had quite clearly defined whom he meant by "others," and quite clearly stated the form he believed follow-up should take:

> I believe that the challenge of Samaritan service, if properly presented, rarely fails to capture young people, body and soul, not only in the Western World. I hear encouraging news about the young behind the Iron Curtain—many of them look westward, with distrust but also with hope. They ask a question which makes us blush: "Are you in earnest about the ideals you profess?" Who shall give an answer? Young men and women who render hard and willing service to their fellow men in danger and in need.

A few months later, visiting in Andover, Hahn gave me a photograph of himself. Part of the inscription, in the form of a charge, was an even more explicit restatement of the thought he had left with the conferees at Harrogate:

> To Josh Miner . . . May he remember that the best service he can render to Outward Bound is to recognize its limits: Outward Bound can kindle the flame but it will be extinguished in many cases unless Outward Bounders, returning to their schools and workshops, are confronted by the challenge and the opportunities to go on active service to help their fellow men in danger and in need. Their resolution to do so will be strengthened if we can build up an aristocracy of service throughout the free world, whose example will create a fashion of conduct.

That "aristocracy of service" was the new institution the 82-year-old Hahn was seeking to invent in the aftermath of his 1968 U.S. safari. The lengthy memorandum he wrote upon his return home and sent to his Outward Bound and other American friends is a kind of testament to all of us who care about the well-being of his institutions. In the memorandum's final paragraph, using the designation *helper* for those performing Samaritan service, he stated the salient, consuming idea one more time:

> One would hope that one day the status of helper would be recognized throughout the Western world—thereby a new and challenging avenue of distinction might be opened. Such development would go far to solve the baffling problem of the "follow-up" for Outward Bound and kindred enterprises.

Henry Brereton said it so well: "Kurt Hahn, who often appears so Victorian in language and manners, belongs in a deep sense to the new age of hope. Like the great artists and scientists, like the astronauts, he is a citizen of global mankind."

Chapter 8

Kurt Hahn

Anthony Richards
Dalhousie University

The phenomenon which has become known as *Hahnism* (Skidelsky, 1976) is the unique approach to experiential education explicated by Kurt Hahn and embodied in the many institutions that he founded, as well as a host of adventure-based experiential education programs, one of which is Outward Bound.

There were four discernible phases in Hahn's life. The first is the period of his childhood, youth, and schooling which eventually took him to universities in Germany and England. This was a time when he was strongly influenced by both family and teachers. The second phase did not begin until he was 34 years of age when he opened his first school in Germany. This is a relatively late age to be starting into the field of education. He would probably have remained with this school, Salem, in Germany, and would not have had an international reputation had it not been for the Nazi movement and Hahn's imprisonment by Hitler. It was the result of this imprisonment and his subsequent release which led him to seek exile in Britain and begin the third phase of his life. This third phase was particularly important because of the number of educational ideas he spawned that led to the establishment of several new schools, programs and indeed institutions. Hahn was in his late 40s when he opened Gordonstoun School in Scotland and Anavryta School in Greece. He also created during his middle age the County Badge Scheme and its outgrowth, Outward Bound. The fourth phase started with Hahn's serious illness at the age of 67, which forced his retirement as headmaster of Gordonstoun. A successful operation in 1955 enabled Hahn to continue to initiate educational projects. The Duke of Edinburgh Award Scheme and Atlantic College were established during this phase, and as an octogenarian he was still active in some of the decision making at various board meetings.

During some of the most turbulent times in recent history with two world wars and educational reform, Hahn was still able to make his mark with a brand of education that has continued to be prominent today. However, it was his unity of purpose without a unity of focus which allowed continual adaptation. One of his weaknesses was his inability to let go and hand the reins over to someone else. Whenever another person or group took over his program (e.g., Outward Bound Trust in 1946), he immediately took this adversity and turned it into an opportunity to create something new. He was a living example of one of his favorite sayings, "your disability is your opportunity." However, in his twilight years he was gracious enough to favorably recognize the variety of agencies which had taken over his programs and ideas.

Hahn was a trained propagandist. His apprenticeship with Prince Max von Baden as a political writer in the German Foreign Office helped him to articulate his position in a very convincing manner. Hogan (1968) felt that Hahn was an "artist with words" and that he was always able to gain "maximum emotional consequence." This was particularly evident in his speeches. His style of presentation utilized aphorisms and anecdotes which were generated from concrete examples. He was often accused of speaking with an economy of truth and inventing statistical evidence when little or none existed. The translation from German to English was not as precise as it might be. This resulted in some of his phrases and expressions being perceived as offensive or radical. For example, in reference to normal adolescent sexual development he used the expressions, "deformities of puberty" and the "poisonous passions." Nevertheless, Hahn made no attempt to moderate these expressions because they had substantial effect and impact during his speeches.

For all the limitations that Hahn had with respect to his language, suspect sources, and dogmatic style, he was still able to impress the "right people." The result was substantial support for his ideas both fiscally and morally. When he was promoting a new idea or program he would leave no stone unturned in order to achieve success. This tenacity of pursuit became one of his trademarks and a notion that pervades all of his programs.

Kurt Hahn was not a prolific writer. Most of his original writings are in the form of transcribed speeches. On several occasions he issued a limited edition of a particular article or would stamp the manuscript "confidential." There appears to be no reason for this other than the fact that he did not want his writing to be made available to the general public for fear that he would be challenged on the grounds that the information was his definitive statement on education. There is no doubt that he had a brand of education that was eclectic in nature but was seen as unique and original.

From the very early days of Salem, Kurt Hahn would say of the school's methods that "there is nothing new." They were borrowed from many sources: from Plato, from Dr. Arnold of Rugby, from Eton, from Abbotsholme, from Hermann Lietz, from Fichte and from Wilhelm Meister. Each of them had proven successful in his own time and Hahn attempted to take the best from each. He was not concerned that some of the sources were not German. As patriotic as he was, he was still liberal enough to accept ideas from other countries provided that they were useful. He had no time for his colleagues who would reject ideas on the basis of their origin and not consider their merit. He would often say, "nor do I sympathize with the continental (German) gentleman who refused to be vaccinated because Jenner was an Englishman" (Hahn, 1940, p. 11).

Hahn was extremely clever at borrowing without copying. His adaptations and application of the elements he borrowed were unique. He had the ability to manipulate and create a new and novel way of delivering an educational experience from common practices such as was evidenced in the English public school system or from the fundamental educational ideas expressed by Plato.

Hahn's conception of education was simple. Its purpose was to develop a righteous man who is vigilant and an active citizen, who has a sense of duty to his fellow man and to God. Whereas this notion was not particularly earth shattering, the process by which he achieved his ends made his educational style effective. So much so that his delivery ideas began to take on the ambience of a philosophy rather than a mere novel teaching method.

In Hahn's writing he seldom refers to academic achievement as being the primary purpose of his schools. In fact, he frequently provides examples of end of term reports which are sent home to parents. In these reports he lists, in his order of importance, the categories in which the teacher is to comment. The evaluative items are public spirit, sense of justice, the faculty of precise evidence, the power to do things right in the face of dangers (e.g., exhaustion, hostile public opinion, skepticism and boredom), imagination, and the power of organization. At the end of the priority list comes Latin, Greek, mathematics and other academic subjects (Hahn, 1947, 1956, 1957).

Educating for active citizenship was fundamental to Hahn's philosophy. He believed that every child was born with innate "spiritual powers" as well as an innate faculty which enables him or her to make correct judgments about moral issues. As the child progresses through adolescence, he or she loses the "spiritual powers" and ability to make correct judgments because of, what Hahn referred to as, the "diseased society" and the impulses of adolescence. In addition, he criticized the "nerve exhausting" practices which were employed in other schools (e.g., examinations). There is, of course, always the counter belief that such powers and conscience are acquired characteristics and not innate, but such beliefs were not Hahn's.

Hahn was obsessed with the social "declines" or social diseases which occurred in his society. These declines have been variously identified by Hahn as:

- decline of fitness due to modern methods of locomotion,
- decline of initiative and enterprise due to the widespread disease of spectatoritis,
- decline of memory and imagination due to the confused restlessness of modern life,
- decline of skill and care due to the weakened tradition of craftsmanship,
- decline of self-discipline due to the ever-present availability of stimulants and tranquilizers, and
- decline of compassion due to the unseemly haste with which modern life is conducted.

Hahn (1934) concluded that the civilization of the day is diseased, often sapping the strength of the young before they can grow up. In 1938 he referred to the "phlegmainousa polis" (the inflamed city) in which youth grow up. The only solution to these problems, Hahn believed, was through education. It is interesting to note that the concerns, and sometimes the criticism of youth in the 1990s are centered on these same declines even though the turn of phrase and manifestation may be a little different. For example, a simple study conducted in 1943 of the outcomes of an early Outward Bound course in Aberdovey showed that the boys returned home some 10 pounds heavier as a result of the good food and exercise. A claim of a modern North American Outward Bound school may be that the participants would return home 10 pounds lighter following a course. The results are opposite but both programs are addressing the first of Hahn's concerns, the decline of fitness.

Each of the "declines" was addressed by Hahn through prescriptive activities which would bring about a collective cure to each disease. His rationale varied according to the group he was addressing or the kind of project at the time. The solution to the six declines appears in the justification for all of Hahn's educational enterprises: Salem School, Gordonstoun School, the County Badge Scheme, Outward Bound, the Duke of Edinburgh Award Scheme, and the United World Colleges. Hahn's solutions to the six declines follow.

The Decline of Fitness

There was widespread "physical illiteracy" around the time that Hahn was developing the curriculum for Gordonstoun School. He believed that it was curable. His solution was to introduce a 45-minute daily physical activity program. Each boy participated in running, throwing and jumping activities. These track and field events had a specific set of standards to be achieved by each boy. The reason for having to work toward these standards went beyond the physical benefits. It was as important for each boy to develop and improve on his weak events as it was to nurture his talents. In fact, the phrase used by Hahn (1961a) was that each boy should "defeat his own defeatism."

Another phrase which has become more popular with Hahn disciples is, "your disability is your opportunity." This occurred frequently in the physical activity program where boys often found hidden talents such as in Hahn's story of a sprinter discovering that he was a better distance runner when a slight injury prevented him from competing in the shorter faster event. The carry-over into the real world allowed many of the boys not to be discouraged by minor setbacks, but to look at them as an opportunity to move in a new direction.

This daily physical education program differed from those of other English public schools which had a strong emphasis and even stronger tradition of team games. Both Salem and Gordonstoun confined their team games to two afternoons per week. This allowed more time for personal development. It was Hahn's experience that this somewhat extensive physical activity program during the morning break did not disturb, but actually enhanced the subsequent classroom work (Hahn, 1938).

Another reason for including an extensive physical activity program was the concern for decline in vital health which was more than a mere absence of illness (Hahn, 1962a). On several occasions Hahn made reference to "underexercise" contributing to coronary thrombosis. He believed that middle-aged men and women could not be expected to take part in regular exercise when the joy of movement has already been extinguished in puberty (Hahn, 1962b).

It is quite easy to see the similarity with the lack of fitness in young people in the 1990s. Also the more recent interest in holistic wellness bears some resemblance to Hahn's notion of vital health. It may be worth rejustifying the physical activity programs in modern schools with the principle that it may contribute to lifelong wellness and healthy lifestyles.

The Decline of Initiative and Enterprise

The decline arose from the inactivity and passive pursuits of young people. Hahn felt that it was akin to a disease which he called *spectatoritis* and credited its origin to the "Americans." He claimed that when a boy sat in a movie theater or listened to the radio, he experienced the thrill of a great adventure and the associated stirring events with unconscious movements of his body and without leaving his seat. He felt part of the action, but Hahn claimed that "the sensation was bogus and transitory but was always hotly desired" (Hahn, 1962b, p. 4). This conclusion has been corroborated in contemporary research on the effect of television on children and youth (Mander, 1978).

The solution to this decline was the introduction of the "expedition" to the curriculum. The expedition into the mountains or the ocean nourished the spirit of adventure. George Trevelyan in a 1943 speech at the christening of the boat *Garibaldi,* at Aberdovey Outward Bound School, said, "without the instinct for adventure in the young men any civilization, however enlightened, must wilt and whither." Hahn was fond of this quote because it illustrated the importance he placed on expeditions that generated opportunities for adventure. He felt that the rigor of expeditions could stretch young boys beyond the track and field activity program. As the training for track and field would help the boy defeat his own defeatism, so the expedition gives the boy the power to overcome (Hahn, 1960). It also revealed the inner worth of the man, the edge of his temper, the fiber of his stuff, the quality of his resistance, the secret truth of his pretenses, not only to himself but to others (Hahn, 1961b).

The expeditions were not always popular with the students despite their value. Hahn relates a story of a boy who had just completed a sailing expedition around the Orkneys. After encountering three gales, he was asked how he enjoyed the adventure. The boy replied: "Magnificently, but not at the time!" This story was used in nearly every speech where Hahn was explaining the virtues of expeditions and adventure as an integral part of the school curriculum.

The Decline of Memory and Imagination

This occurred, according to Hahn, because of an increased pace of life and the rapidly changing political climate of the time. Boys did not have enough opportunity to stop and reflect. There was a need for periods of aloneness. Hahn (1961a) stated that "neither the love of man nor the love of God can take deep root except in aloneness" (p. 15). These times alone were the opportunity to look to the future as well as to reflect.

At Gordonstoun the silent walk to chapel became an important feature for each boy to use to develop his memory and imagination. There were also other activities such as journal writing which would encourage reflection. Most of these opportunities were short in duration, unlike the extended solo often used in the North American Outward Bound schools.

In addition to the opportunity to reflect, Hahn believed that these solo experiences helped to develop memory which was vital. He had a story to illustrate the hazards of a poor memory:

> There was once a famous banker on the Continent who gathered his five sons round his death bed and gave them this piece of advice, "Never tell lies, my boys, your memory is not good enough." If our audiences have a bad memory, and particularly the audiences of politicians, there is a great temptation for the speaker, I won't say to tell lies, but to operate with an economy of truth. (Hahn, 1962a, p. 4)

The Decline of Skill and Care

Because of an increase in technology there was a reduction in the demand for craftsmen. It is the care and pride associated with artists and craftsmen which was disappearing. One of the reasons the Salem students had to spend time with the artisans in the Cistercian Monastery was that craftsmen were far less likely to accept second rate or unfinished work in the same way as the schoolmaster (Hahn, 1934b).

An indication of the extent of this decline is illustrated in Hahn's story of the boy who produced a very shoddy piece of work. Hahn said to him, "Now this is really awful! Aren't you ashamed of yourself?" the boy grinned and said, "It's the genius of the British race to muddle through."

And in his innermost heart he believed that he was contributing to the genius of the race (Hahn, 1961a).

A job of skill often requires a substantial degree of patience. Hahn (1938) referred to the modern boy as having an impetuous lust for quick results. To encourage this patience and pursuit of quality each boy was required to select a project. Extended periods of time were devoted to the project and it was expected that each boy would pursue his task through to excellence. The final product was not necessarily evaluated on its finite level of excellence, but rather the tenacity of the pursuit.

These projects were referred to as "the grande passion" and the idea came about as a result of Hahn's concern about the problems which arise in boys during puberty:

> The discovery of sources of passionate interest can protect the growing young against what have been called the "deforming influences of puberty," resulting in irritability, listlessness, the lack of mental and physical coordination; which some psychologists have regarded as unavoidable symptoms of adolescence. (Hahn, 1965, p. 7)

Hahn believed the psychologists to be wrong. He contended that if a substitute passion could be found, then there was no reason a boy could not pass from childhood to adulthood without being contaminated by an unnatural sex drive (Hahn, 1934):

> If you look around the professions, who would you say has preserved the strength—you might also say the beauty—of childhood? The hunter from the hill, the sailor from the sea. Why? Because their adolescence was guarded by health giving passions. (Hahn, 1938, p. 5)

The Decline of Self-Discipline

In order to overcome this decline, Hahn devised a system of daily exercise and healthy habits known as the "Training Plan." Each student was only permitted to participate in the Training Plan provided that he had proved to the faculty that he could be trusted to complete the daily ritual unsupervised. Each day the students were required to complete all of the following: one warm wash, two cold showers, 30 skips, high jump, running, throwing, no eating between meals, report all illness, account book, and a duty.

The concern by Hahn that self-discipline was declining was spirited by his opinion that the availability of stimulants and tranquilizers was so easy that without self-discipline young people would be "swallowed up" in such things as smoking, drinking, reading undesirable books, indiscriminate listening to the radio, too frequent visits to the cinema, and staying out late (Hahn, 1934).

The Training Plan was created at Salem. When Hahn introduced it to Gordonstoun many people warned him that British children would not respond to the regime. However, the Gordonstoun boys accepted the principle with enthusiasm, and many of the subsequent alumni agreed that it was useful to them in later life. To have experienced a sensible precedent of self-denial proved to be of value to those alumni who were influenced by Hahn. It is interesting to note that when Hahn left Gordonstoun his successors did not understand the rationale for the Training Plan, and it soon became used more as a punishment than a privilege.

The Decline of Compassion

This was considered to be the worst decline of all. The haste with which life was conducted did not allow the time for people to be compassionate. An illustration of the decline is reflected in the story about the time Hahn was driven through Lehrter Station in Berlin in 1945. At this time, there were refugees arriving in cattle trucks, many of them were close to death. The driver of the car was an American sergeant with a kindly, friendly face. While they were driving through the scenes of misery and death he listened to jazz on the radio. He was asked by Hahn's host to turn it off. When Hahn was questioned as to what had happened to the young sergeant, he responded, "He has a dispersed soul which he could not assemble even before the majesty of death" (Hahn, 1947). Hahn therefore looked for deliberate ways of including activities which developed compassion.

The antidote Hahn introduced to counter the decline of compassion was the element of *service*. He was very fond of using the parable of the Samaritan. This provided a metaphor for the service-oriented activities which became an outstanding feature of Hahn's educational programs. At Gordonstoun it was the coast guard service and the volunteer fire brigade; at the Outward Bound Schools it was the mountain rescue teams; and at Atlantic College it was the adoption of the surf rescue service. Kurt Hahn (1962b) believed it to be the supreme task of education to help the young to achieve a balance of power in their inner lives so that the love of man can take charge. The saving of life contributed to this objective.

A cliché which Hahn and many of his supporters used is the concept of an "aristocracy of service." This evolved from an article by William James on the *Moral Equivalent of War*. The title seemed to catch their imagination and was still used many years later in the promotion of American Outward Bound Schools. Whereas James deplored war, he did admit that war satisfied a primitive longing which will never be extinguished: the longing to lose oneself in a common cause that claimed the whole man. Everyone needed a Holy Grail, but it was unreasonable to expect that a war be arranged every time society or an individual

needed to realize himself (Hahn, 1962b). Therefore, a moral equivalent was needed. Hahn maintained that not only was his Samaritan ethic an equivalent, but it was capable of releasing the highest dynamics of the human soul. In every article and speech delivered by Hahn after 1949, the rescue service or Samaritan ethic was always considered to be more than the moral equivalent of war.

These six declines formed the core of all of Kurt Hahn's educational ideas and achievements. Over the past 50 years they have undergone many interpretations but generally are as applicable today as they were in 1933. The fact that most of Hahn's programs and schools are still operating today is testimony to the robustness of his ideas. What was an issue and a need for young people in the 1930s is still current today. In some sense Hahn was ahead of his time in creating a delivery system in education which is pervasive throughout experiential educators today. Of all the sayings that Hahn used, the most famous was the following:

> We believe that it is the sin of the soul to force the young into opinions, but we consider it culpable neglect not to impel every youngster into health-giving experiences, regardless of their inclinations. (Hahn, 1935)

The essence of this statement lies in nonindoctrination yet at the same time nudging the child into action. The most recent clarification by Hahn was in 1967 when he responded to the original manuscript of a book by Robert Skidelsky. He expands the original statement:

> You and I would agree that indoctrination is of the devil and that it is a crime to force anybody into opinions but I, unlike you, consider it culpable neglect not to guide and even plunge the young into experiences which are likely to present opportunities for self-discovery. If you spare the young such experiences, in deference to their wishes, you stunt their natural growth of basic human qualities which they will need for their own happiness and for service to their fellow men. (1967, p. 2)

It seems that most adventure-based experiential education programs, whether they have their roots in Outward Bound or not, all have program goals and objectives that are consistent with Hahn's sentiments expressed in this classic quotation.

In summary it would be fair to say that Kurt Hahn's philosophy of education was somewhat limited in range as compared with some of the "greats." However, he was a master of capturing some profound ideas and presenting them as simple notions. He had a unique talent of being able to rework many statements to suit the needs of the occasion. When he was embarking on a new project which required funding and support, he could present a rationale which was not only inoffensive, but was immediately compelling.

References

Hahn, K. (1934). A German public school. *The Listener*, January 17, pp. 90–92.

Hahn, K. (1935). Report to annual meeting of Gordonstoun School, London, July 18.

Hahn, K. (1938). *Education for leisure*. Conference of schoolmasters and college tutors at Magdalen college. Oxford, UK: University Press.

Hahn, K. (1940). *The love of enterprise, the love of aloneness, the love of skill*. Lecture delivered in Liverpool Cathedral, December 22.

Hahn, K. (1947). *Active citizenship*. Address to Elgin Rotary Club.

Hahn, K. (1956). Juvenile irresponsibility. *Gordonstoun Record, 22*(2), 15–21.

Hahn, K. (1957). Speech at meeting with Friends of Gordonstoun, Admiralty House, London, November 17.

Hahn, K. (1960). Education and changes in our social structure. *BACIE Journal, 14*(1), 1–5.

Hahn, K. (1961a). A cure for the lawless young. *The Sunday Telegraph*, April 2.

Hahn, K. (1961b). *Service by youth*. Address to directors of Bournville Co. Ltd., April.

Hahn, K. (1962a). Unnecessary deaths. *The Listener*, April 26, pp. 715–716.

Hahn, K. (1962b). State of the young in England. *The Listener*, July, pp. 52–53.

Hahn, K. (1965). *Outward Bound*. Address at the Conference at Harrogate, May 9.

Hahn, K. (1967). Letter to Robert Skidelsky, October 30.

Hogan, J. (1968). *Impelled into experience; The story of Outward Bound*. Yorkshire, UK: Educational Publications, Ltd.

Mander, J. (1978). *Four arguments for the elimination of television*. New York, NY: William Morrow and Co., Inc.

Skidelsky, R. (1976). A respectful farewell. *The Encounter, 46*, 86–90.

Chapter 9

A History of the Association
for Experiential Education

Daniel Garvey
University of New Hampshire

As the flight attendant announced our arrival in St. Louis, I awoke from a not-so-sound sleep, gathered my personal belongings from the overhead compartment and floor space in front of my seat, and shuffled off the plane into the airport. Another annual Association for Experiential Education (AEE) conference! Could this possibly be number 16 for the association? My thoughts drifted back to previous gatherings of the association, and as I made my way to the baggage claim area, I privately reflected on these yearly get-togethers and the wonderful memories created during a brief four days every fall.

This conference will be different, not only in the ways that all conferences take on their own character, but because my role within the association has changed. This year, instead of arriving with one piece of carry-on luggage, I have arrived with three suitcases (actually *trunks* would be a better word), because this year I come as the executive director of the association. In addition to several changes of clothes, these trunks contain most of the important records of the AEE; minutes of previous board meetings, bylaws, ballots for the board election, and an assortment of other documents and office supplies.

Driving from the airport in St. Louis to the conference site at the Touch of Nature Environmental Center in Carbondale, Illinois, I attempted to piece together the history of AEE and found I couldn't even be sure of which year conferences were held in certain locations: Was the Portsmouth, New Hampshire conference in 1978 or was it

1979? Placing conferences with their dates was less difficult than attempting to put significant activities of the association within an historical context.

This chapter is an attempt to write a brief history of AEE. I have not said "*The* History" because I expect others who have lived through the development of the association will continue to deepen our understanding of the activities of the past 25 years. In researching this chapter I have attempted to read whatever I could find about the Association for Experiential Education. Of particular help has been the compilation of board minutes pulled together by my friend and former association officer, Betsy Dalgliesh. In addition to the "written word," I have also had formal and informal interviews with Joe Nold, Dick Kraft, Tony Richards, Keith King, Peggy Walker-Stevens, and Jim Keilsmeier, each of whom has played a significant role in the birth and/or continuation of the association. There are many others, to be sure, who could or should have been contacted to gain insight and factual information. I hope this chapter will serve as a beginning and I encourage all who read it to offer their version of history for future updates.

The Association for Experiential Education (AEE) is a member-supported international organization made up of approximately 1,700 individual and 650 corporate and institutional members. The association is committed to the practice and promotion of learning through experience and to the collection and dissemination of information related to the broad topic of experiential education. One of the major foci of the association has been in the area of "adventure education." Since many of our members are involved in the use of experiential techniques in wilderness and adventure settings, the association has maintained a strong commitment to the development of safe practices for adventure programming. In 1980 the Adventure Alternatives Professional Group was formed within AEE. This group has been a powerful collective of practitioners interested in the application of experiential techniques with populations in corrections, mental health, and groups with special needs.

AEE publishes the *Journal of Experiential Education* three times per year, eight books specifically focused on the topic of experiential education and it's application in a variety of settings (including the *Directory of Adventure Alternatives,* edited by Michael Gass, which identified 137 organizations and agencies "providing programs that link therapeutic strategies with experiential practices"), periodic newsletters, and the Jobs Clearinghouse, a listing of positions available throughout North America. In addition to publications, the association also convenes regional and national conferences to help practitioners upgrade their skills and provide a meeting time for like minded people to come together to exchange ideas and renew friendships. Within the association there are four professional interest groups: adventure alternatives, programming for the disabled, schools and colleges, and women in experiential education. The AEE office is located within the school of education at the University of Colorado at Boulder.

The Formation of an Association

The story might begin by placing the birth of the AEE within the context of the "progressive" education movement, as has been described by Albert Adams and Sherrod Reynolds (1985). The purpose of my chapter is to recognize the rich history of experiential education and to focus more directly upon the Association for Experiential Education as a relatively unique adaptation of this educational philosophy. During the late 1970s, Outward Bound began to focus upon teacher training as one way to help influence the direction of the American educational system. The apparent success of Outward Bound programs on previously disinterested students was well-documented and a small group of colleges and universities began to explore the idea of including these techniques within their formal teacher training programs.

In 1968 the Colorado Outward Bound School, under the direction of Joe Nold, began to affiliate with the University of Northern Colorado in Greeley in offering teachers practice. The goal of these "teacher's courses" was to produce a different type of teacher by addressing the criticism that, "methods classes, certification requirements, and

eight-week teacher-training courses, have failed to produce quality educators" (1969). Another program was located at Appalachian State University in Boone, North Carolina. In 1971 Keener Smathers, an assistant professor of secondary education, began to offer a summer teacher-training program which included an Outward Bound course at the North Carolina school.

The success of this program and interest shown by other colleges and universities, led Smathers to write to Henry Taft, president of Outward Bound, Inc., seeking his assistance to help organize a conference which would bring together members of the academic community with staff from the various Outward Bound schools to discuss the value of Outward Bound–type activities at the postsecondary level. Taft responded by sending John Rhodes, program coordinator at Outward Bound, Inc., to work with Smathers at Appalachian State and the two of them planned a conference for February 1974 (cf., Miner and Boldt, 1981). The First North American Conference on Outdoor Pursuits in Higher Education was convened February 10, 1974, at Appalachian State University. One hundred and thirty-six people preregistered for the conference and over 200 attended. One of the attendees, Keith King, who was running his own program at Keene State College in New Hampshire, remembers vividly this first gathering:

> I always took students with me to conferences so I guess there were a dozen or so with me. When I heard about the conference, I just knew I had to go. There wasn't much support for what we were doing, most of us weren't sure if anyone else was trying to teach students this way.

Dave Hopkinson, a student of Keith's recounted to me that he was, "blown away by the experience of being with this exciting group of people at this first gathering."

Henry Taft delivered the keynote address, "The Value of Experience." He ended his talk with the following statement: "Finally, I would hope that some sort of national organization on outdoor experiential education at the college level may evolve from this trailblazing meeting. You are in unexplored territory, and about to be impelled into experience. Good luck" (Taft, 1974). A group of conferees, headed by Alan Hale, presented an outline for a possible national association as a follow-up to the conference. One of the recommendations included the formation of a national steering committee to oversee the development of a future conference and the possibility of a larger association. This first steering committee consisted of Bob Godfrey, University of Colorado; Don Kesselheim, University of Massachusetts; John Rhodes, Outward Bound Inc.; Richard Rogers, Earlham College; and Keener Smathers, Appalachian State University.

The second conference was held eight months later, in October, at Estes Park, Colorado. The organizer of this gathering was Bob Godfrey. The Estes Park conference was noteworthy because of the wide variety of educators who were in attendance. Unlike the previous conference in North Carolina where Outward Bound staff had come together with college faculty, the Colorado conference was attended by "regular classroom teachers."

Reflecting upon this stage of what was to become the AEE, Tony Richards suggested that this inclusion of educators from outside the outdoor pursuits area opened the conferences to a diversity of participants had helped ensure that "you didn't have to be vaccinated with an Outward Bound course to be a member of this group."

Perhaps the most vivid memory of those in attendance at the Estes Park conference was the address delivered by William Unsoeld which he titled "The Spiritual Value of the Wilderness." In this speech, Unsoeld provided a well-articulated rationale for "adventure activities." The effect upon participants was profound. Again quoting Keith King, "We came out of his speech 45 feet in the air, and we didn't come down until we hit New Hampshire."

The 1975 conference was convened by Alan Hale, at Mankato State University. The use of Outward Bound activities on university and college campuses was gaining popularity and the need for a more formal organization was solidifying. Following the 1976 conference, hosted by Bob Pieh at Queens University in Kingston, Ontario, a group of interested participants met and finally pulled together this rather loose group of affiliated individuals and institutions into the Association for Experiential Education. Rick Medrick authored the Articles of Incorporation, which were filed in the state of Colorado on June 17, 1977. The stated purpose of this new association was to "promote experiential education, support experiential educators, and further develop experiential learning approaches through such services as conferences, publications, consulting, research, workshops, etc." The registered agent for the association was Maria Snyder, who was working as a secretary with Joe Nold in his "Project Center" at the Colorado Outward Bound School in Denver (AEE, 1977).

This was the beginning of AEE. The need for college faculty using experiential methods to affiliate, and the financial and emotional support from Outward Bound combined to form a lasting bond which helped create this new organization. Though most of the early members of the association were "cut from the same cloth," AEE would soon move from its university focus to a much broader appeal to mainstream education and to people working with special populations of clients primarily in the fields of corrections and mental health.

The Development of AEE and the Struggle for Survival

A movement starts out with dedication and then, if it is to survive, faces success with

noble resolution to deal with discomforts of size, with the need for professional recognition, with the issues of recruitment, training, the development of curriculum, the business of doing business and the insurance and management expertise this requires. (comment by Arnold Shore reflecting upon the creation of the AEE, 1977)

Thus Arnold Shore aptly described the development of the AEE from 1977–84. The formation of the association was a concrete example of what a group of committed individuals interested in starting a movement within education could accomplish. Having created the AEE, the next question facing the leaders was, "What should this association do?"

The administration of the AEE was the responsibility of the newly organized "coordinating committee," which held its first official meeting April 15–16, 1977, in Denver, Colorado. In attendance at the meeting were, John Rhodes, Dan Campbell, Ron Gager, Rick Medrick and Maria Snyder. The group discussed the need for increased member services and the production of the *Journal of Experiential Education,* which was scheduled to be published soon (AEE, 1978a). In an attempt to more fully use the talents and energies of other interested members of the association, the coordinating committee created four standing committees: (1) membership and promotion; (2) networking, services, and publications; (3) conference; and (4) administration and finance. Much of the current organizational structure in AEE was established during the initial stages of these committee's efforts.

The founders could not rest on their laurels. The 1978 conference was held in St. Louis, Missouri. The choice of this site created substantial difficulties for many of the members, since Missouri had not been one of the states to ratify the Equal Rights Amendment (ERA). During the Annual General Meeting at the conference, a resolution, submitted by Linda Chin representing the Women's Issues Special Interest Group, was unanimously adopted by the membership. This resolution notified the board of directors that a boycott of the conference was taking place, and called for the following action:

1. That the location of subsequent conference sites be chosen in states which had ratified the ERA.
2. That the content of future conferences include concerns particularly relevant to women more extensively than has been done in this year.
3. That efforts be made to eliminate sexist language in the presentations and publications of this association and its conference. (AEE, 1978b)

This resolution called attention to the fact that AEE had an obligation to conduct its activities consistent with the values of the membership. Despite the contributions of several women such as Maryann Hedaa, Sherrod Reynolds, Gruffie Clough, and Maria Snyder in the early development and leadership of the association, AEE was primarily a male organization. Of the 130 people preregistered for the first conference in North Carolina, 17 were women. If AEE was to grow and fulfill the dreams of a broader representation of educators, it was necessary for it to address the problems presented in this resolution.

The next serious attempt to change the composition of the association occurred the very next year, at the Portsmouth, New Hampshire, conference. In the closing moments of the Annual General Meeting, Arthur Conquest was recognized from the floor and addressed the issue of minority representation within AEE. He urged the leadership of the association to seek ways in which those who have been participants in Outward Bound programs, often minority students from urban areas, could also be members of the AEE. Conquest's comments resulted in a 27-point plan created by the board of directors, to help increase the participation of minorities in AEE. Maryann Hedaa assumed responsibility for this endeavor.

One of the more significant problems to face the AEE was looming on the horizon—financial solvency. As the association headed into the 1981 conference to be held in Toronto, there was a $6,288 deficit projected, with $7,531 remaining in the fund balance (AEE, 1981). The need for a financially successful conference was not apparent to the leadership.

When most of the expenses from the Toronto conference were calculated, the association was deeply in debt. President Rich Weider reported the following budget summary to the board of directors during the 1982 gathering:

> In the 1981 budget it was planned to keep $8,000 in a fund balance in case of emergencies. Expenses were cut by $8,000, the *Journal* publication was deferred, bills weren't paid, and the Colorado Outward Bound School wasn't paid, so that with the $25,000 over budget of conference debt and $8,000 administrative bills, the organization entered 1982 with a $33,000 debt. (AEE, 1982a)

In addition to the financial problems facing the association, Stephanie Takis, the executive officer, resigned stating her belief that the AEE could no longer afford to pay someone in her position.

Faced with a substantial debt, the resignation of the executive officer, and the lack of funds to operate or rent an office space, the association was near collapse. Minutes of board meetings from this era reflect the tension and obstacles facing this group.

While no single person could claim to have saved AEE, the imaginative and dedicated activities of Jim Keilsmeier, Peggy Walker-Stevens, and Dick Kraft certainly contributed to its rescue. Without the efforts of these individuals, and the other members of the board of directors, the association would certainly have floundered and collapsed. Dick Kraft, a faculty member at the University of Colorado, offered space within the education department for AEE. The move of AEE from Colorado Outward Bound School (COBS) to the University of Colorado was, in some ways, an appropriate relocation. COBS and the University of Colorado had enjoyed a long history of cooperative activities, including the formation of a jointly run master's in education program. In addition, many of the dominant forces within AEE had either been adjunct faculty in the education department (Bob Godfrey and Joe Nold for instance) or they had studied with Kraft, John Haas, and Stan Ratliff, senior faculty members at the University of Colorado (Jim Kielsmeier, Rocky Kimball, and Tony Richards).

The accounts of the board minutes from this period detail the dedication of a group of determined individuals who were resolved to keep the association alive. Peggy Walker-Stevens arranged her vacation time so that she would be able to journey from New Hampshire to Boulder and work in the office. Keilsmeier and Kraft established the equivalent of martial law regarding the expenditure of money and the operation of the office. The other board members helped subsidize association expenses by covering phone charges and copying costs. The number of yearly board meetings was reduced, and when they met they slept on the floor of a host member's house to help save the costs of hotel rooms.

The efforts of these board members, coupled with a small but well-run conference at Humbolt State University in Arcada, California, convened by Mike Mobley, allowed the leadership and membership of the association to breathe a sigh of relief. At the Annual General Meeting in 1983, Dick Kraft reported "there were 554 people in attendance at this conference and the break even point was 350." He said he had "come to the conference prepared to declare the organization bankrupt, but the success of the conference made that unnecessary" (AEE, 1982b). The financial scare of the early 1980s led to a conservative budget planning process for the mid 1980s, so that the financial stability of the organization continued to grow. Despite the relatively healthy status of the budget, the last of the debts from the Toronto conference was only finally retired in 1987.

The Certification Issue

From the very first meeting in North Carolina, the question of how one determines the relative competence of outdoor instructors has been debated. This question has sometimes been whispered by the membership and at other times shouted from the floor of a general meeting. All discussions concerning the topic of certification were viewed by different factions within the association as biased. To help bring some order to this controversy the board turned to the expert advice of Jed Williamson, Karl Johanson, and a small group of interested practitioners. This group, termed the Safety Committee, forged a near consensus regarding the direction that should be taken by AEE in its efforts to help create and maintain safe wilderness leadership.

In 1984 the safety committee published *Common Peer Practices in Adventure Education*. This document was the culmination of endless hours of negotiation and hard work by the people involved. In addition, it brought the association together in a united effort to determine those techniques and practices which could be mutually agreed upon as contributing to the safety of adventure activities. This publication is perhaps the best compilation of standards in adventure programming available.

Current Times and Future Directions of AEE

The AEE entered a period of growth and maturity marked by a strong financial base and stable leadership. Questions concerning the board and the membership were ones of direction rather than existence. Discussion at board meetings focused on concerns about how the association should be managed. The association began to reach out to like-minded organizations in an attempt to broaden the base of support for mutually agreed upon agendas for educational change. The 1983 conference at Lake Geneva, Wisconsin, was a joint project of AEE, The Council for the Advancement of Experiential Education (CAEL), and The National Society for Internship and Experiential Education (NSIEE). In 1985 AEE became a member of the Forum for Experiential Education, a group of 12 organizations who shared a common commitment to the goal of improving education through the application of a wide variety of experiential education techniques. These outreach efforts, coupled with a more vigorous recruitment program resulted in a dramatic increase in the individual and institutional membership of the association.

At the January 1985 board meeting Dick Kraft submitted his Executive Director's Report:

> With this report, I believe that you will agree with me that the association is now again on solid grounds, so I hereby tender my resignation as executive director, effective on June 30, 1985 or at such time as a new executive director has been appointed.

The board accepted his resignation and moved to hire Mitch Sakofs as the new executive director. Mitch had worked

in the office as associate director with Dick for the previous year and was a natural choice to fill the position. During the next two years, Mitch computerized the records of the association, improved the publication of books and resource materials, and generally systematized the activities of the Boulder office. All of these activities were consistent with the major theme of this period: "the professionalization" of AEE. In 1987 Mitch resigned his position to take a job with Outward Bound, Inc., and was succeeded by Eileen Burke, who assumed the newly created position of association administrator.

The resignation of Mitch Sakofs resulted in a series of prolonged discussions regarding the long-term leadership of the association and the proper role for the board of directors. The result of these discussions was to begin the process of hiring a full-time executive director. Throughout the history of AEE there had been several discussions regarding the possible merits of a full-time executive director, but the association had never been in a financial position such that this could be recommended. Finances had improved to the extent that, in 1987 the association was in a position to hire a full-time director. Rita Yerkes, for the board, began a national search for an executive director in November 1987, and I was hired in August of 1988.

In the past decade AEE has continued to grow and mature. It has developed its program accreditation services, which certifies certain standards of program quality and in general assists in the process of assuring safe and professional delivery of experiential education services. It has continued to encourage and sponsor professional groups, among them Experience-Based Training and Development (EBDT); the Natives, Africans, Asians, Latino(as) & Allied of AEE (NAALA); School & Colleges (S&C); Therapeutic Adventure (TAPG); and Women in Experience Education (WPG). Special interest groups have likewise been supported, among them groups interested in electronic communication and a gays, lesbians, bisexuals and allies special interest group.

In the past, those who comprised AEE were, in large measure, only marginally connected to the educational establishment. Outward Bound instructors and the highly creative classroom teacher have provided a model for many regarding the education that is possible, but they have not been in positions to effect broad-based educational change. Today we are witnessing a new alliance. Large multinational corporations are sending their top executives on training programs that use experiential education approaches. Ernest Boyer, former commissioner of education, writes in his book evaluating the college experience:

> A good college affirms that service to others is a central part of education. The questions we pose are these: Are students encouraged to participate in voluntary service? Does the

college offer the option of deferring admission to students who devote a year to service before coming to campus? Are the service projects drawn into the larger educational purposes, helping students see that they are not only autonomous individuals but also members of an intentional community? And does the faculty set an example and give leadership to service? (Boyer, 1987, p. 294)

Service learning has long been an integral part of experiential education and is one of the major tenets of the Outward Bound credo: "to serve, to strive, and not to yield."

The members of the association are not alone in their view that the educational system is in need of significant change. Conservatives and liberals are interested in listening to a voice which has for many years been only heard by a small group of progressive educators. AEE, and the educational philosophy it represents, will not be a panacea for the ills that have overtaken our educational system, but it may present sound alternatives for some of the problems.

The specific accomplishments of the association are less important than the fact that it exists and supports a different view of educational practice. AEE has evolved from the basic challenges of surviving to solving problems of effective management and finally to a position of leadership in educational innovation. I hope the next person to write the history of AEE will view it as a group that went far beyond an ability to support its members, to an organization deeply involved with supporting change within an educational system which sorely needs it.

References

Adams, A., and Reynolds, S. (1985). The long conversation: Tracing the roots of the past. In R. Kraft and M. Sakofs (Eds.), *The Theory of Experiential Education* (3rd ed., pp. 45–52). Boulder, CO: AEE Publications.

Association of Experiential Education. (1977). Articles of Incorporation filed June 17, 1977, State of Colorado.

Association of Experiential Education. (1978a, April). Minutes from the first meeting of the Coordinating Committee.

Association of Experiential Education. (1978b, September 28). Minutes of the AEE Membership Meeting, St. Louis, Missouri.

Association of Experiential Education. (1981, February). Minutes of the board of directors meeting, Denver, Colorado.

Association of Experiential Education. (1982a, September 8). Minutes of the board of directors meeting, Denver, Colorado.

Association of Experiential Education. (1982b, October 1). Annual General Meeting, Arcada, California.

Association of Experiential Education. (1985, January 31). Minutes of the board of directors meeting, Boulder, Colorado.

Boyer, E. (1987). *College: The undergraduate experience in America.* New York, NY: Harper and Row.

Hawkes, G., and Schulze, J. (1969, Summer). *Evaluation of Outward Bound teachers practica.* Reston, VA: Outward Bound, Inc.

Miner, J., and Boldt, J. (1981). *Outward Bound USA—Learning through experience in adventure-based education.* New York, NY: Morrow Quill Paperbacks.

Shore, A., and Greenberg, E. (1978). Challenging the past, present, and future: New directions in education. *Journal of Experiential Education, 1*(1), 43.

Taft, H. (1974). *The value of experience* (unpublished address).

Chapter 10

The Wilderness Education Association: History and Change

Cheryl E. Teeters and Frank Lupton
Northern Michigan University

The Wilderness Education Association (WEA) was officially founded on October 22, 1977, as the Wilderness Use Education Association (WUEA). Its purpose is to promote the professionalization of outdoor leadership and to thereby improve the safety and quality of outdoor trips and enhance the conservation of the wild outdoors. Since its founding, WEA has undergone several significant changes in its name, organizational structure, headquarter location and scope of program offerings. Despite the changes, the fundamental purpose has remained.

This purpose bears striking resemblance to the missions of Outward Bound and the National Outdoor Leadership School (NOLS). The reason for the similarity is in their common denominator—Paul Petzoldt. Paul Petzoldt, who had been a chief instructor for the first Outward Bound program in the United States and the creator of the National Outdoor Leadership School, was also one of the founders of the Wilderness Education Association. As often happens in life, the events leading to the founding of WEA were quite circumstantial.

In the spring of 1976, Paul Petzoldt met Frank Lupton at a National Recreation and Park Administration student conference in Indiana. Frank Lupton, a professor from the Department of Recreation and Park Administration at Western Illinois University, mentioned to Petzoldt his plan to take students on a 10-week fall quarter expedition to camps and outdoor centers in the Midwest for full university credit. Petzoldt's response to Lupton's plan was to in-

vite the class to Wyoming for a month-long trip in the mountains. He offered to provide equipment and food at a very low cost from his factory and outfitting store in Lander, Wyoming, and to lead the group at no cost for his services. Upon returning to campus, Lupton presented Petzoldt's offer, and the students agreed to do it.

That fall the group, under Petzoldt's leadership, learned basic wilderness living skills, along with ethics, judgment, expedition behavior, and other skills that would later become part of the basic curriculum of the outdoor leadership certification program of WEA. This experience had a great impact on the students and Frank Lupton and plans were made to include the wilderness expedition in the 1977 fall course.

The success of the experience prompted Petzoldt to experiment with similar programs during the summer of 1977. During Petzoldt's travels to universities that fall and winter, he promoted the idea of a month-long wilderness expedition free to students who would help build a large log cabin on his property in Alta, Wyoming. Sixteen students participated in that first program and had a very successful experience.

In the fall of 1977 Petzoldt again led Lupton and his students into the Wyoming mountains. During this expedition, Petzoldt and Lupton discussed at length the future of Western Illinois University's Environmental, Conservation, Outdoor, Education Expedition (ECOEE) program and the need for a program that could educate, train and certify wilderness outdoor leaders. Over the years, Petzoldt had been involved in numerous meetings and conversations relating to the need for some type of standard that could serve as a basis for wilderness leadership certification. While there was some general support for the concept, no consensus had been reached on exactly what should be done or which existing organizations should do it. The seeds of a possible organizational structure and a standard curriculum for educating users and certifying outdoor leaders were planted. They became a reality on Saturday, October 22, 1977.

Petzoldt and Lupton arranged for a meeting at Western Illinois University to discuss the development of a curriculum that could be used to develop standards for certification of wilderness leaders. Petzoldt arranged for Robert Christie, director of Indiana University's Bradford Woods field campus, and Charles Gregory, director of Penn State's Stone Valley Outdoor Center and one of the 16 participants in the summer 1977 program, to be included in the meeting. The meeting ended with the agreement to establish a national or international corporation to be called the Wilderness Use Education Association. These four founders also agreed that national "certifying" programs needed to be established at three levels:

- *skills:* a user's certification for skill competency for wilderness travel;
- *leadership:* a leader's certification for competency to lead others into wilderness areas; and
- *instruction:* an instructor's certification for competency to prepare leaders.

The founders also agreed on basic course content and to establish an organizing committee. The following people were invited and agreed to serve as members of the newly formed Wilderness Use Education Association: Gene Fear, president of the Survival Education Association, Tacoma, Washington; Patrick LaValla, president of the National Association for Search and Rescue, Tacoma, Washington; and Henry Nichol, U.S. Department of Agriculture (retired) Outdoor Recreation consultant, Potomac, Maryland. Robert Christie was selected as chairperson; Frank Lupton became vice chairperson; and Charles Gregory became secretary of the new association.

Charles Gregory prepared a draft for the committee of a *General Course Content Outline*, which included the purpose and 19 program components agreed upon at the founding meeting. The 19 program components became the basis for the 18-point curriculum used in the WEA's present National Standard Program for Outdoor Leadership. The following summarizes the content of the draft that Gregory compiled.

General Course Content Outline: Statement of Purpose

To improve the quality of the wilderness and wilderness experience through education of users and the certification of outdoor leaders.

The outline of the wilderness experience is directed at teaching the basic competencies necessary so the wilderness user will have a safe, enjoyable experience with little impact on the environment.

"The best instructor has a good sense of timing." The following basic content will be taught and practiced some time during the course with flexibility given to the instruction to compensate for variable factors such as weather, terrain and seasonal changes. In order to obtain a Wilderness Use Certification, basic competencies must be met.

The basic competencies included those surrounding:

- expedition behavior,
- environmental ethics,
- trip planning,
- history and culture,
- equipment,
- clothing,
- rations,
- basic camping skills,
- health and sanitation,
- navigation,
- trail techniques,
- weather,
- emergency procedures,
- survival techniques,
- aquatic safety procedures,
- specialized knowledge of one mode of travel,
- supervised leadership experiences,
- judgment in leaders, and
- evaluation (phase I).

Petzoldt added his wisdom to the results of the founding meeting when he wrote a draft of his ideas on the purpose of the Wilderness Use Education Association and sent it to the organizing committee members for their reactions. The content of Petzoldt's draft follows.

Wilderness Use Education Association: Rough Draft of Purpose (December 1977)

The purpose of the association is to encourage enjoyable, safe *use* of our wilderness and the *conservation* of our wilderness through education of the user and group leader.

The above is timely and necessary since laws, regulations, and use restrictions cannot protect the environment against the uneducated user. Most unenjoyable outings, accidents, searches, deaths, and environmental damage can be prevented by education of the user and the group leader. Insurance rates might be lowered for groups having leaders with certified outdoor education. Those selecting leaders for wilderness trips and those individuals depending on the group leader for safety and competence would have a basis for evaluation. Administrators of public lands and others might find such standards useful in planning land use, conservation, and permit issuance.

The association will certify "course leaders" who are capable of planning, outfitting, conducting, and teaching certification courses of at least four weeks' duration in actual wilderness environment. The association has done research with such groups and has developed a course outline of the basics to be taught. These are basic skills, techniques, knowledge, judgment, every outdoorsman (sic) should possess. Those passing courses led by course leaders certified by the association will be certified as having the training and education. Graduates of the courses should be able to plan and execute outings for their lifetime recreational needs and act as leaders and advisers to others.

In addition, this training is a necessary foundation for all who wish to pursue specific outdoor specialties such as outdoor teaching, leading wilderness trips, or hunting, fishing, mountaineering, canoeing, backpacking, skiing, and river running activities. Such training would be helpful to persons managing lands for recreational use and conservation.

The association will inspect courses in the field and improve and change programming as judgment indicates. Certification and the follow-up on activities of certified leaders will be done by the association. Members of the association are acting as individuals who believe that education of the user and group leader is a necessary aspect of wilderness recreational use and wilderness conservation.

Throughout the following fall, winter and summer, WUEA courses were conducted by affiliated colleges and universities and by the WUEA headquarters at the Paul Petzoldt Lodge in Driggs, Idaho. Throughout 1978 and 1979, an advisory committee was formed and, although it was never utilized as much as anticipated, it provided a group of persons who were supportive of the association and willing to give input when requested.

On January 2, 1979, the Wilderness Use Education Association was incorporated in the state of Wyoming as a nonprofit organization, and a board of trustees was established. The original board of trustees included the following persons:

1. Robert Christie, director of Bradford Woods, Indiana University;
2. Eugene Fear, president, Survival Education Association;
3. Charles A. Gregory, director of Stone Valley Outdoor Center, the Pennsylvania State University;
4. Patrick LaValla, president, National Association for Search and Rescue;
5. Frank Lupton, Jr., professor and coordinator of ECOEE, Western Illinois University;
6. Henry Nichol, U.S. Department of Agriculture (retired);
7. Paul Petzoldt, founder of NOLS; and
8. John L. Vidakovich, attorney, Lander, Wyoming.

In 1980 the Wilderness Use Education Association was officially renamed the Wilderness Education Association and Paul Petzoldt was appointed as the executive director at a salary of $12,000. Both the modest stipend and appointment were definitely appropriate. Over the years, Petzoldt had contributed thousands of hours of time and many thousands of dollars to help keep WEA going. He traveled thousands of miles to many university campuses to speak with students, faculty, and administrators about affiliating with WEA. He also spoke at conferences and workshops informing people about the new certification-education program. His efforts brought many students to participate in programs and added to the number of universities that became affiliates of WEA.

In 1984 Sandra Braun was appointed as the second WEA executive director and held this position until 1986. During her tenure, there was a major expansion of programs offered by WEA affiliates and by the headquarters in Driggs, Idaho. It was also during this early time in the association's history that the National Standard Program for Outdoor Leadership (NSP) was more clearly defined. Much effort was expended to refine and standardize the 18-point curriculum that was to be used in the NSP and to develop a more standardized system for evaluation and certification criteria. The result of those initial efforts was a clearer definition of the abilities of a WEA NSP graduate and an accepted body of the required course content for the National Standard Program for Outdoor Leadership. Although the process of revision, refinement and standardization in areas of curriculum, evaluation, and monitoring is seen as an ongoing necessity, the general course content, outlined by the founders in 1977, served as the framework for the 18-point curriculum now in use. The basic abilities of a WEA NSP graduate and the contents of the curriculum are as follows:

Graduates of the NSP are able to:

A. use and teach state-of-the-art minimum-impact camping and travel techniques to move a group through the backcountry with minimum degradation of the environment;

B. exercise good quality judgment and decision-making skills within a leadership position to help avoid potential accident and survival situations;

C. recognize their own leadership abilities and limitations within the context of a group;

D. demonstrate a basic standard of outdoor knowledge and experience based on the WEA 18-point curriculum; and

E. efficiently travel in the wilderness utilizing any one of a number of technical skills such as mountaineering, snow travel, rock climbing, ice climbing, canoeing, rafting, caving, and backpacking.

WEA 18-Point Curriculum Elements:

The WEA 18-point curriculum represents the major skill and knowledge areas in which a qualified outdoor leader should be able to demonstrate a minimum level of competency.

Judgment: Increasing one's ability to exercise good quality judgment in decision making is the overall goal of any WEA program. Judgment involves the ability to utilize a process which enhances the probability of making a decision with a high rate of success.

1. *Decision making and problem solving:* Students will learn decision-making and problem-solving strategies and practice them in a variety of environmental and social conditions.

2. *Leadership:* Students will have the opportunity to apply leadership knowledge when leading their peers in real situations under staff supervision. These structured leadership experiences will require the students to synthesize and apply safety standards, leadership skills, and environmental ethics to a particular situation.

3. *Expedition behavior/group dynamics:* Expedition behavior/group dynamics is a combination of several interrelationships: individual to individual; individual to group; group to individual; group to other groups; and individual and group to multiple users, administrative agencies, and to the local populace. The skillful practice of expedition behavior demands motivation, self-awareness, and other-awareness applied under varying group and environmental conditions. With knowledge of acceptable group behavior and interaction, leaders and students have a better sense of why relations break down and under what circumstances they flourish.

4. *Environmental ethics:* Students will learn the practical and philosophical bases of utilizing the wild outdoor with minimum impact. This area will be introduced and integrated with other curriculum points such as basic camping skills, cooking, equipment, natural history, and health and sanitation. Participants will be exposed to a basic environmental ethic by practicing skills and techniques that promote minimum impact on the environment.

5. *Basic camping skills:* Integrated with environmental ethics, students will learn such basic skills as when and where to camp, fire safety and fire building, establishing shelter, basic cooking, the use of stoves, and how to animal proof the camp.

6. *Nutrition and ration planning:* Through instruction and practice, each participant will be able to adequately plan, package, and cook his or her own rations for a two-week experience. Knowledge of food cost, nutritional value, weight, and where to buy the food at a reasonable cost will be detailed within the program. Emphasis will be placed on low-cost and personally selected foods which allow for variety in self-planned menus.

7. *Equipment/clothing selection and use:* The selection, design, repair, and storage of equipment and clothing will be discussed and practiced. Participants will be instructed in specific equipment and clothing needed for individuals, subgroups, and groups. Design, cost, availability, weight, and quality of equipment will be discussed.

8. *Weather:* Students will receive instruction on cloud formation, basic weather forecasting,

and the implications of the effects of weather on the comfort and safety of the group. Instruction will include reading signs of changing weather and general characteristics of weather patterns in the specific region.

9. *Health and sanitation:* The implementation of proper health and sanitation techniques is essential to the well-being, safety, and comfort of the wilderness user. The subjects of water purification, disposal of human waste, environmentally sound and sanitary dish washing, and preparation of food will be outlined and practiced. Environmentally sound health practices, including bathing and laundry will be taught and practiced.

10. *Travel techniques:* Students will learn to plan for safety, comfort, and group organization while travelling. Pretravel plans which encompass time control, energy control, and climate control will be practiced. Rhythmic breathing, walking techniques, and trail courtesy while hiking will also be taught and practiced.

11. *Navigation:* Navigation is the art of getting from one place to another and understanding how it is done efficiently and safely. Map interpretation, use of a compass, and limiting factors such as weather, physical abilities, and group motivation will be covered and practiced.

12. *Safety and risk management:* Students will learn the most recent techniques of dealing with today's extremely complicated liability and risk management procedures. From insurance forms to liability issues, students will be made aware of programmatic and personal responsibilities.

13. *Wilderness emergency procedures and treatment:* Students will learn to prepare for, prevent, diagnose, and treat injuries common to outdoor travel. Specific skills covered are treatment for broken bones, fatigue, shock, bruises, blisters, hypothermia, hyperthermia, and strains.

14. *Natural and cultural history:* The participants will become more aware of the site's natural and cultural history. Understanding the ecological integrity of an area, particularly flora and fauna, as well as unique geological features, will be emphasized during the program.

15. *Specialized travel/adventure activity:* Depending on the particular emphasis and environment of each program, the participant will be taught special skills in one or more of the following modes of wilderness travel and adventure: mountaineering, backpacking, skiing, canyoneering, canoeing, kayaking, rafting, rock climbing, ice and snow climbing, caving, orienteering, and whitewater river running.

16. *Group processing and communication skills:* Included in this area will be group development, communication skills, conflict resolution, group and individual problem-solving techniques, and learning styles. Included also will be techniques for affecting group motivation such as parties, group games, and initiatives.

17. *Trip planning:* At the end of the program, each student will prepare an effective plan for a group outing for 10 or more days. A standard situation will be selected by the instructors to fit the material covered during the program. Factors included in the situation will be age, size of group, purpose of trip, length of trip, terrain, and mode of travel.

18. *Teaching and transference:* Participants will be given the opportunity to practice teaching techniques and gain skills that will prove invaluable if employed by any of the estimated 8,850 adventure education organizations in North America. Transference is the process of taking what is learned in one situation and applying it to another situation.

Toward the end of Sandra Braun's tenure as executive director, a major debate evolved over the future of WEA. The debate centered around two issues. The affiliates were concerned that headquarter programs were drawing students away from affiliate programs; and the financial resources of the central organization remained inadequate to effectively service and monitor the quality of the courses.

After Sandra Braun resigned as executive director to pursue other interests, WEA headquarters were temporarily moved to Western Illinois University. Frank Lupton, WEA president at the time, functioned as the acting executive director for nearly two years. During this time, WEA became a membership organization, the board of trustees took action to eliminate headquarter programs and to run all programs through affiliates, and the organizational structure changed from a simple wilderness leadership program to a more complex organization with a national administrative office.

In 1987 a $28,000 grant was received from the Adirondack North Country Association through the efforts of Jack Drury. The terms of the grant included moving WEA headquarters to Saranac Lake, New York, to offices provided by North Country Community College. Jeff Brown was hired as the executive director and in June 1988

Jack Drury was elected as the WEA president. While head-quartered in Saranac Lake, the Association became more focused on building an affiliate network and membership base, and on providing professional services for its membership. Changes continued when Jeff Brown left the executive director's post and Mark Wagstaff was hired to fill the position.

WEA experienced significant growth as reflected in Affiliate membership, which rose from 6 to 30 between 1988 and 1992. WEA also sponsored national conferences on leadership, printed newsletters, provided resale items and began a job referral service for members. In 1989 a new program was created to expand the opportunities for educating a broader base of outdoor users. The new (and ongoing) program, a WEA Wilderness Steward course, provided for shorter field time than its companion National Standard Program for Outdoor Leadership, but with a continued emphasis on the elements in the 18-point curriculum. A "graduate" of a wilderness steward course receives a certificate of participation, but is not certified as an outdoor leader. This program helped to expand the affiliate base by providing two levels of affiliation: steward affiliate and national standard program affiliate. The wilderness steward course also helped to expand WEA's ability to more effectively educate the general outdoor user. California State University at Chico was the first Steward Affiliate. During this time, WEA also created the Paul Petzoldt Award for Excellence in Wilderness Education. The first recipient at a 1988 meeting in Saranac Lake was Ernest "Tap" Tapley, a cofounder of NOLS.

In April 1994 the headquarters (national office) moved to Colorado State University at Fort Collins, Colorado. It was also during this time, that WEA experienced more changes in leadership. David Cockrell, professor at Southern Colorado University was elected WEA president; Mark Wagstaff resigned as executive director to pursue graduate studies; and Kent Clement was hired to replace him.

While in Fort Collins, WEA has continued to sponsor national conferences, provide membership services, recruit affiliates and expand program offerings. Two new programs were initiated. One was the Wilderness Education Workshop, a program designed to provide students, adults, children, and professionals from any field with an opportunity to explore the basics of outdoor travel. The 18-point curriculum is used as a guide, but the workshops are tailored to the individual group's needs and wants. The workshop can vary widely in the amount of time required to complete it.

The second program expansion was the development of the Wilderness and Land Ethic Box curriculum. The program was the result of a partnership among the WEA, the Arthur Carhart National Wilderness Training Center, and the Wilderness Education Council of Colorado. It is a K–8 curriculum with integrated educational aids for educating school children about the natural environment us-ing wilderness as a conceptual base. WEA maintained the production and distribution of the Wilderness and Land Ethic Box curriculum until late 1997, when it was turned over to the Wilderness Education Council of Colorado.

The association continues to develop and refine its outdoor leadership training and education program. With the addition of the Wilderness Education Workshop, WEA provides four types of courses:

- *Wilderness Education Workshop:* Described previously.
- *Wilderness Steward Program:* A course, typically 10 days in length, designed to teach participants the basics of judgment and decision-making skills, leadership, minimum-impact camping and travel techniques, and other essential components of the WEA 18-point curriculum.
- *National Standard Program:* A course involving extended wilderness travel (21–35 days are recommended) through which successful graduates may obtain outdoor leadership certification. Such certification qualifies individuals to conduct wilderness education workshops and wilderness steward programs.
- *National Standard Program Professional Short Course:* A course designed for the professional already working in the field of outdoor leadership or related fields who wishes to become a National Standard Program Certified Outdoor Leader. It includes an intense indoctrination to the WEA 18-point curriculum, philosophy, and teaching techniques. These courses are typically 10 days in length and place emphasis on "class" time more than on "moving" time.

The association is also field-testing a refined sequence of instruction through which persons may obtain certifying instructor status. This sequence has been developed to better qualify individuals for instructing the National Standard Program. A portion of that sequence includes an in-depth "classroom" immersion into teaching strategies, assessment and evaluation techniques, and course administration and management.

It has been during this more recent time that the affiliates have begun to take on a more active role in the organizational structure and in the operation of programs. The affiliates sponsor their own annual colloquium to discuss affiliate concerns and issues and to provide recommendations to the board of trustees. In 1996 the board of trustees acted to provide for an affiliate-elected representative to sit on the board. Cheryl Teeters, assistant professor, Northern Michigan University, was elected as the first affiliate representative on the WEA board. Also in 1996, the board of trustees initiated actions to establish a network of standing committees to assist the board in carrying out many of the operating functions of the association.

Another change in leadership occurred in 1996. Kent Clement resigned as executive director to take a teaching position at Colorado Mountain College; Darla DeRuiter served as interim executive director until Jeff Liddle, previously with AEE, was hired in 1997. Chris Cashel, associate professor at Oklahoma State University, was elected as the new WEA president in 1997.

As an organizational structure, WEA is a membership organization that uses a decentralized structure of affiliates to provide its programs, yet maintains a national administrative office. Oversight is through a volunteer board of trustees and its associated standing committees. It is a complex relationship that often has and continues to cause a financial strain throughout the association. Recent board of trustees actions have eliminated the executive director's position for the time being as the Association struggles with funding issues.

This chapter was subtitled "History and Change." That category is certainly true of the Wilderness Education As-sociation. As with many fledgling, nonprofit organizations, WEA has been faced with challenges on many fronts: financial, philosophical, organizational, curricular, and procedural. Some of those challenges continue today and change seems to be on the horizon again. However, some things remain fairly constant. The Wilderness Education Association is unique in the field of Adventure Education and different from other outdoor leadership programs because WEA places its emphasis on developing leadership, judgment, and decision-making skills above and beyond the mastery of technical skills. It has entered the debate over individual outdoor leadership certification by providing outdoor leadership certification. It has provided a forum, through national conferences, for discourse among a variety of agencies and individuals who have a stake in the conservation of wildlands. Above all, the individuals who founded and those who currently comprise the WEA have remained steadfast in their belief in the importance of education in developing leaders and users in order to preserve this country's wilderness areas. The result of this belief is one of the most comprehensive wilderness education and outdoor leadership training organizations in the country—The Wilderness Education Association.

Chapter 11

The National Outdoor Leadership School: 40,000 Wilderness Experiences and Counting

Delmar W. Bachert

Appalachian State University

The National Outdoor Leadership School (NOLS) is a nonprofit school headquartered in Lander, Wyoming, and recognized as the international leader in the field of wilderness-based education and outdoor leadership. NOLS was founded in 1965 to meet a need for instructors who were masters of outdoor living skills and capable of leading others in the wild outdoors:

> A lot has changed in three decades. NOLS has grown and reached out to more than 40,000 students.
>
> The school now runs eight branches and courses on five continents. But much has stayed the same too. We know who we are. We still do real education with real results in a very real place—the wilderness. . . . You can be assured of a quality education that combines excellent instruction, top-notch practical leadership training, the best in skills development, and an outstanding wilderness classroom. (NOLS, 1998a)

The *NOLS 1986 Catalog of Courses* lists four major program objectives: leadership development, outdoor skills, minimum-impact conservation techniques, and expedition dynamics. The 1986 NOLS core curriculum suggests the comprehensive nature of the NOLS learning experience:

- minimum-impact camping and resource protection,
- travel techniques,
- outdoor living skills,
- safety,
- environmental awareness, and
- expedition dynamics. (NOLS, 1986, p. 3)

The 1998 version of the catalog presents both the mission and the core curriculum of the school as they have evolved:

> The mission of the National Outdoor Leadership School is to be the leading source of wilderness skills and leadership that serve people and the environment.
>
> Safety and Judgment: Basic first aid, safety and accident prevention, hazard evaluation, wilderness medicine-related injury prevention and treatment, rescue techniques, emergency procedures. Leadership and Teamwork: Competence, self-awareness, expedition behavior, judgment and decision making, tolerance for hard work, communication, vision and action, small group expeditions, practical leadership opportunities daily. Outdoor Skills: Campsite selection, shelter and stove use, fire building, sanitation and waste

disposal, cooking and baking, nutrition and rations, equipment care and selection, keeping warm and dry, route finding and navigation, backpacking, kayaking, horse packing, sailing, fishing, telemark skiing, caving, climbing, canoeing. Environmental Studies: Leave-no-trace camping and resource protection, ecosystems, flora and fauna identification, geology, weather, astronomy, land management and cultural issues, public service, wilderness ethics. (NOLS, 1998a)

The NOLS experience is the term that students have come to use when describing their adventures in learning with the National Outdoor Leadership School. The aim of this essay is to document and interpret the historical evolution of NOLS. The intent of this documentation is to trace the development of the school and its curriculum and the impact it has had on wilderness education, outdoor leadership, and wilderness management.

The relationship between wilderness education and wilderness management is largely unexplored. Wilderness education can be viewed as a reasonable alternative to regulation as a wilderness management tool. NOLS serves as an excellent case study.

One chapter in this text delves into the significant history of Outward Bound. A subsequent one explores the founding of the Wilderness Education Association. The NOLS story is closely connected to both organizations via the life and work of Paul Petzoldt. A Petzoldt biography, *On Belay: The Life of Legendary Mountaineer Paul Petzoldt*, was written by Ringholz (1997).

The NOLS experience emanates in large part from the lifelong learning of Petzoldt. NOLS was his dream and represents an extension of his life experiences. A glimpse of his accomplishments and lifestyle will prove invaluable to an understanding of the development of NOLS. It will provide a link to the development of the Colorado Outward Bound School and the eventual development of the Wilderness Education Association as well.

Petzoldt claims that it was on his fateful climb of the Grand Teton in 1924, at the age of 16, that he was ingrained with the need to learn as much as he could about the outdoors and how it could be used. He began a career as a climbing guide in the Tetons soon after this ascent. While guiding, Petzoldt had a tremendous opportunity to gather knowledge and techniques from others. He also began to perfect techniques for training climbing guides for the first mountaineering school in America.

The goal of the Petzoldt-Exum School of American Mountaineering differed from European guiding where the object was to get the clients to the top, even if they had to be hauled up. In the Tetons, they tried to educate the clients, to make them into knowledgeable mountaineers— and get them to the summits. Patricia Petzoldt described

the qualities Petzoldt sought in his Teton guides, criteria that would guide the selection of NOLS instructors decades later:

> They were chosen for other qualities as well as their climbing ability. They had to have great strength and endurance, sound judgment, plenty of horse sense, and a knowledge of people. They must be able to cope with emergencies as they arose. And they had to have plenty of patience. They tried to be good hosts as well as good guides. (Petzoldt, 1953, p. 225)

Petzoldt's reputation and skill as a mountaineer and climber continued to grow and develop. He made a double ascent of the Matterhorn in one day. The climb was internationally acclaimed as a "feat of unusual endurance." He made the first ascent of the north face of the Grand Teton in 1936. In that same year, long before winter mountaineering was widely practiced, he made the first winter ascent of the Grand Teton (Petzoldt, 1953, p. 209).

Petzoldt was invited to join the 1938 expedition to K2, the second-highest mountain in the world. In a discussion of the K2 expedition members, Houston describes the factors involved in Petzoldt's selection for the team:

> His great experience with mountain camping, winter weather and climbing of exceptional technical difficulty made him a splendid addition to our group. (Bates et al., 1939, p. 31)

In the 1960s the Outward Bound concept was introduced to America. The involvement in and influence of Petzoldt on the Colorado Outward Bound School (COBS) in its early stages of development were significant. His experience at COBS in turn helped him clarify the need and goals for NOLS. Petzoldt served in three different capacities during the formative years of COBS. In 1962 he was asked by an old acquaintance from the Ski Troops, Ernest "Tap" Tapley, to examine the school's mountaineering practices. In 1963 he became the mountaineering adviser for the school and, in 1964 the chief instructor for COBS. Miner and Boldt (1981) describe his impact:

> Paul brought to the school a superb expertise in his mountain expedition specialty. This was not simply because his involvement exposed instructors and students to the experience-garnered wisdom of a veteran mountaineer of the first rank. It was more particularly due to Petzoldt's having massaged that experience with an analytical turn of mind, that together with his fervor for communication, his love of the wild outdoors and a gift

of communication, made him a fine teacher of wilderness adventuring. (pp. 112–115)

The first effort was made in 1964 to have an instructors' course at COBS. According to Petzoldt (1983), this effort consisted of "Tap (Tapley) taking off with the fellas for a hell of a trip!" During the summer of 1964 Petzoldt openly discussed his intent to start a school in Wyoming. In a debriefing session with one four-man group from C-10, the tenth course at COBS, he stated:

> I'm going to have a school in Wyoming, in the Wind Rivers. Maybe we'll have one Outward Bound course like they have here and maybe we'll have two courses in leadership for older fellas. (Petzoldt, 1964b)

During his tenure at COBS, Petzoldt identified three great needs that would influence the creation of NOLS. The first need was to expose the participants to challenges inherent in a wilderness experience. The second was quality instructors who would meet his standards as outdoor leaders. The third was for a program that would meet the interests of those Outward Bound graduates and others who wanted to progress to greater levels of outdoor skill.

As early as 1963 Petzoldt actually had begun to promote his idea for a Wyoming Outward Bound School. A headline in the *Wyoming State Journal* of July 30, 1963, reads: "Petzoldt believes beginning could be made next year on Outward Bound camp here (p. 12)." In a letter to Josh Miner, founder of Outward Bound in America, Petzoldt (1964a) comments:

> My personal wishes, of course, would be to have an Outward Bound Leadership School here, drawing principally on the students who have finished a course in another Outward Bound school and who, then, are ready to profit by the training that we would give them here to make real outdoor leaders for their communities or, if you wished, for other Outward Bound schools in the future.

The Wyoming Outward Bound School was not to be. Miner was involved not only with supporting the fledgling COBS but the development of both the Minnesota (now Voyageur) and Hurricane Island Outward Bound schools in the mid 1960s. Concern was also expressed about the geographical expediency of another Outward Bound program in the Rocky Mountain region. However, Petzoldt's commitment to an outdoor leadership school never wavered once the idea was firmly established in his mind:

> Both Mr. Tapley and I realized very early in our experience with the Colorado Outward

Bound School that their program could not really come to maturity without instructors with more training and background than they were able to secure in the United States or even from England. Mr. Tapley and I therefore started this school with the idea of supplying good instructors for all outdoor schools and programs. This program should be considered as a crash program in order to raise the standard of outdoor leadership for all groups using the outdoors in America. (Petzoldt, 1965b)

Years later, Josh Miner, the founder of Outward Bound in the United States comments: "I feel that NOLS is one of the great monuments to the success of Outward Bound. I never looked at NOLS as competition. It's a fantastic success story" (Ringholz, 1997, p. 186).

Wilderness, specifically the Wind Rivers Mountain Range of Wyoming, was chosen as the medium in which NOLS would train outdoor leaders. "OUTDOOR LEADERSHIP SCHOOL FORMED HERE," reads a headline of the March 23, 1965, *Wyoming State Journal* published in Lander. Success came quickly for NOLS and its "crash" program. They graduated over 80 students in the summer of 1965. Tapley and Petzoldt shared field leadership and were assisted by six patrol leaders, several with Outward Bound experience. Petzoldt's philosophy is reflected in part by a promotional tape recording he made:

> In order to have outdoor adventure that will compete with the adventure that youth has developed in his own close-knit teenage society, we have to have something that is good. We have to have something that is real adventure: like climbing mountains, like fording wild rivers, like exploring wild country, like facing the storms, like surviving alone in the wilderness. In order to supply this outdoor adventure, at least in order to supply it safely, takes real leaders. (Petzoldt, 1965b)

The *Articles of Incorporation of the National Outdoor Leadership School* elaborate on the purpose of the school:

> The purposes for which this corporation is formed are as follows: to develop and teach wilderness skills and techniques; to develop and teach wilderness use that encourages minimal environmental impact; to develop and teach outdoor leaders. (NOLS, 1965)

A key factor in any successful organization is the personnel. Petzoldt recruited tremendous talent for the school, including Tapley and Rob Hellyer. Both were instrumental in the early success of the school in the field. Also instrumental in backing NOLS were Lander, Wyoming, residents Jack Nicholas, attorney; William Ericson, M.D.; and Ed Breece, legislator. They formed the nucleus of the early board of trustees.

The fee to attend NOLS in the first year of operation was $300 for the 36-day course. The salary of the director was fixed at $650 per month. The school was started with few resources. Petzoldt penned 40 letters a day in early 1965 to gain recruits for the endeavor.

Based on the success of the first summer, plans were laid for 1966. A decision of special significance was made to involve women on the wilderness courses. Petzoldt said: "We expect to expand the course next year. We'll even have a course for girls" (*Wyoming State Journal*, 1965, p. 1). The NOLS experience apparently appealed to women as this comment, made two years later, indicates: "Our women's course was a success and we will have three women's courses in 1967" (Petzoldt, 1967). Soon the gender barriers were merged into a practical and popular coed wilderness experience.

There were other demands early in NOLS' development. One was for a course for younger students. Another was to offer college credit (Petzoldt, 1967). The nature of the program, as well as its initial success, led to rapid expansion. NOLS graduated 83 students in 1965 and nearly 1,000 in 1970. Branch schools were soon established in Tennessee (discontinued), Alaska, Washington, Mexico, Connecticut (discontinued), and Africa. In the 1990s additional branches and programs were established in Patagonia, Western Canada, the U.S. Southwest, Australia and India.

NOLS has been successful, in part, because of the desire of so many young Americans to have a "wilderness experience." It carries with it a certain appeal and represents a rite of passage for many. The wilderness as classroom and the wilderness education it promises offer a stark contrast to the educational institutions and doldrums they may have been experiencing. The NOLS core curriculum promises adventure and a lifetime of skills to be practiced and honed. It suggests for some an *Outdoor Life, Outside* magazine image or lifestyle.

There were other factors in the early and continued success of NOLS. The creation of NOLS was timely. It coincided with the Wilderness Act of 1964. One impact of designated wilderness was to create an increased demand for backcountry experiences:

> Petzoldt thought the Wilderness Act was a great move in the right direction. He had even been in Washington to testify in favor of it. But rules and regulations were not enough to get the job done. Few people knew how to properly use the wilderness they had fought for. Education was the answer. People had to be taught how to enjoy the wild outdoors

safely and without harming it! (Ringholz, 1997, pp. 182–183)

NOLS offered a challenging and appealing package to a growing number of wilderness seekers. The demand for Outward Bound, adapted Outward Bound, and other backcountry programs created a rapidly expanding demand for outdoor leaders. NOLS, unlike Outward Bound, philosophically and practically set out to specifically train a supply of leaders to meet this demand.

NOLS met certain intrinsic needs for many young people in the 1960s. Some were seeking alternatives, seeking immersion into a context of reality. The impact of the wilderness; the explain, demonstrate, and do approach to teaching; the youthful energy and enthusiasm of the instructors (and the Old Man of the Mountains himself), all led graduates to spread the word about the NOLS experience. On campus, at camp, on the trail, this word-of-mouth became NOLS' best advertisement. Employers began to seek NOLS graduates as applicants.

The curriculum was another reason for the school's success. The content and delivery offer those seeking outdoor-related careers a chance to learn from firsthand experience. It suggests an opportunity to become a leader of outdoor pursuits in addition to being a participant. The *must-knows* was the terminology used by Petzoldt to describe what he considered the minimal knowledge and skills that an outdoor leader must possess. The development of judgment was a primary and controversial goal set for NOLS participants. A five-week mountain expedition became the primary "method of education" for delivering the curriculum to the students. Petzoldt (1974) describes both the limitation and the strength of the curriculum:

> While there are many factors of outdoor living that are interesting or enjoyable to know, our primary concern must be immediate protection of the individual, the environment, and the equipment. Thus, time and space limit us to teaching those things which must be known. (p. 23)

The NOLS curriculum was put to the test in the summer of 1965. Petzoldt and Tapley provided primary instruction and leadership with support from patrol leaders Jack Hyland, Jerry Taylor, Bruce Barrus, and Burt Redmayne on the first course (*Wyoming State Journal*, August 17, 1965). Ideas, activities, and techniques were incorporated and others were discarded. The NOLS curriculum was tested and revised in the field. In 1974 Petzoldt published a summation of his work, and the heart of the NOLS curriculum, in *The Wilderness Handbook*. The concepts of wilderness education later received updates in *The National Outdoor Leadership School's Wilderness Guide*

(Simer and Sullivan, 1983) and in Petzoldt's (1984) revision of his book, titled *The New Wilderness Handbook*.

The context and manner in which NOLS delivers the must-knows and attempts to develop judgment is critical to understanding the NOLS experience. The expedition format of NOLS courses is really a special application of the small group process. The process is intense and experiential. The expedition as a mode of education forces both students and instructors to think—and the consequences of their response to challenges in the wilderness are very real. The flow of a lengthy expedition allows for both horizontal and vertical instruction in the practice of skills and techniques, and most importantly allows people to sense the consequences of *their* decision making and judgment.

NOLS is noted for pioneering minimum-impact and no-trace camping techniques. In the early days this was referred to as "practical conservation" by Petzoldt and the course leaders. Peter Simer (1981), past executive director of NOLS, stated:

> An agenda for the next 15 years, aimed at education of the American wilderness user to state-of-the-art techniques, would really only introduce common sense into contemporary American camping. Minimum-impact camping is as essential to wilderness as safe driving habits are to the highway. (p. 3)

Today, NOLS' continuing emphasis on wilderness ethics is reflected in their leadership with the nationally recognized leave-no-trace program, and the *Soft Paths* (Hampton and Cole, 1988) text and video.

An explicit and unique claim of Petzoldt and NOLS' curriculum, in the early days, is that judgment is a basic element in the foundation of a competent and safe outdoor leader and that NOLS attempts to teach it. If the must-knows are the warp then judgment is the woof of the weave that makes up the tapestry of the NOLS experience. All of the skills, abilities, and techniques an outdoor leader can possess are qualified, modified, and tempered in their application by the exercise of sound judgment. Reporting to the board of trustees after the first NOLS courses in 1965, Petzoldt wrote:

> Our theory of teaching corresponding judgment along with techniques was successful, and is one of the important and distinguishing factors between our instruction and other instruction in the field of outdoorsmanship and mountaineering. (Petzoldt, 1965a, p. 3–4)

What has been the impact of NOLS in over three decades of offering a wilderness education, a wilderness experience to over 40,000 participants? Steff Kessler (1983), NOLS instructor and staff director at the time, offers this assessment:

I look for a subtle form of leadership on NOLS' courses—students learning something about themselves as they interact with each other and the wilderness. They are learning to size up situations and intervene in a way that changes reality. Instead of feeling powerless, acted upon by weather, terrain, or group problems, they become actors, problem solvers, using their skills and experiencing the success of their actions.

A NOLS course affords people with the chance to take charge, a chance often denied in our complex, technological society. Instead of passive recipients of events, NOLS students shape their own society and reality within the mountains. What they learn is, I think, transferable to their lives beyond the mountains. (p. 6)

Quincy Van Winkle (1997), another NOLS student-turned-instructor, suggests that a NOLS semester course changed her life. She speaks for many graduates of NOLS:

> I was looking to gain outdoor skills. I wanted to learn to live and navigate in the mountains, I wanted to learn to climb, and I love to ski and was excited to live in and ski on snow for two weeks. I expected to learn these skills; I was going to what I knew was a wilderness school. But the subtle lessons were a surprise—like expedition behavior, leadership, decision making, and judgment. These skills evolved throughout the duration of the semester, slowly taking effect. As I gained more experience, learned more skills, and worked as a team member to achieve goals, I started to grow.
>
> After my semester my family and close friends would say: "You've changed." To hear that you had changed when you felt the same was a little disconcerting and made me self-conscious. What I realized later is that the changes those people closest to me noticed weren't my newly honed wilderness skills, rather it was the influence of the experience as a whole. After my NOLS semester I had become more confident, considerate, motivated and aware of my actions—unbeknownst to me, this was how I had changed. (p. 11)

NOLS represents a unique and powerful contribution to educational innovation in America. It offers an intensity of relevant experience that may take the participant a lifetime of reflection to fully process.

Thirty-two years after founding the school, elder statesman and lifelong learner, Paul K. Petzoldt, comments on the power of the NOLS experience:

> Of course it'll change their lives; it's a wonderful experience coming to NOLS. These kids know about and are concerned with the outdoors. These courses teach kids *how to live the expedition of life.* (Kehoe, 1998, p. 8)

NOLS' future promises to be just as exciting as the past:

> In the summer and fall of 1995 NOLS embarked upon a visioning process to identify the values and goals that would define our future. Six core values were identified: Wilderness . . . Education . . . Leadership . . . Safety . . . Community . . . Excellence. (Palmer, 1998, personal correspondence)
>
> The wilderness educational expedition will remain the core of the school. We will be the primary resource and role model for wilderness and outdoor educators. We will remember that every detail matters and hold true to our core philosophy of excellence from start to finish with our students and our staff. We will remain committed to a community that is welcoming, passionate, and fun. We will not compromise our core values, but will be innovative and nimble enough to modify anything but our core values. We will put more focus on creativity than on growth. (NOLS, 1998b)

This process has resulted in a five-year plan that includes a series of goals to guide the school's immediate future. Growth, as with any successful organization, has always been an issue for the NOLS community:

> We have now laid out a growth plan that blueprints four percent growth per year. . . . We also intend to grow a segment of our program that we refer to as local programs. These are programs that educate individuals indigenous to where we run our international programs. These courses educate teachers and land managers in Kenya, Chile, and Mexico. We also plan to expand beyond our expeditions and bring our message to a wider audience. (Palmer, 1998, personal communication)

Some ways follow in which NOLS is expanding their mission beyond field programming. The effort includes the formation and leadership of the wilderness risk man-agement committee and holding excellent annual risk management conferences. The school has published field texts, including *Soft Paths, NOLS Cookery, Mountaineering, Wilderness First Aid* and the upcoming *Leadership* and *Wilderness Guide.* A career network office has been developed to connect alumni with organizations who want to hire high-quality, experienced staff. NOLS has worked to increase diversity through an extensive scholarship program and special courses for educators at both the domestic and international branches. There has been an increase in professional training for other organizations through specially designed seminars and consultation. NOLS has also established an extensive research program with an advisory board of land managers and university professors (Hampton, 1998, personal communication).

Readers interested in additional information about the history of the National Outdoor Leadership School, a definition of wilderness education, a deeper exploration of the NOLS experience, or the life of Paul Petzoldt are referred to "The NOLS Experience: Experiential Education in the Wilderness" (Bachert, 1987), an unpublished dissertation, and *On Belay: The Life of Legendary Mountaineer Paul Petzoldt* (Ringholz, 1997).

References

Bachert, D. W. (1987). *The NOLS experience: Experiential education in the wilderness.* Unpublished doctoral dissertation, Appalachian State University, Boone, North Carolina.

Bates, R. H., Bursdall, R. L., House, W. P., Houston, C. S., Petzoldt, P. K., and Streatfield, N. R. (1939). *Five miles high: American alpine club American Kharakorum Expedition, 1938.* New York, NY: Dodd, Mead & Co.

Hampton, B., and Cole, D. (1988). *Soft paths: How to enjoy the wilderness without harming it.* Harrisburg, PA: Stackpole.

Kehoe, S. (1998). What's so great about outdoor education?! *The Leader.* Lander, WY: NOLS.

Kessler, S. (1983). Beyond wilderness skills. *NOLS Alumnus,* Fall/Winter, 6.

Miner, J., and Boldt, J. (1981). *Outward Bound USA: Learning through experience in adventure-based education.* New York, NY: Wm. Morrow.

National Outdoor Leadership School. (1965). *Articles of incorporation of the National Outdoor Leadership School, March 4, 1965.* Lander, WY, NOLS archives.

National Outdoor Leadership School. (1986). *Catalog of courses.* Lander, WY: Author

National Outdoor Leadership School. (1998a). *NOLS course catalog.* Lander, WY: Author.

National Outdoor Leadership School. (1998b). *Final draft 5-year field program: The route to 2003.* Lander, WY: Author.

Petzoldt, P. (1953). *On top of the world: My adventures with my mountain-climbing husband.* New York, NY: T. Y. Crowell Co.

Petzoldt, P. K. (1964a). *Letter to J. Miner, Feb. 27.* Lander, WY: NOLS archives.

Petzoldt, P. K. (1964b). *Tape recording, debriefing of C-10 (Tenth course at Colorado Outward Bound).* Lander, WY: NOLS archives.

Petzoldt, P. K. (1965a). *NOLS review and report to the board of trustees.* Lander, WY: NOLS archives.

Petzoldt, P. K. (1965b). *Tape recording, Untitled NOLS promotional slide/tape.* Lander, WY: NOLS archives.

Petzoldt, P. K. (1967). *Letter to J. Miner, Jan. 25.* Lander, WY: NOLS archives.

Petzoldt, P. K. (1974). *The wilderness handbook.* New York, NY: W. W. Norton & Co., Inc.

Petzoldt, P. K. (1984). *The new wilderness handbook.* New York, NY: W. W. Norton & Co., Inc.

Ringholz, R. C. (1997). *On belay: The life of legendary mountaineer Paul Petzoldt.* Seattle, WA: The Mountaineers.

Simer, P. (1981). NOLS director calls for new wilderness agenda. *NOLS Alumnus,* Winter, 3.

Simer, P., and Sullivan, J. (1983). *The National Outdoor Leadership School's wilderness guide.* New York, NY: Simon & Schuster.

Van Winkle, Q. (1997). Just how is it that you've changed? *The Leader.* Lander, WY: NOLS.

Wyoming State Journal, July 30, 1963, p. 12.

Wyoming State Journal, March 23, 1965, p. 1.

Wyoming State Journal, August 17, 1965, pp. 1, 8.

Chapter 12

Project Adventure:
A Brief History

Dick Prouty
Project Adventure

Can any of the insights traditionally gained in a wilderness Outward Bound setting be learned in the course of a twice a week 45-minute high-school physical education program? Can lessons about how to solve problems in a group learned in a physical education class be transferred to cooperative work in a biology class? Can new physical activities be invented to help students to go beyond previously set limits to risk taking? Can public school teachers and counselors learn to use a cooperative style of education which challenges them to be a bit more vulnerable to the students? . . . And learn to like it? Can students help solve problems for groups in their communities, serve real needs, and learn valuable curricula and social lessons in the process?

In 1970 these questions were beginning to show up in the conversations of educators interested in reform. The Outward Bound movement had stirred real interest in using a new set of methods. Jerry Pieh, the young principal of Hamilton-Wenham Junior-Senior High School in Hamilton, Massachusetts, was one of those asking such questions.

As a young graduate student of education, Jerry had helped his father, Bob Pieh, start the Minnesota Outward Bound School in 1962, and had shared the excitement of

those early years. This experience had given Jerry a strong appreciation for the power of the Outward Bound approach. As principal of Hamilton-Wenham Junior-Senior High, Jerry was in a position to examine those questions in a practical way. He and colleague Gary Baker wrote a three-year development proposal to the federal office of education that would try to answer the question of how to "mainstream" the Outward Bound process into a secondary public school setting. He called the new program *Project Adventure.*

In attempting to bring Outward Bound strategies to a school setting, Jerry Pieh was returning to the basic roots of Outward Bound. The founder of Outward Bound, Kurt Hahn, was foremost an educator, with roots in the classical private schools of Germany and Britain. Hahn felt that the classical school curriculum was not enough for the development of the whole child. His work with the Gordounstoun School in Scotland during World War II had led to the establishment of the first Outward Bound School and later to the worldwide Outward Bound school movement. Hahn's original impulse, however, had been to work within the confines of a traditional school. Jerry Pieh sought in his Project Adventure (PA) program to bring these ideas back to the setting in which they were first practiced. This had been done before: Lincoln-Sudbury High School in Lincoln, Massachusetts, had an Outward Bound–type course in the late 1960s, for example. That particular program, however, was taught by Outward Bound staff, not by public school teachers. Such activities, however, tended to be isolated from the standard curriculum and were almost totally dependent on teacher interest. Pieh wanted more than that. He sought to have the Outward Bound *process* become a part of the standard high-school curriculum.

The funding of the Project Adventure grant in 1971 allowed Jerry to hire key staff with Outward Bound backgrounds and to begin the planning of a new curriculum approach. Many teachers were involved in the planning of this grant, and involved themselves in Outward Bound and other training experiences. Teachers, Project Adventure staff, and administrators then set to work writing and experimenting with curriculum. The largest component was focused on tenth grade physical education, but English, history, science, theater arts, and counseling were also explored in the context of what came to be known as "adventure activities."

Bob Lentz was the first director of Project Adventure. Bob had been a teacher, a principal, and had worked at Outward Bound as director of its teacher training programs. Bob also had a deep understanding of the power of the experiential learning process. Here he describes one of his original insights about the effect of an experiential-internship program on students:

> We got back report after report on these kids about what a lively, alert, intelligent, responsible student this is. And you would visit the student on his project and my God, he was alive, and alert and responsible. You'd look through his records and ask teachers about him and the answer you'd get was, "wasn't alive, was lethargic, wasn't alert, wasn't responsible." A kid would come back off his project—for a few days he'd be alive and alert, then his old behavior would come back. That simply said to me, we're missing some vital things here.

Bob found in the Project Adventure curriculum a way to help students become more "alive, alert, and responsible" inside schools, and to institutionalize the process. As Josh Miner and Joe Boldt say in their history of Outward Bound in 1981, "No other innovative educational proposal spinning off from Outward Bound has enjoyed a greater success with the educational establishment than Project Adventure." The reason for this success was the willingness and ability of PA and its staff under Bob Lentz's leadership, to work with teachers and schools, empowering them to institutionalize the curriculum changes.

The nature of these curricula changes were creative and profound, yet not so dramatic that the teachers could not relate them to their existing schedules and class objectives. The original Hamilton-Wenham model was an interdisciplinary concept that focused on the sophomore class. Every sophomore took a yearlong Project Adventure physical education class that went through a sequence of innovative warmups, trust-building exercises, initiative problems and low- and high-ropes course elements. Two basic goals were constantly sought and reinforced: that the students would learn how to solve problems in a group more creatively and efficiently; and that preconceived barriers to what was possible often held both the group and the individual from increasing achievement. Concurrently, the curricula in the sophomore's English, social studies and biology classes had units written by their teachers that reinforced the same goals in pursuit of traditional academic course objectives. For example, a student may have learned that the value of planning to use the resources of the group, and keeping a watchful eye on the time allotted for the task were both necessary to the successful accomplishment of an initiative problem. In biology class, the same student may have put both of those learnings into use again as he or she planned how his or her learning group were to gather data for its investigation of the fresh water swamp behind the high school. The student would finally participate in the adventurous "Swamp Walk" where his or her data-gathering role in the small cooperative learning group of her class would have been negotiated before the trip. Later, the students would use class time to work in groups to prepare the report.

Other classes would have similar experiential units, using cooperative group strategies. Two- to three-day camping trips that used the environment of the camping site to learn course objectives were valuable as peak experiences where students "put it all together." For example, the annual trip to Acadia National Park in Maine allowed the biology students to gather specimens for their saltwater tide pool unit. The Hahn service ethic was honored and fused with learning objectives in cross-age tutoring projects, recycling projects, and other activities done for credited learning classes coordinated by PA staff.

Evaluation

During the second and third year of the grant the program was submitted to a rigorous evaluation by one of the full-time staff members, Mary Smith. Finished during the third year of the program, 1974, the evaluation covered the full sophomore class that took the program each year—224 in 1971 and 231 in 1972. Six instruments were administered preprogram and postprogram application. The instruments were the Tennessee Self-Concept Scale, the School Climate Survey (based on David McClelland's Classroom Climate Survey), two different kinds of student survey, the AAPHERD physical fitness test, and the Rotter Scale of Internal Versus External Control. The specific goals of the evaluation were as follows:

1. to improve self-concept, confidence, and sense of personal competence among participants;

2. to increase psychomotor skills especially in the areas of balance and coordination; and

3. to overcome pervasive passivity, apathy and uninvolvement among students.

The full evaluation report showed strong positive results with statistically significant changes on the Tennessee and the Rotter and consistently strong qualitative data. *Qualitative data* is the evaluation term for those individual reports that come from various types of participants. The following statement is from the qualitative write-up section of the 1974 report: "Not as shy as I used to be but I am still quite shy. Have stayed after school more to get involved in other things. Got up enough courage to stand in front of about 20 sixth grade kids and conduct a lesson." The "change in self-concept" that the evaluation indicates somehow makes more sense through this girl's comments than through the dry numbers. This particular comment from what might be termed a reluctant participant in the physical education component, demonstrates the type of carryover in "involvement" and "courage," to use the girl's own words, I have found to be typical of an average student's participation.

National Demonstration Site Award

The strong evaluation results were responsible for the award in 1974 by the federal Office of Education of National Demonstration School Status and subsequent National Diffusion Network Model program status and funding for dissemination. The National Diffusion Network (NDN) was a new Office of Education program founded on the belief that excellent programs that have had a rigorous evaluation should be shared nationally, with the original teachers of the new program sharing the methods with other teachers directly. From 1974 to 1981 the Hamilton-Wenham School District received a dissemination grant each year from the NDN to subsidize the "adoption" of the PA model by other schools nationally. As director of the PA dissemination effort for the Hamilton-Wenham Schools, Bob Lentz each year set a goal of how many adoptions were likely to occur and how they were to happen.

It is no exaggeration to state that the NDN years literally put Project Adventure on the map nationally. The interest in the PA program was strong anyway, and with a nationally based program with assistance offices and some funding available in each state, the "disseminating" of the PA model was made much easier. The "adoption process," as the NDN language put it, happened in many different fashions. A typical adoption path would be as follows: a teacher would hear of a great new program (PA) from a friend or at a convention; the teacher would call PA and learn about the NDN and about PA workshops offered; the teacher would convince her administrator to contact the nearest NDN state facilitator's office and apply for a grant; the teacher and perhaps several associates would take a five-day PA workshop in either the physical education or academic model; if a ropes course was necessary PA staff would construct it on-site, usually partially funded by the NDN; follow-up assistance and training would occur over the next year. By 1980 over 400 schools in most of the states of the country had adopted at least one component (academic or physical education) of the original PA program at Hamilton-Wenham.

Involvement in the NDN process required that the PA staff be a bit more accountable and rigorous in the spreading of the PA model than they otherwise might have been. Follow-up surveys, tracking of the adoptions numbers, tracking of the "key elements" in place at each site, evaluation of workshops, and a review of the strategies in dissemination efforts that had and had not worked were required on annual reports for funding extensions. The key elements concept was especially helpful. The idea was to identify what elements of the original adoption were responsible for the significant evaluation results, and be able to target the trainings of new teachers and staff at adopter sites so that the evaluation results could in principle be replicated. The key elements checklist was then available to a state facilitator, or anyone, who could visit an adopter and see what was occurring or not. The original Hamilton-Wenham program had been a large and complex effort and most schools would not ever reach that level of adoption. A variety of the key elements checklist as devised by Bob and his staff are still used today by the PA staff as a valuable teaching tool and vehicle to think about what they are really talking about when they say, "Adopt the program."

Key Elements of an Adventure Curriculum

In developing your curriculum, the following components should be an integral part of the final product. It is, however, appropriate to stress some elements more than others, depending on the curriculum you plan. The qualities that make up the adventure approach curriculum include:

1. A sense of adventure, unpredictability, drama and suspense. This tone may emerge from the situation (a cliff, slum, or canoe trip) or from the teacher who builds drama, anticipation, suspense and mystique into the learning experience for students through stories, comments and even humor.

2. A consistently high (but accomplishable) level of expectation demanded and created by both the intrinsic and external forces. Students need to be convinced that not just anyone could have done this, and that the teacher *cares* that the goal is reached.

3. A success orientation in which growth is supported and encouraged and in which the positive is emphasized. Encouragement is one crucial ingredient in resolving the conflict between high expectations and the need for a successful experience.

4. An atmosphere of mutual support in which cooperation, encouragement and interpersonal concerns are consistently present.

5. A sense of enjoyment, fun and the opportunity to laugh at a situation, each other and oneself.

6. An approach to learning which makes use of group problem solving, which allows for a variety of personal contributions and which presents problems that can't ordinarily be solved individually. The rewards are set up for group effort rather than individual success or competition.

7. The use of a learning laboratory that is more complex, more engaging, less predictable and less familiar than a school classroom.

8. The merging of intellectual, social, physical and emotional learning and development.

9. A significant amount of cognitive work related directly to abstractions and questions previously developed in the classroom, or subsequently to be developed.

10. The combining of moments of active involvement with moments of personal and group reflection and evaluation. An awareness that teachable and learnable moments are unpredictable but necessary ingredients in the curriculum.

11. A definite organization and structure which define the limits of the experience and states expectations but within which the participants have freedom to make decisions, choices and even mistakes.

12. An economic and structural reasonableness which allows the curriculum to effectively compete for dollars and other resources within an educational economy which is limited in its resources. Neither too long, too exotic, nor too expensive.

Adventure-Based Counseling

The potential for the use of the Project Adventure activities with the special needs populations of the schools had always been recognized by the PA staff. Self-concept improvement is basic to the needs of most special needs students. Work with these students was not a first priority, however, as the PA model was intended to be a comprehensive school model affecting all the students. But there

was significant work in early years in two ways: first was the Action Seminar at Hamilton-Wenham Regional High School, an interdisciplinary four-period class which drew on a wide mixture of students (outlined under the same title in the Project Adventure book *Teaching Through Adventure*). This class was taught by PA staff members Jim Schoel and Steve Webster. Those students participated in adventure activities, group construction and craft projects and community service. No formal assessment of the students prior to entry was made, but quiet referrals ensured that half the students were experiencing trouble in school and required an "alternative" form of instruction. The action seminar concept was later carried into the Gloucester public schools where it was incorporated as the Gloucester Museum School, and later as Project Alliance.

The second expression of adventure counseling was an outpatient therapy group at the Addison Gilbert Hospital, Gloucester, Massachusetts. Beginning in 1974, Paul Radcliffe, a PA-trained school psychologist, worked under the supervision of Phil Cutter, and teamed with Mary Smith, a PA staff member, to conduct a weekly two-hour adventure group. The hospital therapy group concept, with its intake and consultation process, was subsequently incorporated into the Gloucester Public School's psychological services, and was called the *learning activities group*.

The development of the adventure-based counseling (ABC) process into a curriculum equivalent to the earlier interdisciplinary work at Hamilton-Wenham took place with the funding of a Massachusetts State Department of Education grant in 1980–1983. Paul Radcliffe and Bill Cuff worked with personnel from Gloucester, Hamilton-Wenham, and Manchester, Massachusetts, to refine the process of intake, grouping, staffing, activities selection, and staff training. This development grant was significant in that it put the PA work with special needs students in schools on the same footing as the original PA work. The evaluation was extensive and again showed significant gains on the Tennessee Self-Concept Scale in students in three systems over two years. On the basis of the evaluation, the Massachusetts State Department of Education awarded the program validation as a State Model Program.

The development of the ABC model and its formal evaluation really accelerated a trend that had been there in seed form from the beginning. The NDN had encouraged the dissemination of the PA model beyond schools into all types of *educational service providers,* the bureaucratic term for camps, youth centers, clinics and really any place where an educational function was occurring. The first adventure-based counseling workshop was offered in May of 1979, and the response was strong with over 30 persons attending the four-day workshop. Persons from residential clinics and hospitals, therapeutic camps and drug treatment centers attended, as well as school counselors, psychologists and alternative school teachers. The adaptation of the program's activities to all these sites continued after this workshop, and the movement of the PA outreach into these types of organizations increased.

Transition to Independence

I had first met Bob Lentz in the fall of 1970 when Jim Schoel, one of the original four PA staff, introduced me to him. Jim had been one of my instructors on an Outward Bound teacher practicum course that had been run by the Hurricane Island School out of Bartlett's Island off Maine the preceding summer. As a social studies teacher and director of an experiential education program at the neighboring Manchester schools, I worked closely with both Jim and Bob through the 1970s organizing adventure-type programs in both the Manchester and Gloucester schools. The adventure work was involving, frustrating, and exciting; often all at the same time. When we started an early ABC group in Manchester for kids in difficulty in the junior high, I had some of my most meaningful teaching times. In late 1979 Jim, Bob, Paul Radcliffe and I began meeting to write a grant to develop and refine the ABC model. I enjoyed the challenge of writing the grant, and was intrigued by the possibilities of helping PA grow. I applied for a leave in early 1980 and Bob and I agreed to terms of employment.

In the spring of 1980, Bob Lentz announced that he was resigning as director to assume the principalship of Groves High School in Birmingham, Michigan. After nearly 10 years with Project Adventure at Hamilton-Wenham, Bob was ready for a new challenge. The chance to influence change in a public school in the position that research showed had the most direct influence, the principalship, was just such a challenge. He left Project Adventure in good shape, with a new NDN cycle of funding, the good will of the host school system, a strong reputation for quality, a group of experienced key staff and a system of helping a complex program adoption process happen with minimal problems. Most importantly, he left with a feeling of accomplishment because the original goal of devising a system to mainstream the goals of Outward Bound into schools had been advanced significantly. Not that there wasn't *plenty* of work left to do, he told us.

Karl Rohnke assumed the director's position after Bob left. Karl had been with PA since its start and in many ways was the most well-known staff member. As author of the PA text *Cowstails and Cobras*, Karl had brought to the many readers of that book a real hands-on understanding of the techniques, methods and spirit necessary to implement the physical education curriculum that had started at Hamilton-Wenham. Karl's creative abilities had guided the evolution of the ropes course elements and the games, stunts, and initiatives that were the core of the curriculum. Karl's ability to play and have obvious *fun* in a workshop was invaluable modeling for teachers and staff being trained. Karl enjoyed using these strengths and con-

tinued as director to construct courses, lead workshops and write up new curriculum ideas. Karl was also decisive in letting us know what he did not like about his new role; thinking about budgets, organizational issues and paperwork hassles. He and I agreed about a year after I started that I would assume the director's role, and he would concentrate on what he did best, which was writing, researching new activities and ropes course elements, and leading workshops.

The early 1980s were tough times for education of all sorts. The Reagan revolution was causing increasing cutbacks in funding for schools. The "back-to-basics" movement in public schools was increasing and giving people who wanted to get students to learn in new and creative ways a few more hurdles to jump. Yet, in spite of the mood, the flow of people to training workshops for PA and on to subsequent adoptions continued. The PA budget as part of the Hamilton-Wenham schools in 1981–82 was $345,000, of which only $55,000 was federal money from the National Diffusion Network. The remainder was revenue from workshop fees, ropes course construction and the sale of supplies and books. There were five full-time staff members in the Hamilton offices. In addition, Alan Sentowski, who had been a biology teacher at Hamilton-Wenham and a key early staff member, had started a satellite office in Savannah, Georgia.

In a series of meetings in 1981, PA staff decided with the Hamilton-Wenham administrators that it would be best if PA were to separate from the school. The growth of PA had surpassed expectations of the school, and while justly proud of the spread of their home grown product, they felt it best for the increasing growth to go on separately. The decision to separate seemed to fit for everyone as the PA staff also sensed that PA had the potential to grow in new and important ways and that this could best be done independently. In the next year an amiable agreement was drawn up, a board of directors chosen by me and Karl, and the formal incorporation of Project Adventure Inc. as a nonprofit 501-(c)(3) organization was made in September 1981. The articles of incorporation affirmed that the main purpose of the new corporation was the dissemination of PA programs. We had chosen to continue the basic direction that we had been operating under at the school, but now there was a sense of anticipation that new possibilities awaited.

Steady Growth

The original grant in 1970 had funded a staff of five to work closely with the Hamilton-Wenham staff. The staff of PA in 1981 was six full-time staff, and an additional 10 certified trainers. Certified trainers were encouraged by the NDN as teachers who could teach training workshops nationally with the same "fidelity" as original staff but with more cost-effectiveness. The staff of PA in early 1989 was

37 full-time persons, with a National Certified Trainer staff of 50 that included facilitators with expertise and practical experience in all workshop areas. The growth since separation has been continuous with an increase in revenue each year averaging over 30 percent. The sources of revenue—now they are called *revenue centers*—are in the same categories as they were in 1981 workshop and training, catalogue sales, ropes course construction, and grants and contracts for research purposes. The organization has continued to serve the schools who wanted to expand an existing program or start a new one. The momentum of the word-of-mouth advertising of the existing "installed base" of PA school programs was strong. As teachers and administrators moved on to new jobs, they often took their favorite program with them. Both Jerry Pieh, as headmaster of Milton Academy, and Bob Lentz, as principal of Groves High, had PA help them implement a program. Important new work was also done in urban schools in Cambridge, Savannah, Pittsburgh, Columbus and New York as the ability of PA activities to motivate for achievement and develop group cooperation proved effective for the multiethnic populations of urban schools.

Although work with schools continued to grow, the main reason for the growth of PA was the staff's ability to work with a variety of organizations other than schools and to help them customize a program for their needs. Through the 1980s, PA staff worked with camps, youth agencies such as the Boy Scouts and Girl Scouts, therapeutic agencies, drug and alcohol treatment centers, psychiatric hospitals, colleges, conference centers, corporate training centers, children's homes, job-training centers, outdoor education centers, and state agencies. Throughout this expansion of the audiences that the PA staff served, the continuity of the early training models served as a starting point for new work, and the in-house expertise of the organization contracting with PA for assistance was used to draw out a customized program.

While the range of groups served by PA seems wide, the trainings have followed four generic models: adventure programming, which served physical education and recreation programs; adventure-based counseling, which served therapeutic programs; academic programming, which served classroom academic programs; and staff development programming, which served educational and corporate adult training needs. Project Adventure has an entry level workshop in each area which uses essentially the same activity base with some modifications. Each workshop, however, is taught by PA staff or certified trainers who have experience and expertise in the program area which the workshop is addressing. By the end of each four- to five-day workshop, the participant is ready to design a more expansive program with more specified training, and often is ready to start a modest program in his or her area.

Southern Office

One of the key supports of the growth of PA in the 1980s was the southern office. Alan Sentowski had begun the office at an outdoor education center in Savannah in 1980. The office was moved in 1984 to Atlanta to take advantage of the central location of Atlanta. One of the important groups being served by the southern office in 1984 was the Georgia Department of Youth Services (DYS). Cindy Simpson, a school psychologist, had attended a PA workshop in 1981 and gone on to develop a community-based six-week program for juvenile offenders in the state. Working closely with Juvenile Judge Virgil Costley of Covington, Cindy had developed a program that used a tightly structured adventure-based counseling approach and infused it with academic support, parent counseling, and career counseling. An evaluation of the program from 1983 to 1986 by the Georgia DYS showed that 94 percent of the youths that started the program finished and that the recidivism rate was 15 percent for the three years after the program.

In 1984 Cindy joined Alan Sentowski in the Atlanta office and teamed up with staff associate John Call who coordinated construction and technical trainings. The Atlanta office relocation proved to be a good decision as the small staff began to experience a rapid increase in the demand for PA services soon after the move was made. Alan left PA in June of 1985 to pursue other interests, and Cindy Simpson took over the leadership role. The growth in staff and services rendered has continued and accelerated under Cindy's leadership. The development of innovative community-based direct service models such as Challenge has become a research and development specialty of the southern office. An alternative school model, and a jobs training model were started successfully.

By 1989 the southern office had 16 staff and accounted for about one-third of the total PA budget. All of the functions of the Hamilton office were carried on in the southern office with the exception of the catalogue sale of ropes course equipment and PA publications. The growth was made easier by the move of the office in the summer of 1988 to a new site in Covington, Georgia, 30 miles southeast of Atlanta. With the help of Judge Costly and Pierce Cline, another member of an advisory board that PA had formed for the southern office, Cindy had managed to acquire in 1987 an unoccupied former Elks Club lodge on a five-acre pond. Located on a total of 70 acres, the 12,000-square-foot building was renovated, and housed the Atlanta-based PA staff and programs by the fall of 1988.

Therapeutic Program Growth

The history of PA clearly shows that as the organization works with other client organizations to help them implement a PA program, the resulting customizing process often breaks new ground. The unique issues and needs of the client result in modifications and new designs of existing PA models that often can then be used by other organizations of a similar type that PA helps. This process has clearly been at work in the dissemination of the ABC model. Therapeutic institutions that ranged from public schools to therapeutic camps to counseling centers to residential treatment facilities and psychiatric hospitals implemented a variety of the ABC model in the 1980s.

One of the more important early ABC adoptions was as a result of PA's work with the Institute of Pennsylvania Hospital in Philadelphia. In 1981 four staff of the therapeutic recreation department led by Rick Thomas attended an ABC workshop in Hamilton. A grant by a local benefactor to the hospital, one of the oldest and most respected psychiatric institutions in the country, had paid for the training and later for the ropes course that PA staff constructed on the rolling grounds of the hospital. Under the leadership of Rick Thomas who worked closely with PA staff Paul Radcliffe and Jim Schoel, the Institute began to use the ABC model with a short-term residential adolescent group. The hospital evaluations of the patient's progress in the program were excellent. The therapeutic recreation department has worked with the clinical staff of the hospital to expand the program to other groups including mixed diagnosis adult treatment groups, drug and alcohol groups, and eating disorder groups. The schedules and length of the ABC activities in these groups are somewhat different, but they all occur on the grounds of the hospital and often include the ropes course.

Rick Thomas has some interesting comments on why the ABC model works so well in the hospital setting:

> We want to help patients be more independent, decrease their feelings of helplessness, and get away from the idea that someone else has the secrets about their well-being and who they are. We try to educate patients about their strengths, not looking for pathology. The people we see need experience in doing differently, to experience themselves as different. They're not ready for insight. They need to be brought up to another level before they acquire that. They need to learn by *doing* first. They simply do not have the ability for abstract thinking. Generally, if they do abstract, it is merely a form of intellectualization, with few feelings attached. As Glasser says, "Act differently, even if you don't feel differently."

Rick's comments help explain the power of the ABC model to help the psychiatric patient. The 1980s saw PA work with hospitals and other residential care facilities on an increasing basis. By 1989 PA staff had helped over 100 hospitals implement a variety of the ABC program. The use of an integrated adventure-based hospital program was becoming more widely accepted in the psychiatric field by the end of the 1980s, and the increased refinement of the program was proceeding rapidly. Cindy Simpson from the southern office and Paul Radcliffe from the Hamilton office teamed to lead PA's efforts in this emerging area.

The need for a PA text for the emergence of the ABC field began to be critical as the number of trainings and requests for assistance increased in the early 1980s. In 1985 we received notice that the Culpepper Foundation of New York City had funded our proposal to research and write a new text for the ABC field. The book was written in a collaborative effort with Jim Schoel assuming the lead author position and Paul Radcliffe and I assisting. Jim had one full year funded by the grant to research, interview and write. It took another unfunded year of work by the three of us to complete the book, but when it was finished, we were pleased with the result. We had a text, *Islands of Healing,* that would guide all those workshop participants at the more than 300 institutions of some sort that had an ABC model and others in the field to share the results of more than a decade of development work. It was a fitting complement to *Cowstails and Cobras* and the other PA texts for the other models, and should, we thought, more firmly establish the credibility of the model for all practitioners.

Executive Reach, Corporate Training

In the late 1970s, Karl Rohnke and Bob Lentz had taught education courses at Boston University in adventure education and had met Tony Langston of the faculty. They discussed and planned how to use the PA activities base with the business school classes that Tony was beginning to work with. Tony went on to start a corporate training program at Boston University. The new program, Executive Challenge, found a good reception in the high-tech clients of the Route 128 area in the late 1970s, and quickly became the leader in this new way to work with corporate training: nonwilderness trainings using the range of initiatives, and ropes course elements. Other consultants began to hear of the success of the Executive Challenge model and began to approach PA for assistance in developing a program. As a result of these inquiries, PA staff began to think seriously in 1983 about this emerging area and how it fit into PA's organization.

In the winter of 1984, PA staff received a call from a human resource group at Digital Equipment Corporation. They had heard about PA's programs and wanted PA to design a team-building workshop for their work group. Paul Radcliffe and I worked with the team leader to design a four-day workshop. The result was a great success from the work team's viewpoint. A three-month follow-up visit on-site revealed improved communication, levels of trust, and an ability to take an initiative involving risk with more confidence. A 20-minute video was produced with Digital's help, and was designed for both Digital and PA use.

PA staff did work with other Digital groups as a result of this initial effort, and decided that PA should develop the capability to do corporate training. In 1985 Ann Smolowe joined PA to help develop and market a PA corporate model. Ann had a varied background that included a business school background, three years working for the American Stock Exchange, and a complete thru-hike of the Appalachian Trail. Most importantly, she had a strong desire to bring innovative outdoor training to the corporate setting. Our mutual goal was to develop a PA staff development model that would allow us eventually to have the capability to train others in adventure-based corporate training skills. In addition, we hoped to be able to generate revenue from our direct service efforts with companies to help our overall mission in other areas.

By 1989 PA had developed a significant track record with a number of larger Fortune 500 companies as well as smaller firms. PA had developed customized trainings around the themes of encouraging innovation, culture change initiatives, multiskill retraining, leadership, risk-taking motivation, as well as a more standard team-building option. The ability to train others easily because of PA's overall mission had helped define some of the trainings. Frank Iarossi, president of Exxon Shipping in Houston, had heard Elizabeth Ross-Kanter of the Harvard Business School expound on the need for companies to master change, and had become convinced of the need for his company to begin to change its culture. PA contracted with Exxon Shipping in 1987 to train teams of company facilitators, who in turn led all 1,000 employees through a one-day team building and skill training that was part of a larger week-long training for all employees, designed by an outside consulting firm. Exxon Shipping was on the way to becoming less hierarchical, less rigid, more able to identify problems earlier and work toward their resolution. In a modern technological environment, the super-tanker captain no longer had all the answers or even a knowledge about what many of the problems were. Specialization of knowledge and skills made flexible work team strategies a must.

The Activity Base

All the program models in the world wouldn't work if PA staff did not have an effective arsenal of activities that could be used to accomplish the program aims. The games, prop and nonprop initiatives and challenge ropes course elements that the original staff modified and created for the short 50-minute physical education sessions at Hamilton-Wenham were responsible for the ability of all the subsequent programs to be able to work on-site, indoors if necessary, and to imbue almost any training curriculum with the aims and energy of the PA learning goals. The constant renewing of this activity base and the refinement of the skills training and assessment methods that were necessary as the numbers of adoption sites and participants mushroomed were two key tasks that have helped sustain PA's growth.

One of Karl's strengths is the ability to create new activities and the enjoyment he gets from doing so. An environment of creativity, of pushing for the new modification or of putting together two previously separate things, has been important to renewing our base. Karl also works easily with others creating and likes to give them liberal credit, always important in developing new things. PA now has a 50 element repertoire of ropes course elements, including the following notable PA inventions: Wild Woosey, Mohawk Walk, Proutys Landing, Pamper Pole, Hickory Jump, Seagull Landing and the Flying Squirrel. The first indoor elements were built in the Newburyport, Massachusetts, gym in 1972, and by 1985 every outdoor element had been constructed in some sort of indoor environment also. The refinement of the technology and equipment for the ropes course has been constant with the following at one point being an innovation: galvanized cable, through-bolting, strand vices, telephone poles and accompanying guy technology, custom-made pulley systems for the belay cable and for the zip wire. The invention of new activities was even more pronounced in the initiative and game area, and the publication of *Silver Bullets: A Guide to Initiative Problems and Adventure Games,* was a notable benchmark for the organization. The possibilities continue to expand as PA has become a gathering point for others' ideas in this area.

The direct construction of ropes course elements for others was a service of PA as early as 1972 when Karl built the first PA indoor climbing wall for Newburyport High School. Since then the direct construction of elements for others has become one of PA's key services. PA built over 100 courses in 1998 and provided repair and safety check services at many more. Located all over the United States and in Australia, Singapore, Hong Kong and Europe, these 100 will join the approximately 1,000 courses PA has constructed since it started. PA runs a catalogue supply service for materials to construct courses and to resupply the existing courses with rope and other equipment. One of the more recent developments in the way PA helps people construct has been the creation of the package, Challenge-by-Choice. This is a manual with accompanying two hour video tape and telephone support which gives a willing person the instructions necessary to construct a low ropes course. *Cowstails and Cobras* had construction information of an informal type in several chapters but by the mid 1980s, it was out of date. Construction help is now available from PA only through Challenge-by-Choice or direct service by PA staff. PA is the clear leader in the field of initiative and ropes course design and construction and PA remains committed to continuous improvement in both areas.

The safety of the activity base had always been important. But as the numbers of programs grew, questions on safety and liability issues came more frequently. The second level workshop, Advanced Skills and Standards, first designed and taught by Steve Webster in 1982, was a successful offering that focused on ropes course technical skills, program management and design issues and possible rescue techniques. In 1981 and later in 1986, PA staff conducted a survey of adopting sites and published what was called the Ten and Fifteen Year Safety Studies. Both showed a level of accidents, defined as a day out of school or work through an injury, at a rate below that of the standard public school physical education program. In addition, there were no reported accidents of the severely disabling variety that were everyone's concern. These studies proved valuable when the field of outdoor adventure experienced the general liability crisis of 1985–87 with particular hardness. PA staff were able, with the help of these studies, to forestall many programs from losing insurance, but the problem of obtaining insurance was difficult for some areas of the country. In 1987 with the help of a new site-specific and voluntary accreditation program, PA staff were able to convince a top-rated insurance company to offer liability insurance for all accredited programs. A new generic manual for ropes courses and initiatives has been written by Steve Webster. The accreditation program uses the manual as a guideline for acceptable technical skills and safety issues.

Planning for the Future

In 1985, at the urging of a key PA board member, PA staff worked with an outside consultant to implement a long-range planning process for PA. The staff assessed strengths and weaknesses, looked at mission, set objectives, and designed strategies and action plans to make the objectives happen. After some discussion, PA arrived at this statement of its mission:

> The mission of Project Adventure Inc. is to be the leading organization helping others use adventure education as a catalyst for personal/professional growth and change.

The key phrase is "helping others use." By this, we at PA mean that we consult, train, and empower others to *start, maintain* and *improve* PA program models that use our innovative program base of games, initiatives and ropes course elements. Direct service such as our existing programs with youth at risk, schools, and corporate groups will continue to grow and be a source of important research and development opportunities, and revenue stability; but the primary focus of the organization is to help other organizations use PA models to promote growth and change in their students, clients and organizations.

There is a definite trend worldwide toward incorporating adventure activities into educational and training programs. The main reason for this trend is the recognition that team synergy is a major driving force in both economic productivity and social change possibilities. To help both educational and training institutions address these realities with creative new models is PA's principal long-range goal. PA's unique access to many types and levels of organizations allows us at PA to accent the catalyst role of our mission, and to help communities of interest develop among those we serve. Our focus on a clear mission has helped PA grow strongly since 1985 and it will be even more important to maintain as we head into the next decade. To help this focus, PA staff have begun to use the phrase "bring the adventure home" to describe both the mission goal and the process of encouraging an adventurous challenge-by-choice attitude as a goal of all programs. There are definitely many possibilities ahead and we at PA are committed to continue choosing our challenges with the same spirit of fun and adventure that has been our trademark from the beginning.

Chapter 13

Development Training in the United Kingdom

Chris Loynes
Adventure Education

The use of outdoor adventure for education began in Britain because two men, from very different backgrounds and at different times, felt it was the right thing to do. They were concerned about the moral fiber of young men and saw the outdoor challenge as part of an approach to education that would address the need to develop them physically, socially, morally, and spiritually. The modern equivalent is called *development training,* and it is perhaps appropriate that the current popularity of this approach is so well-founded in the roots of the concept. The two men were Baden Powell and Kurt Hahn.

Baden Powell (usually known as BP) recognized positive benefits of the outdoor life on young scouts while fighting in the Boer War. The ingredients of adventure, challenge, a common purpose, comradeship, and living together were all included in his vision developed from these experiences. On his return to England, BP set out to find a moral alternative. His first experiments in simple camps operating a troop structure with an adventurous program set precedents in methods such as using a residential setting, working in groups, introducing new and adventurous experiences, and self-reliance. Once published in a form eagerly read by boys, market forces soon established the validity of his insights, with the movement blossoming spontaneously.

This was quickly followed by the Guide movement for girls. Often the initiative for the formation of a troop came from the boys who then sought a leader. BP also set standards for leadership being first and foremost interested in the development of young people, understanding their needs, leading by example, delegating responsibility, and using a discovery method of learning. If backwoodsmanship set a bad example in environmental ethics, it was through ignorance rather than by design. The modern Scout and Guide movements are still founded on these essentials and are the largest worldwide voluntary youth movement. The outdoors and the expedition are still major and central parts of their curriculum. Critics point out the paramilitary nature and middle-class appeal of both the Scouts and the Guides. It was a far more egalitarian movement than Hahn set out to achieve.

The expedition was also a central part of Hahn's early thinking being part of the personal development program at Gourdonston School where he was head teacher in the 1930s. In Germany, Hahn was influenced by the *reform-pedagogic,* an attempt to liberalize the German education system in the late 1920s. He experimented with these ideas at Salem School before leaving Germany where he was becoming concerned by the takeover of the reform by the Hitler Youth movement.

In the United Kingdom he joined a small number of independent schools incorporating the outdoors into their curricula. However, the desire to achieve social influence through the hierarchical approach of educating the future leaders of the country came with him and came to dominate what had previously been a much wider range of approaches in the independent school sector including the play philosophy of Hodgkin.

Several voices were raising concerns at the subversion of the anarchic nature of outdoor adventure by educators intent on character building. Tom Price, both a mountaineer and an educator and an early warden of Outward Bound Eskdale, commented on the eternal paradox of combining the opposites of adventure and education in one program. In Germany postwar critiques of Hahn commented that any use of the outdoors was a misuse.

In the 1930s concern with the establishment values of both the scouts and the independent schools was sufficient to give rise to a new movement, the Woodcraft Folk. Still active and widespread throughout Europe the founding ideas were much influenced by stories of the democratic nature of the communities of native American plains people. Simple community living in woodland settings was combined with egalitarian processes of decision making. Programs were driven by the philosophy of exploration, an internally referenced wondering about the world, rather than by the philosophy of challenge, an externally referenced matching up to expectations.

Hahn's Postwar Influence

The pilot program of what was to become the Duke of Edinburgh's Award Scheme, also inspired and initiated by Hahn, took place in Scotland in the 1930s. Called the *Moray Scheme,* it also incorporated an expedition. The overall scheme and its aims bear a striking resemblance to those developed by the Scout movement. The two now work closely together.

It was with Outward Bound (OB) that Hahn made his biggest impact, and OB is really the birthplace of development training. Starting in 1941 with the first school at Aberdovey on the Welsh coast, OB developed month-long adventurous programs incorporating adventure activities, expeditions, community work and working in groups. Challenge, self-reliance, and leadership were key ingredients. The aim was character building, and the forum wild country.

Despite popular opinion, the schools were not elitist, recruiting participants from factories and borstals as well as schools. The mood postwar had changed. This was the time of the Education and Health Acts of Parliament in the United Kingdom. There was a strong desire for a better society, especially for the young. During the war Hahn's first school at Aberdovey was diverted to drown-proofing merchant seamen, hardly a social elite.

After the war, the staff of the first school were largely recruited from the Navy and the programs reflect this influence. The day was full with an early start and late finish. Groups operated in a semimilitary discipline and activities reflected the skills and interests of sailors. The approach did not emphasize athletic achievement, but rather tenacity of pursuit and the education of the whole person.

The second school was in Eskdale, a mountain location, under the influence of the mountaineer and educator Geoffrey Winthrop Young. Staff were a mix of Navy men from Aberdovey and mountaineers. The anarchic traditions of the latter intermixed with the formality of the former to create the full flavor of the archetypal Outward Bound program. This unlikely mix went a long way to help avoid the militaristic and elitist influences of earlier traditions.

Courses for girls began in 1951. Six schools were founded in Britain, of which four remain. There are now many more worldwide.

Outward Bound recognizes that adventure is not something one does, but rather a way one feels—that, as an attitude to life, it is perhaps the best way to encapsulate the kind of relationship a healthy person will have with his or her environment and his or her community. As such, ingredients other than outdoor adventure were included (e.g., community service). The Duke of Edinburgh's Award and, of course, the Scouts and Guides, go even further with personal challenges such as the commitment to a hobby and a fitness test.

The Birth of Outdoor Education in Schools

In 1950 the Derbyshire Local Education Authority founded Whitehall Open Country Pursuits Centre and began a trend that became a rising wave of activity in the outdoors that acquired the name "outdoor pursuits." The increasing number of schools, youth clubs and colleges that became involved during the 1960s initially used land-based activities. Participation was mostly outside school time and thus voluntary in nature. Participants were mostly of average intelligence, fit, motivated and obedient, and the expectations leaders could have of such participants were factors in the kind of experience offered. The aim of such programs was proficiency and self-sufficiency, very different from the personal development aims of OB and the Scout movement. The focus was on the activity rather than the participant. With this emphasis on skill development, teaching styles were heavily directive and inflexible. Early and justifiable concerns about safety tended to reinforce this approach as the best way to ensure the necessary ability for performance in safety.

Field Studies

In parallel with this movement was the development of centers offering field study programs primarily for geography and biology students aged between 14 and 21. This work was pioneered by the Field Studies Council, which by the late 1980s operated 10 centers throughout the United Kingdom. In developing courses for students taking higher school and university subjects related to the environment, the council devised an approach that was quickly adopted by schools. Attendance at a field studies course was the commonest means by which students gain residential experience and participation is frequently required by the examining boards' syllabuses.

Development and Change

Over the last 25 years, the three strands of personal development, outdoor pursuits, and field studies have seen many developments and much change. More young people are involved in a wider range of activities, some of which, like sailboarding and mountain biking, are very recent innovations. Many of the activities have developed offshoots that bear little resemblance to the pure forms from which they sprang. For example, abseiling is often provided as an activity in its own right completely divorced from climbing.

Improvements in the range and standard of equipment now available also permit groups to operate at higher levels of achievement without lowering safety margins. A good example is the change from canvas to glass fiber and now plastic and aluminum canoes. For instance in the 1980s the Ambleside Area Adventure Association (the 4As), a voluntary community group in the English Lake District, had a strong canoeing club working with all ages (in the United Kingdom, *canoeing* is a generic term for the sport, the 4As use kayaks). In competition, the club had trained junior national and world champions and had several members competing in the premier U.K. slalom division. Expeditions include a 100-mile, four-day trip on the Wye, a Welsh river with several rapids, undertaken independent of adults by 12-year-olds, and a sea tour off the Scottish coast with a group whose ages range from 13 to 40. Quality coaching and committed members made this possible, but so did modern materials and designs, without which the progress made with young members would have been impossible, the risks faced on the Wye and the sea unacceptable, and the competition achievements unattainable.

The settings in which activities take place have also diversified. For logistical and financial reasons it is often easier to bring the activity to the client than it is to take the client to the activity in its natural surroundings. Increasingly, adventure activities can be found in the wasteland aftermath of urban renewal, and canals and small reservoirs are being used for water-based sports. The ultimate extension of this has been the creation of artificial environments such as dry ski slopes and climbing walls.

Perhaps the leading example is the Ackers Trust, within a mile of the center of Birmingham, on an old waste tip (garbage dump) where a canal and a railway cross. Nearby are the derelict buildings of the old BSA motorcycle works. The area is characterized by old residential housing, a poor district with a wide variety of ethnic groups represented. The BSA social club was taken over as a community center, the derelict land set aside as a nature reserve and park. The contours of the rubbish heap have been used as the base for a motorbike scramble course and road-training

facility. A trim trail quickly sprouted, followed by a ski slope on the biggest mound of rubbish and a climbing tower was built in the center of the park. There are plans for an indoor equestrian center in an adjacent empty factory. The canal has been dredged (there are more miles of canals in Birmingham than in Venice) and two narrow boats and a fleet of canoes are available. There is open access to the local community as well as educational and recreational groups. The site managers provide supervision where necessary, but prefer to train group leaders in the skills needed to run their own sessions.

The Growth of Development Training

With the raising of the school leaving age in 1974, the experiential approach of outdoor education increasingly found a home in the school timetable as a more relevant way of learning for low-achieving pupils. Also, programs of personal and social education introduced in the past decade in many schools often used outdoor education. This further increased the use of the local environment as the arena for outdoor education. Cumbria Local Education Authority was the first to issue a policy statement on outdoor education:

> Outdoor Education is widely accepted as the term to describe all learning, social development and the acquisition of skill associated with living and journeying in the outdoors. In addition to physical endeavor, it embraces environmental and ecological understanding. Outdoor Education is not a subject but an integrated approach to learning, to decision making and the solution of problems. Apart from opportunities for personal fulfillment and development of leisure interests, Outdoor Education stimulates the development of self-reliance, self-discipline, judgment, responsibility, relationships and the capacity for sustained practical endeavors.

The Authority owned and staffed three residential centers and mounted an in-service training program for teachers to acquire the necessary skills and concepts. They stated:

> Outdoor Education embraces three interlinked areas of experiential learning, through outdoor pursuits, outdoor studies and the residential element.

A curriculum model incorporated these three strands from age 4 to 19, and advisory teachers were appointed to promote and resource its implementation.

Experiential Learning

Few would disagree that outdoor education and experiences in a residential setting have a unique part to play in extending the opportunities for young people to develop, learn and grow, because of the range of opportunities available for experience-based learning. This approach to education and training relies almost totally upon the participants being completely involved in their learning and taking genuine responsibility. They are invited to think, share ideas, make decisions, and exercise independence in the carrying out of activities. However, educationalists assumed that learning automatically occurred as a result of experience-based activities; that having subjected participants to a range of exciting and challenging activities, attitudes are automatically molded or reshaped. There is little evidence to support this assumption, and the realization of this has seen one of the more recent major developments in approach.

If activities are to affect personal and social development and have full impact and more relevance, then there must be opportunities for preparation, evaluation and reflection. This has led to a change in the approach of many leaders, who have adopted a facilitative approach, a long way from the conventional styles of imparting, instructing, and directing. In particular, it requires sensitivity to draw out the personal learning as a result of an activity or experience, not, as one trainer put it: "I do reviewing. I sit them down at the end of each activity and tell them what they did wrong!" This process has become known as *reviewing*.

The Brathay Hall Trust, founded in 1946, was the first residential center to develop this approach and is now widely regarded as a center of excellence. It was responsible for coining the phrase *development training*, and has applied this approach to activities like work experience, as well as to the outdoors—which it regards as only one, albeit potent, of the tools available. Development training is based on Kolb's learning model, "do, reflect, generalize, apply." After an experience, people in the learning group articulate their reactions, reviewing how they worked together, drawing conclusions, and applying these to real-life situations. The tutor facilitates this process by helping members of the group structure their thinking and confront the issues that arise.

The Brathay Hall Trust has found this approach particularly useful in management and leadership training, therapeutic work, and for personal development at times of transition, such as school to work.

Environmental education has also seen development that contributes to development training. Increasingly, project work and excursions are made in the local environment. The approach has shifted from the use of the field as an outdoor classroom to its use as a laboratory applying a discovery method of learning. Environmental education

work in the 1990s takes an issues-based approach. The learning model involved can be summarized as "head, heart and hands," that is, from knowledge and understanding to empathy and action. One Devon school prepares a center spread on community issues for the local newspaper, researched and written by the students.

The primary school curriculum lends itself to work based around outdoor visits. Here are found some of the best examples of curriculum enrichment, with the outdoor experience being integrated into every aspect of the schools' work. Additionally, basic concepts of global and local ecology are being introduced, and environmental awareness is practiced rather than preached.

Residentials and Expeditions

Residential experience as an aid to learning is not a new idea. In 1963 the Newsom Report confirmed the conviction of many teachers that a wide range of activities developed in a residential context provided an abundance of opportunities to enhance and extend learning. Out of it emerged an almost unique environment to promote social and personal development and to bring teachers and young people into closer contact. In the last 30 years, the increasing use of residential centers by schools, youth clubs, and colleges testifies to the rapid demand for such provisions. Significantly, most of the major curriculum initiatives currently being developed stress the potential value of a period of residential experience. Many education authorities have their own centers, often in distant wild country locations. Some schools use other facilities as a base for running their own programs.

A trend has been the acquisition of simple accommodation by individual schools often quite close to home for maximum accessibility. The Peers School in Oxford is an example. The simple hut, on its own wind-generated power and water supplies and two fields from any road, is within half an hour of the school. The rural setting, simple lifestyle, and teaching style are deliberately in contrast with the school environment. Groups can use the center on a part-day or residential basis, and it is built into the curriculum in many ways including field studies, personal and social education, outdoor pursuits, and class tutorial work. In such a setting it is easy to have a different kind of relationship with pupils.

It has also become common to recognize that pupils who are involved in the design of their own experience will learn a great deal more from it due to their investment in the outcome. A Bradford school uses a series of day and multiday journeys designed, organized and carried out by the pupils as the center of a curriculum for low-achieving pupils. Their literacy, numeracy, practical skills and life skills are all focused on the task of carrying out the residential program. This is achieved on a minute budget and no more than a day or two's cycle ride from the school.

The danger has become that the rest of the school's pupils would like the same approach! In Dudley one school has done just that, and pupils carry out a residential program in each year of their school career with increasing amounts of responsibility. However, right from the start each student chooses the activities, the location, and the staff member who will help him or her.

It is apparent that the most effective residential programs are carefully structured to meet predetermined aims and the learning experiences integrated with the curriculum. The use of the residential has also expanded across the age range with many effective examples from the primary sector.

Yet another popular approach incorporating many of the above factors is the expedition. The Young Explorers Trust, the umbrella body of the youth expeditions in the United Kingdom, annually advises and supports many trips. This is the tip of an iceberg, as it only included overseas trips. There will be many more within the United Kingdom. Destinations range around the world with recent venues in Nepal, Peru and China as well as the Arctic, the desert, and the rain forest. Projects range from adventure and field work to community service.

Diversity

Traditionally, most user groups have operated within the structures of local education authorities. However, recent developments have encouraged other groups to use the outdoors for their own, equally valid purposes. Social services, recreation programs and community groups are all part of this growth.

The opportunities to gain proficiency in the skills of an activity are no longer confined to remote and inaccessible outdoor centers but can increasingly be found in the community as part of the recreation department or youth service provision.

Fringe groups only marginally related to mainstream education are becoming increasingly involved in exploiting the potential of the residentials. Where a residential experience is recommended as part of a course, it is often associated with some use of the outdoors as a medium to develop personal effectiveness. IBM ran such a scheme over two years, during which the trainees attended three five-day residentials. The first aimed to develop participants' confidence and their ability to work together. The second explored taking responsibility for standards and making things happen. The last was a chance to reflect on their own abilities and aptitudes and put them into practice. The supervisors of the trainees also attended a residential to experience what the trainees had gone through firsthand and acquire facilitating skills to help them transfer the learning to the workplace.

The Trident Trust, a charity dedicated to bringing development training to programs aimed at helping the tran-

sition from school to work also uses outdoor and residential events. However it takes the wider view of adventure and incorporates community involvement and work experience into the schemes as well.

The social service and the probation service have been exploring the value of outdoor and residential programs for restoring self-esteem and developing positive attitudes in young offenders and children at risk. This is meeting with increasing success, especially when it is linked with continued opportunity for participation back in the community.

Fairbridge, which arose from the successful Operation Drake, forerunner of Operation Raleigh, operates teams of staff in the inner cities of a dozen towns. Its task is to identify disadvantaged young people from all backgrounds and use outdoor programs to give them a new direction and perspective on themselves. After a standard two-week program, there are opportunities for several exciting extension projects and drop-in facilities in the urban center. Some undertake community work and make available a great deal of advice and counseling. Many of the staff are in fact past students of the program. Although the scheme has the advantage of accessibility and street credibility in the towns where these people work they also face the burden of the seemingly insurmountable circumstances of inner cities and their crushing effect on people. Fairbridge is often the only positive opportunity for many.

Studies have shown that a young person placed on an outdoor alternative to custody program will have offended on average 16 times prior to this sentence. The cost up to that point will have been close to £250,000. On that basis if the typical outdoor intervention program diverts between one and three clients a year from crime then its budget is justified. Success rates are known to be several times better than this. However, as with many preventative programs, funding remains an issue.

There are many new programs with therapeutic goals that encourage the mentally and physically handicapped to extend themselves, work toward independence, and mix with able-bodied people. The Calvert Trust in the Lake District aims to give disabled people as equal an access as possible to adventure activities by adapting equipment and appropriate supervision. There is a strong feeling that disabled people have as much right to the benefits of risk taking and challenges as anyone. They often display qualities of determination and courage others cannot manage and delight is always apparent.

Outdoor activities are not just the domain of the young anymore with a number of schemes aimed at increasing participation among the unemployed and retired.

The male-dominated approach to challenge and adventure is also being reassessed. Feminine values are being introduced with a priority on young girls' participation. Outward Bound Eskdale ran the first all-woman course to help participants explore themselves, their attitudes and their capabilities. The Water Activities Centre run by Manchester Youth Service has also addressed female participation by various strategies, including all-girl sessions, changes in teaching style and content, and positive discrimination, all of which have doubled girls' participation in the center over five years. Backbone is an all-woman, all-Black adult youth worker training program. Its aim is to create positive outdoor role models to inspire young Muslim women. Within six months, 12 new leaders had introduced over 150 young women to the outdoors from one town. Up to this point it had been assumed that this group was unreachable or simply disinterested.

Relevance

The impact of diversity has brought about what are perhaps the most important developments in development training to date. There have been fundamental changes in philosophy. The natural environment and its activities have come to be regarded by many no longer as simply a subject to be taught. The outdoors is seen as a medium and the concern is to use it as a vehicle to provide situations for learning with the aim of developing self, social and environmental awareness. The common strands between outdoor and other experiential approaches to development, such as community involvement, are increasingly being utilized. The emphasis is moving from learning about a subject or an activity to the process of learning itself. And the common ground is the sense of adventure. The early thinking of BP and Hahn is undergoing a reappraisal and, with updated values, is being found to be increasingly appropriate as an approach to learning for a modern world.

Section 3

Foundations of Adventure Programming
A Philosophical Overview

What beliefs underlie the approaches to teaching and learning referred to as adventure education? A coherent philosophy establishes a foundation upon which to build theory and action. Does adventure education have such a foundation? What is the role of ethics in this field? How should "good" and "bad" practice be defined? What should be the goals? These and other questions of philosophical importance are touched upon in the essays in this section.

Jasper Hunt finds in Plato the earliest blocks in adventure education's philosophical foundation. Plato was obviously not thinking about adventure education as practiced today, but his thoughts on virtue and experience can be applied by modern practitioners in this arena. So too with Aristotle, William James, Alfred North Whitehead, John Dewey, Kurt Hahn and William Unsoeld. The philosophy of living and theory of knowledge that emerge from the works of these philosophers, Hunt argues, provide adventure education with a sound philosophical heritage.

Hunt and Wurdinger build on the points made in the first essay about the importance of virtue to adventure education. What might define a "good" or "bad" program or a "good" or "bad" practitioner? What should be the "standard of excellence" in this field and who should decide? To what moral virtues is it necessary for practitioners to

adhere? The authors write of honesty, compassion, justice and courage.

The essays by Garvey and Henderson explore philosophical goals that adventure educators might address. Garvey argues that adventure education processes have potential to contribute to the moral development of participants. He reviews principles which might guide program planners and practitioners in including moral development in their programs. Henderson makes the case that if adventure educators tap into the "heritage of adventure" that lies in the history of most places, programs can contribute to participant's "sense of place in a geography that offers hope and faith." Adventures on the trails and rivers, Henderson thinks, can and should add to the "rootedness" and cultural connections to landscape of the adventurers.

This section begins with Priest's attempt to define the key terms used in discussion of adventure education. There is a confusing array of terminology that must be clarified and assumed as discussion in the field progresses. The schema presented here is one attempt to sort out the semantic difficulties. Assumptions about the meaning of terms used in discussion and debate about adventure education and programming must be made, and Priest provides a basis for such meaning in his contribution to this section.

Chapter 14

The Semantics of Adventure Programming

Simon Priest
eXperientia

Outdoor Education

The broad field known as outdoor education encompasses everything from scaling a major Himalayan peak without oxygen, through taking school children outside the classroom for their learning, to bird watching from the bedroom window. Outdoor education has been described as a place (natural environment), a subject (ecological processes), and a reason (resource stewardship) for learning. It has been called a method (experiential), a process (sensory), and a topic (relationships) of learning. However, these explanations have failed to address the facts that outdoor education may take place indoors (trip preparation) and may be concerned with more than ecology (human interactions).

One definition includes all these valid points: outdoor education is an experiential method of learning with the use of all senses. It takes place primarily, but not exclusively, through exposure to the natural environment. In outdoor education the emphasis for the subject of learning is placed on relationships concerning people and natural resources.

This definition implies that outdoor education is more than just learning about nature. Historically, two branches of outdoor education have been identified: environmental education and adventure education. Truly functional outdoor education incorporates aspects of both approaches. Here are explanations of the two approaches in relation to the key point of relationships.

Environmental Education

Environmental education is concerned with two relationships: ecosystemic and ekistic. Ecosystemic relationships refer to the interdependence of living organisms in an ecological microclimate; in other words, basic biological concepts like the web of life, the food chain, and the energy pyramid. Ekistic relationships refer to the key interactions between human society and the natural resources of an environment; in other words, how people influence the quality of the environment (water pollution or strip mining) and how in turn, the environment influences the quality of their lives (clean drinking water or the spiritual beauty of nature).

Adventure Education

Adventure education is also concerned with two relationships, but different ones: interpersonal and intrapersonal. Interpersonal relationships refer to how people get along in a group (two or more people). These include communication, cooperation, trust, conflict resolution, problem solving, and leadership influence. Intrapersonal relationships refer to how an individual gets along with self. These include self-concept, spirituality, confidence, and self-efficacy.

The premise of adventure education is that *change* may take place in groups and individuals from direct and purposeful exposure to: challenge, *high adventure*, and *new growth* experiences. This is not to say that adventure education causes change; just that it highlights a need to change and supports any personal decisions to make changes.

The purpose of adventure education is to bring about an awareness for these positive changes. A subpurpose is to enhance the self-concept and improve social interaction. For these reasons, adventure education has become a powerful tool for modifying the behaviors of many client groups from functionally disabled persons, through individuals who feel socially and personally inadequate, to incarcerated people who are disruptive or destructive to society.

The process of adventure education involves the use of adventurous activities such as recreational pursuits in the outdoors or the so-called artificial adventure environs (ropes courses and group initiatives). These activities are used to provide a group or an individual with tasks to accomplish. These tasks often involve problem solving and challenge. The problem solving requires decision making, judgment, cooperation, communication, and trust. The challenge may take the form of testing one's competence against mental, social or physical risks. To maximize safety, the risk is structured in a manner where it is perceived as being enormously high, while in reality, it is controlled at acceptable low levels.

The product of adventure education is personal growth and development. By responding to seemingly insurmountable tasks, groups and individuals learn to overcome almost any self-imposed perceptions of their capability to succeed. They are able to turn limitations into abilities; and, as a result, they learn a great deal about themselves and how they relate to others.

Outdoor Recreation

Very simply put, outdoor recreation is any activity done outdoors. This broad definition spans the spectrum from gardening, through camping out, to racing cars.

Outdoor Pursuits

Outdoor pursuits are a subset of outdoor recreation. They represent the self-propelled activities performed in an outdoor setting. Some common examples include walking, backpacking, rock climbing, mountaineering, skiing, snowshoeing, orienteering, bicycling, spelunking, sailing, kayaking, rafting, and canoeing. They *do not* include other outdoor recreational activities that are motorized (such as snowmobiling, motorcycling, car racing, and power boating) *nor* animal powered (such as horse riding and dogsledding). While the latter are definitely outdoor recreation, they lack the low-impact environmental philosophy which is expected to go hand-in-hand with outdoor pursuits.

Leisure

Recreational activities take place during an experience known as leisure. In leisure, the process of the experience is the most important part; as opposed to work, where the product is all important. For example, playing music to earn money is work; while playing for the sheer enjoyment is leisure. For an experience to qualify as leisure, it must meet two criteria. First, it must be entered into voluntarily and of free choice; and second, it must be intrinsically motivating in and of its own merit.

Adventure

Adventure is a subset of the leisure experience. For something to qualify as an adventure experience it must meet the two criteria mentioned for leisure, and must meet a third criterium: the outcome must be uncertain. Consider two individuals who go for a walk in the woods. The first is walking because she enjoys getting exercise and likes the outdoors (she is at leisure: free choice and intrinsic motivation). The second is walking because he is placating her, doesn't want to be there, and hopes to get back to the TV as quickly as possible (he is not at leisure: obligatory attendance and extrinsically motivated). If some uncertainty arises, only she is capable of experiencing an adventure. He may become excited and may even enjoy the event, but by definition, the experience cannot qualify as adventurous since he is not at leisure.

Uncertainty

The outcome of an adventure is uncertain when information (critical to the completion of a task or the solution of a problem) is missing, vague, or unknown. For example, on an outdoor journey the outcome is uncertain when the necessary skill or confidence may be lacking; when the leadership influence, task definition, or group morale may appear unclear; and when the weather might be somewhat unpredictable. These conditions all lead to uncertainty through risk.

Risk

Risk is the potential to lose something of value. The loss may lead to physical (broken bones), mental (psychological fear), social (peer embarrassment), or financial (lost or damaged equipment) harm. From moment to moment, no one can be fully sure that a loss will actually occur, hence the uncertainty creating adventure in a leisure experience. Risk is created from the presence of dangers.

Danger

Danger gives rise to risk. They are not the same. Dangers are present in both people and their surroundings. Dangers may be classified as either perils or hazards.

Peril

Perils are the sources of the loss. A lightning bolt is one example. It is the source that leads to the risk of electrocution.

Hazard

Hazards are the conditions which influence the probability or likelihood of a loss actually occurring. An intense thunderstorm is one example. It is the hazard which accentuates the number of lightning bolts.

Human Dangers

Dangers (perils and hazards) may originate from the people in a group. Peer pressure, lack of attention, horseplay, and incompetence are all examples of human dangers. These are said to be subjective or under the control of the group and their leader.

Environmental Dangers

Dangers (perils and hazards) may also come from the natural surroundings. Avalanches, whitewater rapids, poisonous plants or animals, and temperature extremes are all examples of environmental dangers. These are said to be objective or not controllable by the group and their leader.

Accidents

The accident is an unexpected occurrence which results in a loss (illness, injury, or fatality). An accident only becomes an emergency if the group and its leader are not prepared to respond correctly. The potential for an accident occurs if the human and environmental dangers are permitted to occur simultaneously. Kept separate, whitewater rapids and horseplay are just fine; but allowed to combine at the same time leads to the possibility of an accident. This does not mean an accident will always be probable. Accidents can be prevented by effective leadership. However, the concern is not a matter of *will* there be an accident, but *when* will it happen. Be prepared!

Incidents

Incidents or close calls are the unforeseen happenings which do not develop into emergencies. Through effective leadership, the accident is prevented or the conse-quences are reduced. Incidents can be thought of as minor accidents where the losses are acceptable (e.g., cuts, scrapes, and bruises). Acceptability is a personal matter. Acceptable losses to one person, may not be acceptable to another. Death is acceptable to some Himalayan climbers, while a bump on the head may not be to a child's mother.

Risk

Once again, risk is the potential to lose something of value. The risks may be physical, mental, social, or financial. Risk may have two possible values: real and perceived.

Real Risk

Real risk is the true potential for loss: that which actually occurs in an adventure. If no loss occurs, then the real risk was zero. If the person died, then the real risk was extreme. No one can tell with absolute certainty where the real risk lies at any time. However, it can be estimated. Effective leaders with sound judgment and plenty of experience can usually perceive the risk accurately, but not always.

Perceived Risk

The best estimation of real risk is known as perceived risk. For a novice, the perception of risk may be flawed. Fearful people tend to overperceive the risk, while fearless people tend to underperceive it. Only through intensive and extensive experience can a person gain an astute perception of risk.

Competence

An adventurer uses competence (a combination of skill, attitude, knowledge, behavior, confidence and experience) in an attempt to solve the problem or achieve the task. Like risk, it may have two possible values: real and perceived.

Real Competence

Real competence is the true ability of the individual: that which is actually mustered in an adventure. If no loss occurs, then the real competence was sufficient. If the person died, then the real competence was insufficient. No one, not even the adventurers, can tell with absolute certainty where their real competence lies at any time. However, like real risk, real competence can be estimated. Effective leaders with sound judgment and plenty of experience can usually perceive an individual's competence accurately, but not always.

Perceived Competence

The best estimation of real competence is known as perceived competence. For a novice, the perception of competence may be grossly inaccurate. Timid people tend to underperceive their competence, while arrogant people tend to overperceive theirs. Only through intensive and extensive experience can a person gain an astute perception of competence. Perceived competence is closely allied with self-efficacy: a measure of effectiveness and efficiency to perform a competency; in other words, the personal belief that a task can be accomplished or a problem solved.

Facilitated Adventure

The facilitated adventure is used to create astute adventurers. By manipulating perceived values of risk and competence, while keeping real values at acceptable levels, a reasonably well-controlled adventure experience is possible. Depending upon the objectives and precise structuring of such an experience, the misperceiving individuals will slowly come to better recognize real risk and real competence.

Chapter 15

Philosophy of Adventure Education

Jasper S. Hunt, Jr.
Mankato State University

"But," says one, "you do not mean that the students should go to work with their hands instead of their heads?" I do not mean that exactly, but I mean something which he might think a good deal like that; I mean that they should not *play* life, or *study* it merely, while the community supports them at this expensive game, but earnestly *live* it from beginning to end. How could youths better learn to live than by at once trying the experiment of living?

—Henry David Thoreau, 1973, p. 51

The idea of impelling people into adventurous situations in order to gain certain educational goals is not new. There is oftentimes a tendency to view adventure education as a fairly recent development in Western culture. Many people in the field of adventure education, when asked to trace the philosophical development of adventure education, will begin discussing the history of Outward Bound or the Boy Scouts and Girl Scouts or other twentieth-century manifestations. The first thing I want to accomplish here is to argue that adventure education is not a recent educational invention and that an understanding of the philosophy of adventure education must go much further back in history than the twentieth century. This is not the place to do a detailed historical analysis, but some basic issues and sources need to be examined.

Plato, the ancient Greek philosopher, was born about 427 B.C. and died in 347 B.C. During his life of about 81 years, Plato composed many philosophical works. The most famous work was the *Republic,* written in the latter part of Plato's life. On its face, the *Republic* is a treatise about the ideal city-state. However, the *Republic* can also be read as detailed theory of education. In Book 5 of the *Republic* there is a fascinating discussion about the best way to raise children to assume the obligations and responsibilities of adulthood. Specifically, the issue is raised about teaching young boys and girls the virtues needed to assume leadership roles in the city-state. The word virtue should be understood in the sense in which the Greeks used it. To be virtuous for an ancient Greek was to exhibit an excellence demanded by some practice. For instance a virtuous potter would be one who had mastered the art of pottery as evidenced by his or her excellent pottery. Therefore, in order to participate as leaders in the city-state, certain virtues had to be taught to young people, just as certain virtues of pottery making had to be taught to young potters-to-be. The four cardinal virtues needed by the future leaders of the city-state were wisdom, bravery, temperance, and justice.

How best to teach these virtues to young people takes up a major portion of the *Republic*. The issue of participating in war and the defense of the city comes up and Plato offers an interesting proposal for teaching young people the virtues demanded of warriors. Plato writes:

For as for their wars, I said, the manner in which they will conduct them is too obvious for discussion.

How so? said he.

It is obvious that they will march out together, and, what is more, will conduct their children to war when they are sturdy, in order that, like the children of other craftsmen, they may observe the processes of which they must be masters in their maturity, and in addition to looking on they must assist and minister in all the business of war and serve their fathers and mothers. Or have you never noticed the practice in the arts, how for example the sons of potters look on as helpers a long time before they put their hands to the clay?

And later:

What you say is true, I replied, but in the first place, is it your idea that the one thing which we must provide is the avoidance of all danger?

By no means.

And, if they must incur danger, should it not be for something in which success will make them better?

Clearly.

And later:

Still, we may object, it is the unexpected that happens to many in many cases.

Yes, indeed.

To provide against such chances, then, we must wing the children from the start so that if need arises they may fly away and escape. (Plato, 1961, pp. 705–707)

These selections from Plato contain within them several features which I will argue serve as a philosophical foundation for all adventure education in the late twentieth century. It seems obvious to Plato that the best way to learn about what one needs to know for one's maturity, is to experience it directly as a young person. Just as the young potter-to-be needs direct experience with pottery, so does the warrior-to-be need direct experience with war. It is interesting to note what Plato does *not* say here about learning the virtues of a practice. He does not say that one ought to sit the young people in rows and lecture them about either war or pottery. He does not say that the best way to learn these things is to develop a standardized test to examine the retention of facts memorized about the virtues. Indeed, there is a hint of irritation on Plato's part that this subject even needs discussion at all. It is "too obvious for

discussion" says Plato. Plato's interlocutor does not bother to question the point Plato is making about how to teach these things. Rather, the questions asked are about such things as whether complete safety must be guaranteed, what constitutes success, and what must be done if too much danger presents itself to the young people. (I will return to these three questions later.) What is accepted is the notion that the virtues are best learned through direct experience of them by young people.

I do not cite this ancient example because of a desire to root a philosophy of adventure education in preparations for war. I suspect that some of my readers will object to this example because of its connection with waging war. War is not the point. The point is that as far back as Plato the notion was put forth that young people could learn lessons about virtue best by impelling them into adventurous situations that demanded that virtues be exercised.

Another key ancient source is Aristotle (384 B.C.–322 B.C.). Aristotle was a student of Plato, and developed the notion that education should be concerned with the development of virtue in young people. What is interesting to note about Aristotle and the development of moral virtues is his essential agreement with Plato that in order to learn the virtues, one must live the virtues. In Aristotelian language the way one learns a virtue is by the development of right habits:

Neither by nature, then, nor contrary to nature do the virtues arise in us; rather we are adapted by nature to receive them, and are made perfect by habit.

Again, of all the things that come to us by nature we first acquire the potentiality and later exhibit the activity . . . but the virtues we get by first exercising them, as also happens in the case of the arts as well. For the things we have to learn before we can do them, we learn by doing them, e.g., men become builders by building and lyre-players by playing the lyre; so too we become just by doing just acts, temperate by doing temperate acts, brave by doing brave acts.

And later:

It makes no small difference, then, whether we form habits of one kind or another from our very youth; it makes a very great difference, or rather *all* the difference. (Aristotle, 1941, pp. 952–953)

If Aristotle is right about virtues being best learned by the development of right habits and if developing right habits involves education, then it follows that education is connected with the development of virtue. My view is that both Plato and Aristotle are right about education being directly concerned with learning virtue and that this concern with learning virtue is foundational to any philosophy of adventure education.

A similar theme is articulated by a modern writer. William James, the nineteenth-century philosopher and psychologist, wrote an essay titled, "The Moral Equivalent of War." In this essay James argues that war, repugnant as it is, nevertheless brings out many virtues in people in ways that are unique. His point in the essay is to wage a war against war, not to argue for the benefits of war. As James writes:

> The war against war is going to be no holiday excursion or camping party. The military feelings are too deeply grounded to abdicate their place among our ideals until better substitutes are offered than the glory and shame that come to nations as well as to individuals from the ups and downs of politics and the vicissitudes of trade. (1949, p. 311)

James' point is that military feelings represent certain cultural ideals that cannot be met by simple politics or commerce. As he says "better substitutes" must be found to learn the ideals taught through war. In the essay James draws from the military theorist S. R. Steinmetz and lists the following as virtues which are uniquely habituated by war:

> Fidelity, cohesiveness, tenacity, heroism, conscience, education, inventiveness, economy, wealth, physical health and vigor. (1949, p. 319)

James applauds the military virtues. He says:

> Militarism is the great preserver of our ideals of hardihood, and human life with no use for hardihood would be contemptible. Without risks or prizes for the darer, history would be insipid indeed; and there is a type of military character which everyone feels that the race should never cease to breed, for everyone is sensitive to its superiority. (1949, pp. 316–317)

While James applauds the military virtues, he abhors the use of war to teach these virtues. Risk taking is admired by James but the use of war to encourage risk taking is not admired. What is needed, says James, is a substitute for war that will bring out the desired virtues. The substitute which James proposes is impelling young people into adventurous situations utilizing nature as the medium:

> If now—and this is my idea—there were, instead of military conscription a conscription of the whole youthful population to form for a certain number of years a part of the army enlisted against *Nature,* the injustice would tend to be evened out, and numerous goods to the commonwealth would follow. The military ideals of hardihood and discipline would be wrought into the growing fiber of the people; no one would remain blind as the luxurious classes now are blind, to man's relations to the globe he lives on, and to the permanently sour and hard foundations of his higher life.

And later:

> Such a conscription, with the state of public opinion that would have required it, and the many moral fruits it would bear, would preserve in the midst of a pacific civilization the manly virtues which the military party is so afraid of seeing disappear in peace.

And later:

> I spoke of the "moral equivalent" of war. So far, war has been the only force that can discipline a whole community, and until an equivalent discipline is organized, I believe that war must have its way. (1949, pp. 325–326)

One need not agree with James about the conscription issue to see his broader point about using nature-based adventure as a means to moral education and the teaching of virtue in young people. In addition readers who may be offended with James' assumption that the virtues are male ones should remember the cultural context in which these words were written. Conscription and sexism are not the key issues. The use of nature as a means to teach human virtues is the key point. Indeed, war is the enemy for James and he wants to provide an antidote to its allure and acceptability in modern civilization.

As William James was growing old (he died in 1910), across the Atlantic ocean in Germany, a young man emerged who took the philosophical tradition of Plato, Aristotle, and James, and put it into practice. Kurt Hahn, the founder of Outward Bound, should not be omitted from a discussion of the philosophy of adventure education. This is not the place to discuss the life of Kurt Hahn or the history of his educational endeavors. It is the place to outline the key philosophical notions behind his activities in adventure education.

Hahn's thinking about education drew heavily from the Greek tradition outlined here. It was Hahn's view that educators should be concerned with the development of the virtues as well as the traditional academic goals. However, a shift occurs with the advent of Hahn that includes virtues which are omitted in discussions centered around the military and war-based virtues. In an essay about Kurt Hahn, Joshua Miner and Joe Boldt refer to a talk Hahn gave where he was discussing Italian Fascism and the educational virtues embraced by Fascism. Miner and Boldt quote Sir Roger Birley's report of a talk Hahn given in Hamburg, Germany, in 1933 where he referred to Italian, fascistic virtues in education:

> You find that you might be quoting the whole Salem Certificate of Maturity (Hahn's program) with its capacity to endure hardships, to face dangers, a talent for organization, prudence, a fighting spirit, presence of mind, success in dealing with unexpected difficulties. . . . Only one item is and must be missing: *The power of carrying out what is recognized to be just* [emphasis added].

And later:

> We need to be able to feel that as a people we are just and kindly. On this consciousness depends our inner strength. (1981, pp. 30–31)

For Kurt Hahn the fascistic philosophy of using adventure to teach virtue lacked one of the fundamentals articulated long ago by both Plato and Aristotle: justice. Hahn was revolted by the fascistic movements in Italy and Germany with their disregard for justice. Just as William James sought to use nature in the war against war, so, too, did Kurt Hahn want to use adventure education as a tool to arm young people against the allure of fascism and war.

Hahn's educational thought rapidly evolved into the Outward Bound program. I am assuming that readers of this book already know about Outward Bound and I will not, therefore, discuss Outward Bound per se. I do need, however, to mention something, drawing from the philosophy of Kurt Hahn, that is pivotal to a philosophy of adventure education far beyond Outward Bound.

A fundamental philosophical concept that is common to Plato, Aristotle, James, and Kurt Hahn in the teaching of virtue, is that whatever methods are used to instill the virtues are mere *means* to the *end* of virtue. The ultimate goals are not to be confused with the means used to get there. Specifically, as Kurt Hahn's ideas about adventure education matured, the realization that adventure was at the service of much different goals became clear. Kurt Hahn's confederate in the origination of Outward Bound, Lawrence Holt, is credited by Boldt and Miner not only with originating the use of the term *outward bound*, but also, more importantly, with formulating the following philosophical notion:

> *The training at Aberdovey,* Holt said, *must be less a training* for *the sea than* through *the sea and so benefit all walks of life.* [emphasis added] (1981, p. 33)

The wilderness adventure experience does not stand alone in a philosophy of adventure education. Adventure is a mere means to a much loftier end—human virtue. Holt's idea that adventure is a means and not an end is reflected in Plato, Aristotle, and James. In Plato, the young people are taken out to the battlefields in order that they may learn virtues needed for leadership in the city-state; in Aristotle habits are developed in order that virtue be learned; and in James, the use of nature as a teacher is urged in order that war be avoided. The common thread that runs through all of these sources is the importance of adventure as a means and not as an end in itself.

In the initial quotation of this chapter from Plato's *Republic,* three issues were raised that need to be addressed as foundational to a philosophy of adventure education. The three issues were (1) whether all danger should be avoided, (2) what justifies the use of danger in the education of young people, and (3) what to do if too much danger manifests itself. Plato's position on these issues is clear from the quote. From Plato the argument is put forth that no, all danger should not be avoided; the use of danger is justified by making better people; and care must be taken to rescue the young people if too much danger presents itself. It will be helpful in developing a philosophy of adventure education to expand on Plato's ancient advice on these matters by examining these ideas from a modern perspective.

William F. Unsoeld (1926–1979) was a modern adventure educator and philosopher who spent much reflective time responding to the questions raised by Plato. A great deal of philosophical mileage can be gained by outlining some of Unsoeld's thoughts on these issues. In May 1974 Unsoeld gave a talk on adventure education in Kaiserlautern, Germany. During that talk he broached the subject of using risk as an educational tool:

> I've got to put in a pitch for risk. Because, somehow, I see our youth of today being conditioned in the other side of the tracks too much, being warped over here to the conviction that, if it's *risky,* it's *bad.*

And later:

> I think that you pay too great a price when you excise risk from your total economy.

And later:

> We used to tell them in Outward Bound, when a parent would come and ask us, "Can you *guarantee* the safety of our son, Johnny?" And we finally decided to meet it head-on. We would say, "No. We certainly can't Ma'am. We guarantee you the genuine chance of his death. And if we could guarantee his safety, the program would not be worth running. We do make one guarantee, as one parent to another. If you succeed in protecting your boy, as you are doing now, and as its your motherly duty to do, you know, we applaud your watchdog tenacity. You should be protecting him. But if you succeed, *we guarantee you the death of his soul!*" (Unsoeld, 1979)

Of all of the quotations that I could have selected to begin the discussion about Unsoeld's response to Plato's issues, this is probably the most controversial. But space is limited and I want to get to the heart of the matter. Unsoeld agrees with Plato that risk is a legitimate educational tool. Adventure educators in general agree that risk is a legitimate educational tool.

To guarantee that risk has been completely eliminated from an adventure education program would be to contradict oneself. Adventure logically implies risk. But why go forth, adventure, at all? Because that is the nature of reality. When a person lives, he or she goes forth into reality every moment of every day. For a living organism, what will be is never fully predictable. To be is to become. To become means to venture forth into an emergent world. The world of living creatures provides complete safety only in looking backwards. What has faded into the past is safe and predictable because it is the past, and is, therefore, no longer emergent. Unsoeld's comments about risk in education are rooted in the metaphysical notion stated earlier that to be is to become. Alfred North Whitehead had this to say about the process of becoming:

> The world is thus faced by the paradox that, at least in its higher actualities, it craves for novelty and yet is haunted by terror at the loss of the past, with its familiarities and its loved ones. It seeks escape from time in its character of "perpetually perishing." Part of the joy of the new years is the hope of the old round of seasons, with their stable facts— of friendship, and love, and old association. Yet conjointly with this terror, the present as mere unrelieved preservation of the past assumes the character of a horror of the past, rejection of it, revolt:

> To die be given, or attain,
> Fierce work it were to do again.

> Each new epoch enters upon its career by waging unrelenting war upon the aesthetic gods of its immediate predecessor. (1978, p. 340)

Whitehead articulates one of the deepest metaphysical problems of human existence. On the one hand we long for safety and security, to hold on to what we are. Yet, we must live and grow. Literally, not to grow and live means to die. What stands behind Unsoeld's response to the hypothetical mother who wants a guarantee of safety for her son, Johnny, is Unsoeld's understanding that the universe is so constructed, that complete safety is a metaphysical impossibility. To succeed in securing complete safety is to deny reality. As Whitehead puts it:

> The universe is thus a creative advance into novelty. The alternative to this doctrine is a static morphological universe. (1978, p. 222)

It was Unsoeld's view that the denial of reality in the education of young people could only result in the destruction of their souls. It was for this reason that he refused even to attempt to guarantee complete safety to students and parents.

Not guaranteeing complete safety is a far cry from not providing any safety at all in adventure education. Plato recognized this long ago. This issue of impelling students into adventurous situations, while at the same time protecting them from too much danger, presents a point of paradox that must be addressed in a philosophy of adventure education. Too much safety results in killing students' souls. Too little safety results in dead bodies.

Plato's advice on this matter is to "wing the children from the start so that if need arises they may fly away and escape" (1961, p. 467d). The wings that Plato refers to are horses that can be ridden away from danger and towards safety. The importance of providing a means of escape, of protecting student's safety, is critical for adventure education. The deeper philosophical problem of determining how much risk is to be desired and how much safety is to be desired remains to be addressed.

Since I have based the discussion of a philosophy of adventure education in the teaching of virtue, it is useful to seek guidance in resolving the paradox of risk and safety by examining the notion of virtue in more detail. One virtue that most adventure educators hold dear is the virtue of courage. I have never met anyone who denied the desirability of the virtue of courage and I suspect that all adventure educators would agree that courageous people are better than cowardly people. But what does it mean to be courageous?

According to Aristotle, developing the virtue of courage rests upon avoiding two excesses. Too much courage results in recklessness. Too little courage results in cowardice. Aristotle writes:

> Now it is a mean between two vices, that which depends on excess and that which depends on defect; and again it is a mean because the vices respectively fall short of or exceed what is right in both passions and actions, while virtue both finds and chooses that which is intermediate.

And later:

> With regard to feelings of fear and confidence courage is the mean; of the people who exceed, he who exceeds in fearlessness has no name, . . . while the man who exceeds in confidence is rash, and he who exceeds in fear and falls short in confidence is a coward. (1976, p. 959)

It would be a gross misreading of the virtue of courage, at least from Aristotle's perspective, to equate courage with recklessness. For Aristotle, recklessness is as great a vice as is cowardice. Were adventure educators to forget this, then they would fail in teaching virtue. Indeed, they would succeed only in teaching vice.

What prevents the virtue of courage from degenerating into rashness or recklessness? *Safety.* It is my view that one cannot possibly argue for the acceptability of adventure education as a means to courage, and ignore a concomitant commitment to safety, without degenerating into conceptual incoherency. The upshot is that adventure educators are saddled with a very difficult task indeed. On the one hand they embrace risk and on the other hand they embrace safety. What results is a conceptual tension that is, in my opinion, quite healthy. Once again, William F. Unsoeld has an interesting comment on this tension:

> You emphasize safety in a high-risk operation. You emphasize safety, but *you don't kill the risk.* You emphasize safety as a rational man's effort at survival, but we're going to go right ahead and stick our head in the noose . . . that's the game. But we're going to be so careful in doing it, at the same time and that delicate balance, you know, I think it just has to be transmitted all the time. We don't do anything stupid. There's enough out there to get you anyhow. (1976)

The "delicate balance" that Unsoeld talks about demands that adventure educators acknowledge the paradox of adventure and safety as endemic to the profession. Any time that one is forced to keep a balance between two conflicting ideals, there is always the possibility of loosing the balance and giving one too much attention at the expense of the other. Proponents of safety at all costs will be met with resistance by adventure advocates, and proponents of adventure at all costs will be challenged by those concerned with safety. A sort of philosophical checks and balances results that can provide a source of intellectual honesty for all adventure educators. What would be intellectually dishonest would be to ignore the paradox or to dissolve it by embracing one side at the exclusion of the other.

In the final pages of this essay I want to argue that a philosophy of adventure education has implications far beyond the confines of wilderness-based programming. One commonality between Plato, Aristotle, James, Whitehead, Hahn, and Unsoeld is the importance that the virtues be *lived* in order that they be *learned*. Adventure education provides a vehicle which enables students to live the virtues. Fundamentally, this idea of living in order to learn presupposes a theory of knowledge which has applicability far beyond the teaching of the moral virtues.

There is a marvelous quotation from Thoreau which leads in nicely to the broader applications of adventure education:

> Which would have advanced the most at the end of a month,—the boy who had made his own jackknife from the ore which he had dug and smelted, reading as much as would be necessary for this, or the boy who had attended the lectures on metallurgy at the Institute in the mean while, and had received a Rodgers' penknife from his father? Which would be most likely to cut his fingers? To my astonishment I was informed on leaving college that I had studied navigation! Why, if I had taken one turn down the harbor I should have known more about it. (1973, pp. 51–52)

The contrast Thoreau presents between learning about knives from listening to lectures, then being presented with a knife as a gift, and building his own knife from scratch is striking. So is Thoreau's reaction to being informed that he had studied navigation while in college. Thoreau thinks there is a difference between learning *about* knives and learning *about* navigation and knowing knives and knowing navigation. This difference illustrates precisely what I mean by a broader application of adventure education far beyond the confines of wilderness adventures.

To equate learning with sitting passively in a lecture hall or classroom and regurgitating facts back to a teacher who talks 95 percent of the time is the antithesis of adventure education. To measure scholastic aptitude by scores obtained from students filling in the proper computer bubble responses to questions posed in a booklet is the antithesis of adventure education. In either case, what is rewarded is a student's ability to make safe, predictable answers. For a student to attempt any sort of creativity is to risk, not genuine adventure, but censorship and punishment. I will label the sort of education that Thoreau refers to as the conservative theory of education in contradistinction to adventure.

The conservative theory of education assumes that knowing is a simple matter of listening plus mental cogitation. Adventure educators argue that knowing is much more complex than the conservatives assume.

A philosophical source that I have not yet mentioned is John Dewey. Dewey spent a great deal of time and effort on the issue of knowledge and the implications of a theory of knowledge for education. In opposition to the dominant conservative trend, Dewey argued that the quest for knowledge is itself an adventure. For a person to think at all implies adventure, according to Dewey:

> It also follows that all thinking involves a risk. Certainty cannot be guaranteed in advance. The invasion of the unknown is of the nature of an adventure; we cannot be sure in advance. The conclusions of thinking, till confirmed by the event, are, accordingly, more-or-less tentative or hypothetical. (1916, p. 148)

Thinking for John Dewey is primarily forward looking and is not restricted to the confines of the past. Although the past sets the stage for the future, the past does not provide the starting point for thought. Thought begins and is rooted in the process of inquiry. Inquiry is a disciplined response to a situation that is indeterminate and which demands intellectual resolution:

> Inquiry is the controlled or directed transformation of an indeterminate situation into one that is so determinate in its constituent distinctions and relations as to convert the elements of the original situation into a unified whole.

And later:

> Inquiry and questioning, up to a certain point, are synonymous terms. We inquire when we question; and we inquire when we seek for whatever will provide an answer to a question asked. (Dewey, 1938, pp. 104–105)

A key idea in this quotation from Dewey is his analysis of what constitutes an indeterminate situation. In Dewey's theory of knowledge an indeterminate situation is not just a mental state of confusion. Rather, an indeterminate situation is one which is rooted in the actual world of a person. Dewey writes:

> A variety of names serve to characterize indeterminate situations. They are disturbed, troubled, ambiguous, confused, full of conflicting tendencies, obscure, etc. It is the *situation* that has these traits. *We* are doubtful because the situation is inherently doubtful. Personal states of doubt that are not evoked by and are not relative to some existential situation are pathological. (1938, pp. 105–106)

If a necessary condition for thought to occur at all is the existence of situations of the type that Dewey describes, then it follows that adventure is intimately bound up in thought as such. Whenever educators impel students into indeterminate situations in order to facilitate thought, they are using adventure as a means to thought. To ask a student to question any aspect of his or her world is to risk many things. The complete security of the settled past is abandoned in favor of an uncertain future opened by inquiry. The exercise of the human imagination is fundamentally an exercise of adventure when it reaches out to an uncertain future. If to think is to inquire, then to think is to risk being wrong.

If adventure is an effective means for learning virtue, then I want to argue that it is a good means for learning other things as well. As adventure education shows its effectiveness in the moral education realm, it gains additional justification for branching out into other educational areas. Thoreau thought that there was more to knowing navigation than his professors at Harvard imagined. Most adventure educators would agree with him.

There is no way to impel students into indeterminate situations without impelling them into adventure. Whenever a student encounters situations that are incomplete and which demand inquiry, he or she is faced with uncertainty and with possible outcomes that are not preset. Outcomes that are not preset are oftentimes intolerable for those whose highest educational aspirations are toward safety and predictability.

As I write this chapter, the American educational establishment has been in the grip of conservative educational reformers for nearly eight years. Most of the reforms have involved increased emphasis on student passivity, rote memorization, standardized testing, and other reforms which seek to eliminate adventure from education. The very things that Thoreau criticized about his own education have become the centerpieces of much of recent educational reform. Where Thoreau and Dewey encourage questioning and risk taking by students, many current reforms encourage unquestioned acceptance of authority and the elimination of risk from education. Instead of the existentially real, indeterminate situations that Dewey writes about, students are too often being given material that is dead, wooden and far removed from their own experiences.

My goal here is not to offer a critique of recent educational reforms. It is to make the point that a philosophy of adventure education includes a theory of knowledge that has applicability in many other areas of education. Kurt Hahn was not primarily an outdoorsman. His main concern was with education in general and with the use of adventure as a broad educational tool. Earlier in this chapter I discussed adventure as basically a philosophy of living. The philosophical implications of adventure education reach into the very core of civilization and what direction the modern world will take. Alfred North Whitehead discusses adventure as foundational to the positive directions the modern world might take:

> But given the vigor of adventure, sooner or later the leap of imagination reaches beyond the safe limits of the epoch, and beyond the safe limits of learned rules of taste. It then produces the dislocations and confusions marking the advent of new ideals for civilized effort. A race preserves its vigor so long as it harbors a real contrast between what has been and what may be; and so long as it is nerved by the vigor to adventure beyond the safeties of the past. Without adventure civilization is in full decay. (1933, p. 279)

Whitehead suggests that a philosophy of adventure is vital to the prevention of the decay of civilization. A philosophy of adventure education, therefore, has much to offer the broader social context in which it occurs. In this sense, adventure educators can lay claim to a philosophical heritage that is arguably one of the sources of the preservation and endurance of a vital and alive civilization.

References

Aristotle. (1941). Nicomachean ethics. In R. McKeon (Ed.), *The basic works of Aristotle* (Book 2, Chapter 1). New York, NY: Random House.

Dewey, J. (1916). *Democracy and education.* New York, NY: The Free Press.

Dewey, J. (1938). *Logic: The theory of inquiry.* New York, NY: Irvington.

James, W. (1949). *Essays on faith and morals.* New York, NY: Longmans, Green and Co.

Miner, J. L., and Boldt, J. (1981). *Outward Bound USA.* New York, NY: William Morrow Co.

Plato. (1961). Republic. In E. Hamilton and H. Cairns (Eds.), *Plato: Collected dialogues* (Book 5, 466e–467e). Princeton, NJ: Princeton University Press.

Thoreau, H. D. (1973). *Walden.* Princeton, NJ: Princeton University Press.

Unsoeld, W. F. (1974). *Outdoor education.* Lecture given at Kaiserlautern, May 1974. Olympia, WA: Copyright 1979 by Jolene Unsoeld.

Unsoeld, W. F. (1976). *Outdoor education.* Lecture given at Charles Wright Academy, November 1976. Olympia, WA: Copyright 1979 by Jolene Unsoeld.

Whitehead, A. N. (1933). *Adventures of ideas.* New York, NY: The Free Press.

Whitehead, A. N. (1978). *Process and reality* (Corrected Edition edited by D. R. Griffin and D. W. Sherburne). New York, NY: The Free Press.

Chapter 16

Ethics and Adventure Programming

Jasper S. Hunt, Jr.
Mankato State University

Scott D. Wurdinger
Ferris State University

The goal of this chapter is to convince readers that ethical issues are intimately bound up with every aspect of adventure education, and that ethics must be dealt with by adventure education practitioners. It is not our intent to deal with specific issues or to suggest ways of resolving ethical conflicts when they arise. Rather, it will be enough to present a case for the inclusion of ethics within the broader scope of adventure education in general. Once this crucial first step has been taken, the details of ethics will follow naturally for practitioners in the course of their professional lives (Hunt, 1986).

In Hunt's other chapter in this book, "Philosophy of Adventure Programming," he spent some time on the Greek origins with particular attention paid to the concept of virtue as a key educational goal of adventure educators. The idea of virtue will be used in this chapter to outline our case for the inseparability of ethics from the study and practice of adventure education.

Adventure education is not an abstraction with no concrete manifestations in actuality. To talk about adventure education is to talk about programs that do things with human beings. Students are taught. Budgets are formulated. Staff members are hired and trained. Programs are implemented. In short, adventure education manifests itself in the actual world of human affairs. Therefore, it is useful in articulating the argument for the inclusion of ethics in adventure education and to root ethics within the context of actual programs. Our assumption is that all ad-

venture programs share certain generic features and that ethics can be grounded within these generic features.

Any adventure education program that is developed will have certain activities, procedures, and policies that will be used to achieve the goals of the program. The goals of the program constitute the end or ends toward which the program aims. The ends will vary from program to program, but the very fact that a program exists implies some end towards which the program aims. So the first generic trait of all adventure programs is that they all have ends toward which they aim.

Ends are not achieved from nowhere. Ends are achieved by putting together activities that lead toward ends. These activities constitute the means by which the program operates. It is impossible to arrive at an end without doing something to get there. The second generic trait that all programs share is the use of means to get to ends.

For instance, a program may have as its end the development of sound judgment by its students. Developing sound judgment as a surgeon is very different from developing sound judgment as a mountaineering leader. Good judgment is not a generic skill that is applicable to any situation. Rather, good judgment resides within the scope of a range of activities with discernible boundaries. One does not teach judgment skills in mountaineering by putting students in hospital operating suites. The point is that the activities used to achieve desired ends will define a program as much as the existence of the ends themselves.

Therefore, all adventure programs are partially defined by the *practices* that they employ as means to their desired ends. The term *practice,* as we use it here, is a technical one and is crucial for grounding ethics within adventure education. Philosopher Alasdair MacIntyre (1984) describes a practice in the sense in which we are using it here:

> By "practice" I am going to mean any coherent and complex form of socially established cooperative human activity through which goods internal to that form of activity are realized in the course of trying to achieve those standards of excellence which are appropriate to, and partially definitive of, that form of activity, with the result that human powers to achieve excellence, and human conceptions of the ends and goods involved are systematically extended. Tick-tack-toe is not an example of a practice in this sense, nor is throwing a football with skill; but the fame of football is and so is chess. (p. 187)

Coiling a climbing rope is not a practice in MacIntyre's sense, but teaching rock climbing is. Just as I can be an excellent surgeon or a poor surgeon, so too can I be an excellent adventure educator or a poor one. The goods or "standards of excellence" achievable by a surgeon, a football player, or an adventure educator are goods attainable only by those who participate in the practice of medicine, football, or adventure education. Participating in a practice presents the practitioner with the potential of achieving various goods, excellences, which inhere in the specific practices.

The use of the term *goods* is open to a confusion that should be mentioned. MacIntyre (1984) makes a distinction between goods that are internal to a practice and goods that are external to a practice. Suppose, for illustration, that an adventure education program was to hire an instructor who was primarily seeking employment in order to finance a personal mountaineering expedition. The instructor does an adequate job, is appropriately compensated, and goes on the expedition as a result of the pay. The good which the hypothetical instructor receives is the money. There is no reason for this instructor to do more than the minimum required in order to be paid for the job done. Indeed, if the instructor can do less than is called for, and not get caught, then the instructor still receives the pay and can be called successful. This sort of good achieved by the instructor is what MacIntyre calls a good external to a practice.

Internal goods, on the other hand, are goods attained purely because of the excellence achieved by participating fully in a practice. An adventure educator pursuing internal goods will receive personal satisfaction by being recognized as achieving a level of excellence only attainable by participating in the practice. This does not mean that internal and external goods are mutually exclusive. An adventure educator who is well-paid financially may at the same time receive internal goods from a job well-done.

Thus, it makes sense to talk about a good or bad adventure educator. Presumably what is desired is good adventure educators rather than bad ones. This is where ethics begins to emerge as inherent to the very core of what it means to participate in the practice of adventure education. Practices logically imply standards of excellence for practitioners to measure themselves against. As MacIntyre (1984) argues:

> A practice involves standards of excellence and obedience to rules as well as the achievement of goods. To enter into a practice is to accept the authority of those standards and the inadequacy of my own performance as judged by them. It is to subject my own attitudes, choices, preferences and tastes to the standards which currently and partially define the practices. (p. 190)

I may aspire to achieve excellence as a baseball player. However, I am only able to hit the ball if I am allowed five strikes at the ball, instead of three. The point of MacIntyre's quote is that inherent to achieving the label of "a good baseball player" is the idea that I am only allowed three strikes at bat. Any more than three strikes and I am no longer playing baseball. The three-strike rule provides a standard of excellence by which my performance is judged. If I am to achieve excellence as a baseball player, it will only be possible insofar as I conform to the standards as the goods internal to the practice of baseball.

It is at this point that the transition can be made to the discussion of virtue. Since the teaching of virtue is foundational to the philosophy of adventure education (Hunt, 1990; Wurdinger, 1997) and adventure educators are teaching virtue to others, does it not make sense that they are themselves virtuous? Therefore, the next step in discussing ethics in adventure education is to describe what it means to be a virtuous adventure educator.

If someone achieves levels of excellence set by a practice, that individual may be called a virtuous person. In formulating the definition of virtue, MacIntyre (1984) writes:

> But what does all or any of this have to do with the concept of the virtues? It turns out that we are now in a position to formulate a first, even if partial and tentative, definition of a virtue. A virtue is an acquired human quality the possession and exercise of which tends to enable us to achieve those goods which are internal to practices and the lack

of which effectively prevents us from achieving any such goods. (p. 191)

The first step, then, in formulating a conception of a virtuous adventure educator is to look at the practices that make adventure education what it is. For it is only as a person functions within the practice of adventure educa-tion that he or she can attain the status of a virtuous adven-ture educator. The achievement of goods internal to the practice of adventure education is the key to achieving virtue in this context.

There is often a tendency to restrict discussion of prac-tices to purely technical practices. In other words, a prac-tice could be limited to articulating the standards of excel-lence purely in terms of such things as hard skills, soft skills, and other technical skills needed to function as an adventure educator. If this was the case, then virtue in ad-venture education would reduce to the mastery of purely technical skills and the issue of ethics would, therefore, convert to a discussion of technical skills. I have mastered these technical practices, therefore I am a virtuous adven-ture educator, one could argue. This argument would be valid as far as it goes. Certainly, mastering the internal technical goods of the practice of adventure education is a vital part of the virtues of adventure education. But there is more to virtue than just technical practices.

Aristotle discusses two kinds of virtue that are very helpful:

> Virtue too is distinguished into kinds in ac-cordance with this difference; for we say that some of the virtues are intellectual and oth-ers moral, philosophic wisdom and under-standing and practical wisdom being intel-lectual, liberality and temperance moral. (McKeon, 1941, p. 952)

And later:

> Virtue, then, being of two kinds, intellectual and moral, intellectual virtue in the main owes both its birth and its growth to teach-ing (for which reason it requires experience and time), while moral virtue comes about as a result of habit whence also its name *ethike* is one that is formed by a slight varia-tion from the word *ethos* (habit). (McKeon, 1941, p. 952)

Aristotle makes the distinction between intellectual virtue and moral virtue. Knowing how to perform the tech-nical practices of adventure education falls under the um-brella of intellectual virtue. The intellectual virtues, how-ever, cover only part of the territory of virtue. A moral virtue is one which must be developed in order that the

intellectual virtues be guided and controlled toward their proper ends. For example, I may achieve the excellence of making good safety judgments about appropriate techni-cal rock-climbing routes to do with students. Suppose how-ever, that I am lazy and therefore evade doing these routes because they make my job more difficult. My laziness becomes a character flaw within me that gets in the way of my exercising the intellectual (technical) virtue of being a good rock-climbing educator. Unless I develop the moral virtue of industriousness as well as the intellectual virtue of good technical rock skills, then I will never achieve the internal good of being an adventure educator who utilizes rock climbing as an educational practice. Without the moral virtue I could become a rock-climbing instructor but I could not become a good rock-climbing instructor.

According to Aristotle, therefore, ethics becomes the formation of the right habits needed to guide the intellec-tual virtues:

> This, then, is the case with the virtues also, by doing the acts that we do in our transac-tions with other men we become just or un-just, and by doing the acts that we do in the presence of danger, and being habituated to feel fear or confidence, we become brave or cowardly. (McKeon, 1941, p. 953)

And later:

> Thus, in one work, states or character arise out of like activities. This is why the activi-ties we exhibit must be of a certain kind; it is because the states of character correspond to the differences between these. It makes no small difference, then, whether we form hab-its of one kind or another from our very youth; it makes a very great difference, or rather all the difference. (McKeon, 1941, p. 953)

If MacIntyre is right about virtue being a necessary ingredient for achieving goods internal to practices, then the virtues become essential for practitioners to achieve their ends. If Aristotle is right that ethics is the develop-ment of right habits needed to guide the intellectual vir-tues, then it seems reasonable to conclude that in order to have a practice of adventure education, ethics and virtue are needed as inherent to the practice.

You may wonder at this lengthy justification for the place of ethics within the practice of adventure education. Many may assume that ethics obviously have a place within adventure education. Our experience is that even to jus-tify the place of ethics within the practice of adventure education is difficult with many practitioners.

A young adventure educator, that had been employed by a reputable adventure education program, described the following scenario. The belay method used on their high ropes course utilizes the Y Tail (also called the Lobster Claw) technique to protect students from falling to the ground. As with all such belay methods, it is necessary for instructors to be prepared to effect the rescue of a student who might fall from the course and is unable to get back on the course unaided. In order to be able to effect a fast rescue, the course has a "rescue box" that contains all of the necessary gear for a rescue high up on the course.

During staff training, the young man raised the question of how instructors should respond to students who might ask, "What is the box for?" The instructor was worried that students, if told what the box was for, might become overly fearful, since the presence of the box might be a constant reminder of the possibility of falling off the course and of a rescue. The senior staff member present during the staff training replied that of course the instructor should tell students that the box contained "maintenance gear" in order to avoid scaring students unnecessarily. The instructor then asked the senior staff member if giving such a deceptive reply would be an ethical thing to do. The senior staff person became irritated and retorted that ethics did not have anything to do with it. He said that it was a policy issue and that he did not have time during staff training to deal with ethics.

Presumably the senior staff member wanted his instructors to be good instructors. Yet when confronted by the problem of determining what constitutes a good instructor, the senior staff member precluded the attainment of a good internal to the practice of adventure education. Without time allowed to discuss the problem of deceptive replies to students' questions, the moral virtue needed to guide the intellectual virtue of being competent to run a ropes course with students was left out of the picture. Therefore, the practice of adventure education taught to the young instructor was an incomplete practice.

The moral virtues that are a part of the practice of adventure education are not an option to practitioners. To leave out the moral virtues and attempt to practice adventure education as a purely technical enterprise is impossible. If such an attempt is made, the moral virtues will be present in programs but they will be unconscious and assumed to be true without being acknowledged. Unconscious assumptions in ethics are problematic at best. At worst they can produce bad practices and bad practitioners. To return to the example of the rescue box, no judgments were made about whether or not lying to students about such things is good or bad. Maybe the policy promulgated by the senior staff member was the right one. *The point we do make, however, is that the senior instructor's refusal to deal with the ethical issues was intellectually incoherent and irrational.*

As a practical matter one might ask at this point, where does one go to find the virtues needed to resolve problems like the rescue box issue? It is one thing to recognize the problem for what it is. It is another thing to try to rationally resolve the problem. In the end, students either are told the truth about rescue boxes or they are not.

Practices and the virtues needed to realize the goods internal to the practices do not come out of nowhere. Every practice emerges out of a history that gave rise to the practice. The modern physician is the heir to the practice of medicine with a long history. Modern physicians do not practice medicine the way the ancient Greeks did, but they do turn to Hippocrates, an ancient Greek physician, for guidance in pursuit of what it means to be a virtuous physician. The Hippocratic Oath is not simply an oath. It is a moral connection with the history of the practice of medicine. It is a reminder to the modern physician that there are virtues attendant to the practice of medicine to which he or she had better pay attention. Failure to do so can result in the physician only attaining external goods and never achieving the internal goods open to medical practitioners.

Alasdair MacIntyre (1984) has this to say about the importance of history to practices:

> What I am, therefore, is in key part what I inherit, a specific past that is present to some degree in my present. I find myself part of a history and that is generally to say, whether I like it or not, whether I recognize it or not, one of the bearers of a tradition. It was important when I characterized the concept of a practice to notice that practices always have histories and that at any given moment what a practice is depends on a mode of understanding which has been transmitted often through many generations. And thus, insofar as the virtues sustain the relationships required for practices, they have to sustain relationships to the past—and to the future—as well as in the present. (p. 221)

One thing that might be a great aid to the people involved in the issue of the rescue box would be to look back and think about what has defined and sustained the student-teacher relationship in adventure education in the past. The question could be faced about the role of truth-telling as a virtue for the practice of adventure education. Has lying to students enabled practitioners of adventure education to achieve the internal goods of the practice in the past? Has truthfulness been an aid or an impediment to the practice of adventure education throughout its history? In short, has honesty been considered a virtue in the history of adventure education? If it has, then modern practitioners need at the very least to take account of this. If honesty has not been a virtue and lying has been a virtue, then this ought to be taken into account.

In addition to historical sources, practitioners can turn to the current practices of their fellow practitioners for guidance in recognizing the virtues. To enter into a practice is to enter into membership in a community of other practitioners. When I am deciding to install a belay system in a high ropes course that I use in my professional life, I consult other practitioners about the latest development in ropes course belay techniques. Checking on such things as safe belay techniques would fall under the heading of an intellectual virtue for Aristotle. There is no reason why one could not check with one's fellow practitioners for guidance in the moral virtues as well.

This need not imply that other practitioners are always right about their views on moral matters. The same holds true for technical issues. There is a good deal of disagreement about what the safety standards should be for belays on high ropes courses. Check with a variety of practitioners and there will not be a consensus on many technical issues. The same holds true for moral virtues.

However, certain virtues will be common for all practitioners both in the technical and moral areas. For instance, there may be disagreement about the best belay techniques, but there will be no disagreement that students should have a belay when on a high ropes course. Agreeing that a belay is needed in the first place, at least sets the stage for the ensuing argument about the best technique to use.

The same holds true for moral virtues. Without the sharing of certain fundamental moral virtues by all practitioners, the practice of adventure education would be impossible in the first place. For instance, the practice of adventure education would cease to exist if practitioners were dishonest, were cowardly, or unjust. How could I possibly value a colleague's opinion about safe belay techniques if I was unsure about whether or not I was being told the truth about my colleague's opinions about safety? A precondition for entering into a practice is that practitioners be honest with each other. It is for this reason that the medical profession, for instance, is so harsh on practitioners who publish phony research results in medical journals. Physicians who treat patients based on false research data risk endangering the health of their patients. To harm a patient is to violate the very nature of the practice of medicine. Therefore, honesty becomes a cardinal virtue in the practice of medicine. Without honesty, there would be no practice of medicine. The same holds true for the practice of adventure education.

An adventure educator who is a coward would be unable to practice adventure education. It was argued in the chapter on philosophy of adventure education that adventure logically implies risk. Eliminate the risk and the adventure is eliminated. Therefore, a practitioner who is a coward and as a result denies risk, is unable to achieve the internal goods of being an adventure educator. How much risk is morally acceptable within the practice of adventure education is debatable, but the acceptability of cowardly practitioners is not debatable.

Justice is another virtue essential for the practice of adventure education. Without concern for what one is due, for what is fair, practitioners would be unable to function. Suppose a student was to pay for an adventure education program and was told upon arrival that it was all a joke, there really was no course, and that, in addition, there would be no refund of money to the student. Although this is a bit outlandish to consider, the point is that without some conception of justice and fairness guiding the practice of adventure education, there would be no reason not to do such things.

The same can be said of the virtue of compassion. Kurt Hahn is on record as believing that compassion was one virtue that must be common to all adventure education programs. To impel students into adventurous situations in order to learn the virtue of compassion in a compassionless manner, or under the tutelage of a practitioner who lacked compassion, would render adventure education absurd. If compassion is a fundamental virtue that students should be learning from adventure education, then it is essential that virtue permeate the entire practice of adventure education.

The presence of the virtues within the practice of adventure education does not eliminate moral conflict or controversy from the scene. Some practitioners might be tempted to conclude that the acceptance of the moral virtues would render ethical decision making easy. This is not the case. It might be a very difficult matter indeed to determine within a given context what the virtuous course of action might be. Decisions must be made on a case-by-case basis as to what the various virtues demand. Problems like when does courage become recklessness, when does honesty become brutality (must I really tell Aunt Alice that the new dress she has just purchased and of which she is so proud is hideous in my opinion?), and when does compassion become mere sentimentality must be faced. These are not easy problems to solve. The important point to gain is that the virtues at least provide a standard from which to operate when facing specific difficulties. I may decide not to be totally honest with Aunt Alice about my opinion of her new dress, but I at least confront that problem with the virtue of honesty as the standard to which I turn to and from which I depart.

We have included three cases to illustrate the variety of situations where ethical issues manifest themselves in adventure-based activities. The first comes from a wilderness-based context. The second comes from a school-based context, where the word *adventure* is based upon an experiential model of learning. The third comes from non-wilderness-based adventure programming. Our goal with these cases is simply to point out the presence of ethical issues and dilemmas within real contexts. We make no attempt here at exhaustive analysis. We are content to this point to have readers recognize ethical matters for what they are.

Case Study One—1996 Mount Everest Tragedy

In May of 1996 five individuals—a postal worker, a Japanese businesswoman, and three climbing guides—died while climbing Mount Everest. According to Krakauer (1997) there were numerous variables that may have led to this disaster such as guide competition, notoriety, reputation, inexperience, and timing to name a few. For the purpose of this case study we will examine several of these issues. However, for a more detailed account of this expedition readers should refer to *Into Thin Air: A Personal Account of the Mount Everest Disaster* by Jon Krakauer (1997), and *The Climb* by Anatoli Boukreev and G. Weston DeWalt (1997).

Rob Hall, leader of Adventure Consultants, and Scott Fischer, leader of the Mountain Madness guide service, left camp four for the summit of Mount Everest with their clients and Sherpas in the middle of the night on May 9, 1996. In total there were 30 climbers with these two guide services that began the final push for the summit. According to Krakauer (1997) several individuals were still climbing upwards well beyond a previously agreed upon turnaround time late in the afternoon on May 10. He states that "predetermined turnaround times were egregiously ignored" (p. 273), which may have been the main factor contributing to this tragedy.

These guides had obviously achieved a very high degree of excellence in their professional practice. They had learned the skills necessary to guide clients up and down some of the most dangerous mountains in the world, so why had they ignored one of their most basic rules that would govern the activities of the summit day? Both Fischer and Hall had established a climbing protocol to begin the summit push early in the morning and to descend quickly back to base camp before afternoon storms rolled in. A specific turnaround time had been discussed by Hall's group. This time was considered sufficient for the protection of the welfare of the climbers. In this case, the turnaround time was a rule that depended upon the virtue of faithful adherence to it, in order that an internal and external good might be achieved. Since these guides did not make it down alive, one can only speculate why they had ignored this fundamental rule.

Did the desire for external goods overshadow this rule which was designed to accomplish both external and internal goods? According to Krakauer (1997), Hall's and Fischer's guiding services were definitely in competition with one another. At the time of the expedition, clients were paying up to $65,000 each for the guide service. Such a large sum of money would seem to place tremendous pressure on the guides to get their clients to the top. Furthermore, clients with this type of cash are in limited supply, which meant that any favorable publicity from the expedition could potentially increase their clientele. Krakauer, sent to Everest to write an article for *Outside* magazine, was a highly sought-after client by these two guide services. He notes in his book that "like Hall, Fischer didn't bother trying to hide the fact that it wasn't me he was interested in, but rather the collateral publicity and advertising" (Krakauer, 1997, p. 67). There were other notable individuals like Sandy Hill Pittman who were providing media coverage that may have inadvertently influenced the guides' decision to keep climbing long after the 2:00 P.M. agreed upon turnaround time on May 10, 1996. This suggests that there was competition for clients and that the external good of money may have influenced the guides' decision-making processes.

Another external good that may have influenced these guides is reputation. Both Fischer and Hall were extremely concerned about getting themselves and their clients to the top of Everest. Their reputations were at stake, and failing could adversely affect their businesses, especially if one party succeeded and the other did not. "Likewise, having failed to get anybody to the top in 1995, it would have been bad for Hall's business if he failed again in 1996, especially if Fischer succeeded" (Krakauer, 1997, p. 273). Like competition, reputation was a variable that may have clouded their decision-making processes.

There were other factors that influenced the guides' decision making; however, it appears that external goods such as money, fame, publicity, and reputation may have kept Hall and Fischer from exercising one of the most basic rules governing their professional practice on this expedition of descending by 2:00 P.M. Would they have turned around if external goods had not played such a significant role in this particular expedition?

One is also forced to consider whether or not people with minimal mountaineering skills are even capable of achieving the internal goods obtainable by participating in the practice of Himalayan mountaineering. It is arguable that the clients, with very few exceptions, had no business whatsoever even attempting Mt. Everest. For instance, suppose an individual were to take an intense interest in the practice of football. And suppose further that he or she was able to buy his or her way onto an NFL team for one game in order that he or she could have pictures on the wall picturing himself or herself in full NFL regalia, with pictorial proof of having actually played in a regular NFL game. The individual plays in the game, survives it due to careful shepherding by his or her fellow players, and then claims to have obtained the internal goods of the practice of professional football. But has he or she really experienced internal goods? The analogy of professional football with an Everest climb illustrates the problematic situation of claiming internal goods in practices where one has no portfolio or right to participate in that practice.

A key factor in the analysis of the ethics of this tragic case is the role of oxygen deprivation (hypoxia) in the decisions that were made. An argument can be made that an ethical analysis that might be persuasive in a fully functioning human being, would be less forceful when applied to people who are not thinking rationally, due to a state of hypoxia, which would render the principal actors less than completely morally accountable. In other words, the case could be made that Fischer and Hall made their decisions, not because of an excessive concern for external goods, but because of the mind-robbing effects of high altitude and exhaustion.

Finally, it is appropriate in this case study to point out the achievement of virtues of heroic proportion both by the guides and by some of the clients. That Rob Hall, for instance, died as a direct result of his attempting to aid his stricken client rises to an extremely high level of a key moral virtue—courage. Similar acts of courage evidenced themselves throughout this expedition both by guides and by clients. Thus one can see that this case is extremely complex in its mix of virtues and vices. Internal and external goods germane to the practice are interwoven in a manner which defies simple judgments and analysis.

Case Study Two—University-Sponsored Building Contest

Jim, a university professor, wanted to hold a hands-on competition that would promote experiential learning, and at the same time promote a friendly rivalry between the recognized student organizations on campus. He put together a proposal for a spaghetti bridge-building competition and submitted it to his dean who thought it was a great idea. A committee was formed to discuss the rules and logistics of the competition. Jim came to the first meeting with a list of the rules which follow:

1. Only recognized student organizations housed within the seven colleges may participate.
2. Structure will be assembled at the site of the contest in a one-hour time slot.
3. The bridge must span 24 inches in length and will be supported by two tables at either end.
4. Weight will be applied to the bridge at the center by hanging a container below the bridge and adding 25 ml. of water every 20 seconds until the bridge breaks.
5. The winner will be the bridge that can support the most amount of weight.

Sally, a representative from the student affairs office was deeply disturbed with rule number one because it excluded 70 percent of the university's student population. She suggested that all students should have an opportunity to participate, and that the competitive nature of the activity be minimized by awarding a variety of prizes for categories such as lightest, strongest, most beautiful, and

ugliest. Jim disagreed. He argued that Sally's ideas would dilute academic excellence, and that the competition would not be taken seriously by the academic community. He also argued that the university often excludes students from participation in a number of other activities and cited collegiate sports as an example. The debate continued for two hours without reaching a decision.

Who's Virtuous?

Sally believes all students should have the right to participate in the competition so her intention is admirable, but do her ideas promote intellectual and moral virtue in the students? It is arguable that the activity of the bridge-building contest is not a practice in the sense in which MacIntyre uses the term *practice*. On the other hand the bridge-building contest could be accounted a practice as a part of the overall practice of engineering or construction management or some other existent practice within the university. Being a university professor would be to participate in the practice of education. Promoting academic excellence through such an activity may be considered an internal good of this profession. One of the standards of this practice revolves around teaching excellence, and such a competition would promote and enhance teamwork, communication, and problem-solving skills. One could argue that Jim is practicing virtue-based ethics because he is upholding the standards of his professional practice by promoting academic excellence through intellectual competition.

Furthermore, one could argue that Jim is also concerned about promoting the intellectual and moral virtues. Intellectual virtues such as precision and problem-solving strategies are required of individuals working together to build a complex weight bearing structure. Moral virtues such as cooperation, compassion, and fairness would also need to be practiced in order for a group to be productive and effective. They may also have to exercise patience, not only in the actual building process, but with fellow classmates as well.

Sally believes all students should have the right to participate in the competition. She could argue that the level of competition might actually increase if more groups were allowed to participate. It seems likely that as the pool of participants increases, so would the possibility for greater diversity and creativity in the bridges that are built. The logistics of organizing such a contest would be challenging, but it may increase the level of competition. Sally's position raises an important question. Is competition necessary to promote the virtues? On one hand it seems that participants could practice the virtues through the activity without it being a competition. However, if professors like Jim are correct about achieving academic excellence through this activity, their standards and rules should not be compromised.

A larger problem that Sally may have to face is giving prizes to all participants. The standards and rules for building the bridges might become a less important consideration for the groups. The competition may then become a fun social event, which has its merits, but exercising the virtues may not be one of them. If everybody gets a prize (external good), then what is the point of the "contest"?

Drawing from the distinction between internal and external goods it is possible that in the ethical conflict in this example resides the question of whether or not the presence of competition with its attendant external goods (e.g., prizes) in fact increases the likelihood of an increase in internal good. If the presence of competition will probably, or even potentially, increase the probability of increased achievement of internal goods, then Jim may have the stronger argument over Sally. However, such a claim by Jim rests upon empirical assumptions that may not in fact be true. The same can be said of Sally's claim that removing external goods from the overall activity will not detract from the achievement of high internal goods. It is possible that it will be deleterious to the achievement of internal goods by removing the reward of the prizes. If this were the case, then an argument could be made that Sally's restructuring of the bridge-building contest has damaged it's potential for teaching the virtues to the participants.

What would you do if you were on this committee? What position would you take?

Case Study Three— Money Versus Quality

The Association for Challenge Course Technology (ACCT) is a relatively new association in the field of adventure education. It was formed to promote and develop safe practices within the challenge course industry. It consists of a general membership and voting board members who are some of the leading vendors in the field (ACCT, 1997). Their primary charge as an association appears to be to oversee a set of construction standards for builders, as well as develop and oversee technical facilitation standards for instructors. Board members, who have paid a substantial fee to sit on this board, have had a tremendous influence on ratifying construction and technical facilitation standards.

Some argue that this presents an ethical dilemma. ACCT voting board members, who consist of a minority of total ACCT members, are determining standards for the majority. In order to have voting privileges one must go through a rigorous, very expensive peer review, and if accepted, pay a substantial yearly fee. The problem is if one wants to have voting privileges one must pay large fees.

One argument is that board members are behaving ethically because they have taken on the responsibility of establishing and maintaining important standards for the

field. As MacIntyre notes, "to enter a practice is to accept the authority of those standards and the inadequacy of my own performance as judged by them" (p. 190). This suggests that a professional practice is at least partially recognized by having a set of standards that are upheld by the field. The challenge course industry is housed within the field of adventure education and the standards established by ACCT appear to be recognized by this field. What group of individuals are better suited to establish challenge course standards than the experts themselves? The cost to build challenge courses that meet these standards may be more than what programs expect; however, programs should realize that it usually is expensive to purchase a product or service from vendors that have achieved a high degree of excellence in their field.

In addition, one could also argue that board members are ethical because they are more concerned with the internal goods of this industry, as opposed to the external goods. The primary reason for organizing themselves into an association was to promote safe practices for the entire field. In this particular instance, safe practices are a means of achieving internal goods. Goods such as excellent challenge-course design and appropriate equipment use are internal and may be achieved only by becoming a challenge-course builder. A tremendous amount of time was dedicated to developing these internal goods, which suggests that board members are less concerned with external goods such as money and fame.

On the other hand, one could argue that ACCT's board members are primarily interested in maintaining a small voting board in order to control a young, emerging practice with the potential for great financial gain (external goods). Why should vendors have to pay this fee in order to have their votes count? Shouldn't all vendors have an opportunity to voice their opinions? When external goods, such as control, cloud one's ability to develop and maintain reasonable standards that are safe and fair for all, problems may arise.

Aristotle, in his discussion of the virtues, warns that the virtues are not rigid edifices that take away the burden of thoughtful decision making from people. The very nature of ethics as the science of right action precludes neat, tidy, thoughtless answers to complex and difficult problems. To thoughtlessly apply the virtue of honesty in my interaction with Aunt Alice and ignore the virtue of compassion would be an improper use of the virtues.

Another warning that adventure education practitioners ought to take note of is the too-easy identification of the virtues only with the virtues of the past. There is no reason to think that the virtues of adventure education are contained in a neat "Sears and Roebuck catalogue of ethics" someplace. As the relatively young practice of adventure education grows and develops, new and different virtues will need to be recognized and practiced.

There is always the potential for the virtues that are accepted by practitioners to equate directly to the interests and needs of those in power and with what we will call the *ethical establishment*. In the practice of slavery, for instance, a virtuous slave is one who submits well to his or her master. It could be the case that, on the contrary, a virtuous slave is one who works with all his or her might to end the practice of slavery or in some way change it. Of course, most slave owners would hardly recognize this possibility of the virtuous slave as the most rebellious one! Practitioners need to be careful that the ethical standards which develop not be allowed to result in a static, self-satisfied tool to maintain the status quo as an end in itself. The classic example that comes to mind are the Old Testament prophets who attacked the dominant interests and demanded a reexamination of what it meant to be a virtuous Hebrew. Every practice needs its "prophets" to shake things up.

Our final recommendation for practitioners of adventure education is that they take the time to discuss what they are doing within the contexts of their various programs. While there are some generic features common to all adventure education programs, there will also be differences between programs that might demand different virtues from practitioners. However, unless time is taken to think about these issues, thoughtful recognition and resolution of specific issues cannot happen.

We have made no attempt to list what we think the virtues are for the practice of adventure education. Readers should not conclude that since we mentioned justice, honesty, courage and compassion in this chapter that we are implying that these are a complete set of the virtues. Far from it, we do think these four virtues are common to all adventure education programs, but they hardly represent a complete picture. It is only within the context of a much wider discussion that an adequate account could be given of the virtues essential to the practice of adventure education. We will be content here if we have convinced readers that there is at least something worthy of consideration in the issue of ethics in adventure education.

References

Association for Challenge Course Technology. (1997). *Voting Members List.* Purcellville, VA: Author.

Boukreev, A., and DeWalt, G. W. (1997). *The climb.* New York, NY: St. Martins Press.

Hunt, J. (1986). *Ethical issues in experiential education.* Boulder, CO: Association for Experiential Education.

Hunt, J. (1990). Philosophy of adventure education. In J. Miles and S. Priest (Eds.), *Adventure education* (pp. 119–128). State College, PA: Venture Publishing, Inc.

Krakauer, J. (1997). *Into thin air: A personal account of the Mount Everest disaster.* New York, NY: Vallard Press.

McIntyre, A. (1984). *After-virtue* (2nd ed.). Notre Dame, IN: University of Notre Dame Press.

McKeon, R. (Ed.). (1941). *The basic works of Aristotle.* New York, NY: Random House.

Wurdinger, S. D. (1997). *Philosophical issues in adventure education* (3rd ed.). Dubuque, IA: Kendall/Hunt Publishing Co.

Chapter 17

Outdoor Adventure Programming and Moral Development

Daniel Garvey
University of New Hampshire

Outdoor adventure programs have a great potential to be used to improve the moral development of participants. I believe many of the conditions necessary to improve moral reasoning and action are present in outdoor adventure programs. We can employ a variety of methods to accomplish this goal, but first we need to elevate moral development to a primary goal within our programs. Once this is done, strategies can be undertaken to use our programs as a vehicle for improving moral development.

What Is Moral or Just?

"Before considering how outdoor adventure education can be used to improve the moral reasoning of participants, we need to be clear about the broad concept of moral development and morality itself" (T. Bruce, personal communication 1997). Fortunately, or unfortunately, discussions of morality are often confined to the religious domain. But the question of morality is fundamentally an issue of how we are to act in a social system where our needs and desires may be in conflict with those of other people. Defining moral action has been the focus of ethicists and philosophers for more than 2,000 years. For the purpose of this chapter, the definition offered by Rest and Thoma (1996, p. 1) provides a framework to understand moral development and judgment: "Moral judgment is a psychological construct that characterizes the process by which people determine that one course of action in a particular situation is morally right and another course of action is wrong."

The concept of morality is rooted in the social condition in which we all live. Because we live in groups, what any person does has the potential to affect others. For example, if we live in a crowded area, and we want to play our music loud, we would disturb the peace and tranquility of our neighbors. If we decided to discard our trash on the side of the road, we might be rid of the trash, but it would negatively affect others. In these examples, our behavior would be in conflict with the behavior and expectations of others. Understanding what behavior is appropriate in complex social settings is often a vexing problem. Improving our moral development and moral reasoning skills provides a framework to better understand complex social interactions. As James Rest has said: "The function of morality is to provide basic guidelines for determining how conflict in human interests are to be settled and for optimizing mutual benefit of people living in groups" (Rest, 1986, p. 1).

Outdoor adventure education provides many opportunities to illustrate a problem containing a moral dimension. For example, imagine a group of participants are taking part in a winter backpacking trip in the White Mountains of New Hampshire. The group expects to be in the field for seven days. The weather is unusually cold for this time of year. On day five, one of the participants becomes angry, and wants to leave the program because of a conflict in the group. The group is in a remote location. The instructor determines that to safely walk this participant out of the woods, the entire group would need to accompany the participant and instructor to the designated pick-up point. Such a walk-out would result in the group being at the trailhead one day early for the completion of the course. Some people are interested in leaving the course early, and are happy the disgruntled participant might need to be walked out. Some participants do not want the trip to end, and are in favor of making the unhappy student as content as possible until the anticipated end of the program, thus remaining in the field. Other participants are looking to the instructor for leadership and guidance in this matter.

Faced with the above scenario, how should the people in this group decide what is correct? Do they place the needs of the unhappy participant first? Should they consider the agreed upon goals of the group at the beginning of the program, and try to accomplish their goal of remaining seven days in the woods? How should the participants weigh their own personal feelings about being out for two more nights? Clearly, not everyone on this trip will have their personal expectations fulfilled. The activity of ordering and selecting the course of action to be taken, is the process of moral reasoning.

Jasper Hunt has made significant contributions to our understanding of the unique place moral decision making occupies in the outdoor adventure education field. In *Ethical Issues in Experiential Education* (1990), Hunt outlines a few of the general belief systems that members in our example group could use to help them organize the complexities of the problem they face, and make a decision. Regardless of the system of thought used, most of the participants will question what should be done. This process of questioning and deciding is a process used by all of us as we attempt to navigate through our social world of freedom and responsibility.

It is beyond the scope of this chapter to suggest what is moral in any given situation. A moral decision must be based on the particular factors that are present at the time, and the implications that are likely to result from our action or inaction. It is important to state however, I believe some behaviors will be more moral (right) than other behaviors, when we are dealing with a moral dilemma. The relativist stance, that every act can be viewed as equally moral or immoral depending on your individual perspective, is rejected, because our actions follow our thinking. In order for us to act in a more moral way, we must focus upon improving how we think about complex social situations. Moral reasoning has a direct connection to moral action.

The Need for Education to Be Concerned With Moral Development

Helping ourselves and others learn the most appropriate action to be taken in a given situation may be the highest goal of education in general, and outdoor adventure education in particular. In every society, the principle role of education is the transmission of cultural norms and expectations to the next generation. The teaching of particular subjects or facts are secondary to the socialization that the institution of education provides for society. I believe this socialization should include the teaching of those skills and techniques that are necessary for people to understand and resolve complex social situations, where the needs of individuals and groups of individuals may be in conflict.

John Dewey (1938) perhaps the most important educational philosopher from the United States, wrote of the need for democratic education as a means to help ensure the highest principles of social order. His democratic theme was connected to moral development of students because he believed that the institution of education needed to behave in a moral fashion in order to help promote the moral development of the students socialized within its walls. Dewey linked democratic education and freedom, as a means to help students understand their rights and responsibilities to act in a moral way.

In a more contemporary light, we need only listen to the news to hear of a recent example of the lack of moral judgment. A young high-school student in 1996 gave birth to a baby at a dance, and left it in the wastebasket while she returned to the dance floor and resumed her evening activities. Random gang violence is common, and unintended victims are murdered because they were in the wrong place. Political and religious celebrities are often exposed for their immoral behavior. These are but a few examples that cause some concerned educators to believe that programs which include moral development are needed. Perhaps education that stops at subject content, or self-discovery, is inadequate for the world many of us live in.

I believe the field of outdoor adventure education has a place in developing the moral reasoning of participants. In order to connect outdoor adventure education and moral development theory, I will address four interrelated questions:

1. Should we focus on moral reasoning in our outdoor adventure programs?
2. If we decide we should address moral reasoning, whose values should we use?
3. If we attempt to influence moral reasoning through outdoor adventure activities, is there any reason to assume we could be successful?

4. How would we alter our programs if increasing moral reasoning were the highest educational outcome we were seeking?

Should We Focus on Moral Development?

We already teach morals and values either intentionally or unintentionally in our programs. In everything we do, for and with the participants, we are modeling what we hold to be the most appropriate behavior in a given situation. We display a respect for the natural environment and the people in our programs because these are values we hold, and our actions usually reflect these values.

But should we make the teaching of moral reasoning a more intentional part of the adventure education curriculum? I believe we may be delinquent in our responsibility as educators if we do not teach these things. The rather unique educational setting of outdoor adventure education provides a wonderful environment for the development of moral reasoning, and an opportunity to practice new behavior that is influenced by this new moral development. More will be offered later to demonstrate the relationship of moral development to outdoor adventure education.

Whose Values Will Be Taught?

There is little possibility of gaining a consensus regarding the moral code to teach. Some would favor a religious approach, while others might conclude a morality rooted in secular experiences would be more important. Regardless of the moral system ultimately used, we must all conclude that faced with any decision that affects ourselves and others, there is no logical reason to assume that all possible actions are equally appropriate. Some decisions we make, and the resulting actions we could take, have a higher moral value than others. Rather than teaching a particular set of values, we would be better serving our participants if we helped them understand the process of making reasonable moral decisions. Perhaps we can't agree on a system of morals, but we might be able to agree that certain patterns of reasoning are more likely to result in a moral decision than other patterns of thinking. Outdoor adventure education can be used to help participants understand this process of moral thinking. We may not all agree on the philosophic orientation used to determine just and unjust acts, but we should agree that some system will probably be better than no system.

If We Were to Attempt to Influence Moral Development, Is There Any Reason to Assume We Could Be Successful?

Conrad and Hedin (1985) pretested and posttested 4,000 students using Rest's *Defining Issues Test* and found a significant increase in moral reasoning in those students who had participated in an outdoor adventure program. Little research beyond this attempts to link outdoor adventure education with moral development.

It is possible, however, to examine some of the research that is related to outdoor adventure education and gain an educated prediction of whether outdoor adventure education might influence moral development. Many of the characteristics that have been found to improve moral reasoning in other studies are present in the unique methodologies and processes used in outdoor adventure education.

Piaget (1923) believed that as children we develop the capacity to have thoughts as we interact with our physical and social world. As we attempt to understand ourselves as distinct from the world around us, we learn from interacting with the objects that are in our world. At first, these are physical objects, such as other people, and things in our world. As we develop, we begin to expand our thinking about our self and others, based on the social norms and customs to which we are exposed. In other words, look closely at the objects and social structures a child has been exposed to, and you might have a key to understanding the thinking process of that child.

Moral development is a cognitive process similar to the processes to which Piaget was referring. Because moral development is a cognitive process, it is influenced by experiences with the physical and social world. The rather unique environment in which many outdoor adventure education experiences take place provides an educationally rich setting to gain the skills needed to improve moral reasoning.

The outdoor setting has the potential to be important in the development of moral reasoning for three reasons. First, the groups that are formed as we take our participants into the outdoors are often intended to allow the best in the individual to emerge, while still maintaining the high functioning of the group. Kohlberg (1985) wrote of the concept of "just communities," in which the behavior of the individuals is raised to a higher level by virtue of their affiliation with the group. Because the groups' moral values are more developed than most of the individuals that make up the group, the individual persons' moral reasoning is increased, simply by being part of the group. The values and norms necessary for groups to function safely and effectively in the outdoors have a great potential to create this "just community." The necessity for people to get along, share resources, be concerned with the welfare of other participants, and view their personal behavior in the context of the group, helps create the conditions for a "just community." The moral development of individuals taking part in outdoor adventure education experiences may be increased simply because they are part of a group that must, often for the safety of each person, act in a reasonably ethical fashion.

The second reason to predict that outdoor adventure education has the potential to improve the moral development of participants is linked to the types of people who choose to enroll in such programs. Rest offered a composite picture of the personality characteristics often found in people who develop their moral reasoning and judgment:

> The people who develop in moral judgment are those that love to learn, who seek new challenges, who enjoy intellectually stimulating environments, who are reflective, who make plans and set goals, who take risks, who see themselves in the larger social context of history and institutions and broad cultural trends, who take responsibility for themselves and their environs. (1986, p. 57)

People with this profile are drawn to novel educational experiences such as outdoor adventure education, study abroad, and service-learning education programs because these venues allow for the challenge and stimulation they value. In a previous study (Garvey, 1991), I found those college students enrolled in an off-campus experiential global study program showed significantly higher moral reasoning skills at entry to the program than the population of college students in general. Not every person taking part in an outdoor adventure program possesses this profile. It would be fair to say that those self-selecting outdoor adventure education experiences have a stronger predisposition for seeking challenging and stimulating environments than the population in general. By offering programs that provide an opportunity for individuals who possess these personality characteristics to assemble, we help create an environment for moral development to occur.

The third reason why outdoor adventure education may have a positive effect on moral development is because the unique setting in which these activities takes place causes participants to examine some of their previously held beliefs and attitudes. In a meta-analysis of the conditions that appear to be essential in order for an increase in moral development to occur Rest (1986, p. 32) offered the following summation: "Change in one's cognition comes from experiences that do not fit into one's earlier (and simpler) conceptions. Cognitive disequilibrium is the condition for development." Outdoor adventure settings are often intended to help create this sense of disequilibrium. We chose an outdoor setting for participants because it is novel and strange. The participants are in an environment where their previously held beliefs about themselves and others may

need to be examined and modified in order to succeed. In addition, the natural consequences of their behavior while in an outdoor setting is often more readily apparent. They may learn to act differently and think differently because the consequences of not doing so can be uncomfortable, or even dangerous. For example, a youth who has developed an oppositional stance to *all* authority figures, may face some very uncomfortable consequence should he or she apply this opposition to all of the suggestions offered by his or her outdoor trip leader. A young person who is wet and cold in the morning because he or she would not listen to the advise of the trip leader regarding how to set up a tent during a rainstorm, may have an opportunity to reexamine his or her assumptions about authority figures, because the result of not listening to the advise of the trip leader has caused the young person discomfort.

The strangeness of the program location causes individuals to develop new response patterns to problems they face. Often, habitual responses to problems are inadequate in an outdoor setting. For example, faced with a disagreeable social situation, a participant may have developed a coping mechanism of withdrawal, pouting, and noninvolvement. This may frustrate those around the participant, and cause them to stop making the participant feel uncomfortable. This personality trait may be highly effective in the person's day-to-day life, but he or she might seriously reexamine this strategy when cold weather is the cause of his or her discomfort and pouting and noninvolvement will only cause him or her more discomfort.

Outdoor adventure education has a high potential to influence moral development because it meets several of the conditions that have been found to enhance moral development. Future research will provide important information on the unique ways in which outdoor education interacts with the construct of moral development. But based on the associated success of related activities, we should be encouraged to investigate this connection between outdoor adventure education and moral development.

If We Assume Outdoor Education Has the Potential to Influence Moral Development, How Would We Plan and Conduct Our Programs to Achieve This Result?

The question of our ability to positively effect moral development, if we choose to do so, requires a much deeper understanding of the various components that are present when one attempts to act in a moral way. Rest's (1986) model for the essential characteristics of moral action offers a clear guide. Rest argues that in order for a person to act in a moral way, four constructs are present. I will list Rest's four constructs, and offer an example from the outdoor adventure field:

1. *The person is aware his or her actions have an impact on others, and that the way he or she acts can influence the welfare of others.* For example, as I load my packs for the first time, I am unaware that I'm carrying twice as much of the chocolate candy as other members of my group. At the first nights' camp, I make the discovery that no one else knows I have most of the candy. I love chocolate, and know the food will not only be enjoyable, but it will add to my performance during the trip. I would satisfy the first process of moral reasoning if I understood that by eating all of the candy I could impact on the well-being of others.

2. *The person defines an appropriate moral course of action for the situation.* I understand that eating all of the chocolate might have a negative effect on others, so I decide to give the chocolate to the group. An inappropriate response might be to throw the excess chocolate in the woods, so we would all be equally deprived.

3. *The person values moral action more than other often competing needs and desires.* I see the impact I can have on the other members of the group. I have a plan that is appropriate for the situation. However, I must value my need to act in a moral way, more than my need for the chocolate. So, I really want the candy, but I give more importance to doing the correct thing in this situation. Many people know what they should do to be acting in a moral way; however, they value something else more than acting in a moral way, and their behavior reflects this choice.

4. *The person executes the moral act.* I see the moral dimension of the problem. I have an appropriate plan. I value moral action over other competing needs and desires. I must still act. If I have all the understanding required to fulfill the first three processes, but do nothing with the chocolate, other than think about the dilemma this is causing, I have not satisfied the conditions of a moral act.

In theory, for our programs to adequately effect the moral development of participants we would construct activities that allow participants to understand and practice the skills necessary to accomplish Rest's four conditions for moral action as detailed here. Each of the four conditions could be isolated and program activities designed to improve participants' understanding and progress in each area.

For example, activities could easily be devised to help participants learn the impact their individual behavior was having on the welfare of the other members of the group. A simple activity such as "group juggle" could be framed so that participants were encouraged to focus on their responsibility to the member of the group to whom they will be tossing a ball or other object. If the person to whom you are going to pass the ball is having difficulty keeping up with the activity, is it appropriate to continue to send balls in his or her direction? Participants could be encouraged to put themselves in the role of the befuddled group member. Does the function of the group improve if this person continues to receive additional balls, when he or she is already dropping the ones being sent his or her way? Ultimately, the participants could learn that for the group to succeed, each individual must take responsibility to help control not only his or her personal success, but also the success of the other group members. Activities framed and processed in this manner could help participants gain insight into the first of Rest's conditions for moral action: *"The person is aware his or her actions have an impact on others, and that the way he or she acts can influence the welfare of others."*

This simple example illustrates the potential for outdoor adventure activities to foster a deeper understanding of the moral action needed from participants to succeed in an activity.

Blasi (1980) established that moral reasoning is directly related to appropriate moral behavior. As we increase our moral reasoning, we have the potential to act in more moral ways. The ideal outdoor adventure program would start from the orientation that moral reasoning and moral behavior are linked, and this link is in two directions and interactive. Improving moral reasoning leads to an increased sophistication in how to resolve moral problems, which influences our behavior. Likewise, behaviors we are engaged in have the potential to influence our moral reasoning. The connection and interdependence of thought *and* behavior, acting on each other has been under represented in both our practice and the literature.

Designing a Moral Development Program

Reimer, Paolitto, and Hersh (1990) have created a curriculum development model that can be modified to form a framework for including moral development into outdoor adventure programs. They offer 10 activities that will be useful in creating outdoor adventure education experiences which address moral development:

1. *Develop a rationale for moral development.* Understand the basic concepts of moral development and the unique needs of the client group being served. Care must be taken to

match the intended activities to the developmental stages of the participants. A group of eighth grade students will require a different program model than a group of corporate executives. The program should review its current objectives. For example, are the current program offerings intended to help participants increase communication skills, trust, or team effectiveness? If the current objectives are related to, but different from, the goal of increasing moral development, how can the design and activities be modified or adapted?

2. *Identify moral issues that may arise in the program.* Whether it is a one-day ropes course activity, or a semester-long program, there are issues that can be expected to arise that will provide a vehicle for moral reasoning and action. These can be identified by staff and used as a powerful teaching tool to enhance the moral development skills of participants.

3. *Help relate or transfer the inherent moral issues in an outdoor adventure program to the participants' lives.* Participants can be asked to connect the experiences they are having when they face moral issues in an outdoor adventure program with real-life situations they face at home. Helping participants understand that their behavior in a program will be a mirror to help them reflect on their real-life behavior is an essential part of the process of moral development.

4. *Select activities that promote participants taking the role of "another."* It is important that we help participants move from a self-centered posture to one where they can imagine the world from another's perspective. Asking participants to view experiences from the vantage point of others in the program will help them see how their behavior could be seen in a different way than it was intended. Outdoor adventure activities have the potential to naturally encourage participants to be dependent on each other for comfort and safety.

5. *Model and facilitate the acquisition of higher order moral reasoning skills.* Leaders should be aware of the conscious use of themselves as members of the group. Staff should explain their rationale for decisions they make. The goal is to help participants appreciate the breadth of views that can exist when faced with a moral dilemma, and that these often competing views can be ordered, from a moral perspective, to yield the best resolutions. Using the issues and problems that are created in every outdoor adventure program as the tool, staff can help participants improve their reasoning through dialogue and experimentation with different approaches.

6. *Create opportunities for participants to address their personal moral dilemmas.* Although there will be issues shared by the entire group, there are also personal moral dilemmas that individuals in the group may have. Participants should be encouraged to use other group members, including staff, to help resolve these dilemmas. It is often the case that participants begin to connect their experiences in an outdoor adventure program with problems they are having in their real life. These connections can be used to help educate participants about the moral reasoning they are using. Once a participant's resolution pattern has been opened for discussion and comment, staff and other participants can offer solutions that may encourage and increase in moral reasoning for the participant faced with the dilemma, as well as the other members of the group.

7. *Work with a colleague as cofacilitator.* The creation, conducting, and evaluation of the program will be greatly enhanced by involving others in our work. The perspective offered by another staff member when we, as staff, face our own moral dilemmas is essential for sound decision making. As staff we are subject to our own personal biases and limitations when dealing with complex moral issues that arise during the course. By using the coinstructor as a sounding board, we will raise our moral-reasoning skills and make better decisions on behalf of the participants. Staff should attempt to be in agreement on the action to be taken, and the rationale that supports this action. A failure to be consistent with staff decisions will reinforce the notion that moral reasoning is a relative concept. This will retard the moral development of most participants, particularly young people.

8. *Pilot test the intended activities.* If a program is going to include one or more activities intended to focus on the broad issue of moral reasoning or action, these activities should be pretested with a "safe" group. We must be fairly sure how participants are likely to respond to our intended activities and their sequence before we use these experiences in an actual program. Groups of staff can be

asked to take part in our intended activities so we can gain valuable feedback on the design and execution. As with all areas of outdoor adventure programming, we should be as intentional as possible, as we link our choice of activities and the sequence to the intended program goals.

9. *Allow students to act on their reasoning.* The notion of natural consequence is important in the development of moral reasoning and action. Where possible, we should help create situations where participants are allowed to act in a way that is consistent with their reasoning, and where they can receive feedback from the group. We should also help create experiences that will give participants an opportunity to try new and different ways of responding to moral issues. One of the values of outdoor adventure programs is that they promote risk taking. This risk taking should extend to the area of allowing participants to risk other forms of thinking and action when faced with moral issues.

10. *Commit to continued staff renewal and development.* One of the most important findings of Rest and others who have researched moral reasoning is the inability of individuals to understand moral reasoning that is beyond their personal stage of moral development. People tend to believe their solutions to moral issues are the best available, and they discredit more advanced moral reasoning when it is in conflict with their own. The implication of this tendency is obvious. If staff do not attempt to raise or maintain their moral reasoning skills, they will be unable to appreciate or understand superior reasoning in other staff or participants. Since staff have the potential to control power within the program, the moral development of participants may be greatly enhanced or retarded by the positions staff take when faced with moral dilemmas. We should therefore commit to the development of staff, so they are increasing their moral reasoning, thus creating a model for participants.

Conclusion

Outdoor adventure education programs have a great potential to be used to improve the moral reasoning and action of participants. The theory and research that exists in related areas suggests outdoor adventure education, because of its unique characteristics, will influence moral development. I have given examples of why outdoor adventure education should be used to improve moral development and an outline of 10 steps to take if improving participant's moral development is a program goal.

References

Blasi, A. (1980). Bridging moral cognition and moral action: A critical review of the literature. *Psychological Bulletin, 88,* 1–45.

Conrad, D., and Hedin, D. (1985). *Executive summary: Experiential education evaluation project.* Minneapolis, MN: Center for Youth Development and Research University of Minnesota.

Dewey, J. (1938). *Experience in education.* New York, NY: Macmillan.

Garvey, D. (1991). *The effects of cross-cultural experiences on the moral development of a select group of college students.* Unpublished doctoral dissertation, University of Colorado, Boulder, Colorado.

Hunt, J. (1981). Dewey's philosophical method and its influence on his philosophy of education. *Journal of Experiential Education, 4*(1), 29–34.

Kohlberg, L. (1985). The just moral community approach to moral education in theory and practice. In M. W. Berkowitz and F. Oser (Eds.), *Moral education: Theory and practice* (pp. 27–88). Hillsdale, NJ: Erlbaum.

Piaget, J. (1923). *The language and thought of the child.* New York, NY: Harcourt, Brace.

Reimer, J., Paolitto, D. P., and Hersh, R. (1990). *Promoting moral growth: From Piaget to Kohlberg* (3rd ed.). Prospect Heights, IL: Waveland.

Rest, J., and Thoma, S. J. (1996). *Designing and validating a measure of moral judgment: Stage preferences and stage consistency approaches.* Unpublished paper, University of Minnesota, Minneapolis, Minnesota.

Chapter 18

Every Trail Has a Story: The Heritage Context as Adventure

Robert Henderson
McMaster University

> There is something exciting in the first start even upon an ordinary journey. The bustle of preparation—the act of departing, which seems like a decided step taken—the prospect of change, and consequent stretching out of the imagination—have at all times the effect of stirring the blood and giving a quicker motion to the spirits. It may be conceived then with what sensation I set forth on my journey into the arctic wilderness. . . . Before me were novelty and enterprise; hope, curiosity, and the love of adventure were my companions; and even the prospect of difficulties and danger to be encountered, with the responsibility inseparable from command, instead of damping rather heightened the enjoyment of the moment.
>
> —George Back (1970, p. 256)

These words would pull the heartstrings of any adventurer today, but the date and place suggest this was no "ordinary" adventure. This was no ordinary "stretching out of the imagination."

George Back's 1833 exploration into the central barren grounds of the Canadian Arctic was unquestionably an adventure then and remains an unquestionably adventurous route for today's traveler. The river run remains an opportunity to put one's competence to task with the risk inherent in the travel. Such adventure travel experiences rarely, hopefully can never, fall into that problematic category of adventure without risk that is possible with overly structured safety criteria and a watered-down adventure curriculum. Most adventure travel programs maintain the qualities of novelty and enterprise and deliver the goods in line with George Back's explorations: for adventure is a state of mind. The risk is real and is a modern-day goal in itself. We share this quest for adventure without historical precursors, though rarely was this a goal in itself in former times. But there are other goals available for the modern explorer—the cultural explorer.

Then, in 1833, the stretching out of the imagination was a wide-eyed stare into the unknown—the never recorded. This quest upstaged any concern for common sense and safety, though at all times common sense and safety would have governed Back's conduct. As compared to some cohorts such as Sir John Franklin's string of misadventures, George Back's safety record proves his attention to safe conduct. The modern adventure can recapture this drive for the unknown, granted maintaining the more easily found sensibility for common sense and safety. But another quality can be carried along today that brings an added dimension of "prospects of change and consequent stretching out of the imagination."

This quality embodies an affinity with what has passed before, tapping a rich heritage of adventure on the trails and waterways of those lands whose natural integrity has remained relatively intact. This abstract sense of related-ness—being part of history—being within the ways of a tradition, is something extra, complementing and perhaps creating the adventure spirit. The feeling of "fit" with the experience of another person, George Back, and the fit into the "mindscape" of another time serves to enrich the present reality and warm the spirits of the land. As Sigurd Olson (1969) said, "and when they did (seek these spirits), the land glowed with warmth and light." Such spirits—whether native, voyageur, pioneer, cowboy, mountain man, or early recreationalists—can become celebrated partners on the trail, a companionship of past and present. This in itself can be that quality of adventure sought on the trail—an-other kind of unknown, perhaps part of an evolution of what is the adventure of the trail.

Such stretching of one's aspirations bespeaks the po-tential that awaits the cultural explorer, who, added to or growing out of the adventure at hand, brings a poetic imagi-nation for the sharing of time and place, a sublime expres-sion of imprinting with a time, person, or travel style. Such connection is not accessible everywhere and at all times, but it is accessible as a compliment to modern adventure far more than we avail ourselves to it. We make things beautiful, adventurous, and vital with our imagination. It is with imagination that adventure finds its starting point and its further depth; its added qualitative dimensions. George Back's bustle of preparation describes his imagi-nation at work. Today the adventurer and/or adventure edu-cator can pull the same heartstrings. As Canadian novelist Peter Such (1978, p. 9) has said, "We all need a sense of our past, and how our present and indeed our future grow out of it, to see ourselves as part of that continuing tradi-tion as it keeps evolving and not separate from it," and we need imaginations for this in keeping with the poet Wallace Stevens' (1942, p. 150) reminder that, *imagination*—"we have it because we don't have enough without it."

A Journal Excerpt

Huddled around an evening fire before a difficult height of land watershed crossing, we sat staring and wondering into the fire. Would years of historical use have maintained a worn portage trail, or is this today only an obscure, poorly marked waterway connection? Would we even find such a trail? Would our loads be too heavy for our stamina? For some, this might have been the last straw, a turning back point due to the frustration of an adventure gone wrong. Leonidas Hubbard, a 1903 adventurer's misadventure in Labrador, springs to mind. This adventure turned to pure adversity on the "wrong" trail. Many other such stories from the past creep into our present. P. G. Downes' 1940s description of a challenging portage and searching for trails, and Grey Owl's narrative of getting lost (misdirected) are tales for the telling by the fire this night. These stories we keep alive by the fire, creating a tangled web of heritage

context; preserving oral tradition with the drama of a ca-noe travel legacy composing our present adventure.

> How we were part of the verb to explore. . . .
> The search being not for a material thing as
> much as it is for an attitude or a quality of
> imagination. (Perkins, 1983)

We were part of a scene that has been repeated for all first-timers through this canoe route and countless other routes. Our maps did not place us out of context; they helped define the context. How many have huddled by a fire at this campsite with the same sense of adventure and apprehension for the long height of land portages ahead? For fleeting moments, the shared humanity was comfort-ing, revealing an added depth to our adventure. In the morning the portage trail we would seek was "their" trail. They were real and we were living their story. For every trail has a story! Whether specific in nature or only gen-eral to the broad sweep of history and the land, the bush is alive with the stories that await our imagination as told in travelers' journals, from old-timers or simply from an old trailblaze marking a now forgotten height of land portage. When on "their" trails, the travelling was no longer only imaginative and reflective. Their trails had become our trails, "as part of a continuing tradition." The real physical adventure of sweat and struggle with a load on a now rarely used trail was matched with the real awareness of ourselves on a historical continuum of human spirit on the land and of the environmental histories of the land tied to people over time.

The Specific Heritage Context

Retracing George Back's trip down the river that now bears his name with his journal in hand is an example of a spe-cific in-context challenge that is less demanding for the imagination compared to general themes. To share an ad-venture with an 1833 group through a largely unchanged landscape, aware of the similarities of circumstance and yet not naive to the differences dictated by water levels, modern equipment, and modern knowledge and tempera-ments, is to be at all times thinking about and fusing past and present. Here is a twofold adventure; one physical and one visionary or mythical.

One need not be in the Arctic for such adventure. The voyageur canoe routes and horseback treks into mountain passes can offer the same insights with "real people" in context with specific stories and unknowns to explore. Lewis and Clark on the Missouri, William Butler on the Voyageur waterways, LaSalle on the Mississippi, and Mary Schaffer and John Colter in the Rocky Mountains are among the many possible personalities with whom one may share common ground and a common quest for adventure; yet for today's explorer, the trail is also graced with the genius of this past. Questions arise, such as from what vantage point would this sketch have been drawn? What inspired a particular journal entry? Where is the old gravestone so meticulously recorded by another? Such retracing of experiences bring history to direct interpretation. Thinking in terms of education, the experiential moment takes one from studying history to realizing "that history is me" (Brown, 1971). In short, the particular fascination with experiencing the similarities and differences with the likes of explorers George Back, William Butler, and John Colter, is itself an adventure.

The affinity can also be discovered with a specific out-of-context nature. The Bennett Outdoor Education Centre in Edmonton, Alberta, has a program where school groups study the specific circumstance of David Thompson's 1812 winter discovery of the Athabasca Pass. Thompson's hired canoe men mutinied and with great difficulty finally ascended this northern gateway to the Pacific.

School groups capture this moment on the steep ravine slope behind the center with a mock Thompson dressed the part shouting orders to browbeat mock voyageurs. The exercise can be an initiative task of hauling weighted sleds up a pitch or the challenge of freighting gear over the Athabasca Pass, the major obstacle in the Atlantic-Pacific fur trade, while putting up with the belittling, arrogant Thompson. In both cases the imagination is stirred. In the latter, additional questions arise that create an enlarged context and a story quality to the immediate task. Such questions may be, why was Thompson belligerent to his men? Why attempt the pass in the winter months? Why this pass anyway? The answers for these questions and more are solvable puzzles that again bring history and adventure alive. Such questions bring travel literature and adventure into an experiential package. The asking brings the experience alive in a specific context of Thompson on the Athabasca without the specific setting.

What we experience is not the initiative alone, but the experience exposed to our methods of questioning that may include the specific context of a David Thompson, the voyageur, the Piegan Indians, and the life on the land of that time. All the various players must become involved as the questioning becomes more complex and demanding. Imagination here exposes a broader perceptual and conceptual method of questioning. One's sense of the unknown is given a broader base or grounding. Carefully chosen interpretive questioning strategies of educators keep the past within reach for all ages.

The General Heritage Context

This bridging of past and present is also accessible in a most general sense, without specific places, people, and times. Picture a beautiful winter's day! Somewhere in the Canadian Shield, you ascend a steep, forested ridge on snowshoes, through three feet of snow to arrive at a level ridge top. Intentions had been to get a distant view, but the forest blocked all possibilities. The large pine of this area have been cut, so climbing a tree would not help. You walk the ridge awhile, then slowly descend. No adventure, no real success, little physical challenge to your endeavors and yet you feel wonderful, having stretched some needed quality inside yourself. Utter contentment. Your climb was merely recreational. You were not a timber cruiser of the past identifying particular timber in the wood lots; not a surveyor overcoming land obstacles; not a native hunter using the ridge to hunt moose where less snow prevails, offering choice winter moose habitat; not an explorer trying to use a vantage point to discern any future course. You were none of these, yet they are all stored fuel for the imagination. They were all with you. With each step of your snowshoe you connect with the spirit of this technology so brilliantly adapted to such winter terrain—so necessary for all of the above. Each step with your snowshoes puts you deep into the romantic prints of its past and its utility. As Sigurd Olson (1956, p. 77) has said of the snowshoe's close cousin, the canoe, it "makes you a part of all it knows." Here the travel mode captures a general flavor of the experiences of the nameless people, places, stories, and mostly with a time when snowshoe was king and of course, at times, it still is. Some of the wisdom of this technology comes with such steps, confusing your present with an adventure of possible relatedness where no adventure seems apparent. Your adventure now is one of sensitivity and "homeness," comfort and sense of place in the bush (not wilderness) with knowledge of those who passed before. This is not the wilderness, but a homeland; it demands less aggression and more sensitivity. Your adventure demands that you know something of the stories of the technique you are using, stories of its past travelers and stories of the changing landscape. The Norwegians have a word, *friluftsliv,* to convey the notion of "a way home to nature" (Faarlund, 1993). It is suggested here that this genuine meeting of nature unfettered by an agenda of conquest or objectified study is enhanced by the slowly garnering of the ways and traditions on the land and the stories therein to broaden your frame of reference.

Briefly, how does the educator bring to students, the adventure of the past rendered as a felt experience? Some pretrip reading and presentations to provide an orientation for travel is obvious if possible. During the experience of travel, one can "pepper" the experience as appropriate with stories, historic readings and/or quotes from earlier travelers, introducing items of clothing and technology used in certain circumstances and the use of ceremonies.[1] More specifically, such peppering may include the wearing of a voyageur sash for the long portage, the distribution of a shot of rum following a height of land portage or that point

---

[1]Thanks to Molly Baker for a conversation where the notion of peppering the experience found solid expression.

on the trip when the group is furthest from the trailhead, the reintroduction of old wisdoms such as the use of snow messages—a sign language using formations of sticks—the reintroduction of language mostly lost to modern ways and times that relate to travel, the leaving of an offering at a native rock art site. Mostly though, the power of story is the most potent compliment to the travel itself. For example, when all are huddled together using the sleds and toboggan loads for shelter from the stiff wind on the open ice, the time is right to tell the story of Peter Freuchen's mishap on the open Arctic plain. He, in a similar predicament, was, with time, encased within his makeshift shelter. As the story goes, caught in a blizzard, he covered himself with his sled and later contemplated digging himself free (as the newly piled snow had encased him) by using his own excrement as a fashioned dagger (1935, pp. 407–411). A gripping story indeed.

It takes awhile to amass the readings, stories and general knowledge of early travel technique but with one's first acquisition can come the beginning of the shared moments of heritage interpretation.

For the educator, the challenge can be to impart the touch of this imagination in others so that snowshoes (canoe, horseback) are not just snowshoes, but doorways to this notion of "being" history. Whether general or specific in context, adventure on the land may offer this potential of relatedness to a larger reality. Contemporary Canadian painter Ivan Eyre has said of art:

> When I look at a painting it isn't only the painting that I see, but the thing that I am. If there is more in the painting than I am, then I wouldn't get it. (Woodcock, 1981)

This is also true of adventure education and travel in a heritage context. With travel in settings (where natural integrity remains relatively intact) such as the north shore of Lake Superior specifically, much of the Canadian Shield, Rocky Mountains, and Arctic Barren Grounds generally—where the travel mode has a rich heritage such as horseback outfitting, snowshoeing, and canoeing—with travel that can tap the insights and adventures of others through journals and stories; with all of these, it is not only the adventure that is available, but an added thing that is in each of us. Part of each of us desires to be grounded in a heritage, to see ourselves as reflections of a past, yet evolving! We all desire a sense of place in a geography that offers hope and faith. This helps define who we are.

It is because there are so many cultural explorers adding this "grounding" to their travel experiences through study and exploration that it seems possible to say, "We do see it," for there is not more in the adventure than we are. Because if there were more in adventure than we are, then we wouldn't get or see it; and we can *get* these sleeping stories of the past, ready to be awakened with our imaginative qualities. Gregory Bateson has said:

> In choosing our beliefs we are therefore also choosing the images that will guide, create, and pull us along with our culture, into the future. The world partly becomes—comes to be—how it is imagined. (Bateson, 1972, p. 11)

We can hope that adventure education helps us choose images that add a feeling of relatedness to our heritage on the land so that we evolve from a sole adventure frontier perceptive of many of those we study to a grounding, a homeness that comes with a sense of past and roots. "The continuity and context of this sort of physical and mythical [well-storied] reality is even more essential to humanity than adventure in the realm of the unknown" (Franks, 1981, p. 191). We take the indigenous people's spirit, and the "discoverers," explorers and settlers' spirit with us as best we can and evolve through it to a modern rootedness, a more *connected* culture to our landscape. Hopefully, we can merge our immigrant status with a more indigenous one. Being history, this abstract magical affinity, taken in fleeting moments captured whole, helps us see who we are and all we are. It helps us see that history is in me and I am in history. From this perspective, one of heritage, the self gains images of caring, respect, awareness of culture and diversity and how we all must evolve *with* and *within* our landscape.

The stretching out of the imagination we share with George Back can tap two unknowns: the physical adventure of risk-testing competence, and the well-storied adventure of the self stretching its boundaries of time and place. In both there is great promise.

The Australian aborigines relate to their homeland through a labyrinth of invisible pathways known as songlines or dreaming tracks. Perhaps the North American Native pictographs and petroglyphs served much the same end. More literally, these pathways are the "footprints of the ancestors who sang the world into existence" (Chatwin, 1987). The songlines provide direction for the young man's walkabout or vision quest, a cultural rite of passage where ecological maturity or grounding in nature is imparted. The cultural explorer, adventurer, and educator can channel a mythical association of self and landscape toward a beautiful, caring adventurous imagination. Canoeist, artist, and filmmaker Bill Mason called such connections "the song of paddle" (Mason, 1988, p. 2). Sigurd Olson called it "the ancient rhythms" (1969). Though we remain of largely immigrant status with the modern concept of "wilderness," if we approach our travel and adventures within a historical context, the songlines can exist for us in the North American landscape. Every trail and waterway has a story. These stories can sing to us as echoes along our travels. These are the bush travelers' dreaming tracks that, when listened to, can help sing a new "first start upon an ordinary journey." We learn to travel more "within" the land, more "of" the land.

Bibliography

This list serves as an enticer—to draw the adventurer into the rich treasure chest of historical writings. The sources provided pertain to themes presented within the text.

Bakeless, J. (1950). *The eyes of discovery: The pageant of North America as seen by the first explorers.* Philadelphia, PA: J. B. Lippincott Co.—The adventures of North America's first explorers, including LaSalle and Lewis and Clark.

Blevis, W. (1973). *Give your heart to the hawks: A tribute to the mountain men.* Los Angeles, CA: Nash Publishing.—The mountain men story. Great campfire reading, including John Colter's travels.

Butler, W. (1891). *The great lone land, A narrative of travel and adventure in the north-west of America, 1872* (14th ed.). London, UK: Sampson Low, Marston and Co.—An early adventure tourist travels across the Canadian western interior. Also see William Butler's *The Wild North Land,* for a winter travel account.

Davidson, J. W., and Rugge, J. (1988). *Great heart: The history of a Labrador adventure.* New York, NY: Viking.—The complete story and travels of the Hubbard-Wallace expeditions in Labrador.

Downs, P. G. (1988). *Sleeping island.* Saskatoon, Saskatchewan: Western Producer Prairie Books. (Original work published 1943).—A northern traveler's bible. The journal entries of a man who experienced the ending of the north that was.

Grey Owl. (1936). *Tales of an empty cabin.* Toronto, Ontario: MacMillan.—Stories, philosophies and curious ties of the Canadian Shield.

Martin, C. (1978). *Keepers of the game: Indian animal relationships and the fur trade.* Berkeley, CA: University of California Press.—An attempt is made to understand the native world-view and the spiritual affects of European contact on culture.

Merrick, E. (1989). *True north.* Lincoln, NE: University of Nebraska Press. (Original work published 1942.)—A classic account of snowshoe travel in Labrador from a man who "got out" and got into the bush.

Nisbet, J. (1994). *Sources of the river: Tracing David Thompson across western North America.* Seattle, WA: Sasquatch Books.

Schaffer, M. (1980). *Old Indian Trails of the Canadian Rockies.* Banff, Alberta: The Whyte Foundation.—Exploration in the Canadian Rockies by a sensitive, self-effacing Quaker woman explorer.

Thompson, D. (1971). *Travels in western North America, 1784–1812* (V. G. Hopwood, Ed). Toronto, Ontario: MacMillan Co.—The opening of the western interior of North America as told by the one man who could make such a claim.

Wallace, D. (1977). *The lure of Labrador wild.* Portugal Cove, Newfoundland: Breakwater Books. (Original work published 1905.)—The firsthand account of an epic misadventure.

Davis, R. C. (Ed.). (1996). *Lobsticks and stone cairns: Human landmarks in the arctic.* Calgary, Alberta: University of Calgary Press.—Short detailed character sketches of a variety of well-known and lesser known travelers.

References

Back, G. (1970). *Narrative of the arctic land expedition to the mouth of the Great Fish River, and along the shores of the Arctic Ocean in the years 1833, 1834, and 1835.* Rutland, VT: Charles E. Tuttle Co. (Original work published 1836).

Bateson, G. (1972). *Steps to an ecology of mind.* New York, NY: Ballantine.

Brown, G. I. (1971). *Human teaching for human learning.* New York, NY: Penguin.

Chatwin, B. (1987). *The songlines.* New York, NY: Penguin.

Faarlund, N. (1993). Nils Faarlund. In P. Reed and D. Rothenberg (Eds.), *Wisdom in the open air.* Minneapolis, MN: University of Minnesota Press.

Franks, C. E. S. (1988). Canoeing: Toward a landscape of the imagination. In J. Raffan and B. Horwood (Eds.), *Canexus: The canoe in Canadian culture.* Toronto, Ontario: Betelgeuse Books.

Freuchen, P. (1935). *The arctic adventurer.* New York, NY: Farrar and Rinehart.

Mason, B. (1988). *Song of the paddle: An illustrated guide to wilderness camping.* Toronto, Ontario: Key Porter Books.

Olson, S. (1956). *The singing wilderness.* New York, NY: A. A. Knopf.

Olson, S. (1969). *Open horizons.* New York, NY: A. A. Knopf.

Perkins, R. (1983). *Against straight lines: Alone in Labrador.* Boston, MA: Little, Brown & Co.

Stevens, W. (1942). *The necessary angel: Essays on reality and the imagination.* New York, NY: Vintage Books.

Such, P. (1978). *Vanished peoples: The Archaic Corset and Beothuk people of Newfoundland.* Toronto, Ontario: NC Press.

Woodcock, G. (1981). *Ivan Eyre.* Don Mills, UK: Fitzhenry and Whiteside

Section 4

The Social Psychology of Adventure Programming
The Nature of the Experience

This section takes up questions dealing with the psychology of having an adventure and of helping others grow from such experiences. Such questions as what is adventure and why are people attracted to adventure are considered. So too are questions about what happens psychologically to people in the process of having an adventure, and how do leaders and educators help participants in educational processes using adventure derive the most learning and personal growth from these experiences.

Quinn approaches the question: why adventure? He dissects the adventure experience and finds subjectivity, discovery, desire, striving, uncertainty, excitement, fun, exhilaration and growth. The world can be a small and narrow place, he argues, unless one seeks to explore. Adventure is exploration, which requires extension of self. This extension leads to growth, which feels good, leads to further exploration, and thus do people move toward fulfillment.

The Csikszentmihalyis carry the analysis further. Their concept of flow is well-known, and they present it again here in the context of adventure and adventure education. Flow is a useful way of describing and understanding the elements of the adventure experience—of what happens to a person in such an experience. The Csikszentmihalyis' research yields insight into why people seek adventure and what they gain from it.

This analysis can be complex and confusing, and Priest attempts to diagrammatically present a simple model of the adventure experience, a conceptual model based partly on the work of the Csikszentmihalyis. He explains how risk relates to competence in the adventurer, and what the various outcomes of the adventure experience may be. He reveals the positive and negative feedback loops that may be set off by adventure experiences. His approach yields useful visualizations of this experience.

Klint offers a review of what developmental psychology has revealed about the value of adventure education. What effect does it have on self-concept, self-efficacy and perception of confidence? She concludes that research has given insight into the outcome of the adventure experience, but much work needs doing to understand the learning process involved. What specific elements of the adventure experience produce which results? There may be much work to do, says Klint, but at least past inquiry gives clear direction to future research.

Martin concludes this section with an examination of how practitioners might use the understanding of the learning-through-adventure process that is emerging from theory and research. Focusing on attribution and self-efficacy theory applied to a specific adventure education situation, Martin explains how the practitioner might apply available theory to understand the dynamics of the situation and to achieve the most desirable outcome. He makes a convincing case that the more one knows about theory and research, the greater the likelihood the best decision will be made in the field situation.

Chapter 19

The Essence of Adventure

William Quinn
Northern Illinois University

Goethe said: "Whatever you can do or dream you can do, begin it. Boldness has genius, power and magic in it."

Adventure. Adventure speaks of beginning, boldness, and power. Adventure connotes participation and active involvement in life. An adventure, a quest, begins because of a human desire, a drive to experience that which is hidden and unknown. "We are attracted by a deep forest or lake because it gives the impression that there is some truth to discover, some secret to abduct from the heart of the object. It is the eternal seduction of the hidden" (Dufrenne, 1973, p. 398). The discovery, the unveiling, is the recompense of the adventurous seeker. A desire for adventure may have directly contributed to the emergence of the human species from equatorial Africa untold eons ago. Rober Ardrey (1976), in *The Hunting Hypothesis,* contends that a primordial sense of adventure stimulated early humans to discover and inhabit the world. He stated:

> The magnet of our nature commanded that we investigate certain blue Ethiopian hills, and what lay beyond. And so in the vast concourse of time we moved on past the veto of desert, into the chill of winters that our equatorial existence had never anticipated. But we did not go back. And that is what is so interesting. (p. 135)

Ardrey believes that the ancient drives of simian curiosity and propensities of predation combined together to create the desire for adventure in the human species. He continued:

> There had to be ancient winds within us, old primate curiosities, newer predator demand for exploration. These were not so much the biological consequences of cultural advance, but very old biological demands—that inhabit us still, to become a dominant quality in the life of our species. Adventure. (p. 136)

Adventure does not lie only within the objective natural world. It lies deeply within oneself, within the spiritual, emotional, and intellectual spheres of personhood. An adventurous undertaking need not always be outwardly evident. High, dangerous, or spirited adventure may exist privately and be outwardly unobservable. Consider the appearance of two chess players engaged in an important match. Outwardly, they are as stoic as possible, but inwardly they are functioning intensely.

The question remains as to what the essence of adventure is. It is a desire for a something, a condition, which is absent. It is a process which begins with the acceptance of a situation where one knows one will need to call upon one's own *supposed* talents and spontaneously, irrevocably, act upon them. During the process of accepting the idea of placing oneself in a tenuous situation, one *must* harbor doubt as to the adequacy of one's ability. Without question, when complete confidence and competence reign, adventure cannot exist. Yet the essential feeling of adventure varies in degree. The stranger the new ground trodden upon, the further one goes beyond one's imagined talents, the more intense and profound the adventure becomes. Duration is a functioning part of the feeling of adventure. The longer the final outcome remains obscure, the closer one comes to the edge, the deadline, before culminating action resolves conflict, the more concentrated and reverberating the adventure becomes. Yet there are no final outcomes, only episodes.

The price of failure is always the same—there is loss. However small or great depends upon what has been originally risked. Loss, the result of error, may be physical (the skinning of the knee or the forfeiture of life), emotional (hurt feelings or the shattering of self-confidence), intellectual (a missed exam question or a situation where one's ideas are compelled to crumble), social (a lonely afternoon or ostracism by peers), or spiritual (a momentary lapse into indifference or the devastation of cherished beliefs). Inevitably, there is casualty.

But what is a life that is dominated by the fear of pain? If pain appears as an archenemy, an intruder to be avoided at all costs, a person would be restricted to asking, "Would this action I am contemplating hurt?" rather than, "Would it be good to take a chance in this way?" To the person who assumes a risk, pain, if it does occur, will not feel less, but will matter less. There is so much more in the striving that matters (Kohak, 1984). The essential feeling of the striving is what Mitchell (1983), and Csikszentmihalyi (1975) before him, described as flow. The flow state refers to a "kind of personal transcendence" (Mitchell, 1983, p. 153), brought on by engaging in activity solely to inculcate the inherent rewards of that activity. But this explanation is not enough. Mitchell further elucidates the idea by describing the flow state as one where "a level of involvement such that consciousness at hand and the doing of it blend, that action and awareness become indistinguishable" (p. 154). The flow state, or personal transcendence experienced when risk is courted and met, describes a reason for inviting adventure into one's life.

The price of success may be even more harrowing. Triumph carries the requirement to continue for anyone honest to himself. As Eugene O'Neill (in Ferguson, 1980) put it:

> Those who succeed and do not push on to greater failure are the spiritual middle classers. Their stopping at success is the proof of their compromising insignificance. . . . Only through the unattainable does man achieve a hope worth living and dying for— and so attain himself. (p. 673)

If a climber hasn't fallen, he or she hasn't climbed; and if a canoeist is dry, he or she hasn't paddled. Real fear comes from knowing that there is no honest place to hide. But O'Neill has missed something—the knowledge that through adventure, peace is obtainable. Maybe its duration is ephemeral, and feelings of peace certainly vary from person to person, but peace is an outcome of adventure. D. H. Lawrence (1936) stated, "Peace is the state of fulfilling the deepest desire of the soul. It is the condition of flying within the greatest impulse that enters us from the unknown" (p. 117–118). To fly, wrapped in an impulse from the unknown towards the unknown, lies close to the heart of the experience of adventure. Peace comes from confidence gained and the fulfillment of success. "When a man yields himself implicitly to the suggestion which transcends him, when he accepts gently and honorably his own creative fate, he is beautiful and beyond aspersion" (Lawrence, 1936, p. 671). He is also enmeshed in adventure and will soon be at peace. The reward of peace is the difference between adventure and thrill seeking. The thrill seekers find no peace.

In our contemporary society accolades are heaped upon those who, through their personal adventuring, achieve the stupendous and visibly great deeds. Grand adventurousness is recognized in those who confront death while seeking excitement. The price of a mistake is so great. Scaling Everest, diving to the ocean depth, mushing to the North Pole, or leaping from airplanes is perceived as adventure to most onlookers and may well be perceived as adventure by the participant. William James (in McDermott, 1968) expressed an essential quality of adventure which is apparent through obvious risk:

> The element of precipitousness, of strength and strenuousness, intensity and danger. What excites and interests the looker on at life, what the romances and the statues celebrate . . . is the everlasting battle of the powers of light with those of darkness; with heroism reduced to its bare chance. (p. 648)

He continues with the ideas which describe adventure and remind us again of O'Neill:

> Sweat and effort, human nature strained to its uttermost and on the rack, yet getting through alive, and then turning its back on success to pursue another more rare and arduous skill—this is the sort of thing the presence of which inspires us. (p. 648)

Visible actions of a stupendous nature catch the public eye because of the immediacy of confrontation and the extremity of the price of failure. A real sense of urgency is felt. However, there are magnificent adventures in human lives that are not applauded because of their commonality, even though these undertakings are no less compelling. Raising children honestly, choosing a career faithfully, maintaining a marriage continually, now these are adventures! I have seen adventure in the deep darkness of my daughter's eyes, in the recesses of my mate's feelings, and in the expressions of those whom I served.

To engage in adventurous activity and to fail will necessitate some sort of loss. But what is the price of choosing not to seek or purposely avoiding tenuous situations? The price is torpidity, and the result is stagnation. One must actively seek an adventurous way of life; otherwise there is only a small and narrow world to explore. A diminutive existence then ensues. D. H. Lawrence (1936) conceptualizes:

> We all must die. But we need not all live. . . .
> We may refuse to live, we may refuse to pass
> into the unknown of life; we may deny our-
> selves to life altogether. . . . Unless we sub-
> mit our will to the flooding of life, there is
> no life in us. (p. 673)

So the answers to the questions, why risk, why engage the possibility of penalty and discomfort, and why approach one's personal limit, become obvious. Without actively seeking, without attempting to, and going beyond what one already knows one can accomplish, there is no growth. Strenuousness of mind, heart, and body engenders growth. Where there is no growth, where stagnation is the rule, a human being offers nothing, either to one's self or to society.

Even without regard to any of these thoughts, without conceptualizing the need for adventure in one's life, individuals would still seek it. Adventure is courted because it is rewarding, exciting, fun and exhilarating. Taking part in some discovery about oneself and one's environment is pleasurable. Self-knowledge is always an outcome of adventure, be it happy or sad, uplifting or degrading.

But the emotions that precede and lead to exhilaration and excitement are often fear, hesitation, and apprehension. Again, one is mired between an enlivened state and a static, stagnant existence. The catalyst is the need for committed action. So, the frightening question comes back again. Granted that I am the master of my own destiny, how shall I fulfill that destiny (Novak, 1970)? Why

scale that rock wall to the east? Why make that national presentation? Why complete a doctoral dissertation? One is inevitably drawn back to the desire for the hidden, the inexplicable human urge to experience that which is just out of range of prior background, to supplement insight with experience previously unknown.

Rene Daumal (1967), in *Mount Analogue,* expresses the feeling thusly:

> You cannot stay on the summit forever; you
> have to come down again—so why bother in
> the first place? Just this; what is above knows
> what is below, but what is below does not
> know what is above. One climbs, one sees,
> one descends; one sees no longer, *but one
> has seen* [emphasis added]. (p. 103)

As a result of an experience like this, one also has a broader base from which to attempt to see again, and again. An attitude that permits a person to seek adventure in life feeds upon itself and renews itself. Any life worth living is worth living with the advent of a venture.

References

Ardrey, R. (1976). *The hunting hypothesis.* New York, NY: Atheneum.

Csikszentmihalyi, M. (1975). *Beyond boredom and anxiety.* San Francisco, CA: Jossey-Bass.

Daumal, R. (1967). *Mount analogue.* San Francisco, CA: City of Lights Books.

Dufrenne, M. (1973). *The phenomenology of aesthetic experience.* Evanston, IL: Northwestern University Press.

Ferguson, M. (1980). *The Aquarian conspiracy.* Los Angeles, CA: J. P. Tarcher Inc.

Kohak, E. (1984). *The embers and the stars.* Chicago, IL: University of Chicago Press.

Lawrence, D. H. (1936). *Phoenix, The posthumous papers.* New York, NY: Viking Press.

McDermott, J. (Ed.). (1968). *The writing of William James.* New York, NY: Random House.

Mitchell, R. G. (1983). *Mountain experience: The psychology and sociology of adventure.* Chicago, IL: University of Chicago Press.

Novak, M. (1970). *The experience of nothingness.* New York, NY: Harper and Row.

Chapter 20

Adventure and the Flow Experience

Mihaly Csikszentmihalyi and Isabella Csikszentmihalyi

University of Chicago

It has not been easy for the human race to survive. Through millions of years our ancestors have been challenged by all kinds of trials and tribulations: ice ages, saber-toothed tigers, droughts and diseases. If we are still here, it is because they were able to develop a superb array of survival tools. Some of these are well-known: our complex brain, our nimble fingers, our ability to cooperate, and of course the various technologies these made possible, ranging from the taming of fire to the splicing of genes. But there is one advantage we know less about, even though it must have been indispensable to our ancestors in their long struggle to survive in a mysterious and dangerous environment. This advantage is the enjoyment we derive from exploring the unknown and confronting the unexpected.

During the course of evolution, we have learned to enjoy those activities that are necessary for individual survival and the reproduction of the species. Human life would have disappeared long ago from earth if we did not derive pleasure from food and sex. Physiological rewards have been built over time into our bodies so that we may feel good when we do what needs to be done. But man does not live by bread alone. To survive in an unpredictable and dangerous environment, human beings must also enjoy a certain amount of novelty and danger.

And this is indeed the case. Some day we shall be able to document exactly the physiological benefit that "adrenaline rushes" provide rock climbers or sky divers, or the release of endorphins that a "runner's high" brings to the nervous system of athletes. In the meantime, even though we lack an understanding of the biological mechanisms, it is quite clear that facing the challenge of the unknown is generally felt to be pleasurable by most people. The "spirit of adventure" is not dead, and it must have been strong and healthy through the endless stretches of nameless centuries in which our ancestors struggled to gain a foothold on the earth.

In our studies, we have found that people involved in adventurous pursuits such as rock climbing (Csikszentmihalyi, 1975; Mitchell, 1983), solo long-distance sailing (Macbeth, 1988), polar explorations (Logan, 1985), spelunking (Massimini and Carli, 1986), and a variety of similar endeavors, report a state of optimal experience we have called *flow*. To understand why adventure is so attractive, it is important to understand what happens to people when they experience flow.

Characteristics of the Flow Experience

Flow describes a state of experience that is engrossing, intrinsically rewarding, and "outside the parameters of worry and boredom" (Csikszentmihalyi, 1975). Since its introduction some 14 years ago, the flow concept has been applied theoretically in a variety of disciplines, including psychology, cultural anthropology, and sociology. Its impact has probably been strongest in the study of free time:

play, sports, leisure, and recreation (Csikszentmihalyi, 1969, 1975). On a wider level, the cumulating research from these years has resulted in its application in educational, clinical, and commercial settings (Csikszentmihalyi and Csikszentmihalyi, 1988).

The flow concept emerged from observing and interviewing people who expended much time and energy on activities that provided few extrinsic rewards such as money or recognition: artists, rock climbers, dancers, music composers, amateur athletes, high-school basketball players (Csikszentmihalyi, 1975). Their answers suggested a common set of characteristics that constituted a feeling of enjoyment, well-being and competence that distinguished their particular involvement from the less satisfying events common to most of everyday life. Since what motivated the activity usually seemed not to be external rewards but the activity itself, the conclusion was that it was *the quality of the subjective experience itself* that made the behavior intrinsically rewarding.

What are the elements of the flow experience that make it a desirable and motivating state? Certainly a crucial one is the level of absorption of the person with the activity. In a flow state there is characteristically a total involvement with the chosen activity, one which typically offers constant challenges that have to be met with appropriate skills, and the ability to match these provides immediate and gratifying feedback. An underlying assumption of flow-producing activities is that they "are ways for people to test the limits of their being, to transcend their former conception of self by extending skills and undergoing new experience" (Csikszentmihalyi, 1975, p. 26). Although ideally flow would be the result of pure involvement, some people need other inducements, such as competition, extrinsic rewards (money, recognition, or the prestige and glamour associated with certain activities), and the risk involved in physical danger, to get involved in flow activities. But when the activity itself becomes the goal, when it becomes a flow-producing experience, the following characteristics are what make it worthy of repetition to the participant:

1. A person in flow knows clearly what must be done, and gets quick feedback about how well he or she is doing. Goals and means are logically ordered, so that it is possible to foresee the results of alternative actions. A tennis player always knows she must return the ball to the opponent's court, and the goal of a chess player is to mate the opponent's king before his own is mated. The many ambiguities of everyday life are banished. However, in flow there is no pause to evaluate the feedback, the person is too involved with the experience to reflect on it. Action and reaction have become so well-synchronized that the resulting behavior is automatic. This is true even in endeavors that are not as clear-cut as those of a tennis or chess player. A composer of music and an explorer set for themselves tasks that are much more open-ended; however, they must have within themselves certain internalized goals that allow them to recognize positive feedback. For instance, the composer's goal is to write down certain chords and harmonies imagined in the mind; if the notes sound right when played back, the feedback is positive. The explorer may not have a specific goal in mind, but each day some objective must be set and achieved. Without knowing whether they are doing well, neither could feel the enjoyment that makes their efforts a flow experience.

2. Because goals and feedback are so clear, the flow experience involves a merging of action and awareness. A person in flow has no dualistic perspective: there is awareness of the actions but not of the awareness itself. All the attention is concentrated on the relevant stimuli, and one stops being aware of oneself as separate from what is being engaged in. This feeling was aptly described by an expert rock climber in our sample: "You are so involved in what you are doing [that] you aren't thinking of yourself as separate from the immediate activity. . . . You don't see yourself as separate from what you are doing." A dancer described her feelings when a performance is going well in very similar terms: "Your concentration is very complete. Your mind isn't wandering, you are not thinking of something else; you are totally involved in what you are doing. . . . Your body is awake all over. . . . Your energy is flowing very smoothly. You feel relaxed, comfortable, and energetic." Although the flow experience may appear effortless, it often requires strenuous physical exertion or highly disciplined mental activity. For this reason it is difficult to maintain for any length of time without at least momentary interruptions.

3. This merging of action and awareness is made possible by a third characteristic of flow experiences: a centering of attention on a limited stimulus field. To ensure that people will concentrate on their actions, potentially intruding stimuli must be kept out of attention; i.e., one's consciousness is "narrowed" so that irrelevant stimuli are excluded. In play and leisure activities, the rules of the game tend to perform this function. In less structured activities, certain routines and settings facilitate the limiting of the stimulus field and the keeping of attention on what is going on.

The important thing is that irrelevant information is weeded out. A mountaineer describes the results of this complete focusing of attention on what is going on: "When you're [climbing] you're not aware of other problematic life situations. It becomes a world unto its own, significant only to itself. It's a concentration thing. Once you're into the situation, it's incredibly real, and you're very much in charge of it. It becomes your total world." A basketball player expresses the same idea: "The court—that's all that matters. . . . Sometimes on court I think of a problem, like fighting with my steady girl, and I think that's nothing compared to the game. You can think about a problem all day but as soon as you get in the game, the hell with it!" And a dancer sums up the benefits emerging from this centering of attention on a limited stimulus field: "I get a feeling that I don't get anywhere else. . . . I have more confidence in myself than any other time. . . . Dance is like therapy. If I am troubled about something, I leave it out of the door as I go in [the dance studio]."

4. A consequence of this intense concentration is a fourth characteristic of the flow experience, often described as "loss of ego" and "self-forgetfulness." When an activity completely involves a person with its demands for action, the self which serves to negotiate between a person's actions and those of others is no longer necessary. Although in some situations a person may lose touch with his own physical reality, in others there may be a heightened awareness of internal processes. What is usually lost in flow is not the awareness of one's body or of one's functions, but only the self-*construct*, the "I" as the actor or intermediary that a person learns to interpose between stimulus and response. A person making a difficult ascent has to concentrate on his mountain-climber role in order to survive and cannot afford to bring into question any other aspect of his self. Even the possible threat from the mountain itself does not intrude because a good climber feels well-equipped to face the challenges presented to him, and does not need to bring the self into play. The loss of the sense of self is sometimes accompanied by a feeling of union with the environment, whether it is the mountain one is climbing, or one's team, or even the universe. The sense of time may also change: hours may seem to pass by in minutes, or the intensity of the concentration and

the heightened awareness may give seconds a feeling of incredible depth and infinity. This lack of preoccupation with the self, this loss of self-consciousness paradoxically allows people to expand their self-concept: what emerges is a feeling of self-transcendence, of the boundaries of the self being expanded. Thus a good violinist, surrounded by the stream of sound she helps to create, may feel she is part of the "harmony of the spheres." A climber may begin to feel a sense of kinship developing between fingers and rock, between the vulnerable body and the surrounding stone, sky, and wind. An ocean sailor during a long night watch will begin to feel that the boat is an extension of himself, moving to the same rhythms and to a common goal. In each case the person becomes part of a concrete system of action greater than the individual self. This expansion of one's being, accompanied by a successful matching of skills to challenges, is deeply enjoyable, and at the same time it produces a person enriched by new achievements and a stronger confidence.

5. People in flow feel potentially in control of their actions and of the environment. Rather than an active awareness of control, one ceases to worry about losing control, as one often does in real life. This feeling is true even in situations where the objective dangers are quite real—hang-gliding, deep-sea diving, spelunking, race car driving, rock climbing—yet they are seen as predictable and manageable. Risktakers often claim that their enjoyment comes not from the danger itself, but from their ability to minimize it, from their feeling that they are able to control potentially dangerous forces. Rock climbers must always be aware of two types of problematic situations: "objective dangers" such as falling rock, drastic drops in temperature, sudden storms, even avalanches; and "subjective dangers" related to the climber's lack of skill, such as being unable to correctly estimate the difficulty of a rockface in relation to one's ability. Yet the whole point of climbing is to avoid objective dangers as much as possible, and to eliminate subjective dangers entirely by rigorous discipline and sound preparation. As a result many good climbers maintain that their mountaineering exploits are far less dangerous than crossing a busy street in a large city: they feel that the objective dangers presented by the crowds, buses, and taxi drivers are less predictable than those

on a mountain, which can be overcome by skills. Sailors who have circumnavigated the earth's vast oceans alone on a small boat have expressed the same types of feelings. It is this confidence of being able to exercise control through one's skills that not only makes flow experiences enjoyable but also ensures a desire for their repetition.

6. The final characteristic of the flow experience is its autotelic nature. The components of the flow state are usually so enjoyable and psychically rewarding, and so unlike the drudgery of most of life, that there is a desire to repeat activities that produce the flow experience. Even if initially done for extrinsic reasons, the activity becomes intrinsically rewarding. Some surgeons get so involved in their work that they volunteer their services to local hospitals while on vacation because they find using their skills more enjoyable than sitting on a beach. Children forced to take music lessons may in time get to enjoy playing music for its own sake if they begin to hear the results of using their skills. The same happens to high-school mathematics students who are able to match their skills to the increasingly complex problems being presented in the classrooms.

The Importance of the Flow Experience

Why is the flow experience important? Probably because it provides a key to understanding the strivings of the self and illustrates the human search for an improved quality of individual well-being. The fact that many flow activities are rarely extrinsically rewarded, or at least not rewarded to the extent of the effort involved, illustrates the fact that man needs more than the fulfillment of genetically programmed needs. Both Csikszentmihalyi (1975) and Mitchell (1983) have shown that persons with jobs and statuses viewed as highly desirable by others look for flow experiences outside their everyday work and social settings. Moreover, as modern life becomes more and more complex, feelings of apathy on the one hand and alienation on the other may become even more widespread, and increasing numbers of persons will strive to find situations in which they feel that what they do is of their own choice and under their own control.

An extreme example of this search for improved experience are the full-time ocean cruisers studied by Macbeth (1988), many of whom feel that everyday life contains meaningless goals, alienates the person from the rhythms of nature, and is antagonistic to the autonomy of the individual. In ocean cruising they find the sense of fulfillment and enjoyment of life that was missing in their previous endeavors. As a result they go so far as to drop out of society to pursue an autotelic but solitary *lifestyle* that they feel gives them autonomy and choice, and enhances their identity and sense of competence. These, of course, are the same goals that are central to *activities* such as rock climbing, chess playing, or adventure seeking; the difference is that such flow experiences are rarely pursued full time. Most people will continue to find their flow experience in free-time activities, although some are lucky enough to find it on their jobs. Other people, who may possess what we call an "autotelic personality," are actually able to structure flow into compulsory activities such as school or work—situations to which many others respond with boredom or frustration. Ideally, of course, school and work, which take up so many years of a person's life, would be structured to provide flow experiences to a maximum number of people (Delle Fave and Massimini, 1988; Rathunde, 1988).

Flow and Adventure Education

Where does adventure education fit into the picture? Certainly it responds to the human desire for novelty, discovery, uncertainty, and problem solving. The pursuit of these attributes assumes that people are motivated by intrinsic rewards, in addition to extrinsic rewards based on physiological drives, stimulus-response, and social conditioning. Hebb (1955), Berlyne (1960), and others have introduced into modern psychology the idea that organisms need to do more than satisfy preprogrammed needs, that an optimal level of stimulation is also needed. One may extrapolate from this position that a person will enjoy an activity if it offers a pattern of stimulation not ordinarily available in the environment; it must also have been freely chosen (deCharms, 1976; Deci and Ryan, 1985), and allow the person to use his physical, sensory, or intellectual potential in a new or challenging way. However, this does not explain why certain activities are considered enjoyable and others are not.

By interviewing participants in "autotelic" activities in our pilot studies, we were able to separate eight items that were regularly cited as reasons for enjoying such activities. These items were then introduced to the later sample groups studied, who were asked to rank their particular activity according to a questionnaire containing both intrinsic and extrinsic reasons for enjoying the activity (Csikszentmihalyi, 1975). The "autotelic factor" of each activity was determined by the ranking given to each reason. The eight factors were:

1. the enjoyment of the experience and the use of skills;

2. the activity itself: the pattern, the action, the world it provides;
3. friendship, companionship;
4. development of personal skills;
5. measuring self against own ideals;
6. emotional release;
7. competition, measuring self against others; and
8. prestige, regard, glamour.

Adventure participants would probably rank the reasons for the activities they undertake in an order very similar to that given by rock climbers (Csikszentmihalyi, 1975) and full-time ocean cruisers (Macbeth, 1988), who rated "the enjoyment of the experience and the use of skills;" and "the activity itself: the pattern, the action, the world it provides," as the two top items. Adventure activities, having few extrinsic rewards, are a way of challenging oneself to participate in experiences that are removed from everyday opportunities, that may use skills not called for in daily routines, or conversely, as a way of developing skills that one admires and would like to acquire. The milieu in which these skills are practiced—the environment as well as the individuals sharing the same interests and goals—is probably also an important factor. The importance of the other items is likely to vary with the person and the particular activity being engaged in.

Like participants in other autotelic activities, adventure participants are searching for a peculiar state of experience, an experience that is rarely accessible in everyday life. As Mitchell (1983) has pointed out in connection with the choice of mountaineering as an avocation, "the key concept, the desirable condition, the sought-after goal of climbing is the social-psychological condition of flow." What is being sought is the experience corresponding to an unusual match between person and environment. The challenges and skills in question are based on real elements of the situation—such as the waves confronting the sailor—but what effectively determines the quality of the experience is the person's subjective estimation of what the level of challenges and skills are at any given time.

The flow model suggests that to derive enjoyment from life reliably requires the ability to get into flow, stay in it, and make the process evolve. This in turn depends on a capacity to structure interaction with the environment in a way that facilitates flow. Specifically the characteristics of the autotelic experience correspond to capacities to (1) focus attention on the present moment and the activity at hand; (2) define one's goals in an activity and identify the means for reaching them; and (3) seek feedback and focus on its informational aspects. In addition to these abilities, the dependence of enjoyment on a balancing of challenges and skills suggests the importance of a capacity to continuously adjust this balance by using anxiety and boredom as information, and identifying new challenges as

skills grow. Being able to tolerate the anxiety-provoking interactions that test one's skills also appears to be important. Finally, other attributes are likely to have an effect outside of the particular interaction; among these would be the ability to delay gratification, which is necessary for the eventual enjoyment of activities that require a significant investment of energy before they start providing intrinsic rewards. Clearly all of these are important in adventure activities. As Priest and Baillie (1987) have pointed out, good adventure education consists of an accurate evaluation of both the environmental dangers being pursued (risk) and the individual ability of each participant to confront them (competence). It is the careful matching of risk and competence in situations of progressing complexity that produces the experiences characteristic of the flow state. Eventually those who are able to find enjoyment in adventure activities made on purpose to provide autotelic experiences, are more likely to begin finding flow in other areas of life as well. Indeed, a new range of activities may be opened to them as avenues for enjoyment. And when people derive enjoyment from their daily lives, they will spend less time feeling apathetic, anxious, or bored.

This ability to match ever-complexifying skills and challenges produces feelings of enjoyment and achievement that lead to a stronger and more confident sense of self. Over the millions of years of evolution, humans have been challenged by many trials. Rather than giving up, they have met these head-on, and have even managed to derive pleasure from facing the unknown and the unexpected. By being able to turn adversity into flow experiences, they have managed to control nature and to free themselves from many of the constraints imposed by the need to survive. However, at each stage of development, after having found a comfortable adaptation to the environment, humans have not been content to rest on their achievements but have kept pushing on to new frontiers, led on by the enjoyment of the unknown. At present, when we are faced with a daunting array of possibilities for action, the ability to find flow may be as big a challenge as mankind has ever encountered before.

References

Berlyne, D. E. (1960). *Conflict, arousal and curiosity.* New York, NY: McGraw Hill.

Csikszentmihalyi, M. (1969). The Americanization of rock climbing. *University of Chicago Magazine, 61*(6), 20–27.

Csikszentmihalyi, M. (1975). *Beyond boredom and anxiety.* San Francisco, CA: Jossey-Bass.

Csikszentmihalyi, M., and Csikszentmihalyi, I. S. (1988). *Optimal experience: Psychological studies of flow in conscious.* New York, NY: Cambridge University Press.

deCharms, R. (1976). *Personal causation: The internal affective determinants of behavior.* New York, NY: Academic Press.

Deci, E. L., and Ryan, R. M. (1985). *Intrinsic motivation and self-determination of human behavior.* New York, NY: Plenum Press.

Delle Fave, A., and Massimini, F. (1988). Modernization and the changing contexts of flow in work and leisure. In M. Csikszentmihalyi and I. S. Csikszentmihalyi (Eds.), *Optimal experience: Psychological studies of flow in conscious* (pp. 193–213). New York, NY: Cambridge University Press.

Hebb, D. O. (1955). Drives and the CNS. *Psychological Review, 62,* 243–254.

Logan, R. D. (1985). The flow experience in solitary ordeals. *Journal of Humanistic Psychology, 25*(4), 70–89.

Macbeth, J. (1988). Ocean cruising. In M. Csikszentmihalyi and I. S. Csikszentmihalyi (Eds.), *Optimal experience: Psychological studies of flow in conscious* (pp. 214–231). New York, NY: Cambridge University Press.

Massimini, F., and Carli, M. (1986). La selezione psicologica umana tra biologia e cultura. In F. Massimini and P. Inghilleri (Eds.), *L'esperienza quotidiana* (pp. 65–84). Milan, Italy: Franco Angeli.

Mitchell, R. G. (1983). *Mountain experience: The psychology and sociology of adventure.* Chicago, IL: University of Chicago Press.

Priest, S., and Baillie R. (1987). Justifying risk to others: The real razor's edge. *Journal of Experiential Education, 10*(1), 16–22.

Rathunde, K. (1988). Optimal experience and the family context. In M. Csikszentmihalyi and I. S. Csikszentmihalyi (Eds.), *Optimal experience: Psychological studies of flow in conscious* (pp. 342–63). New York, NY: Cambridge University Press.

Chapter 21

The Adventure Experience Paradigm

Simon Priest
eXperientia

Paradigms are merely conceptual models and theories designed to view and explain phenomena in life. One such perspective, the adventure experience paradigm (Martin and Priest, 1986), was designed to interpret adventure experiences. Based on the works of Ellis (1973), Csikszent-mihalyi (1975) and Mortlock (1984), the paradigm is diagrammed in Figure 21.1. Before reading on, a review of the definitions given in the chapter on semantics is now warranted.

Note the model has two axes: those of risk (the potential to lose something of value) and competence (a synergy of skill, knowledge, attitude, behavior, confidence, and experience). Recall from the last section on philosophy that challenge is the interplay of risk and competence. In this model, five such conditions of interplay are shown. The condition which is expected or results depends upon the balance of risk and competence.

When risks are low, and competence is high, a condition termed *exploration and experimentation* exists. Using the common activity of canoeing, this is likened to practicing paddle strokes on a calm lake. As risks increase, and/or competence decreases, the conditions of *adventure, peak adventure,* and *misadventure* occur. Returning to canoeing, these would be respectively analogous to paddling on gentle moving water, successfully running a fierce rapid, and dumping overboard in whitewater. These four conditions are acceptable learning opportunities for any adventurer. Learning basic skills, applying them to a challenging task, testing one's limits on the razor's edge, and having

to deal with the consequences of error are the mainstay of education from and through adventure.

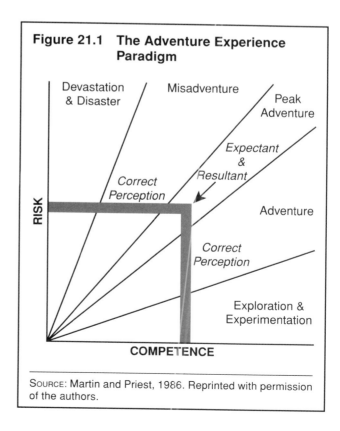

Figure 21.1   The Adventure Experience Paradigm

However, the fifth condition of *devastation and disaster* is a place where few adventurers choose to tread. Occurring when risks are high and competence is low, this frightening condition should have no role in educational experiences. People may learn from misadventures, from which they may recover, but deaths result in negative adventure experiences and seek only to reverse the educational merit of adventure.

The key to an experience being adventurous, then, is uncertainty of outcome (Priest and Baillie, 1987). In fact, adventure is simply leisure with uncertainty (Carpenter and Priest, 1989). The uncertainty comes from the risks inherent in the activity and becomes challenging when a person applies his or her competence against the risks in an attempt to resolve that uncertainty. Furthermore, people tend to select risks which balance their competence in order that they may achieve optimal arousal (Ellis, 1973), a state of flow (Csikszentmihalyi, 1975), and/or peak adventure experiences (Priest, 1987).

For these reasons adventures are personally specific (based on personal competence) and situationally specific (based on situational risks). In other words, an adventure for one person, in a particular place, at a given time, may not be adventure for another, or for the same person in a different place or time. Like leisure, adventure is purely "a state of mind" (Mitchell, 1983)!

The state of mind concept dictates human behavior and, in turn, is driven by human perceptions of reality. Hence, both risk and competence (the two axes of the model) may be thought of as having two possible values: real and perceived. Unfortunately for most people engaged in adventures these are often not the same value. Novices tend to misperceive the risks and competence of an adventure experience. Two types of such novices are common.

First, the timid and fearful people overperceive the risk (this is going to be dangerous) and underperceive their competence (I can't do this). If we consider that the perceptions of these people to dictate their expectations, then they are likely expecting a condition of misadventure (Figure 21.2). Also, if the real values of risk and competence dictate the actual outcome, then a condition like exploration and experimentation may result. This adventure experience is undesirable; because, when left to their own accord, the timid and fearful will miss their opportunity to experience a self-actualizing adventure and this is a shame.

Second, the arrogant and fearless people underperceive the risk (this is going to be a breeze) and overperceive their competence (I can do this the best). Again, if we consider that the perceptions of these people to dictate their expectations, then they are likely expecting a condition of adventure (Figure 21.3). Also, if the real values of risk and competence dictate the actual outcome, then a condition like devastation and disaster may result. This adventure experience is equally if not more undesirable than the previously mentioned one; since the arrogant and fearless

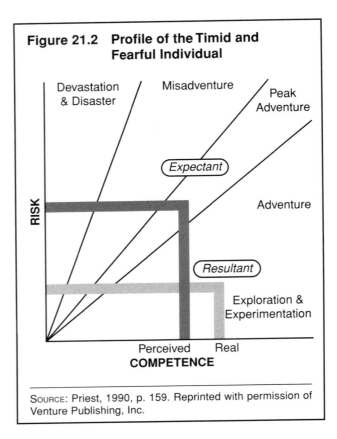

Figure 21.2 Profile of the Timid and Fearful Individual

SOURCE: Priest, 1990, p. 159. Reprinted with permission of Venture Publishing, Inc.

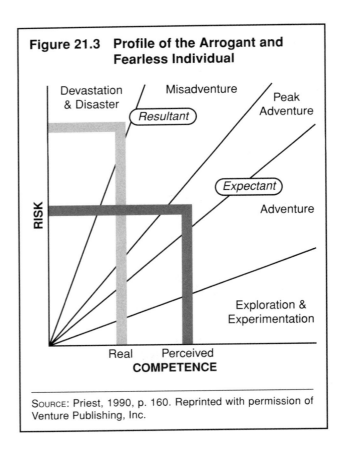

Figure 21.3 Profile of the Arrogant and Fearless Individual

SOURCE: Priest, 1990, p. 160. Reprinted with permission of Venture Publishing, Inc.

will injure themselves and may likely take some other adventurers with them and this is unacceptable.

These kinds of shortcomings are often avoided by experienced adventurers. Through repeated exposure to the risks and by repeated application of their competence, these people have become astute: accurate in their perceptions. Hence, one goal of adventure education should be to create astute individuals: people who correctly perceive the situational risks and their personal competence, plus seek adventure experiences where the two variables are matched for a peak adventure.

The solution to the problems elucidated here are known as the facilitated adventure experience. Through structured and controlled experiences under the supervision of a facilitator or leader, people can make advances toward astuteness. These experiences are said to be structured, since the facilitator sets up the level of challenge as a custom fit for the individual; and are said to be controlled, because the risks which are manipulated are strictly the perceived values (the real values are maintained at acceptable and/or low levels). The key to the operation is the facilitator, who must be sufficiently experienced and astute enough to perceive the risks and the people's competence more accurately than they can. Two examples are shown in Figures 21.4 through 21.7 (page 162).

By way of illustration, consider a timid and fearful man on a high ropes traverse. The facilitator has structured an experience where this person is asked to walk across a tightrope 50 feet above the ground with only a rope strung from the far tree for balance and support. Based on perceived values, he is expecting a misadventure or, even worse, devastation and disaster! In actuality, the real values are quite different, since he is belayed (protected by a safety line). After considerable coaxing and assistance from the facilitator, he completes the traverse with the accompanying feeling of elation. The facilitator assists him in reflecting on his adventure and after some thought and discussion he now realizes that the task was not so dangerous and that he really was capable enough to complete it. This learning may later transfer to daily living concerns, where perhaps the man expresses timid and fearful behaviors when meeting new people.

As a second case, take an arrogant and fearless woman on a rock climb. The facilitator has structured an experience where she is asked to climb a particularly difficult route which has previously been the topic of some bragging on her part. Based on perceived values, she is expecting exploration and experimentation or, at best, mere adventure! In actuality, the real values are quite different, since she is belayed (protected by a safety line), but the facilitator has chosen a very difficult route and expects her to fail. After considerable effort, she has fallen off the crux of the climb repeatedly and is exhausted. The facilitator now assists her in reflecting back on her misadventure and after some thought and discussion she realizes

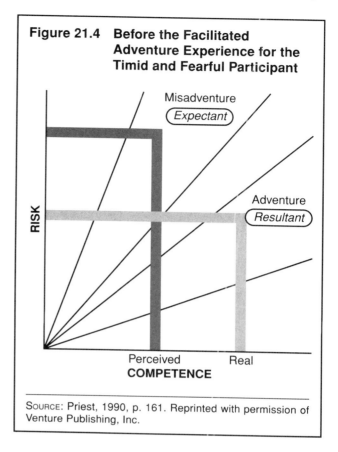

Figure 21.4   Before the Facilitated Adventure Experience for the Timid and Fearful Participant

SOURCE: Priest, 1990, p. 161. Reprinted with permission of Venture Publishing, Inc.

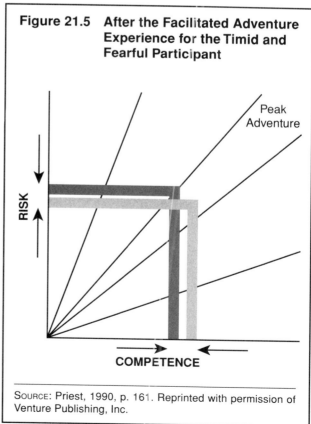

Figure 21.5   After the Facilitated Adventure Experience for the Timid and Fearful Participant

SOURCE: Priest, 1990, p. 161. Reprinted with permission of Venture Publishing, Inc.

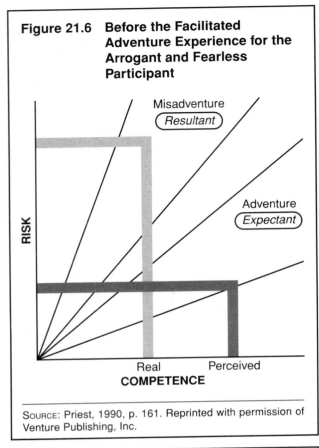

Figure 21.6   Before the Facilitated Adventure Experience for the Arrogant and Fearless Participant

Misadventure
(Resultant)

Adventure
(Expectant)

RISK

Real   Perceived
COMPETENCE

Source: Priest, 1990, p. 161. Reprinted with permission of Venture Publishing, Inc.

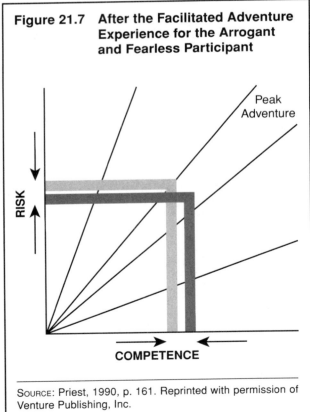

Figure 21.7   After the Facilitated Adventure Experience for the Arrogant and Fearless Participant

Peak Adventure

RISK

COMPETENCE

Source: Priest, 1990, p. 161. Reprinted with permission of Venture Publishing, Inc.

that the task was indeed more difficult than she expected and that she really was not as good as she was saying. This learning may later transfer to daily living concerns, where perhaps the woman expresses arrogant and fearless behaviors when working on projects as part of a small group.

These types of facilitated adventure experiences are repeated in different contexts, but with similar structuring and control. The upshot is that people slowly shift their perceptions toward becoming "in-tune" with reality: they slowly become astute! With astuteness often comes improvements in self-concept and in socialization. The interpersonal and intrapersonal relationships benefit from such adventure experiences. The paradigm described in this chapter helps visualize how this takes place.

References

Carpenter, G., and Priest, S. (1989). The adventure experience paradigm and nonoutdoor leisure pursuits. *Leisure Studies, 8*(1), 65–75.

Csikszentmihalyi, M. (1975). *Beyond boredom and anxiety.* San Francisco, CA: Jossey-Bass.

Ellis, M. J. (1973). *Why people play.* Englewood Cliffs, NJ: Prentice-Hall.

Martin, P., and Priest, S. (1986). Understanding the adventure experience. *Journal of Adventure Education, 3*(1), 18–21.

Mitchell, R. G. (1983). *Mountain experience: The psychology and sociology of adventure.* Chicago, IL: University of Chicago Press.

Mortlock, C. (1984). *The adventure alternative.* Cumbria, UK: Cicerone.

Priest, S., and Baillie, R. (1987) Justifying the risk to others: The real razor's edge. *Journal of Experiential Education, 10*(1), 6–22.

Priest, S. (1987). Modeling the adventure experience. In R. Yerkes (Ed.), *Outdoor education across America: Weaving the web* (pp. 7–12). Las Cruces, NM: ERIC CRESS.

Priest, S. (1990). The adventure experience paradigm. In J. C. Miles and S. Priest (Eds.), *Adventure education* (pp. 157–162). State College, PA: Venture Publishing, Inc.

Chapter 22

New Directions for Inquiry Into Self-Concept and Adventure Experiences

Kimberley Ann Klint
eXperientia

The adventure experience has been attributed with the potential for enhancing human development in the physical, cognitive and affective domains (Ford and Blanchard, 1985). Benefits associated with the adventure experience in the physical domain include increased levels of strength, cardiovascular and muscular endurance, and feelings of well-being. Cognitive development centers around development of an enriched body of knowledge associated with a variety of topics including the environment, safety skills and activity skills. Finally, self-concept, senses of achievement and motivation, and stress control represent some of the affective components which may be influenced by an adventure experience. This latter area is of particular interest to many adventure programmers. If adventure experiences can indeed enhance affective development, then planned adventure experiences could be considered attractive alternatives to therapeutic programming and human development.

The notion that adventure experiences offer opportunities for affective development is not new. The Outward Bound Movement has been the guiding ship for adventure education around the world since its conception in 1941 (Wichmann, 1976). The original aim of the movement was to build character and develop survival skills in young seamen. These goals directly address all three areas of human development: affective, cognitive, and physical. The initial Outward Bound experiences were deemed a success, and soon Outward Bound programs were established around the world. Other adventure programs also were

initiated, many modeling themselves after the Outward Bound program. The Outward Bound Movement came to North America in 1963.

Since its conception, the Outward Bound experience has been subject to the researcher's microscope. In particular, researchers have tested Outward Bound's claim that it is an experience through which personal growth and self-perceptions are enhanced (Ewert, 1983). Support for this hypothesis has been forwarded on repeated occasions. An Outward Bound experience has been found to enhance self-confidence and other self-perceptions (Fletcher, 1970; Hendy, 1976; Lee and Schoder, 1969; Nye, 1976; Stremba, 1977; Wetmore, 1972), reduce recidivism (Kelly and Baer, 1969), enhance motivation levels (Kolb, 1965), and enhance self-actualization (Vander Wilt and Klocke, 1971). The benefits of adventure have not been limited to the Outward Bound experience since similar results have been associated with many other adventure programs (cf., Ewert, 1983).

These studies are to be commended because they have attempted the difficult task of gaining quantitative understanding of affective development while maintaining the integrity of the adventure experience. Unfortunately, as with many compromising situations, these results paint a far from complete picture. Study findings support the hypothesis that the adventure experience can influence affective development. However, they fail to provide clues as to how this influence is developed, and more importantly, what aspects of the adventure experience are salient to the development of affect. In other words, there is understanding about what adventure experiences can potentially accomplish, and yet there are few insights as to how these potentials are fulfilled. Future research needs to move away from identifying products associated with adventure experiences and towards understanding the process. The testing of theoretical frameworks could provide a starting point for such studies. The purpose of this chapter is to review theories of self-concept which may be applied toward understanding the adventure experience.

Self-Concept

Self-concept is a generalized term referring to the mental image one creates about one's self. Other terms such as self-esteem, self-efficacy, self-confidence, and self-image refer to specific aspects of the self and sometimes their meanings overlap. For example, self-esteem refers to satisfaction and confidence in oneself, while self-confidence connotes confidence in one's abilities and powers to accomplish a goal or task.

Interest in "the self" as an influential factor of behavior dates back to the first century B.C. (Ewert, 1983). However, notions about how "the self" was involved were not crystallized until William James (1890) posed a theory of self-concept. He hypothesized that self-concept was related to achievement. He proposed that one's feelings of worthiness were a function of the ratio of one's actual achievements to one's aspirations. According to James, affect was viewed as central to the development of self-concept.

Cooley (1902/1956) challenged James' hypothesis that achievement and affects were the underlying aspects of self-concept. Cooley argued that social interactions were fundamental to the development of "the self." He felt that a sense of worth was developed through one's perceptions of how significant others felt about behaviors and appearances. In other words, self was a "looking-glass self," created from the information received from others.

Mead (1934) expanded Cooley's theory to include a cognitive perspective. Mead stated that sense of self was developed through a cognitive process, involving interpretation of self in the social context. Rosenberg (1979) further elaborated upon the notion that self-concept was associated with cognitive processes. However, Rosenberg suggested that the cognitive processes involved with self-concept development changed with the maturation process. Specifically, younger children rely on different information and processes in their self-concept development compared to older children and adults.

Many other theories of self-concept development have been forwarded; however, they are too numbered to described here. Many of these theories have expanded on one small aspect of the fore-described theories. However, acknowledgment of these theories is important since they encompass the fundamental principles of self-concept, as we currently understand it (Weiss, 1987). These principles include:

1. Self-concept is a function of social interactions.
2. Self-concept is multidimensional.
3. Affect is associated with the development of self-concept.
4. The degree to which successes and failures influence self-concept is a function of the importance one attributes to the activity.
5. Self-concept levels influence motivation levels.

It was suggested at the beginning of this chapter that further understanding into how self-concept is affected through the adventure experience should start with theoretical frameworks. However, quantitative research relies on theories which are testable and theories which are broken down into variables with identified constructs and relationships. Very few theories of self-concept meet these requirements. Fortunately, there are a few testable theories which include a self-concept component in their explanation of another human phenomenon such as motivation. These theories may be useful as a starting point for understanding the process of self-concept development in the adventure experience. These theories include Bandura's (1977) theory of self-efficacy and White's (1959) model of effectance motivation and its expansion into Harter's (1978, 1981) theory of competence motivation.

Self-Efficacy

Bandura's (1977) theory of self-efficacy is a cognitively based explanation of the motivational process. The theory revolves around ones' feelings of self-efficacy under mastery conditions. Self-efficacy is defined as the strength of an individual's belief that he or she can successfully accomplish a task which tests ability levels. According to Bandura, self-efficacy is based upon information derived from internal or external sources. Levels of self-efficacy, in turn, influence future mastery attempts through choice, effort, and persistence. Thus, perceptions of self-efficacy levels play the central role in the motivational process.

Self-efficacy has three dimensions. These are magnitude, generality and strength. These dimensions hold important implications for mastery performances. Magnitude of self-efficacy levels is influenced by perceptions of task difficulty. If a number of related tasks were ordered according to difficulty levels, one's efficacy expectations may only include the simple tasks, or it may be extended to include the more difficult tasks. In other words, one individual may hold expectations for success with only the simple tasks, while another person may believe that success will be achieved for all the tasks, including the most difficult tasks. Generality refers to the degree to which one limits or extends self-efficacy levels to different situations. For example, one may limit efficacy expectations to identical tasks, while another may generalize expectations for success to a range of situations. Finally, the strength dimension refers to how long one will hold on to high expectations for success despite contradictory information. For example, one with a weak strength dimension may lower self-efficacy levels after one failure, while one with a strong strength dimension may maintain high self-efficacy levels in the face of many past failures.

In summary, high self-efficacy expectations may be defined by strong degrees of magnitude, generality and strength. One may have low self-efficacy levels if magnitude, generality and strength dimensions are weak, and the task is novel. Intermediate levels of self-efficacy are determined by an interaction among the three dimensions.

Bandura's theory also states that self-efficacy levels are determined by the cognitive interpretation of information derived from four possible sources. These sources include performance accomplishments, vicarious experiences, verbal persuasion, and physiological arousal. Performance accomplishments refer to an individual's past experiences of success and failure in mastery experiences. Success increases mastery expectations, while repeated failures decrease expectations. The effects of single failures on expectations depend upon timing and circumstances. Failures early in learning tend to be more influential than failures in later stages. Also, failures that are later overcome by increased effort levels can strengthen self-efficacy levels to a greater degree than failures overcome by chance. Information gained through performance accomplishments is thought to be the most influential and stable source of information because it is based upon actual experiences.

However, actual experiences are not the only means in which information about self-efficacy is gained. Vicarious experiences can also provide meaningful information. Thus, observing another pursue similar mastery attempts without negative repercussions can enhance the observer's efficacy expectations. The modeling effects of vicarious experiences are relatively weak and unstable influences on self-efficacy. However, the more similar the actor is to the observer, the stronger the modeling effect is.

Efficacy expectations can also be affected by verbal persuasion. Again, this source of information is relatively weak compared to actual experience. However, in combination with vicarious or aided experiences, verbal persuasion can be a mobilizing factor. On the other hand, verbal persuasion followed by failure can have detrimental effects on self-efficacy levels.

Finally, physiological arousal levels can provide valuable information about self-efficacy. Since high arousal levels usually undermine performance, persons experiencing high anxiety levels might expect failure. Additionally, expectations for failure can further elevate arousal levels since the anticipation of failure may confirm thoughts about personal inabilities. Thus, arousal levels can influence self-efficacy levels, particularly for individuals who use arousal states to assess perceptions of vulnerability and stress.

In summary, expectations for success are enhanced if an individual has a history of success with similar tasks. The observation of others experiencing similar success, verbal persuasion from social sources, and low arousal levels may increase self-efficacy levels to a lesser degree. Finally, these four sources can influence self-efficacy levels independently or interactively.

According to Bandura, efficacy expectations determine performance through choice or avoidance of activities, the amount of effort associated with mastery attempts, and how long effort will be sustained in failure or stressful situations. Self-efficacy levels can influence one, two or all three of these motivated behaviors to different degrees. Bandura also suggested that the relationship between self-efficacy and performance is reciprocal: elevated efficacy expectations influence performance, and performance outcomes, in turn, influence self-efficacy levels.

In conclusion, Bandura's theory hypothesizes some possible antecedents and consequences of self-efficacy levels. Researchers in many different fields have applied Bandura's theory in attempts to understand how specific experiences influence self-efficacy levels. To date, only one published study has applied Bandura's theory to the adventure experience.

Brody, Hatfield, and Spalding (1988) investigated the generality dimension of the self-efficacy construct. Specifically, they were interested in how the levels of perceived self-efficacy developed through rappelling (a perceived high-risk adventure pursuit) were generalized to other perceived high-risk adventure pursuits such as rock climbing and scuba diving, as well as everyday potentially stressful situations like speaking to a group of strangers or coping with test anxiety. The study involved 34 male undergraduates with no experience in high-risk outdoor activities. The experimental group was exposed to two two-hour sessions of rappelling instruction. The other group received no treatment. The results revealed that self-efficacy levels associated with rappelling were enhanced after the treatment. More importantly, the perceived increase in self-efficacy was generalized to the other high-risk adventure activities, but not to the everyday potentially stressful activities. The authors concluded that the generalization of self-efficacy levels can extended to similar activities.

This study marks one direction future inquiry testing Bandura's theory of self-efficacy in the adventure context can take. It has moved beyond describing consequences of adventure experiences and provides insight to how these consequences, namely increased self-concept levels, are developed.

Perceived Competence

White's (1959) model of effectancy motivation offers another perspective on the motivational process. It is a simple model which states that behavior is the result of an "urge to competence." More specifically, individuals are motivated toward mastery attempts because they wish to have an effect on their environment. If a mastery attempt is achieved by a competent performance, then the urge is satisfied by feelings of efficacy or pleasure. These feelings of efficacy, in turn, increase or maintain effectance motivation. If motivation levels are increased, then future mastery attempts are initiated. Figure 22.1 displays White's model of effectancy motivation.

White's model was revolutionary because it challenged earlier notions that behaviors were instinctive. However, the theory was not operationalized, and thus, it could not be tested. Almost 20 years later, Harter (1978, 1981) built White's framework into a theory of competence motivation. It should be noted that Harter's theory is a developmental theory. It was specifically developed to understand the motivational process in maturing children. However, the directions in which Harter moved away from White's basic theory should have implications for understanding adult behavior. Harter expanded White's model to include the effects of social and interpersonal factors, as well as the effects of positive and negative experiences. She also hypothesized that the motivational process is domain specific. Figure 22.2 shows a model of Harter's theory of competence motivation.

The construct of perceived competence is one of the central components of Harter's theory. It is also the construct related to self-concept. According to Harter, perceived competence is a domain-specific measure of self-esteem. Thus, one develops a perceived competence level for each domain that one is involved with. This is in contrast to earlier theories which discuss a general sense of self. Harter also suggested that perceived competence levels were influenced by many factors: success or failure after mastery attempts; perceptions of control; motivational orientation; positive or negative reinforcement and approval from significant others; and characteristics of the task. In turn, perceived competence levels, in conjunction with perceptions of control, influence affective responses and effectance motivation. Effectance motivation levels are then associated with future mastery attempts.

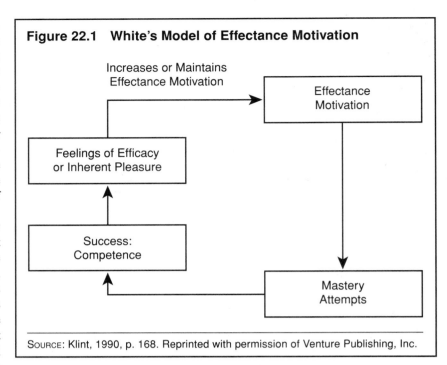

Figure 22.1   White's Model of Effectance Motivation

Source: Klint, 1990, p. 168. Reprinted with permission of Venture Publishing, Inc.

The complexities of Harter's theory may best be explained through an example. Suppose an individual decided to attempt a new rock climb route. If the level of route difficulty matches the skill level of the climber, then the task is described as optimally challenging. Achievement of optimally challenging tasks has a greater impact

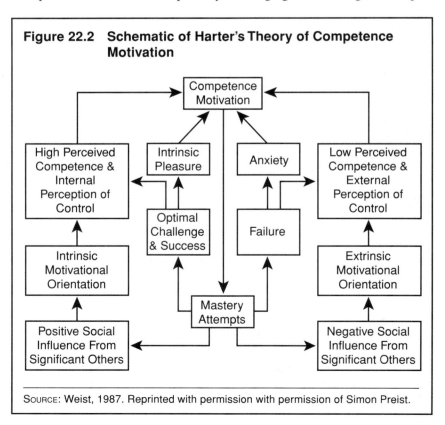

Figure 22.2   Schematic of Harter's Theory of Competence Motivation

Source: Weist, 1987. Reprinted with permission with permission of Simon Preist.

on self-perceptions. If the climber is successful in the attempt, then positive affects such as enjoyment or intrinsic pleasure are experienced. Additionally, success can increase levels of perceived rock-climbing competence and enhance the likelihood that internal perceptions of control are developed. In other words, the climber attributes the success to internal sources like effort and ability. The climb attempt can also receive positive reinforcement and approval from significant others like climbing friends. If this is the case, then the information provided in the reinforcement is internalized to develop self-reward systems. Specifically, the climber develops an intrinsic motivational orientation, meaning that the climber chooses activities which provide self-satisfaction and meet self-determined standards of performance. An intrinsic motivational orientation further enhances perceived competence levels and internal perceptions of control. These self-perceptions augment affective reactions such as pleasure. The combination of positive self-perceptions and affects, in turn, increase motivational levels. The climber is likely to attempt the task again.

On the contrary, failure in the climbing attempt can diminish motivational levels as negative affects and self-perceptions are experienced. Repeated failure eventually reduces perceived climbing competence levels, and might lead to external perceptions of control. In other words, the climber may attribute the failure to external reasons such as difficulty of the route or that bad luck was involved. Additionally, the lack of reinforcement and approval from significant others may result in the development of extrinsic motivational orientation. The climber may begin to choose routes which meet other people's approval and strive to meet external standards of performance. An extrinsic motivational orientation tends to decrease perceived competence levels and enhance external perceptions of control. Decreasing self-perceptions and negative affects such as anxiety, in turn, decrease effectance motivation. The climber may not attempt that particular route again.

This generalized explanation of Harter's theory does not suggest that a single success or failure experience has an immediate effect on future motivation levels. Past experiences play an important role in the process. However, self-perceptions are probably modified to a slight degree with single experiences.

To date, Harter's theory has not been tested in the adventure domain. This can be partially attributed to the fact that the theory and the instruments created by measuring various variables are directed toward children between the ages of 7 to 16 years of age. However, this theory could form the basis of adventure experience research since it is testable and many of the constructs have been operationalized. Further, many of the instruments have been modified to domain-specific versions. For example, the perceived physical competence scale developed by Harter has been modified to sport-specific scales in basketball, baseball, soccer, and gymnastics.

Future Research

Inquiry into the adventure experience needs to move into the next stage, from describing the product to understanding the process. It was suggested that theoretically based research could serve as a starting point for these future inquiries. However, the call for theoretically based research on the adventure experience does not mean that experimental research designs are the only direction to follow. The theories presented in this chapter were offered because they identify some of the elements apparently involved in the development of self-concept.

Future inquiry based upon Bandura's theory can focus upon which information sources are associated with the adventure experience, and more importantly, which of these information sources are involved in the self-concept changes which result from adventure experiences. Further inquiry can investigate which of the three dimensions of self-efficacy are most susceptible to change in the adventure experience. Additionally, the meaning or implications of changes in these self-efficacy dimensions are worthy of future inquiry.

White's and Harter's theories of competence motivation can also provide a valuable framework for theoretical research. Again, Harter's theory designates antecedents of perceived competence. These include success and failure, degree and type of reinforcement from others, motivational orientation, and perceptions of control. Inquiry into the adventure experience can examine which of these factors are associated with the experience and which factors are related with changes in perceived competence levels. Additionally, inquiry can explore which of these factors influence perceived competence levels to the greatest degree and how the influences of these factors can be maximized in the adventure experience.

In summary, the quantitative and theoretical researchers can test these theories in the adventure context by creating situations which isolate the selected factors. Thus, they can begin to identify which aspects and how the adventure experience influence self-concept levels. This, in turn, would allow adventure programmers to enhance the adventure experience by focusing upon these salient factors.

However, future inquiry into self-concept development in the adventure experience is not limited to quantitative research. The self-concept theories of Bandura, White and Harter can also serve as starting points for qualitative researchers. The hypotheses of these theories can function as the first working hypothesis in an emergent design (see Lincoln and Guba, 1985). The inquirer can then purposefully seek knowledge which supports or refutes the working hypothesis. The additional information will gradually allow the inquirer to modify the working hypothesis so that it conveys the essence of self-concept in the adventure context. Eventually, the inquirer should create an understanding of self-concept as relates to the adventure experience.

This context-specific understanding of self-concept can then be quantitatively tested by a quantitative researcher.

The theories of self-concept can also assist the qualitative inquirer by identifying respondents from qualitative study. For example, the inquirer can use the quantitative instruments developed to measure specific aspects (variables) of a theory. The inquirer can then purposefully select respondents whose answers support the theoretical hypothesis, as well as those whose answers are unpredictable. This type of respondent selection will facilitate the development of a context-specific understanding of self-concept development in the adventure experience.

In conclusion, inquiry needs to move forward towards an understanding of *how* the adventure experience influences human perceptions and behavior. However, this inquiry process does not need to start in square one. The body of knowledge created by social psychology can serve as a departure point. The theories of Bandura, White and Harter, among others, probably have application to inquiry into the adventure experience. Both quantitative and qualitative inquirers can benefit from the works of our social psychology peers. Both types of inquiry can be combined to create a holistic understanding of the essence of the adventure experience; an essence which can be communicated with those not yet enlightened.

References

Bandura, A. (1977). Self-efficacy: Toward a unifying theory for behavioral change. *Psychological Review, 84,* 191–215.

Brody, E., Hatfield, B., and Spalding, T. (1988). Generalization of self-efficacy to a continuum of stressers upon mastery of a high-risk sport skill. *Journal of Sport Psychology, 10,* 32–44.

Cooley, C. H. (1956). *Human nature and the social order.* Glencoe, IL: Free Press. (Original work published 1902).

Ewert, A. (1983). *Outdoor adventure and self-concept: A research analysis.* Eugene, OR: Center of Leisure Studies, University of Oregon.

Fletcher, B. (1970). *Students of Outward Bound schools in Great Britain: A follow-up study.* (ERIC Document Reproduction Service No. ED 050 325).

Ford, P., and Blanchard, J. (1985). *Leadership and administration of outdoor pursuits.* State College, PA: Venture Publishing, Inc.

Harter, S. (1978). Effectance motivation reconsidered. *Human Development, 21,* 34–64.

Harter, S. (1981). A model of intrinsic mastery motivation in children: Individual differences and developmental changes. In W. A. Collins (Ed.), *Minnesota Symposium on Child Psychology* (Vol. 14, pp. 215–255). Hillsdale, NJ: Erlbaum.

Hendy, C. (1976). *Outward Bound and personality: 16PF profiles of instructors and ipsative changes in male and female students 16–19 years of age.* Unpublished doctoral dissertation, University of Oregon, Eugene, Oregon.

James, W. (1890). *The principles of psychology.* New York, NY: Henry Holt.

Kelly, F., and Baer, D. (1969). *Outward Bound: An alternative to institutionalization for adolescent delinquent boys.* Boston, MA: Fandel Press.

Klint, K. A. (1990). New directions for inquiry into self-concept and adventure experiences. In J. C. Miles and S. Priest (Eds.), *Adventure education* (pp. 161–172). State College, PA: Venture Publishing, Inc.

Kolb, D. (1965). Achievement motivation training for underachieving high-school boys. *Journal of Personality and Social Psychology, 2*(6).

Lincoln, Y., and Guba, E. (1985). *Naturalistic inquiry.* Beverly Hills, CA: Sage

Lee, R., and Schoder, H. (1969). Effects of Outward Bound training on urban youth. *Journal of Special Education, 3*(2).

Mead, G. H. (1934). *Mind, self and society.* Chicago, IL: University of Chicago Press.

Nye, R., Jr. (1976). *The influence of an Outward Bound program on the self-concept of the participants.* Unpublished doctoral dissertation, Temple University, Philadelphia, Pennsylvania.

Rosenberg, M. (1979). *Conceiving the self.* New York, NY: Basic Books.

Stremba, R. (1977). *A study of the relationship between participation in an Outward Bound program and changes in self-esteem and locus of control.* Unpublished doctoral dissertation, Indiana University, Bloomington, Indiana.

Vander Wilt, R., and Klocke, R. (1971). Self-actualization of females in an experimental orientation program. *National Association of Women's Deans and Counselors Journal, 34*(3).

Weiss, M. (1987). Self-esteem and achievement in children's sport and physical activity. In M. Weiss and D. Gould (Eds.), *Advances in pediatric sport science, Vol. 2.* Champaign, IL: Human Kinetics.

Wetmore, R. (1972). *The influence of Outward Bound school experience on the self-concept for adolescent boys.* Unpublished doctoral dissertation, Boston University, Boston, Massachusetts.

Wichmann, T. (1976). *Affective role expectations for delinquent youth in environmental stress-challenge programs.* (ERIC Document Reproduction Service No. ED 156 394).

White, R. (1959). Motivation reconsidered: The concept of competence. *Psychological Review, 66,* 297–333.

Chapter 23

Practical Stories in a Theoretical Framework

Peter Martin
La Trobe University

I started teaching people to climb long before I started lecturing, reading and researching adventure education. I can clearly remember the opening classes in my master's degree where I was introduced to the book by Mihaly Csikszentmihalyi, *Beyond Boredom and Anxiety* (1975). What struck me most about Csikszentmihalyi's work was that it made sense to me as a rock climber. It made sense because Csikszentmihalyi helped develop the groundedness of his writing and research with direct reference to practice and practitioners, many of whom were climbers:

> The task at hand is so demanding and rich in its complexity and pull that the conscious subject is really diminished in intensity. Corollary of that is that all the hang-ups that people have or that I have as an individual person are momentarily obliterated. . . . It's one of the few ways I have found to . . . live outside my head. (Rock climber quoted in Csikszentmihalyi, 1975, p. 43)

His description of the "flow experience" (p. 36) put into words for me what I had personally known, through the direct experience of climbing, for almost a decade. I identified closely with the comments made by climbers— as a consequence I was intrigued by the academic synthesis which enabled the evolution of the concept of flow and my understanding of the flow experience, and how I gained it, was enhanced.

I now lecture in outdoor and adventure education at a university. One of the important points I like to remember from my experiences with the flow concept, is that theory is a construction of reality. At least in the study of human behavior, what comes first is observation or attention to some phenomena, after which an inquiring mind begins to interpret and develop constructs to examine or explain the phenomena more closely. Csikszentmihalyi describes how his research into flow developed:

> The ideas presented here began to crystallize in my mind about a dozen years ago, as I was observing artists at work. One thing struck me as especially intriguing. Despite the fact that almost no one can make either a reputation or a living from painting, the artists studied were almost fanatically devoted to their work . . . nothing else seemed to matter so much in their lives (p. xi).

What I have come to conclude in my own work with students is that the links between theorizing about adventure and adventure itself need to be inextricably linked and understood in terms of the way each complements the other. I like to remind myself that good theory in adventure education improves educational outcomes, enables more directed learning, and helps to minimize unnecessary risks. In a reciprocal way, good reflective practice can help interpret and also generate theory, which in turn assists future practice. I have found that if students can understand theoretical constructs in terms of their own practical adventure experiences, and vice versa, then they seem to take off on a developmental spiral of theorizing and application of theory in practice which seems unending. To this end, this chapter is aimed at telling practical stories within a broader framework of theoretical understanding.

My first realization in writing here, is that it is impossible to relate a practical story that can somehow illuminate all theory of interest to adventure education; even if it was, I couldn't do it. The approach I wish to take will therefore be eclectic and purposive—I have chosen theory which I think helps illuminate practice, picking and choosing from the gamut of different ideas that have been proffered as explanatory of human behavior. The position I wish to establish at the outset is that theory must make sense in practice, it must gel with the experiential trial-and-error knowledge that practitioners have distilled and evolved over time. It must be pragmatic. After all, theories about say, how people form opinions of their own competence to complete a rock climb, are just that, theories. Researchers, philosophers, and poets can't know for sure what goes on inside my head when I'm standing below the overhang tied onto the sharp end of a climbing rope. A theory about human behavior is essentially a researcher's best guess, albeit an informed one, about what a person is thinking or feeling during various circumstances. Because it is a guess, it is also an interpretation of reality. Any practical story is also an interpretation of reality. Selecting the theory and context to relate here is my first act of interpretation. My interpretations are based on my experience as a lecturer and instructor and are grounded in my interpretations of research, which I have eclectically chosen, driven by my view of pragmatic relevance to adventure education and the reality of limited time and space. The context of my story is abseiling, the theoretical perspectives are attribution theory and efficacy theory.

The final abseil was one that had a reputation. When David came to the last wall he balked. He had descended two short, easy angled walls already, but there was no way he was going over the edge here. The drop was not huge, perhaps a little over 20 meters, but it disappeared into a dark hole. The bottom was hidden from above by an overhang. David knew enough about abseiling to know that the last part of the descent would be away from the cliff, hanging in space. He knew his full weight would be on the rope, his feet helpless to take any load off his hands gripping the rope. He knew he was a bit heavier than the other kids, and felt less comfortable supporting his own weight. . . . He wasn't going to do it.

The brief story described here is pretty typical of the issues faced by adventure educators, where students are confronted with a challenge and begin to wonder about their own competence to safely complete the task. As practitioners we have developed strategies to work through situations such as this. (You may have dealt with this exact situation yourself. Before I consider what theoretical perspectives have to offer here, it's worth noting what you would do, the options you might exercise in this circumstance; given you want David to feel empowered and self-competent.)

One interesting idea from the adventure education literature which could be applied to this situation is the model of Competence for Human Risk-Taking Behavior proposed by Priest (1993). Priest's model is a graphic representation, or diagram, which incorporates several important theoretical perspectives on human behavior (Figure 23.1). To follow David's story through the Priest model we need to go back and look at what happened prior to David's arrival at the final abseil.

David has already abseiled twice before in the program. After the first abseil he just felt relieved to be down. David didn't really understand what was going on—nor how he really managed to get down at all—he'd been pretty scared. The wall was short and low angled enough that he could have pretty much walked straight back up it, if he wished— which he did not! The instructor had taken much of David's weight on the safety line. There had been plenty of very specific instructions about how to complete the task . . . "feet apart, weight in your harness, shoulders back;" and lots of encouragement "good effort, you're doing well. . . ."

At this stage we are at point 2 in the Priest model— "sufficient competence performed"—although who determines success and by what definition is problematic (1993, p. 51). After his first abseil David will have formed a set of understandings which help him explain his abseiling experience—these are called attributions. Research suggests we all do this, frequently, as a way to help us make sense of the world around us. Attribution theory in social psychology research has developed into a substantial body of knowledge, beginning with Heider's causal analyses of perception in 1954 (Weary, Stanley, and Harvey, 1989). We make attributions for both ourselves (self-attributions) and for others with ourselves as observers (observer attributions). In forming attributions we utilize two prime sources of data: information about the person (internal attributions) and information about the situation or environment in which behavior takes place (external attributions) (Weary et al., 1989). My description made of David, from

Figure 23.1   A Theoretical Model of Competence Effectance for Human Risk-Taking Behavior

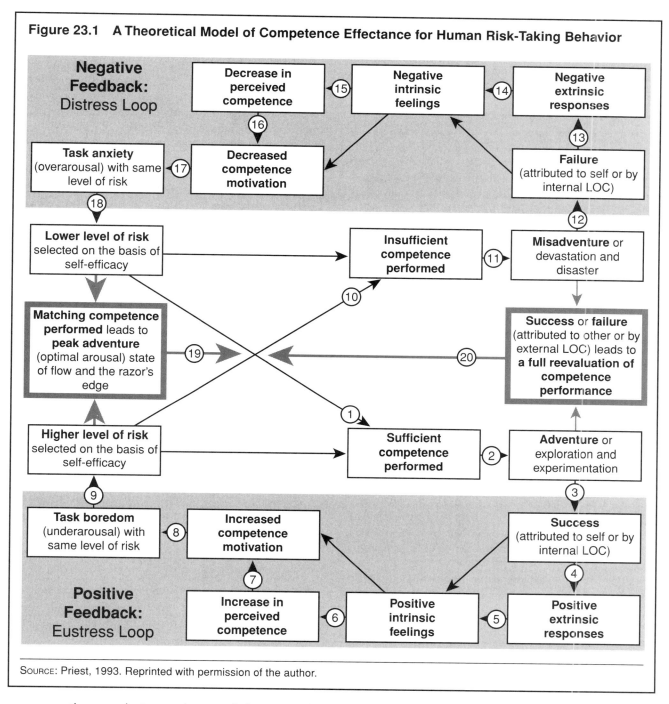

Source: Priest, 1993. Reprinted with permission of the author.

my perspective as an instructor, is a set of observer attributions. In my story I have attributed David's performance to internal factors about David and external factors about the situation.

> *(He) didn't really understand what was going on, . . . he'd been pretty scared . . . the wall was short and low angled. . . . The instructor had taken much of David's weight. . . . There had been plenty of very specific instructions about how to complete the task.*

David has also made a set of self-attributions to explain his experience. What they are I can never be certain, but similar external and internal sources are available. An external attribution would see David attributing his completion of the abseil to factors outside himself, such as the instructor's advice or safety line. An internal attribution would acknowledge David's own skill, strength, weight or attitude in shaping the outcome.

> *The second abseil was at a different site. The wall was higher. David seemed really scared*

of the height, he seemed very worried with how he could control his descent. Again the instructor explained and encouraged, although this time another student controlled the safety rope. David descended in erratic jerks. He looked unable to develop a feel for the rope and how much friction was needed to control his descent. David's luck held; he made it to the bottom.

What attribution does David make? If he judges his experience to be a successful one and does so due to his own abilities, he moves onto the pathway described by Priest as a "positive feedback: eustress loop" (1993, p. 51)—a loop which will see him gain in motivation and competence before eventually becoming bored and moving on to more difficult challenges. Alternatively, if David perceives his abseiling as unsuccessful, or successful only because of external agents such as luck, then he, at best, is forced to reevaluate his own competence, at worst, embarks on a "negative feedback: distress loop" ending in lowered perceptions of competence, task anxiety and avoidance (1993, p. 51). The Priest model describes possible pathways, it is the intent of this chapter to consider the practical options that an instructor can choose to help influence which of those pathways is traveled.

In my description of David's abseiling I have implied a set of observer attributions which seek to explain or make sense of David's behavior. As a teacher an important part of my job is to observe and draw such conclusions about causes of a student's behaviors. For the second abseil, my description explains David's poor performance by his apparent lack of skill and fear of heights—both are internal observer attributions. I have described David as the author of his actions, rather than an actor in a controlling environment.

How does David interpret the situation? Perhaps he has also begun to shift his self-attribution to more internal sources—"my skill level is really low, I don't understand this, I'm too heavy, I'm not strong enough." Again as an instructor I can never be certain about what my students think; but making such judgments is a necessary, indeed essential, part of teaching.

Before I go back to consider the action I might now take with David as he hesitates at the top of the third abseil, I need to reflect on the judgments I have already made. I have presented the description of events so far as facts, in much the same way as I might relate details of a teaching event to a colleague over lunch. But clearly they are not facts. I have told a story, my interpretation of events. My observer attributions are primed to fundamentally influence how I will relate to David at the top of the last abseil, but are they trustworthy? In attribution theory jargon, are my attributions "stable," unlikely to change, or are they "unstable," tentative and easily altered? Importantly also for teaching, are the attributions due to causes which are

"controllable," within David's control such as how much he is concentrating, or are they due to "uncontrollable" factors, such as David's body weight (Weiner, 1986). Was David *really* scared? Did he *really* not understand what was happening and *clearly* lack the basic skills to abseil, or were other external factors influential? Attribution theory research concludes I should consider three main factors prior to determining the trustworthiness of my attributions: consistency, consensus, and distinctiveness (Weiner, 1986).

Consistency asks if the behavior is consistent over time, from one event to the next. In David's case how many abseils are required to satisfy the instructor that David is fearful is still judgmental. However, it is hardly likely that only two abseils are sufficient to satisfy aspects of consistency—my judgments of David's poor ability may have been too hasty.

Consensus seeks to determine if the observed behavior is also evident for others in the same setting, or would be expected by others in the setting (normative). During the abseil session were other participants similarly fearful and confused? This aspect has not been part of my story, but should have been. One of the reasons that true consensus is not applied is that a "false consensus effect" occurs where the instructor may subconsciously ignore the behavior of other participants and substitute their own false consensus information by seeing their own behavior as typical (Kelley in Vaughan and Hogg, 1995, p. 59). False consensus information is derived by the instructor assuming that under similar circumstances they would be behaving in a particular way, which they then adopt as the norm. The need for instructors to be wary of this tendency, and to therefore deliberately seek true consensus information through accurate observation of other participants, is essential.

Distinctiveness is a test to determine the influential element(s) in the behavior. Is David fearful and slow to learn skills in other situations or is it just something about abseiling? How did he behave during the canoe session, the ropes course or in the dining room?

As an instructor, I can only make sound judgments about the causes of a participant's behavior (observer attribution) if I have applied tests of consistency, consensus, and distinctiveness to observations about both the person and the situation. My story is incomplete here; I suspect some of my past teaching judgments may have been also.

Biases in Attributions

As well as the need to gain additional information to help determine the accuracy of an observer attribution, research has identified several biases in the way we determine causal attributions. We apparently tend to oversimplify causal explanations and to put too much weight on the salient readily observable, rather than hidden, factors (Zimbardo and Leippe, 1991, p. 93). Also "there is an attributional bias that is so pervasive and so full of implications that it has been dubbed the fundamental attribution error" (Ross in Zimbardo and Leippe, 1991, p. 93). The fundamental attribution error is that observers tend to overestimate the influence of internal factors and underestimate the importance of situational factors. Although there is evidence to suggest that cultural aspects have influence here, at least in Western culture (Fletcher and Ward, 1988) it seems that human nature is such that we lay causal explanation or blame at the feet of the person, more readily than we identify extenuating circumstances. An extension of the fundamental attributional error is what has been called the actor-observer effect which refers to propensity for observers, such as teachers, to attribute other people's behavior to internal factors, while attributing their own behaviors to external environmental factors. This is particularly the case for failure situations (Chen, Yates, and McGinnies, 1988).

Attribution biases is one of those junctures between theory and practice where important implications exist for those in the field. In David's case, I may have sought only superficial obvious and easy explanations, or my observations may have inappropriately concentrated on David's performance rather than the surrounding context. Informed by this knowledge I could reevaluate my observations and attributions. Perhaps I could have observed the following:

> *The safety rope, controlled now by a novice student, was too tight, then too loose, it sent mixed messages to David as he struggled to determine just how much friction he needed to apply to control his descent. He had earlier watched a student's descent suddenly restricted by the safety rope so that his feet dropped too low and he smashed his shins into the wall—David feared a similar situation.*

The task of accurately determining causal factors is daunting, yet is a common aspect of instructors' work. Our observer attributions influence how we relate to participants; however the pathways actually followed are determined by participant's self-attributions. As instructors we are therefore also faced with the task of helping students make appropriate self-attributions.

Self-Attributions?

One of the outcomes I seek through adventure education is that participants develop a stable controllable internal self-attribution of success from outdoor involvement. In this situation participants would see themselves as competent to safely participate in a life involving continued interactions with the outdoors. I consider this the first step in gaining other pervasive outcomes concerned with appropriate sustainable human nature relationships (see Chapter 60, Critical Outdoor Education and Nature as a Friend). A stable controllable internal self-attribution of success

from outdoor involvement leads to the positive, eustress loop described by Priest (1993, p. 51).

However, having students all departing an adventure experience with stable internal controllable self-attributions of success, seems pretty much a dream to me. The actuality of teaching is that I often seem faced with the reality of disparate outcomes, precipitated by varying factors, for diverse participants. In such a scenario judging how to help participants form appropriate self-attributions becomes a critical teaching issue.

As discussed earlier, attributions can be internal external, stable unstable, controllable or uncontrollable. When considered with attributions for either success or failure, this provides for a set of diverse possible self-attributions following any experience (Table 23.1, page 174).

Not withstanding the comments already made with respect to observer attribution and attribution biases, instructors are often able, by virtue of experience, to make accurate judgments about the causes of participant's behaviors. Encouraging particular self-attributions from participants demands this.

While the options from Table 23.1 (page 174) may initially look confusing, the choices for the instructor come down to two essential questions about internal or external attribution:

1. *Should I encourage an* internal *attribution here?* An internal attribution will be laying causal explanation with the participant. This may be appropriate if the person has control over his or her capacity to improve but needs encouragement to reapply himself or herself or work harder, if he or she has succeeded deservedly, or if the person needs to be encouraged to understand his or her limitations.
2. *Should I encourage an* external *attribution here?* An external attribution lays causal explanation with the situation. This may be appropriate if the person has reached the limit of his or her capabilities, if he or she has succeeded without effort or application, or if the situation was not as it initially seemed and was, or became, beyond his or her control.

As an example, in David's case if I had judged that he was quite capable of completing the task to a higher standard, then I may encourage an internal attribution. "David, you seem pretty tense, and seem to be gripping the abseil rope too tightly. You have a good basic position but. . . ." I could then give specific information to help David modify his behavior. The power to change lies within David's capacity to understand and apply modifications to his actions. The attribution I am encouraging here is internal, unstable and within David's control. With assistance in recognizing the aspects he is already doing well, I am hoping David will be motivated to accept the challenge.

Table 23.1   Possible Self-Attributions Following an Adventure Experience

Type of Cause		Outcome Attributed to, for Example:	
		If Fail:	**If Succeed:**
Unstable	External, Uncontrollable	• Bad luck • Little shame, low influence on future action	• Good luck • Little pride, next time? • Can decrease motivation
Unstable	External, Controllable	• Attention to poor advice • Reevaluation of self and source of advice, positive influence on future action	• Advice understood • Some pride, transfer to learning possible
Unstable	Internal, Uncontrollable	• Illness, phobia, hormonal • Little shame, expect improvement in future with changed situation	• Buzz of adrenalin, euphoric mood • Enjoyment, some motivation for future
Unstable	Internal, Controllable	• Insufficient effort • Some shame, expect future improvement if motivated to do so	• Hard work, effort • High satisfaction, increased self-efficacy • Increased motivation
Stable	External, Uncontrollable	• Difficult task • No shame, but little expectation of future success	• Easy task • Some pride, some motivation to harder task, potential boredom
Stable	External, Controllable	• Poor choice and/or description of task • Little shame, some motivation	• Consistent good advice • Little pride, expect future success if linked with advice
Stable	Internal, Uncontrollable	• Wrong body size/shape • Some shame, decreased motivation	• Right body size/shape • Some satisfaction, pride, increased motivation
Stable	Internal, Controllable	• Low ability, poor fitness • Shame, future task avoidance	• High ability, good fitness • High satisfaction, stable high self-efficacy • Expect future success

Alternatively, if I had judged a participant to be beyond the limit of his or her present ability and unlikely to improve, I may encourage an external attribution. "Good try, but I think this is too hard for you at the moment." A comment such as this attributes the outcome to an external cause (difficult task). It has hinted at the possibility of future change but not without implying significant future effort. In adventure activities I consider it important that participants understand that not all activities will be within their capabilities, especially in the short term. Realistic feedback on the difficulty of the task compared to participant's ability is essential in helping to develop participant astuteness in determining the competence-risk balance (Martin and Priest, 1986).

Self-Efficacy

I will now return to David at the top of the third abseil. David has completed two earlier abseils, he has a set of attributions to explain his experiences so far. As he con-

templates his immediate future abseiling, research suggests he will form two sets of expectations: self-efficacy expectations and outcome expectations. Efficacy expectations are concerned with questions such as, how effectively will I be able to perform this task? Outcome expectations are concerned with questions such as, what outcomes will occur, what will happen here (Bandura,[1] 1997, p. 21)? While attribution theory has researched and described the way people develop causal explanations for past behavior, self-efficacy theory is the body of knowledge and research concerned with how people contemplate future behavior. Although debate exists between the two theoretical perspectives, I find both have something to offer the practitioner.

Outcome expectations are a judgment of the likely consequences of participation. David will be imagining

[1] Albert Bandura is the author of multiple works on self-efficacy. His book, *Self-efficacy: The Exercise of Control* (1997), summarizes decades of research and writing on self-efficacy. It is perhaps the definitive contemporary work on the subject.

the outcomes of abseiling: positive outcomes, such as excitement, peer recognition, and self-satisfaction will become incentives to participation. Negative outcomes such as fear, ridicule, or self-condemnation will become disincentives (Bandura, 1997). However, achieving any outcome ultimately depends on David's performance, and that is largely a function of his sense of self-efficacy, of how effectively he will be able to complete the abseil.

Self-efficacy is concerned with an individual's judgments about himself or herself as actors in a complex world. Self-efficacy is interested explicitly with self-judgments of capacity. (This differs from self-esteem, which is concerned with issues of self-worth.) Self-efficacy has been shown to influence personal health and well-being, levels and extent of motivation, and demonstration of ability (Bandura, 1997). As a theoretical construct which describes human behavior it is profoundly relevant to adventure educators.

Self-efficacy is not just a person's description of his or her own performance, rather, self-efficacy expectations are formed from subjective inferences. As an example, research repeatedly illustrates that self-efficacy exerts an effect on performance somewhat independent of real ability levels (Bandura, 1997). What is of direct relevance to outdoor instructors is that induced levels of self-efficacy lead to subsequent behavior change in that direction (Bandura, 1997). If David believes he is no good at abseiling then he will not persevere, will give up readily in the face of difficulties and uncertainty. As a consequence his sense of self-efficacy with respect to abseiling will be reinforced. On the other hand, if David has high self-efficacy, he will endure difficult situations longer, try harder, and work with more assuredness. As a consequence he will greatly improve his chances of success, therefore consolidating his sense of efficacy. The need for instructors to gain an understanding of how participants determine self-efficacy levels is therefore compelling.

Sources of Self-Efficacy

Self-efficacy information is derived from four main sources of information: prior performance, vicarious performance, verbal persuasion, and emotional arousal (Bandura, 1997, p. 79). *Prior performances* or "enactive mastery experiences," are the most influential in determining self-efficacy (Bandura, 1997, p. 80). Participants look back at previous experiences to help determine how they will perform future actions; this makes sense. However what is important is that participants determine their ability based on their own perceptions of the prior performance, not the performance itself judged by some objective measure. It is the participants' self-attribution that will have most influence on their expectations. In a teaching situation the same level of performance may raise, lower or leave unaltered, self-efficacy expectations within a group, depending on how the performance was individually attributed.

Self-efficacy does not fluctuate wildly with every momentary success or failure; rather, people develop views of themselves and their own capabilities, and as a result self-efficacy is quite resilient (Cervone and Palmer, 1990; Newman and Goldfried, 1987). Even in novel experiences, such as first time abseiling or canoeing, people will develop self-efficacy expectations based on their perceptions of relevant prior experiences. In terms of enabling participants to learn and grow from adventure experiences, one of the challenges for instructors then becomes the very resilient nature of self-efficacy beliefs. This is particularly the case for those participants low in self-efficacy. Albert Bandura, who has conducted much research in the area of self-efficacy, could well be talking about the potential value of adventure education for at-risk youth, in his following comments about the resilience of self-efficacy:

> Self-beliefs that have served a protective function for years are not quickly discarded. People who doubt their coping efficacy are more likely to distrust their success experiences than to risk more involving encounters with threats they doubt they can adequately control. When experience contradicts firmly held beliefs of weak efficacy, people resist changing their views of themselves if they can find grounds to discount the diagnostic value of the success experience. In such instances, producing enduring, generalized changes in personal efficacy requires powerful confirmatory experiences in which people successfully manage, under diverse conditions, task demands that far exceed those commonly encountered in everyday lives. They hold their efficacy beliefs in a provisional status, testing their new knowledge and skills before raising their judgments of what they are able to do. As they gain increasing ability to predict and manage potential threats, they develop a robust sense of efficacy that serves them well in mastering new challenges. (Bandura, 1997, p. 83)

The importance of prior mastery performances in shaping self-efficacy leads to important practical implications. Instructors have long known of the need for a slow sequenced progression in skill learning, but a slow sequenced progression is also vital for the shaping of self-efficacy. Initial success must exist if participants are to have a point of reference upon which to build future expectations of competence. A slow progression may not in itself be sufficient. In David's case the progression was inadequate because he had not had the opportunity to establish an appropriate internal causal explanation for his earlier abseiling experiences. David would have been better served by opportunities to repeat his abseiling experience at the same site, perhaps several times, before moving on to a more complex or difficult task. By enabling students to undertake additional performances they have the opportunity of shifting their self-attribution to a more internal cause, such as their own skill development. With a more internal attribution they can then begin to move around the positive eustress loop of the Priest model (Priest, 1993, p. 51). When students have mastered the task, and aspects of task familiarity shift student's reactions towards "boredom" outcomes then it is time to move on (Csikszentmihalyi, 1975, p. 49).

Within this framework of sequenced progression and repeat performances, the instructor can begin to increasingly attribute successes to the participant by highlighting the competent aspects of performance. In addition, as the sequence progresses the instructor actually does less to facilitate the experience. Participants slowly take charge of more and more aspects of the activity as both their ability and concentration capacity allows.

I will now apply this thinking to David's abseiling experience. During his first abseil David was guided, quite necessarily, by specific direct instruction. He would have made at least a degree of external attribution to account for the instructor's advice. Instead of moving on to the next abseil site, had David been allowed to repeat his performance, this time with decreasing amounts of instructor assistance, then it is more likely that his attribution would have become more internal, finding causal explanations in his own ability rather than the instructor's coaching. While repeat performance opportunities may have been appropriate for David, they may not have been necessary for others in the group.

Vicarious performance is also an influential source of self-efficacy information. Although grading systems exist for some outdoor adventure situations, most activities lack any objective measures of competence. In situations such as these, participants often refer to achievements or actions of other participants to help determine the effectiveness of their own actions (Festinger, 1954; Suls and Miller, 1977). Within any group there always seems to be some form of either overt or covert comparisons between different levels of performance.

Vicarious performance refers to participants gaining virtual experience through some other form, such as watching a demonstration. In terms of helping participants develop positive self-efficacy expectations, performance modeling becomes a powerful tool. Through watching others perform a task, participants can begin to see themselves in the same situation, prelearning skills, but also conceiving of themselves as actors in context. The common remark of "if he (she) can do it, so can I" is more a subconscious reference to perceived self-efficacy, than it is a comment on observed performance. The power of vicarious experience on self-efficacy works in both directions. A failed performance by a person perceived to be similarly competent, despite significant efforts, serves to lower one's

own self-efficacy—unless one notices an error, in which case efficacy can actually be enhanced. Vicarious performance is particularly powerful in shaping self-efficacy when the task is novel (Takata and Takata in Bandura, 1997).

The practical implications of the power of vicarious experiences in helping to shape self-efficacy are enticing. Demonstrations and the use of models are effective in raising expectations of success, but only if the actor is perceived to be similarly skilled to the participants. Often when I demonstrate a particular climbing move my students respond by saying "that's okay for you but what about me, I don't have your height, experience, or confidence." As a consequence, I often use fellow participants as effective models. Usually those who volunteer to take this role will already have a high sense of efficacy for the situation—the chances are they will give successful demonstrations and help inspire others in the group more effectively. Interestingly, research suggests that people may gain more from watching models struggle to overcome problems with effort, compared to observing a highly skilled performer who may hide his or her actions beneath a competent flowing performance (Kazdin, 1973). A coping model who exhibits confidence in the face of difficulties is also modeling an attitude or disposition as well as specific skills (Zimmerman and Ringle, 1981).

Within adventure education vicarious performance can occur through a diversity of ways. The use of video sequences, narrative extracts, participant testimonials, case studies, even reading texts can help participants form positive self-efficacy expectations. Personally my own efficacy in mountaineering is helped by reading accounts of climbers who have maintained well-being despite extreme environmental conditions. Similarly, accurate preactivity visualization activity has been shown to have a positive effect on participant's performance—an outcome potentially linked to gains in self-efficacy (Murphy and Jowdy, 1992).

In any vicarious experience episode participants will draw their own meanings and significance from any modeling or demonstration; it is therefore helpful if a knowledgeable instructor cues participants to the aspects which deserve most attention; this leads to an additional source of efficacy information—verbal persuasion.

Verbal persuasion is another means by which people are influenced to believe they have the capabilities to succeed. For instructors verbal persuasion is a commonly utilized tool, even though it is less influential than the options already discussed. Talk is cheap. Most verbal persuasion comes as either feedback after a performance or as encouragement prior to a performance. Research has indicated that in terms of feedback, information which highlighted achievement had the most influence upon self-efficacy, more so than feedback linking achievement with effort (Shunk, 1984). When providing feedback to participants it is relevant to note that:

Dwelling on formidable aspects weakened people's belief in their efficacy, but focusing on doable aspects raised self-judgment of capabilities . . . the higher the perceived self-efficacy, the longer individuals persevere on difficult and unsolvable problems before they quit (Bandura in Schwarzer, 1992, p. 7).

The more the persuasive feedback raised children's beliefs in their efficacy, the more persistent they were in their efforts and the higher the level of competence they actually achieved (Bandura, 1997, p. 103).

Participants, especially adults, are quite skilled at determining authenticity of feedback. Overinflated verbal persuasion is quickly discredited by repeated action that falls short of what was described. Leaders who inaccurately anticipate the levels to which participants can rise serve to alienate themselves from participants, as well as sending failed expectation messages and lowering efficacy. Provision of praise for mediocre performance can also be paradoxical, being interpreted as devaluing performance and again lowering self-efficacy (Meyer, 1992). This is a common point of discussion for women's participation in adventure activities where instructors frequently tend to set lower expectations compared to male performance levels. The most powerful verbal persuasion needs to be towards performance levels within reach of participants—I think this is something all experienced instructors do instinctively, and very consciously as part of the building of programs.

When I take a group of students to a cliff for a climbing session, I need to be clear that the activities I am constructing are achievable. Verbal persuasion becomes easier if I am convinced that the skills and experiences that my students have already accrued have placed them in good stead to succeed in this new situation. As well as attempting to generate high levels of self-efficacy, I am consciously structuring programs to enable success experiences to be built. I deliberately avoid placing students in situations where they are repeatedly likely to fail, or to succeed only with a high degree of instructor intervention. In a diverse group this demands I know the strengths and weaknesses of my students and work at having students measuring success in terms of their own improvements rather than their competition with others. To this end I often avoid contexts which have all students completing the same climb.

Emotional arousal is the fourth determinant of self-efficacy levels (Bandura, 1997). Mood states, excitement, fear, anxiety, lethargy, all influence a participant's view of how effectively he or she will be able to complete a task. As an example in climbing, the sewing machine leg, where a climber exhibits rapid twitching of leg muscles while balanced on a small hold, does little to instill confidence in the ability to succeed.

Research has clearly identified the existence of optimal arousal conditions for generation of optimal performance. The inverted-U function of performance against arousal is well-known (Ellis, 1973, p. 90). Developing strategies that enable participants to manipulate arousal levels to maximize performance is worthwhile. For participants who are overaroused and showing signs of stress, specific exploratory strategies are appropriate (Berlyne, 1960). Specific exploration encourages participants to narrow their field of perception and concentrate on the immediate and most relevant aspects of the task. Instructors can assist participants here by helping them select the most important aspects, as often less skilled performers are unable to determine the most pertinent factors. The raising of arousal levels is less compelling for adventure education situations, although enjoyment levels have also been associated with optimal arousal (Ellis, 1973). A diversive exploration strategy, where participants are encouraged to more widely explore their circumstances or environment is one option for increasing arousal. The creation of artificial challenges, such as climbing blindfolded, are also options here.

Summary

In summary, information used to judge the capacity to complete a task can be derived for past performances, vicarious performances, verbal persuasion and/or emotional arousal. How this information is then processed and weighted varies with cognitive processes and reflective thought. A role exists for instructors to cue participants to information which will increase the chances of them making positive self-efficacy determinations. Drawing parallels to past performances, encouraging various forms of vicarious experience, and appropriate verbal responses need to become as much a part of an instructor's teaching repertoire as outdoor skills. As David stands atop the third abseil contemplating his future actions, faced with the challenge of a descent over an overhang, he needs to seek out coping strategies that enable him to reach a positive conclusion with respect to his self-efficacy to complete the descent. The four sources of efficacy information can be used as evidence for constructing coping strategies. If David begins to recognize how he may cope with the task then his self-efficacy will increase. If David has not developed the ability, or is not encouraged to recognize the ability to cope with the task, then self-efficacy will decrease. An instructor's role then, is to assist David to realize he has the skills to cope with the task by cueing into aspects of past performance, vicarious performance, verbal persuasion or arousal.

In the End

David is still standing on the top of the third abseil! The choice to abseil must ultimately be his own. To force David to abseil would be to unsettle his most fundamental sense of self-efficacy, his capacity to shape his own well-being, to control the events that shape his life. While we all recognize that contextual issues impinge on our lives, our continued mental health relies on us being able to see ourselves as competent actors in a complex world. Forcing David to abseil against his strongest wishes can do significant harm; if there is nothing else we can learn from theoretical perspectives, we should at least acknowledge that option and respect David's right to say, "No."

Teaching is both a craft and a moral endeavor. There are choices I need to make all the time as a teacher: what to say, what to do, how to do it. The responsibility of working with people outdoors is significant—in terms of moral obligations to participants and to the environment. I can improve my chances of making the right choice, doing the right thing, by being open to the fusion of theory and practice. Being aware of how research can inform my actions in the field and how my practical reflections and discussion with colleagues can help make sense of theory. It is to that end that this essay has been devoted.

References

Bandura, A. (1997). *Self-efficacy: The exercise of control*. New York, NY: W. H. Freeman and Company.

Berlyne, D. (1966). Curiosity and exploration. *Science, 153*, 25–33.

Cervone, D., and Palmer, B. (1990). Anchoring biases and the perseverance of self-efficacy beliefs. *Cognitive Therapy and Research, 14*, 401–416.

Chen, H., Yates, B., and McGinnies, E. (1988). Effects of involvement on observers' estimates of consensus, distinctiveness and consistency. *Personality and Social Psychology Bulletin, 14*, 468–478.

Csikszentmihalyi, M. (1975). *Beyond boredom and anxiety*. San Francisco, CA: Jossey-Bass.

Ellis, M. (1973). *Why people play*. Englewood Cliffs, NJ: Prentice-Hall.

Festinger, L. (1954). *A theory of cognitive dissonance*. Evanston, IL: Row, Peterson.

Fletcher, G., and Ward, C. (1988). Attribution theory and process: A cross-cultural perspective. In M. Bond (Ed.), *The cross-cultural challenge to social psychology*. Newbury Park, CA: Sage.

Kazdin, A. (1973). Covert modeling and the reduction of avoidance behavior. *Journal of Abnormal Psychology, 81*, 87–95.

Martin, P., and Priest, S. (1986). Understanding the adventure experience. *Adventure Education, 3*(1), 18–21.

Meyer. (1992). Paradoxical effects of praise and blame on perceived ability. In W. Stroede and M. Hewstone (Eds.), *European review of social psychology*. Chichester, UK: Wiley.

Murphy, S., and Jowdy, D. (1992). Imagery and mental practice. In T. Horn (Ed.), *Advances in sport psychology*. Champaign, IL: Human Kinetics.

Newman, R., and Goldfried, M. (1987). Disabusing negative self-efficacy expectations via experience, feedback and discrediting. *Cognitive Therapy and Research, 11*, 401–417.

Priest, S. (1993). A new model for risk taking. *Journal of Experiential Education, 16*(1), pp. 50–53.

Schwarzer, R. (Ed.). (1992). *Self-efficacy: Thought control of action*. Washington, DC: Hemisphere.

Suls, J., and Miller, R. (1977). *Social comparison processes: Theoretical and empirical perspectives*. Washington, DC: Hemisphere.

Vaughan, G., and Hogg, M. (1995). *Social psychology*. Sydney, Australia: Prentice Hall.

Weary, G., Stanley, M., and Harvey, J. (1989). *Attribution*. New York, NY: Springer-Verlag.

Weiner, B. (1986). *An attribution theory of motivation and emotion*. New York, NY: Springer-Verlag.

Zimbardo, P., and Leippe, M. (1991). *The psychology of attitude change and social influence*. New York, NY: McGraw-Hill.

Zimmerman, B., and Ringle, J. (1981). Effects of model persistence and statements of confidence on children's self-efficacy and problem solving. *Journal of Educational Psychology, 73*, 485–493.

Section 5

The Learning in Adventure Programming
The Experience Cornerstone

The essence of adventure education—of any approach to education—is learning. How might educators wishing to use the process of adventure for learning best achieve the learning objectives they have set for their students? What does the literature of education contain that might be useful to adventure educators? What is research in this field suggesting that program planners need to consider in developing programs that will have the most significant educational effect?

Kraft, in the introductory essay, inquires into what learning theory offers to adventure educators. He briefly reviews the behaviorist, social, cognitive, and developmental theories of learning. What have Gardner, Dewey, Piaget, Coleman and Resnick offered that might help adventure educators? Kraft notes that adventure educators often think the work of educational theorists in the laboratory is of no relevance to them. Not so, he argues. If the aim is to conduct the best learning experience, then insight must be gleaned from all available sources. Kraft does a brief but comprehensive job of suggesting where the best gleaning may be done.

Wurdinger and Priest explore theories and models involving the organization of the experiential learning experience. A key question is where the experience optimally should be in the learning process. Should it come before the learner encounters theory about the phenomena he or she is encountering, or should it come after? They also look to theorists such as Dewey, Coleman, Gager, Kolb and others, to review what has been suggested as the optimal ordering of the major elements of the process. They conclude that no hard-and-fast order suits all situations, but suggest that a sequence involving an encounter with a problem, theorizing about solutions, and application of theory seems a widely applicable general approach.

Fine provides an overview of the major stage theories of human development in the domains of psychomotor, psychosocial, cognitive, and moral development. Practitioners, he argues, should consider the life stage of the participants when designing programs. There are several major ideas about what the stages are, and concerns have been expressed about the simplicity and cultural biases of the major theories, but Fine thinks that several general considerations may be derived from the literature which will be helpful in adventure program design. He summarizes these.

Bisson provides a comprehensive review of theory about and research into the problem of identifying the optimum sequence of learning activities in adventure programming. He explains the importance of careful sequencing, reviews sequencing models that have been described, and concludes that there is no ultimate sequencing scheme suited for all situations. There are, though, common developmental phases in most models, and he offers a multi-layer sequence model which displays these common elements and which offers an approach that might be useful in most adventure education programs.

Hammerman and Knapp address practical consideration in their contributions. The former explains the inquiry approach to teaching and learning, and provides examples of how it can be applied in adventure education settings. Knapp suggests how leaders can help participants process their experience. He offers guidelines for helping people internalize meaning from experience. This is not a task, he notes, to be taken lightly. The facilitator is "playing with fire," and there is much to know in order to do the job correctly. He offers many suggestions on how to do this critically important work.

In the penultimate essay, Gass addresses the critical issue of transference of learning. How can learning experiences during adventure serve the learner back home? What can adventure educators do to increase the long-term effect of the experiences they facilitate for their students? Gass reviews relevant theory, then offers a model for transfer. His discussion comes down to specific techniques useful for enhancing transfer.

In the final chapter, Priest and Gass outline several facilitation techniques as they have evolved through the history of adventure programming. As with all sections of this book, the authors here can only suggest the vast array of ideas and methods that might be useful for understanding the challenges of learning through the experience of adventure. The purpose here is to suggest general directions in which adventure educators might travel in their search for insight and resources for their task.

Chapter 24

Experiential Learning

Richard J. Kraft
University of Colorado

Everybody experiences far more than he understands. Yet it is experience, rather than understanding that influences behavior.
—McLuhan

Introduction

Despite the repeated calls over the Reagan-Bush era for a "return to the basics," generally interpreted to mean the formal classroom with its traditional reading, writing, arithmetic, classics, Shakespeare, American history, and Western civilization, experiential learning is alive and well as we head towards the twenty-first century. McLuhan gives us a clue as to why experiential learning has always been and will continue to be a major, if not *the* major, way in which most of us attempt to make sense of our universe. Vicarious and symbolic forms of learning dominate our schools and classrooms, but it would be foolhardy to claim that these are the only, or even the dominant, ways in which we as human beings learn. In this brief chapter, I shall attempt to explore a few of the philosophical and psychological relationships between experience and learning.

Educational psychologists usually define learning as "a change in the individual caused by experience" (Slavin, 1986, p. 104). Change can and does obviously occur in the formal classroom as the result of such educational interventions as the lecture, laboratory, discussion, recitation, and testing. On the other hand, it is equally obvious that change in the individual or in behavior can and does occur in the nonschool environment, and thus learning is not something confined to the school, nor only that which occurs under certified teachers and in interaction with state approved curricula and textbooks.

It is only in this century that learning in the formal school setting became the dominant mode for the majority of persons in the "developed" world, and it is only in the past quarter-century that a majority of children throughout the Third World have had their learning formalized and curricularized in the classroom. The purpose of this essay is not to deny that important learning does occur in the traditional school setting, but to look at what learning theory, educational philosophy, the psychology of learning, theories of intelligence, and research on learning can tell us about how learning occurs in the nonschool environment.

Learning theories are generally divided into two principal types, behavioral and cognitive. Observable behavior in or outside the classroom is the major focus of the behavioral theories, while the mental processes individuals use to learn and remember information or skills is the focus of the cognitive theories. Adventure educators and others who use "real-life" experiences as their major teaching or learning tool, often ignore or denigrate what laboratory learning theorists have discovered, not recognizing that our carefully programmed outdoor experiences or work-study apprenticeship programs make use of the same principles of learning, only in a different setting. We also hope, as evidence is slim, that these nontraditional learning environments will result in greater, more beneficial behavioral change, greater learning, longer retention, and all the other points made so cogently in the learning laboratory.

Behavioral Learning Theories

Numerous principles of behavioral learning theories can be found in the practice of adventure and other forms of experience-based learning. The principle that behavior changes according to its immediate consequences is perhaps the most important in both classroom and nonclassroom learning environments. In the adventure setting, countless examples of the immediacy of consequences can be given through such things as ill-fitting boots leading to blisters, improperly tied knots leading to injury or death in a fall, a tent being washed away if set up in a streambed, dehydration from lack of prepared water, and literally hundreds of other examples.

The use of positive and negative reinforcers, rewards and punishments, has been well-documented with laboratory animals, with students in the classroom, and in the wilderness. While researchers in the laboratory reward rats with pellets of food, and teachers use such positive reinforcers as stars and grades, or aversive stimuli such as tests or various punishments, outdoor adventure educators can and do use rewards such as praise for an activity well-done, or a wide range of positive or negative reinforcers when working in therapeutic settings with alcoholics, drug abusers, and delinquents. The ropes course setting may differ from a psychiatrist's office, a detoxification center, or a locked youth facility, but the basic behavioral principles remain the same. While adventure educators may not be as overt, as specific, or as well-planned in the behavioral conditioning process as B. F. Skinner (1968) or Ivan Pavlov, the basic principles remain the same.

Social Learning Theory

Albert Bandura (1969), in his social learning theory, uses the basic principles of the behaviorists, but suggests that we also learn vicariously through modeling or imitating other's behavior. In social learning theory not all learning is shaped by consequences, but rather can be directly learned from a model. Bandura suggests that there are four phases to this form of learning: attentional, retention, reproduction, and motivational.

The attentional phase in which the learner is presented with appropriate cues and novelty is used to motivate the student to pay attention. In adventure education, such activities early in a course as crossing a Burma Bridge, participating in cooperative games or initiatives, or the group leader setting the metaphor (Bacon, 1983) are examples of the attentional phase.

In the retention phase the instructor models the behavior and encourages the student to imitate and practice the behavior. Knot tying in preparation for a belay and paddling technique in preparation for the rapids are among the many examples in which adventure educators model the behavior and then have students practice it, before getting into the more dangerous setting.

The reproduction phase is the time in which students match the instructor's behavior and their ability is assessed. Adventure educators pride themselves in their instruction of behaviors which have obvious meaning for the learner, and which must be properly performed or individual or group disaster might result. Assessment is immediate, as the raft might turn over or the tent blow away if the appropriate behavior has not been learned.

In the final motivational phase, the learners model the appropriate behavior because they believe that in doing so they will increase their chances of being reinforced. Whether reinforcement comes in the form of praise from the instructor, in the successful climbing of a rockface, or in more traditional classroom reinforcements, the learning process is the same.

Cognitive Learning Theories

As with the behavioral learning theories, only a cursory overview will be provided, and only those aspects of the theories that appear to relate to adventure education will be discussed.

Information processing theories attempt to analyze by what process information is absorbed and how students can be helped to retain the information. Short-term and long-term memory are an important part of the research. Information from the senses (sight, hearing, touch, smell, taste) meets the sensory register, and if nothing happens in the first few seconds, it is rapidly lost. Adventure educators pride themselves in using "all the senses" in their work, and while the research evidence is limited, it would appear that the memories of many of the experiences that are part of our adventure programs would be retained much longer than the less profoundly moving experiences in the classroom. What is learned or remembered, however, has never been carefully researched, and it would behoove experiential educators to limit their claims.

Space does not permit any discussion of critical cognitive learning research on perception, attention, automatization, levels of processing, or verbal learning. Schema theory, however, attempts to deal with questions of meaningful learning as opposed to rote learning, and holds that long-term memory is enhanced when information fits into an existing schema. Outdoor, adventure, and other experiential educators constantly raise the importance of schema in helping their students to learn new skills or function in new environments. Without well-developed schemata, the learner in any environment is involved in rote or "meaningless" learning. The memorization of the names of trees, without the ability to place them in a broader schema based on leaves, needles, size, color, bark or a variety of other criteria, is rote memorization and in most cases will not lead to longer term memory.

Experiential educators also pride themselves in the teaching of concepts, not unrelated facts, and in addition often claim greater transfer of learning and problem-solving skills than is found in the typical classroom setting. There is once again little research on the transferability of skills learned in the wilderness to one's home, school or community, although some of the recidivism studies on delinquents would appear to point towards such a transfer. Problem solving and critical thinking are major areas of research by cognitive psychologists, and the educational reform movements of the 1980s are unanimous in their advocacy of these important areas. It is in these areas that experiential educators make their greatest claims, and would appear to lead in pedagogy. Rather than deal with abstract mathematical problems in a textbook, the experiential educator seeks to place the student in a setting which forces appropriate problem-solving behavior. Rather than develop critical thinking skills unrelated to the real life of the student, the experiential educator places the learner in an environment in which those skills can be used to solve problems around him or her.

The Theory of Multiple Intelligences

Howard Gardner, in his influential book *Frames of Mind* (1983), defines intelligence as the "ability to solve problems or to create products, that are valued within one or more cultural settings." He goes on to propose eight distinct criteria for an intelligence and seven human competencies. Among other critiques of traditional IQ measurements, Piaget's developmental stages, and information processing research, he suggests that they emphasize linguistic or logical-mathematical intelligences to the near total exclusion of forms of intelligence.

Reviewing the basic biological research, Gardner concludes that there are seven distinct intelligences:

1. mathematical-logical—the ability to organize thoughts sequentially and logically;
2. verbal-linguistic—the ability to understand and express ideas through language;
3. bodily-kinesthetic—the gaining of knowledge through feedback from physical activity;
4. musical—sensitivity to tone, pitch and rhythm and the ability to reproduce them;
5. visual-spatial—the ability to learn directly through images and to think intuitively without the use of language;
6. interpersonal—the ability to notice and make discriminations regarding the moods, temperaments, motivations and intentions of others; and
7. intrapersonal—having access to one's own feeling life.

Space does not permit a detailed discussion of Gardner's research criteria, but he makes a strong case that all seven intelligences meet certain biological and psychological specifications, and that all can and have been isolated in various parts of the brain.

Gardner and other educators are only just beginning to discuss the pedagogical implications of his theory, but some of them for experiential adventure educators are quite clear. Gardner outlines the forms of education and intelligences used in nonliterature societies and discusses the use of linguistic and musical skills in oral verse, spatial intelligence in sailing, numerous examples of bodily-kinesthetic intelligence in the work in the village or tribal settings, and many interpersonal skills passed on throughout the tight knit group. He points to the transitional "schools" of the rites of passage or initiation rites, bush schools and the apprenticeship systems, and their emphasis on a range of intelligences. The modern scientific secular school, however, concentrates its efforts on the logical-mathematical intelligence, with some lesser emphasis on the interpersonal and linguistic.

If Gardner's theory continues to gain acceptance among educators, it is likely to affect the way the public schools look at learning and intelligence. Experiential educators have always felt uncomfortable with the near total emphasis in traditional education on the logical-mathematical and linguistic skills, and have sought to provide a more holistic learning environment. Gardner's theory provides a solid research rationale for the wide variety of bodily-kinesthetic activities used in adventure programs, and for the wide range of interpersonal and intrapersonal activities which form such a critical part of the pedagogy for both the therapeutic and nontherapeutic outdoor education programs. Rites of passage and apprenticeships, found in traditional societies have been resurrected by experiential educators as having relevance in the late twentieth century, and with the current emphasis in education on critical thinking and problem solving, adventure educators and others dealing with the role of experience in learning, can justifiably take the lead in providing a range of learning activities which use all the intelligences.

Dewey and Progressive Education

John Dewey and the Progressive Educational Movement in the 1930s took seriously the role of experience inside and outside the schools. The 1960s and early 1970s educational reform movements also attempted to bring the world into the classroom and reconnect the school with the broader society. Following a decade of "back to the basics" and a return to traditional education, the 1990s have been a period of time in which experiential learning both inside and outside the classroom has be looked upon with greater favor, if still not with the same consideration as the more traditional information assimilation and symbolic and vicarious learning approaches which still dominate our schools. With the massive failure of the schools to reach the "forgotten half" of the students, particularly among the poor and minorities, a few researchers, psychologists, educators, and a few public policymakers are returning again to some of the basic ideas of experiential learning. It appears that American education is still going through periodic swings of its educational pendulum, and that many of the ideas which focus the argument go back almost a century to the original writings of Dewey, or even two centuries to Rousseau and other European writers. Perhaps the pendulum will stop when educators admit the need for both symbolic and vicarious learning which is predominantly classroom-based and for experiential learning, which involves all the senses, all the intelligences, and a range of learning environments.

While Dewey warned against unjustified dichotomies, he differentiated between progressive and traditional education in his 1938 classic *Experience and Education* (pp. 19–20):

> To imposition from above is opposed expression and cultivation of individuality; to external discipline is opposed free activity; to learning from texts and teachers, learning through experience; to acquisition of isolated skills and techniques by drill, is opposed acquisition of them as means to attaining ends which make direct vital appeal; to preparation for a more-or-less remote future is opposed making the most of the opportunities of present life; to static aims and materials is opposed acquaintance with a changing world.

Dewey also warned that experiences could be miseducative if they prevent further growth or lead to callousness or lack of sensitivity. Growth must be physical and moral, not just intellectual. Dewey constantly emphasized the social aspects of learning and the importance of learning contributing to the good of the society, not just narcissistic pleasure. He emphasized the need for rigor and discipline in learning, whether in the classroom or on a mountain top. Adventure educators and other advocates of experience-based learning, would do well to heed Dewey's warnings, or we shall surely be condemned to further swings of the pendulum.

Piaget and Developmental Theory

Part of the impetus for the revival of experience-based learning in the 1960s came from the work of Jean Piaget (1952), the Swiss psychologist, whose work on the devel-

opmental stages of cognitive growth emphasized the importance to active learning and concrete experiences. Piaget's theory of development holds that there are four interrelated factors that influence mental development:

1. physical maturation;
2. experiences that involve handling, moving, and thinking about concrete objects;
3. social interaction, particularly with other children; and
4. equilibration which results from bringing the other three factors together to build and rebuild mental structures.

Piaget went on to delineate the stages of growth as from 0–2 years of age sensorimotor control; 2–4 extracting concepts from experience; 4–7 intuitive thought; 7–11 concrete operational thought; and 11–15 formal or abstract operational thought.

The implications of Piaget's theory are critical for experiential educators of children and adults, as it posits the active nature of all learning, that children learn best from concrete experiences, and that even adolescents and adults who are capable of formal abstract thought, need concrete experiences in order to develop new physical knowledge. Some research on Piaget's stages would appear to indicate that many adults remain at the concrete operational stage for much or most of their learning. Elementary educators in the United States, Britain, and other countries have been profoundly influenced by Piaget's work, but his warnings about overemphasis on symbolic learning and rote memorization and the need for active physical and social interactions with one's environment have generally been ignored by secondary, higher, and adult educators. Adventure educators, who spend a majority of their time providing experiences that involve active, concrete learning in interaction with the physical environment and in social interaction with members of the group, have taken a leadership role in the 1990s in putting into practice in adult learning environments the ideas of Piaget.

Coleman: Information Assimilation Versus Experiential Learning

James Coleman (1977) differentiates between the information assimilation process of the regular classroom and the experiential learning process. In the traditional classroom information assimilation model, the student generally receives the information through a symbolic medium such as a lecture or book, and then assimilates and organizes the information so that the general principle is understood. Inferences are then drawn to a particular application of the general principle and the learner finally moves from the cognitive and symbol-processing sphere to the sphere of action where the knowledge gained is actually applied. Critics of contemporary education, such as Paulo Friere the Brazilian philosopher, suggest that modern schools seldom get past the third step of Coleman's model, or what Friere calls the reflective stage, and into the world of action, where genuine change occurs.

Coleman suggests that the experiential learning process occurs in almost a reverse sequence and at least initially does not use a symbolic medium for transmitting information, as the information is generated through the sequence of steps itself. The steps in the experiential learning process then are to carry out an action in a particular instance and see the effects of that action. Understanding the effects in a particular instance and the consequences of the action, the learner then moves towards an understanding of the general principles involved, and finally applying through action what has been learned in a new circumstance.

Coleman suggests that schools use the information assimilation model to a far greater extent than the experiential model, as it can reduce the time and effort needed to learn something new. On the other hand for children, adolescents or adults who have not mastered the complex systems of symbols used in reading, mathematics and other disciplines, the information assimilation model leads to almost guaranteed failure, as they are unable to translate the learnings into concrete sequences of action. The traditional learning model also is dependent on artificial and extrinsic motivation, as action (the intrinsic motivation) comes at the end of the learning sequence.

The experiential learning mode on the other hand is a time-consuming process because it involves actions sufficiently repeated that the learner is able to generalize from the experience. Ideally, it uses no symbolic medium and consequences follow actions immediately. Motivation is intrinsic, as actions with real consequences occur as the first step in the learning process. Finally, experiential learning appears to be more deeply etched into the brain of the learner, as all learning can be associated with concrete actions and events, not just abstract symbols or general principles.

It is difficult to generate research evidence backing Coleman's theory, as most evidence of learning is shown through pencil and paper tests, which are dependent upon mastery of symbolic media. When a mechanic cannot explain in writing what needs to be done to repair an automobile, but can carry out the necessary work, or when a rock climber cannot explain the physical motions needed or the physics of his activity, but can climb a 5.12 rockface, one is faced with the question of behavioral evidence versus "book learning."

Resnick: Learning in School and out

Adventure educators face the challenge of "proving" the efficacy of the learning which occurs on their courses using traditional symbolic research models, or in creating new models which document what has been learned.

One indication of the pendulum swing once again towards experiential learning in the final decade of the twentieth century is the growing interest on the part of the educational research establishment on what is learned "in school and out." Lauren Resnick, in her 1987 Presidential Address to the prestigious American Educational Research Association, explicated some of the differences between "practical and formal intelligence." Using research by anthropologists and psychologists in such disparate settings as navigation practice on U.S. Navy ships, black market lottery bookies in Brazil, mathematics knowledge among dairy workers, and arithmetic performance by people in a Weight Watcher's program, Resnick (1987) concludes that school learning differs from other learning in four basic ways:

1. individual cognition in school versus shared cognition outside;
2. pure mentation in schools versus tool manipulation outside;
3. symbol manipulation in school versus contextualized reasoning outside school; and
4. generalized learning in school versus situation-specific competencies outside.

Resnick suggests that school learning often becomes a matter of manipulating symbols rather than connecting with the real world. It often becomes the learning of rules disconnected from real life, and concludes that:

> There is growing evidence, then, that not only may schooling not contribute in a direct and obvious way to performance outside school, but also that knowledge acquired outside school is not always used to support in-school learning. Schooling is coming to look increasingly isolated from the rest of what we do.

She also suggests that there is growing evidence that there is little direct transfer from in-school to out-of-school use. Before experiential educators get too excited with these statements, however, she also suggests that much of the situation-specific learning which occurs in our experiential programs can be very limiting, with little transferability to other settings.

With the shift away from apprenticeship models in both the trades and the professions towards formal school settings, Resnick suggests that technical, management and professional education are adhering to too great an extent on forms of teaching found in the traditional classroom and that there is too little engagement with the "tools and materials of work," and more time given to theory than to developing truly expert performance skills. She concludes that we need to help students gain skills for learning even when optimum conditions do not exist. We need learners who can transfer skills from one setting to another and who are adaptive learners. The discontinuity between the worlds of school and work suggests that we should not focus so much on "symbols correctly manipulated but divorced from experience." Successful schooling must involve socially shared mental work and more direct engagement with the referents of symbols. Schooling should begin to look more like out-of-school functioning and include greater use of reflection and reasoning.

Resnick has clearly laid out the challenge for adventure and other experiential educators in coming years. With claims of an educational process that is dependent on shared cognition, skills directly related to real-life settings, learning in environments that demand a wide range of reasoning skills, and a range of specific competencies which provide immediate feedback and are transferable to other life settings, experiential education would appear to be uniquely poised to help overcome the current deficiencies of both traditional schooling and much of vocational-technical training as it occurs today. The rapid growth in adventure programming for the criminal justice system, many public schools, businesses, therapeutic centers, teacher training universities and in youth leadership, to name but a few of the institutions now using the methodology, would appear to indicate a growing acceptance of this form of experiential learning. The challenge now is to carefully document what is being done and its therapeutic and learning effects.

Conclusions

In this brief overview of experiential learning, we have attempted to provide insights from only a few of the many philosophers, psychologists, educators and researchers who have spoken to the issues of the role of experience in learning. If space permitted we would have gone into learning style theorists such as Kolb (1976), McCarthy (1980) and Gregore and Ward (1977), who provide valuable insight into how learners differ in both style and emphasis. Friere (1973), with his naming, reflecting, and acting has developed a pedagogy for liberation that is sweeping the Third World, while Kurt Hahn (1970) developed the theory and practice underlying the Outward Bound schools, and Maria Montessori (1972) gave her name to a whole pedagogy based on concrete experiences. Many experiential educa-

tors have looked to humanistic psychologists such as Maslow (1968) and Rogers (1969) for insight into personal growth, group processes, and openness to new experiences.

In conclusion, perhaps the educational systems in the United States have finally come of age in their recognition that not all children, young people or adults learn in the same manner or at the same speed. They have begun to learn that the insights gained form adventure programs and other experiential learning environments have great potential for use in the mainstream of our educational settings, whether in schools and colleges, in therapeutic programs or in the worlds of business and industry.

References

Bacon, S. (1983). *The conscious use of metaphor in outward bound*. Denver, CO: Colorado Outward Bound School.

Bandura, A. (1969). *Principles of behavior modification*. New York, NY: Rinehart and Winston.

Coleman, J. A. (1977). Differences between experiential and classroom learning. In M. T. Keeton (Ed.), *Experiential learning: Rationale characteristics, and assessment* (pp. 49–61). San Francisco, CA: Jossey-Bass Publishers.

Dewey, J. (1938). *Experience and education*. New York, NY: Collier Books.

Friere, P. (1973). *Pedagogy of the oppressed*. New York, NY: The Seabury Press.

Gardner, H. (1983). *Frames of mind: The theory of multiple intelligences*. New York, NY: Basic Books, Inc.

Gregore, A. F., and Ward, H. B. (1977). A new definition for individual. *NAASP Bulletin*.

Hahn, K. (1970). *The educational thought of Kurt Hahn*. London, UK: Routledge and Kegan Paul Ltd.

Kolb, D. A. (1976). Management and the learning process. *California Management Review*, Spring.

Maslow, A. H. (1968). Some educational implications of humanistic psychologies. *Harvard Educational Review*, *38*(4).

McCarthy, B. (1980). *The 4 MAT system*. Arlington Heights, IL: Excel, Inc.

Montessori, M. (1972). *Spontaneous activity*. New York, NY: Schocken Books.

Piaget, J. (1952). *The origins of intelligence in children*. New York, NY: Basic Books.

Resnick, L. B. (1987). Learning in school and out. *Educational Researcher, 16*(9), 13–20.

Rogers, C. (1969). *Freedom to learn*. Columbus, OH: Charles E. Merrill.

Skinner, B. F. (1968). *The technology of teaching*. New York, NY: Appleton-Century-Crofts.

Slavin, R. E. (1986). *Educational psychology: Theory into practice*. Englewood Cliffs, NJ: Prentice-Hall.

Chapter 25

Integrating Theory and Application in Experiential Learning

Scott D. Wurdinger
Ferris State University

Simon Priest
eXperientia

Authors such as Boud, Cohen, and Walker (1993) and Weil and McGill (1993) are exploring new ground and raising important questions about experiential learning. For instance, Boud and colleagues (1993) suggest that it is elusive because experiences are continually being reconstructed, and therefore, it is difficult to determine where the learning process begins and ends. They also confront the notion of objective knowledge by suggesting that learners make their own meaning from an experience. Careful analysis of experiential learning may be difficult, but is necessary if we wish to improve upon teaching methods.

To help clarify the meaning of experiential learning, Henry (1993) sent out a questionnaire and discovered two broad-based definitions; one claiming that all learning is experiential, and the other suggesting it is a sequence consisting of specific components. Although the first definition raises some interesting questions, it is not the definition we are most concerned with in this chapter. The sequence of experiential learning, however, is rich with practical application for adventure educators wishing to employ such methodologies.

This chapter will trace the history and evolution of sequential models of experiential learning, and will outline a new model called proactive experiential learning which includes a problematic situation requiring an active search for a solution. This model suggests that three elements—a problematic situation, theory, and application—must be present to qualify as experiential learning, and that the process may require moving back and forth be-

tween theory and application several times before the problem is solved. It is proactive rather than reactive because the learning process is triggered by a problematic situation which initiates an active search for a solution.

History and Evolution of Experiential Learning

Dewey (1916) was one of the first thinkers to articulate a sequential order to the learning process. The "method of intelligence" or "reflective experience" includes the following steps (p. 150):

1. perplexity or confusion,
2. a careful survey of all the variables that define the problem,
3. developing a tentative hypothesis or plan which may be tested,
4. testing the hypothesis, and
5. reflecting on the experience for later use.

Dewey's learning sequence included both theory and experience. One is presented with a problem that requires developing a speculative plan (theory), which is then followed by direct interaction with the subject matter (experience). He developed this theory because the education system at the time was lacking in hands-on experience:

For one has only to call to mind what is sometimes treated in schools as acquisition of knowledge to realize how lacking it is in any fruitful connection with the ongoing experience of the students—how largely it seems to be believed that the mere appropriation of subject matter which happens to be stored in books constitutes knowledge. (Dewey, 1916, p. 342)

According to Dewey (1938), an educative experience entailed testing theory. Learning was less likely to occur when theory was presented without opportunities to test it. For instance, if college students in an outdoor education class are provided with pedagogical theory but never allowed time to practice teaching, how will they know whether the theory is valid? Likewise, one may experience teaching but be unable to adjust methods and subject matter to fit the students' needs. In both cases learning falls short. Learners must be given opportunities to test information, and develop theories about how to change their practices if they are not working.

Coleman (1976) added to Dewey's ideas by neatly summarizing the comparative differences between experiential learning and information assimilation (Figure 25.1). Information assimilation, which is often associated with traditional education, begins with receiving data in the form of symbols such as numbers in a book or words in a lecture. In the second step, the information is assimilated and general principles are formed. The inference of a specific application from general principles is the third step, implying cognitive intelligence or the ability to apply learning. The fourth and final step is application which is where the learner tests the information to determine its usefulness. For instance, a student listens to a lecture on how to use a map and compass for wilderness travel. From this lecture he or she formulates principles about such things as map reading and compass declination. Specific applications might include using map and compass in dense forests, mountainous terrain or paddling lakes and rivers.

The last step is applying general principles by actually using map and compass in a wilderness setting.

Experiential learning on the other hand, reverses the four-step sequence of information assimilation. This model begins with action and moves to observation of the effects of that action. Coleman (1976) suggests that understanding the cause and effect allows one to predict the outcome of situations having the same set of circumstances. An instructor using this methodology would begin a map and compass session with a direct experience. For instance, students could be given maps and compasses and told they must find their way from point A to point B on a map. During this exercise they would experience several trials and errors, allowing them to gather important information about map and compass use. The principles learned from the experience could then be applied to other similar wilderness settings.

Gager (1977) developed the experiential learning process flow. His model focused on the psychological effects of the learning process. The learner is placed in a demanding situation that requires action and decision making. This necessitates the mastery of a new skill which satisfies ego needs and self-esteem. The experience is then followed immediately by another challenge, which is similar to the previous challenge. Reflection, the last step, allows one to examine performance and speculate on how the experience might apply to a broader range of experiences. Whitewater canoeing for instance, places one in a demanding situation that requires action and on-the-spot decision making. Developing these skills leads to feelings of accomplishment. Another challenge, like canoeing a more difficult river which may require using new equipment, is then presented. Once accomplished, individuals reflect on what they learned about themselves and how it can be applied to other life experiences.

Pfeiffer and Jones's (1980) view of the experiential learning process for group facilitators includes five steps. Step 1 involves the action of doing or "experiencing" in order to generate information for analysis in subsequent steps. Step 2 incorporates sharing reactions to and observations from the experience in what is termed *publishing*

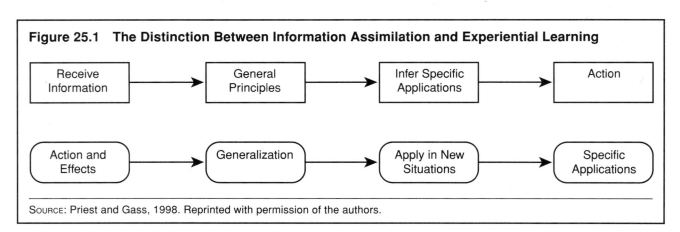

Figure 25.1 The Distinction Between Information Assimilation and Experiential Learning

Receive Information → General Principles → Infer Specific Applications → Action

Action and Effects → Generalization → Apply in New Situations → Specific Applications

SOURCE: Priest and Gass, 1998. Reprinted with permission of the authors.

or is likened to data input. Step 3 includes the systematic examination of the experience during "processing" by discussing the patterns and dynamics that arise from the reactions and observations. The combined publishing and processing steps can be thought of as "an *inductive* process: proceeding from observation rather than from a priori 'truth' (as in the *deductive* process). . . . Inductive learning means learning through discovery" (p. 3–4). Step 4 infers principles about the real world by "generalizing" from the publishing and processing steps. This step makes the learning truly pragmatic by matching its relevance to reality. Step 5 infers "applying" new action and planning more effective behavior on the basis of the generalized principles. The cycle is complete when the participant applies the information in a new situation.

Kolb's (1984) model also begins with concrete experience but he expands upon the previous models by stating that the observations are assimilated into a "theory" from which new implications for action can be deduced (Figure 25.2). These implications or hypotheses then serve as guides in acting to create new experiences. For instance, the experience of flying a kite can be used to formulate theories on how to build a better kite. This means that one experience is used as a foundation for future experiences.

Dewey's ideas have been utilized in one form or another in all these models, but they have also been expanded upon creating more fully developed learning theories. The next section will analyze these models and show that they lack certain components important to the experiential learning process.

Analyzing Experiential Learning Models

These models raise several questions. Are all the models experiential? All the models I've discussed including Coleman's (1976) information assimilation combine theory and experience. Therefore, one could argue that information assimilation is an experiential learning model as well. In fact, Dewey's reflective experience, which is often thought of as the cornerstone of experiential education, is quite similar to information assimilation in that it begins by gathering information and ends with testing this information against reality.

Can learning occur without combining theory and experience? If learning is defined as the ability to remember information which is what may happen when reading a book, watching a videotape, or listening to a lecture then it can occur without this combination. Formal education is a series of experiences including such things as reading books, going to lectures and movies, taking tests, discussing ideas in the classroom, participating in labs, doing projects, and going on field trips. Some of these activities require active participation, while others are mostly passive. Some require hands-on involvement and others simply listening to what is being said. If one defines knowledge as the ability to recall information, then learning can occur without combining theory and experience.

This suggests that there may be a difference between learning from an experience and experiential learning. To illustrate, I recently read an article about ways to enhance teaching practices and learned how to use a tool that can point out problems with methodology. According to these models, learning does not become experiential until I take the tool and actually apply it in my own classroom. I may learn from the experience of reading the article, but the learning does not become experiential until I use it.

However, if knowledge is defined as the ability to apply information, then information assimilation may fall short. When a learning environment is dependent upon a symbolic medium it becomes theory rich, which minimizes the amount of learning taking place:

> For children, adolescents or adults who have not mastered the complex systems of symbols used in reading, mathematics and other disciplines, [this] model leads to almost guaranteed failure, as they are unable to translate the learnings into concrete sequences of action. (Kraft, 1990, p. 180)

This criticism is also echoed by employers, who frequently state that students know a lot, but have difficulty doing anything with it (Little, 1981). This suggests that students may learn from formal education experiences, but the learning may not mean anything until they apply it in reality.

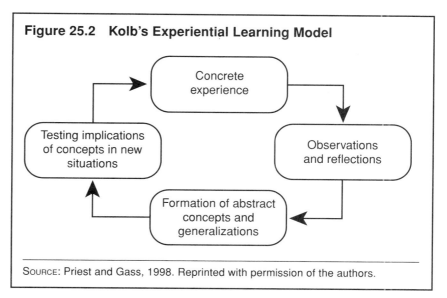

Figure 25.2   Kolb's Experiential Learning Model

Concrete experience

Observations and reflections

Formation of abstract concepts and generalizations

Testing implications of concepts in new situations

SOURCE: Priest and Gass, 1998. Reprinted with permission of the authors.

Joplin (1981) notes that when given an opportunity to use theory, it "emphasizes a student's ability to justify or explain a subject rather than to recite an expert's testimony" (p. 20).

Does it matter where experience falls in the sequence? Kolb, Coleman, and Gager all suggest that concrete experience is the starting point in the experiential learning process. But according to Dewey (1916), it doesn't matter whether one starts with a concrete experience or theory, learning may occur as long as they are both present and there is a connection made between the two, which can then be applied to future experiences. For instance, he states that "when an activity is continued into the undergoing of consequences, when the change made by action is reflected back into a change made in us, the mere flux is loaded with significance" (p. 139). Here, experience comes first and learning occurs because a connection is made between the activity and the consequences that result. But with the reflective experience, the sequence begins with an indeterminate situation that requires using theory to solve a problem. With the reflective experience one must understand theory first, in order to solve a problem. This suggests that the learning process does not have to begin with a concrete experience. It may begin with theory, and as long as the cycle is completed learning will occur. Dewey implies that experience is a necessary condition to the learning process, but not sufficient.

The models where experience comes first may also be effective as long as they are applicable to future experiences. When one is impelled into an experience that includes a problem or challenge, it creates desire to solve the dilemma. When this happens it enhances one's level of motivation. Initiating learning through problem solving is an attempt to influence or control one's environment and provides impetus to complete all the steps in the learning cycle. The learner becomes actively engaged in the experience from which theoretical principles are then generated. These principles may then be applied to future problem posing experiences. In either case what is important is completion of the learning cycle. Theory without experience is incomplete because ideas need to be put to practice to verify their significance. Likewise, experience without theory is inadequate because it does not allow individuals to take what they have learned and apply it to future experiences.

These models may serve different purposes. When theory is presented first, it gives students an opportunity to take information and test it against reality, thus finding out for themselves whether the theory is useful or meaningful. When experience is presented first, it provides hands-on opportunities that may require on-the-spot problem solving. Students learn to think on their feet, and acquire new information which may then be used in future experiences. In both cases the end result is education, which implies that these models may be effective if carried to their ends.

Are there times when theory should precede experience or vice versa? In certain situations it is extremely important to understand some theory before engaging in an experience. For instance, in the field of adventure education it is important for future educators to understand theories associated with learning and motivation which will then allow them to avoid numerous trial-and-error experiences. Examples in other fields such as medicine are even more dramatic. Imagine providing treatment to an injured victim without any theory? Using the information assimilation process is extremely important in situations where error is not permissible. It bypasses the need for learners to repeat centuries of miseducative experiences.

The experience first models have their place as well. Dewey (1916) suggests that the teacher should first provide the student with something to do rather than something to learn, and that the activity be uncertain or problematic (p. 154). This allows students to experiment and discover things on their own. When possible students should be allowed to make mistakes so that they can "act intelligently next time under similar circumstances" (Dewey, 1916, p. 27). It may be more time-consuming when experience is at the beginning of the cycle, but it may also be more effective in the long run. Coleman (1976) believes that such learning is retained longer because it is equated with concrete experience rather than abstract symbols, but it also requires greater effort. Students experience something and if the problem is not solved, they have to develop a new plan and then test it again. The goal behind this process is for students to discover answers on their own, which may require several trial-and-error attempts before they are successful. This is quite different than information assimilation where students are given answers and then asked to reproduce them, which theoretically should only require one attempt.

Is one starting point more effective than another? The answer to this question depends on the context of the situation. A wilderness instructor wishing to avoid hypothermia and frostbite should present students with theories associated with cold weather injuries before they actually experience winter camping. Similarly, instructors in teacher education courses might want to discuss learning theories and motivation techniques so that future educators can avoid making costly mistakes once they begin teaching. On the other hand, educators teaching cooperative learning games and critical thinking skills may decide to impel students into experiences that require hands-on learning and then draw out key principles through reflection. In either situation, educators need to consider a number of variables such as safety concerns, overall objectives, and age level before determining which model they wish to employ.

What are the critical elements in the experiential learning process? If a primary goal of education is to prepare students for life after school, then they should be exposed to problematic situations that emulate life outside the classroom, and be provided opportunities to test their ideas against reality while they are still in school. One may learn about theories, and even discuss and question these theories in the classroom, but these learnings will not become experiential until they are tested in situations that have real-life consequences. Therefore, three critical elements of experiential learning are a problematic situation, theory, and application.

Proactive Experiential Learning

Proactive experiential learning is initiated with a problematic situation that requires an interplay between theory and application while searching for a solution to the problem. Initiating the learning process with a problem or challenge is a critical component that differentiates experiential learning from other types of learning (Wurdinger, 1997). Problematic situations are those that throw learners into perplexity and engage their intellect and emotions. They are situations that have meaningful consequences and are relevant to the student's life outside the classroom. With this model, theory is defined as a speculative plan to solve a problem. The process of developing a plan may require collecting information from sources such as books, articles, lectures, videotapes, and past experiences. Application is the implementation of theory. The application stage entails testing theory for the purpose of achieving meaningful ends. Application is different than practice because it affects the learner on a personal level. For instance, there is a difference between practicing math equations to complete some homework and using these equations to balance a program's budget. The latter situation has personal meaning, whereas the former may be busywork that must be completed before the next class.

The learning models discussed earlier suggest learning occurs through a one-way sequence that moves from one stage to the next until the process is completed. One problem with this notion is, one may have to return to previous stages before a solution is discovered. A plan may look good on paper, but during implementation one may come across unanticipated problems that will necessitate a return to theory. The new model suggests that one may move back and forth between theory and application in order to find a solution (Figure 25.3). Teaching a one-day team-building program to a group of children represents a relevant problem for a class of adventure education students. Students will have to formulate a speculative plan which may require gathering information on presenting and debriefing various team-building activities. During the application stage they may discover that the activities or debriefing techniques do not work the way they intended, which may necessitate a return to theory. Students may have to make

several attempts before they discover a solution to the problem. Once a problem is solved, it may then be used to solve future problems.

Some of the previous models imply that there may be a lengthy time interval between the theory and practice stage. With information assimilation for example, it may be several years before theory is actually applied. Such is the case with teacher education programs that do not provide opportunities for students to practice their craft until the fourth or fifth year of college when they do their student teaching. The new model indicates learning is more likely to occur when there is a shorter time span between the theory and application stages. For instance, in a semester-long college course, students should be given a problem and then allowed time to work through the proactive experiential learning process. Due to the time constraints of formal education, it is difficult to engage students in experiential learning every class period. However, students should be allowed opportunities to apply theory at appropriate times during a semester-long course.

Another pitfall with some of the previous models is the lack of problem solving. Students in formal education settings are often given information and answers for the purpose of avoiding potential problems during the application phase. For instance, in a teacher education methods course students are given information on how to use different teaching techniques once they become a teacher. This approach relies heavily on memorization and reproduction. Students must remember the theory and then reproduce it at a later point in time when it is needed.

The new model promotes problem solving. It begins with a problem that may lead to other problems during the application stage. For instance, teaching students how to apply John Dewey's theory of education presents a difficult problem. Students will first have to read books and probably struggle to understand the theory. This may require several readings mixed with discussions. Applying this theory may present new problems and questions. Will it work with large groups? Does it take different learning styles into consideration? How does one evaluate hands-on learning that takes place outside the classroom? When individuals are required to apply theory they may be confronted with unexpected problems that require on-the-spot problem solving.

Self-directed learners are able to develop their own problematic situations, but in many cases teachers need to guide this process to enhance the potential for meaningful

Figure 25.3 Proactive Experiential Learning

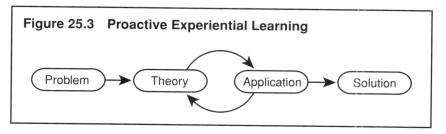

learning outcomes. Some implications for teachers wishing to use proactive experiential learning include providing learners with relevant problematic situations, allowing time to go back and forth between the two phases so that a solution may be reached, and making sure the time phase between theory and application is relatively short.

Some of the more meaningful problems or challenges are those that have to be applied outside the classroom. Such experiences tend to be more relevant because they have real consequences. They are also more effective in promoting problem solving because students are learning to think on their feet. Educators can raise questions, hold discussions, and have students do presentations in the classroom which may promote thinking, but learning becomes most relevant to students during the application stage when they are testing theory that impacts upon their lives. Therefore, teachers wishing to employ this method should help design learning situations that require application, and then be sure to provide time and opportunities for students to carry out these experiences.

References

Boud, D., Cohen, R., and Walker, D. (1993). *Using experience for learning*. Buckingham, UK: Open University Press.

Coleman, J. S. (1976). Differences between experiential and classroom learning. In M. T. Keeton (Ed.), *Experiential learning: Rationale, characteristics and assessment*. San Francisco, CA: Jossey-Bass.

Coleman, J. S. (1979). Experiential learning and information assimilation: Toward an appropriate mix. *Journal of Experiential Education, 2*(1), 6–9.

Dewey, J. (1916). *Democracy and education*. New York, NY: The Free Press.

Dewey, J. (1938). *Experience and education*. New York, NY: Collier Books.

Gager, R. (1977). As a learning process . . . It's more than just getting your hands dirty. *Voyageur, 1*. Boulder, CO: Association for Experiential Education.

Henry, J. (1993). Meaning and practice in experiential learning. In S. Weil and I. McGill (Eds.), *Making sense of experiential learning: Diversity in theory and practice*. Buckingham, UK: Open University Press.

Joplin, L. (1981). On defining experiential education. *Journal of Experiential Education, 4*(1), 17–20.

Kraft, R. J. (1990). Experiential learning. In J. C. Miles and S. Priest (Eds.), *Adventure education* (pp. 175–183). State College, PA: Venture Publishing, Inc.

Kolb, D. A. (1984). *Experiential learning*. Englewood Cliffs, NJ: Prentice-Hall.

Little, T. (1981). *History and rationale for experiential learning* (Panel Resource Paper #1). Washington, DC: National Society for Internships and Experiential Education.

Pfeiffer, J. W., and Jones J. E. (1980). *The 1980 annual handbook for group facilitators*. San Diego, CA: University Associates.

Preist, S., and Gass, M. A. (1998). *Effective leadership in adventure programming*. Champaign, IL: Human Kinetics.

Weil, S., and McGill, I. (1993). *Making sense of experiential learning: Diversity in theory and practice*. Buckingham, UK: Open University Press.

Wurdinger, S. D. (1997). *Philosophical issues in adventure education*. Dubuque, IA: Kendall/Hunt Publishing Co.

Chapter 26

Stage Development Theory in Adventure Programming

L-Jay Fine
California State University at Fresno

Importance of Existing Stage Development Theory in Adventure Education

Designing adventure programs has always been as much art as science. We rely on our intuition and experience to provide activities in harmony with the readiness (skills, ability, and maturity) of participants. But do we know whether a group of 10-year-olds rafting down a class III river will work as a team to make it through critical rapids? By what basis can we assert that an adjudicated youth will have the cognitive skills to reflect appropriately during a two-day solo? Isomorphic learning (using metaphors) is a complex way to mirror an adventure activity with a situation or challenge the client has in daily life. The cognitive ability needed to make these connections and then apply them may be quite high. How can we claim the client grasps higher levels of thought?

As our sophistication in processing adventure activities increases, so too will our need to understand development and life stages of our clients. A wealth of research exists in comparable fields such as education, psychology, and sociology describing development and, subsequently, the potential readiness of individuals at various stages in their lives. Development theory proposes that a human being is, in fact, a human becoming. Individuals follow a path over the course of their lives where coping skills generally diversify and improve. Although we all progress dif-

ferently, development is often in concrete, identifiable stages providing an optimistic view of human potential and growth.

After reviewing several theories on human development, an adventure educator should have further insight into the capabilities of his or her clients. It is also hoped that we can avoid reinventing the wheel by borrowing those theories which apply directly to our field. The well-worn credo of eminent social-psychologist Kurt Lewin says it best: "Nothing is so practical as a good theory" (Schoel, Prouty, and Radcliffe, 1988, p. 16).

To maintain accountability in our profession, educational opportunities through adventure must be based on sound research. A danger befalling the practitioner is the ever-tempting reliance on cloned adventure experiences. If the Trust Fall works for teenagers then it must for pre-teens. Stage theory allows the practitioner to consider the participant's life stage in program considerations. This not only fosters better use of educational objectives but may also create safer experiences. Csikszentmihalyi (1975) described the flow experience as a balance between a person's perceived competence and the challenge at hand. When they are not congruent then either boredom or anxiety ensues. When balance is struck the flow experience provides enriched perception, orientation to the present, and absence of fear. For the educator this translates to an enhanced learning experience. This notion of balance is critical in adventure education. Invariably we will be pushing our clients outside their comfort zone. However, if we want them to benefit and learn from the activity we must seek a balance between their life stage and the type and degree of challenge. Here the concept of optimal dissonance (the perfect challenge) comes into play, designing experiences just beyond the scope of the client perceived capabilities.

Stage Development Theories

Stage development theory spans the life from cradle to grave. However, the ages from around eight to later adulthood are most relevant to adventure educators and discussion will be limited to those ages. Development occurs in four domains: psychomotor, psychosocial, cognitive, and moral. Of course, creating artificial divisions among psychomotor, psychosocial, cognitive, and moral development is arbitrary and potentially deceiving since they interrelate. For example, cognitive skills increase from adolescence to adulthood largely because one's inner life is in less turmoil. This concept of reality testing asserts that as we become more emotionally autonomous we are more able to accurately comprehend reality (Colarusso, 1992). Therefore, psychological growth directly affects cognitive development.

In order to constitute a stage development theory it should include the following components:

1. The theory should describe general issues confronting the individual.
2. It should refer to qualitatively different behavior patterns. These should be distinguishable and identifiable when contrasted with other stages.
3. It should follow an invariant sequence.
4. It should be, though rarely is, culturally universal (Freiberg, 1987).

Psychomotor

Human development follows concrete steps in a variety of domains. Psychomotor development is the most obvious. A child crawls before he or she walks. Muscle control, strength, and endurance progress in complex but identifiable increments throughout childhood and into one's twenties. Psychomotor learning refers to learning skills that involve a mental component (psycho) as well as physical movement (motor). There are three types of psychomotor development: (1) object-motor (climbing, canoeing), (2) language-motor (speech), and (3) feeling motor (painting) (Gallahue and Ozmun, 1995).

By the time a child is seven, most gross motor skills have developed and he or she is ready to enter what Gallahue and Ozmun (1995) labeled the *specialized movement phase*. Within the phase are three stages: transition, application, and lifelong utilization stage.

Transition (8–10 years). At around eight the child is ready to combine and apply fundamental skills previously developed and start testing performance in sports and recreational activities. It is exciting for the child simply to combine skills; emphasis on competition and specialized skills should be postponed.

Application (10–14 years). Children are becoming more selective of activities around 11 years. Increased emphasis is placed on form, skill and accuracy in advanced games and sports (Gallahue and Ozmun, 1995). Where rock climbing could be introduced at the transition stage, skills to enhance performance could be offered at this stage.

Lifelong utilization (14 years and above). The foundation laid in the previous stages helps determine the success of ongoing participation in physical activities throughout life. This stage emerges at around 14 years and continues for the duration of one's life. Principally, participants refine skills and select activities where they exhibit talent and are able to fit them into their daily lives. For the adventure educator, high-level skills such as scuba diving, flying, climbing, and kayaking become excellent opportunities for lifelong recreation experiences with diverse skill use and ongoing challenges.

Other concerns about psychomotor development inevitably emerge for the adventure educator such as gender differences and changes brought on during adolescence. Gender differences in strength do not happen until puberty. Indeed, girls commonly surpass boys in growth for a time prior to adolescence. Uneven growth spurts occur during adolescence for both sexes, but primarily males, creating some awkwardness. However, this is offset by enhanced strength and motor-skill development which increases the greatest between ages 12 and 16. Therefore, teens are capable of engaging in sequentially more difficult challenges.

In terms of adventure experiences it seems important to deemphasize strength differences and design experiences requiring balance, coordination, and stamina. Perhaps the most important consideration in designing adventure experiences is not to worry about psychomotor levels. Rafting, climbing, hiking, and canoeing are great equalizers in terms of ages. They offer a chance for cross-generational experience and groups, with a few exceptions, should not be segregated simply on the basis of psychomotor development.

Psychosocial Development

Psychological development theory began with Freud's identification of the id, ego, and superego. From conflict between the id ("I want to") and the superego ("I should do") emerges the ego. A healthy ego establishes a balance between the inner drive and the conscience. An unhealthy ego causes repression often manifesting in physical or behavioral problems. The most important implication for adventure education is the inherent adaptive function of the ego. The ego provides the drive for mastering our environment and, most relevant to the adventure field, it manifests our insatiable curiosity and need to explore (Scarr, Weinberg, and Levine, 1986).

The pioneering work in stage development by Carl Jung and Abraham Maslow provides a strong framework for more specific theories. Jung approached development as a process of individuation. Similarly, Maslow viewed growth as developing toward self-actualization. In achieving individuation or self-actualization the individual would find harmony with his or her environment and self-acceptance. With Maslow, one would meet basic needs (physiological), relationship needs (sense of belonging) and, eventually, some fortunate souls realize self-actualization.

Applying Maslow to adventure education might prove difficult. Often basic needs are not perceived as being met in outdoor activities. Yet, who is to say that higher needs are not? More useful applications of theories on development come from Loevinger, Erikson, Piaget, Perry, Kohlberg, and Selman. These researchers proposed specific stages of development with direct implications to adventure education curricula.

Loevinger's Ego Development

Continuing Freud's examination of the ego, Jane Loevinger defined "impressionistic descriptions" of stages (1976, p. 13). Loevinger's theory paints with a broad brush to include cognitive, social, and moral domains under the aegis of ego development. Although it does not provide the convenience of concrete age distinctions one can readily see that character development would unlikely fall in a specific chronological pattern. Nonetheless, her stages do illustrate the sequence in which an individual develops and the age breakdowns can be suggested as the result of her research.

Conformist (12–15 years). The young teenager cannot distinguish between rules, norms, or convention. If someone's appearance or actions fall outside the conformist's group then that person is not accepted. On the downside, this leads to stereotyping largely on race, age, sex, and nationality. However, this is a critical stage in that one no longer views the world strictly from his or her perspective. This is the stage of belonging. One accepts that one's welfare is directly attributable to the welfare of the immediate group, usually the family. The conformist adopts rules, not out of fear of punishment, but because he or she recognizes the benefit to the group. Research shows that conformity to peers peaks around ninth grade. Regardless, bigger issues are most heavily influenced by parents and mentors (Scarr et al., 1986).

An individual at this stage has a simple inner life. He or she would only express feelings in terms of "happy, sad, glad, joy, sorrow and love" (Loevinger, 1976, p. 18). The adventure educator might feel frustrated from discussions on feelings with inadequate replies.

Cooperation is important to the conformist. However, if one did not experience trusting relationships earlier in life he or she may take a "self-protective course" (Loevinger p. 17). Self-protection is identified in the person who externalizes and projects blame: "The reason we couldn't get dinner ready is because the stupid stove wouldn't light and Jimmy wasn't helping." Exhibiting intense competitive behavior is another sign of self-protection.

Conscientious-conformist (16–22 years). There begins an increase in self-awareness as the young teenager enters early adulthood. One's inner life is still simplistic. Feelings are vague and difficult to articulate. Typically they are expressed as lonely, homesick, and most often, as self-conscious. The individual internalizes a sense of responsibility and is able to establish long-term goals (temporal perspective changes). This higher level is more concerned with doing the right thing than simply following rules.

This person is not deterministic; he or she recognizes that he or she has choices and rights. Unlike in the lower stages, work is no longer seen as drudgery. Unless the work is routine or boring it is viewed as positive with achievement being an end in itself.

Autonomous (22–40 years). This stage is labeled autonomy not simply because one is more in control but because one recognizes the importance of freedom in all people. This person copes well with inner conflict, does not see the world through polarities (but recognizes the complexity of situations), and places high value on personal relationships.

Integrated (41 years and above). The highest level is also the most difficult to describe according to Loevinger. She explains this by the rarity it is attained, the subjective nature of the researcher (how can someone describe a level he or she has not attained), and the nuances and subtleties of this stage. Her best definition was simply equating it with Maslow's self-actualized individual.

Erikson's Stages of Human Development

Since Freud examined conflict between the id and super-ego as stemming from psychosexual tension there is little direct value in his work for adventure educators. A more applicable use of conflict-resolution stage theory comes from Erikson. Erikson's psychosocial perspective is more in line with the curricula objectives in adventure education.

In many ways Erikson provides the most important overview of life stages for adventure education because it allows the facilitator an idea of the general issues his or her clientele are facing. Erikson separated the steps more along age lines asserting that at each stage individuals go through a psychosocial crisis. Of the eight stages he proposed the first and the latter six are most applicable to adventure educators. If earlier conflicts are not resolved in a positive way then problems may emerge in later stages. This is particularly a concern with Erikson's initial stage of *trust versus mistrust*. Trust is such a vital component of adventure education, yet, it is conceivable that it would be very difficult to resolve something so deep rooted during adventure activities.

Middle school (8–12 years). During the middle-school years the child wrestles with *industry versus inferiority*. The child aspires to develop skills and is beginning to learn teamwork. Achievement and success is of utmost importance. Adventure experiences teaching specific skills such as canoeing and climbing build self-esteem by making the child feel able and useful.

Adventure activities focusing on team-building skills are important but need to be approached cautiously. Team maturity is a stage of development. A child unable to work in a team is not deviant but merely not ready for group work. This is not to say that this child does not value his social group. Therefore, one can see the need to gradually introduce team concepts and allow children to progress at their own pace.

Early adolescence (13–17 years). Entering early adolescence, the challenge is *group identity versus alienation*. The young teen seeks peer approval and wants to fit in. Adventure activities can be more challenging, a longer duration, and group-oriented. Teamwork is very satisfying so the challenge of the adventure educator may be to provide lone time, an opportunity for reflection.

Later adolescence (18–22 years). The college age manifests the challenge of *individual identity versus roles diffusion*. The question of who am I becomes more pronounced. Values, autonomy, and seeking one's path are the focal points at this stage. Adventure experiences can focus on initiation, rites of passage, and goal setting. There is probably no state in a person's life where adventure education is more valuable. In our secular society, deprived of formal rituals, outdoor activities can assist in facilitating the transition from youth to adulthood.

Early adulthood. The crisis for this stage is *intimacy versus isolation or stagnation*. The young adult internalizes the needs of another as equal to one's own. Although intimacy may be practiced earlier, it is not sustainable until this stage. At this stage one's ego is more in check. Clients demonstrate an ability to delay gratification, control impulsive and aggressive behavior, and direct energy towards work (Colarusso, 1992, p. 145). Failing to find intimacy, the young adult runs the risk of being isolated and self-absorbed into midlife.

Middle adulthood. *Generativity versus self-absorption* becomes the issue through one's midlife. Nurturing relationships and giving of oneself to social issues indicate a healthy transition from young adulthood. Jung talked of this stage as the emergence of wisdom. Adventure educators should take advantage of individuals in their forties and fifties for their desire and ability to be mentors for younger participants. This can prove to be a win-win situation for all involved.

Late adulthood. The final stage proposed by Erikson was *integrity versus despair*. Essentially this is the time when individuals look back on their lives. The person who fears death, blames circumstances and others for how life turned out, and feels hopelessness, has taken the path of despair. Conversely, the older adult who accepts responsibility for the way things turned out and reviews the good with the bad in an objective light experiences integrity. As more adventure activities are provided for this age group facilitation techniques should be developed that go beyond recreation and education (e.g., ecotourism) and foster personal development.

Selman's Stages of Interpersonal Reasoning

Robert Selman (1976) addressed the manner in which people interpret interpersonal relations. Selman's work has tremendous implications for adventure education. Much of what we stress emanates of relationship issues. For example, if the child has not matured to the level of discerning the nuances of relationships then it may be improper to expect an ability to work in teams. His work focused on elementary age to the young teenager.

Self-reflective role taking (8–10 years). The child can only interpret interpersonal relations under specific situations. There is difficulty in seeing two or more perspectives though the child can understand other's expectations. Adventure activities could introduce concepts of trust and teamwork but should focus more on skill acquisition. Small groups and pairs may offer a gradual introduction to the complexities of relationships. Specific problem-solving activities may be preferable to ones which elicit strong emotional responses.

Multiple role taking (10–12 years). Taking on the third view (perspective of another) is developing in the child at this stage. This is the preferable stage for providing team-oriented activities. Empathy often emerges as the most powerful insight from adventure activities and individuals can now begin to articulate this at their level.

Social and conventional (12–15 years). Clients at this stage understand many of the subtleties involved in relationships. They are able to take a societal view where actions are judged by how they influence all individuals. Individuals are more likely to be team-mature as a result of empathy skills.

Cognitive Development

Perhaps the most important domain regarding a client's development is in cognitive processes. Creating sophisticated metaphors will be in vain if your client cannot grasp the connections. Indeed, an awareness of your client's cognitive stage may dictate the processing technique one would use. For example, one technique for debriefing adventure experiences uses Bloom's Taxonomy (Gass and Priest, 1997). Addressing the last three levels (analysis, synthesis, and evaluation) requires abstract thinking which may be difficult for someone at a concrete level (knowledge, comprehension, and application). Cognitive ability, in this context, is not indicative of intelligence but simply refers to the development stage.

Piaget's work with children demonstrated that they learn in distinct steps. The concept of conservation is not something automatically grasped by young children. Knowing that pouring a liquid from a short container into a long container results in the same amount of liquid is simply not understood by a young child. Piaget studied cognitive development up to the young teenager, noting that at each stage significant patterns in learning could be documented. The two stages of most interest to the adventure educator are the concrete and formal operations.

Concrete operations (7–11 years). The child's ability to think logically and perform tasks mentally without the actual object begins the most important stage to cognitive development. Adventure experiences become more feasible at this stage because the child can grasp skills prior to the experience. Though the level of abstract thinking is limited, the child will admit to not understanding (at the previous stage this will not occur and the child may claim to understand something he does not). Again, skill-oriented activities such as sailing or canoeing can be used at this stage.

Formal operations (11–15 years). A child learns to think abstractly and reason at a higher level in the early teens. Piaget observed that three different thought processes emerge: interpropositional thinking (seeing relationships), combinatorial analysis (systematic approach to problem solving), and hypothetical-deductive reasoning (Frieberg, 1987, p. 356). More sophisticated problem-solving activities can be facilitated for groups at this stage.

Perry's Cognitive Levels

Continuing Piaget's work to the later stages of development was William Perry. He furthered research on Piaget's concrete and formal operation stages by studying how young adults reason. His work has profound implications for processing initiatives and other adventure activities. In its essence, he found that individuals learn to assimilate knowledge at four levels: *dualistic, multiplistic, relativism,* and *commitment to relativism* (Barrow, 1986, p. 21).

Dualistic. At this level the client only recognizes between right and wrong. This can be a frustrating level for the facilitator. The aim for clients at this level may simply be to move them up to a larger world-view; that there may be many solutions to a problem and many ways to view a situation.

Multiplistic. After a client successfully crosses the "poison peanut butter pit" on the ropes course, he asks: "How are you supposed to do this?" This question seems odd in light of the fact that he got over just fine. This person accepts that there is more than one answer to a problem but cannot see that there is not *one* correct answer.

Relativism. The relativist thinker is able to see that solutions to problems are situational. Clients offer creative solutions to initiatives and are able to look at each problem in its own light. Thinking becomes more organized and analytical.

Commitment to relativism. At this stage the client internalizes relativism but also forms strong opinions and values. Essentially, he sees the big picture and where he stands in it.

The first three levels offer the adventure educator a unique opportunity to expand perspectives on problems and individual issues.

Moral Development

The child does not begin life with a readiness to obey, or even understand, social rules and laws. He must be socialized. The infant begins life with a completely egocentric view of the world. Moral development involves a decentering and an increasing appreciation of the views and rights of others. A child thinks and perceives differently at successive stages. Piaget tells us that the child aged seven to twelve is still concrete in his or her thinking; that thought is oriented toward concrete things and events in the immediate present. This child, then, is mainly concerned with the real rather then the potential (Breger, 1974). Values and personal responsibility are themes which emerge throughout adventure education curricula. Just as facilitators need to be concerned with the client's cognitive ability they should not assume that all people are at the same moral level or even view moral dilemmas in similar ways. The seminal work of Piaget and Kohlberg give important insights into specific moral development stages.

Piaget

Piaget's studies on young children initiated tremendous interest in the moral as well as the cognitive development of children. He noted progress at around seven to eight years through a stage he labeled *morality of cooperation* (Scarr et al., 1986).

At this age, the child is no longer bound to the authority of adults. He is more able to work cooperatively and is more flexible in establishing rules with peers. The adventure educator can foster the development of this stage by offering freedom for groups to create rules for activities and self-guidance.

By 11 or 12, the child starts to look at the intentions of the transgressor, not simply the transgression. For example, before the child reaches this stage someone who stole food on the canoe trip would be no worse then the person who forgot to pack the food. Morality changes from authority to autonomy.

Kohlberg

Lawrence Kohlberg continued Piaget's studies into adolescence. He found that moral development followed three major stages: preconventional, conventional, and postconventional. No ages have been assigned to the various stages. Although the earlier stages generally emerge before ones' teen years, it is important to recognize that many of our clients operate at low-morality levels and that is precisely why some are involved in our adventure programs. As such, the value of Kohlberg's morality levels cannot be overstated in adventure education.

Preconventional. Punishment is the determining factor for those at this morality level. Concern is strictly on whether one gets caught, not on the ethical dilemma of the transgression. Within this context can be two substages: *punishment-obedience orientation* and *instrumental relativist.* The former responds simply to punishment to change behavior while the instrumental relativist will obey rules when he or she sees that it will provide some benefit.

Conventional. Society and the social group dictate moral and ethical behavior at this level. Entering this level the individual seeks to impress others with a *good boy– nice girl orientation.* Advancing to this stage the individual recognizes the need for social order and accepts that fixed rules must be established and obeyed.

Postconventional. Higher level morality emerges with this social contract stage. Rules are based on mutual agreement but the right of the individual must be taken into account. At the highest level moral decisions should be based on consistently applied self-chosen principles.

Problems and Concerns With Stage Development Theory

There are many who question the validity of set stages. Environmental theorists such as Bandura (Turner and Helm, 1983) claim that extrinsic influences such as modeling behavior are far more likely to create behavioral changes than passing through invariant stages. In contrast with stage theory are the environmental theories proposing that we develop in response to external influences—a nature versus nurture argument.

Designing adventure programs based solely on stage theory would be both foolish and risky. Like any theory, it should be used as a foundation. It is a model we can use in our thinking and program development. Several concerns about stage theory have been discussed in the literature. Perhaps the most strident attack is the notion that development is culturally neutral. Piaget studied primarily middle-class, European children. Kohlberg studied afflu-

ent college students. Though many attempts have been made to broaden the diversity of study subjects, the case can be made that there is a cultural bias inherent in the theories. Indeed, only recently has gender been considered a factor in development. For example, moral development in girls tends to follow a different path than boys (Freiberg, 1987).

Another concern in the use of stage theory is the assumption we ascend in a consistent, sequential manner and that reaching the highest level is our ultimate aim. Attaining higher stages is not a race, there is no brass ring. What we need our clients to realize are the opportunities available in all types of growth. A person who is developing to his potential becomes more autonomous, independent, and free of determinism. A diversity of skills emerges to assist in tackling life's challenges.

Regardless of the researchers' school of thought, little argument exists on whether we develop in concrete ways through our life. To mitigate some of the cultural bias, it may be best to view the development along life stages opposed to strict age definitions. Loevinger stated quite tersely in her tome on ego development: "The question most often asked—What age does each stage correspond to?—I shall not answer" (1976, p. 13). In order to facilitate the use of these theories, age parameters were given. But these are simply broad parameters.

Summary

A cookie-cutter approach to adventure programming has many disadvantages, not the least of which is safety. Adventure education is a powerful tool; anything powerful enough to help is powerful enough to harm. Age and life stages need to have a significant consideration in program design.

Applying principles of human development theory should aid the practitioner in several ways. Though many criticisms can be levied against stage developmental theory, it would be a mistake to disregard it. A thoughtful practitioner can identify the weaknesses inherent in its simplicity and cultural biases and design properly sequenced and age-appropriate adventure activities.

The following is a partial list of considerations one might use in designing adventure education curricula based on stage development:

1. Middle-school age children have the basic psychomotor skills required for the physical nature of adventure pursuits but may be deficient in cognitive and social skills. Focus on teamwork needs to be carefully presented. Ten-year-olds are capable of the same physical tasks as a college age individual. The scope and depth of the skill would be different but by the time a child is in middle school

essential physical development and coordination has taken place. Therefore the limitation in designing adventure education activities would lie more in the cognitive and social domains.

2. Trust levels are developed early in life. It may be that this will be difficult to work on at any age if they were not resolved early in a person's life.

3. Since adventure education is about creating experiences which push people beyond preconceived limitations, perhaps this should include pushing them to higher developmental levels. Of course we as facilitators do that regardless of intention but having an idea of their current level we might create what is known as optimal dissonance. Figuratively speaking, we can nudge them into the next level or make them aware of the opportunities at this level.

4. People develop throughout their life. With the graying of baby boomers, more adventure activities will be demanded at older ages. Instead of just offering recreational and educational adventure experiences, we also need to develop processing techniques which cater to the psychosocial developmental needs of older participants.

References

Barrow, J. C. (1986). *Fostering cognitive development of students*. San Francisco, CA: Jossey-Bass.

Breger, L. (1974). *Instinct to identity*. New York, NY: Prentice-Hall.

Colarusso, C. A. (1992). *Child and adult development: A psychoanalytic introduction for clinicians*. New York, NY: Plenum Press.

Csikszentmihalyi, M. (1975). *Beyond boredom and anxiety*. San Francisco, CA: Jossey-Bass.

Frieberg, K. L. (1987). *Human development: A life-span approach* (3rd ed.). Boston, MA: Jones and Bartlett Publishers, Inc.

Gallahue, D. L., and Ozmun, J. C. (1995). *Development: Infants, children, adolescents, adults* (3rd ed.). New York, NY: McGraw-Hill.

Gass, M., and Priest, S. (1997). *Effective leadership in adventure programming*. Champaign, IL: Human Kinetics.

Loevinger, J. (1976). *Ego development*. San Francisco, CA: Jossey-Bass.

Scarr, S., Weinberg, R. A., and Levine, A. (1986). *Understanding development*. San Diego, CA: Harcourt Brace Javanovich.

Schoel, J., Prouty, D., and Radcliffe, P. (1988). *Island of healing*. Hamilton, MA: Project Adventure.

Selman, R. L. (1976). Social-cognitive understanding: a guide to educational and clinical practice. In T. Likona (Ed.), *Moral development and behavior: Theory, research and social issues*. New York, NY: Holt, Rinehart, and Winston.

Turner, J. S., and Helm, D. B. (1983). *Life span development* (2nd ed.). New York, NY: Holt, Rinehart, and Winston.

Chapter 27

Teaching by Inquiry

Donald R. Hammerman
Northern Illinois University

Inquiry is by no means a new approach to learning. Socrates, Plato and Aristotle are said to have employed inquiry as a means to provoke comprehension on the part of their followers. Inquiry is time-consuming. It involves a high degree of interaction between teacher and learners. The teacher or leader is the asker of questions, not the one who gives answers. Students rely on their own observations and analysis of data. The teacher stimulates the learning process by posing questions to students causing them to think about (a) what they have observed, (b) what is likely to occur next, and (c) a course of action or steps to pursue in order to bring about a certain action or solve a particular problem.

The term *inquiry* is often used synonymously with exploratory learning, discovery learning, problem solving and Socratic questioning. While being closely related and containing elements that reinforce and complement one another, inquiry, discovery, and problem solving are not one and the same. The process of inquiry can lead to discovery, to making inferences, to arriving at generalizations and drawing conclusions. These elements, in turn, can be a part of the problem-solving process.

Inquiry Training

Inquiring or inquiry is a very natural way to learn. It is the way most of us go about learning on our own outside of formal learning situations. We pose questions like: I wonder why? How did this happen? How does this work? What do you suppose would happen if?

In a more formal sense inquiry training refers to a model for teaching students some of the techniques and applications of scientific or scholarly inquiry pioneered by J. Richard Suchman. In Suchman's model students are usually presented with a puzzling or discrepant event and then invited to direct their questions to the teacher. This reverses the traditional role of teacher asking and students parroting back information gleaned from the textbook. The students must test their hypothesis by framing questions which can only be answered with a yes or a no.

Picture the following scenario:

> A group of wilderness campers is out for a day's trek in the Colorado Rockies. They have paused for a brief lunch break just below timberline seeking shelter from the biting wind before continuing on to the summit. One of the group poses the question: "Why do the trees not grow above this elevation?" Rather than launch into a long-winded verbal explanation, the leader turns the question back to the group: "Why do you think there are few trees beyond this point?" The following dialogue ensues:

HIKER: As we've climbed there has been a definite drop in temperature. Does climate have something to do with it?

LEADER: Yes.

ANOTHER HIKER: The air also feels much drier up here than down below, am I right?

LEADER: Yes.

HIKER: Other than for a few patches of old snow here and there, there is no running water; that would seem to support the lack of moisture theory, right?

LEADER: Correct.

HIKER: The few trees remaining as we approach timberline are definitely smaller and more thinly spaced. Does this mean a much shorter growing season at this altitude?

LEADER: Yes.

HIKER: Why are most of the trees just above us gnarled and deformed?

LEADER: Rephrase your question please so that I can answer it with a yes or a no.

HIKER: I've noticed that the wind is blowing harder up here. Could that deform a tree over a period of time?

LEADER: Yes.

Thus the questioning-answering process continues until basic concepts are grasped or a puzzling situation is solved.

Instruction Through Inquiry

The traditional approach to imparting "skill knowledge" is through lecture-demonstration, i.e., I'll teach you what you need to know about this specific skill by showing you what to do and explaining how to do it. In situations in which the safety of the participant is of paramount importance this is usually the most efficient procedure. Inquiry techniques can be employed in combination with lecture-demonstration without diminishing the effectiveness of the instruction. In fact, in most cases, by varying instructional strategies and introducing techniques such as inquiry and problem solving, learner involvement is increased and student interest heightened.

As my first example I will consider the teaching of specific canoeing skills, namely, some of the basic canoe strokes. All of the essential safety instruction concerning launching the canoe, proper seating or kneeling position, and what to do if swamped, will already have been covered. Now we are ready to handle the canoe on water. Beginners usually experience difficulty in keeping the craft moving in a straight line. Thus it is essential to begin with basic strokes that will enable paddlers to move the canoe forward in a straight line, and then proceed to strokes for changing direction and reversing direction. The traditional mode of teaching would have the instructor demonstrating and giving appropriate verbal explanation.

Consider the following scenario employing inquiry process along with lecture-demonstration as an alternative. In this example, two students are in each canoe; one in the bow, the other in the stern—canoes gathered in front of the instructor on a quiet lake.

INSTRUCTOR: To move the canoe forward it works best if the sternperson and bowperson paddle on opposite sides of the canoe. Place your hands on the paddle like this and take long, smooth, strokes [demonstrates]. Now try it. [Students try this for a few minutes.]

INSTRUCTOR: Now both of you paddle on the same side of the canoe and see what happens. [Students try this for a few minutes.]

INSTRUCTOR: This is the sweep stroke, and this is reverse sweep. [Demonstrates both strokes.] With bowperson and sternperson paddling on opposite sides once again, see what happens when one of you sweeps and the other reverse sweeps. Make the canoe move in different directions. [Canoers experiment for a while.] Now let's review. Bowperson paddle on the right, sternperson on the left. To change direction to the right what stroke should the bowperson use and what should the sternperson do?

ANSWER: Bowperson reverse sweeps, while sternperson sweeps.

INSTRUCTOR: To move the canoe to the left which stroke would each paddler use?

ANSWER: Bowperson sweeps; sternperson reverse sweeps.

Students practice these maneuvers changing from one side of the canoe to the other until they get used to the feel of both strokes from a left-handed and right-handed paddle position:

INSTRUCTOR: In running a river it is sometimes necessary to veer the canoe quickly in one direction or the other in order to avoid a rock, a submerged log, or some other hazard. To do this the bowperson does a bow rudder [demonstrates] or a cross-bow rudder [demonstrates] while the sternperson executes a broad sweep stroke on the opposite side [demonstrates]. Bowperson, assume paddling on the left side of the canoe, and you wish to veer left, which stroke would you use?

ANSWER: Bow rudder.

INSTRUCTOR: What should the sternperson do?

ANSWER: Sweep on the right.

INSTRUCTOR: Bowperson, you are still paddling on the left, but you need to veer quickly to the right. What do you do?

ANSWER: Cross-bow rudder.

INSTRUCTOR: And the sternperson?

ANSWER: He either does a reverse sweep on the side on which he or she has been paddling (the right) or switches to the opposite side and uses a broad sweep.

These maneuvers are practiced by both paddlers on each side of the canoe and in both the bow and stern position. Additional examples of inquiry-type questions are: "What will happen if you use this stroke in the bow and this one in the stern? If you want to turn your canoe around to reverse direction, what combination of strokes would you use?"

Other basic strokes such as the draw stroke and the J-stroke can be presented in similar fashion. These examples should suffice, however, to demonstrate that it is possible to present some basic skill information by incorporating questions and inquiry into the lecture-demonstration process.

For the next example to illustrate how teaching by inquiry can be applied to adventure education I assume that a small group of backpackers has set off on a week to 10-day trekking expedition in the western Rockies. This involves moving from site to site every day or so. Once beyond the trailhead the trip leader must map out daily hiking routes. The leader who wishes to use inquiry teaching methods and involve participation in the decision-making process might conduct a discussion along the following lines:

LEADER: Tomorrow we intend to break camp and move to a new site on the other side of the mountain. [At this point the leader brings out a topographic map and compass.] Let's map out a route that will be scenic and not too vigorous since we're just at the start of our trip and still adapting to the altitude.

HIKER: The shortest route appears to be straight over this pass.

LEADER: Yes, you're right; that is the shortest line in distance, but what kind of climb is it? [The group members examine the map and determine that they are at an elevation of 7,000 feet, and the pass is situated at about 9,800 feet.]

LEADER: That may be a little more than we want to tackle on only our second day out. Are there some alternative routes?

HIKER: What if we followed this stream through the valley between the two mountains?

LEADER: That's a possibility. Let's figure out the distance. [They check the scale on the map.]

HIKER: It looks to be about nine miles with little change in elevation. We should be able to handle that easily.

LEADER: I agree. And an added advantage is that we'll always be close to a water supply. Why is that a good idea?

GROUP: Because we need to take in plenty of fluids at these elevations to keep us from dehydrating.

Later that day the group approaches its destination and must begin searching for a suitable campsite. The trip leader continues the teaching by inquiry process:

LEADER: What factors do we need to keep in mind in selecting our campsite for tonight?

GROUP: We want to be sheltered from the wind. We want to locate the tents so they catch the early morning sunlight. We want to be fairly close to our water supply.

LEADER: Which direction would our tents face? Where should the cooking area be set up? Where should we locate the latrine?

Thus the instruction continues with the leader subtly providing certain bits of information and guiding learning to acquire additional information and grasp other concepts by having the participants confront real-life situations and come up with appropriate solutions.

Additional Considerations

In adventure education there are some skills that are so technical—where procedures are so exact, and where safety is at such a high premium—that there is little room for teaching by inquiry. An example of this would be in the realm of rock climbing where certain basic skills must be acquired; safety measures must be adhered to exactly, and in the interests of efficiency there is usually a best way to do it. In situations like this there is no question as to the most efficient method—straight demonstration and explanation.

Once the basic skills are learned and a certain amount of proficiency attained, however, some inquiry may be applied to help a group investigate and/or solve a particular problem. For example, "Now that we know what we know, which specific climbing techniques will work best in getting around this ledge or in ascending this crack?" Or returning to our previous section on canoeing. "Which design works best in various conditions, i.e., large bodies of water as opposed to rivers; fast water as opposed to smooth water?" "What are the advantages of a longer canoe versus a shorter canoe or the reverse under different conditions?" "What are the advantages of a broader beamed canoe versus a narrow beamed craft?" "Round-bottomed versus flat-bottomed?"

A Final Word

Adventure to some is a state of mind, not so much a place or a physical risk as a mental challenge. One can find adventure in the most unlikely places—in the midst of a teeming metropolis or in a secluded ocean cove as well as on a wild river or on a mountain peak. The wise instructor and leader recognizes the value of allowing learners to experience the joy and thrill of learning by themselves.

Chapter 28

Sequencing the Adventure Experience

Christian Bisson
Northland College

We must remember that the most important thing is sequencing. Then, we must remember that there is no sequence.

—Tom Smith

Anyone modestly concerned with transmitting information is intuitively aware of the importance of sequencing. For example, when writing a letter, an article, or a book, it will be easier for the reader to understand if the written information is organized in a logical and sequential manner. Lectures, presentations, and lessons abide by the same rule.

This omnipresence of "sequences" in our lives exists for a good reason. One could argue that because of the way we understand and perceive time, we are bound to a linear perception of what happens around us. This means that we will always experience life in a successive order of events, words, and thoughts.

Despite the fact that events are compelled to occur in a linear fashion (i.e., past, present, and future), we can plan the sequence before it occurs and therefore take some control over the way we exchange information with each other.

Perhaps the most universal and commonly used sequence is the classic "story line" sequence which includes a beginning, a middle, and an end. Sequences also exist in linear model (i.e., from simple to complex and vice versa) and in a circular model (i.e., from general to specific then back to general). For whatever reason a specific sequence is adopted, the bottom line is that sequences are an intrinsic part of human learning and development. Educators certainly do not escape this reality. Since education often involves transmitting information or presenting experiences, whether we like it or not, sequencing plays an important role in our profession.

Uniqueness or Universality

Sequencing has been defined as the act of "paying attention to the order of activities so that the order is appropriate to the needs of the group" (Schoel, Prouty, and Radcliffe, 1988, p. 35). The literature also suggests that one of the most important programming components of an adventure-based learning experience is the selection of activities and the order in which these are presented (Anderson and Frison, 1992; Nadler and Luckner, 1992; Priest, in press; Roland and Havens, 1983; Rohnke, 1989; Rohnke and Butler, 1995; Schoel et al., 1988; Smith, 1991).

Consequently, specialists and practitioners in this field tend to agree that adventure activities should be sequenced in a logical manner in order to reach specific educational goals (Bisson, 1997). In addition, a variety of authors have addressed not only the importance of sequencing, but also the common belief regarding the uniqueness of each adventure sequence.

For instance, Schoel et al. (1988) argued that "a good sequence for one group may not work for another. There is no exact formula" (p. 77). Like Schoel et al. (1988), several other authors have expressed the importance of customizing a sequence specific to the nature and needs of each group (Rohnke, 1989; Rohnke and Butler, 1995; Smith, Roland, Havens, and Hoyt, 1992). In essence, the popular argument is that there is no magical recipe for sequencing—each group requires a unique and customized set of activities.

However, despite this argument, when we look carefully at a few of the most commonly known prescribed sequences in our literature, apparent similarities can be found in their overall progression. What is even more astonishing is that these similarities exist even though the prescribed sequences were originally customized for different populations such as people with disabilities (Roland and Havens, 1983), patients in mental health institutions (Roland, Summers, Friedman, Barton, and McCarty, 1987; Roland, Keene, Dubois, and Lentini, 1987), children with behavioral disorders (Robb and Ewert, 1987), youth in counseling programs (Schoel et al., 1988), adult corporate training programs (Priest, Attarian, and Schubert, 1993), and general populations (Rohnke, 1989).

This last observation somehow contradicts the common assumption regarding the uniqueness of each sequence. Consequently, a dilemma arises between uniqueness and universality. On one hand, it is argued that program planning should remain flexible to allow for customization, yet on the other hand, it seems that a certain universality exists between sequences prescribed for distinct groups.

In my opinion, both conditions often coexist. However, before explaining this position on sequencing adventure activities, I believe it is important to look more carefully at the evolution of the prescribed sequence models that shared the observed similarities.

The Sequential Process

The sequential process model was developed at the Vinland National Center in Minnesota during the early 1980s. Roland and Havens's (1983) "sequential process" model for people with disabilities included five levels: (a) awareness activities, (b) group cooperative games, (c) individual initiative tasks (i.e., the adapted low ropes course), (d) group initiative tasks, and (e) high adventure activities.

Overall, it seems like the sequential process proposed by Roland and Havens (1983) progressed by alternating individual- and group-oriented activities. It is also important to point out that this alternating process has not been strongly encouraged by others, and eventually, Roland himself modified his own sequence to create a more group-oriented progression.

The Experiential Challenge Program

Later on, Roland, Summers, et al. (1987) proposed another five-step model named the *Experiential Challenge Program* (ECP). This model included the following steps: (a)

goal setting, (b) awareness, (c) trust, (d) group problem solving, and (e) individual problem solving. The ECP was originally designed for patients in mental health institutions, but soon was adapted to other settings (Smith et al., 1992). The steps were presented in a pyramidal structure (Figure 28.1) to express the progressive nature of the model. The pyramid also illustrates that each step establishes a foundation for the following level of activities. For instance, step one serves as the foundation for the rest of the sequence, and so on.

The Activity Process Model

Soon after the publication of the ECP sequence, the model was slightly modified and adapted to a different setting. This time, Roland, Keene, et al. (1987) traded the image of the pyramid for a circular model. The reason for this change was that now each step of the ECP included activities that contained components from all the other steps. For instance, they argued that an activity such as the Trust Circle (i.e., better known as the Willow in the Wind) includes not only trust, but also cooperation from the spotters and initiative from the "faller." This new model (Figure 28.2) was called the *Activity Process Model* (Roland, 1993, p. 199; Roland, Keene, et al., 1987, p. 69).

In this new conceptualization of the ECP, the core of the circle bears the term *challenge activities,* and represented the fundamental nature of the program. The five stages or programmatic levels were placed in a circle around the core to indicate that each level shared common adventure components such as communication, cooperation, and trust. The next circle indicates that "debriefing"

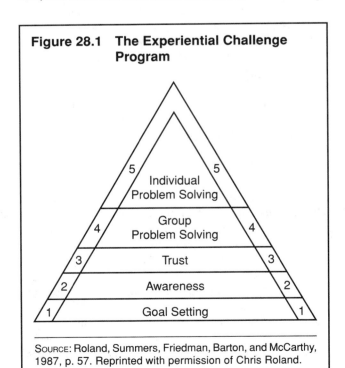

Figure 28.1   The Experiential Challenge Program

5 5 Individual Problem Solving
4 4 Group Problem Solving
3 3 Trust
2 2 Awareness
1 1 Goal Setting

Source: Roland, Summers, Friedman, Barton, and McCarthy, 1987, p. 57. Reprinted with permission of Chris Roland.

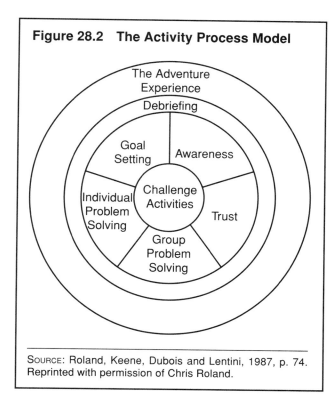

Figure 28.2   The Activity Process Model

SOURCE: Roland, Keene, Dubois and Lentini, 1987, p. 74. Reprinted with permission of Chris Roland.

The Challenge Education Sequence

Inspired by Roland, Keene, et al.'s (1987) and Roland, Summers, et al.'s (1987) work, Robb and Ewert (1987), and later Robb and Leslie (1987) proposed an adventure sequence of their own to work with children displaying behavioral disorders. Their sequence model was titled the Challenge Education Sequence (CES) which included seven steps: (a) goal setting, (b) awareness, (c) trust, (d) cooperative activities, (e) problem solving, (f) group challenge, and (g) adventure activities. The CES model was presented as a staircase to illustrate the progressive nature of the sequence (Figure 28.3). The first three steps of the CES are identical to the first steps of the ECP presented earlier in this chapter. The fourth step differs from Roland, Keene, et al.'s (1987) and Roland, Summers, et al.'s (1987) sequences by introducing a new category titled "cooperative activities."

In the CES, Robb and Ewert (1987) seemed to have returned to a sequential progression that inserted individual challenge activities within group-challenge tasks. This way, scheduling "problem-solving" activities after "cooperative activities" and before "group challenge" shifts the task orientation of the participants from focusing on the group, to focusing on the individual, to again focusing on the group.

This insertion of individual-oriented tasks between group-centered tasks is at least intriguing since it appears that individual challenges are most often introduced at the end of a program because it is assumed that the group will then be ready to offer greater psychological support (Priest, 1996). In this vein, some authors (Priest, 1996; Schoel et al., 1988) also argue that personal problem-solving activities, such as the low-ropes-course events, can promote

or "processing" was performed throughout the experience. The outer circle—the adventure experience—represented a sixth level in the form of a traditional outdoor pursuit activity (i.e., rock climbing and rappelling).

Roland, Keene, et al. (1987) explained that the realm of the adventure experience constituted a perimeter where all levels of the inner core can be integrated. For instance, rock climbing is presented to encourage goal setting, awareness, trust, group problem solving, and individual problem solving. Therefore, for the participants, the adventure experience represents a peak experience. After gaining the necessary skills and attributes during the first part of the program, they could, if ready, participate in a more global and concrete adventure experience. On this issue, Roland (1993) wrote:

> The key concept was that the "inner core" had been initially developed while the "outer core"—the adventure experience—was developed later. This perimeter was thus dependent on the core, but the core was not dependent on the perimeter. (p. 205)

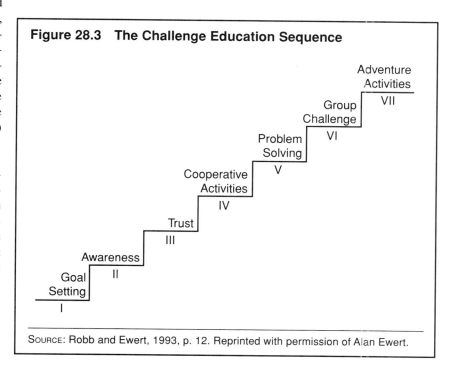

Figure 28.3   The Challenge Education Sequence

SOURCE: Robb and Ewert, 1993, p. 12. Reprinted with permission of Alan Ewert.

group cooperation because they require group members to physically spot and encourage each other during the execution of the task.

While Robb and Ewert (1987) optimized the work of Roland and Havens (1983); Roland, Keene, et al. (1987); and Roland, Summers, et al. (1987) on the development of a prescribed adventure sequence, another group of practitioners developed a sequence of their own. This group of practitioners (i.e., Project Adventure, Inc.) had perhaps the greatest influence on the development of adventure programming in North America for the past 20 years. Their perception of a correct sequence is therefore critical.

Project Adventure's Trust Fall and Spotting Exercise Sequence

All of Project Adventure's publications emphasize the importance of sequencing in adventure programming (Rohnke, 1989; Rohnke and Butler, 1995; Schoel et al., 1988). They strongly adhere to the idea that there is no right or wrong sequence and that each group requires a customized progression (Rohnke, 1989; Rohnke and Butler, 1995; Schoel et al., 1988). However, they also advocate the use of a three-step fundamental introductory sequence. This short sequence is known as "the Trust Fall and spotting exercise sequence" (Rohnke, 1989; Schoel et al., 1988). The three steps include (a) icebreaker and acquaintance activities, (b) deinhibitizer activities, and (c) beginning trust and spotting activities (Rohnke, 1989; Schoel et al., 1988). Schoel et al. (1988) indicate that the Trust Fall sequence, as it is often referred to, is fundamental to the Project Adventure curriculum because it assures psychological and physical safety by developing trust and mutual caring among the members of a participating group.

The sequence is also seen as a preparatory stage before involving the group in more challenging activities. Schoel et al. (1988) recommend introducing the Trust Fall sequence before attempting the low- and high-ropes-course activities. On the preparatory aspect of the Trust Fall and spotting exercise sequence, Rohnke (1989) wrote: "This sequence takes the group from icebreakers, to deinhibitizers, to the trust activities so that the group is prepared for the [group] initiatives" (p. 10). Rohnke also explained that the sequence allows the instructor to accomplish two goals. First, it helps with the development of group cohesion in a gradual, nonthreatening manner; and second, it helps to develop the spotting skills of each participant. Spotting is an integral and essential safety procedure used during group initiatives and low-ropes-course elements. Basically, it is a "human safety net provided by other people for the persons doing an activity" (Webster, 1989, p. 7).

As explained previously, the Trust Fall and spotting exercise sequence is only an introductory sequence for a much larger progression. However, it is important to note

that Project Adventure does not suggest that these activity categories are a definitive sequence. Nevertheless, Schoel et al. (1988) enumerate these categories of activities in an order that, to many practitioners and scholars, appears to be a valuable sequence. Consequently, the following sequence: (a) icebreaker and acquaintance activities, (b) deinhibitizer activities, (c) trust and empathy activities, (d) communication, (e) decision making and problem solving, (f) social responsibility, and (g) personal responsibility (Schoel et al., 1988, p. 69) has often been adopted as a standard sequence for many adventure programs (James, 1991; Priest, 1996; Rohnke, 1989). For the sake of clarity, I will refer to this sequence as the *Project Adventure sequence*.

Project Adventure Sequence

The Project Adventure (PA) sequence starts with the three steps explained in the previous section (i.e., icebreaker and acquaintance activities; deinhibitizer activities; trust and empathy activities). Additional categories of activities then introduce more group-oriented and individual-oriented challenges. Explanations of these categories follow.

Communication. Developing effective and respectful communication skills is the main objective of this step in the PA sequence. Schoel et al. (1988) mentioned that it is important to prepare the group to work together before placing them in complex problem-solving activities. They wrote:

> [Communication activities] provide an opportunity for group members to enhance their ability and skill to communicate thoughts, feelings, and behaviors more appropriately through activities which emphasize listening, verbal, and physical skills in the group decision-making process. (p. 69)

The reader will see later that this stage of the sequence can be considered a "team tool" (Priest et al., 1993) to be developed before attempting challenges that will require effective communication within the group.

Decision making and problem solving. The fifth step in the PA sequence introduces initiative activities (i.e., problem solving) which require the group to come up with effective ways of finding solutions to various problems. The problems are often physical and require cooperation, trust, and effective communication. Schoel et al. (1988) suggests that the members of the group have to learn to support each other while participating in a trial-and-error problem-solving process. The activities associated with this step are often presented in a sequence of their own, from the simple to the more complex.

Social responsibility. Although this step is identified using a somewhat generic title, the objective of this category of activities is quite specific. According to Schoel et al. (1988):

[Social responsibility activities] provide a setting wherein group participants can build upon previous gains in areas of acquaintances, trust, communications, and decision making, to develop skill in assessing and working effectively with the strengths and weaknesses of individuals in a group. (p. 72)

Activities in this category are often presented as individual tasks or skills to be performed for the benefit of others. Spotting, belaying, community service, and first-aid skills are a few examples of activities within this category. However, most adventure programs use only low-ropes-course activities to promote social responsibility. As explained earlier, spotting is an integral part of an individual low-ropes-course challenge and therefore becomes an ideal task underlining social responsibility through group support.

Personal responsibility. The seventh and final step of the PA sequence presents the group with more challenging individual tasks. High-ropes-course activities, rock climbing, and rappelling are classic examples of activities found at this stage of the program. The objective of these activities is to present challenges that will develop persistence, determination, and self-confidence in each participant (Schoel et al., 1988). Although these activities mainly focus on the individual, they can also require a degree of group support.

Also, as mentioned earlier, the PA sequence is perhaps the most known and accepted adventure sequence used today in adventure programming due to the popularity of books like *Islands of Healing* (Schoel et al., 1988) and *Cowstails and Cobras II* (Rohnke, 1989). Parts of the PA sequence can be found in programs for diverse populations such as in adventure therapy (Kimball, 1986), physical education (Anderson and Frison, 1992), and corporate adventure training (Priest et al., 1993).

The Corporate Adventure Training Sequence

The Corporate Adventure Training (CAT) sequence introduces categories of activities similar to the PA sequence. The CAT sequence includes five general categories: (a) classroom sessions, (b) socialization games, (c) group initiatives, (d) ropes courses, and (e) outdoor pursuits (Priest et al., 1993). The CAT sequence also includes two other general categories, "client visitations" and "other adventures," respectively placed at the beginning and end of the adventure program. For the purpose of this chapter, only four of the general categories will be discussed.

Socialization games. The socialization games category includes two specific types of activities: (a) familiarization and (b) deinhibitization (Priest et al., 1993). Like in the PA sequence, these two first steps are designed to help participants get to know each other while increasing their level of comfort within the group.

Group initiatives. The second category of activities includes team tools and team tasks (Priest et al., 1993). Team tools correspond to the trust and communication category of the PA sequence (Schoel et al., 1988). This set of activities focuses on the specific skills required to work efficiently as a group. Here trust and communication are the more common aspects. On the other hand, team tasks can be compared to the decision-making and problem-solving step of the PA sequence (Schoel et al., 1988). Activities in this subcategory present physical problems (i.e., initiatives) that require cooperation, planning, and group consensus.

Ropes courses. In this category, individuals participate in low- and high-ropes-course activities. The low-ropes-course activities are similar to the social responsibility phase of the PA sequence, while the high-ropes-course activities match the personal responsibility phase of the PA sequence (Schoel et al., 1988). Both subcategories contain activities that focus mainly on individual challenges that encourage group support. To that effect, group support on the low ropes course is often less psychological (e.g., through verbal encouragement) than physical (e.g., by spotting), as opposed to the high ropes course where group support is typically more psychological and less physical. Since most programs either do not allow students to belay each other on a high ropes course or use a static belay system (i.e., the participant is responsible for his or her own safety), the role of peer support is reduced to psychological encouragement. However, if a participant receives a belay from his or her peers, the support becomes both physical and psychological. For instance, in the activity called *Flying Squirrel* an individual is vertically hoisted up using a rope and pulley system activated by the group (Rohnke, 1989). The group here provides strong physical and psychological support.

Outdoor pursuits. The last category of activities in the CAT sequence includes traditional outdoor pursuit activities that are either activity based or wilderness based. In activity-based activities, the participants are introduced to outdoor pursuits that can be experienced in one day such as rock climbing, kayaking, or orienteering. Wilderness-based activities, on the other hand, last at least two days and are the equivalent of an expedition designed to integrate everything the group has learned up to that point. In other words, wilderness-based activities are the final test, or culminating experience, as suggested by Schoel et al. (1988). The outdoor pursuit category matches the "adventure experiences" of the activity process model (Roland, Keene, et al., 1987) or the "adventure activities" of the challenge education sequence (Robb and Ewert, 1987).

Common Phases Among Prescribed Sequences

After analysis, it becomes obvious that the CAT sequence has been strongly influenced by the prescribed sequences that preceded its appearance in the literature. This influence can be found across all of the prescribed adventure sequences presented in this review. As expressed at the beginning of this chapter, it is my contention that all of these prescribed sequences share similarities in their progression. To enhance these similarities, I have classified the various categories of adventure activity into four large, group-related, phases: (a) group formation, (b) group challenge, (c) group support, and (d) group achievement. Each of these phases represents a distinct activity focus. An analysis of these focus areas will help clarify the nomenclature used to identify the phases.

Group formation. Phase one of the classification refers to categories of activities such as goal setting, awareness, cooperative games, trust, communication, icebreaker, deinhibitizer, and socialization games. The focus of this phase is quite apparent. All of the activities used at the beginning of the prescribed sequences are designed to help the members of a new group get acquainted with each other. Their progressive set of activities allows the participants to experience fun in a safe social environment. In addition, some of the initial activities are purposefully designed to develop trust and communication skills among participants.

Group challenge. The second phase includes activities that are designed to challenge the group. Various appellations, such as group initiative tasks, group problem solving, group challenges, decision making and problem solving, and team tasks, are used to identify activities that present the group with physical or mental challenges. To resolve these challenges, the group must make decisions while cooperatively recognizing the need for leadership and followership. All of the prescribed sequences presented have included this type of category of activities. Most of them were introduced before the personal challenge activities and after the initial group formation activities. Only two prescribed sequences, the sequential process (Roland and Havens, 1983) and the challenge education sequence (Robb and Ewert, 1987) introduce their set of group challenge activities after having led the group through a series of personal challenges. All other prescribed sequences introduce the personal challenge activities after the group challenge phase.

Group support. The personal challenge activities encountered in the low- and high-ropes-course events are often used at the end or near the end of an adventure program. It seems that the prescribed sequences have all included this category of activities in the last segment of their progression. Professionals in this field have called it individual initiative tasks, high-adventure activities, individual problem solving, social and individual responsibil-

ity, or simply, low- and high-ropes activities. Regardless of their appellation, these categories of activities are quite similar because they require not only self-confidence and determination from the participant, but also psychological support and compassion on the group's part. Given that this study was mainly concerned with the development of group cohesion, the term *group support* was chosen to indicate this particular phase in the adventure sequence.

Group achievement. The final phase of the model is used to represent the category of activities that extends the adventure into the realm of traditional outdoor pursuit activities. This may include short-term canoeing, backpacking, and/or mountaineering expeditions, to name a few. The categories are titled adventure experiences, adventure activities, and activity-based or wilderness-based pursuits activities. Because these activities require more time and commitment from the participants, they are not present in all of the prescribed sequences. However, when present, they are invariably placed at the end of the experience.

The phases I have just described summarize the progressions suggested by the most commonly prescribed sequences. These phases are principally concerned with the various developmental stages that a group will experience as the adventure program unfolds. The phases could be regrouped into three large groupings: (a) the "group formation" and "group challenge" phases are group-oriented activities which are introduced at the beginning of the sequences, (b) the "group support" phase is a collection of individual-oriented activities which are introduced near the end of the sequences, (c) the final "group achievement" phase which involves traditional outdoor pursuit activities and/or expedition-type experiences are another group-oriented set of activities which are introduced at the end of the sequences.

Sequencing Group Development

Adventure programming has often been associated with small group development (Ewert, 1992; Kerr and Gass, 1995) and team building (Bronson, Gibson, Kichar, and Priest, 1992; Priest, 1996). Whether the goals of the adventure program focus on skill development or social growth, or have a therapeutical application, groups participating in these programs often experience various stages of group development (Kerr and Gass, 1995).

Group development was defined by Sarri and Galinsky (1974) as "changes through time in the internal structures, processes, and culture of the group" (p. 72). In addition, Sarri and Galinsky (1974) offered three dimensions to the changes in the life of a group: (a) social organization of the group (i.e., changes in the patterns of participants status among the group); (b) activities, tasks, and operative processes of the group (i.e., changes in the decision-making processes inside the group); and (c) culture of the group (i.e., norms, expectations, values, and purposes shared by the group members). These dimensions are important not only because they change during the life of a group, but because the members undergo these changes with a certain regularity. In fact, these changes are considered so recurrent that they can be classified into phases or stages of development (Sarri and Galinsky, 1974).

Stages of group development have been proposed by several authors of small-group research. The models proposed over the years have varied from three to eight stages of development (Johnson and Johnson, 1987). Still, despite the lack of consensus between the models, there are some important similarities (Tuckman, 1965).

Tuckman reviewed 50 studies on group development which had been conducted with a variety of groups (e.g., therapy groups, sensitivity groups, natural and laboratory groups). After a thorough classification process which included variables such as (a) setting in which the studies were conducted, (b) the social realm in which the group behavior fell at any point during the life of the group, and (c) the position of the group in a hypothetical developmental sequence or stage of development, Tuckman eventually identified four stages of development common to all small group experiences. He called these stages *forming, storming, norming,* and *performing.*

Forming. During the forming stage, the participants usually experience a period of uncertainty in which they try to determine their status with the group and the group's norms (Tuckman, 1965). Some members search for leadership amidst confusion and anxiety. There is more of a willingness to please each other at this stage than during the storming stage.

Storming. During the storming stage, the participants engage themselves in interpersonal conflict as some of them might resist the influence of the group (Tuckman, 1965). During this stage, while reacting to situations with little independence or initiative, group members may show negative behaviors and test the limits of the leaders (Schoel et al., 1988).

Norming. During the norming stage, the participants establish a greater level of cohesiveness and commitment towards group cooperation and task accomplishment. The members of the group accept the establishment of new group norms and appropriate behaviors (Tuckman, 1965). Now the group begins to use its own strengths and to take pride in its accomplishments. Members become more independent and willing to work towards accomplishing goals (Schoel et al., 1989).

Performing. In the performing stage, the participants are able to perform tasks with proficiency and flexibility (Tuckman, 1965). The unified group members compliment each other by using the strengths of all members (Schoel et al., 1989).

Finally, Tuckman's developmental sequence is subject to some conditions that will influence the rate of progression through the stages. One of these conditions relates to the duration of the group's life. Groups that form for only a few hours a day or a week will progress slower in the developmental sequence than those that are formed and remain as such for several consecutive days. Another condition influencing the rate of progression is the specificity of the task performed. Conditions of intense experimental control might increase the rate of development while a group left on its own without specific tasks to accomplish might take longer. Even though Tuckman (1965) identified these conditions and their influence on the rate of progression, he did not specify the duration for each phase or the entire process.

Research on Sequencing and Teamwork

Priest's (in print) study on sequencing and teamwork clearly indicated the effect of sequencing on the development of teamwork among adults. Using a series of variations on the corporate adventure training (CAT) sequence, Priest designed a study that tested 8 different sequences. Table 28.1 (page 212) illustrates the variations performed on the CAT sequence.

Priest found that all subgroups improved their teamwork as a result of the 10-week CAT program. Improvement ranged from 50 percent to 70 percent on a 100 percent scale. Variation in the degree of teamwork improvement was attributed to the order of activities. Priest, then, indicated that teamwork in some subgroups began to improve immediately while in others it started with a slight decline before increasing. He concluded that:

> The greatest gains in teamwork were achieved from the group-oriented activities like socialization, group initiative tools and tests, and low ropes course with spotting [group support]. Individually oriented activities, such as high ropes courses, orienteering and rappelling, were powerful adjuncts to the group-oriented activities, provided they followed in sequence and did not precede the later.

So in Priest's study, sequence B displayed the most uniformity and greatest increase in teamwork with activities such as socialization, group initiative tools, group initiative tests, and the low ropes course displaying significant differences at $p < .05$ in *post hoc* comparison. These findings are important because they are the first to support the assumption that the sequencing of adventure activities can have either a positive or a detrimental effect on the way adventure program participants develop teamwork skills and attitudes.

Table 28.1 Variations on the CAT Sequence

	Week 1	Week 2	Week 3	Week 4	Week 5	Week 6	Week 7	Week 8	Week 9	Week 10
Group A	GSI	Class	Social	Tools	Tests	Low	High	O'ing	Rapp	APC
Group B	GSI	Social	Tools	Tests	Low	High	O'ing	Rapp	Class	APC
Group C	GSI	Tools	Tests	Low	High	O'ing	Rapp	Class	Social	APC
Group D	GSI	Tests	Low	High	O'ing	Rapp	Class	Social	Tools	APC
Group E	GSI	Low	High	O'ing	Rapp	Class	Social	Tools	Tests	APC
Group F	GSI	High	O'ing	Rapp	Class	Social	Tools	Tests	Low	APC
Group G	GSI	O'ing	Rapp	Class	Social	Tools	Tests	Low	High	APC
Group H	GSI	Rapp	Class	Social	Tools	Tests	Low	High	O'ing	APC

APC = Action Planning and Closure
GSI = Goal Setting and Introduction
Class = Classroom Lectures
High = High Ropes Course
Low = Low Ropes Course

O'ing = Orienteering Course
Rapp = Rappelling
Social = Socialization Game
Tools = Group Initiative Tools
Tests = Group Initiative Tests

Source: Adapted from Priest, Attarian, and Schubert, 1993, p. 12.

Research on Sequencing and Group Cohesion

In 1997 a panel of 25 professionals in adventure education was used to establish a "hypothetically correct sequence" (Bisson, 1997). Using a modified Delphi questionnaire, I invited scholars and practitioners on this panel to develop a "hypothetically correct sequence" that would promote the development of group cohesion among sixth grade students participating in a five-day residential outdoor adventure program.

After three rounds, the modified Delphi questionnaire indicated that the following sequence of categories of activities could be accepted as a hypothetically correct sequence. This sequence of categories of adventure activities was:

1. acquaintance activities,
2. deinhibitizer activities,
3. communication activities,
4. trust activities,
5. group problem-solving activities,
6. individual low-ropes-course events,
7. individual high-ropes-course events, and
8. outdoor pursuit experience.

My study was twofold. First, it established a hypothetically correct sequence, and second, it measured the effects of this sequence on the development of group cohesion among students participating in a traditional outdoor adventure program. Group cohesion results for the hypothetically correct sequence were also compared to the results from a group that received an "altered sequence" and a control group that participated in an environmental education residential program.

In the second phase the Group Development Assessment (GDA) questionnaire developed by Jones and Bearley (1994) was used to determine the level of group cohesion among subjects. The GDA included four phases identified as dependency, conflict, cohesion, and interdependence. Of those, only the mean scores of the cohesion phase were used for data analysis.

My finding suggested that the hypothetically correct sequence appears to be effective at developing group cohesion among participants. Second, although the altered sequence was effective at developing group cohesion, it was significantly less effective than the hypothetically correct sequence. Finally, it appears that participating in a residential outdoor adventure program was more effective at developing group cohesion than participating in an environmental education program.

The Multilayer Sequence Model

This chapter reveals four important observations. First, it indicated that sequencing was perceived as one of the most important programming factors in adventure-based learning. Second, it pointed out the generalized belief that adventure sequencing could not be reduced to one ultimate or universal sequence. Third, it also demonstrated that most prescribed sequences, although different in length, nature, and context, share some common developmental phases. And fourth, it reported that appropriate sequencing has a direct effect on the development of teamwork (Priest, in print) and group cohesion (Bisson, 1997).

In light of this new information regarding sequencing, it appears that a balance between extreme flexibility and rigid universality in adventure sequencing is still the subject of a profound contention, these two perspectives create a false dichotomy that keeps the debate over adventure sequencing lingering and unresolved. Hence, we must entertain an alternative and more encompassing notion about sequencing.

Arguing for some flexibility has merit because, evidently, each adventure learning group is composed of people with different personalities and is submitted to a particular set of group dynamics. It is therefore reasonable to tend toward keeping the sequence of categories of adventure activities as flexible as possible so as to adjust the type and order of these categories of activities to the needs of each group.

On the other hand, some universality has not only been demonstrated by the obvious similarities found between the various prescribed sequences in our field, but most importantly, it has been supported by numerous research studies on small group dynamics. These studies suggest that most newly formed groups will experience a series of behavioral phases that are predictable and, somehow, common to the social maturity of any group.

From this rationalization, a new theory emerges which can be explained as follows. Adventure programming can be composed of three distinct types of sequences, each operating at a different level in a planning continuum. At one end of the continuum one would find a level of "flexible planning" that relates to the "microsequence." The other end of the continuum would contain a level of "fixed planning" relating to the "macrosequence." While the middle of the continuum would contain a level of "mixed planning" corresponding to the "mesosequence" (Figure 28.4).

In other words, the microsequence would refer to the adventure activity per se (e.g., Spider's Web, Tension Traverse, Human Knot). This sequence would be flexible

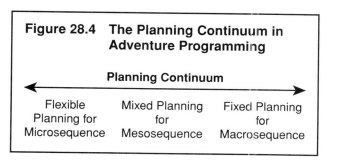

Figure 28.4　The Planning Continuum in Adventure Programming

Planning Continuum

| Flexible Planning for Microsequence | Mixed Planning for Mesosequence | Fixed Planning for Macrosequence |

in nature and could be modified at any time by the adventure educator in response to the needs of a particular group.

The macrosequence would represent the phases the group experiences throughout its development. These phases were introduced earlier in this chapter as (a) group formation, (b) group challenge, (c) group support, and (d) group achievement. These phases, representing the macrosequence itself, would imply that some categories of adventure activities should be integrated and introduced in a specific order according to the social development of the group. In other words, the macrosequence would include a fixed plan of categories of adventure activities that would operate as catalyzers for the social maturation of a group. This would also mean that because of its rigidity, no phase of the macrosequence could be bypassed.

Conclusion

This chapter presented in its opening a popular remark from Tom Smith. Smith often said that sequencing is the most important thing but that there was no sequence. After reviewing Priest's and Bisson's studies on sequencing and group attributes, it seems that Smith is right when asserting that sequencing is an important programming component of any adventure-based curriculum. Moreover, if we accept the multilayer sequence model we can also accept Smith's argument that "there is no sequence." Since it is quite possible that Smith was referring to the microsequence when arguing that there is no "magical sequence," it is then possible to subscribe to his remark on sequencing.

Although the model proposed in this chapter helps alleviate the dissonance between rigid planning and flexible planning, more studies on sequencing are needed to confirm or refute the proposed model. In addition, more inquiries are needed to see if sequencing has also an effects on other popular programming outcomes such as trust building, problem-solving skills, and leadership skills.

References

Anderson, G. S., and Frison, D. (1992). The hidden value of adventure-based programs: A reflection. *CAHPER Journal, 58*(2), 12–17.

Bisson, C. (1997). *The effects of varying the sequence of categories of adventure activities on the development of group cohesion.* Unpublished doctoral dissertation, University of Northern Colorado, Greeley.

Bronson, J., Gibson, S., Kichar, R., and Priest, S. (1992). Evaluation of team development in a corporate adventure training program. *The Journal of Experiential Education, 15*(2), 50–53.

Ewert, A. (1992). Group development through experiential education: Does it happen? *The Journal of Experiential Education, 15*(2), 56.

James, L. (1991). Add a little adventure: An introductory adventure program. *Pathways, 3*(4), 24–29.

Johnson, D. W., and Johnson, F. P. (1987). *Joining together: Group theory and group skills.* Englewood, NJ: Prentice-Hall, Inc.

Jones, J. E., and Bearley, W. L. (1994). *Group development assessment: Facilitator guide.* King of Prussia, PA: Organization Design and Development, Inc.

Kerr, P. J., and Gass, M. A. (1995). A group development model for adventure education. In K. Warren, M. Sakofs, and J. S. Hunt (Eds.), *The theory of experiential education* (pp. 285–296). Dubuque, IA: Kendall/Hunt Publishing Co.

Kimball, R. O. (1986). Experiential therapy for youths: The adventure model. *Children Today, 15*(2), 26–31.

Nadler, R. S., and Luckner, J. L. (1992). *Processing the adventure experience: Theory and practice.* Dubuque, IA: Kendall/Hunt Publishing Co.

Priest, S. (in print). The impact of sequencing on teamwork development in a CAT program. Manuscript submitted for publication in *The Australian Journal of Outdoor Education.*

Priest, S. (1996). Thoughts on managing dangers in adventure programs. *Australian Journal of Outdoor Education, 1*(3), 15–21.

Priest, S., Attarian, A., and Schubert, S. (1993). Conducting research in experiential-based training and development programs: Pass keys to locked doors. *The Journal of Experiential Education, 16*(2), 11–20.

Robb, G. M., and Ewert, A. (1987). Risk recreation and persons with disabilities. *Therapeutic Recreation Journal, 21*(1), 58–69.

Robb, G. M., and Leslie, J. (1987). *An introduction to alternative learning environments for behavior disordered children.* Martinsville, IN: Bradford Woods Outdoor Education Center.

Rohnke, K. (1989). *Cowstails and Cobras II: A guide to games, initiatives, rope courses, & adventure curriculum.* Dubuque, Iowa: Kendall/Hunt Publishing Co.

Rohnke, K., and Butler, S. (1995). *Quicksilver: Adventure, games, initiatives problems, trust activities and a guide to effective leadership.* Dubuque, IA: Kendall/Hunt Publishing Co.

Roland, C. C. (1993). Experiential challenge program development in the mental health setting: A case study. In M. Gass (Ed.), *Adventure therapy: Therapeutical applications of adventure programming* (pp. 195–208). Dubuque, IA: Kendall/Hunt Publishing Co.

Roland, C. C., and Havens, M. D. (1983). *A sequential approach to challenging activities with persons who are disabled.* Loretto, MN: The Vinland National Center.

Roland, C. C., Keene, T., Dubois, M., and Lentini, J. (1987). *Experiential challenge program development in the mental health setting. The Bradford Papers Annual, Volume III.* Martinsville, IN: Bradford Woods Outdoor Center.

Roland, C. C., Summers, S., Friedman, M., Barton, G., and McCarthy, K. (1987). Creation of an experiential challenge program. *Therapeutic Recreation Journal, 21*(2), 54–63.

Sarri, R. C., and Galinsky, M. J. (1974). A conceptual framework for group development. In P. Glasser, R. Sarri, and R. Vinter (Eds.), *Individual change through small groups* (pp. 71–88). New York, NY: The Free Press.

Schoel, J., Prouty, D., and Radcliffe, P. (1988). *Island of healing: A guide to adventure-based counseling.* Hamilton, MA: Project Adventure, Inc.

Smith, L. J. (1991, July). A passionate challenge. *Camping Connections,* 6–11.

Smith, T. E., Roland, C. C., Havens, M. D., and Hoyt, J. A. (1992). *The theory and practice of challenge education.* Dubuque, IA: Kendall/Hunt Publishing Co.

Tuckman, B. W. (1965). Development sequence in small groups. *Psychological Bulletin, 63*(6), 384–399.

Webster, S. E. (1989). *Ropes course safety manual: An instructor's guide to initiatives, and low and high elements.* Dubuque, IA: Kendall/Hunt Publishing Co.

Chapter 29

Six Generations of Facilitation Skills

Simon Priest

eXperientia

Michael A. Gass

University of New Hampshire

Introduction

Since reflection is the key to deeper learning that leads to more lasting change in adventure programming, anything that a "facilitator" does to enhance reflection before, during, or after an experience is called *facilitation*. Facilitation comes in many forms and its evolution can be traced through six distinct generations of skills. These six generations are summarized in Table 29.1 in order of occurrence (about every decade or so since the start of recent adventure programming history) and in order of sophistication, complexity, and difficulty (Priest and Gass, 1997).

This chapter examines each of these generations in more detail and provides examples using the common group initiative called *Spider's Web*. Spider's Web is elastic chord strung between two posts to look like a giant web with openings large enough to pass a person through. *Rules: Group members should be passed through different openings, from one side to the other, without touching the strands. Contact with a strand wakes the spider, which bites and causes one to start over. A repeat contact sends the whole group back to the beginning.*

Six Generations

Letting the experience speak for itself is a method found in numerous adventure programs where clients are left to sort out their own personal insights. When properly sequenced and well-designed, the inherently enriching qualities of adventure activities serve to lead clients into their own insights and discoveries through "learning and doing." This approach is fine, provided that identified or prescriptive intrapersonal and interpersonal goals are not sought. Clients may well have a good time and possibly become

---

Table 29.1   Six Generations of Facilitation Skills

Decade	Generation	Explanation
1940s	Letting the experience speak for itself	Learning and doing
1950s	Speaking on behalf of the experience	Learning by telling
1960s	Funneling or debriefing the experience	Learning through reflection
1970s	Front-loading (by direct method) the experience	Direction with reflection
1980s	Framing (by isomorphic method) the experience	Reinforcement in reflection
1990s	Front-loading (by indirect method) the experience	Redirection before reflection

proficient at new skills, but they are less likely to have learned anything about themselves, how they relate with others, or how to resolve certain issues confronting them in their lives. In letting the experience speak for itself, the leader would *not* look to add any insights regarding the Spider's Web exercise when the experience was completed. If any comments were made, they might pertain to how much fun the experience was and encourage the group to move on and try the next event: "That was great! Good job! Now let's try something new and different."

In an effort to enhance programming efforts, several programs have implemented the second generational approach of *speaking on behalf of the experience*. Here the leader (often in the role of an expert) interprets the experience for the clients, informing them of what they had learned and how they should apply their new knowledge in the future. This second approach of "learning by telling" can be well-suited to role plays and simulations where results are predictable and reproducible time and time again. However, in the adventure experience, groups bring unique behavioral history to bear on the way they act under stress. The results from these experiences also seem to be more unpredictable and unique. Due to this uncertainty, client learning is generally quite varied and personal. Telling individuals what they received from an experience can cause problems by disempowering and alienating them, or can possibly disconnect the leader from clients, thus hampering their future learning opportunities.

In speaking for the experience, the leader would provide the group with feedback about their general behaviors after the activity was completed: what they did well, what they need to work on, and what they learned from the exercise. Examples of such statements might include:

- You've learned to cooperate by virtue of working together and succeeding.
- Your communication is poor, everyone is talking and no one seems to be listening to anyone's ideas.
- The level of trust seems to be improving, since no one appeared to worry about being picked up by the others.
- You could have benefited from having a coordinator for this activity!

One solution to the problems arising from telling has been to encourage "learning through reflection" styles that enable clients to discover learning after the experience. As clients bring up issues to work on or state personal commitments to change, they are more likely to follow through if they possess ownership over such issues. By asking questions, instead of telling, ownership is much more likely. This idea has given rise to the third generational approach of *debriefing the experience*. Here clients are asked to reflect on each adventure activity and discuss

points of learning that they believe took place. Obviously, if an experience is to have true meaning for clients or if they are going to make use of new learning, then they should be invested in the experience and prepared to bear responsibility for their actions or how they functioned during the experience. In this model, clients learn under the guidance of a questioning leader, who helps the group members to discover their own learning. Although numerous methods of debriefing exist, the most common approach in North America is the group discussion.

One example of a successful debriefing approach is *funneling* the use of sequenced questions to funnel learning from the broad experience to the narrow change. In debriefing the experience, the leader would foster a group discussion concerning the details, analysis, and evaluation of the group's behavior following activity completion. Sample questions of this funneling style might include:

- What happened?
- What was the impact of this?
- How did that make you feel?
- What did you learn from this?
- What aspects for this activity were metaphors of your life? and
- What will you do differently next time? in this order.

Since reflection is typically accomplished after the experience, a number of leaders have concluded that benefit may be added by directing the clients before the experience even begins. This kind of thinking has led to the fourth generational approach of *directly front-loading the experience*. *Front-loading* is a term used for highlighting (or loading) the learning prior to (or in front of) the experience. In most adventure activities, leaders typically brief clients before the experience by explaining how the activity should work (tasks, rules or safety concerns), and then debrief them afterwards by guiding reflective discussions. However, in the fourth generation, front-loading is held just prior to engaging in the adventure as a kind of extra "prebriefing" where the leader emphasizes several key points, such as:

1. *revisit*—what behaviors or performances were promised and learned from the last activity,
2. *objectives*—the aims of the activity and what can be learned or gained from this experience,
3. *motivation*—why experiencing the activity might be important and how it relates to life,
4. *function*—what behaviors will help bring about success and how to optimize these, and
5. *dysfunction*—what behaviors will hinder success and how to overcome these barriers.

In essence, the clients are focused toward certain distinct learning outcomes assessed as determined by the leader. By loading the learning up front, debriefing simply becomes "direction with reflection" and a reemphasis of learning rather than a reactive discussion as in earlier generations. In front-loading the experience, the leader would introduce Spider's Web with the same logistical briefing as usual. In addition to this, the leader would add a series of questions to focus the learning prior to the activity:

- What do you think this exercise might teach you?
- Why is learning this important?
- How might your learning help you in the future? and
- Do you recall from past exercises what each of you wanted to work on in situations like this?

Since this front-loaded prebriefing has already covered many of the topics usually held in debriefing, the concluding discussion can concentrate solely on changes.

A fifth generation of facilitation involves *isomorphically framing the experience* and is still a relatively uncommon approach in adventure programming. Recall that metaphors are the analogous connections made by clients between the adventure experience and their real lives. *Isomorphs* are the parallel structures added to the adventure experience by the leader so clients are encouraged to make certain metaphoric linkages. For example, when leaders use the word *marriage* to describe a canoe, they are purposefully creating an isomorph with the intention of linking the skills of tandem paddling to the difficulties of living with a partner. When strong linkages are meaningful and relevant, client motivation is increased and transfer of learning is usually enhanced. If the leader can "frame" (or introduce) an activity with several isomorphs, which paint a mirror image of reality for the clients, then any changes they express in the similar adventure experience may match the change desired for daily living. When this framing is successfully accomplished, transfer will also be effective, since the dynamics and processes of the two experiences will not be that different. Again, only a little debriefing is needed afterwards, becoming "reinforcement in reflection," since clients discuss the close similarities and immediately see the obvious connections (if a strategy works here, it can work in real life too).

In isomorphic framing, the leader would address the briefing in terms of the similar structures between the adventure and corresponding present life experiences of the client. For example, with a group working in a company warehouse, the Spider's Web might be transformed into:

a distribution network (the web) through which goods and services (team members) are passed from the warehouse (one side) to

the customer's many outlets (other side). Passage takes place along unique routings (openings) and contact with the network (brushing up against a strand) damages the goods and services which means they need to be returned to the warehouse. If damaged goods and services are purposely passed on to the customer, then all shipments will be refused by the customer and returned to the warehouse to be fixed and shipped again!

If this form of briefing is close to a mirror image of the workplace and current reality of this organization, then the debriefing need only focus on reinforcing the needs of the organization that were attained by accomplishing the activity and on those that weren't achieved due to particular shortcomings.

Even more rare than any other generation of facilitation are instances involving *indirectly front-loading the experience*. It is used only as a last resort: when all other approaches have failed, only in the clients' best interests, and for the purpose of addressing continuing problematic issues. For example, the harder a client tries to eliminate an unwanted issue, the more it occurs; or the more a client tries to attain a desired result, the more elusive this result becomes. Indirect front-loading can take several *paradoxical* forms: (1) double binding, (2) symptom prescription, (3) symptom displacement, (4) illusion of alternatives, and (5) proactive reframing.

An example of double binding for a problematic group with sexist behaviors follows:

> Most . . . groups who attempt the Spider's Web tend to do it in a particular way. At the beginning, they mill around a bit with lots of people offering their suggestions. After some time a couple of dominant males tend to start the group off. They get a few men to the other side of the web and then throw the women through like sacks of potatoes and often with embarrassing remarks about female anatomy disguised as humor. Then the same group of dominant males decides how to do the hardest part [of the task] which is getting the last few people through. Afterwards, during the discussion of the exercise, everyone agrees that the leadership was more-or-less sexist and there are various emotional reactions to that. There are other ways to do the Spider's Web. . . .

Stated in this way, the front-loaded double bind is positive and a win-win situation is created. If the group chooses to perform the task in a sexist manner, then they "win" because their true behaviors will become painfully obvious and the awareness or denial of the group's sexist behavior will be heightened for the debriefing. If the group chooses to perform in a nonsexist and equitable manner, then they also "win" since they have clearly demonstrated that they can act differently and may continue to do so in the future. One way brings dysfunction to the forefront of discussion, while the other breaks old habits and provides new learning. With this indirect front-loading technique, the leader has positively "bound" this resistant client group into a unique learning opportunity. The approach is one of "redirection before reflection" as the debriefing part is simply an opportunity to punctuate key lessons gained before and during the experience rather than after it.

Conclusion

Recall that adventure programming can be categorized on the basis of whether the primary focus for learning and change emphasizes feelings, thinking, functional behavior, or dysfunctional behavior. In *recreational* adventure programs, where having fun, learning a new skill, and being entertained is the purpose, the first and second generations tend to be the most appropriate facilitational approaches. In *educational* adventure programs, where understanding new concepts, enriching the knowledge of old concepts, and generating an awareness of the need for change is the purpose, the third generation is the most commonly used method of facilitation. In *developmental* adventure programs, where improving functional behavior and training new and different behaviors is the purpose, third, fourth and fifth generations appear to fit best. In *therapeutic* adventure programs, where reducing dysfunctional behavior and conditioning less negative behaviors is the purpose, the fifth and sixth generations are the most effective techniques.

Outdoor leaders have a responsibility to their adventure programs (which provide a service) and to their customers (who consume that service) to be clear on the level of facilitation they can provide. For example, the reputation and credibility of the profession suffers when a customer requests therapy (with the intent of getting specific prescriptive behavioral change for the clients), but the program provides education (with a more general focus of learning new ideas), and the leader offers recreation (with little or no facilitation)! Anyone using these six generations of facilitation has the responsibility to consider the type of program he or she can offer, which generation is most appropriate to that program and how his or her choice of approach will impact his or her clients. Failure to do so can damage the reputation of the entire profession.

Reference

Priest, S., and Gass, M. A. (1997). *Effective leadership in adventure programming*. Champaign, IL: Human Kinetics.

Chapter 30

Processing the Adventure Experience

Clifford E. Knapp
Northern Illinois University

What is of greatest consequence in a person's life is not just the nature and extent of his or her experiences but what has been learned from them.

—Cousins (1987, p. 16)

You do not learn by doing, . . . you learn by thinking—acting—thinking—acting, etc. In and of itself, doing, like experiencing, can be a mindless affair.

—Sarason (1984, p. 224)

Introduction

Every moment of life is an experience. Some moments bring pain, pleasure, boredom or a variety of other emotional responses. Some experiences are planned and others seem to just happen to people. In order for experiences to be more than mindless affairs, they must have meaning that enables us to behave in useful ways in the future. Put briefly, we need to learn from them.

Whitehead (1929) in *The Aims of Education* stated that "the problem of education is to make the pupil see the wood by means of the trees" (p. 18). Adventure educators can assist their participants in acquiring better lives through helping them identify "trees" of knowledge in the woods of experience. These trees consist, in part, of the intrapersonal and interpersonal skills needed to function alone and with others.

Leadership involves more than merely selecting outdoor tasks such as canoeing, backpacking, soloing, or climbing a 14-foot wall. Leadership also entails conducting these tasks safely and skillfully, as well as facilitating the process of making sense from what is learned. This act of processing or helping others internalize meaning from experience has also been described as debriefing, reflecting, analyzing, and generalizing, or simply sharing outcomes from the activity. Traditionally, this event occurs in a group gathered together to verbalize about personal feelings, thoughts, and human interactions under the guidance of an adventure educator.

Walter and Marks (1981) define processing as "primarily a discussion of the completed activity [which] . . . provides detail, order, and meaning to the participants' experiences" (p. 166). The principal facilitation tools are observing, listening, providing feedback, questioning, and structuring activities to help participants reach the program objectives.

Ways of Learning

Koziey (1987) contrasts two ways of learning. He describes the traditional, deductive model used in most schools as the "learn-look-do" (p. 20) approach in which students *learn* about something (usually through hearing or reading), then *look* at someone else applying it, and sometime later *do* what has been learned. An alternative inductive model, more appropriate to adventure education, is the do-look-learn approach which provides for discovering truths that have been personally assimilated through experience. During the *look* or reflection phase of this model, participants "examine the subjective experience of doing the activities, and then determine what happened, how it happened, and what forces were present which influenced the way things happened" (p. 21). In the *learn* phase of this model, participants internalize "through extrapolating data to other real-life situations; through the use of theoretical inputs for understanding processes and activity;" and "through making decisions about how insights gained can be utilized for personal growth or for being effective in the world" (p. 22). Particularly during the *look* and *learn* phases of Koziey's model, facilitators can assist learners by helping them process the experience.

Underlying Assumptions About Processing

In describing the theory and practice of processing experiences, several assumptions have been made:

1. Skilled facilitators can assist participants in gaining understandings from human experience through the application of effective processing techniques.
2. Human relations process skills can be practiced and learned best through interactions with others in a controlled group setting.
3. Much of the group learning that takes place can be applied to situations outside of the group if the participants are assisted by skilled leaders.
4. Stress-producing outdoor challenges and the accompanying processing sessions can provide the necessary stimuli for making lasting life changes.

These assumptions indicate the underlying premise of this section: adventure educators must possess group processing skills in order to expand the personal meanings of outdoor experiences for participants and attain the program objectives.

Hard and Soft Skills

Adventure educators generally accept the need to develop both hard and soft skills. The hard skills are defined as the technical competencies needed to conduct physical activities skillfully and safely. A few examples are setting up a system for belaying a climber, cooking a meal, or paddling a canoe. The soft skills are defined as the human relations competencies needed to guide personal growth and achieve group unity. A few examples are empathizing

accurately with others, resolving a conflict, or drawing out individual feelings. Perhaps the term *soft skills* originated because of the stereotypical image of females as being physically "soft" and also skilled in listening, expressing feelings, cooperating, maintaining relationships, and nurturing others. Whatever the semantic roots of the term, adventure educators agree that men and women need hard and soft skills to be complete and effective leaders. The overall skill of conducting a processing session consists of a variety of soft skill components.

Because human group interaction is a complex phenomenon, creating a comprehensive list of soft skills is difficult. Gardner (1983) divided human relations skills (which he termed personal intelligence) into two categories—intrapersonal and interpersonal. Intrapersonal skills permit "access to one's own feeling life" (p. 239) to guide personal behavior. Some examples are becoming aware of feelings, affirming personal worth, recognizing personal power, and taking risks. Interpersonal skills include those that allow individuals "to notice and make distinctions among other individuals," especially their moods, temperaments, motivations, and intentions (p. 239). Some examples are communicating thoughts and feelings, empathizing, interpreting nonverbal language, cooperating, and listening to others. Adventure educators can help the "participants develop and practice these skills in outdoor settings and provide guidance in applying them to other life situations."

Suggested Group Norms for Community Building

Norms, or standards of behavior, can only be suggested, not mandated. However, the designated leader is usually given a considerable amount of power in determining the norms under which the group will operate. The following norms have been shown to increase the probability that a caring and trusting community will form:

1. Confidentiality should be preserved within the group.
2. Participation in the group activities should be encouraged as much as possible.
3. Participants should ask for what they need and want although they should not expect to get all they ask for.
4. Participants should speak for themselves rather than assume that they can speak for others in the group.
5. Discussions should focus on the "here and now" as much as possible rather than include frequent references to other people and situations outside the group.
6. The dignity of everyone should be respected by avoiding putdowns and encouraging validations.

7. Participants should be encouraged to take appropriate risks in order to promote positive changes.

8. Participants should be in charge of designing their own plans for personal growth.

9. Participants should demonstrate openness and honesty with their thoughts and feelings whenever possible.

10. The privacy of the group members should be respected at all times.

Barriers to Community Building Objectives

Building a supportive community involves learning and applying intrapersonal and interpersonal skills. In order to function effectively, a group needs to adopt a set of enabling norms that promote unity. Many adventure leaders agree that certain behaviors inhibit the attainment of a sense of community. These behaviors could be described as "restricting" norms. For example, the following norms generally impede the formation of caring communities: dishonesty, competition, rigidity, mistrust, avoidance of conflict, defensiveness, pessimism, and criticism. One goal of the facilitator is to influence the norms operating within the group so that they become enabling rather than restricting.

The Role of the Facilitator in Processing

The facilitator's role is to create situations in which participants encounter opportunities to learn about themselves and others through direct experience. Facilitators should make it easier for the group to form a supportive community. Facilitators cannot do this for the group, but their knowledge and interventions can help the process along. Groups usually pass through various predictable stages before they reach a state of unity in which the members work well together. Facilitators first outline the tasks (i.e., climbing a mountain, pitching a tent, or using a map and compass to find a destination) to be accomplished. Sometimes participants already have these hard skills, but often they need to be taught or perfected. These tasks are designed to help participants reach the program objectives established by the sponsoring institution. The difference between the tasks and the objectives must be clear to both the leaders and the participants. In ideal situations the group members usually prefer to complete the task (i.e., fording a river) *and* to achieve certain program objectives (i.e., cooperating, building trust, or gaining self-confidence). However, if the group fails to successfully cross the river (assuming that no one is hurt or drowned), the objectives can still be met. If completion of the task is viewed as the sole end in view and the objectives are ignored or minimized, the benefits to the participants will be limited. The role of the facilitator during the processing phase of the experience is to help the participants reach as many objectives as possible, whether the tasks are completed or not. According to Jordan (1987), "An overly aggressive or autocratic leader or an overly lackadaisical or laissez-faire leader may inhibit both the number and quality of participant contributions" (p. 74). "The leader should take care not to inadvertently tell participants how they are functioning and feeling, but rather probe and verbally guide the participants into discovering their own emotions and attitudes" (p. 74). "Throughout the discussion it is important that the leader maintain an open and caring attitude towards all group members. By being attentive to his or her own nonverbal language, tone of voice, and choice of wording the leader will develop a better understanding of the group" (p. 76).

Facilitators must also be aware of and capitalize on both the content (what is discussed) *and* the process (what is communicated nonverbally) in order to maximize the participants' learning. By being attentive to the content *and* process involved in the experience, the facilitator will be better able to guide the development of the group from a collection of individuals into a cohesive community.

Preplanning the Processing Phase

Some preplanning can be accomplished if leaders have access to some information about the participants beforehand. This preliminary data can be obtained through personal contact or written documentation. Knowing certain facts about the population such as age, gender, special needs, physical disabilities, purposes for attending, or behavioral characteristics can be helpful, although even this is insufficient to fully plan the processing session. Facilitators may want to prepare a list of questions related to some predictable issues that may arise. For instance, many individuals in newly formed groups have difficulties communicating effectively, deferring judgments about others, listening, cooperating, respecting human differences, trusting others, and leading or following others. Preplanned lists of questions have limitations, however, they can prove useful as checklists for what to look for. (*Note:* For examples of preplanned questions organized under various objectives, see "Designing Processing Questions to Meet Specific Objectives" [Knapp, 1984].)

Additional Group Issues to Process

One of the most difficult dilemmas for leaders is deciding what issues to process. If guiding a community is the main focus, then any barriers to achieving this goal become crucial group issues worthy of time and attention. Some additional group issues to watch for and process are:

1. participation and/or involvement in group activities;
2. level and style of influence exerted by individuals;
3. group decision-making methods (i.e., voting, consensus seeking, or domination by a verbal minority);
4. expressions of belonging or feeling rejected (group membership);
5. the extent to which feelings are openly expressed;
6. the amount of putdowns and critical comments;
7. obvious attempts to control others against their wills;
8. evidence of low self-esteem and lack of confidence;
9. unresolved conflicts;
10. aggressive or hostile behavior; and
11. unwarranted gender stereotyping.

Facilitators should design a plan of action to achieve preselected objectives, but must always be flexible enough to alter the plan if necessary. The best preparation for processing the group experience is a thorough understanding of psychological and sociological principles as they occur in structured adventure situations.

Suggested Steps in Processing

Step 1—Establishing Rapport, Norms, and Ground Rules

After the group members have been prepared for participating in the outdoor task, they should be oriented to the purpose of the processing sessions. Facilitators need to establish a rapport with the participants and should outline some minimal behavioral expectations. Individual leadership style and philosophy dictate the extent to which the group is instructed about the objectives, expected norms, and ground rules prior to the activity. Participants need to feel safe both physically and psychologically and therefore some ground rules are helpful in the beginning of the session. Insisting upon the importance of respecting confidentiality and individual privacy, giving permission to not participate verbally, and prohibiting verbal putdowns helps the group members to develop feelings of safety. The facilitator must create and maintain a humane climate in the group or honest expressions of thoughts, feelings and actions are inhibited.

Step 2—Observing, Reporting, and Questioning

When group members interact as they move toward completing assigned tasks, there are literally hundreds of human content and process observations that can be made. Facilitators need to identify the relevant issues to process. The program objectives are important guides in making these decisions. In these matters there is no substitute for experience and sound professional judgment. Group issues can range from those which are relatively nonthreatening to those which are potentially volatile and values sensitive. For example, issues that can be emotionally powerful include those related to gender stereotyping, flagrant disregard for safety rules, personal competence and self-esteem, or deeply held prejudices. Facilitators should always be alert to incidents which evoke strong feelings in the participants. The leader has the responsibility to make key observations and to report them to the group or raise questions so that key issues will become more apparent to the participants. Usually, these observations are directed first toward concrete behavior and not to the inferences drawn from these actions. For example, when a participant stays physically apart from the rest of the group, this act is merely described or probed through questioning. It is risky to interpret the reasons for a person's separation from the group. Identifying and discussing factual observations are less problematical than trying to uncover the underlying motivations for these behaviors. Later in the session, when more trust and mutual support have developed, the facilitator can ask for feedback about the feeling associated with the behavior. Hammel (1986) suggests that *Bloom's Taxonomy of Education Objectives Handbook I: Cognitive Domain* (Bloom, 1959) can guide the sequence of the processing session. This method involves becoming aware of the concrete aspects of the experience first (eliciting information about knowledge, comprehension, and application) through directed questions such as what happened when . . . or how did you feel when . . . (p. 22). Next, the group could examine the more abstract ways of thinking about the experience such as analysis, synthesis, and evaluation by answering questions such as do you see any patterns, have you learned anything about yourself, or what was the highlight for you (p. 22).

Step 3—Other Types of Facilitator Intervention

This step is somewhat more controversial and not always included in a typical processing sequence. Some types of facilitator interventions are especially applicable to the more contrived situations involving group initiatives or ropes challenge courses. Some facilitators may choose to stop the group before the task is completed to process certain interactions while they are still vivid. If a participant contributes a significant element to the solving of a group problem, the action could be stopped to process it. In another instance, if the group demonstrates a restricting norm, the action could be stopped to discuss the situation and to suggest a more appropriate enabling norm. Another type of facilitator intervention is to respond to specific behaviors by changing the rules for completing the task. For example, if one of the physically strong participants always contributes to the group in that way, the facilitator could create a hypothetical situation in which that person "breaks" both arms. This would force the group into a different problem-solving strategy and would provide that physically strong person with opportunities to contribute in other ways. Alternative ways to "disable" the participants are to render them temporarily blind (using blindfolds), mute, or deaf (using ear plugs) in order to change the dynamics of the group.

Step 4—Summarizing, Evaluating, and Reaching Closure

The final step in the processing sequence is to help the group summarize, evaluate, and transfer the adventure program to future situations. This phase can be done at the close of a short two-hour session or at the end of a 26-day course. Reaching closure is important for participants, especially if they have achieved a sense of community and developed strong feelings for each other. When people feel cared for, trusted, and supported by others, they often want to bid others farewell through a structured celebration or ritual. Even if the group remains intact upon returning home, closure activities can relate to leaving the place and completing a valuable program. Part of the closure ceremony involves helping the participants transfer and apply what is learned to other settings. Closure activities can be as simple as allowing everyone an opportunity to verbalize the high points of their time together or to plan how they will apply what they learned at home or as complex as writing and performing a poem, song or skit which captures the positive experience or developing and signing a self-contract related to proposed personal attitudinal and behavioral changes. Sometimes participants may plan their own activities for accomplishing closure. However the closure phase is achieved, this step is important to include before the group disbands. Adequate time should be devoted to discussing the transition from the group experience to the situation back home. Usually the norms established in the group are different from those operating outside of the group. Participants should be cautioned about assuming that everyone in other settings have fully accepted norms such as expressing feelings openly, listening by reflecting back what is heard, taking behavioral risks in order to grow, or validating each other in verbal or nonverbal ways. The participants' gains from the adventure experience can be erased if they encounter problems of rejection or hostility in back-home situations. Potential re-entry problems need to be addressed with care in order to ease the transition from one group culture to another.

Alternatives Modes for Processing

Although the traditional image of a processing session is a leader-led group of people sitting in a circle discussing the impact of the experience, other methods for acquiring personal meaning should be considered. Smith (1987, pp. 34–37), outlines several other ways that allow participants to process their experiences:

1. *Relaxation, centering, and introspection.* Provide time, either in silence or with background music or natural sounds to reflect on the experience. Sometimes controlled breathing and relaxation exercises can help to create the conditions necessary for quiet introspection and learning.

2. *Special places.* Assign special places outdoors for participants to "become one" with the environment, and to process their experience. They can be asked to find special objects such as a tree or rock to use as sounding boards for a "conversation" with nature.

3. *Solos.* Direct participants to spend time alone outdoors. This period can be as short as several minutes or as long as a few days. They can also use this reflection time alone to eat or to watch a natural event like a sunrise or a bee pollinating flowers.

4. *Guided fantasy.* Provide verbal input in order to influence the thoughts and feelings of the participants. The monologue could take the form of a story that has relevance for the group and evokes mental images related to the impact of the experiences on the individuals.

5. *Journal writing.* Direct the participants to write about their experiences in a structured or unstructured way. Use sentence stems, diagrams, and other written thought stimuli to trigger appropriate responses or to suggest stream-of-consciousness writing to record insights and questions.

6. *Small groups.* Suggest that participants share in several small groups, which usually permit more verbal interaction and feelings of belonging. These sessions can be open ended or structured to varying degrees. If a group issue such as how decisions are being made arises, the participants can divide into trios or pairs to talk about good and poor decision-making examples observed in their group.

Developing A Code of Ethics for Processing Adventure Experiences: A Self-Inventory

Directions: The following statements are possible components of a personal code of ethics for processing adventure experience. A code of ethics is a set of ideas which establish a standard for what is right and good. Read the statements through once and then rate them on a scale using the numerals, 0, 1, 2, 3, 4, or 5 (0 equals no value as a component of a code of ethics and 5 equals an essential part of a code of ethics).

1. Select educational objectives that you are qualified to process.
2. Share the educational objectives with the group.
3. Find out as much as possible about the group members prior to working with them.
4. Allow adequate time for doing and processing each activity.
5. Share the expected ground rules and norms of behavior for the group.
6. Stress the importance of maintaining confidentiality among the participants.
7. Respect a participant's right to remain silent or to "pass" during the processing session.
8. Respond to participants in ways that enhance their self-esteem and build their confidence.
9. When possible, avoid opening up traumatic issues in the lives of the participants unless you have the time and expertise to adequately follow up.
10. Limit the giving of advice about how people *should* live their lives.
11. Provide opportunities for all participants to meet their needs in the group.
12. Continually learn more about psychology, communications, and group dynamics through personal involvement in groups, reading, lectures, and other means.
13. Provide time to discuss the transition from the group to back-home situations to help participants apply newly acquired knowledge and skills.
14. Be cautious about "pushing" participants beyond the limits they choose for themselves.
15. Intervene when an important group issue surfaces in order to help the participants understand the dynamics of the situation.
16. Begin the processing session with a clear plan for reaching specific objectives, but remain flexible and open to change.
17. Create a rapport with the participants and build a climate of safety and support.
18. Devote time and attention to group issues and avoid spending time on your own personal issues.

What other essential components of a personal code of ethics would you add to this list?

Some Cautions to Consider

Interacting with people who express thoughts and feelings in stressful group situations can be as dangerous as playing with fire. Leaders must have a clear picture of what they wish to accomplish, their own skill levels, and as much information about the participants as possible. Processing, as conducted in most adventure settings, is not designed as a therapy session. Participants are not there to be healed of mental disabilities in most situations. The leader is not there to heal himself or herself either and should not take "group time" to raise and pursue personal emotional issues. If leaders feel intense emotions or bring in burdensome problems from outside the group, they should not conduct the processing session until these distracting feelings or problems can be put aside. A cofacilitator is usually helpful to take over in these extreme cases. Knowing one's limitations is just as important as knowing one's strengths. Facilitators can only suggest more gentle slopes in reaching life's mountain peaks; they cannot do the climbing for the participants.

Summary

Processing the experience is part science and part art. This section has attempted to delineate some of the science of processing so that facilitators can develop clearer objectives and use more precise methods. Because processing the experience involves making on-the-spot judgments based on new factual information and intuitive predictions, all the steps cannot be outlined in cookbook fashion. If adventure educators focus carefully upon who is in the group, how they interact as they complete their tasks, and the objectives they would like to achieve, the art and science of processing experience will be practiced more effectively.

References

Bloom, B. S. (Ed.). (1956). *Taxonomy of educational objectives handbook I: Cognitive domain.* New York, NY: David McKay Company, Inc.

Cousins, N. (1981). *Human options: An autobiographical notebook.* New York, NY: W. W. Norton and Company.

Gardner, H. (1983). *Frames of mind: The theory of multiple intelligences.* New York, NY: Basic Books, Inc.

Hammel, H. (1986). How to design a debriefing session. *The Journal of Experiential Education, 9*(3), 20–25.

Jordan, D. (1987). Processing the initiative course experience. *The Bradford Papers Annual, II,* 73–78.

Knapp, C. E. (1984). Idea notebook: Designing processing questions to meet specific objectives. *The Journal of Experiential Education, 7*(2), 47–49.

Koziey, P. W. (1987). Experiencing mutuality. *Journal of Experiential Education, 10*(3), 20–22.

Sarason, S. B. Quoted in Smith, V. (1984) Book review: Schooling in America, scapegoat and salvation. *Phi Delta Kappan, 66*(3), 224–225.

Smith, T. E. (1986). Alternative methodologies for processing the adventure experience. *The Bradford Papers Annual, 1*, 29–38.

Walter, G. A., and Marks, S. E. (1981). *Experiential learning and change: Theory design and practice.* New York, NY: John Wiley and Sons.

Whitehead, A. N. (1929). *The aims of education and other essays.* New York, NY: The Macmillan Company.

Chapter 31

Transfer of Learning in Adventure Programming

Michael A. Gass
University of New Hampshire

As seen throughout this text, the growth of adventure experiences has produced a wide variety of applications. Some of these applications have been used to provide and/or enhance leisure or recreational experiences. The focus of these types of experiences is on the activity itself, and while there may be application to future recreational experiences, the major intent of these activities is on the leisure experience.

However, when the focus of adventure experiences is on educational or therapeutic goals, the intent of the process pertains not only to the immediate activity, but also on the relation of the experience to future issues for the participant. The true value or effectiveness of the program lies in how learning experienced during adventure activity will serve the learner in the future. Dewey (1938) goes as far as to say that this quality of application to future learning "discriminates between experiences that are worthwhile educationally and those that are not" (p. 33). This aphorism is especially true for adventure education and therapy programs. Whether it has been a juvenile offender developing more appropriate social behaviors, a freshman student obtaining a more beneficial educational experience at a university, or another program where adventure is used as a valid educational or therapeutic medium, the credibility of programs using a challenging environment is based upon the positive effects they have on their students' or clients' futures.

This effect that a particular experience has on future learning experiences is called the transfer of learning or

simply *transfer*. Not only is transfer important for adventure education programs, it also has been identified as critical for the support, continuation, and/or livelihood of such programs. For example, when describing the value of adventure programming as a milieu used to prevent delinquency, the U.S. Department of Justice (1981) states that:

> Despite having some plausible theoretical or correlational basis, wilderness programs without follow-up (transfer) into clients' home communities should be rejected on the basis of their repeated failure to demonstrate effectiveness in reducing delinquency after having been tried and evaluated. (p. 2-77)

While transfer is critical to the field of adventure education, probably no other concept is so often misunderstood. Much of the confusion plaguing the transfer of learning has resulted from two main factors. First is the concern that the initial learning usually takes place in an environment (e.g., mountains) quite different from the environment where the student's future learning will occur. Second is the lack of knowledge concerning the variety of methods available to promote transfer. Neither of these problems are limited to adventure education, but there are certain theories, models, and techniques that pertain directly to the field and can assist in eliminating much of the confusion surrounding the topic and enable individuals to strengthen the transfer of their program's goals.

Theories Concerning Transfer

Concerning the application to adventure education, three central learning theories pertaining to transfer exist that explain how the linking of elements from one learning environment to another occur (Figure 31.1). Bruner (1960) describes the first two, specific and nonspecific transfer, in attempting to show how current learning serves the learner in the future:

> There are two ways in which learning serves the future. One is through its specific applicability to tasks that are highly similar to those we originally learned to perform. Psychologists refer to this specific phenomenon as specific transfer of training; perhaps it should be called the extension of habits or associations. Its utility appears to be limited in the main to what we speak of as skills. A second way in which earlier learning renders later performance more efficient is through what is conveniently called nonspecific transfer, or, more accurately, the transfer of principles and attitudes. In essence, it consists of learning, initially, not a skill but a general idea which can then be used as a basis of recognizing subsequent problems as special cases of the idea originally mastered. (p. 17)

The following example from a student's notebook serves to illustrate the use of specific transfer in adventure education:

> Today during the class we learned how to rappel. Initially I was quite frightened, but I ended up catching on to the proper techniques and enjoying it quite a bit! One thing that helped me in learning how to rappel was the belaying we did yesterday. With belaying, our left hand is the "feel" hand while the right hand is the "brake" hand. With rappelling, it is the same; our left hand is the "feel" hand and our right hand is used to "brake" our rappel and control our descent.

In this example, the student's previous experiences of specific hand skills learned while belaying positively affected her ability to learn the necessary and correct hand skills of rappelling. Figure 31.1 illustrates these events occurring—the initial stage of learning how to belay, the development of the proper and safe habits while belaying, and finally, the use of these skills while rappelling.

The next example from another student's notebook highlights what Bruner describes as nonspecific transfer, or the use of common underlying principles in one learning situation to assist the student in a future learning experience:

> (As a result of the wilderness course) I've seen myself developing more trust in my friends at school. The no-discount policy helps me quite a bit, but I think what helped the most was learning how I receive as well as give support to others. I felt that this was the most important thing I learned (while on the wilderness course).

In this second example, the student has taken the common underlying principles that she learned about developing trust (i.e., receiving and giving support from and to others) from the wilderness course and generalized those principles and attitudes to a new learning situation (i.e., school). This ability to generalize by the learner is crucial for nonspecific transfer to occur. Figure 31.1 shows the connection of two learning situations by common underlying principles or nonspecific transfer. In this example, the student, through an initiative such as the Willow Wand exercise supplemented with a no-discount policy, learns valuable principles and attitudes about developing trust in peer relationships. She takes these principles, generalizes them, and transfers them to a new learning situation, such as developing meaningful relationships at school based on trust.

The third transfer theory associated with adventure learning also requires the student to generalize certain principles from one learning situation to another. But the principles being transferred in this theory are not common or the same in structure, but are similar, analogous, or metaphorical. The following passage illustrates a student making the connection between the similar underlying principles of canoeing and his group working together:

> There has been a certain jerkiness in the group. It's like the progress of a canoe. When the people on each side paddle in unison, with each person pulling his weight, the canoe goes forward smoothly. If certain people slack, or if there is a lack of coordination, progress becomes jerky. The canoe veers (from) side to side. Time and energy are wasted. (Godfrey, 1980, p. 229)

In this particular situation, the student is not using the principles of efficient canoeing for future aquatic learning experiences. He is instead transferring the concepts or principles of canoeing as metaphors for another learning experience that is similar, yet not the same.

This third type of transfer, metaphoric transfer, is also illustrated in Figure 31.1. Here the student takes the similar underlying principles mentioned in the previous

Figure 31.1   Three Theories of Transfer in Adventure Education

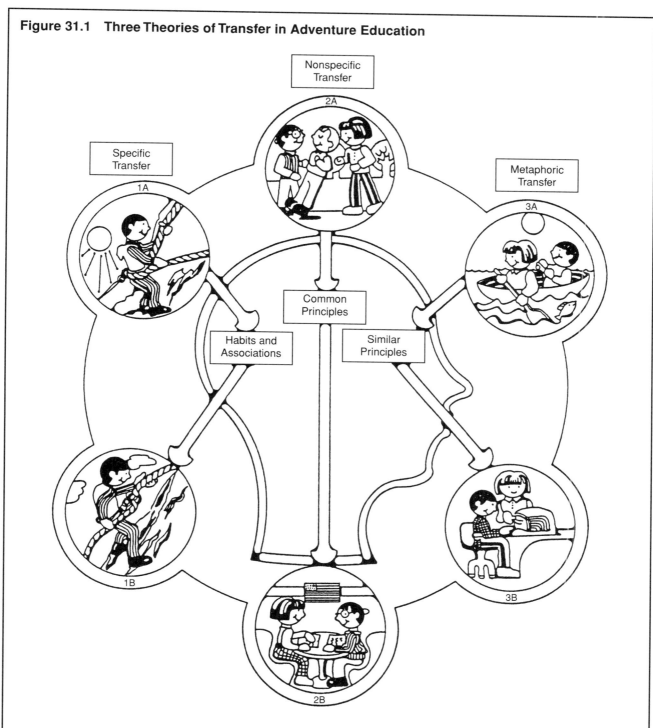

The above diagram illustrates how learning in adventure education is linked to future learning experiences. In the first theory, specific transfer, the learner takes the habits and associations acquired during a previous experience (Diagram 1A—the hand skills of belaying) and applies them to a new experience to assist him in developing a new skill (Diagram 1B—the hand skills of rappelling.) In the second theory, nonspecific transfer, the learner generalizes the common underlying principles received from a previous experience (Diagram 2A—developing trust from an initiative game) and employs them in a new learning situation (Diagram 2B—developing trust with peers at school). The third theory, metaphoric transfer, shows the learner transferring the similar underlying principles from canoeing (Diagram 3A) to working with other individuals in a business corporation (Diagram 3B).

SOURCE: Gass, 1990, p. 202. Reprinted with permission of Venture Publishing, Inc.

example, generalizes them and applies them to a future learning experience with similar elements. The future learning experience represented in Figure 31.1 (page 229) for metaphoric transfer is a group situation where the necessity of everyone working together efficiently is vital (in this case, working for a business corporation).

One individual who has done a great deal of investigation into the use of metaphoric transfer with adventure learning is Stephen Bacon. In the following passage, he further explains how using experiences that are metaphoric provide a vehicle for the transfer of learning:

> The key factor in determining whether experiences are metaphoric is the degree of isomorphism between the metaphoric situation and the real-life situation. Isomorphism means having the same structure. When all the major elements in one experience are represented by corresponding elements in another experience, and when the overall structure of the two experiences are highly similar, then the two experiences are metaphors for each other. This does not imply that the corresponding elements are literally identical; rather, they must be symbolically identical. (Bacon, 1983, p. 4)

A Program Model for Transfer

When reviewing the three transfer of learning theories discussed previously, it can be seen that the key to increasing transfer often lies in the selection or design of appropriate learning activities and the teaching methodology. One of the major faults of adventure education has been the lack of planning for the transfer in either of these areas. Transfer must be planned, much in the same manner as an educational objective or a properly planned learning skill.

Figure 31.2 portrays the learning process of an adventure program interested in procuring positive transfer for a student. As seen in the model, once the needs of the student and the goals of the program are properly identified and matched, learning skills, activities, teaching strategies, and transfer models and techniques are planned. A strong emphasis is placed on providing the connection between the present and future learning environments to increase the amount of transfer which will occur. Note that throughout the program if the needs of the student change, the model directs the instructor to assess these changes and adapt new learning activities and transfer elements to the student's new behavior. At the completion of the adventure experience, follow-up activities are also used to enhance positive transfer.

Factors and Techniques That Enhance Transfer of Learning

Given the information in Figure 31.2 for programming transfer, what are some of the factors or techniques adventure educators can use to assist them in increasing the transfer of their students' learning (shown by step 4 in Figure 31.2)? Many researchers have presented exhaustive lists of elements which can lead to positive transfer, but some of these are unalterable (e.g., genetic factors concerning intelligence) while others have little application to the "non-traditional" atmosphere where most adventure learning takes place.

As stated in the program model, it is necessary for adventure educators to select not only the proper transfer of learning theories, but also the techniques and activities involved with the increase of transfer applicable to their program. Ten techniques adaptable to the transfer of learning occurring with adventure activities are presented here as examples. Many other techniques exist and should be selected for their ability to transfer the goals of the specific program and what theory of transfer one is using.

1. *Design conditions for transfer before the course, program, or learning activities actually begin.* Several steps can be done prior to a learning experience that can aid in the transfer of learning from an adventure activity. Examples of these steps include:

   a. Identify, develop, or establish a commitment to change in the student.
   b. Have a student set goals for the experience.
   c. Write and set tight learning objectives for the student in the program.
   d. Place the plans and goals made by the student in writing to create a stronger commitment for transferring the learning.
   e. Plan adventure experiences based on their ability to enable students and clients to transfer learning from the adventure experience into their future experiences.

Each of these steps illustrates the need for instructors of adventure education and therapy programs to think and plan proactively. Using such conditions enhances the strengths of using adventure experiences for educational or therapeutic goals.

2. *Create elements in the student's learning environment similar to those elements likely to be found in future learning environments.* Learning environments with strong applicability to future experiences have greater potential for a more positive transfer of learning. The following example of a "youth at risk" in a wilderness program shows how elements of the program were created to assist him in transferring a behavior, in this case, a greater self-concept, into a subsequent learning environment:

Throughout the course, Kurt was presented with a variety of challenging tasks. He overcame strong personal fears and doubts and succeeded at many of the tasks that required a great deal of initiative. The staff noticed that after he had developed a stronger belief in himself, he was especially zealous on tasks that required a great deal of trust and responsibility (e.g., belaying). Throughout the course, the staff continued to place Kurt in progressively more difficult situations that demanded a strong, realistic belief in himself as well as other members in the group. Many of the discussions at night were about the relationships between the elements they faced as individuals and as a group in the wilderness and how these elements mirrored the situations they would encounter when they returned to their communities.

Other learning behaviors are often presented in a similar manner to increase their relevance and application to future learning environments for students. Certain programs have found that by approaching problem-solving and decision-making skills in a general manner, their students succeed in creating elements valuable for future use (Gass, 1985, p. 5).

3. *Provide students with the opportunities to practice the transfer of learning while still in the program.* There was probably no better time for Kurt to practice the skill to be transferred (i.e., an increased self-concept) than during the adventure experience. The variety of contexts in which to

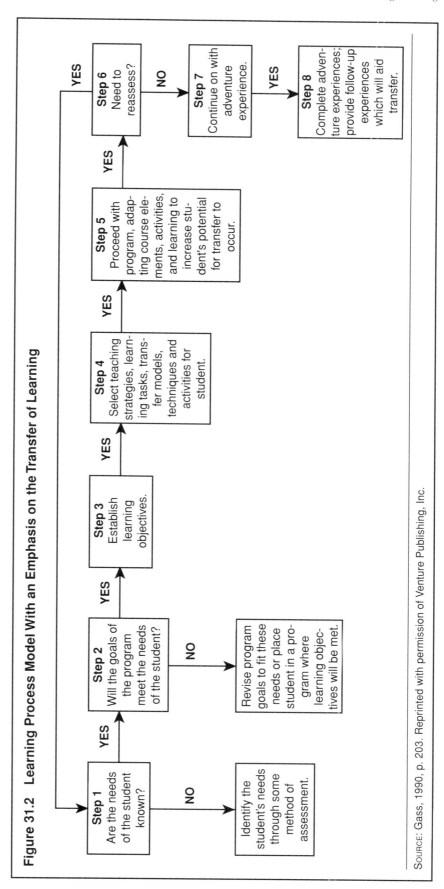

Figure 31.2   Learning Process Model With an Emphasis on the Transfer of Learning

Source: Gass, 1990, p. 203. Reprinted with permission of Venture Publishing, Inc.

practice transfer, the number of times Kurt could practice transferring the skills, and the strong support within the group that developed during this outdoor adventure program all helped Kurt focus on necessary generalizing and conceptualizing skills. These skills proved valuable in strengthening his ability to transfer these skills for future learning situations.

4. *Have the consequences of learning be natural— not artificial*. One can think of the consequences of learning as either being natural or artificial:

> Natural consequences are those that follow or would follow a given act unless some human or human system intervenes. Artificial consequences follow or would follow a given act, if, and only if, some human or human system anticipates or responds to the initial act and causes the artificial consequence or modifies a natural consequence. (Darnell, 1983, p. 4)

Superficially viewing the field of outdoor education, one would think that all learning taking place in the outdoors would have natural consequences. Unfortunately, far too often this is not the case. Whether it has been from an "overly" caring instructor or an overpowering one, too often the student becomes dependent on, is shielded by, or anticipates the instructor as a reinforcer of learning. Once the course is over and the reinforcer (i.e., the instructor) is removed from the student, learning behavior is severely hampered or terminated. In this way, with artificial consequences the result of learning transfer is extremely limited.

However, if outdoor programs could make their students' learning more experiential, natural consequences would be more likely to occur. This would result in the stronger formation of learning behaviors likely to be available in future learning situations, hence, increasing the amount of transfer. Some experiential learning techniques that could foster the development of natural consequences include relying upon the students' intrinsic rather than some external source of motivation; placing more responsibility for learning on the student (see #8); and not shielding the learner from the consequences of his or her learning, whether they be positive or negative.

5. *Provide the means for students to internalize their own learning*. The ability for a student to internalize his or her own learning creates the concepts and generalizations central to the transfer process. Adventure educators have differed to a great extent on how this is best accomplished. Many believe that by getting their students to verbalize or place their own learning into words, the internalization of the concepts to be transferred is increased through self-awareness and reflective thinking (Kalisch, 1979, p. 62). Others feel that conscious efforts such as verbalizing are secondary to other methods of internalization, such as the

subconscious development of metaphors for transfer (Bacon, 1983, p. 2).

Methods that enable students to internalize learning behaviors from adventure programs often use reflective processes to aid internalization. An example of one method often used by adventure education programs that increases transfer through reflection is the "solo" experience. Certain programs feel that such an experience, when appropriately implemented, reinforces the learning that occurs in the adventure program and helps students and clients to identify how they are going to use the experience in the future (Gass, 1985, p. 6).

6. *Include past successful alumni in the adventure program*. Sometimes the incorporation of successful alumni in courses or programs assists in the transfer of learning for students and clients. The following examples demonstrate how one program uses this technique:

> By listening to how these alumni used the skills they had learned from the program in their lives, students began to envision how they might use elements of the program in future situations. While not always advisable or possible for some programs, many individuals felt this "vicarious" method of planning future transfer strategies aided in the transfer of learning for students. (Gass, 1985, p. 5)

7. *Include significant others in the learning process*. The inclusion of other individuals closely associated with the student's or client's learning process has often been found to heighten the transfer of learning (Gass, 1985, p. 2). Some of the persons used to fill this vital role have been peers, parents, counselors, social workers and/or teachers. The following example illustrates how one program includes significant others in the learning process to provide positive transfer for a student:

> Before Cristina participated on the adventure portion of the family therapy program, several objectives were established for her family, counselor and school teacher—as well as herself. Cristina and her family met with the staff, other participants and their families prior to the adventure experience in order to familiarize both the students and the parents of the reasons for their participation on the course. Another reason for this meeting was to inform them of possible changes in the student that could occur. The program continued to stay in close contact with Cristina's family in order for them to adjust to and support possible changes in Cristina's personality and behavior.

Cristina also created several "goal contracts" in a pretrip meeting with the assistance of a staff member in the areas of personal, family, school and peer development. The contracts were discussed on the course and monitored monthly, with proper adaptations, for the next six months. These contracts were agreed to and supported by Cristina's family. Cristina's teacher also participated on several portions of the wilderness course, enabling him to support, reinforce, and try and use the observable changes during the adventure program with Cristina in the classroom.

8. *When possible, place more responsibility for learning in the program with the students or clients.* Many programs, especially those invested in teaching adventure education experientially, believe that placing more responsibility with the student in the program not only increases his or her motivation to learn but also his or her incentive to apply the learning in future experiences. Examples of this range from some programs involving students in the planning of food menus to other programs that have students organize and conduct an entire adventure experience on their own. Certain programs have implemented strong service components that have a definite focus on future experiences outside of the adventure experience (MacArthur, 1982, pp. 37–38) and enhance the self-responsibility within the student which could lead to a greater transfer of learning.

No matter what techniques programs use to involve their students and clients in the planning and operations of an adventure learning experience, their involvement should depend on their ability to accept responsibility for learning and their willingness and desire to do so. A person that willingly accepts responsibility for learning will transfer information much more readily than an individual who approaches such a task with a sense of indifference or resentment.

9. *Develop focused processing techniques that facilitate the transfer of learning.* In many adventure education programs, processing, debriefing, and facilitating are often used to enrich a student's learning experience. The length and intensity of these debriefings can differ from a quick and informal sharing of the day's occurrences to a lengthy and formalized discussion of a particular incident with a specific set of rules and guidelines. Despite this vast difference in the application of techniques, there are certain general characteristics that, if included in the processing of an experience, will assist in the transfer of learning. Some of these characteristics are:

a. Present processing sessions based on the student's or client's ability to contribute personally meaningful responses. Use feedback that is well-intended, descriptive, specific, and directed toward positive change.

b. Focus on linking the experiences from the present and future learning environments together during the processing session. This can often be accomplished by actually contracting with the students for this to occur.

c. When possible, debrief prior to and throughout the learning experience and not just the end of it. This allows students to continually focus on the future applicability of the adventure experience.

10. *Provide follow-up experiences which aid in the application of transfer.* Once a student begins transferring learning, the presence of follow-up activities (e.g., continued communications, feedback on learning decisions, processes and choices) serve to heighten transfer abilities. Again, one reason for this might be the positive effects of reflection between learning situations. Reflection gives the student the opportunity to see and evaluate the results of past learning behaviors, garner learner motivation and plan future learning strategies and directions.

Conclusion

As educators who use the outdoors and challenging situations to help students to learn more efficiently, we all aspire to teach our students something usable; and therein lies the value of our program. But unless we assist our students in providing our own linkages, bridges and connections to their learning, the utility of much of the education we care and work so hard to bring about is put away in the equipment room along with the ropes and backpacks. As we strive to become better educators and proponents of the value of adventure education, let us look upon transfer as a device to excite students by showing them the future value of their current learning experiences. This motivation, provided by the opportunity to use their learning again, can furnish one of the strongest incentives for our students' continued learning and the field's success.

References

Bacon, S. (1983). *The conscious use of metaphor in Outward Bound.* Denver, CO: Colorado Outward Bound School.

Bruner, J. (1960). *The process of education.* New York, NY: Vintage Books.

Darnell, D. K. (1983). *On consequences, learning, survival, and "the good life."* An unpublished report. Department of Communications, University of Colorado.

Dewey, J. (1938). *Experience and education.* New York, NY: MacMillan Publishing Company.

Gass, M. A. (1985). *Strengthening adventure education by increasing the transfer of learning*. Durham, NH: University of New Hampshire. (ERIC Document Reproduction Service No. 255 335).

Gass, M. A. (1990). Transfer of learning in adventure education. In J. C. Miles and S. Priest (Eds.), *Adventure education* (pp. 199–208). State College, PA: Venture Publishing, Inc.

Godfrey, R. (1980). *Outward Bound: Schools of the possible*. Garden City, NJ: Anchor Press, Doubleday.

Kalisch, K. (1979). *The role of the instructor in the Outward Bound process*. Three Lakes, WI: Honey Lakes Camp.

MacArthur, R. S. (1982). The changing role of service in Outward Bound. *Journal of Experiential Education, 5*(2), 34–39.

Section 6

The Leadership of Adventure Programming
A Most Critical Ingredient

Leadership is a critical element in any field of activity, but especially so in one like adventure programming where the safety of participants is of central concern. Adventure, by its nature, involves elements of risk and uncertainty. It occurs in environments containing both objective dangers like falling rocks and lightning, and subjective ones like fear and irresponsibility of participants. Outdoor leadership demands many skills, especially judgment. This last is an intangible quality that is very difficult to teach and to assess. One may not know whether he or she has it until a situation demands it. If judgment is lacking, disaster may be the result.

The authors in this section tackle, from various angles, the problems of defining good outdoor leadership and of educating and training good leaders. Priest starts off again with definitions useful for understanding the discussion, and then examines the nature of hard, soft, and meta skills.

Raiola and Sugerman examine the state of leadership training in colleges and universities. They note a dramatic increase in the number of higher education programs in outdoor leadership and summarize where they are and what they are teaching. An outdoor leadership development continuum is described, and the authors suggest and summarize an outdoor leadership curriculum that involves nine elements. They argue for a balance in leadership instruction between "training" and "education," the former involving the learning of techniques, the latter developing an understanding of when and why the techniques can and should be used.

The adventure programming profession has wrestled since the 1970s with the challenge of assuring the quality of leadership and programs across this diverse field. Gass reviews the history of this effort, describing how and why the movement to certify instructors has been unsuccessful and explaining the emergence of a more successful effort to certify and accredit programs. He explains the four-phase accreditation process of the Association for Experiential Education (AEE) which is the most fully developed and widely used process to date.

Mitten concludes the section with discussion of the nature and importance of an inclusive community in adventure programming. Noting that some, such as women and nonwesterners, have not in the past been included sufficiently in adventure programming activities, she offers suggestions on how the situation may be improved. The emphasis is upon creating a trip setting that is supportive and nurturing for *all* participants.

Chapter 32

Outdoor Leadership Competencies

Simon Priest
eXperientia

Definitions

Adventure programming requires competent outdoor leaders to avoid accidents, reduce damage to the environment, and maximize client learning. For our purposes, leadership is defined as a process of influence. A leader is one who influences others to create, identify, work toward, achieve, share, and celebrate mutually acceptable goals. Therefore, anyone in a group can be a leader and exercise his or her leadership influence. However, the outdoor leader is someone who has been appointed by a sponsoring agency and is in charge of the group. This means being morally and legally responsible for ensuring individual safety, protecting the surrounding natural environment, and facilitating personal change (Priest and Gass, 1997).

Several studies into what it takes to be an effective outdoor leader found reasonable agreement on the necessary competencies. An analysis of these findings has led to the brick wall model of hard, soft, and meta skills for outdoor leadership (Figure 32.1, page 238) (Priest and Gass, 1997). Hard skills tend to be solid, tangible, measurable, and easy to train and assess; while soft skills tend to be amorphous, intangible, difficult to measure, and tough to train or assess. Meta skills are higher order core abilities which serve to integrate the hard and soft skills and bind them together in a workable synergy. Hard and soft skills are bricks in the wall. Meta skills are mortar holding

those bricks together, thus strengthening the wall of outdoor leadership. The wall sits atop a strong foundation of theoretical understanding such as the breadth and depth of concepts covered in this book.

Hard Skills

Technical skills are competencies in the actual adventure activities or outdoor pursuits being led. Two examples may include being able to climb at a certain level or standard and being able to paddle a particular grade or class of whitewater. In order to maintain group control during these activities, outdoor leaders need to be able to perform at a proficiency higher than that of the group members, thus giving them a safety margin or "cushion of competence."

Safety skills are those competencies necessary to enjoy the adventure activity in a safe and prudent manner. Examples of safety skills include navigation, survival, weather interpretation, body temperature regulation, first aid, accident response, search and rescue.

Environmental skills are those competencies necessary to prevent damage to the natural surroundings. Examples of these skills include practicing and encouraging minimum-impact travel and no-trace camping, modeling behaviors such as carrying out the garbage and not crosscutting switchback trails.

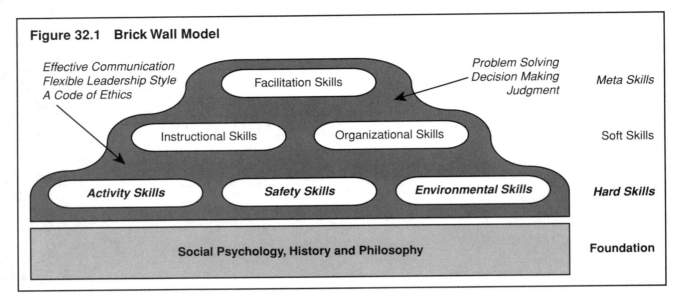

Figure 32.1 Brick Wall Model

Effective Communication
Flexible Leadership Style
A Code of Ethics

Problem Solving
Decision Making
Judgment

Facilitation Skills — Meta Skills

Instructional Skills — Organizational Skills — Soft Skills

Activity Skills — Safety Skills — Environmental Skills — Hard Skills

Social Psychology, History and Philosophy — Foundation

Soft Skills

Organizational skills are those competencies that permit a leader to plan, prepare, execute, and evaluate experiences for the specific needs of particular client groups. For example, outdoor adventure leaders need to manage risks; arrange transportation, food and lodging for a group; schedule activities; select routes; plan contingencies; and secure the necessary permits, equipment, and clothing to make the experience a success.

Instructional skills are those competencies required to appropriately teach people technical skills related to the activity, environment, and safety. For example, teaching skiing technique in a series of progressions, learning safety by the inquiry or discovery approach, and effective use of instructional aids to teach environmental concepts are all important instructional skills.

Facilitation skills are those competencies fostering productive group dynamics, so clients can work toward completing tasks, while developing their relationships. For example, outdoor adventure leaders may need to resolve conflicts, communicate effectively, and foster personal trust and group cooperation. They need to know how to debrief and guide reflection on adventure experiences to generate conditions for optimal change with people.

Meta Skills

Flexible leadership style means knowing how, why, and when to express differing leadership styles. For example, under most conditions, the decision making of a group is actually democratic or shared. At other times, like in an emergency, leaders must be autocratic: giving orders and expecting them to be carried out. However, when the experience is progressing well, the leader may be abdicratic: abdicating or delegating responsibility to the group. These examples highlight the need for outdoor leaders to flex their leadership style to suit the circumstances.

Experience-based judgment is required when leaders confront situations where pertinent information is unknown, missing, or vague. By considering past experiences and utilizing sound judgment, outdoor adventure leaders can appropriately substitute predictions for the unknown, missing, or vague information. This type of judgment becomes extremely important when the act of delaying a decision (in hopes that new information will become available) might result in further compounding the problem. Sound judgment comes from surviving past judgment calls (good or bad), analyzing those successes and failures, and applying learning from the analysis to future situations. In turn, this requires that outdoor leaders gain plenty of intensive and extensive field experience. Possession of a great base of experiences in no way assures sound judgment on the part of anyone; but lack of experience cannot possibly provide the critical foundation required for the interpolation or extrapolation of uncertain information.

Problem-solving skills can be creative or analytical, since a combination of both might be best. Outdoor leaders need to follow analytical processes to recognize a problem, define the crux, anticipate the outcome, identify several possible solutions, select the most probable one, put it into action and evaluate its effectiveness. They also need to be able to use creative techniques such as brainstorming, extended effort, attribute listing, forced relationships, and deferred prejudice.

Decision-making skills enable leaders to select the most probable option from a collection of possible ones. Outdoor leaders need to be capable of diverging or building up a range of options and then converging or narrowing down that range to pick the best option by using methods such as gathering, weeding, organizing, weighting, and choosing.

Effective communication is a process of information exchange between two or more people resulting in behavioral change. A message of the information (in the form of ideas, actions, or emotions) is transmitted along a pathway of audio, visual and tactile channels. Outdoor leaders need to be able to generate, encode, link, send, transmit, receive, decode, and interpret such messages. They need to be able to use paraphrasing, impression checking, and behavior description feedback to reduce the interference of noise, and to confirm that the message received was indeed the same as the message sent.

Professional ethics refer to the moral standards and value systems that outdoor leaders have and adventure programming demands. For example, challenge-by-choice is an ethic that defines adventure programming. People have the right to choose their level of participation in activities and not be coerced in doing an action they are unwilling to perform. Similarly, outdoor leaders hold enormous power over their clients and certain ethics guide leaders away from possible abuses of this power, such as deception, secrecy, or sexual contact with clients.

Reference

Priest, S., and Gass, M. A. (1997). *Effective leadership in adventure programming.* Champaign, IL: Human Kinetics.

Chapter 33

Outdoor Leadership Curricula

Edward Raiola
Warren Wilson College

Deborah Sugerman
University of New Hampshire

One of the exciting and, at times, frustrating elements of participating in the field of outdoor adventure education and recreation involves the issue of ensuring that practicing professionals function with competence, safety, and prudence. There is no doubt that camp directors, program supervisors, and administrators need competent and qualified people in charge of their outdoor adventure programs: they all want skilled, safe, knowledgeable staff. Whether one is a parent sending a child to a camp that offers adventure-based programming, a student enrolled in a stress-challenge course or the director of a therapeutic wilderness-based program for troubled youth, there is a concern about the quality of the staff who lead such programs. Are the leaders knowledgeable and competent enough to provide a safe and enjoyable experience? Do they meet the minimum qualifications to handle such positions as adventure educator, canoe guide, ropes course instructor, or rock-climbing specialist?

The past decade has seen extraordinary growth in the use of the outdoors for educational, recreational, and human service programs. Increasing numbers of people have found the outdoors a wonderful place to arouse sensitivity, learn practical living skills, shape values, expand cognitive understanding, develop commitments, and strengthen personalities. As the demand for outdoor activities increases, there is a need for highly skilled outdoor leaders and administrators—professionals who have knowledge and skills gained from many disciplines and a variety of life experiences.

The field of outdoor adventure education is interdisciplinary in that it provides educational, recreational, and therapeutic experiences for people in dispersed recreation areas. It deals with people and the natural environment and requires knowledge, ability, and skills sufficient to operate in that environment in a safe manner with minimum impact. This field also requires understanding of and competence in group process, learning theories, leadership, program planning, administration, and a wide variety of outdoor skills.

Individual leaders and administrators of outdoor programs must understand specific characteristics of the people with whom they work, such as age group traits, socioeconomic characteristics, and developmental levels. This awareness will help in understanding behavior and developing appropriate activities and experiences. Leaders are responsible not only for designing and administering outdoor recreational programs, but also for teaching specialized outdoor recreational skills and observing the participants' interpersonal relationships.

Research in Outdoor Leadership

During the last 25 years, there have been a number of studies pertinent to outdoor leadership education. Cousineau (1977), Swiderski (1981), and Buell (1983) all identified specific competencies deemed necessary for outdoor leaders. Each of these studies stressed that the education and preparation of competent outdoor leaders is comprised of a variety of components (e.g., experience in the field, leadership ability, skill development, and training experiences).

While several studies identify specific leadership competencies and course topics, the majority have been built from conceptual theory and have not been tested or evaluated. Shiner (1970), Mendence (1979), Simmons (1982), and Priest (1988) developed and recommended theoretical programs for the education and training of outdoor leaders in a higher education setting. Each of the studies strongly recommended that the programs be interdisciplinary in nature and that there be classroom as well as field experiences.

Building on the work of Green (1981), Raiola (1986) used an interdisciplinary approach to establish, test, and evaluate a curriculum for outdoor leadership education. Respondents in the study included not only experts with both higher education and field experience in outdoor recreation, but also students who were leaders-in-training. Based on the responses of panel members and students, a review of the literature, and the limitations set forth in the study, nine elements emerged as preferred curriculum content for outdoor leadership education (Figure 33.1).

Current Practice

After having reviewed the research, it is appropriate to look at what is actually happening in terms of current practice. More and more colleges and universities are offering wilderness-related courses and outdoor leadership curricula. In 1987 the National Recreation and Park Association–Society of Park and Recreation Educators curriculum catalog listed 17 colleges and universities which indicated the inclusion of outdoor leadership related courses or degree programs in their curriculum. The same catalog in 1997 listed 41 programs, an increase of 141 percent.

Sugerman (1997) looked at 15 colleges and universities in the United States that offered four-year academic degree programs in outdoor leadership. A review of these programs revealed interesting information. There did not seem to be a typical school at which programs were offered; degree programs occurred in both large universities and in small schools and in both public and private institutions.

There was no agreement as to what to call these degree programs, as the titles differed tremendously from school to school. Titles included Wilderness Leadership, Outdoor Leadership, Outdoor Leadership and Instruction, Experiential Education, Adventure Education, Outdoor Education, Outdoor Adventure Education, Outdoor Recreation and Adventure Recreation.

The department in which the degree programs were housed varied greatly between schools, and tended to impact the courses within the program. Out of the 15 schools, 9 (60 percent) were located in health, physical education and recreation (HPER); recreation management; or leisure studies departments. Two programs were located in kinesiology or exercise science, one in environmental sciences, and three in outdoor or adventure education or leadership.

Required coursework within degree programs also varied. Some schools tended to require courses strictly related to outdoor leadership such as technical skills, group process, leadership, and administration. Other schools stressed coursework in the natural sciences and education. Programs within HPER departments tended to have community-based recreation courses required as well as outdoor leadership courses. Sugerman calculated the percentage of credits in each curriculum that were specifically outdoor leadership-focused and found a range from 22.2 percent to 86.8 percent.

There is much variation in the current degree programs which is based on the mission and goals of the program, the influence of the department in which the program is housed and the philosophy of the college or university in which the program is located. The following describes four selected programs that are representative of the variety and focus of current curricula.

The outdoor recreation option at Eastern Washington University is one of three options in the recreation and leisure services department including therapeutic recreation and recreation management. The outdoor recreation option is geared to train students in outdoor leadership and resource management to eventually work for public and private organizations including government and commercial agencies. Students in the option are required to take a core of recreation courses required of all majors in the department and in addition must take technical skills courses in backpacking, canoeing, whitewater rafting, and search and rescue along with wilderness second-aid and outdoor leadership.

The outdoor education program at the University of New Hampshire is located within the Department of Kinesiology. The option is one of five in the department including exercise science, physical education pedagogy, athletic training and sports studies. Students are trained in the management and educational and/or therapeutic uses of physical activity in the natural environment. These goals are achieved by having students complete coursework in technical skills, wilderness emergency medicine, outdoor leadership, theory of outdoor education, administration, and field-based experiences. In addition, students develop a specialized area focusing on a current professional application in outdoor education. Areas in which students specialize tend to occur in education, business, therapy, therapeutic recreation, or management. Students are also required to document a minimum of 100 days of "face-to-face" outdoor leadership experiences before completing an academic internship.

Figure 33.1   Content of Outdoor Leadership Curriculum

Based on the consensus of objectives, the review of the literature, and the limitations set forth, the following nine elements emerged as preferred content of the outdoor leadership curriculum.

1. *Leadership style:* This element of the curriculum identifies topics, information, and practices that will enhance the knowledge, skills, and abilities of the student to develop his or her own leadership style. Topics:
   a. General knowledge related to leadership styles.
   b. Characteristics of the leader.
   c. Responsibilities of the wilderness leader.

2. *Judgment/objective-subjective:* This element serves to identify topics, information, and practices that will help students to develop their own judgment and decision-making ability for outdoor leadership. Topics:
   a. Characteristics of sound judgment.
   b. Potential problems of poor judgment.
   c. Process for learning sound judgment.

3. *Trip planning and organization:* This element identifies topics, information, and practices that will help students to enhance their knowledge, skills, and abilities in program planning, organization, and evaluation for outdoor leadership. Topics:
   a. Common elements of program planning.
   b. Considerations of activity and site selection.
   c. Evaluation tools for outdoor programs.
   d. Common elements of successful wilderness programs.

4. *Environmental issues:* This element identifies topics, information, and practices that will enhance the student's skills and abilities in minimum-impact practice and environmental considerations that affect wilderness programs. Topics:
   a. Philosophy of minimum-impact practice.
   b. Common problems of overuse.
   c. Minimum-impact practice and procedures.
   d. Common hazards in wilderness trips
   e. Procedures and practice to minimize hazards.

5. *Risk management:* This element identifies information and practices that will enable students to become aware of the safety and legal issues associated with outdoor leadership, and to develop emergency plans and procedures. Topics:
   a. Common risks in outdoor programming.
   b. Steps in risk management for outdoor programming.

   c. Legal liability and standard of care.
   d. Release forms and acknowledgment of participation.
   e. Emergency policies and procedures.

6. *Instructional principles:* This element identifies information and practices that will enhance the knowledge and abilities of students to teach and present material in an outdoor setting. Topics:
   a. Introduction to learning styles.
   b. Elements of experiential education.
   c. Opportunities and limitations on instruction in an outdoor setting.
   d. Teaching techniques for wilderness programming.

7. *Navigation:* This element identifies information and practices that will help students to enhance their knowledge, skills, and abilities in map and compass use for outdoor leadership. Topics:
   a. Topographic map symbols and uses.
   b. Compass use.
   c. Use of map and compass.
   d. Planning routes.

8. *Group dynamics:* This element identifies topics, information, and practices that will help students enhance their knowledge, skills, and abilities to work with small groups in outdoor settings. Topics:
   a. Techniques for communication and problem solving.
   b. Common interpersonal issues associated with wilderness programs.
   c. Opportunities and limitations of problem solving with small groups in an outdoor setting.

9. *Nutrition:* This element identifies information and practices that will help students to enhance their knowledge, skills, and abilities related to menu planning and preparation for outdoor programming. Topics:
   a. Components of a balanced diet.
   b. Practical nutrition for wilderness leaders.
   c. Organizing, planning, and preparation of food for outdoor programming
   d. Techniques for food preparation in the field.

Warren Wilson College, located in Asheville, North Carolina, offers a degree in outdoor leadership studies. The degree, which is housed in the outdoor leadership department, is designed to prepare students for a leadership role in the professional field of outdoor adventure education. Students focus on facilitation and experiential education methodologies while taking courses in technical skills such as backpacking, canoeing, rock climbing, and group initiatives, interpersonal and leadership skills, and program

planning and administration. In addition, students take supporting coursework from a variety of disciplines including psychology, sociology, biology, and education. Students are encouraged to take other supporting coursework based on their career interests and needs. Experiential fieldwork includes a supervised practicum and an internship. Students may also work in conjunction with North Carolina Outward Bound to complete an intensive instructor development curriculum.

Northland College is located in Ashland, Wisconsin, and offers a degree in adventure education within the outdoor education department. The emphasis of the program is to prepare students for instructional positions with public and private adventure agencies. Through the curriculum, students develop a broad range of experiential teaching strategies and a strong background in safety management, environmental ethics, and technical and interpersonal skills. Students take a variety of coursework including technical skills, group process, teaching techniques, recreation leadership, and practicum experience. In addition, students are encouraged to develop a minor to enhance their professional development. Choices for minors include environmental education, Native American studies, earth science, biology or business. Students have the opportunity to take courses in blocks, which offer a more intensive, experiential program.

Sugerman concluded from her study that a more in-depth look at higher education curricula would be an important step in defining what constitutes excellence in outdoor leadership training and education.

Striking a Balance

When considering the components of outdoor leadership development, it is helpful to distinguish between "training" and "education." Such a distinction illuminates the necessary interplay of skill mastery, in the technical sense and the evolution of a larger context of knowledge with which to practice skills. If one thinks of training as the learning of techniques, whether of fire making, rope handling, or map and compass navigation, one can view education as the process through which the student comes to understand the appropriate use of technique, as well as the implications of such use.

Through this framework, the need for a balance of training and education in the preparation of outdoor leaders becomes self-evident. One also may become aware that the development of a good leader, much like that of a good writer, psychologist, or teacher, is an ongoing process.

In the pilot and ongoing testing and evaluation of the curriculum for outdoor leadership (Raiola, 1986, 1996), some of the stages of this ongoing process become evident (Figure 33.2). At the beginning of the course, the students were at a level of "unconscious incom-

petence" relative to their skills and understanding. That is, they were largely unaware of the aspects of capable leadership and were unable to demonstrate these aspects. As they were introduced to the curriculum objectives, they progressed into a level of "conscious incompetence," where the components of effective leadership became known to them, as did their lack of skill and experience.

Over time, the students moved into a state of "conscious competence." With deliberate attention, they were now able to perform competently the tasks of outdoor leadership, yet the degree of self-scrutiny required to do so led to awkwardness. Often, each step of a procedure had to be thought through in order to achieve the desired result.

By the end of the course of instruction, most of the students had arrived at a level of "unconscious competence" relative to most of the curriculum objectives. They had integrated the educational and training experiences to the extent that they could perform their duties competently without constant thought. Their automatic responses had become reliable, and the groundwork for future refinements of their expertise was in place.

Each of these leaders that moves out into new situations and is required to encompass new learning, will pass

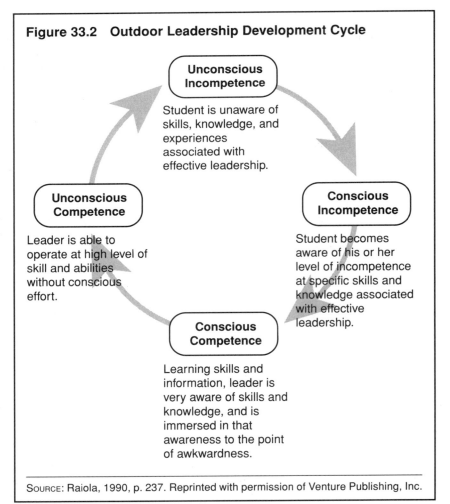

Figure 33.2   Outdoor Leadership Development Cycle

Unconscious Incompetence
Student is unaware of skills, knowledge, and experiences associated with effective leadership.

Conscious Incompetence
Student becomes aware of his or her level of incompetence at specific skills and knowledge associated with effective leadership.

Conscious Competence
Learning skills and information, leader is very aware of skills and knowledge, and is immersed in that awareness to the point of awkwardness.

Unconscious Competence
Leader is able to operate at high level of skill and abilities without conscious effort.

SOURCE: Raiola, 1990, p. 237. Reprinted with permission of Venture Publishing, Inc.

through the four stages illustrated in Figure 33.2. This developmental movement, though broadly defined, is subjective in nature and individual to each person; some students move through this process much faster than others.

This process, in terms of leadership development, is generally the same for each person and is a continuing, lifelong evolution as one grows and absorbs new knowledge. Optimally, an outdoor recreation curriculum will provide students with both the fundamental skills and knowledge for beginning their maturation in this field of endeavor, and a sense of themselves as representatives and teachers of the values and ethics of the outdoors.

The education and training of competent and sensitive outdoor leaders and educators have some important social and political implications for the use of and general attitudes toward the natural environment, and thus, the minimization of environmental degradation through use. Highly skilled and aware outdoor leaders are a major resource for the reeducation of the increasing numbers of people who are discovering the outdoors. By creating outdoor experiences that embody values of preservation and conservation of nature and promoting, through role modeling, a nonabusive relationship with one's environment, an outdoor leader has a unique opportunity to shape the practices and attitudes of the public.

In terms of choosing which curriculum objectives should be included in a model outdoor leadership curriculum, the studies cited earlier offer specific recommendations for content as well as sequencing. It is our view that the application of specific curriculum content should be chosen by individual outdoor recreation educators. For example, the nine elements that emerged as preferred content of the outdoor leadership education curriculum should be considered as guidelines for a college-level outdoor leadership course. The objectives are not listed in a sequence that reflects a recommended preference for presentation. Rather, they are listed as a guide for the outdoor recreation educator. It is important to note that organizing curriculum objectives around the common threads of *concepts, values,* and *skills and abilities* related to outdoor leadership will help to provide continuity, sequence, and integration in order to reinforce each aspect and produce a cumulative learning effect. The interplay of these organizing principles is considered by us to be critical to the success of any curriculum.

References

Buell, L. (1983). *Outdoor leadership competency: A manual for self-assessment and staff evaluation.* Greenfield, MA: Environmental Awareness Publishers.

Cousineau, C. (1977). *A Delphi consensus on a set of principles for the development of a certification system for educators in outdoor adventure programs.* Unpublished doctoral dissertation, University of Northern Colorado, Greeley, Colorado.

Fuller, S. K. (1985). A camp director's view. *Camping Magazine, 57*(6), 25–26.

Green, P. J. (1981). *The content of a college-level outdoor leadership course for land-based outdoor pursuits in the Pacific Northwest: A Delphi consensus.* Unpublished doctoral dissertation, University of Oregon, Eugene, Oregon.

Mendence, D. J. (1979). *An integrated-interdisciplinary model in outdoor education for higher education.* Unpublished doctoral dissertation, University of Northern Colorado, Greeley, Colorado.

NRPA/SPRE. (1997). *Recreation and parks education curriculum catalog.* Alexandria, VA: National Recreation and Parks Association.

Priest, S. (1988). Outdoor leadership training in higher education. *Journal of Experiential Education, 11*(1), 42–47.

Raiola, E. O. (1986). *Outdoor wilderness education: A leadership curriculum.* Unpublished doctoral dissertation, The Union for Experimenting Colleges and Universities.

Raiola, E. (1990). Outdoor leadership curricula. In J. C. Miles and S. Priest (Eds.), *Adventure education* (pp. 233–237). State College, PA: Venture Publishing, Inc.

Raiola, E. (1996). Outdoor leadership education: Review and analysis of a nine-year study of a college level curriculum. In M. L. Phipps (Ed.), *Proceedings of the 1996 Wilderness Education Association's national conference for outdoor leaders.* Nashville, TN: Tennessee Department of Environment and Conservation.

Shiner, J. W. (1970). *Developing professional leadership in outdoor recreation.* Unpublished doctoral dissertation, State University of New York, Syracuse, New York.

Simmons, G. (1982). *An outdoor adventure education baccalaureate degree curriculum and activities model.* Unpublished doctoral dissertation, University of Northern Colorado, Greeley, Colorado.

Sugerman, D., and Raiola, E. (1997). *Twenty-five years of outdoor leadership education: The past, present and future.* Paper presented at the 1997 International Conference of the Association for Experiential Education, Asheville, North Carolina.

Swiderski, M. J. (1981). *Outdoor leadership competencies identified by outdoor leaders in five western regions.* Unpublished doctoral dissertation, University of Oregon, Eugene, Oregon.

Chapter 34

Accreditation and Certification: Questions for an Advancing Profession

Michael A. Gass
University of New Hampshire

As professions mature and evolve, several mechanisms of operation often develop. Some of these mechanisms include establishing and maintaining integrity through identified codes of conduct, the demonstration of competence by passing certain standards, the assumption of responsibility for the profession as a whole, and some method of sanctioning by the professional community (e.g., Kultgen, 1988). With the emergence of adventure programming as a profession, questions on how the field might deal with such issues have often become the center of debate. No longer have such questions revolved around whether or not these efforts should be done, but how they might be best accomplished (e.g., Bassin et al., 1992).

Probably the two best expressions of such efforts have come in the form of certifying individual professions as competent and accreditating the programming practices of competent adventure programs. While this chapter centers on examining this evolutionary process in and from a North American perspective, you need to be aware that exhaustive dialogues concerning evolving professionalism, certification, and accreditation are currently in the forefront of thinking around the world, most notably in Australia, Great Britain, and New Zealand (e.g., Priest and Gass, 1997a).

Factors and Indicators Influencing the Professionalism of Adventure Programming in the United States

Adventure programming in North America has undergone many dramatic and rapid changes over the past 35 years. Priest and Gass (1997a) have identified some of the indicators of this growth to be:

- increasing numbers of adventure programs;
- expanding applications of adventure programs for specific populations;
- greater public acceptance of adventure programming as a valid profession;
- increase in the number of adventure programming organizations;
- increase in artificially constructed adventure environments for programming; and
- increase in the level of research and program evaluation.

What has been interesting to observe with this growth in adventure programming are several related factors that have a direct bearing on the future growth, acceptance, and possibly even the continuance of the field. Some of these factors include:

- an increasingly litigious society;
- a better educated insurance industry;
- limited access to insurance coverage (e.g., in the spring of 1997 Markel Insurance Company—the second largest provider of insurance for adventure programs in the United States—decided not to renew insurance policies of stand-alone ropes/adventure courses);
- increasing government regulation concerning access and use of natural resources (e.g., Joshua Tree National Park and Red Rock Canyon Conservation Area);
- decreasing levels of federal, state, and local funding to support the sustenance and protection of natural environments;
- establishment of or an increase in fees to use wilderness areas;
- increasing levels of technological advances and their influences on programming as well as client expectations (e.g., cell phones, global positioning systems, more advanced extrication systems used in rescues); and
- the development of external "watchdog" groups (e.g., Michelle Sutton Memorial Fund Inc., which addresses inappropriate practices of wilderness therapy camps).

Methods of Verifying Professionalism: Certification and Accreditation

To address such developments, a number of strategies have emerged in the adventure programming industry. Probably the first to be considered was the certification of individual leaders. Certification can be defined as a process guaranteeing that certain minimum standards of competency have been met or exceeded by a professional as evaluated by a certifying agency (Senosk, 1977). The idea of certifying adventure professionals was to provide a "means to [ensure] that only qualified people may systematically engage in the formal teaching and/or leading of individuals in the outdoor adventure situation" (Ewert, 1985, p. 17).

A movement to certify individual instructors began in the late 1970s in the United States. Led by Paul Petzoldt and some colleges and universities that offered adventure programming, dialogue in the late 1970s was followed by the formation of the Wilderness Education Association (WEA) outdoor leader certification program in 1980. WEA enjoyed initial advances as being an accepted form of verifying leaders with appropriate judgment to deliver safe and quality wilderness programming. However, its influence on the field has faded and as an organization it is currently experiencing a downturn in operations.

Why has such an effort failed to prosper at this time? It certainly was not due to monetary support or professional effort. Some of the best minds in the North American adventure programming field focused much of their professional careers and talents on trying to see this effort or similar ones succeed for more than 15 years. At least at the current time, the certification of outdoor adventure leaders has not evolved as an effective answer to the problems facing adventure programming for a number of reasons.

One problem was the ability to adequately identify and assess the so-called *soft* and *meta* skills; the "people-oriented" elements such as instruction, facilitation, and communication skills of leadership (Priest and Gass, 1997a). These elements of outdoor leadership are much more difficult to train and assess than technically oriented *hard* skills such as activity, safety, and environmental skills. Note that there are several other certification schemes in North America that currently are experiencing stronger degrees of success (e.g., American Mountain Guides Association [AMGA], Wilderness First Responder [WFR] trainings), but these programs center primarily on certifying specific associated technical skills, and not the soft or meta skills of outdoor leadership.

The idea that certification was the "answer" to client safety or environmental protection was also critically flawed. Consider a most capable outdoor leader with excellent judgment working in a program with old equipment, outdated educational philosophies, unethical client treatment, and a large group travelling through a dangerous and very fragile area. Whether this leader is certified won't make any difference in avoiding accidents or preventing damage to nature for this substandard program (Priest and Gass, 1997b).

In many ways, certification also failed because it was unable to examine adventure programming in a true systemic manner. Geographical diversity (e.g., different environments) and programming differences (e.g., varying client groups, differing program lengths) made the development of one set of standards for all programming formats often impossible.

While certification was being considered, another form of professional assessment was also developing. Evolving out of a number of sources with their roots in the Outward Bound system (e.g., Wade, 1983; Wade and Fischesser, 1988) as well as through several documents produced by the Association for Experiential Education (Johanson, 1984, 1985, 1987; Priest and Dixon, 1990), program accreditation was formalized in the early 1990s as a method for programs to provide greater benefits for their organizations and clients. Some of the targeted benefits for accrediting programs include:

- achieving appropriate standards of professional care without programs losing the flexibility to decide how standards can be met;

- stimulating an internal learning process within the organization to enhance risk management and program quality efforts;
- receiving an external and objective perspective on program operations and risk management;
- providing program participants with a level of quality assurance;
- providing a marketing tool for attracting clients;
- providing external regulating agencies (e.g., federal and state governments) with a level of quality assurance;
- receiving access to natural resources and programming areas where external agencies require accreditation for entrance;
- providing insurance providers with a level of quality assurance;
- receiving discounts on insurance premiums; and
- becoming associated with programs that have made a commitment to hold themselves out to the greater community as possessing standards valued by the field.

Accreditation retains the strengths of individual certification without being bound by some of its weaknesses. For example, accreditation (1) provides adventure programs with the ability to achieve standards without losing the flexibility to decide and design how these standards are met; (2) takes a "systemic view" of the process of adventure programming rather than dividing it into individualized categories; (3) encourages improvement through internal and external review; (4) assures clients, agencies, and the custodians of the lands that a program has clearly defined and appropriate objectives, and (5) maintains conditions under which their achievement can be reasonably met.

Two studies assessing the professional opinions of certification and accreditation have been conducted in the United States and their findings seem to be consistent with the trends highlighted here. In one study surveying professional opinions of certification and accreditation process of adventure leaders, Bassin et al. (1992) found that 62 percent favored program accreditation over individual certification (38 percent). These researchers also found that those individuals who commented on their preference of program accreditation over individual certification "felt that accreditation was the only viable alternative to certification because more professional credibility would be gained and there would be less dependence on the unpredictable human part of the equation (of leading adventure experiences)" (p. 25). This was similar to results found in a study by Cockrell and Detzel (1985) where 70 percent of professionals surveyed supported the idea of program accreditation over individual certification.

The Association for Experiential Education Accreditation Process

The Association for Experiential Education (AEE) Accreditation Process possesses four phases—the initial application, self-assessment phase, on-site evaluation phase, and formal accreditation and continuation of accreditation phase. Within each of these phases are 17 sequential steps prospective programs follow on their way to becoming accredited. These steps include (van der Smissen and Liddle, 1997):

Phase I—Initial Application
- Step 1: Organization contacts the AEE Staff Accreditation Administrator.
- Step 2: AEE provides materials: Cover Letter, Fact Sheet, Preliminary Application, and Organization Profile Form.
- Step 3: Organization completes Preliminary Application and Organization Profile, pays preliminary application fee, and receives current *Manual of Accreditation Standards for Adventure Programs, Self-Assessment Workbook* on disk, and *Policy and Procedures Manual.*
- Step 4: Organization attends Accreditation Workshop (registration included in the fee paid in Step 3; this fee does not include food and lodging for the workshop).

Phase II—Self-Assessment
- Step 5: Organization undertakes self-assessment process.
- Step 6: Organization submits self-assessment report with formal application and fee within 18 months of processing the Preliminary Application (Step 3).
- Step 7: Liaison Accreditation Council members and AEE Staff Accreditation Administrator review report, in general, for completeness.

Phase III—Evaluation
- Step 8: Accreditation Council with Organization forms on-site review team, and establishes time schedule.

Step 9:   Team conducts on-site review and reports findings to Accreditation Council.
Step 10:   Accreditation Council liaisons review the findings of the on-site review team.
Step 11:   Accreditation Council sends the report to the Organization for response.
Step 12:   Organization submits a response to Council.

Phase IV—Formal Accreditation and Continuation of Accreditation
Step 13:   Accreditation Council (entire) reviews the Organization response.
Step 14:   Accreditation Council formally acts (see types of action).
Step 15:   Organization evaluates the process.
Step 16:   Organization submits annual status report and pays annual fee.
Step 17:   Organization applies to Accreditation Council for renewal of accreditation.

The accreditation manual (Williamson and Gass, 1993, 1995) is designed in a sequential fashion, focusing on both the technical aspects of adventure experiences as well as the teaching and ethical practices used by programs. Chapter one addresses philosophical, educational, and ethical concerns, focusing on program management and operations, ethical considerations, environmental concerns, and universal access considerations. Chapter two addresses risk management, including guidelines on safety policies; risk management plans; communications protocols; search, rescue, emergency aid, and evacuation procedures; staff: participant ratios; safety reviews; and written procedures. Chapter three addresses staff qualifications, covering areas concerning hiring, qualifications, skills and training, and conduct. Chapter four addresses transportation, concentrating on ground, water, and air transportation methods.

Chapter five addresses land technical skills, covering areas concerning hiking, running, initiative games, high- and low-ropes-challenge courses, orienteering, bike touring, mountain biking, bouldering, artificial wall climbing, top rope and lead rock climbing, rappelling, caving, river crossing activities, snow shoeing, ice climbing, mountain snow and glacier travel, cross-country and backcountry skiing, mountaineering, and solos. Chapter six addresses water technical skills, directing attention to personal floatation devices, flat water canoeing and kayaking, whitewater canoeing and kayaking, river rafting, ocean kayaking, sailing, snorkeling and scuba diving. Chapter seven addresses air technical skills, concentrating on parapente, hang glid-

ing, and parachuting. Chapter eight addresses environmental, emergency, and cultural skills, targeting concerns with service projects, camping, remote travel, expeditions, international considerations, and emergency response training. There is also a reference section that includes a report/scoring card and bibliography.

All of the sections within each chapter are designed in a sequential fashion, with each standard presented in a "general" structure followed by more specific details. A lettering system exists in each section and is structured in the following manner:

A. General—provides for any overview of items not covered under the other letters.
B. Environmental Understanding—examines a program's knowledge of the areas of operations as they relate to risk management and appropriateness of activities. "Environments" include wild and natural areas, towns and cities, and constructions—such as ropes courses and artificial climbing walls.
C. Human Understanding—examines a program's knowledge of participants' abilities, health, and readiness for the activities.
D. Conducting the Activity—examines how the program presents and operates each activity.
E. Emergency Procedures—examines the program's preparedness to respond to accidents, which can include damage to property, illness, injury, fatality, lost persons, and near misses.
F. Clothing and Equipment—examines a program's understanding of the appropriate clothing and equipment for activities, including maintenance, repair, replacement, and how to improvise if necessary.
G. Nourishment—examines a program's understanding of how to provide for adequate food and water requirements for given activities and environments.

Some standards include an explanation to help interpret the desired intent for the personnel from the adventure program and the reviewers. The following example is from the clothing and equipment area of the section addressing high- and low-ropes-challenge courses:

13.F.01 Participants wear appropriate clothing and equipment.
Explanation: When protective gear (e.g., helmets, harnesses) is used on elements requiring it, each piece is securely and properly fastened. Proper wheelchairs are used/provided for participants needing them. If helmets are worn by people on the challenge course, then they are also worn by belayers.

One of the most important features of the accreditation process is the program self-assessment stage (Step 5). During this stage, programs are supplied with a computerized disk that leads the program through a systematic self-examination procedure on its strengths and weaknesses. The purpose of the self-assessment is to lead programs to collect, review, and record appropriate materials related to the administration of adventure-based, experiential education organizations and document concepts, policies, and actions of such programs in writing (van der Smissen and Liddle, 1997).

Conclusion

The growth of adventure programming and its increasing intersection with traditional agencies (e.g., educational institutions, government regulating bodies, therapeutic organizations) has led to standardizing certain methods of practice. This phenomenon, combined with requests for ways to verify program quality and the management of risk (e.g., from various constituents, including parents, administrators, funding agencies, other professionals, participants) has resulted in several efforts to provide a means of quality assurance. Probably the two most developed efforts replying to such a need have been efforts to certify individual professions as competent and accreditate the programming practices of competent adventure programs. Currently in North America, certification efforts seem most successful when targeted toward addressing competence in specific technical skills. Program accreditation seems better suited when addressing broader, systematic, comprehensive, and more dynamic issues in leading adventure programs.

References

Bassin, Z., Breault, M., Fleming, J., Foell, S., Neufeld, J., and Priest, S. (1992). AEE organizational membership preference for program accreditation. *Journal of Experiential Education, 15*(2), 21–27.

Cockrell, D., and Detzel, D. (1985). Effects of outdoor leadership certification on safety, impacts, and program. *Trends, 22*(3), 15–21.

Ewert, A. (1985). Emerging trends in outdoor adventure recreation. In G. McClellan (Ed.), *Proceedings—1985 national outdoor recreation trends symposium II.* Atlanta, GA: USDI National Park Service.

Johanson, K., et al. (1984). *Common/accepted peer practices in adventure programming.* Boulder, CO: Association for Experiential Education.

Johanson, K., et al. (1987). *Common/accepted peer practices in adventure programming* (2nd ed.). Boulder, CO: Association for Experiential Education.

Johanson, K., et al. (1989). *Common/accepted peer practices in adventure programming* (3rd ed.). Boulder, CO: Association for Experiential Education.

Kultgen, J. (1988). *Ethics and professionalism.* Philadelphia, PA: University of Pennsylvania Press.

Priest, S., and Dixon, T. (1990). *Safety practices in adventure programming.* Boulder, CO: Association for Experiential Education.

Priest, S., and Gass, M. A. (1997a). *Effective leadership in adventure programming.* Champaign, IL: Human Kinetics, Inc.

Priest, S., and Gass, M. A. (1997b). Trends and issues. *Journeys, 2*(4), 13–21.

Senosk, E. M. (1977). *An examination of outdoor pursuit leader certification and licensing within the United States in 1976.* Unpublished master's thesis, University of Oregon, Eugene, Oregon.

van der Smissen, B., and Liddle, J. B. (1997). *Accreditation of adventure-based experiential education programs policy and procedures manual.* Boulder, CO: Association for Experiential Education.

Wade, I. (1983). *Alternative to certification programs.* Unpublished manuscript.

Wade, I., and Fischesser, M. (1988). *The safety review manual: A guide to conducting safety reviews for assessing and upgrading safety in outdoor adventure programs.* Greenwich, CT: Outward Bound USA.

Williamson, J., and Gass, M. (1993). *Manual of accreditation standards for adventure programs.* Boulder, CO: Association for Experiential Education.

Williamson, J., and Gass, M. (1993). *Manual of accreditation standards for adventure programs* (2nd ed.). Boulder, CO: Association for Experiential Education.

Chapter 35

Leadership for Community Building

Denise Mitten
eXperientia

Introduction

The United States was founded on discontent and rugged individualism. As people moved out into the frontier, their experiences encouraged individualism, competition, and egalitarianism among men. Men formed temporary relationships based on shared goals. In some areas, communities came and went with mining and lumbering success or not. Culturally, in North America, community building has been based more on economic need rather than intentional relationships.

Historically, the notion of community members and therefore the sense of community has been based on Frederick Jackson Turner's model of rugged individualism on the frontier (Potter, 1962). David Potter (1962) pointed out that Turner's model was deeply sexist. Though the frontier experience did encourage individualism, competition, and egalitarianism among men, it denied women alternatives to marriage, and hence encouraged quite another set of character traits for women (Manning, 1992). American liberalism, like adventure education, is deeply influenced by this sexist frontier picture as the normative person. Communities, then, may not have been sensitive to the needs and experiences of women and non-Western males.

Since its inception, and with the influence of Turner's model, the field of adventure education has been teaching people about communities. The wilderness was the teacher and students learned to accept and defeat challenges and to work together as a team to accomplish tasks such as

mountaineering and boating feats. Kimball and Bacon (1993) see troubled youth as "needing a reinitiation into cultural norms" (p. 19) and adventure therapy provides an "educational process where adolescents are initiated into the prosocial values that form the basis of the Western culture" (p. 19).

In the past, this notion of a normative person as being an individual to corral into a group either by a strong leader, peer pressure, the threat that success depended on teamwork, or, more recently, by leadership techniques known by names such as telling and selling, left out the experience of most women and some non-Western groups (Manning, 1992). However, with a bigger than ever influence of women in the corporate, political, and adventure education arenas, as well as an understanding by many men that the historical ways of leadership and decision making are obsolete for today's world, leadership and therefore community building has changed significantly.

As a result of this awareness, in the last couple of decades, intentional communities have blossomed. More people want to live in a community, not just for economic need but also for the nurturing and caring relationships that can come from living in a community.

Similarly, a more recent goal of many outdoor programs and adventure education is for participants to have positive group experiences including creating positive relationships and bonds among participants. This community may be temporary, but it provides a valuable arena where people can share and learn. With a positive group experience to serve as a model, participants can return home and re-create communities in healthy ways for themselves. In replicating this experience and in forming other communities sensitive and responsive to the needs and desires of many different people, leaders and participants in adventure education programs are transforming the world into a place that welcomes them as they are.

This chapter will describe philosophical underpinnings and leadership practices that can be used by practitioners to help develop a healthy trip community. I will share a group stage model and a leadership perspective designed to help leaders recognize and highlight the strengths of group members that in turn helps create a positive and pleasurable learning environment and community. After being part of these temporary communities of one day to several weeks, people returned home stronger and often with a commitment to build community that they want.

The Importance of Community Building

Most people have a need to feel connected and therefore they make connections. Especially on an outdoor adventure, connections contribute to participants feeling safe and secure. Establishing relationships or friendships is a learned behavior. People form relationships in the ways they know how. Their relationship skills often originate from their family experiences. For many people, group membership is an unconscious means of regaining the security of the family (Freud, 1922). Freud concluded that people join groups simply because they have been in groups since infancy and that people join groups for less-than-rational reasons. Exploratory studies of long-term, emotionally intensive groups, such as families, therapeutic groups, and combat units, reveal processes that are consistent with Freud's hypotheses (Billig, 1976; Janis, 1963).

Our culture influences families and therefore individuals and the reverse is also true. It is an accepted notion that our culture has become more violent in the last few decades. Children are more at risk for suicide and violence towards one another as well as engaging in other socially unacceptable behavior. In our society some people come from families where they have learned to base relationships on unhealthy factors. Some people learn unhealthy relationship skills from families who connect around secrets, crisis, or abuse of another family member(s). These people may see others liking them when there is a crisis and people have to interact with them and they feel needed, or when they can focus negative energy on something or someone else. They feel little or no liking based on self-worth or respect by others. They use power over someone or something to feel good about themselves. Some people may have low self-esteem and build themselves up by tearing other people down or by patronizing less competent people. For example, if they survive a week in the woods, they feel good because they have conquered or beaten nature.

Unhealthy or dependency relationships are reactions against an outside stimulus—a thing or a person that is disliked, a treatment perceived as negative, or various evils that should be fought. Those who have learned this type of dependency bonding often have low self-esteem and these unhealthy relationships reinforce low self-esteem (Clarke, 1978). Unhealthy connections can divide a group, create unsafe conditions, or cause people to compete for food, shelter, and protection. This form of relationship is exemplified more by what one is "against" than by what one is "for."

Unhealthy relationships discourage people from feeling good about themselves and from valuing their and other's differences. Unhealthy relationships discourage people from pursuing individual goals simultaneously to the group goals, and can trap individuals in unhealthy subgroups. If participants connect to survive the wilderness, they are making a connection in reaction to an outside stimulus. In this case, connecting in order to survive supports the idea that wilderness is bad, evil, something to be afraid of, something to be conquered or even fought. These connections often are maintained only as long as the fight goes on and the crisis continues. During trips, it is easy to increase perceived risk, invent hardships, create stress that produces intense emotional outbreaks, or accomplish feat after death-defying feat that may, as a planned goal or as a side-effect, define group member relationships, as well as maintain a closeness and excitement (high) that comes with this type of bonding (Mitten, 1986). However, this type of programming models to the participant that these factors are necessary for relationships and in their families and work situations these factors may not be functional.

In contrast, healthy relationships, connections based on mutual respect, trust, and experience with one another, can add to group cohesiveness, enable people to feel good about themselves, and give them opportunities to grow. In healthy relationships, people come together for positive reasons and then establish connections or friendships. Healthy connections come from individuals *acting* on their own desires, rather than *reacting* to an outside stimulus. When people form healthy connections they enter relationships where they maintain a separate identity and individual responsibility, yet can still function well in a group and feel a sense of inclusion. Such relationships often begin with common interests, shared experiences, learning together, or accomplishing tasks in an atmosphere of mutual respect and trust. In a healthy group, members have the skills to eliminate barriers to the accomplishment of the group's goals, to maintain high-quality interaction among members, and to overcome obstacles to the development of a more effective group (Johnson and Johnson, 1991). Trips are also safer, because people in healthy relationships feel secure and speak up if they are cold, tired, hungry, or have other concerns.

It takes time to develop the trust and respect necessary for healthy relationships. In outdoor situations, people tend, as soon as the experience begins, to strive to establish connections with each other, and relationships can rely on dependency rather than trust and respect. Components that help mitigate people's impulse for instant intimacy and influence connections to be healthy and respectful are the leaders modeling healthy connections by their own examples, the trip pace, and the program philosophy. In groups, healthy relationships among participants and between the leaders and participants, as well as with the humans and nature can facilitate open communication and rapport, which help build support systems and group cohesiveness. The trip can be a safe and powerful experience for the participants and relationship models experienced on the trip can be replicated at home.

Practitioners and leaders in adventure education work with people, at least some who have learned unhealthy ways of relating. In therapeutic populations, most of the participants will have limited relationship-building skills and therefore limited community-building skills. Therefore leaders in adventure education are teaching relationship- and community-building skills by their program design and most importantly by how they form relationships with their participants. To truly help group members learn positive community-building skills, it is useful to examine one's own beliefs about communities and relationships.

Putting It Together Consciously (What We Want in a Community)

Many leaders in adventure education are in this field because of their commitment and desire to help people enjoy the outdoors and find greater personal freedom through learning more about themselves. Many leaders have been conscious about how they have wanted to relate to their group members and to nature. Through my work for almost two decades at Woodswomen, Inc., I, with the help of the staff, took this consciousness and began to focus on the group dynamics and leadership aspects that seemed to reliably develop the community we desired.

Some important relationship themes emerged that, when present, seemed to help establish the community environment we found successful. These themes relate to Noddings' ethic of care and involve a morality grounded in relationship and response (Mannings, 1992). Creating ways for these themes to reliably emerge on trips guided our trip or program process. Important themes include:

- Seeing and experiencing ourselves as working with nature and in community with nature. This serves as an action metaphor for human relationships. This includes appreci-

ating biodiversity and using state-of-the-art low-trace traveling and camping techniques. We discourage conquering or adversarial attitudes and we do not foster adversarial or duality language. We work with the challenges that inevitably come up when traveling in the outdoors with good cheer and resourcefulness.

- Being in the outdoors because we enjoy and appreciate nature and not using the natural environment as a testing ground to prove competency or create situations to take risks. Using the outdoors as a testing ground would be inconsistent with the respectful and comfortable connections with nature that we want to foster. The process and how that impacts participants and the natural environment is as important as the accomplishment.

- Believing that constructive, safe leadership can take a number of forms and that there are many different ways to learn skills and be outdoors. My experience is that this skill development is far more important than mere accomplishment or "survival." Many women find their self-esteem heightened after learning outdoor skills that help them be comfortable and safe in the outdoors.

- Creating an atmosphere that felt safe—emotionally, spiritually, and physically; an atmosphere supportive of differences in participants' needs and consistent with the belief that individual needs are varied, valid, and possible to meet.

- Striving for collaboration as much as possible, by sharing information, decision-making processes and, when appropriate, decision making.

- Focusing on group members' strengths and believing that women and other minority people's strengths are an asset to programs. People do not need to be changed to fit into adventure programs or "taught" in order to be good enough outdoors.

- Respecting and valuing each person for who he or she is, as well as the special gifts and contributions he or she offered. For example, canoe portagers are respected for their contributions, just as the people gathering firewood are respected for their contributions, and just as guitar players are respected for their contributions. Additionally, all people are respected for giving the gift of bringing themselves to the trip.

- Believing that individual goals and accomplishments are different and special to each person and within the context of the trip, encouraging individuals to define their own goals and accomplishments.

Philosophical Underpinnings or Early Women Pave the Way

As it turns out, the values, described previously, that were incorporated into the Woodswomen program, reflected many of the same values that early women adventurers described. In 1955 the first recorded women's Himalayan expedition took place. Three Scottish women, with Sherpas, explored an unknown section of the Himalayas. Monica Jackson and Elizabeth Stark wrote about their adventure with their comrade, Evelyn Camrass, in their book *Tents in the Clouds: The First Women's Himalayan Expedition* (1956). They were extremely modest about their impressive venture. They wrote about the specific planning they did about group dynamics and how the team wanted to be in a community in the mountains. Four women were going to be on the expedition. Very close to the departure date, illness prevented the fourth team member, Esme Speakman, from going. However, she was already so much a part of the community established in planning their trip that the other three commented that they always thought of her as part of the expedition. They highly valued her contributions and gifts, even though that did not include being on the actual trip. They shared leadership in a collaborative manner and built in structures, for example a tent rotation pattern, that allowed each woman alone time every third night. In their book, Jackson and Stark wrote about their community and connections with each other as well as the land and how they respected the local people and their traditions traveling with them.

Miranda (1987) found similar values focusing on relationships, community, and the person as she researched the history of the camping movement of the late 1800s. Miranda said that women camp leaders wanted their programs to emphasize "the aesthetic and spiritual kinship of girls to nature and to one another." This program emphasis was in response to the women camp leaders' belief that due to the effects of urbanization women's lives were going to change. These leaders wanted women to have tools to thrive in the change and so made the girls' camps "into excellent social incubators for what would become a new type of woman, the politically active citizen." Contrary to these values, Miranda (1987) found that at the same time men's response to the effects of the industrial age was to organize boys' camps that could help boys recapture some of their rugged individualism. Competition, challenge and conquering the wilderness were general themes of boys camps in the 1800s.

In the past 20 years, many women's programs have emerged. Not all, but many of these programs incorporated the values articulated here. Women resonated with

the program design. Starting as early as 1982, Yerkes and Miranda asked women what drew them to these groups. They found that fun, laughter, and sharing common interests were top priorities for the women. These women enjoyed an atmosphere where they felt they could try new skills unencumbered by gender expectations (if there were no men in the group, then women could steer the canoe, make the fire, pitch the tent, and the like). Women also said they went on these outdoor trips specifically to feel empowered, to relax, to gain a sense of renewal, to network, and to find spiritual healing and a connection with nature. All of these benefits are enhanced because of the "community" that develops on trips.

Arlene Blum wanted to climb mountains. She had climbed successfully in coed groups and also was a leader in shaping the women's mountaineering community. In 1977 she organized the first American and first women's climb of Annapurna, one of the tallest peaks in the Himalayas. In her book, *Annapurna: A Woman's Place,* Blum (1980) talks about the women's community while preparing to climb, climbing, and after the climb. From that women's experience sprung many more women's mountaineering expeditions. Blum is clear that the process which included community building is important to the group members. She and her teammates even met with a psychologist before the trip to explore feelings and explore how they wanted to form community on the trip.

On women's trips, the community that forms can help women feel safe to work with fears. On a Colorado River raft trip, four women said they chose the trip because they were afraid of water and wanted to use this trip to explore their fears. Their hope was that after the trip their fears would limit them less. They said they chose an all-woman trip because they believed they would have the freedom to express their feelings and get support when they needed it (Mitten, 1992a).

While many mixed gender trips offer forums to express fears and feelings, I think these women and others have clearly indicated that early women's programs paved the way in creating trips where emotional safety and women's strengths were valued. In such a positive sense, as more women have entered the adventure education field, the field has become more relationship-focused.

A number of the themes and values articulated here also have been identified in teaching and therapeutic relationships. Many researchers have tried to identify teaching styles of "good teachers." If a "best" teaching style can be defined, then it can be taught and replicated. If good teachers can be replicated then students can learn more. Interestingly, one study of a large number of people found that what makes a "good" teacher cannot be quantified or defined as a style. Good teachers came in all shapes, sizes, philosophical beliefs, teaching styles, and the like. Some teachers were dynamic in nature, some low key. Some teachers lectured only, others used interactive techniques, some used films, some used discussions, some used debate. The teaching style was not as significant as the relationship between the teacher and student.

The subjects had common responses: "I believed that who I was, what I said/did mattered to my teacher;" "I felt heard;" "I felt recognized;" "I felt wanted;" "I felt cared about." Under those relationship conditions they learned.

The researcher also asked about poor teachers and their teaching style. Again, the teachers' style was not related to learning as much as the relationship with the student was. The subjects said, "I felt invisible. I don't think the teacher cared about me."

Similar to group therapy in a clinical setting, for outdoor therapeutic experiences to be positive and result in desired behavioral changes there have to be positive relationships between leaders and participants. Research has shown that successful therapists establish relationships with clients that offer them "high levels of accurate empathy, nonpossessive warmth and genuineness" (Truax and Carkhuff, 1967). In a therapeutic context patients who believe that they are liked by their therapist can then more easily trust the therapist and the therapeutic process as well as have a feeling of safety in the process (Parloff, 1961; Rogers, 1959; Seeman, 1954).

Therefore, extending this to an outdoor therapeutic environment, there has to be a relationship that includes acceptance and trust between the leaders and the participants for participants to be able to develop self-esteem and learn healthy relationship-building skills. If leaders focus on the leader and participant trust and establish that bond, then the therapeutic process can occur. This can include the participants making internal changes that can lead to behavioral changes.

Power Differences

We expanded our thinking about power. It is important to understand that participants on outdoor trips can be dependent on leaders not only for the physical needs of how to tie into a climb or where and how to make camp and what food to eat, but also for the social needs of being welcomed and cared for. All of these needs are often viewed by participants as crucial to their survival. When participants believe that a leader holds a key to their survival, the leader has a great deal of power and there is a hierarchy. Even highly skilled people can feel scared and give up agency to the leader in an adventure education program.

We sought out people who had thought about power differences in regard to client respect and safety, and borrowed from their work in the area of ethics and power (Lerman and Porter, 1990; Noddings, 1984; Peterson, 1992). Feminist therapy was rich with information because feminist therapists have acknowledged power differences and researched how to deal with power differences responsibly (Lerman and Porter, 1990). Feminist therapists be-

lieve that "a focus on ethics is a focus on power and how it is used and shared in the process and practices of therapy" (Lerman and Porter, 1990, p. 1).

This focus recognizes the need for therapists or leaders to continually be aware of the power differential between the client and therapist [or the participant and leader] so that power will not be abused and emphasizes minimizing misuse of power, maintaining the dignity of the individual client, and better understanding how the client therapist relationship can truly benefit the client.

Because outdoor trips are typically informal settings, the power difference between leaders and participants has sometimes been minimized. The phrase "the outdoors is a great equalizer" is not true for leader and participant relationships and is probably not true for groups of participants. Women participants may bring less activity skills than men on mixed trips. Men typically have an internal locus of control for success and an external locus of control for failure. Women tend to be the opposite. These gender differences often cause power differences among participants.

Many people coming to adventure education programs will come with increased feelings of insecurity because of the newness and unfamiliarity of the setting which can accentuate the power differences that already exist between leaders and participants. Some leaders may overlook the power differences between themselves and participants if participants are professionals, including doctors, lawyers, teachers, or have significantly higher incomes than the leaders. Combining appropriate understanding of inevitable power differences and working with the power differences between and among participants on trips with an ethic of caring works well to actualize the values outlined above.

In relationships on adventure education trips, using an ethic of caring, the greater responsibility belongs to the leader. This includes maintaining what Peterson (1992) refers to as a professional boundary. When leaders maintain this professional boundary, participants are better able to attend to their own needs and learning. It is important for participants to feel comfortable being in a learning role and in that role sharing their needs and possibly fears. These tasks or roles are often made easier for participants with responsible use of power by leaders, including maintaining a professional boundary. If the boundary is blurred, participants may try to do what they believe the leaders want and thus are distracted from their own learning.

What This Means for the Leadership

There were many challenges in creating a leadership model that was consistent with our desired themes. In some ways we had to challenge the very core of common notions about leadership. One concept that remained constant is that successful leaders projected a genuine feeling of comfort and ease in the outdoors and especially in the area chosen for the trip.

We came to a belief, perspective, or paradigm that *leadership is a relationship,* teaching is a relationship, facilitating is a relationship. The event is about the relationships one forms rather than results. We are often asked, what kind of leader are you, democratic, authoritarian, laissez-faire, situational? We take tests to see our leadership style preferences. I think this information is useful—to a certain extent. Then we need to know how to lead with our heart and model building healthy, caring relationships.

These healthy relationships are based on caring. Noddings (1984) described this as an ethic of caring that involves a morality grounded in relationship and response. At the heart of this ethic is the maintenance of the caring relationship.

Caring and understanding of others aids in their personal empowerment. When people feel empowered, it is easier for them to choose to change and learn new behaviors and skills. Leaders' understanding and ability to engage in healthy relationships is integral to positive group cohesion and often influences the ability of group members to increase their self-esteem.

Describing what caring means in this sense is integral. Caring involves stepping out of one's own personal frame of reference into another's, and is characterized by a move away from self. One makes an internal commitment to promote another's well-being and does this by learning about and understanding the other person. In an ethic of caring, respect for diversity—including diversity of experiences—is implicit. In an ethic of caring intimacy is achieved without annihilating differences. Noddings (1984) also says that since people are so different there is no simple formula that describes what to teach leaders and students about caring in order to care meaningfully for persons.

Ways Leaders Display Caring

Participants need to know that they can depend on the leader in case of an emergency and for reliable information about safety and risk. At the beginning of a trip and of new activities, leaders can explain safety considerations. They can tell participants that as leaders they will be clear whether a suggestion is for safety (in which case *do* it) or if it is simply a suggested alternative way to accomplish a task. This promotes a feeling of security, makes it easier for people to learn new skills, and enables them to handle routine activities comfortably and safely.

The leader can encourage participants to say if they feel unsafe and to acknowledge and affirm when a person makes a choice for his or her feeling of safety. A person might say, "I don't think I want to paddle those rapids this afternoon—I just don't feel up to it." Leaders might ac-

knowledge that this person's decision is *not* irrational and may well avert a potential disaster. Often one's intuitive feelings, when valued, provide important information.

Because leaders need to establish trusting relationships with participants, it means leaders cannot pull surprises (except birthday parties), even in the name of building character or creating a learning situation. Participants should have a good idea of the course content before arriving, including information about the route, packing suggestions, and what to expect in physical exertion, bugs, and weather. Answers to the myriad questions from group members at the beginning of a trip need to be given in a direct, patient, and positive manner.

Leaders can encourage participants to feel included in the group, which is very different from "belonging to a group." If an individual feels like he or she belongs to a group, he or she will be less likely to recognize or attend to his or her own needs. The person may feel pressure to comply with pervasive group norms, which can result in him or her feeling inhibited and not included at all. Feeling included is simply feeling that he or she has a right to be there, and is welcomed and accepted just as he or she is today.

Another gesture that builds individual security is giving each participant his or her own amount of high-energy snack food. For some individuals this personal food helps provide a feeling of confidence that they will be able to meet trip challenges. These efforts to create a comfortable atmosphere and encourage participants to take care of their own needs decrease the stress that participants feel. My experiences confirm the assertions of stress management courses, that the less stress participants feel, the better able they are to cope with new activities, participate as a constructive group members, and handle challenging physical situations.

Delight in group diversity and recognize differences. The melting pot theory that we learned in the fourth grade really isn't true. It assumes that everyone turns out White, middle class, heterosexual, and male. On one trip, an extremely novice participant decided that the leader might benefit from learning Yiddish. This made the participant feel more equal by being able to offer a skill and contribute to the group. Meanwhile, the leader had great fun practicing and using Yiddish and the other group members experienced differences being affirmed.

Reinforce that a "sunset watcher" can be as important as a "fire builder." Equal is not that we each carry 55 pounds, but rather that we all contribute appropriately. One woman may carry a limited amount due to a weak back, but she may cook a little more often, or sing wonderful songs as the group portages. Often, given the space and support, participants who feel secure and cared about will equal out the trip tasks.

In order for participants to internalize experiences as their own, they have to choose it and acknowledge that they choose it. One way to offer genuine choice in a program is to have a flexible and reoccurring schedule rather than one day to carry a canoe or not, to learn knots or not. For example, on a three-week canoe trip, one could have some portages most days, need to build fires or use stoves each day, and paddle varied distances. It may be on Day 12 that a participant decides to portage his or her first canoe, or Day 1 when he or she jumps in to help with cooking, or Day 6 when he or she is really tired and decides to sleep through breakfast. The leaders can encourage participants and be active themselves. Leaders can invite participants to go fishing with them. Perhaps in private, ask Joan or Ed if she or he would like to carry a canoe or if one of them would like to paddle with a leader to learn stern. If there was only one day when participants would be able to climb because of location, one might start learning the knots and talk about some concepts several days before. This can ease the stress for some people who need to know about what is coming up and ease the stress for people who need to have a significant amount of time to learn knots and make the day more manageable.

Another way to add program flexibility is to use a coleading system (have a high leader to participant ratio), which gives leaders the option of subdividing groups of people. This encourages individual choices and immediately gives group members more flexibility. Some of the group members can start moving early to catch the sunrise. Or some group members may want to take the high road and the others the low road.

How to Build a Group— Creating Healthy Group Cohesion

Over 100 theories have been advanced by group dynamists seeking to describe the kinds of developmental changes seen in most groups (Forsyth, 1990, p. 77). Group dynamists agree that groups change over time and that conclusions taken at Time 1 may not hold true for conclusions taken at Time 2. Changes occur at both the group level and the individual level. At the group level there are patterns of growth and change starting with the formation of the group and continuing through its life cycle to dissolution. At the individual level in group socialization there are patterns of change in relationship among the individual members of the group and the group itself.

The developmental changes a group goes through is linked to the purpose of the group or why the group was formed. A problem-solving group develops somewhat differently from a sensitivity-training group, for example.

Most group development models have two basic approaches. The first is *recurring-phase models* or *cyclical models* which assert that certain issues tend to dominate group interaction during various phases of group development, but that these issues can occur later in the life of the group. This can also be referred to as a thematic approach to group development (Napier and Gershenfield, 1989, p. 479).

The second, *sequential-stage* or *successive stage* theories seek to specify the typical order of the phases of group development. The amount of time in each phase is determined by the leader's direction or nondirection, skills and emotional strengths of the members. Some groups never progress beyond early stages.

Over the years I have come to believe that using a multidimensional model can help a leader help group members form a cohesive yet individual affirming group. The model borrows from Tuckman's (1965) sequential stage model. My model has more dimensions than his model and I have changed the nature and therefore name of some of the stages from the way Tuckman presented them. The stages do not have discreet beginnings or endings. With deliberate guidance from the trip leader, group members successfully achieve each of the stages and individuals feel included, but not ruled by the group process (Mitten, 1986).

In my model, the leader is a conscious role model. He or she understands that, especially in a new setting, participants are watching him or her for direction and guidance. This looking to the leader in no way diminishes the participants. After one decides to participate in an outdoor program, it is useful behavior to look to the leader for guidance. It is the leader's responsibility to use this power caringly and to value the skills and competencies the participants bring. Lehman (1991) writes about this model and relates it to Terry's ethical leadership concept. Mitten's model is described here:

> *Forming:* During the initial stage of the trip the leader models inclusivity and information sharing. Participants learn about each other and trip expectations. The leader is setting the tone for attitudinal norms and rules (if any) for structural norms.
>
> *Sorting:* During this stage participants learn more about necessary tasks—when to camp, canoe, climb, mountaineer, be environmentally appropriate, and so forth. Information about how tasks are done and who does the tasks is shared. Some classic group dynamists say that this stage can be conflictual. They say that group members react to having been dependent in the initial stage and now issues of counter dependence and negativity toward the leader are expressed. My model differs significantly here. In my experience, if the leader sets a tone for inclusivity and collaborative leadership (often modeled by having coleaders) then there may be no power and authority issues to lead to conflict. If

power has not been misused, then most members find power accessible as they feel ready to embrace it. If the leader has been successful in setting a tone for inclusivity in the forming stage, then people will likely have not put on a positive front or have what some dynamists call a honeymoon phase that ends. There will be conflict in every stage. The leader sets the tone for working with the origins of conflict: (1) unclear communication, (2) role ambiguity, or (3) a values difference and resolving the conflicts accordingly.

Norming: This stage is really another dimension. From the forming stage the group's norms have been encouraged and established. I suggest that if a group has 12 members, then by this stage there are 13 members. Norma (a compilation of the norms) has been built. Norma may be part of every member or part of no member. Norma is formed by the leaders' actions and the chemistry of the group members, and the mix of the chemistry of the group members and the leaders. There are structural norms. For example, we take off our shoes before getting into the tents at night, or we eat breakfast at 7 A.M. There are attitudinal norms. For example, group members are supportive to one another, or there is lots of healthy laughter.

Performing: During this stage the group members can function as a team and accomplish tasks. For example, without help from the leader, camp can be packed up and canoes packed. Contrary to other outdoor models, in this model the leader does not step back or become less to the group. Her role does shift so that she can be helpful to group members in different ways. For example, the leader may help members who want to climb an extra pitch instead of helping with the stove and dinner.

Differentiating: This stage is also another dimension. After the members gain a certain level of competency as described in the performing stage, differentiating tends to be displayed more. Differentiation can be seen as doing different activities and being and believing differently. By definition differentiation behavior is positive and not rebellious. Differentiating is the sense that participants know that their needs and wants are valid and they can ask for what they want from themselves, other group members, and the leaders. Group members can feel free to express who they are and expect to be accepted for who they are. For example a member can say, "I know we have to get up at 5 A.M. to complete the climb we want to do, but I want you to know how hard that is for me." Or a woman can talk about her lesbian partner, Jewish heritage, children, or male partner without fear of dismissal or rejection. This notion can also be contrary to some models of group development that at least imply that individual sacrifices have to be made for the good of the group. My experience is that setting a tone that allows for differentiation keeps a trip safer. Members say when they are hungry or tired without grunting through it and becoming weak and perhaps unsafe. Of course there are times when one may be hungry or tired and one has to wait because of safety concerns, but being able to freely express needs and ask for what one wants makes those times more bearable. This process of differentiating can be different for each member. Some members arrive being able to ask for what they want, even in a new circumstance. Other women are encouraged by Norma, and learn, at least on this trip, to ask for what they need and that is positive for the group. It is another dimension because like the norms, this attitude or phenomena has been building or developing since the inception of the trip.

Closure: This stage is the conscious act of ending the trip. Having a concrete closure can be a powerful gift to all the group members. Closing and validating the experience for what it was can help members go on to have other group experiences taking with them ideas they learned from this experience. They can keep some of the pieces they liked about the norms created and in a new group they may use skills to change norms they didn't like.

During all of the stages leaders can be helpful in the kind of caring relationship they form with participants and the skills they teach. Mitten (1995) discussed the ways that personal affirmations can help build healthy group cohesion. Individuals hearing caring and genuine affirmations patterned after Jean Clarke's (1979) developmental affirmations can feel more of a sense of inclusion and permission to learn at their own pace and in their own style. This affirmation process can help group members accomplish incredible tasks. For example, I once led a women's mountaineering expedition in the Himalayas. Some of the women on the trip had very little mountaineering experience. On the trip, we took the time to teach at a pace comfortable to each woman. The result was that the group members reached 18,000 feet. All the women experienced personal bests and our American team gained a higher altitude on that peak than any other team at that time in the season (Mitten, 1992b).

Summary

We live in a world that is fraught with violence. The experience also provides a concrete model of a community experience that many people want to replicate. I have been privileged to be a part of many women's outdoor trips. I believe that women often join these trips with high expectations of community and connection with the natural world. Leisure professionals and outdoor trip leaders can be instrumental in helping trip participants create a trip that meets these important needs. Leaders need to understand power differences, be able to form healthy relationships with participants, and understand participants' expectations. In summary, leaders help create a positive atmosphere for relationships to develop by creating a trip setting that feels emotionally, spiritually, and physically safe. Mitten (1985) said that in a supportive and nurturing trip environment, participants often responded by feeling good and having fun which led to:

- taking the initiative to try new activities and skills,
- reaching out to others,
- cooperating as individuals to accomplish group tasks and goals, and
- allowing themselves to recognize and fulfill their wants and goals.

Group cohesion to the extent that it is wanted by the participants is achieved and the women participants know they are just fine as they are.

Reference

Billig, M. (1976). *Social psychology and group relations*. New York, NY: Academic Press.

Blum, A. (1980). *Annapurna: A woman's place*. San Francisco, CA: Sierra Club

Clarke, J. I. (1979). *Self-esteem: A family affair*. Minneapolis, MN: Winston Press.

Forsyth, D. (1990). *Group dynamics* (2nd ed.). New York, NY: Harper and Row.

Freud, S. (1922). *Group psychology and the analysis of the ego*. London, UK: Hogarth.

Jackson, M., and Stark, E. (1956). *Tents in the clouds: The first women's Himalayan expedition*. London, UK: Collins.

Janis, I. L. (1963). Group identification under conditions of external danger. *British Journal of Medical Psychology, 36*, 227–238.

Kimball, R., and Bacon, S. (1993). The wilderness challenge model. In M. A. Gass (Ed.), *Adventure therapy:*

Therapeutic applications of adventure programming. Dubuque, IA: Kendall/Hunt Publishing Co.

Lehman, K. (1991). *Integrating ethics and leadership: A journey with woodswomen*. Master's thesis, College of St. Catherine, St. Paul, Minnesota.

Lerman, H., and Porter, N. (1990). *Feminist ethics in psychotherapy*. New York, NY: Springer Publishing Company.

Manning, R. C. (1992). *Speaking from the heart: A feminist perspective on ethics*. Lanham, MD: Rowman & Littlefield Publishers, Inc.

Miranda, W. (1987). The genteel radicals. *Camping Magazine, 59*(4), 12–16.

Mitten, D. (1985). A philosophical basis for a women's outdoor adventure program. *Journal of Experiential Education*, Summer, 20–24.

Mitten, D. (1986). *Meeting the unknown: Group dynamics in the wilderness*. Minneapolis, MN: Woodswomen, Inc.

Mitten, D. (1992a). The American team. In R. da Silva (Ed.), *Leading out: Women climbers reaching for the top* (pp. 201–217). Seattle, WA: Seal Press.

Mitten, D. (1992). Empowering girls and women in the outdoors. *The Journal of Physical Education, Recreation, and Dance*, Vol. 63, No. 2, pp. 56–60.

Mitten, D. (1995). Building the group: Using personal affirming to create healthy group process. *Journal of Experiential Education, 18*(2), 82–90.

Noddings, N. (1984). *Caring: A feminine approach to ethics and moral education*. Berkeley, CA: University of California Press.

Parloff, M. (1961). Therapist-patient relationships and outcome of psychotherapy. *Journal of Consulting Psychology, 25*, 29–38.

Peterson, M. (1992). *At personal risk*. New York, NY: W. W. Norton & Company.

Potter, D. (1962). American women and the American character. *Steton University Bulletin, LXII*, 1–22).

Rogers, C. (1959). A theory of therapy, personality and interpersonal relationships. In S. Koch (Ed.), *Psychology: A study of a science* (Vol. 3, pp. 184–256). New York, NY: McGraw-Hill.

Seeman, J. (1954). Counselor judgments of the therapeutic process and outcome. In C. Rogers and R. Dymond (Eds.), *Psychotherapy and personality change*. Chicago, IL: University of Chicago Press.

Truax, C., and Carkhuff, R. (1967). Toward effective counseling and psychotherapy: Training and practice. Chicago, IL: Aldine Publishing Company.

Tuckman, B. (1965). Developmental sequence in small groups. *Psychological Bulletin* (63) 384–399.

Yerkes, R., and Miranda, W. (1982). Outdoor adventure courses for women: Implications for new programming. *Journal of Health, Physical Education, and Dance, 53*(4), 82–85.

Section 7

The Management of Adventure Programming
Administering the Resources

Discussions of leadership in adventure education and programming, and in outdoor pursuits in general, usually examine the challenges of field leaders. Behind each field leader, of course, lies leadership of another sort—that which creates, maintains, and develops the organization. Such leadership offers different challenges and satisfactions than those facing the field people, but is no less critical to the success of adventure education. The essays in this section examine general topics central to organizational leadership and management.

All programs start with an idea, and many end there. Costello offers a few hints on how to get off the starting line. Do a realistic assessment of your possibilities, prepare an action plan, determine the finances, and start. When the start is made there will be a tremendous work load, as Watters testifies. A successful program requires long hours, thorough planning and emotional commitment. Tight budgets, politics and protocol will produce much stress on staff, and burn-out will be a real risk. Burn-out can and must be avoided. Watters correctly points to personnel management as perhaps the most critical ingredient of successful program administration.

Squarely facing every adventure program administrator are the challenges of safety and risk management. The next two essays tackle these problems. Terry Brown provides an overview of risk, arguing that while it must be a part of adventure programming, it must also be managed. Drawing from a world of thought about this dilemma, he suggests processes that achieve effective and responsible risk management. What emerges is a good overview of this thorny territory, with practical ideas as to how to do this necessary if complex and often tedious work so necessary to keep clients safe and the litigious society at bay.

The chapter by Betty van der Smissen and "Reb" Gregg is a primer on how to think about and address the problem of liability in adventure program management. They argue that liability can be managed and should not be an obstacle to programming, and then proceed to explain the concepts and principles that need to considered. These include legal concepts like standard of care, primary and secondary assumption of risk, and comparative negligence, among others. Risk management planning and implementation as a path toward avoiding liability are explained and advice on what should be included in these processes is offered. They conclude with a summary of the alternative strategies that are available for resolving disputes. There is a philosophy of risk, which van der Smissen and Gregg describe, and they point out that the goal of adventure programming cannot be risk-free activity, but it can be "activity free of risk and dangers that are unknown or unacceptable to the provider and the participant." They offer much good advice on how this essential condition may be achieved.

Warner next takes a comprehensive look at the challenge of program evaluation. Such evaluation was lacking in early stages of the development of the field, but lessons are being learned and he shares some of them. Evaluation is, he argues, simply good programming. It not only indicates whether or not program outcomes are being achieved, but is essential to program development. Warner reviews psychological and structural obstacles to evaluation and suggests how they may be overcome. Strategies include the training of future practitioners in the importance and practices of evaluation, the hiring of staff with commitment to reflection and evaluation, and the building of evaluation into the program as a program development tool. A line item for evaluation must also, of course, be built into the program proposal and the budget.

Evaluation is one process, research quite another, as Priest points out in the final essay in this section. Program administrators may not do the research, but they must be cognizant of what research is telling them about what strategies do or do not work, and what outcomes are demonstrable. As Priest notes, "research can prove how and why adventure works and evaluation can improve the way programming works." Those who must administer and sustain programs need the service of both researchers and evaluators. Priest provides a primer on research, explaining inquiry paradigms and basic concepts of research. His essay is a general overview and aims to clarify the nature of the research enterprise and its importance to administration and practice of adventure programming.

Chapter 36

Starting Your New Outdoor Program

Phil Costello
Project USE

Many individuals involved in instructing and managing adventure programs reach a point in their career when they consider the possibility of starting their own program. In some cases, usually after being involved with a number of different adventure education programs, and developing different skills along the way, an individual will consider taking on the challenge of starting and managing his or her own program. In all cases, the start of a program begins with an idea.

The Idea Stage

Many individuals reach a point where they have an idea for a program they would like to develop. Some of these ideas will prove to be solid and should be developed, others will need a lot of adjustment and still others should be dropped.

How do you know if your idea has a good chance of making it?

1. Develop and write your first program description. Include a clear and specific purpose of your idea as well as goals and objectives.
2. Put together a list of six to eight people you would like to have review your idea. Send them your written description in advance, then meet with them and discuss your idea in detail. Ask each of these individuals to suggest others who should review your idea.
3. Find out if any groups, organizations or individuals in your area are already involved in activities similar to your idea.
4. Do some basic research to find out if the services you want to offer are needed.
5. Begin to think about whether or not you want to have one or more partners to help develop your ideas.
6. Review your work thus far and rewrite your program description.

The Action Plan

If you consider all of the information discussed thus far and you feel ready to further develop your idea, you will need to begin to consider some of the organizational options. There are a wide range of possible ways to structure a program. The following are points to consider regarding four options:

1. Incorporate as a profit-making corporation:

   a. Good points:

      - maximum amount of control;
      - you could develop a marketable business and eventually sell it at a profit; and

- better chance of getting back any personal investment.

   b. Bad points:

- very difficult to obtain funding from private foundations;
- some school systems and organizations prefer working with non-profit organizations;
- will not qualify for surplus food and equipment; and
- tax payments.

2. Incorporate as a nonprofit corporation:

   a. Good points:

- tax exempt status;
- donations are tax deductible;
- bulk mailing permit;
- eligible for surplus government food and equipment;
- eligible for private foundation funding; and
- high degree of control.

   b. Bad points:

- limited lobbying ability;
- board of trustees control overall program;
- regulation of earnings and fees; and
- if corporation dissolves, all assets must be given to another non-profit organization.

3. Develop your program under the "umbrella" of a larger organization. A number of successful organizations were initiated as smaller programs operating under the umbrella of larger existing corporations with the "goal" of eventually "spinning off" to become their own program. In each state there are a number of private educational corporations that are involved with contracting with the federal and state governments for their services. Once your written program is refined, locate a private educational corporation in your area and present your idea to them. You may want to seek out a corporation with a strong network of contacts that would be helpful to you for developing your program, that may not be heavily involved in experiential education, but is receptive to the concept. This arrangement may be beneficial to the larger corporation by giving it new services to market.

   a. Good points:

- fairly easy to initiate;
- least difficult way to obtain proper insurance coverage;
- very efficient way to develop a client market;
- highly probable that you will survive first two years; and
- good intermediate step to being on your own.

   b. Bad points:

- you will not have complete control of your operation; and
- could be difficult to disengage and "spin off" on your own, especially if your program is successful.

This option has a great deal of potential, but problems can occur if there is not a clear agreement regarding expectations, ownership of assets, long-range planning, and accumulated deficits or surpluses.

4. Develop your idea in a tri-school arrangement. Sell your idea to three or four schools or a mixture of several schools and a college or university. Base your program in one of the schools and provide services to each school. Develop a "menu" of all the possible program ideas including services to special needs groups: potential dropouts, disruptive and disabled students.

   a. Good points:

- client base in central area;
- potential for impact; and
- community-based.

   b. Bad points:

- you would have to sell to three schools in same general area;
- if one of the schools wouldn't adopt your program, you might have to incorporate; and
- change in school administration could change status.

Getting off the Ground

Once you determine the direction you want to go with your idea, such as incorporating as a private nonprofit corporation, you will be anxious to get started and will want to jump in with both feet immediately. However, it is recommended to work for one full year prior to going operational. A preferred arrangement would be to have a full-time position and a stable financial base for the year before going on your own.

"Preflight" Checklist

1. If you decide to incorporate, check with state officials to identify all legal requirements for proper compliance. Requirements for profit and nonprofit corporations vary from state to state.
2. Begin to develop an advisory board of key individuals that are interested in your program. Eventually you will want representatives from law, banking, medicine, education, and fund raising.
3. Develop diverse funding possibilities rather than relying on one or two sources. Explore federal, state, private foundations, donations and client sources for developing an income base.
4. Most private foundations will not support a new organization for several years, but if they think you are a potential candidate for funding, they will watch the progress of your program.
5. Select primary and secondary clients on which you would like to focus:

    *   public elementary, middle and secondary schools;
    *   independent schools;
    *   colleges and universities;
    *   alternate education programs;
    *   special populations;
    *   teacher training;
    *   juvenile justice system: corrections, probation, residential centers, youth agencies;
    *   adult and continuing education programs;
    *   youth groups, clubs, church groups, local recreation programs;
    *   families, parents and children;
    *   open enrollment courses for youth and adults;
    *   corporations: management training; employee courses; and/or
    *   military organizations and units.

6. Develop and run a series of one-day invitational programs that will enable key people, including potential funding sources, to meet and spend time with people to whom you plan to offer services.
7. Do not rely on letters, phone calls or mailings to establish yourself with clients. Make it a priority to meet personally and spend time with people to whom you plan to offer services.
8. Seek advice from others in the field before preparing your first public relations materials.
9. If you conduct any programs during your preflight stage, be sure they are of the highest quality possible. Begin to develop a reputation as a strong, reliable, professional program regardless of the status of your program.
10. Research possible locations where you will be able to conduct your programs—federal land, state parks and forests, and private outdoor centers are possible locations. Some private landowners are more than willing to have programs conducted on their property.
11. Approximately a dozen states have a Camp Safety Act Program usually administered by the state department of health. Check to see if your state has a Camp Safety Act Program as this will have a major effect on your program.

Considerations

Many outdoor programs that managed to get off the ground did not last long for two primary reasons: (1) lack of capital to invest in starting up the program; and (2) poor overall management of the program.

Capital Investment

Obviously, the more money you have to get started, the easier it will be. If your capital is limited and you do not want to take out a bank loan, you can still make it work, but you will need to operate on a strict budget and stick to it. If your capital is limited for start-up, you will need to develop skills for scrounging, bartering, checking out surplus property, and requesting donations from equipment companies.

Management

As your program starts to grow, get to know every aspect inside and out. Find out how much it costs to operate every aspect of your programs so you will be able to make decisions to help you survive. As you discover aspects of program management that you don't enjoy and tend to put off, check yourself to be sure these areas get covered.

Insurance

The insurance market changes every year. During most of the 1980s, it would have been nearly impossible for a new small program to obtain insurance. Currently, in 1988 it is less difficult, but still not a simple task. A good place to start is by contacting other experiential education programs and talking with their insurance agents. Do some shopping. Check out different sized programs from various parts of the country. Some states have regulations regarding the minimum amount of liability insurance required to operate an adventure program.

Scrounging

A great deal can be accomplished through scrounging and bartering. Equipment companies, lumber yards, and corporations are generally willing to help but they should be approached personally. While scrounging can prove beneficial, the down side is that it is time-consuming and sometimes needs to be a low priority for the use of your time.

Be willing to take risks! Keep your sense of humor!

Chapter 37

Management and Administration of Outdoor Programs

Ron Watters
Idaho State University

Since the heady, hectic days of outdoor programming in the mid to latter part of the 1900s, a slow, maturing process has settled upon the field. The field is still young, of course, and full of promise for meaningful experiences for participants and stimulating job opportunities for professionals. But the field has come to a point where most program directors find themselves wearing the hat of an administrator more than that of an outdoor educator.

It's not because those of us in the position dreamed of shuffling papers. Rather, it is a necessity brought on by the changing nature of outdoor education and society. Outdoor employees are seeking reasonable salaries and benefit packages. Participants want quality instruction and services. Upper level administrators ask for travel requisitions, risk management plans, and written justifications of the program. And the legal profession continues to cast its menacing shadow over programs.

All of these and more require our attention in an administrative and managerial capacity. And, like any form of management, the style utilized is dictated by the service or product provided. In our case, the service is outdoor recreation, and there are management procedures and techniques particular to the field which are helpful in running outdoor operations. I won't attempt to cover the entire topic in the limited space this chapter, but I will touch on a few key areas that I've found helpful in my 25 years in the field. One of those areas is the most vexing, yet rewarding part of outdoor management: personnel.

Personnel Management

The nice thing about outdoor education is that it attracts good people, willing to devote inordinate amounts of their time and energy. Certainly, there are a few misguided souls who would be better off in more sedentary positions. But on the whole, it has been my experience that finding the right people is not the problem. Rather, the challenge of personnel management in outdoor programs is dealing with the overenthusiastic and eventually overworked employee.

Outdoor program jobs are far different than the typical working situation of eight to five. A staff member might work a full weekend on a backpack trip, then be back in the office on Monday morning . . . and then work several evenings teaching kayaking during the week . . . and then work the next weekend. It's not unusual during the height of ski or summer seasons for a employee to work four or five weeks without a break.

Upon hearing about such work hours, the standard layman's impression is "well, it's easy work. He's just out playing." Certainly it's play, but it's other people's play. And that is the catch. There's a big difference between personal recreation and recreation that is done for the benefit of others. Even in the least structured of all styles of outdoor trips, the common adventure trip, outdoor program staff are burdened with the responsibility of helping guide the democratic process within groups. Democracy even within small groups is never easy, and dealing with personality conflicts within the unsettling environment of the outdoors can be (and is) wearing. When you're doing it every weekend, it's work.

What is at the heart of the matter is an emotional commitment to the job and the participants. Some trips go smoothly, of course, but others are different. Like a raft with a slow leak, an outdoor staff person staggers home at the end of emotionally demanding trips, flaccid and deflated. Often the next morning he or she will be back in the office, cleaning up the van, putting away gear and tying up the loose ends. Throw several of these trips together, and with time, burn-out enters the picture and quietly does its damage.

The cure, of course, is time off. Outdoor program directors need to keep an eye on how much their staff is working and watch for the signs of burn-out. A little time off to enjoy one's own personal recreation or to do something different can greatly improve employees' outlook and productivity.

The method in which time off is given will depend upon the appropriate protocol of the sponsoring institution. In my situation, for years we were able to provide time off on an informal basis. The idea was if you worked a weekend you took two days off. Stricter state requirements now require us to record compensation (comp) hours. It is difficult to calculate the number of hours outdoor program employees work when they're on trips, but generally giving eight hours compensation for each extra day beyond a regular five-day week is accepted as fair. For instance, a person working a weekend trip receives 16 hours of comp time (eight for Saturday and eight for Sunday). This method requires greater paperwork, but from procedural standpoint most personnel departments will be more comfortable with it than informal methods.

A number of outdoor program directors and employees have indicated to me that they are unable to accumulate compensation hours. However, in Idaho, where I work, the state has determined that compensation hours should be granted to those in outdoor work (including Conservation Officers working for the Fish and Game Department) in order to be in compliance with the Fair Labor Standards Act. If you are not presently on the comp hour system, then it may be wise to check with your personnel department. According to the act, certain positions, occupations and trades are exempt from the comp hours provisions of the law. A review of those exempt positions, however, does not include anything which would resemble an outdoor program job (U.S. Department of Labor, 1975).

It is very important that your superiors, the people who are above your program, understand the amount of time and emotional commitments being put in by your staff. I'll talk about communication with superiors later in the chapter, but you need to make a concerted effort to remind those in authority of the good work and dedication put

forth by your staff. With this understanding, your superiors can set the record straight to higher administers.

Program Planning

I don't want to state the obvious, since everyone's fully aware of it. But it won't hurt. Plan carefully. Assiduous planning is key to a smoothly functioning program. While there are various stratagems than can be employed, I found that two elements greatly assist the process. One is regular staff meetings and the other is a large calendar with lots of space to write down ideas. The regular staff meeting (once a week) is used to touch base with everyone, to find out how trips went and to generate ideas for upcoming events.

I would suggest scheduling the planning meeting early in the week, since the staff can make last minute preparations of activities occurring later that week. For specific days, Monday is OK, but Tuesday is better. Mondays are often poor days since staff members who have just worked the weekend come into the meeting tired. Tuesday seems to be a much more energetic day, and staff members are more enthusiastic and better inclined toward rolling up their sleeves.

The large planning calendar comes to meetings as well. As ideas are discussed, they are penciled in on the calendar. The calendar serves to remind staff members about events coming up, publicity that needs to go out, and rooms to be scheduled. By using pencil, the calendar is easily altered and updated. When it comes time to print out schedules, the calendar serves as a convenient rough draft.

Volunteer Management

Few in the outdoor program business have the luxury of working with liberal budgets. Often funding is tight and there's little to spare. Thus methods must be found to stretch hard-earned funding dollars. The use of volunteers is one such method.

Volunteers can serve many functions in an outdoor program. They can help organize and take out-trips, run workshops, conduct evening programs, help with disabled programs or even assist with office duties. Those with programs at universities have a advantage here. The student population on a college campus serves as a great pool from which young, enthusiastic volunteers can be drawn.

But volunteers don't necessarily need to be young or come from the campus. Volunteer resources are available in any community. Take evening programs, for instance. A good many emergency room doctors are more than happy to do sessions on emergency first-aid procedures in the backcountry. A geologist might be interested in doing a program on the geology of a popular climbing area. A member of a nearby ski patrol likely could be talked into doing a program on avalanche safety. Even the local insurance agent might turn out to be a good prospect for a program, particularly one who has just returned from a trek to Annapurna. It's a pleasant marriage. Volunteers are happy to do their program and share their knowledge and skills and you're happy to have the free offering.

Some volunteers require extra time, particularly those who will be assuming coordinating or leadership positions in the program. Many programs have found the extra time spent training to be well worth the effort. The University of California–San Francisco is an example of a program that provides training for volunteer coordinators in its successful common adventurer trip program. Handicapped programs throughout the country provide training programs and utilize volunteers extensively in such programs as skiing, rafting, sailing, and horse riding.

Before unleashing dozens of volunteers, let me issue a warning. Volunteers are not a cure-all. Many prospective volunteers are initially enthusiastic, but when the routine work begins, they suddenly disappear. Others are simply unreliable. It takes work to interest the right people, and once the right people are found, it takes more work to cultivate and keep them motivated. Show personal interest in volunteers. Follow up good helpers with phone calls. Invite volunteers to social events, like a pizza evening after a day of ski touring, or the annual Christmas party at the end of the year.

People who volunteer do so not only for the personal satisfaction of helping others. There are other reasons, and oftentimes, it is the other reasons that are most important. They may have a need to be a part of a group. They may get an ego boast from being in a leadership position. Or they may enjoy the extra recognition and prestige that comes from leading. It is an understanding of these other motivations which can help you keep volunteers on track and enthusiastic. One tenet of volunteer management is to always give recognition. Don't be afraid to be profuse. Making the extra effort to compliment and say thanks over and over will pay many dividends. If you keep that in mind, you'll have a windfall of volunteer help in your programs.

Program Recordkeeping

There's little joy in it. Nobody looks forward to it, but directors of outdoor programs more than anyone need to keep good records—for good reason. Good recordkeeping shows a level of sophistication. By having data on participation, results of participation satisfaction surveys, or an analysis of costs and benefits, you are in a much better position to justify the expenditure of funds for your program. Programs with no records or poorly tabulated participation figures appear, even though they might not be, loosely organized and poorly run.

Recordkeeping need not be taxing as long as it is done on a regular basis. I utilize the weekly staff meeting as a time to keep records up-to-date. While the staff meeting is underway, a master data sheet can be passed around and

members of the staff can update their entries for the past week. A variety of records can be kept, but at the very least, good participation records should be maintained. Even if your sponsoring agency or institution doesn't require one, prepare an annual report with total numbers of participants and information on the year's highlights.

The journal method is one way of collecting records and information as the year progresses. The journal, which is basically a scrapbook, can include participation figures, copies of news releases, photographs from trips and complimentary letters from participants. At the end of the year, the annual report can be easily prepared by paging through the journal and picking out significant events. The journal, if left in a prominent place in the outdoor office, also serves as a good promotional tool. People stopping by the office invariably pick it up and page through it.

Politics of Outdoor Programming

The smoky, sultry world of politics is probably the last arena in which an outdoor program director wants to get involved. But the political arena described here is not the sultry kind, nor is it the kind that involves the surreptitious jockeying and power positioning that sometimes takes place within the bureaucracy of institutions. Rather, this is about its more subtle form: the wise, tactful, and artful way of getting things done.

When you are in charge of an outdoor program, how tactful your approach is often means the difference between good administrative support and poor administrative support. Or put more practically, it's the difference between a good budget and a poor budget.

Artful politics involves the understanding of power structures within institutions. One way of categorizing institutional power is to look at it from the perspective of two dimensions (Banning and Sherman, 1988). One dimension is authoritarian power. Authoritarian power is that which is assigned by the institution. The power that your superior possesses to hire, supervise you, or to approve your budgets has been given to him or her by the institution. Most institutions have flow charts showing the network and chains of authoritarian power.

The other dimension of power, influential power, is not assigned by the institution. This kind of power comes through personality, tact, and persistence. It also comes through friendly contacts, respect for work, and logical and compelling proposals. And if it's carefully nurtured and used, influential power can effect positive change.

Outdoor programs are always low on the authoritarian power scale. It's never more obvious than by looking at the institutional flow chart where the rectangular box housing the outdoor program appears at bottom of the page—if it appears at all. It is, then, influential power which must be utilized by outdoor program directors. The development and use of influence doesn't happen overnight. It takes time.

What is important is that you understand your institution's protocols and the chain of command in which you fit and who, in that chain, are the key people. Make friends with those above you. Keep it on a business level, but friendly. No one likes to deal with negative people. Keep supervisors, especially your immediate supervisor, informed of your program's activities. When supervisors hear from you on a regular basis, they become comfortable and stay comfortable with your program. That's the way you want supervisors to be. If they are not familiar with the program, you'll have little support when chips are down.

Administrators higher in the chain of command are more difficult to reach. But nevertheless, you should take advantage of occasional opportunities to make contact when they present themselves. If the community newspaper runs a complimentary article on your program, you may wish to send a higher administrator a copy of the article. Supervisors and presidents like good press—and good mail. When you have enthusiastic participants who just had a wonderful time on a trip, have them drop a line to the president.

Sometimes help comes from unexpected corners. Our program occasionally runs climbing demonstrations for high schools around the area. At one of the out-of-town demonstrations we learned that a teacher who helped organize the event was a state senator on a key legislative committee. When we found this out, we asked if he wouldn't mind dropping a line to our immediate supervisor and the president of the university. He didn't mind, and ended up writing a complimentary missive on legislative letterhead.

A year later, I submitted a proposal for extra funding which was considered by the president of our university. The extra funds were sorely needed in our handicapped program. In the end, we were successful in obtaining the extra funds. Did the letter from the legislator help us? One can never be certain. There are many factors that influence decision making in an organization, but I'm convinced it helped.

Become familiar with how decisions are made in your institution. When developing funding proposals, start with your immediate supervisor and work up through those above. You'll find that there are appropriate times and routes to take. Much of how you tailor your approach will be guided by your experience and by the experiences of those who have been in the system for long time.

Always keep a wary eye. If the timing is not right, proposals can backfire. An outdoor program in Utah floated a proposal, which was approved by its student senate, to expand its operations. Unfortunately, it came at a time when the president of the university was beginning a campaign of cost-cutting. It also came at time when a local rental shop in town had complained to the administration that the outdoor program was unfairly competing with it. The result: the proposal was rejected and the program was trimmed back. Fortunately, funding was later restored, but for a time the very survival of the program was in question.

I give this example not to discourage you, but as a warning that organizational politics can be risky, and you need to build a network of friends, constantly seek opinions and advice, and be ready to retreat when things aren't right.

Keep at it and keep coming up with ideas and trying them out. Eventually, something will click, and you'll have a success. With time and a little luck, you'll be able to increase the budget, provide better pay for your staff and improve services to your participants. That's when playing politics becomes worth it.

References

Banning J. H., and Sherman R. (1988, November). The politics of change: A different view of working together. *ACU-I Bulletin*, p. 4.

U.S. Department of Labor. (1975). *Defining the terms "executive," "administrative," "professional" and "outside salesman" : Regulations Title 29, Part 541 of the code of federal regulations* (WH Publication 1281). Washington, DC: Government Printing Office.

Chapter 38

Adventure Risk Management

Terry J. Brown
Griffith University, Australia

Adventure education is a profession of risk taking, but of risk taking with a purpose. The exposure to a variety of risks in an outdoor context produces an uncertainty of outcome which is central to the adventure experience. Such uncertainty sets the scene for challenge, commitment, cooperation, exhilaration, problem solving and clear, unambiguous feedback which may produce learning, growth, transformation and the realization of human potential. The specific benefits of participation in adventure experiences include:

- increased self-esteem,
- increased self-confidence,
- the exhilaration of overcoming or facing challenges,
- a sense of achievement and well-being,
- opportunities for cooperation and team building,
- awareness of new life priorities,
- volitional control,
- environmental awareness and advocacy, and
- improved health.

These outcomes are addressed elsewhere in this text and have been widely recognized in the adventure literature (Ewert and Priest, 1990; Haddock, 1993; Hunt, 1995; McAvoy and Dustin, 1990; Meier, 1990; Robinson, 1992). The fundamental risk management questions which confront adventure educators are:

- Do the benefits of adventure outweigh the risks? and
- What level of risk is acceptable?

Accidents happen, and in the outdoor recreation sector today they have a high profile and attract quite sensational media attention. This, together with an increasingly litigious environment and risk-averse society, has forced providers to avoid some outdoor recreation activities (Cuskelly and Sessoms, 1989) or to control for risks to the point where challenge is lost and where many of the benefits of participation cannot be expected to occur (McAvoy and Dustin, 1990). Risk management aims to address the risk-benefit paradox through actions applied to minimize risk and optimize the potential for personal development outcomes. After all, as Bertrand Russell observed, "a life without adventure is likely to be unsatisfying, but a life in which adventure is allowed to take whatever form it will, is likely to be short."

Acceptability of risk is in the eye of the beholder. Adventure educators must be seen to care for their clients and an appropriate goal for the profession would be to ensure a level of real risk equivalent to, or less than, that associated with normal life activities.

This chapter outlines the conceptual basis of risk management and provides practical advice on the development of risk management plans. Definitions are clarified, understandings from adventure accident data are revealed and the sources of risk are discussed. The Adventure-REACT

Model (Brown, 1995a) is introduced as a framework for risk management and as the basis of a risk management protocol incorporating a range of risk control strategies aimed at achieving optimal participant safety. Legal liability issues are addressed in another chapter.

Risk Definition

Some confusion exists about the terminology associated with risk, its sources and management. Even within the technical risk management literature there is a level of disagreement. The reader is referred to an earlier chapter on the semantics of adventure education for a more comprehensive range of definitions which are applicable to the following discussion.

Risk management is the systematic application of management policies, standards and procedures to the tasks of identifying, analyzing, assessing, treating and monitoring risk. The prime objective of adventure risk management is to minimize the potential for physical, social, emotional, or financial loss arising from participation in an unusual activity in an unfamiliar environment with unknown outcomes. Risk is the potential to lose something of value, or simply a potential accident. It is formally represented by the equation:

$$Risk = (Probability \times Magnitude) + Public\ Outrage$$

Risk arises from the dangers associated with a particular activity, and these dangers may be linked to environmental characteristics at the site where the activity is conducted or to the type and manner in which any equipment is used or to the characteristics of the participants. Traditionally, risk was considered to increase with the increasing chance of a damaging event occurring and with the growing severity of possible outcomes or losses. However, more recent research (Sandman, Weinstein, and Klotz, 1987; Sandman, Miller, Branden, and Weinstein, 1993) has acknowledged the potential for the level of community response toward accidents to enhance risk evaluation, and particularly the risk of litigation. Outrage is likely to be greater in circumstances where:

- activities are unfamiliar within the community;
- participants are under the care of a professional organization or leader;
- professional standards are compromised;
- participants are uninformed of possible dangers; and
- the community is predominantly risk averse and motivated to apportion blame.

This means that adventure educators must *be* professional and *be seen* to be professional. Fortunately levels of professionalism within the outdoor adventure sector have increased in recent years with greater industry accountability and the adoption of quality management principles, including the development and application of contemporary risk management techniques. The advantages of this trend have already been recognized in the sport sector within Australia, where risk management implementation has been found to reduce both the frequency and magnitude of lawsuits (Cuskelly and Auld, 1989).

Risk Responsibility

Everyone is responsible for risk management: the adventure provider or organization for establishing a safety culture; managers for developing appropriate programs and establishing risk assessment and control procedures; leaders for implementing safety strategies; and participants for being proactive in the care they demonstrate for their own and other's safety. The balance of shared responsibility between a provider and participant is not constant. It can be expected to vary according to a range of factors, including type of adventure activity, nature of the environmental setting, and level of experience of the participants.

The Risk Control Spectrum (RCS) is a useful concept for highlighting the shared relationship for adventure safety responsibility. It establishes a framework for the provision of a range of adventure recreation opportunities reflecting a spectrum of self-reliance required by participants. The RCS was developed by Parks Canada (Sparkes, 1996) and is based on the Recreation Opportunity Spectrum (ROS) methodology introduced by the U.S. Forest Service (Clark and Stankey, 1989).

The RCS framework specifies a range of "public safety zones" which are based upon particular recreation opportunity setting characteristics and the potential for selected participant risks to dominate in each zone. Varying activities, degrees of remoteness, and requirements for different levels of participant self-reliance are associated with the zones. Also, various degrees of risk control intervention and search and rescue response are features of the different zones. These relationships are shown in Figure 38.1. The RCS acknowledges that differing degrees of agency risk management intervention and expected self-reliance of participants are associated with the range of opportunities available to clients in a given natural area or between different activity sites.

The RCS system raises the notion of "voluntary assumption of risk" (Hanna, 1991) and the fact that at the extreme of wilderness adventure education, participants may be given almost total responsibility for management of their experience, well-being, and safety.

Risk Data

There is now general recognition that a clearer picture of the real risks associated with adventure activities, and more informed risk management decisions can be made with reference to hard facts about accidents and incidents occurring in the outdoors. This position is reflected in the fact that eight papers on this issue were presented at a Wilderness Risk Management Conference in the United States (Wilderness Risk Managers Committee [WRMC], 1995). Recordkeeping at the organizational level is essential, though the ideal database would be a national outdoor incident data gathering system compiling information on all outdoor accidents, including minor injuries and even close calls. The rationale for comprehensive data collection is supported by an American industrial study (Bird and Germaine, 1987) that found that many incidents or close calls had similar causes to accidents producing injury or property damage. The research resulted in the Accident Ratio Triangle Theory which suggests that for every major injury there would typically be 10 minor injuries and up to 600 near misses. This theory is illustrated in Figure 38.2 and has subsequently been supported in studies of outdoor recreation accidents in New Zealand (Haddock, 1992) and Australia (Brown and Wood, 1997). Hence there is significant potential for much to be learned from close calls that could mitigate against the occurrence of serious events. The specific benefits of instituting an incident database include:

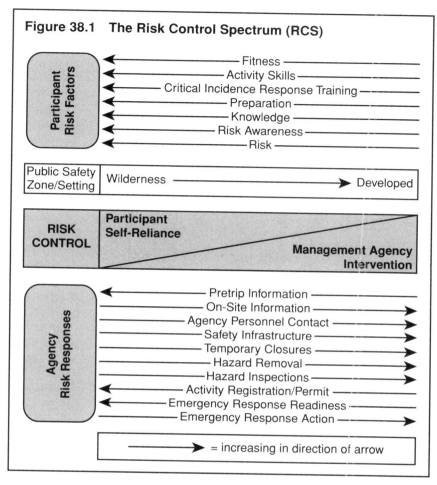

Figure 38.1   The Risk Control Spectrum (RCS)

- Acknowledging incidents and accidents so we can learn from them.
- Efficient notification of an event for communication to appropriate authorities.
- A comprehensive and systematic understanding of the nature, circumstances and outcomes of an incident or accident.
- An awareness of victim demographics and hence the identification of participants most at risk.
- Informing the decision-making process relating to appropriate management strategies aimed at minimizing accident occurrence.
- Promotion of professionalism in the outdoor industry and an enhanced quality of outdoor experiences.

In summary, the main advantage of centralized and standardized records is the facilitation of better quality risk management decisions associated with various programs

or activities. Also comparisons can be made between different outdoor activities and with risk exposure in other areas of life.

A number of national incident databases already exist. In the United States there is the National Safety Network, currently administered by the WRMC (Priest, 1996).

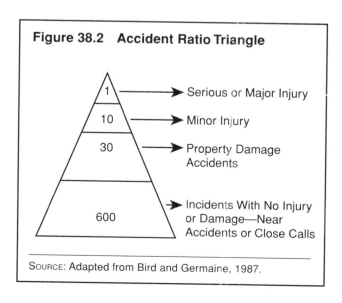

Figure 38.2   Accident Ratio Triangle

1 → Serious or Major Injury
10 → Minor Injury
30 → Property Damage Accidents
600 → Incidents With No Injury or Damage—Near Accidents or Close Calls

Source: Adapted from Bird and Germaine, 1987.

In New Zealand there is the Outdoor Safety Institute database (Haddock, 1993), and in Canada the Occurrence Tracking Information System (OTIS) set up by Parks Canada in 1990. In Australia, the National Injury Surveillance Unit (NISU) based at Flinders University in Adelaide collects regional accident data, but is limited by grouping all outdoor adventure related injuries in a broad category of "other sport or leisure activity."

Many individual outdoor organizations have well-developed incident reporting systems in place. For example the Outward Bound organization and the National Outdoor Leadership School (NOLS) in the United States, and the New Zealand Mountain Safety Council have collected accident and incident data since the early 1980s. Analyses of data collected to date have revealed a number of interesting findings (Brown, 1996; WRMC, 1995). These include:

- Many outdoor adventure programs subject clients to lower levels of risk than would be normally experienced in everyday living. This may be attributed to implementation of appropriate safety procedures, training and equipment.
- Injury rates in organized outdoor programs are substantially less than in many organized sports.
- Supervised outdoor experiences are safer than other activities engaged in by urban youth.
- Injury rates have steadily declined over the past decade.
- The risk of serious accidents in the outdoors is very low.
- Males are more likely to be involved in incidents than females.
- Drowning has been the most frequent cause of death in Outward Bound programs in the United States.
- The most common cause of accidents is the human factor, with adverse weather also being significant and equipment failures rare.
- Benefits gained from participation in outdoor experiences outweigh the relatively low risks involved.
- Incidents in outdoor programs typically reflect poor hygiene, minor joint injuries and soft tissue wounds.
- Incident rates amongst independent adventure participants need to be recorded and investigated.
- Injury rates appear to be highest for whitewater paddling, caving and Nordic skiing.
- For certain activities, such as rock climbing and caving, instructor incidents have been more common than those for clients. This may relate to the more active, up-front lead-ing role required for these activities and the generally higher exposure to dangers.
- Mountaineering fatalities in New Zealand involve equal numbers of experienced and inexperienced participants and 92 percent are related to errors of human judgment and could be considered avoidable.
- Fourteen percent of outdoor fatalities in New Zealand occur on paid commercial trips.
- Whitewater kayaking causes relatively few life-threatening or major injuries, though numerous minor to moderately serious maladies such as blisters, muscle strains and sprains, and submersion trauma are associated with this activity.
- Of the annual total of about 70 caving incidents in the United States per year most result from caver falls, equipment problems and rockfalls.

Findings such as these help to place adventure risk in perspective for the broader community and indicate to providers what types of accidents seem to be occurring to whom and under what circumstances. This information highlights where energy and resources should best be directed to achieve optimal client safety.

Risk Sources

A recent study investigating visitor accidents in Uluru–Kata Tjuta (Ayers Rock–Mt. Olga) National Park in central Australia (Brown and Wood, 1997) revealed that the sources of visitor risk in the park could be attributed to groups of hazards associated with the park environment, visitor attributes and visitor preparation for their intended activities in the park. This has relevance to the broader outdoor recreation context and the relationship is illustrated in Figure 38.3 for adventure education activities. The presence of certain risk factors at a given time and place will predispose participants to a predictable level of risk exposure. Essentially, the more risk factors that exist within and between risk groups the greater the potential for an accident to occur.

During a low element ropes course activity for example, the presence of a single risk factor such as poor fitness may cause an incident to occur. However if additional factors are added, such as a strong determination to succeed on the element, slippery footwear and inadequate supervision or spotting, then a damaging fall is virtually a forgone conclusion. According to prior research (Curtis, 1995), it is likely that the number of factors present in each risk group are likely to have a multiplier effect on risk exposure rather than an additive one. Hence, two risk factors in each of the hazard groups will produce a risk exposure of eight (2 x 2 x 2) times rather than six (2 + 2 + 2) times.

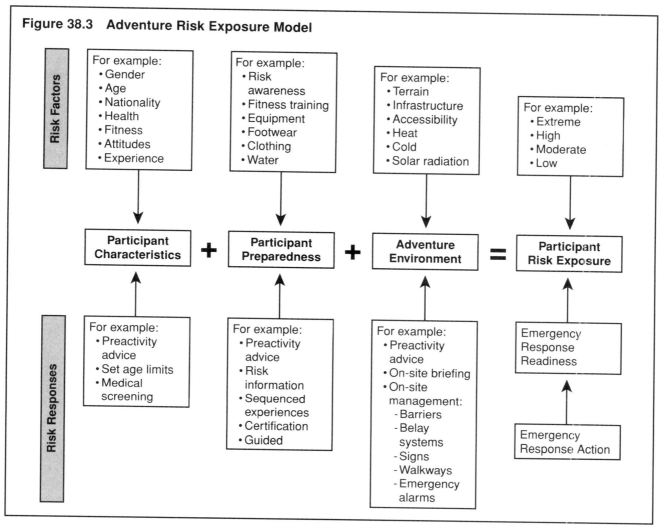

Figure 38.3   Adventure Risk Exposure Model

The Adventure Risk Exposure Model highlights the need for adventure education organizations, managers, leaders and participants to address a range of risk responses aimed at mitigating the multiple risk factors that are revealed through incident data analysis. Such proactive risk control measures should constitute the basis of an adventure risk management plan. Also, in the event of an accident occurring, emergency response procedures will need to be in place and capable of rapid implementation.

Risk Management Process

Effective risk management requires a systematic approach to the development of a plan aimed at controlling the range and impact of potential losses associated with adventure activities. Ewert (1983) conducted some early conceptual research in this area. More recently a number of useful practical strategies have been devised to assist adventure education providers develop risk management plans for particular activities and settings. Some writers took the components of Ewert's Decision Package Model (1983)

and used them to create checklists to assist with the planning process (Ford and Blanchard, 1985; Peterson, 1987). Others have systematically and comprehensively addressed a sequence of steps that lead to the development of a practical risk management plan. These steps include:

- risk identification (hazard assessment),
- risk evaluation (frequency, severity),
- risk adjustment or control (retain, reduce, transfer, avoid),
- risk management plan (choices), and
- plan evaluation and update (monitoring).

One prominent example of this type of risk management framework is the Visitor Risk Management (VRM) Process developed by Parks Canada (Sparkes, 1996). It is a seven-step process designed to facilitate production of public safety plans for particular national parks or historic sites. It represents a practical visitor management tool which complements a range of visitor management strategies adopted by Parks Canada over the past decade. For specific outdoor activities conducted at specific locations for specific clients, the Adventure-REACT Model describes the process leading to the production of a detailed risk management plan (Brown, 1995a). The model represents a decision-making system which aims to highlight the position and potential relevance of a range of factors in the risk management process. It incorporates a number of key leadership attributes which may influence risk management decisions; notably knowledge, experience and judgment ability.

The components of the Adventure-REACT Model of managing risk are represented in Figure 38.4. The framework was adapted from the risk behavior research of MacCrimmon and Wehrung (1986), and the acronym, REACT, represents the recognition, evaluation, adjustment, choice and tracking phases of risk management. Normally the model would be applied as part of the broader planning process that takes place prior to engaging in an adventure activity. The process could also take place *in situ* when confronted with an unexpected or modified danger encountered during an activity. In fact, the model should be representative of the sequential steps any experienced outdoor leader or adventure manager would follow naturally to assess the riskiness of a given situation.

In simple terms, for any given *adventure activity,* the first step in the "management process" is the *recognition* of all the potential risks associated with the range of possible dangers. This requires an astute *awareness* of the activity, the environment and the clients on the part of the manager or leader. The next stage is to *evaluate* each potential risk in terms of the probability and magnitude of possible consequences. At this stage specific *knowledge* about the skills and equipment involved, the environmental setting and the group's characteristics will need to be drawn upon.

Trained *judgment* is necessary to allow the best decision to be made concerning opting in or opting out of the activity. The decision to opt in may be premised on the desire to make *adjustments* to the identified risks. This is achieved through gaining more *information* about the situation and dangers, gaining more *time* to allow for more reflection and hopefully a better decision, and gaining more *control* via the appli-

cation of technical and planning expertise to allow the risks to match the desired exposure. This "risk structuring," or assessment process may require progressive reevaluation of the risks involved according to a leader's or group's knowledge base, field *experience,* and judgment ability associated with a particular activity.

Eventually the *choice* is made to take on a portfolio of risks in association with an appropriate risk management plan which will result in particular *outcomes.* The choice at this stage then, is not whether to opt in or opt out, but to choose from the range of alternatives that present themselves. *Tracking* of events during implementation of the activity will allow for progressive review and reassessment

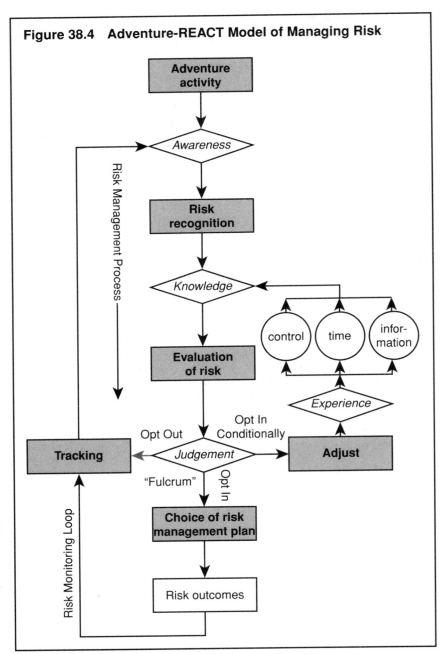

Figure 38.4   Adventure-REACT Model of Managing Risk

if necessary, thereby providing for flexibility and a dynamic component to the model.

Judgment is the central focus, or "fulcrum," of the Adventure-REACT Model. Good judgment will allow the right decisions to be made under the prevailing circumstances. The importance of judgment in decision making is well-documented in the outdoor adventure literature. Cain and McAvoy (1990) consider the vital attribute of any outdoor leader to be the ability to make quality decisions, based on good judgment, that work, are safe, protect the environment, and accomplish the purpose of the activity or trip. They consider judgment to be the "glue" which cements all the other competencies of outdoor leadership. Likewise, Priest (1990) rates judgment with a similar status, and it is generally agreed that the basis of "sound" judgment is knowledge and experience which has been subjected to reflection. Hence the attributes of knowledge, experience and judgment in the model do not work in isolation at various stages, but together in a synergistic manner within the "risk structuring loop." This should allow for the optimum management choices to be made according to the objectives and nature of the adventure activity.

Risk Management Plan

The output from the risk management process for a particular adventure activity or experience is the production and implementation of a comprehensive risk management plan. The results are probably best summarized in a "risk assessment and management matrix" such as the example shown in Figure 38.5 (page 280).

The first step in the matrix is to document all possible dangers arising from the environmental setting for the activity, the equipment used and the people involved. Second, the potential risks associated with each danger are listed. Each risk is then subjectively, though professionally, assessed to rate its probability of occurrence and the magnitude of possible consequences. This third step may present a significant challenge in itself but the leadership qualities of knowledge, experience and judgment should contribute to a realistic and astute assessment. On the other hand, despite the best efforts of prior planning, certain social and psychological factors may act to inhibit a realistic on-site perspective of hazard assessment once the activity is in progress (Haddock, 1993; Priest, 1996). These factors include:

- inappropriate attribution—"I'm not to blame";
- situational familiarity—"It can't happen to me";
- relaxed concentration—"It's all over now";
- smelling the barn—"The end is nigh";
- risky shift—"Safety in numbers"; and
- bad judgment—"I know best."

The fourth step in the matrix is to specify the desired control strategies aimed at reducing or eliminating identified risks, and the fifth step requires an acknowledgment that a particular strategy was adopted. Finally, continual improvement of the plan is encouraged through an evaluation of the outcomes of the activity.

The risk management matrix is only one component of a comprehensive plan for adventure risk management. Additional sections should include information on the activity itself, an emergency response protocol and an activity or route plan (Tasmanian Outdoor Leadership Council, 1996). Required adventure activity information should comprise a cover sheet and include:

- name of organization,
- type of activity,
- commencement date and time of activity,
- date and approximate time of return,
- location,
- names of instructors and/or leaders,
- total number of people on activity,
- necessary staff and leader skills,
- aims of the activity,
- experience of participants,
- medical conditions of participants, and
- medications required and carried by participants or leaders for any of the identified medical conditions.

The emergency response protocol should document a proposed approach to critical incident management in the event of an accident occurring, and would include:

- accident management approach,
- first-aid provisions,
- emergency communication options,
- evacuation options,
- "home base" contact details,
- police phone numbers,
- local hospital and/or doctor phone numbers,
- other relevant contact numbers (e.g., park ranger, accommodation facility),
- group's mobile phone number, and
- location of nearest phone to group in the field.

An activity or route plan should include:

- descriptions of the activity or route of travel;
- a map of the area if appropriate, with route marked;
- locations of proposed campsites or other accommodation;
- possible route or activity alternatives;
- potential escape routes; and
- transport arrangements.

Figure 38.5 Risk Assessment and Management Matrix

Activity Type: **Rock Climbing**

Activity Location: **Vista Bluff**

Activity Date: **27 June 1999**

Item Number	Recognized Dangers (hazard/peril)	Risk Items (potential accident, injury or other loss)	Risk Assessment (rate probability and magnitude as high, medium or low, e.g., ProbH MagL)	Control Strategies (to reduce or eliminate risk)	Strategy Adopted? (yes/no)	Evaluation of Outcomes (strengths/improvements)
A. ENVIRONMENT (factors that impact on the activity)						
Example	Loose cliff-top surface	Rock impact, falling	ProbM MagH	Physical check; attach to safety line within 2 m of edge	Y	No incident. Maintain vigilance; brief clients
1						
2						
3						
B. EQUIPMENT (resources that impact on the activity)						
Example	Failure/faults: ropes & tape slings	Falling	ProbL MagH	UIAA approved; less than 3 years old; good condition	Y	Minor rockfall onto rope; thorough check before continuing use
4						
5						
6						
C. PEOPLE (attributes that impact on the activity)						
Example	Client emotional health problems	Emotional trauma; reduced self-concept	ProbM MagM	Prior screening	Y	No incident. Maintain vigilance; be empathetic; debrief if necessary
7						
8						
9						

Compiling all this information may appear as a somewhat daunting task, though a systematic approach involving electronic storage in a database should expedite the process and facilitate regular updating of risk management plans. Also, the generic nature of much of the information should readily permit the adaptation of existing plans to new activities, locations or clients. Considering the increasing climate of litigation, the suggested protocol clearly records and displays the safety precautions that have been set in place, and therefore serves to define the desired or appropriate safety standard for a given adventure education context.

Risk Control Strategies

Risk control relates to the adjustments that can be made in an activity to minimize risks for participants and staff, and ensure the greatest degree of safety without compromising the objectives and potential benefits of the activity. Four general management options are available to deal with risk (Hanna, 1991):

- *Retention:* Organization assumes the consequences of any loss; Primarily for low probability or low-consequence losses.
- *Reduction:* Employment of safety measures to reduce the frequency and/or potential for a loss. For example, the use of trained staff and safety equipment.
- *Avoidance:* Making a conscious decision not to accept the risk associated with a situation. This may involve not operating an activity under the given circumstances, or removing an unacceptable risk such as a hazardous tree from a campground.
- *Transference:* Usually used to manage risks that occur infrequently, but when they do occur have catastrophic consequences. The most common forms of transference are insurance and liability waivers.

Organizations would typically adopt a combination of measures in each of these categories and above all, liability insurance is essential. The most common approach employed in adventure programs is the reduction of identified risks through implementation of a range of safety strategies. Most adventure education providers now document their adopted safety strategies in comprehensive procedural manuals (Brown, 1995b; Camp Fire Inc., 1993). Alternatively, a number of very useful generic guidelines are available (Curtis, 1998; Jack, 1995; Priest and Dixon, 1990). Clearly, safety cannot necessarily be guaranteed by a set of rigid standards. It also depends very much on a particular mental attitude which develops with competence and experience. Also, there are many objective hazards over which little or no control can be exerted. These include the weather, sudden rockfall, or a tree fallen in a river for example.

Ideally, safety strategies should reflect current professional best practice and include measures in the areas of primary, secondary and tertiary safety (Dynon and Loynes, 1990). Primary safety includes all the appropriate steps that should be taken prior to engagement in any activity to ensure that everything possible has been covered to prevent an accident happening. Relevant procedures and standards are specific to each activity, setting and client group but should include consideration of the following issues:

1. Staff Expertise:

   a. Qualifications:

      - certification,
      - training, and
      - experience.

   b. Staff to client ratios
   c. Preparation:

      - fitness and health;
      - program goals;
      - activity schedule;
      - activity organization;
      - leadership arrangements; and
      - empathy, insight and initiative.

2. Equipment:

   a. Clothing:

      - appropriate and
      - comfortable.

   b. Technical and protective:

      - personal items,
      - group items,
      - transportation,
      - acceptable quality standard, and
      - maintenance.

   c. Safety:

      - first aid,
      - repair kit,
      - whistle,
      - pocket knife, and
      - food.

3. Procedures:

a. Client preparation:

- briefing,
- training,
- fitness and health, and
- medical screening.

b. Group control:

- set appropriate physical and behavioral limits.

c. Emergency response plan
d. Suitability of venue and activity

Secondary safety considerations include the resources necessary to respond to any accident or mishap. This requires a clear critical incident management plan to be in place (Tasmanian Outdoor Leadership Council, 1996), including preparation for the following:

- *Staff responsibilities and tasks:* on-site; home base (24 hour contact); incident coordinator.
- *Protocol for communication of events to staff, relevant authorities and other persons.*
- *Preincident, during incident and postincident documentation:* medical disclosure; patient monitoring chart; accident report form.
- *First-aid procedures and protocols:* action plan.
- *Search and rescue procedures and protocols:* objective; communications; weather and topography; time frame for survival; search area; resources; time factors.
- *Evacuation policies and procedures:* patient status; urgency; resources available; evacuation modes.
- *Procedures for managing a fatality:* record all details; preserve accident scene; protect body; care for remaining group; contact police.

Tertiary safety involves actions taken some time following an accident and includes:

- *Long-term patient care:* once a patient has been immobilized and is awaiting evacuation.
- *Management of the remaining group:* decision on continuation of activity; emotional reaction of self and group; need for critical incident stress management.
- *Administrative follow-up:* handling the media; further counseling; incident reporting; collating all information relevant to the incident; writing a factual report on the accident

and preceding events; preparation for any inquest or inquiry; organizational review of the incident and adjustment to risk management plan.

Emotional Safety

With the progressive increase in adventure therapy programs has come the awareness that attention to physical risks is only one facet of risk management. The management of psychological impacts on clients is of equal importance. Past research has approached this issue. For example, Ogilvie (1989) identified some of the possible psychological outcomes for participants who engage in adventure activities either willingly (self-motivated) or by being forced when a fear of failure or sense of boredom exists. Also, Peart (1991) recognized the importance of "empathy and insight" as leadership qualities and incorporated these into a classification of leadership types.

More recently, Vincent (1995) has addressed the meaning of "emotional safety" and the factors which may assist leaders in regulating the level of emotional safety for program participants. Twenty-six factors were found to influence an individual's level of emotional safety and these were grouped into the four areas of:

- specific techniques used by instructors,
- instructor skills and abilities,
- the physical environment, and
- group composition.

There is scope for much more research in this area of risk management, especially focusing on identifying the most appropriate level of emotional safety to achieve desired outcomes for particular groups of clients.

Emotional safety is also compromised by a person's psychological response to witnessing or confronting an accident. This produces "critical incident stress" (Tasmanian Outdoor Leadership Council, 1996) which can overwhelm the capacities of a person to cope with an incident. This risk issue relates to the grief reaction that typically results from encountering a seriously or fatally injured person. Such occurrences highlight the need for understanding, recognizing and managing the health impacts of critical incident stress.

Grief is the evolutionary emotional and behavioral train of reactions set in motion by the loss of a loved one or by involvement in a traumatic event (Wilkerson, 1985). Participants and others may experience trauma and grief following the treatment and evacuation of a seriously injured or deceased companion. Such trauma is likely to be greater amongst clients, staff and amateur rescuers with limited encounters of real-life accidents. The reaction cycle associated with grief usually proceeds through a sequence of protest, despair, detachment and recovery. The manifestation of these stages and the timing of the cycle will vary considerably for different individuals. If the rescuer is not afforded the opportunity to work through his or her stress reactions it is possible that the extreme condition of posttraumatic stress disorder will result. This is a debilitating and protracted neurosis requiring extensive professional therapy. Whatever the degree of stress reaction, it is important to acknowledge that this is a normal response.

Critical incident stress may result in general dysfunction or an incapacity to engage in certain tasks. Typical signs and symptoms include physical conditions such as nausea, dizziness, headaches and sleep disturbance; cognitive impairments like disorientation, difficulty making decisions, memory problems and distressing dreams; and emotional trauma such as anxiety, depression, wanting to hide, and anger. Management options include:

- Selection of leaders according to appropriate physical condition, technical expertise, and personality characteristics.
- Preparation of staff to encounter victims or dead bodies. This will involve professional critical incident management training to provide simulated accident experiences and the development of anticipatory grief as a buffer to real-life exposure.
- Allow staff to choose how closely involved they wish to be with a rescue operation.
- Allow staff and clients adequate time to eat and rest after a rescue.
- Encourage opportunities for postincident strenuous aerobic exercise to relieve tension and achieve greater muscular relaxation. Also promote regular physical training for staff to maintain a high level of fitness.
- Conduct a critical incident stress debrief within 24 to 48 hours after the rescue. This may necessitate facilitation by a professional counselor if senior personnel in the organization do not feel competent to handle potential outcomes.
- Following physical and emotional recovery, the leaders and management should objectively critique the accident and evacuation in order to learn from successes and mistakes which contribute to an improved emergency response plan in the future.
- Provide access to professional grief and trauma counseling for individual clients and staff members as required.
- Make staff and clients aware of ways they can help themselves (e.g., resting, talking, keeping active), and each other (e.g., listening, assisting with tasks, empathizing) to alleviate the emotional impact of a traumatic event.

Conclusion

Life in general is risky, it just so happens that adventure education actively promotes challenge and therefore exposure to risks! This chapter has explored the paradox of adventure risk management and provided practical strategies for effectively managing risk associated with adventurous activities and experiences. The objective of risk management in adventure education cannot be the elimination of all dangers and risks. The meaning of adventure and its well-documented powerful effects on human development suggest a more appropriate goal of achieving maximum value for participants within an environment of manageable risk. Reaching this goal requires risk management to be meshed with experience management, where the level of risk control is a function of the outcomes desired from the experience.

The notion of both professional and public acceptance for a spectrum of risk control options according to program objectives, client needs, and environmental setting requires acknowledging risk management as not only a technical exercise but also a social issue. Responsible risk management therefore requires community education and justification for exposing people to real risks, as well as general industry acceptance and agreed standards of professional practice.

It may be more useful to practice risk-benefit management where the task of risk recognition is matched with identification of program objectives; risk evaluation by outcome assessment; risk control by experience design; and risk management strategies by opportunities for challenge. The increasing professionalism of the adventure education sector over the past decade has reaped enormous improvements in client safety and particularly in the reduction of serious injury and fatalities. The challenge ahead is to maintain this trend without compromising the spirit of adventure.

References

Bird, F. E., and Germaine, G. R. (1987). *Practical loss control leadership: The conservation of people, property, process and profits.* Loganville, GA: Institute Publishing.

Brown, T. J. (1995a). Adventure risk management: A practical model. *Australian Journal of Outdoor Education,* 1(2), 16–24.

Brown, T. J. (1995b). *Safety procedures and guidelines for outdoor adventure activities.* Brisbane, Australia: Griffith University.

Brown, T. J. (1996). Adventure risk management research—Review and action. In *Proceedings of the national conference: Risk management in the outdoors* (pp. 40–72). Launceston, Tasmania: Outdoor Recreation Council of Australia.

Brown, T. J., and Wood, J. (1997). *Uluru–Kata Tjuta national park: Visitor risk management assessment and visitor safety plan*. Brisbane, Australia: Griffith University Centre for Leisure Research and EDAW (Aust.) Pty. Ltd.

Cain, K. D., and McAvoy, L. H. (1990). Experience-based judgment. In J. C. Miles and S. Priest (Eds.), *Adventure education* (pp. 241–250). State College, PA. Venture Publishing, Inc.

Camp Fire, Inc. (1993). *Management of risks and emergencies: A workbook for administrators*. Kansas City, MO: Author.

Clark, R. N., and Stankey, G. H. (1989). The recreation opportunity spectrum: A framework for management, planning and research. In R. Graham and R. Lawrence (Eds.), *Towards serving visitors and managing our resources. Proceedings of a North American Workshop on visitor management in parks and protected areas* (pp. 127–158). Waterloo, Ontario: Tourism Research and Education Centre.

Curtis, R. (1995). *Outdoor action guide to outdoor safety management* [On-line]. Available: www.princeton.~oa/safety/safemen/html.

Curtis, R. (1998). *The backpacker's field manual*. New York, NY: Three Rivers Press.

Cuskelly, G., and Auld, C. J. (1989). Retain, reduce, transfer or avoid? Risk management in sport organizations. *The ACHPER National Journal*, March, 17–20.

Cuskelly, G., and Sessoms, H. D. (1989). An investigation of selected risk management practices among local government park and recreation departments in North Carolina. *Journal of Park and Recreation Administration, 7*(1), 26–40.

Dynon, J., and Loynes, C. (1990). Legal liability and risk management in outdoor training. *Journal of Adventure Education and Outdoor Leadership, 7*(2), 9–12.

Ewert, A. (1983). The decision package: A tool for risk management. *Parks and Recreation*, April, 39–41.

Ewert, A., and Priest, S. (1990). Leisure in the natural environment—Past, prologue and promise. *The Journal of Physical Education, Recreation and Dance, 61*(4), 34–35.

Ford, P., and Blanchard, J. (1985). *Leadership and administration of outdoor pursuits*. State College, PA: Venture Publishing, Inc.

Haddock, C. (1992). Accident and incident reporting . . . As a way of reducing and minimizing accidents. In *Step outside: Proceedings of the second New Zealand national outdoor education conference*. GP Print Ltd.

Haddock, C. (1993). *Managing risks in outdoor activities*. Wellington, New Zealand: New Zealand Mountain Safety Council Inc.

Hanna, G. (1991). *Outdoor pursuits programming: Legal liability and risk management*. Edmonton, Alberta: The University of Alberta Press.

Hunt, J. S. (1995). Risk-benefit analysis. In J. Gookin (Ed.), *Wilderness risk management: Proceedings of the 1995 wilderness risk managers conference* (pp. 51–56). Estes Park, CO: National Outdoor Leadership School.

Jack, M. (1995). *Strategies for risk management in outdoor and experiential learning*. Lindfield, Australia: The Outdoor Professionals.

McAvoy, L. H., and Dustin, D. L. (1990). The danger in safe recreation. *The Journal of Physical Education, Recreation and Dance, 61*(4), 57–59.

MacCrimmon, K. R., and Wehrung, D. A. (1986). *Taking risks: The management of uncertainty*. New York, NY: The Free Press.

Meier, J. (1990). A lot can happen in 12 years! *The Journal of Physical Education, Recreation and Dance, 61*(4), 36–38.

Ogilvie, K. (1989). The management of risk. *Journal of Adventure Education and Outdoor Leadership, 6*(4), 30–34.

Peart, R. (1991). Safe leadership in outdoor education part 2: Effective leadership. *Journal of Adventure Education and Outdoor Leadership, 8*(4), 21–25.

Peterson, J. A. (1987). *Risk management for park, recreation and leisure services*. Champaign, IL: Management Learning Laboratories.

Priest, S. (1990). Everything you always wanted to know about judgment, but were afraid to ask! *Journal of Adventure Education and Outdoor Leadership, 7*(3), 5–12.

Priest, S. (1996). Thoughts on managing dangers in adventure programs. *Australian Journal of Outdoor Education, 1*(3), 15–21.

Priest, S., and Dixon, T. (1990). *Safety practices in adventure programming*. Boulder, CO: The Association for Experiential Education.

Robinson, D. W. (1992). The risk recreation experience: Subjective state dimensions and the transferability of benefits. *Journal of Applied Recreation Research, 17*(1), 12–36.

Sandman, P. M., Miller, P. M., Branden, P. J., and Weinstein, N. D. (1993). Agency communication, community outrage, and perception of risk: Three simulation experiments. *Risk Analysis, 13*(6), 585–598.

Sandman, P. M., Weinstein, N. D., and Klotz, M. L. (1987). Public response to the risk from geological radon. *Journal of Communication, 37*(3), 93–108.

Sparkes, J. (1996). *Visitor risk management handbook*. Ottawa, Ontario: Parks Canada, Department of Canadian Heritage.

Tasmanian Outdoor Leadership Council. (1996). *Managing risks and critical incidents in outdoor programs*. Hobart, Australia: Department of Tourism, Sport and Recreation.

Vincent, S. M. (1995). Emotional safety in adventure therapy programs: Can it be defined? *The Journal of Experiential Education, 18*(2), 76–81.

Wilderness Risk Managers Committee. (1995). *Wilderness risk management: Proceedings of the 1995 Wilderness risk managers conference*. Estes Park, CO: Author.

Wilkerson, J. A. (1985). *Medicine for mountaineering* (3rd ed.). Seattle, WA: The Mountaineers.

Chapter 39

Legal Liability and Risk Management

Betty van der Smissen
Michigan State University

Charles "Reb" Gregg
Liddell, Sapp, Zivley, Hill, and LaBoon

How many times have you heard "Adventure programs are too 'risky'!"—and your desire to conduct adventure activities is denied by your policy board or top administrators? One need not fear liability, if one understands better (a) the philosophy and role of risk, (b) the basic legal concepts related to liability, (c) the protective shield that excellent risk management can provide, and (d) the alternative strategies for resolving a dispute. This chapter sets forth some fundamental considerations and principles to enable the reader to gain better understanding.

The Philosophy and Role of Risk

Any change of position, any adventure, any exploration into new places, ideas or activities is risky. Everyone—everything—on this planet is exposed to risk. People continue doing what they do with their lives because their experience has been that the rewards outweigh the risks. Individual experiences may validate the real relationship between the risks taken and the losses avoided; or one may simply be lucky. As Peter Bernstein observes in his *Against the Gods:*

> the real trouble with this world of ours is . . . that it is nearly reasonable but not quite. It looks just a little more mathematical and regular than it is . . . ; its wildness lies in wait. (1996, p. 331).

The value of risk has been eloquently described by Priest and Brown elsewhere in this volume. A reading of the observations of these authors on the subject is important for the adventure programmer. Suffice it to say here that risk sharpens and enhances the learning experience. It stimulates and provides focus; it is the "stuff" of life; it is a value in itself.

While the adventure education industry seems to understand well the value of risk to the individual, it has not paid as much attention to the inevitability of injury and loss which flows from risk. Risk and "safety" (literally, freedom from loss or harm) are mutually exclusive. Safety cannot be guaranteed and should not be promised. Accidents will happen in good programs and under circumstances supervised by competent people.

The adventure education profession has a responsibility to declare and protect the certainty and value of risk, and the possibility of harm. If it fails to do so, the providers in the industry will become insurers against every disappointment suffered by the people served.

Risk and Services Offered

A responsible program will analyze its services—what it does, where it does it, and with whom—and then it will reduce the risks to those which are essential to the goals of the program, manage them, and inform the participants of them. A program has two general areas of risk: (1) property loss and personal injury to participants, and (2) financial or other loss to the organization (provider) that may result from those personal losses.

Program data—your own and that of similar programs—may be used to measure the severity and frequency of losses incurred in an activity, under the supervision of certain staff members, and in certain environments. Near misses and evacuations, and an analysis of reports of these occurrences, are good sources of information about what might happen in the future. An activity producing an undesired risk occurrence which is severe and frequent should be stopped—do not continue. Occurrences which are not severe and are rare do not require a great deal of attention. The best risk management skills must be reserved for those severe occurrences that are rare, and those not severe occurrences that are frequent. Insurance is considered essential for potential happenings which are frequent and severe and should be considered for those which are frequent although not severe and severe but not frequent (Figure 39.1).

Risk and Types of Conduct

Liability arises from the conduct of the provider (program sponsor, leadership) and may be reduced by the conduct of the participants. Different risks arise from different behaviors. If the risks encountered in an activity are placed on a continuum, in the order of a provider's responsibility for the resulting loss or injury, they would range from criminal, intentional, gross negligent, and ordinary negligent acts of the provider, on one end, to the acts of the participant—contributory fault for injury, reckless disregard, intentional and criminal acts—on the other. In the middle would be the inherent risks of an activity and "acts of God"—the provider is not negligent, nor is the participant contributing any fault to injury (Figure 39.2).

Criminal acts are felonies and misdemeanors, which are prosecuted by the government on behalf of the victim and society. The individual committing the crime is individually responsible for the act. (However, see the discussion on security as a function of supervision.) Intentional acts, *torts,* also generally are the responsibility of the individual committing the act. These usually are "intentional,"

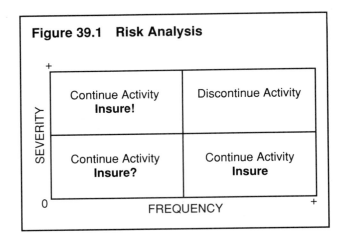

Figure 39.1   Risk Analysis

"willful and wanton" or "willful and malicious" acts, such as assault and battery, invasion of privacy, and defamation.

The risks most often encountered in adventure programs arise from the acts and events which fall in the middle range of this continuum and include, generally, the careless conduct of the people involved—contributory fault of participants and negligence of the staff of the provider—and the inherent (unavoidable) risks of the activity, including environmental or contextual hazards which simply "come with the territory."

Inherent risks. Inherent risks are those which are such an integral part of an activity that they cannot be removed without changing the basic nature of that activity. For example, whitewater canoeing has certain inherent risks which are different from the inherent risks of a ropes course, a climbing wall, a hike in the woods, camping, or scuba diving.

Lightning and falling rock may be alleged to be inherent risks of an outdoor adventure, but a court might ask to be convinced that the provider, or the participant, took reasonable steps for protection from the lightning or falling object. The provider and the participant should have some understanding of lightning as part of the environmental conditions, and failure of the provider to properly protect the participant or failure of the participant to seek protection may be considered ordinary negligence or contributory fault, respectively. Precisely the right decision in an outdoor setting, in the context of a variety of acts of nature and other contingencies, cannot always be expected. Arguably, in hindsight, a decision may be wrong, but a

Figure 39.2   Provider and Participant Liability by Types of Acts

Provider				Participant				
criminal act	intentional tort	gross negligence	ordinary negligence	inherent risks	contributory fault	reckless disregard	intentional tort	criminal act
				"acts of God"				

judge or a jury might, after hearing the circumstances, consider the decision, at the time, to have been reasonable. Generally, inherent risks are those which do not include a human element, but rather, are an aspect of the activity and its environment. Most states allow a provider to be relieved of any responsibility for an injury caused by an inherent risk.

To provide relief to providers and place responsibility on the participant when engaging in recreational adventure activities, some state statutes describe the inherent risks of a specific activity (e.g., skiing, equine, whitewater) or describe generic risks associated with all outdoor recreation activities (e.g., "hazardous recreation" statutes for public entities in California and Illinois). Part of the purpose of such statutes is to give a provider, accused of causing harm, an opportunity to avoid liability by showing the court that, as a matter of law, the risk was a reasonable and foreseeable part of the activity which the participant knew or should have known, appreciated and consented to. In any event, while the provider may avoid liability for inherent risks of an activity, the provider still must provide the service without negligence, e.g., ski lifts, supervision, instruction (see later section on assumption of risk).

The provider of an adventure program may extend the challenge to the individual participating and, thus, enlarge the inherent risks of ordinary outdoor activities and the environment. Such risks should be clearly understood by the participant and the provider.

Careless conduct. Also roughly in the middle of the risk-behavior continuum is the ordinary negligence of the provider and the contributory fault of the participant—essentially, careless conduct that produces foreseeable results, causing injury or property loss. Whether the conduct is sufficiently careless to create liability depends on whether the behavior was that of a reasonable person, similarly situated. In the case of an adventure program provider, the test would be whether the leader or organizer acted in accordance with the standards of the profession—really, a "reasonable adventure program professional" standard (see later section on standard of care).

When ordinary negligence is enhanced to gross negligence, usually any statutory immunity available to the provider is negated and the provider is liable to the injured participant. And, when a participant is careless toward the safety of a coparticipant, referred to as reckless disregard, intent to injure is implied, and the individual becomes liable to the coparticipant.

Risk management focuses on those risks occasioned by the ordinary negligence of the provider and the contributory fault of the participant. An analysis of a program's risks and reasonable efforts through a good risk management plan to reduce the risks to a level which is acceptable will benefit both the participants (they are less likely to be hurt) and the provider (it is less likely to suffer a financial loss from a claim). Adequate disclosure of risks produces a better informed, and perhaps more careful, participant. Correspondingly, the participant who discloses emotional or physical characteristics which may effect performance allows the provider to identify these additional risk factors and better care for that participant in certain situations.

A provider which conducts its affairs with "one eye on the courthouse" is not paying proper attention to business. As is true of any profession, fear of failure produces failure. The law is designed to protect those who adhere to the standards of their profession—the "reasonable professional" test. So, while there can be no guarantees, if a sound program is conducted, which is fair to the participants, utilizes the premises and the environment responsibly, and operates in accordance with established standards, the legal issues generally will take care of themselves. This does not mean that a provider will never be sued, but operating in this way gives the best chance of a satisfactory experience for the provider and its participants.

So, to summarize, adventure programs are risky. Providers understand the value of risk. Providers also must understand the inevitability of the injuries and losses which those risks produce. The responsible provider will identify the acceptable risks, disclose them to the participants, and manage them to the standards of the profession. The goal of an adventure program is not a risk-free activity. Rather, it is an activity free of risks and dangers that are unknown or unacceptable to the provider and the participant.

Some Legal Concepts

There are certain legal concepts basic to understanding liability and risk management. In this section only three will be set forth—the standard of care, assumption of risk, and allocating financial responsibility by contract.

The Standard of Care

There are three criteria for determining whether a provider performed the appropriate standard of care to protect the participants: (1) the reasonable and prudent professional, (2) the foreseeability of unreasonable risks, and (3) industry standards.

Often one hears about acting like "the reasonable and prudent person." What one must add to that phrase is "for the situation," and the situation in adventure activities requires *a reasonable and prudent professional.* When one accepts a responsibility, the expectation is that the task will be performed according to accepted standards or practices of the profession. The standard is not determined by the background of the person in charge, such as experience, skill, credentials held, maturity, or knowledge. There is not one standard for beginners and inexperienced persons and another for persons of some years of experience. The participant is owed a duty to be protected from unreasonable risk of harm regardless of who is in charge. The specific standard of care required is situational and has three determinants:

    a. the nature of the activity, whether simple or complex (the leader must have appropriate skill and knowledge suitable to the "level" of the activity);

    b. the type of participants, whether exuberant youngsters, the physically disabled, those capable of deviant behavior, the elderly, or others (the person in charge must understand the clientele and know how to work with them); and

    c. the environmental conditions (whether it is hot and humid, a Class V river, the presence of lightning, a muddy field, or slippery floors the leader must be able to "read" the environment and know what to do to protect the participants).

The standard of care also is determined by the *foreseeability of unreasonable risk of injury.* Under the circumstances which existed (the situation) could a reasonable and prudent professional have foreseen or expected or anticipated that the participants would be exposed to an unreasonable risk of injury? If so, there is a responsibility to act to protect the participant. For example, if there is a rainstorm with lightning, a reasonable and prudent professional with a group of youngsters on a hike or on a river would foresee potential injury to the participants, and would act to get the hikers to a safe location (not under high trees!) and the canoers off the water. On the other hand, if a group of youth were properly racing in a swimming pool and a 14-year-old dived into the pool, hitting and injuring one of the racers, there would be no improper supervision. In fact, in such a situation, the court said that because the youth watching had always behaved well, it was not foreseeable that this youth would dive into the racers. It must be emphasized, though, that the standard is foreseeability by a professional, not the ordinary person.

A third dimension of the standard of care is the *industry standard.* What is considered by the professionals in the adventure program field to be the best or recommended way to conduct an activity? In a lawsuit expert witnesses will be brought in to testify as to what the industry considers proper practice and the jury will determine whether or not what was done was in accord therewith. The AEE *Manual of Accreditation Standards for Adventure Programs* sets forth desirable practices for technical skills for 30 land, water, and air activities. Other literature, as well as presentations and discussions by experienced professionals at workshops and conferences, also can provide guidelines. *It behooves every professional to keep up on the best and latest practices of the profession.*

Assumption of Risk

Assumption of risk is a legal concept integral to understanding the responsibility of the participants. There are two types: primary assumption of risk and secondary assumption of risk.

Primary assumption of risk. Primary assumption of risk is based on the *consent* of the injured party and is a bar to recovery (no award for injury). There are three essential components of such consent. First, the participation must be "free and voluntary;" the individual must not be coerced into participating. Second, the individual consents only to those risks which are inherent in the activity, that is, are integral to the activity and without which the activity would lose its character. For example, if a person were injured while whitewater canoeing when the canoe flipped over, such activity would be considered inherent in the activity. It is not conceivable that one could go through whitewater, especially in a learning stage, without flipping over—that is why "rescues" are practiced before one goes whitewater canoeing. However, the participant does not assume risks occasioned by the negligence of the provider, such as defective equipment or improper instruction. The third component for valid consent has three aspects: knowledge of the activity, understanding in terms of one's own condition and skill, and an appreciation for potential injuries. Under ordinary circumstances, the participants do not assume any risk of an activity or condition of which they are ignorant, and thus, the leadership must make every effort to properly inform and instruct. Knowledge of the activity means knowing the nature of the activity and the basics for participating. The understanding aspect is difficult for leaders, as the participants need to be able to use their knowledge about an activity and the conditions under which it is being engaged in, and assess their own skill competence and physical and emotional condition, as well as understand the prerequisite safety precautions and why. Appreciation extends to awareness of possible accidents and resultant injuries, both minimal and catastrophic. The courts have required a great deal of leadership regarding these three aspects. Communicating with participants, in addition to oral instructions, can include the application form or an agreement to participate, videos, printed information on brochures and handouts, and signs. Adventure program providers seeking to attract participants may not always be entirely accurate in their communications. Their marketing often does not present an adequate picture of the perils to be encountered—brochures become more enticing and photographs more likely to reflect only the happiest of experiences.

If participants are experienced and highly skilled, they should be cognizant of the risks when they consent to participate. On the other hand, if participants are beginners, it is important that the provider gives appropriate instructions and supervision as the participants are learning. Sometimes in regard to offering activities, it is suggested that only beginning activities should be offered to reduce liability. The opposite is true—the more experienced persons who participate in advanced activities have a greater knowledge about, understanding of, and appreciation for the activity, thus assuming the inherent risks to a greater extent than would a beginner.

Primary assumption of risk can be either *implied*—that is, knowing the risks to be encountered, one participates anyway—or *express,* usually a written or oral statement saying specifically that the inherent risks are assumed. In some literature and in a few jurisdictions, the term *express assumption of risk* may be used synonymously with waiver; however, a waiver is a contract not to hold the provider liable for ordinary negligence and usually has nothing to do with inherent risks (see later section on waivers). The term *informed consent* also is often used synonymously with primary assumption of risk, for indeed the participant must both be "informed" and must consent; but informed consent really came from the medical and research fields, indicating that the client or subject is informed of the "treatment" to be done and what results can be expected therefrom.

Secondary assumption of risk and contributory fault. Secondary assumption of risk is really contributory negligence or fault of the participant, in that it is not an acceptance of the inherent risk of the activity, but goes to the *conduct* of the participant, which contributes to the injury. Such behaviors could include, for example, failure to obey rules, to follow directed skill progression, to heed warnings, to properly use safety devices, or to follow the sequence of instructions (directions) given by the leader. Previously in the majority of states, any amount (even one percent) of contributory negligence or fault by the injured would bar recovery of any award to the injured. But in the 1990s less than half a dozen states still adhere to this point of view and most states have merged contributory fault into the concept of comparative fault. If the provider (the defendant in a lawsuit) expects to have available contributory fault as a defense, two practices are essential. First, the provider must set forth appropriate rules, give proper warnings, and instruct as to desirable practices. The participant must be informed orally or by written statement as to expected behaviors. Second, there must be a documentation system of just what was "informed" and the practices of the provider in the conduct of activities or services, as well as the behavior or conduct of the participant (see later information-documentation system section).

Concept of comparative negligence or fault. Comparative negligence is not really a defense, but a method of apportioning an award for damages—how much should the plaintiff receive? The jury determines the percentage of fault attributed to the plaintiff (the injured participant) and the percentage of fault for all defendants and others (provider, leadership) aggregated; then, the award is made in respect to the ratio of fault. There are two methods provided in the various state statutes. About a dozen states

have what is called the *pure form,* that is, the plaintiff can receive whatever percentage the defendant was at fault. For example, if the plaintiff was 10 percent at fault and the defendants 90 percent, the plaintiff would receive 90 percent of the award. Or, if the plaintiff was 80 percent at fault, only 20 percent of the award would be received. The other method is the "50-50" approach. Some states say if the plaintiff's fault is "not greater than" the defendant's fault, then the plaintiff may receive the proportionate amount of the award; otherwise no award. Other states will say the plaintiff's fault must be "not as great as" or "less than" the defendant's in order to receive any pro rata share (plaintiff does not receive an award if fault is equal to that of defendants). But whichever the state statutory language, the basic holding is that when the plaintiff contributes more than 50 percent of the fault toward the injury, then there is no award. For example, if plaintiff is 60 percent at fault, there is no award. But if the plaintiff is 40 percent at fault and aggregate defendant fault is 60 percent, the plaintiff receives 60 percent of whatever was awarded by the jury. Thus, the defendant seeks to establish as much contributory fault on the part of the plaintiff as possible, making the documentation system essential.

Warnings. The foregoing is based upon the participant having sufficient information to make an informed decision to agree to participate and assume the inherent risks (*consent*) or to engage in an activity in a certain manner, notwithstanding the circumstances (*conduct*). Integral to providing this information are warnings.

The essence of *warnings* is communication to the participant as to how one engages in an activity, what is required to avoid an unreasonable risk of injury, or the condition of the physical environment, including equipment, and the modifications desirable to help prevent injury. There are four criteria for communicating a warning:

1. obvious and direct; cannot be subtle;
2. specific to the risk; cannot be generalized, but must indicate the risk;
3. comprehensible, in language understandable by the one being warned; and
4. location, at the point of hazard, or at the time when such warning is appropriate.

Warnings can come in various forms of communication, including oral instruction, video, pictures, posters, literature, and signs. Often it is desirable to use more than one form for emphasis and reinforcement. Warnings are essential in all aspects of programs and services—in skill instruction, appropriate use of safety equipment, condition of the snow or river, for example. Books and articles on individual activities provide further guidance regarding warnings specific to that activity. Because warnings regarding how to participate to reduce the likelihood of injury are so pervasive, it is understandable that *warnings have become one of the most important risk management tools.* However, the provider, to utilize warnings to show secondary assumption of risk, must keep complete records of the warnings and the behavior (conduct) of the participant related thereto, specifically when and in what manner the participant ignored or "violated" the warning. Thus, again, the importance of the information-documentation system is again evidenced.

Agreement to Participate forms. Agreement to Participate forms can be utilized both to provide information regarding the nature of the activity and appreciation of possible injury, which provides a base for an assumption of risk defense, and to set forth expectations for the participant, an element in secondary assumption of risk. Usually an Agreement to Participate form has three sections. The first describes the activity so that the participant has some knowledge thereof and an understanding of what capabilities one must have to appropriately participate. It also sets forth in a positive way an appreciation of the possible consequences of participation in terms of injury. The expectations of the participants, the second section, include behavioral policies, such as those related to drugs, drinking, and smoking; discipline and group responsibilities; and a directive to follow the leader's instructions. The third section describes special requirements, such as skill level or physical condition, equipment and clothing, physical disability or health concerns (e.g., food allergies, bee stings, recent injuries not healed or stamina not at full strength), and insurance. While Agreement to Participate forms are not a contract, and should not be confused with waivers (exculpatory clauses), they do give some documentary evidence of an effort to inform and educate the participant. Even though participants may be minors, they should sign the form, as it is they who are to understand about the activity and the expectations, both as related to the activity and their behavior. To have parents also sign serves as an excellent public relations device. Such forms can be included as part of a regular application or registration form and do not have to be on a separate sheet, as often waivers are.

Allocating Financial Responsibility by Contract

The adventure programmer may use a number of contract techniques for avoiding or shifting to another the financial responsibility for legal liability losses.

Covenant not to sue. It is common for the provider to seek from participants assurance that the provider will not be sued for injuries or other losses which result from inherent or other risks of the activity. A careful provider will have the participant acknowledge a description of those risks.

Express assumption of risk. Similarly, the provider will seek protection from claims that arise from risks of the activity, which are reasonably expected by the provider

and which are understood and expressly assumed by the participant. The participant agrees to take part in the activity in the face of that understanding. When these assumed risks go beyond the inherent risks of the activity, the document is usually referred to as a waiver.

Waivers. Some providers seek from an adult participant a waiver or release, in advance, of claims for injury or loss arising from their negligence. It is a contract between the provider and the participant not to hold the provider liable for injuries which may occur during participation due to the ordinary negligence of the provider. Most states hold waivers valid, if properly written. The participant must be of majority age and must sign voluntarily. Three key principles for valid waivers are (a) explicit, clear language that covers all aspects of activity participation and injury from whatever cause, including negligence; (b) the format provides for conspicuousness of the exculpatory (waiver) language in a print size that is easily readable; and (c) entered into knowingly and voluntarily (no coercion). Usually waivers are not held valid for minors on the basis that they cannot contract, although they may ratify a waiver (contract) upon reaching age of majority (for minors, see section on Agreements to Participate).

Consider again the risk-behavior continuum (Figure 39.2, page 286). The areas of contention when it comes to an agreement between the participant and the provider regarding who is liable for what, are inherent risks and the negligent acts of the provider. Courts do not allow a provider to be relieved for conduct more than simple or ordinary negligence.

Some might argue that it is reasonable for the provider to be liable for the inherent risks of an activity (presuming the provider knows these risks better than the participant); but the law provides otherwise. Inherent risks are those which do not depend on the particular knowledge of the participant. The presumption is that the participant knows that there are a bundle of risks which cannot be eliminated without changing the nature of the activity—falls on moguls in downhill skiing, for example.

The justification or rationale for a provider seeking protection for its negligent acts has been described previously. Particularly in these litigious times, many programs feel they cannot trust to a judge or jury the determination of what is a negligent act.

Ordinarily, avoidance or allocation of financial responsibility for losses will be set out in a document which incorporates the assumption of identified, including inherent hazards and risks; and a release and waiver of claims arising from other categories of risks, including the negligence of the provider or coparticipant.

Indemnification. In some circumstances, a promise is made to protect the provider if certain claims are brought which the parties agree are more properly defended by someone other than the provider (perhaps the participant or a parent, guardian or sponsor).

Such indemnities are utilized often with third parties who are willing to absorb the financial responsibility for the loss of another. A careful provider will buy insurance, for example. The insurance company essentially is indemnifying the provider against certain categories of claims which might be brought against it. A provider which contracts for the performance of certain services may logically expect to be indemnified by that contractor for losses which occur under that contractor's management. Some providers ask parents for indemnity from potential claims of or on behalf of a minor participant. This means of protection from minors' claims has not been satisfactorily tested in the courts.

Legal advice should be sought concerning which of these methods of shifting financial responsibility best suits your program—insurance, assumption of risk, waiver and release, and indemnities. Be aware that certain public land managers, including the National Park Service, may limit your use of these techniques for avoiding financial responsibility.

The Risk Management Plan

It is imperative that each agency, organization, business enterprise or other corporate entity offering adventure programs have a risk management plan, up-to-date and implemented. Accreditation Standard 5.A.02 requires a written risk management plan. (*Note:* All references to standards are from the AEE *Manual of Accreditation Standards for Adventure Programs.*)

What risks are we managing? There are two types: the risk of *financial loss* and the risk of *personal injury,* including pain and suffering and loss of capability to perform both work-related tasks and personal enjoyment tasks. Financial loss most frequently is addressed by shifting liability through contract, particularly the purchase of insurance, employment of independent contractors, lease arrangements with indemnification, or exculpatory clauses (waivers) in membership, participation, or use contracts. The approach outlined in this section is the amelioration of personal injury risk exposures through operational policies and practices.

A risk management plan is more than safety checklists—although safety is important (see the previous chapter by Brown). It is the systematic analysis of one's operations for potential risks or risk exposures and a plan to reduce the severity and frequency of such exposures. It is an integrating opportunity, integrating many operational elements.

Risk management *plans have three primary parts:* (1) the analysis of risks, (2) the policies and procedures for reducing the risks, and (3) the implementation of the plan. Risk assessment must be very thorough and encompass the entire operation—risks related to property, to business operations, to personnel, to participants. The focus of this section, however, is on the participant experience only.

There must be operational practices and procedures set forth in detail and specific to all aspects of the operation. Of course, each organization will offer its own activities and services and, thus, risk management details will vary from organization to organization. For this reason, only a generic outline of tort liability–related aspects to be covered in the risk management plan is set forth here. There are three major aspects: the environmental conditions, the conduct of the activity, and the supervision of participants. Many of the aspects are required for accreditation and such standards are designated at the appropriate topic.

Environmental Conditions

There are three aspects to environmental conditions: the natural environment, equipment, and areas and facilities.

Natural environment. The most obvious aspect of adventure programs is that of the natural environment. The leadership is expected to know about the elements of the natural environment essential to a particular program or activity or sport in order not only to protect participants from exposure to unreasonable risks but also to heighten the quality of the experience for the participant. The natural environment may be the primary "challenge" in an adventure program and, thus, it is important that the participants have some understanding about the environment for their comfort in participating and to enable them to better care for their own safety. Participants must have sufficient knowledge about the outdoors to make informed decisions. In the AEE *Manual of Accreditation Standards for Adventure Programs,* each activity has a section titled Environmental Understandings.

The leadership must be knowledgeable about the natural environment, the hazards of the environment for program activities and the hazards of the environment in the vicinity in general. While it is true that the recreation user statutes limit liability of the landowner, they only do so if there is no fee charged; the use of the land must be gratuitous. The concept of "open and obvious" has helped landowners particularly, and also those who utilize the outdoors. There is no liability for those hazards which are open and obvious; however, *to identify such a hazard must be within the experience of the participant.* For example, bodies of water today, in nearly all jurisdictions, are not considered an attractive nuisance for children, because the dangers of water are considered within the experience of children. Dangers not "open and obvious," when known to the landowner, must be identified and warned against. A warning regarding natural hazards, to be useful, must have the same attributes as warnings related to activities: obvious, not subtle; specific as to what the danger is; comprehensible to those to whom directed; and located so people can easily see it.

Equipment. A second aspect of the environment is equipment. All adventure programs have specialized equipment, whether it is personal clothing and equipment or group equipment. Again, the AEE *Manual of Accreditation Standards for Adventure Programs* for each activity has a section titled Clothing and Equipment. Equipment must be appropriate to the activity and especially to the size of the participants. There must be adequate protective devices and instructions on how to fit or use. Equipment must be in good condition and appropriate to the activity for protecting the participants. It must be "fitted" on or to the participant, where size is important; and, also, there must be instruction how to use and care for the equipment. Where canoes, ropes, and other equipment are used, they must be systematically checked often for defects or signs of wear and unserviceability. Frequency and type of use must be recorded for "safety" items (e.g., ropes, logs) subject to deterioration.

Transportation by vehicle is a part of the equipment dimension, too. Is the vehicle in good condition? Has it recently had a maintenance check? And, are the drivers qualified and have the appropriate licenses? Is there proper and sufficient supervision en route (e.g., on the bus) and is the route established and checked out? Is transportation provided for all participants or only those who do not have their own? What is the policy regarding participants riding with other participants and the use of parents' and volunteers' cars? How do you protect against a child being picked up by an "unauthorized" person? One way to avoid liability for transportation accidents is to have participants convene at the site of the event or activity; that is, no transportation is provided by the organization.

Areas and facilities. Areas and facilities is the third aspect of environmental conditions. A number of adventure activities have specialized areas and/or facilities. Also, in resident facilities, the layout and design, especially rest rooms and shower areas; architectural barriers for the handicapped; and layout of activity areas for safety and supervising, must be given special attention. Further, vehicular and pedestrian traffic pattern and flow should be diagramed and assessed for ease of supervision, for entry control, and for personal safety, especially hidden and/or dark areas. Premises liability for areas and facilities is an important element in legal liability. The liability arises primarily from the condition (maintenance) of the premises. Organizations are held liable for both constructive and actual notice of a hazardous condition; that is, whether the staff person in charge actually saw the dangerous condition or, if he or she had done his or her job in inspecting, would have seen it. Thus, a maintenance inspection system is essential. As to the maintenance of areas and facilities, remember, *premise-related injuries are the responsibility of* both *the owner of the premise and the activity sponsor!* Further, all appropriate permits must be obtained for use of lands and rivers, and regulations followed (see Standard 5.A.12).

There must be an inspection records and system, which has four elements. Maintenance is everyone's job, so the first element is *general employee maintenance inspections;* it must be built into the job description for each of the employees and volunteers. The second element is a *formal checklist* of what to look for related to the condition of the areas and facilities. This should be a detailed list, checked regularly, dated, and signed. Of course, when dangers are noted, they must be corrected. How much time does one have to correct a dangerous condition? It depends on the density of use, the likelihood of an injury, and severity of injury, if one might occur. *Critical parts inspection,* those things that need a specialist to check (e.g., the pool filtration system, the climbing ropes, your transport vehicles), is the third element. The fourth element addresses the tendency to overlook those things worked with most frequently and closely; get a pair of "external eyes." Have someone who is not as familiar with your operations, whether it's a consultant or fellow professional in another organization, come over and take a look at your environment.

Supervision

Supervision is one of the most important legal responsibilities in the provision of adventure programs. There are two types of supervision, general and specific. General supervision is that provided to oversee an activity area, whereas specific supervision is that directly related to individual participant instruction and care. Specific supervision is addressed in the sections on individual activities of the AEE *Manual of Accreditation Standards for Adventure Programs* and other literature resources. This section deals with general supervision in a generic manner. The focus is supervision of participants, not of staff.

The *supervisory plan* is a critical dimension of risk management. It must be written, communicated to the leadership, and incorporated into the staff in-service program. A supervisory plan should be written in terms of *functions (activities) and areas, not by position descriptions!* For example, it might be said that Fred is in charge of the waterfront and Sally is the canoeing instructor—but that is *not* a supervisory plan. There must be a plan for the waterfront (an area) stating how the area is to be covered at all times, as well as how each function or activity (e.g., free swim, swimming or canoeing instruction, scuba diving) will be covered. Or, if there is "free time" for participants or travel unaccompanied by the leader, how are the different areas to which they may go or the activities in which they may participate supervised? The assignment of personnel to cover an area or function must consider the number of staff necessary, the competence of the person for that specific task, and the suitability of the person to handle clientele (e.g., physically handicapped, juvenile delinquents, physically "out-of-shape," adults). Also, how "closely" one supervises participants may be a matter of the provider's mission, e.g., if an objective of the program is to develop self-reliance and have the participant learn to be "on one's own," then the supervision would be more at a distance. Of course, there must be appropriate training for the participants and assessment of the abilities of the participant before a participant engages in activity with minimal or distant supervision.

There are five functions of general supervision:

1. *Management of behavior.* This includes discipline policy and procedures, as well as dealing with drug abuse, child abuse, intoxication, and antisocial behaviors. How does one discipline a participant? When are the participants just having fun or engaged in "horseplay"? When do such acts become rowdiness, and how does one curb such behavior before it results in serious injury? What does one do if a participant appears to have "reckless disregard" for the safety of others. What should be done if someone has drugs, alcohol or firearms, or commits other "forbidden" acts (see Accreditation Standard 5.A.05). Further, when large events occur, there must be policies and procedures for crowd control.

2. *Rules and regulations.* Be cautious of having too many rules and regulations established. Only those rules and regulations which are essential for the safety and well-being of the participants should be established. Too many rules and regulations cause problems for both the leadership and the participants—no participant can abide by all the rules if there are too many, nor can the leadership enforce so many. However, at all times, it must be understood both by leaders and participants that should conditions warrant, additional rules and regulations for the safety of the participants may be established by the leader. *Rules and regulations which are established, but not communicated or enforced consistently and fairly, might as well not have been established.* Communication means that the rule or regulation must be made obvious to the participant for whom it was intended and must be comprehensible in terms of the participant's understanding (maturity and language). Furthermore, the risk against which the rule is protecting should be made known. Communication may be through several media, such as postings, handouts, program brochures, videos, lectures and discussions, as long as the appropriate information is communicated. One should not overlook applicable local, state, and national laws and regulations (see Accreditation Standard 5.A.14).

3. *Dangerous situations and conditions.* The supervising leadership must be alert for activities being conducted in a dangerous manner (see Conduct of Activity) and physical conditions which are hazardous (see Environmental Conditions). Action must be taken to reduce the likelihood of injury due to such dangerous participant conduct or environmental hazards (see Accreditation Standard 5.A.01).

4. *Security (protection against criminal acts).* Security and safety of persons and property from criminal activity is especially important in today's society, and one must take precautions where there is foreseeability of kidnapping, physical violence, robbery, shootings, or rape. Of particular importance is the screening of personnel. Nearly all states now require criminal background screening of personnel who work with children, as a precaution against child abuse. If an organization does not do appropriate screening and a staff member, either employee or volunteer, physically or sexually abuses a child, a disabled person, or the elderly, the provider may be liable.

5. *Emergency procedures.* Emergency procedures are especially important for adventure programs and the preparation for this supervisory function cannot be overemphasized. There are three considerations—preparation prior to (anticipating) an emergency, preparation for properly dealing with an emergency when it happens, and preparation for the aftermath of an emergency—and each must be carefully addressed in the risk management plan (see standards 5.A.06, 5.A.07, 5.A.08, 5.A.09, 5.A.10, and 5A.13.).

Prior to an emergency (e.g., "accident injuries," tornadoes, floods, fire, runaway children, external violence) there must be well-established policies and procedures and most importantly, proper arrangements. Appropriate procedures must be set out—for both staff and participants—as to who does what, including how one notifies the families of the participants and the other participants in the program who were not involved in the emergency. Arrangements must be made with local law enforcement, fire department, 911 support services, and hospital and medical personnel. Where are the emergency medical treatment permissions for minors kept and have appropriate arrangements been made with hospitals en route for trips? Transportation accommodations, including helicopters and rescue teams, if needed, must be addressed. Medical insurance coverage must be known for each individual (participants and staff) and especially volunteers, as they often are not covered by providers. A *crisis management plan* also is integral to planning for emergencies, not only to outline how to work with participants in the case of a catastrophic accident but also how to work with their families and their lawyers.

During the emergency the tasks of different personnel should be well-established, but this will not be the case unless there has been prior appropriate training in first-aid and rescue techniques, and properly equipped first-aid kits and appropriate rescue equipment are available. This stage encompasses the initial rendering of lifesaving first aid, the sequence of personnel to continue on-site care through to the hospital, if needed, e.g., emergency medical technician, 911 personnel, nurse, physician, and media contacts.

Following the immediate emergency, the plan must direct how to correctly fill out an accident form, properly handle the media, and debrief the participants and staff. The crisis management plan may need to be activated.

Accident reporting forms and procedures are integral to any risk management plan. There are four types—accident forms, treatment (not on-site first aid) or rehabilitation forms, statistical reporting forms, and insurance forms—which should be distinguished and the role of each known. A treatment form is usually used when a program has the capacity to follow-up on an injury, e.g., a resident facility with a health center or when treatment and/or rehabilitation is provided, such as an athletic training program in a sport camp. Then excellent records need to be kept of the treatment given to the injured. Statistical reports are usually requested for keeping of records by state or national agencies or organizations. Such forms usually are composed of "check-off" responses regarding the accident—what activity, which body part injured, what type of injury, causes, and area located. Insurance forms, of course, are those from an insurance company. However, the form of most interest in risk management is the accident form, which provides needed and valuable information about the circumstances of the injury, so one can reconstruct what happened. Many adventure programs also record "near-misses." Such information may be helpful in making a program more risk free, if any needed "corrections" are made immediately and if used in in-service education of staff. However, it is cautioned that a long list of "near-misses" on record, even if corrected, can provide evidence of careless leadership in a lawsuit.

Information necessary on an accident form to be useful in assessing risks, for a claim or a lawsuit, includes:

a. identification information, e.g., full ID information on the injured, the person in charge, date and time of day of accident, event, witnesses and address, insurance;

b. location of accident, i.e., a specific diagram—where were the witnesses, the leaders, other participants;

c. action of injured, i.e., what was the injured actually doing (only facts should be given,

e.g., one would say that the injured was running and fell, not was running, stepped in a hole, and broke her leg, for the latter may not be fact but presumptions);

d. activity context (relates to secondary assumption of risk, the conduct of the injured)—had the injured done this activity before, had there been instruction and warnings;

e. preventive measures by the injured—what could the injured have done to prevent the injury (e.g., the injured may actually say, "Oh, I've done it many times and I just slipped," "Oh, you told me not to . . . ," or "If I'd only followed your instructions"); *never attempt to describe what the provider could have done to have prevented the accident—this might be construed as an admission of negligence,* and invariably this issue requires careful study by a variety of experts;

f. procedures followed in rendering aid; and

g. disposition—physician diagnosis, what happened to the individual following the injury, such as return to participation?

Accident records should be maintained in the documentation system for the state statute of limitations period, plus two to three years, after the participant reaches the age of majority.

Conduct of Activity and Knowing the Participants

It is the legal responsibility of the leadership to know and understand the participants and to conduct the activity in accord therewith. This aspect of the risk management plan deals with the conduct of the activity itself, with considerations related both to the specific activity and to the participants.

One of the most essential aspects relates to the *maturity and condition of participants,* that is, their age, developmental stage, size; physical, emotional and social maturity; skill and experience; and mental and physical capability. Also, do they have a temporary state or condition, physical or emotional, or any permanent disabilities which must be considered as related to the specific activity. What health disclosures are essential and who is responsible for appropriate consideration thereof? Are there any disabilities which must be accommodated under the Americans With Disabilities Act (see standards 5.A.15, 5.A.16)?

Consideration must be given to the *adequacy of instruction and the learning progress,* including skill and judgment progression, instruction for safety, rules for participant conduct in the sport or activity, protective devices and equipment, and rules and regulations of the sport or activity. Is there adequate instruction and progression? Are the participants properly informed about the nature of the activity and its inherent risks? Participants who do not understand the nature of the activity, do not comprehend the risk with regard to their own condition and skill, do not appreciate the potential injury, and *do not assume the risks of the activity* (see primary assumption of risk). Are participants warned about what injury might occur if they do not follow instructions? Warnings are the foundation of secondary assumption of risk or contributory fault defenses to a claim and can decrease an award to the plaintiff under comparative fault statutes (see comparative fault). Having an Agreement to Participate form (see previous section) with a client can be a valuable asset both in public relations (people understand more completely what they are getting into) and risk management, as he or she gives some documentary evidence of an assumption of risk (see standard 5.A.04).

Implementation of Risk Management Plan

A risk management plan that people spend a lot of time producing is valueless unless it is implemented. The critical components of implementation are a risk manager, an information-documentation system, a public relations program, and monitoring or assessing the performance of the plan.

Risk manager. Every organization should have a person designated as *the risk manager.* To say all personnel are responsible for risk management is inadequate because "everybody's business is nobody's business!" *There must be a specific person responsible for overseeing risk management.* This would be a specific position in larger organizations (providers) or an assigned responsibility in smaller organizations. The director may want to take such responsibility. It is this person's responsibility to see that a risk management manual (which for many adventure programs may be "The Manual") is prepared and regularly updated. Personnel not only must be oriented to risk management practices and procedures, but also supervised to see that such are carried out. There should be active interaction between employees, administrators, and supervisors (see standard 5.A.03).

Information-documentation system. The risk manager also oversees the information-documentation system, which is an integral part of all risk management and essential to defense in any lawsuit. An analysis of the data provides a basis for the management of risks. The information to be included is extensive, and should include information on participants, e.g., applications, waivers, health and accident forms; operations information, e.g., staff personnel files (including evaluations and certifications); permits and contracts with land managers; risk management policies and procedures, insurance; and program data and docu-

ments, e.g., emergency plans, brochures and information on programs, courses, and workshops, safety records, and especially information on specific events in the field, e.g., program or course log—progressions, weather, maps and routes, significant events which occurred, incident and near-miss reports, evacuation reports, students' separation statements, debriefings, student evaluations, administrative evaluations. It also is desirable to keep a library or file of pertinent articles, standards, books, et al.

The use of the information-documentation system should be carefully controlled; however, it can be a valuable resource when working with leadership, media, attorneys, or insurance companies. There also should be an established document retention policy.

Public relations program. A public relations program should be directed toward the concerns of risk management. It is well-known that an irritated, unsatisfied customer or participant is prone to bring legal action much quicker than a person toward whom care, concern, and taking care of "minor" expenses are exhibited.

Monitoring and assessment of performance. There, too, must be monitoring of the plan. The effectiveness and cost-efficiency of risk management practices must be systematically evaluated and adjustments made, as appropriate. Neither the implementation of the plan nor assessment of its effectiveness just happens.

Is the time and effort it takes to make and implement a risk management plan worth it? Indeed it is, if you do not want to have "the specter of liability" haunt you. Think it's too expensive? It's not nearly as expensive as a lawsuit. A risk management plan also encourages professional practices and increases employee and volunteer pride, loyalty, productivity, and confidence. It promulgates good stewardship of human, financial, and physical resources and, most importantly, enhances the experience for the participant.

Resolving the Dispute

A broken promise, a personal injury or some other event has, let us suppose, given rise to a real or imagined claim. A controversy arising from an injury or loss follows a predictable pattern. Inevitably, the injured party will at least consider a lawsuit. However, many people in the outdoor industry have no idea how a lawsuit begins, develops or ends. Nor do they understand the roles of the insurance carrier or an attorney in settling a claim. Further, most people are not aware of alternatives to a lawsuit, such as mediation or arbitration. Settlement by negotiation, mediation or arbitration is the cheapest, least adversarial, and the quickest solution to a dispute, and should be explored as soon as it is clear that the matter will not go away.

Initial Negotiation

Customarily the claim is presented to the offending party, the adventure program provider, for example, by a telephone call or letter. The aggrieved participant or family representative might not attempt to resolve the dispute personally and, instead, may enlist the services of an *attorney* immediately. The first thing the adventure program hears or reads about the claim may come from an attorney.

Whatever the source, this initial expression of disappointment or anger will probably include some request or demand for relief—an apology, refund, credit toward participation in a future program, or monetary satisfaction.

Any such claim should be immediately reported to your *insurance carrier,* which usually will provide a defense, even if it does not agree immediately to pay losses suffered by you. The relationship which you have with your insurance carrier will determine how active you will thereafter be in dealing with the person who is complaining. Clearly the insurance company has a stake in the outcome of your negotiations, to the extent that the insurance company's funds are implicated (that is, your retention or deductible is exceeded). Be very cautious about committing, without the approval of your insurance carrier, to any exchange of information or any settlement which involves the funds of the insurance carrier. It would be rare if a suit were filed before the demand for satisfaction, aforementioned, has been sent to you, and you have had an opportunity to respond. But it can happen.

Receipt of this demand may fairly be regarded as an invitation to attempt to *negotiate* some settlement of the dispute, and you should not hesitate to suggest such negotiations. Usually the complaining party will be willing to talk.

Mediation and Arbitration

If and when negotiations break down, or a lawsuit is threatened or appears inevitable, either party may suggest that the dispute be referred to some neutral person or panel for resolution, by mediation, arbitration or other means. Agreement to Participate forms or other documentation between the participant and the provider may require that one or another such method be at least attempted.

Mediation is, as the term implies, a process in which a neutral third party attempts to bring the parties to an agreement, somewhere between their respective positions. Most states have laws which protect the confidentiality of the process. In some states, courts may order the parties to a lawsuit to mediate.

Arbitration is a more formal process, in which a person or panel hears the parties' positions, and perhaps witnesses, and rules for one party or the other.

Going to Court—The Lawsuit

If the parties cannot agree on an alternate means of resolving the dispute, or if such means fail, the dispute will be placed in the hands of the court by a formal *complaint* or *plaintiff's original petition.* This document tells the court, and a jury if one is requested by a party, the basis of the claim of the injured person, who thereafter is referred to as the *plaintiff* or *complainant.*

The target of the claim (adventure program provider), called the *defendant* in the lawsuit, has an opportunity to respond to the complaint. The requirements of this *response,* or *answer,* will vary from state to state, and are often different in a federal suit than in a state court suit. Generally the response will give the position of the defendant and usually will raise certain defenses. Defenses might include a claim that the conduct of the plaintiff contributed to the accident, the plaintiff has waived its claim by means of a written agreement, or the accident arose from inherent risks or risks which were expressly assumed (see legal concepts section). The answer may be accompanied by a *counterclaim,* if the defendant feels that the plaintiff has somehow harmed the defendant.

The filing of an answer provides another opportunity for the parties to attempt to negotiate a settlement. Failing that, the parties engage in what is called *discovery,* which is a formal procedure for collecting information from the other side and, often, from persons or entities who are not parties to the lawsuit. State laws control what questions may be asked and what documents collected. Evidence may include testimony from persons with information about the incident (in questions and answer form, under oath, known as a *deposition;* admissions; and answers to written questions, known as *interrogatories*), and requests for documents. Generally the scope of these inquiries and requests is very broad—seeking information and documents that may not themselves be admissible in court, but may lead to admissible evidence.

After adequate time for discovery, the matter will be tried to a judge, or to a judge and jury—the trial. The judge applies the law, assisted by briefs or legal memoranda prepared by the attorneys for the parties, urging their respective clients' views. The jury decides the facts.

If the facts are not in dispute, a party who believes the law is on its side may file a *motion for summary judgment* (or similar proceeding) which may dispose of the case before trial. An example of such a motion may be a claim that an accident was the result of inherent risks. In many states such a circumstance provides a full defense to the defendant, who would be entitled to summary judgment and, subject to appeal, an end to the case.

Ordinarily the party who loses is entitled to an appeal and sometimes the appeal may move through more than one level of appellate courts in a state. Even this late in the process, a responsible attorney will seek opportunities to settle the dispute. Some jurisdictions, in fact, require mediation of matters on appeal. The benefits of settlement are obvious, and always should be explored. State laws will determine if and under what circumstances a winning party may be entitled to its attorney's fees. Do not assume that the losing side will have to pay the winner's attorney's fees.

Selection of a good attorney in these matters is critically important. Hopefully the provider (defendant) has already enlisted the help of a variety of professionals in insurance, medicine and law. A trial attorney should be selected who can adequately defend a claim against you. This may require some collaboration with the insurance company.

The provider's (defendant's) board of trustees or directors and the management will have to decide whether to fight the lawsuit or seek an early settlement. Again, this decision will have to be made in consultation with the insurance company. Matters which might be considered are the time required to prepare and try the case, the distractions to staff; any "matter or principle" to be preserved; whether it is felt that the publicity which will attend the trial can be tolerated (that is, what is the impact of the publication of the negative allegations of the plaintiff; provider's financial resources [including insurance] for responding to the claim; and, of course, the quality of the defenses and of the plaintiff's claim).

Where the suit is tried, and the laws which are applied, can be quite important. Applicable laws and the attitudes of juries vary from state to state. Counsel should be consulted to determine whether one can contractually bind a participant to resolve the dispute in a certain jurisdiction, using the laws of that state. Ordinarily the jurisdiction which is chosen must have some reasonable connection to the relationship between the provider and the participant.

Legal Responsibilities Require Professionalism

After reading this chapter, you might say, "Oh, why bother, I can never fulfill all the legal responsibilities—it's just not worth all the 'hassle.'" *Wait*—go back and review the responsibilities. Are most providers already doing most of the suggested operational practices? The legal responsibilities are nothing more and nothing less than current professional practices—which all should be doing anyway. This chapter can be used as a self-assessment of present practices and a determination of where one excels and what needs more attention.

One should *not* fear liability, but be confident in the quality of one's operational practices and move forward positively and with enthusiasm. Leaders should act professionally and serve with pride! Do not deny youth or adults the opportunity to engage in challenging and exhilarating adventure activities because of a preoccupation with legal liability.

Reference

Bernstein, P. (1996). *Against the gods*. New York, NY: John Wiley & Sons, Inc.

Williamson, J., and Gass, M. (1993). *Manual of accreditation standards for adventure programs*. Boulder, CO: Association for Experiential Education.

Chapter 40

Improving Program Quality Through Evaluation

Alan Warner
Acadia University

Adventure-based experiential education traces its roots across a century of critical philosophers and educators from William James, to John Dewey, to Kurt Hahn, not to mention the broader contributions from aboriginal cultures. However, as an educational field with a sense of definition and self-awareness, it is a young movement that was only organized in the early 1970s. Evaluation and research questions inevitably only started to surface in the 1980s, once proponents began to give some definition to their approaches and expected outcomes. The 1990s have brought a dramatic growth in the profile, and the quantity and diversity of programming in experiential education. With this growth has come an increased expectation of quality and accountability from consumers, funding agencies, and educational stakeholders. The discipline has entered "adolescence." Will its rapid growth, enthusiasm, and successes be another passing educational fad due to a lack of ongoing attention to quality and critical reflection? Or will the experiential education field build on its successes and develop a solid knowledge base of what works, how and why it works, and how it can be improved? Effective evaluation provides the means to learn from experiences, both successes and failures. It will be a critical element in determining the broader acceptance and development of the field.

What lessons have been learned from previous work with respect to how evaluation can best contribute to the field? What are the present challenges in producing valu-able evaluation efforts? Where are the obstacles? Each professional, program, and institution needs to examine these questions and generate answers and strategies which will encourage continual quality improvement in their endeavors in the field.

Past Lessons

Move Beyond Talk

Calls for more attention to evaluation and research were a constant refrain throughout the 1970s and 1980s while in practice the evaluation and research literature was weak (Cason and Gillis, 1994; Conrad, 1979; Conrad and Hedin, 1981; Ewert, 1995; Priest, Attarian, and Schubert, 1993; Shore, 1978). The 1990s have seen an increase in published evaluation research with an increasing level of sophistication (e.g., Doherty, 1995; Priest and Gass, 1997). Yet the work has been undertaken by a limited number of university researchers and prominent organizations with a large resource base. Broader surveys of program evaluation activity in the field by acknowledged service providers consistently indicate a low percentage of organizations which are actually engaged in ongoing evaluation and research work with respect to their programming. Recent national surveys have indicated that more that 80 percent of wilderness orientation programs for university students, more than 80 percent of adventure programs for substance abusers, and more than half of wilderness therapy programs were not conducting systematic evaluation work (Davis-Berman and Berman, 1996; Davis-Berman, Berman, and Capone, 1994; Gass and McPhee, 1990). Why? Evaluation has not traditionally been a priority relative to service, program development, and fund raising. It requires an organizational resource base which is still in its early phases of development. Underlying these practical issues has been an important psychological dimension: experiential educators have a strong sense of mission and belief in their work. The zeal and energy which it takes to chart new educational directions does not necessarily breed critical reflection and self-analysis.

Quality Work Takes Quality Effort

Early evaluation projects most frequently involved giving program participants pretreatment and posttreatment questionnaires in order to document positive changes across the program on key personality traits and attitudes, particularly self-concept (Ewert, 1983; Priest et al., 1993; Shore, 1978). Much of the evaluation work was devoted to one-shot outcome studies conducted by researchers from other disciplines, frequently graduate students in education or psychology who were completing thesis requirements. From a scientific point of view, the evaluation designs were weak although the multitude of positive results tended to bewilder reviewers into concluding that there is a documented improvement in self-concept as a result of intensive outdoor adventure programs. From a discipline perspective, too much time and effort was devoted to conducting poorly controlled outcome studies on psychological variables. A few strong studies could have accomplished the same task, leaving more time and resources to be devoted to other issues.

The past decade has produced some evaluation and research studies which have devoted more attention to understanding the process and components of program effectiveness rather than simply focusing on outcomes (e.g., Phipps and Claxton, 1997; Priest, 1995). Yet despite these examples, a wide range of programs are still not engaged in learning through evaluation.

Take Responsibility for Your Own Learning

The past low priority and narrow focus of evaluation research resulted in programs contracting out work to researchers from other disciplines. But by relinquishing responsibility for defining evaluation approaches and borrowing evaluation expertise and methodology from others, experiential education has been dominated by evaluation criteria which are philosophically out of tune with experiential theory and practice. As an experiential educator, one must question whether assessment techniques which measure abstract traits and concepts, and depend on verbal and cognitive skills, should be the primary means of evaluating experiential education programs committed to learning through concrete action and experience (Warner, 1984a). These types of evaluation studies have had pragmatic advantages for administrators in that they do not interfere with programming, yet they have produced "clean" numerical results. Ironically, even when these evaluation designs are well-controlled, many social scientists question the value of only relying on psychological tests because of their empirical deficiencies in reliability, validity, and ability to predict behavior (Abelson, 1972; Rappaport, 1977).

Evaluation researchers trained within the field have been gaining experience and expertise over the past decade. There are now examples of quality work and alternative evaluation methods being put into practice (Gordon, 1994; Raffan and Barrett, 1989). However, there will never be enough university research specialists within the field to conduct evaluation work across all programs, and there will inevitably be differences in perspectives between researchers and practitioners. Practitioners and administrators have to take responsibility for their own evaluation projects if their programs are to develop.

These past lessons have been well-recognized in the experiential education literature (Cason and Gillis, 1994; Ewert, 1995; Hamilton, 1979; Priest et al., 1993; Warner, 1984a). Given the theory and principles of experiential education, the lessons are common sense: move beyond talk, quality work takes quality effort, and take responsibility for your own learning. The development of specialist evaluation and research expertise within the field provides a valuable resource, but the question remains as to whether the vast majority of practitioners and programs are ready to appreciate these lessons, benefit from the resources and take on the responsibility to make evaluation happen. Broad-based evaluation efforts are essential if the field is to learn from the past and build a stronger foundation of quality programming.

Present Challenges

Integrate Action and Reflection

Program evaluation is fundamentally a tool for critical reflection but has not been used in this way given the past focus on one-shot evaluation studies. To be meaningful, evaluation needs to be built into the program from the outset, setting up an action-reflection learning cycle for program staff and administrators. For example, experiential education practice typically involves leaders processing activities with participants either immediately or at the end of a day. Programs are processed by staff at their conclusion, if not before. An important but simple evaluation process could involve asking participants after each program activity or session to assess the value of their experience on a three-point scale along with a brief comment. The rating process would contribute to the program experience by communicating to participants that they have a role in program evaluation. If the ratings were collected across instructors and programs, staff would have a valuable tool to look at what is working and where there are difficulties. New hypotheses may be generated which in turn require follow-up and/or encourage program innovations. Taking the extra step of writing down ratings allows one to capture patterns beyond the words of the more articulate participants and staff.

The systematic documentation of participants' feedback on a regular basis is extremely simple and yet can literally transform programming by requiring educators to continually examine their own assumptions, methods, and presumed outcomes for learners. For example, Brookfield (1996) gave a brief critical incident questionnaire to students in his university course on a weekly basis and as a result was able to identify problems before they escalated into disasters, promote critical reflection among students, build trust, identify the value of differing teaching styles for different students, and identify specific areas where he could benefit from additional training. Systematic monitoring of critical incidents on adventure courses run by the Santa Fe Mountain School uncovered the connection between the survivors of sexual abuse experiencing flashbacks and participation in blindfold activities (Gray and Yerkes, 1995).

A simple regular feedback system is not a startling idea and it will not "sell" a program. However, over time this process promotes quality and ultimately the program's credibility. In fact, the field has been quick to take steps to monitor physical safety issues (Hale, 1990). However, a systematic monitoring must involve a range of program and leadership elements and outcomes if there is to be critical reflection and continual improvement in quality (Braverman, Brenner, Fretz, and Desmond, 1990).

In order to move toward using evaluation as a program development tool, integrating action and reflection, practitioners must take a greater responsibility for program evaluation efforts, both independently and in conjunction with researchers. Practitioners are more in touch with the practical realities of the work and have a greater vested interest in maximizing the impact of the evaluation efforts. Researchers, even those working within the discipline, tend to be less concerned with direct program impact and more focused on theory, long-term program development, and the accumulation of knowledge.

Practical evaluation ideas often come from thoughtful practitioners. For example, Heinrichsdorff (1987) proposes a methodology whereby participants and staff develop their own evaluation criteria at the start of each program. She suggests that this approach immediately clarifies staff and participant expectations, ensures relevant

outcome criteria are assessed, and starts the process of participants and staff taking joint responsibility to realize their goals. At the end of the course, the participants and staff already have an investment in providing meaningful data, and there is a greater likelihood that the results will be cycled back into the program. A rigorous, quantitative expert in research methodology would quickly shoot holes in this approach: where is the control group, how can one trust biased self-reports, and so on. But these concerns may not be the priority in program efforts to improve specific practices where there is no intent to generalize to other settings. The goal is to promote program development rather than pronounce on outcome. Integrating action and reflection can develop a positive spiral in terms of practitioner involvement in evaluation work. If practitioners begin to see that evaluation efforts provide valuable information to them, they in turn will put more commitment and energy into evaluation, which in turn will create more successful projects.

Take a developmental approach to evaluation. A developmental approach involves asking different types of questions at different stages in program development. Initially, the focus is on "formative" or "process" evaluation questions as one works to build the program: who are the participants, what are their needs, what are the goals, do the activities really address the program goals, and how and why do specific activities work? The need to define priorities for evaluation work initiates an invaluable process of critical reflection by program staff. Staff must carefully revisit the program's goals and objectives in order to determine exactly what the program is trying to accomplish and what is most important. Frequently goals were originally established in a general way to satisfy external agencies and never revisited, while in other instances the program may have drifted over time and the stated goals no longer match the practices. Evaluation can put a program back on track before there is even any attempt to collect information.

Once a program has a clear and coherent framework for program delivery, then there is value in examining outcomes, though process data is typically still needed to interpret the results. There is little point in drawing firm conclusions or generalizing from outcome data before a program has a consistent and coherent structure. Unfortunately, experiential education as a discipline inverted this pattern by relying on outcome strategies in its early phase of development.

Focus on the Process

Experiential educators are moving beyond the simplistic belief that experiential education is inherently good for everyone under all circumstances. What are the principles, theories, and processes which combine to build the most effective programs for specific types of participants? In recent years published evaluation efforts have shifted from the preoccupation with general outcomes to work that evaluates specific processes. For example, Doherty (1995) examined processing and facilitation styles in a one-day ropes course program and found that a facilitation approach that framed metaphors before an activity resulted in longer term positive outcomes than styles which only emphasized transfer to real-life situations in the debriefing. The results of this type of study are much more valuable to practitioners than work which simply notes general increases in self-concept. It promotes further reflection on facilitation styles and potential experimentation in practice, resulting in further improvements in quality and additional evaluation efforts.

In another study of program variables, Drebing, Willis, and Genet (1987) looked at how a participant's level of anxiety impacts on program satisfaction, self-reported learning, and the person's relationship with the leader. The results indicated that anxiety has a unique relationship with each of these variables. With further work, one might begin to identify appropriate levels of anxiety for specific types of program goals, participants, and activities. Mitten and Dutton (1993) have examined these issues with respect to outdoor leadership with female survivors of sexual abuse, suggesting that this group requires special considerations in relation to their experiences of fear and anxiety. The authors' reflections are drawn from their personal leadership experience but programs could go further to document practically through evaluation the strengths and weaknesses of the recommended approaches with this group of participants in a more systematic manner. Practitioners and researchers have complementary strengths and need to work together to improve programs. Practitioners often have implicit, experience-based theories of how and why specific practices may work. In turn, researchers can help practitioners articulate and test theories while integrating them with previous work.

Emphasize the Quality of the Experience

Valuable knowledge can be gained by carefully analyzing the components of experiential programs, but since the emphasis in experiential education is on the whole person, there would seem to be some inherent limitations in subdividing people into traits or programs into units and goals. Most experiential educators would not accept the premise that the whole person is equal to the sum of his or her parts (traits), much less that the whole program is equal to the sum of its individual activities. Critics of behaviorist educational approaches note that experiential education "is not a series of activities done to a learner" (Delay, 1996, p. 80). Learners actively extract and construct meaning from their experiences. By only focusing on the quantifiable effects, the holistic, qualitative experience may be

missed. For example, documenting changes in participants across a program on scales of moral reasoning and self-esteem does not provide great insight into the process and implications of the changes for participants in terms of their experience. Instead, one may better come to understand the development of moral values and the impact of experience on them through the use of personal interviews and narratives (Beringer, 1990).

There is a need to shift at least some of the evaluation effort to documenting the nature of both the individual's experience and the total program experience. Qualitative and naturalistic evaluation and research methods are probably best equipped to contribute to this task and need greater emphasis (Henderson, 1993; Kolb, 1991: Rowley, 1987). Qualitative work typically involves the researcher implementing program evaluation with a broader approach based on program participation, observation, and/or interviews. The evaluator attempts to integrate information from various sources into a description and analysis of the program. The experience of a program is conceptualized as a subjective, complex, and interactive phenomena which needs to be assessed in a holistic fashion. One of the advantages of this approach is that the subjective nature of the work is immediately evident whereas subjective values are often hidden in the "objective," quantitative model. Of course the very subjective aspect of the qualitative model may be viewed as a limitation.

In recent years, there has been much philosophical debate in the program evaluation field over the relative merits of the qualitative and quantitative models (Henderson, 1993; Smith and Glass, 1987). At a practical level, it seems reasonable to conclude that both approaches have their place in a new field which needs to address a wide range of questions (Braverman et al., 1990). For example, an experienced participant observer, intent on critically documenting and assessing the experience of a program and the individuals within it, can provide a wealth of new ideas, hypotheses, and information that can be cycled back into the program and the experiential education literature. The observer is in a position to ask questions and raise issues beyond the limits of the program ideology which staff typically adopt, even when they are critiquing and reflecting on their efforts. The challenge is the need to focus on the quality of the experience in a holistic fashion.

Problem Solve With Multiple Strategies

The development of participants' problem-solving skills is a key element of many experiential education programs. Effective problem solving involves having a wide range of strategies at one's disposal and then tailoring them in a flexible fashion to the specific issue or situation. Effective program evaluation requires a similar approach and the past work has brought home the limitations of relying on only a few strategies for all situations. Braverman et al. (1990) has illustrated the use of three very divergent strategies of evaluation in the same ropes course program (program monitoring, an experimental study, and a naturalistic inquiry) in order to obtain a holistic perspective of the program.

A wide range of resources are available which can be used to generate alternative evaluation strategies. Kolb (1991) has examined the potential applications of the literature in education, sociology, and anthropology on naturalistic inquiry (Goetz and LeCompt, 1984; Guba and Lincoln, 1985) to the evaluation of experiential programs. From an opposing philosophical direction, there are several decades of work in the field of applied behavioral analysis which takes a very scientific approach to defining treatments and assessing change (Kazdin, 1994). For example, sophisticated behavior observation procedures can be used to evaluate changes in participants' problem-solving skills across a program on initiative tasks (Warner, 1984b). Peer evaluation is another approach which has been used to assess a range of educational programs and seems particularly compatible with experiential education philosophy (Gordon, 1994; Kaufman and Johnson, 1974; Wiggins, 1973). One might document changes in participants' perspectives of their peers as a tool to analyze group dynamics and leadership styles. Portfolios represent another rich source of information about what participants have learned and how they have experienced a course, be it at the elementary or university level (Gordon, 1994; Hamm and Evans, 1992). Finally, journals are a key element in many experiential programs and there is an extensive literature on extracting themes and insights from open-ended writing (Raffan and Barrett, 1989; Carney, 1972). For example, a careful analysis of self-oriented statements in participants' journals may shed light on changes in self-perception across an experience. In brief, the field should ask a broad range of questions with a diversity of approaches.

Learn From the Consequences

Experiential practice attempts to set up learning situations where feedback and consequences are direct, natural, and concrete. If a group of adolescents cannot work together to cook a meal on a wilderness trip, they do not eat. What if the same learning model was applied to program decisions? If the participants do not demonstrate an increase in cooperative behavior by the end of the program, the program must be changed. Both examples are simplistic but the notion is that at some point one does need to be concerned with practical outcomes. Ultimately, for many programs, particularly those working with troubled participants, program goals aim at changing behavior. There is a need to shift the focus in outcome evaluation from looking at changes in attitudes to documenting accomplish-

ments and changes in behavior which can be related back to process-oriented evaluation data. For example, some adventure programs claim that troubled adolescents become more cooperative and socially responsible as a result of their program experiences. There are numerous possibilities for testing this notion by assessing practical behaviors. Do the young peoples' drinking patterns change as the result of their experiences? Do they become more active in work and recreation activities? Defenders of these programs faced with negative results on these measures could argue that one is being unrealistic to expect changes in participants' behavior back in their home environments with intensive, short-term programs. Probably they would be correct, but then the challenge posed by the negative results would be whether the program could do more to reintegrate young people into their home communities and create quality follow-up experiences (Hutton-Durgin and McEwen, 1991; McCabe and Harris, 1979).

On the other end of the participant spectrum, why couldn't evaluation work examine whether there is an increase in cooperative behavior in the workplace after a corporate team-building adventure program, rather than only relying on a team development inventory? There are more obstacles to this sort of evaluation project—it takes more time, requires more cooperation from the corporation, and is more intrusive with respect to participants. Yet in the programming sphere experiential educators often reframe obstacles as challenges. Should any less be expected of evaluation efforts when there would be benefits for the participants, the organization, and the experiential program?

Personal growth measures are important in assessing outcome, but there is also great value in measures which focus on social change or community development. Action research efforts can produce significant outcomes for the community while promoting growth among students. There are a wide range of examples of success stories in the environmental field where committed young people in experiential-based programs have brought about significant changes in organizational policies or community structures (i.e., Grant, 1996–97). Service learning programs provide another example of the importance of documenting broader outcomes such as the number of hours of service and the practical contributions to the community by participants. The focus should be on what the program is trying to achieve, whether it is a change in participants, a school, or a community.

It may seem contradictory to argue both for increased evaluation emphasis on program process and experience, and also for a shift to practical behaviors and accomplishments to assess outcome. In fact, the two approaches complement each other. Behavioral outcome evaluation will only provide meaningful information if it can be connected to information about program processes and experiences in a longitudinal way. For example, Ross and

McKay (1976) developed a sophisticated behavior modification program in a juvenile corrections facility for difficult female offenders. Their initial results were dramatic in terms of a greatly reduced recidivism rate for participants relative to a comparison group. They repeated their program twice with a few "minor" changes, and in these instances the recidivism rates of the participants jumped to a level which was even higher than the standard treatments. After a careful review of the program process and experience, the investigators recognized that it was the peer therapist aspect of the original treatment which was the key factor in the initial success, not the more prominent behavior modification procedures. They then dropped the behavior modification program entirely and developed the peer therapist model. As a result, they were able to repeat the very significant decrease in the recidivism rate that had been documented initially. Without the process data, their outcome information was misleading. Outcome data becomes valuable to the extent that it is connected to information about how the program works.

Obstacles to Productive and Broad-Based Evaluation

The previously mentioned challenges for evaluation are common sense from the perspective of an experiential educator. What could be more logical than to integrate action and reflection, focus on the process, emphasize the quality of the experience, problem solve with multiple strategies, and learn from the consequences? Unfortunately, it is a relatively easy task to define the needs relative to implementing them. Specific researchers and organizations have made significant progress in publishing creative ideas and model studies along these lines over the past decade, but broader survey studies indicate that only a minority of programs are actually even engaged in systematic evaluation (Davis-Berman and Berman, 1996; Davis-Berman et al., 1994; Gass and McPhee, 1990). It is not a coincidence that these directions are still relatively uncharted despite the fact that they seem like common sense. The challenge is to overcome the psychological and structural issues which are the roadblocks to moving in these directions.

Psychological Obstacles

One quality of strong leadership is the ability to believe in what one is doing, otherwise participants will not identify with the program's values and goals. The very powerful role of the self-fulfilling prophesy has been well-documented in the education literature (Rosenthal and Jacobson, 1968). Outcome research in mental health has indicated that the type of theoretical treatment approach adopted by a therapist can be far less important in predicting outcome than the extent to which the therapist believes in the spe-

cific approach (Yalom, 1985). Practitioners need to believe in themselves, both to survive psychologically in intensive programs requiring high energy, and to ensure the success of their programs.

Unfortunately, this need to believe has a dangerous flip side. Implicitly, often unconsciously, it can be translated into "I am a helpful person, therefore, I would not do anything to hurt anyone, therefore, what I am doing is helpful." Most leaders are keen to make adjustments in programs when they identify trouble spots, but are they willing to step beyond their own biases, paradigms, and ideologies? The role of evaluation in providing a new perspective is often proclaimed, but when push comes to shove, the energy and priority is not there to make the evaluation happen. In part, it is leaders' need to believe in what they are doing which results in evaluation receiving a lower priority relative to other tasks. On the other hand, if one waited until a program approach was proven to be absolutely effective before implementing it, very little, if anything would get accomplished. There is a middle road but experiential educators more often tend to err towards too much implicit faith in themselves and their work.

A second psychological issue which blocks practitioners from getting more involved in evaluation and research efforts is the tendency of researchers to use jargon and sophisticated technical procedures which obscure the nature of the evaluation process. Practitioners are implicitly convinced that they do not have the expertise to define program evaluation efforts. Recently, in the early stages of a research design course for practicing teachers, the professor introduced the notion of frequency polygons and histograms. After five minutes, one teacher pointed out to the others that the professor was simply talking about line graphs and bar graphs which are elementary school mathematics concepts. By the end of the course, the same teachers had gained a very different perspective of the research enterprise and their ability to undertake evaluation and research work in their own settings. They had learned the jargon such that they could review and identify fatal weaknesses and shoddy work in articles published in some of the most "respectable" education journals. Prior to the course, they would not have dreamed of drawing such conclusions, much less reading these "difficult" articles. The sophisticated academic jargon is particularly intimidating when researchers are quick to criticize what they perceive to be the biased evaluation efforts of others in scientific terminology. However, they often fail to acknowledge the inadequacies and weaknesses in their own approaches. Often, the simplest designs produce the most meaningful results.

The key ingredients to defining an evaluation are knowing the phenomena, identifying the key issues, and defining potential evaluation strategies in a creative, logical, and thoughtful fashion. One does not have to conduct major research projects to produce meaningful evaluation data for a particular setting. The priority is to build evaluation and reflection into the program, regardless of the scale of the project. Researchers do have technical expertise which can be necessary and valuable, but typically the expertise is more relevant to the question of how to implement a specific strategy rather than deciding what issue should be addressed and what strategy developed.

Structural Obstacles

Structural issues within the experiential education field combine with practitioners' beliefs to further restrict evaluation efforts. A legitimate complaint among practitioners is that there is simply no time available for evaluation given other responsibilities. Experiential education organizations are often run on a shoestring and/or programs are spearheaded by committed individuals within larger organizations which do not even recognize the person's experiential activities as his or her primary job responsibility. Evaluation requires the allocation of staff time at an organizational level which can only come at some sacrifice to other priorities and services.

There are also typically few incentives and payoffs to the practitioner for evaluation from an organizational perspective. Significant recognition does not often result from the write-up of an evaluation report or a research article. Instead, evaluation may be seen as taking time and resources away from service, while neither generating funds nor having a dramatic short-term impact. Moreover, given the negligible impact of past evaluation work on program development, organizations may have some experience to justify relegating evaluation to a low-priority endeavor. Complimenting the pressures on practitioners are the academic pressures on university-based researchers. Although they have incentives for doing research and writing in terms of career advancement, the pressure can become extreme to the point that the priority becomes the amount of work one has published rather than the quality. Numbers of quick and easy studies can score points with tenure committees. Yet, more carefully developed longitudinal efforts that have meaningful returns to local programs and take more time and effort, do not gain an equivalent level of academic recognition. Practitioners and academic researchers are under different types of pressures which can detract from quality evaluation efforts, and in turn, quality programs.

Confronting the Obstacles

Developing a meaningful and constructive program evaluation and research base involves overcoming the psychological and structural obstacles. As a young field, experiential education has an opportunity to avoid the alienating research versus practice dichotomy which is entrenched in other disciplines. For example, classroom teachers typically ignore their technical research literature because it seems irrelevant to day-to-day activities. Some teachers

do not view evaluation or research as essential or even helpful to good practice. One key element to addressing the psychological roadblocks involves integrating research and practice in the training process. If future experiential educators are given a firm grounding in program evaluation and research as a part of their training to be practitioners, it may help them to constructively question their practices while building confidence in their ability to define and develop evaluation strategies. Moreover, evaluation and research teaching responsibilities must not be farmed out to someone from another field. These topics must be taught by an experiential educator in an experiential fashion, addressing relevant examples, methodologies, and issues. Only then will students integrate their evaluation and research experience with their practical work. The ideal standard for undergraduate and masters research should be meaningful, small scale efforts, that can impact on specific practices, rather than independent studies which can be published. A diversity of approaches, qualitative as well as quantitative, need to be addressed.

The leadership in training innovations will have to come from the stronger, cohesive programs which offer an integrated degree in experiential education. Unfortunately, in many places, experiential education is taught across a few courses by faculty who are working within a broader department or division. These faculty often do not have control over courses taken by students with experiential education interests. However, leadership from the integrated degree programs can have a substantial impact on the field while individual faculty can include evaluation and research topics as sections of practical courses.

The structural obstacles must be confronted by practitioners through their programs and institutions. Inevitably, some time and resources committed to other priorities must be shifted to evaluation work. Over the long run these initial shifts can bring better programs and save resources. Many organizations are recognizing that the traditional outdoor program staffing strategy of utilizing high energy, committed, young instructors to run very intensive courses, has serious shortcomings in terms of instructor burn-out and turnover. By the time instructors have gained experience and are more able and willing to recognize the limits of their missionary zeal, they turn over. Organizations lose the staff who are probably in a better position to identify and put priority on meaningful evaluation projects. Experienced staff are more likely to see the long-term benefits of putting short-term energy into evaluation. Finally, at the initial hiring level, more priority might be placed on hiring staff with a strong commitment to reflection and evaluation.

Another means for organizations to increase their emphasis on evaluation is to carefully integrate meaningful procedures into new program proposals and build the cost in as a budget line. Given the increased push for accountability in education and social programs in recent years, evaluation is one item that granting agencies are more amenable to supporting. Programs may also pool resources, cooperate with universities, and/or build and utilize larger networks as a means to increase priority on program evaluation without making unacceptable sacrifices in other areas. At an administrative level, these strategies demand creativity, commitment, and communication. The return can be substantial for quality program development.

Putting the Ideas Into Practice

The psychological and structural obstacles will only be overcome through long-term efforts to change organizational and university structures at the local level, though broader networks and publications can facilitate the process. But what are the key questions for those committed and able to develop evaluation projects now? The fundamental question is why evaluate? The priority should be program improvement, rather than to meet external grant criteria, or to justify and sell the program. In the long run nothing sells better than quality!

The second issue is to consider the developmental stage of the program and its present level of sophistication. What types of evaluation projects will feed back information and contribute to action? For example, assume one is developing a pilot program to build multicultural awareness and sensitivity among high-school youth. It includes a short-term, intensive summer experience in a camp setting followed by participants working together in small, independent teams to put on multicultural events in their home communities during the subsequent fall season. How could one build evaluation into the program? A key program issue would involve participants developing the planning skills and the teamwork to put on the community events. One could expect participants to keep journals throughout the process of planning and running the community events in order to document their teamwork and accomplishments. By working with the participants to develop a meaningful planning process during the summer camp, one could ask that specific information be included in the journals: number of meetings, number of community participants, and quality of the team process. One could even assist participants to develop their own evaluation strategy for their event which in turn would contribute to an overall program evaluation. Valuable information could be generated if priority is placed on getting participants to follow through with their journal recordings and if there is a careful analysis of the collected information. One would have a record of program accomplishments, some numerical indicators of impact on the community, and insights into the team process. The requirements of the evaluation also promote meaningful practice: use of a journal, development of planning strategies, and participant reflection and evaluation of his or her work. This approach is more time-consuming than only administering a couple of pretreatment and posttreatment

attitude questionnaires, but the return in the long run is much higher. Questionnaires might be used in conjunction with this approach, but their value would come in relating their results to the other types of data.

This scenario provides one example for a program at an early stage of development. One could envision a similar evaluation process for a more developed corporate team-building program in which the follow-up task was an important practical project in the workplace. In this instance, a cooperative partnership with the corporation would be essential, but it would receive a benefit in terms of being able to identify the outcomes of its staff development training programs. Moreover, the reflection process would likely promote positive outcomes for participants in itself. On the other hand, a well-entrenched program may benefit from a broader, more rigorous evaluation process with comparison groups or repeated measurements over time. The key is to tailor the approach to the needs of the program.

A third issue and trap which frequently appears in program evaluation work is an attempt to make the program and the resulting evaluation be all things to all people. A proposal for an adventure program for a delinquent population promises improvements in self-esteem, socially responsible behavior, cooperative attitudes, problem-solving skills, and empathy for others. The evaluation then ends up involving innumerable questions and sections on a great range of topics. The result is a little bit of information about everything and not much of substance about anything. The root of the problem is often with the program's lack of clarity and specificity in defining goals. The evaluation process, rather than condoning this approach, can be used to raise questions: what are the key goals and how exactly will the program provide experiences which will help participants achieve their goals? There must be a clear vision of the program before one can identify the options for evaluation.

A final issue is the recognition that good work takes time. One needs to assess the extent of what a program can achieve in terms of the time, energy, and resources available. A small, well-implemented project, in which information is carefully analyzed and cycled back into programming, can start a positive spiral by involving staff in the process and creating opportunities for further work. However, intensive evaluation strategies which may seem exciting in their initial stages, can reinforce negative attitudes if the initial enthusiasm falls off and there are not the time and resources to carry the project through to completion. In short, one needs to be realistic about what can be accomplished and creative about tapping additional resources. The critical issue when pulling in external resources is to ensure that the people who will be using the information maintain involvement and control over what will be done and how the evaluation will be conducted.

The priorities for effective evaluation will not be achieved in the short term. It is a major challenge to integrate action and reflection, focus on the process, emphasize the quality of the experience, problem solve with multiple strategies, and learn from the consequences. The psychological and structural obstacles are substantial and there are no quick and easy answers. Practitioners' strong faith in their practices, and sense of helplessness with respect to research, are attitudes embedded in who they are as people. The organizational pressures and reward structures which inhibit quality work are rooted in institutions that are often beyond the control of experiential educators. However, as more practitioners and researchers work to put the ideas into practice at the local level, the discipline will be strengthening its evaluation and research base, and the process of change will gain momentum. It is a major challenge, but that is a key ingredient at the start of the experiential learning cycle.

References

Abelson, R. (1972). Are attitudes necessary? In B. T. King and E. McGinnes (Eds.), *Attitudes, conflict, and social change.* New York, NY: Academic Press.

Beringer, A. (1990). Understanding moral development and environmental values through experience. *Journal of Experiential Education, 13*(3), 29–34.

Braverman, M., Brenner, J., Fretz, P., and Desmond, D. (1990). Three approaches to evaluation: A ropes course illustration. *Journal of Experiential Education, 13*(1), 23–30.

Brookfield, S. (1996). Experiential pedagogy: Grounding teaching in students' learning. *Journal of Experiential Education, 19*(2), 62–68.

Carney, T. F. (1972). *Content analysis: A Technique for systematic inference from communications.* Winnipeg, Manitoba: University of Manitoba Press.

Cason, D., and Gillis, H. L. (1994). A meta-analysis of outdoor adventure programming with adolescents. *Journal of Experiential Education, 17*(1), 40–47.

Conrad, D. (1979). *Experiential education: A summary of the theoretical foundations and a critical review of recent research.* St. Paul, Minnesota: Center for Youth Research and Development, University of Minnesota.

Conrad, D., and Hedin, D. (1981). National assessment of experiential education: Summary and implications. *Journal of Experiential Education, 4*(2), 6–20.

Davis-Berman, J., and Berman, D. (1996). Using the wilderness to facilitate adjustment to college: An updated description of wilderness orientation programs. *Journal of Experiential Education, 19*(1), 22–28.

Davis-Berman, J., Berman, D., and Capone, L. (1994). Therapeutic wilderness programs: A national survey. *Journal of Experiential Education, 17*(2), 49–53.

Delay, R. (1996). Forming knowledge: Constructivist learning and experiential education. *Journal of Experiential Education, 19*(2), 76–81.

Doherty, K. (1995). A quantitative analysis of three teaching styles. *Journal of Experiential Education, 18*(1), 12–19.

Drebing, C. E., Willis, S. C., and Genet, B. (1987). Anxiety and the outward bound process. *Journal of Experiential Education, 10*(2), 17–21.

Ewert, A. (1983). *Outdoor adventure and self-concept: A research analysis.* Eugene, OR: Center of Leisure Studies, University of Oregon.

Ewert, A. (1995). Research in experiential education: An overview. In R. J. Kraft and J. Kielsmeier (Eds.), *Experiential learning in schools and higher education.* Boulder, Colorado: Association for Experiential Education.

Gass, M. A., and McPhee, P. J. (1990). Emerging from recovery: A descriptive analysis of adventure therapy for substance abusers. *Journal of Experiential Education, 13*(2), 29–35.

Goetz, J. P., and LeCompt, M. D. (1984). *Ethnography and qualitative design in educational research.* Orlando, FL: Academic Press.

Gordon, R. (1994). Keeping students at the center: Portfolio assessment at the college level. *Journal of Experiential Education, 17*(1), 23–27.

Gray, S., and Yerkes, R. (1995). Documenting clinical events in adventure therapy. *Journal of Experiential Education, 18*(2), 95–101.

Grant, T. (1996–97). Youth in action: Tipping the legislative balance. *Green Teacher, 50,* p. 13.

Guba, E. G., and Lincoln, Y. S. (1985). *Naturalistic inquiry.* Beverly Hills, CA: Sage.

Hale, A. (1990). *Annual review—1989: National safety network.* Belfontaine, OH: National Safety Network.

Hamilton, S. (1979). *Evaluating experiential learning programs.* Paper presented at the Annual Meeting of the American Educational Research Association.

Hamm, M., and Evans, D. (1992). Portfolios: A valuable tool for reflection and assessment. *Journal of Experiential Education, 15*(1), 48–50.

Henderson, K. A. (1993). The yin-yang of experiential education research. *Journal of Experiential Education, 16*(3), 49–54.

Heinrichsdorff, A. M. (1987). Course evaluations: Creating a self-fulfilling prophecy. *Journal of Experiential Education, 10*(2), 47–49.

Hutton-Durgin, C., and McEwen, D. (1991). Troubled young people after the adventure program: A case study. *Journal of Experiential Education, 14*(1), 31–35.

Kaufman, G. G., and Johnson, J. C. (1974). Scaling peer ratings: An examination of the differential validity of positive and negative nominations. *Journal of Applied Psychology, 59,* 302–306.

Kazdin, A. E. (1994). *Behavior modification in applied settings.* Toronto, Ontario: Brooks/Cole Publishing Company.

Kolb, D. (1991). Meaningful methods: Evaluation without the crunch. *Journal of Experiential Education, 14*(1), 40–44.

McCabe, B. A., and Harris, B. (1979). *Keeping the flame alive: The role of follow-up in therapeutic adventure programming*. Paper presented at the Annual Conference of the Association for Experiential Education, Portsmouth, New Hampshire.

Mitten, D., and Dutton, R. (1993). Outdoor leadership considerations with women survivors of sexual abuse. *Journal of Experiential Education, 16*(1), 7–13.

Phipps, M., and Claxton, D. B. (1997). An investigation into instructor effectiveness. *Journal of Experiential Education, 20*(1), 40–46.

Priest, S. (1995). The effect of belaying and belayer type on development of interpersonal partnership trust in rock climbing. *Journal of Experiential Education, 18*(2), 107–109.

Priest, S., and Gass, M. A. (1997). An examination of "problem-solving" versus "solution-focused" facilitation styles in a corporate setting. *Journal of Experiential Education, 20*(1), 34–39.

Priest, S., Attarian, A., and Schubert, S. (1993). Conducting research in experience-based training and development programs: Pass keys to locked doors. *Journal of Experiential Education, 16*(2), 11–20.

Raffan, J., and Barrett, M. J. (1989). Sharing the path: Reflections on journals from an expedition. *Journal of Experiential Education, 12*(2), 29–36.

Rappaport, J. (1977). *Community psychology*. Toronto, Ontario: Holt, Rinehart, and Winston.

Rosenthal, R., and Jacobson, L. (1968). *Pygmalion in the classroom*. New York, NY: Rinehart & Winston.

Ross, R., and McKay, H. B. (1976). Adolescent therapists. *Canada's Mental Health, 24*, 15–17.

Rowley, J. (1987). Adventure education and qualitative research. *Journal of Experiential Education, 10*(2), 8–12.

Shore, A. (1978). *Outward Bound: A reference volume*. Greenwich, CT: Outward Bound, Inc.

Smith, M. L., and Glass, G. V. (1987). *Research and evaluation in education and the social sciences*. Englewood Cliffs, NJ: Prentice-Hall, Inc.

Warner, A. (1984a). How to creatively evaluate programs. *Journal of Experiential Education, 7*(2), 38–43.

Warner, A. (1984b). Using initiative games to assess group cooperation. *Journal of Experiential Education, 7*(1), 42–43.

Wiggins, J. S. (1973). *Personality and prediction: Principles of personality assessment*. Don Mills, Ontario: Addison Wesley.

Yalom, I. (1985). *The theory and practice of group psychotherapy* (3rd ed.). New York, NY: Basic Books.

Chapter 41

Research in Adventure Programming

Simon Priest
eXperientia

In the late 1970s, Endeavour Enterprise (not a real name) was generally acknowledged by many professionals as an effective and innovative adventure program. Sponsored by its local government and funded by tax dollars, EE received court referred young people, who were at risk of imprisonment if they continued their present actions. Over two decades, EE changed the lives of countless youth and put them on the road to becoming productive members of society.

In the early 1990s, financial cutbacks brought an end to this top-rated program. Despite numerous protests from the staff and participants of EE, the powers that be cancelled this program and refused to fund any similar programs that provided wilderness "holidays for criminals." While EE claimed to make an important difference, and many experts agreed it did, EE could not present evidence of its impact. It could not prove that its recidivism rate was lower than other programs or that its program cost less than prison and other treatment alternatives.

The very real program described here had not bothered to conduct any program research or evaluation and so, like many others, suffered a very real end to its prosperity. Toward the turn of the century, increasing numbers of pro-grams are being terminated around the world due to funding cutbacks. A main reason for their inability to defend their end, can be traced to a disturbing lack of *inquiry* (research or evaluation) conducted by the profession. Adventure programming has failed to create a unique body of knowledge (one criterion for any profession). Therefore, the adventure programming profession sits on the fringe, unable to claim that it does much good. More research is needed to demonstrate effectiveness and establish credibility. More evaluation is needed to reform practice and enhance methodology. *Research* can *prove* how and why adventure works and *evaluation* can *improve* the way programming works.

Paradigms

While research proves and evaluation improves, these two forms of inquiry are conducted by people working under a set of philosophical beliefs called *paradigms* or worldviews of truth and understanding. A paradigm is a representative model of how one perceives reality, how one interprets the complexities of knowledge, and how this collection of philosophical assumptions about reality in turn influence how one seeks to acquire knowledge. In research and evaluation, a pair of paradigms prevail: positivism and naturalism (Klint, 1988). The positivistic paradigm also goes by the name of the scientific, reductional, or rationalistic paradigm. The naturalistic paradigm also goes by the names of the interpretive, phenomenological, or holistic paradigm. Their principle differences are summarized in Table 41.1 (after Klint, 1988). Each paradigm holds unique philosophical assumptions about the nature of reality (ontology), the nature of values (axiology), the nature of causality (attribution), and the nature of knowledge (epistemology).

People who prefer *positivism* are primarily interested in description, explanation, prediction, control, and verification of cause and effect relationships. They contend that knowledge is cumulative, and that experimentation is the ideal method of gaining that knowledge. Positivists believe in a single objective reality and, although people may perceive reality differently, they all perceive from the same base of reality. They presuppose that this single reality can be discovered by breaking it down into its constituent parts, independently studying these pieces and assuming that the whole is simply the sum of its parts.

People who prefer *naturalism* are primarily interested in revelation and comprehension of meaning within the actual context of the situation being studied and without

Table 41.1   Comparative Table of Inquiry Paradigms

Characteristic	Positivistic Paradigm	Naturalistic Paradigm
Other names	Scientific, reductional, rationalistic.	Interpretive, phenomenological, holistic.
Main purposes	Description, explanation, prediction, control, and verification of causality.	Revelation, creation, comprehension, and construction of meaning within context.
Attribution (the nature of causality)	Cause and effect relationships.	Causality *cannot* explain outcomes.
Ontology (the nature of reality)	Knowledge is cumulative. Single objective reality with different perceptions of the same base of reality. Single reality can be broken down into parts and a whole is simply the sum of its parts.	Reality *cannot* be fully known. Multiple realities are subjectively constructed or created. Reality comes from the arrangement of data into meaningful patterns and reality doesn't exist until perceived so. Synergy: whole is greater than parts.
Axiology (the nature of values)	Unbiased and value-free, objective, outcomes protected from influence.	Bias laden and value bound, subjective, outcomes impacted by inquirer's choices.
Epistemology (the nature of knowledge)	Inquirer is kept separate from knowledge.	Inquirer is entwined with knowledge.
Outcomes	Nomothetic and generalized by researcher, removed from context as much as possible, and presented as statistical tables.	Ideographic and transferred by reader, bound by societal or cultural contexts, and presented in thick rich description.
Preferred methods	Usually *quantitative* (before qualitative) rigorous fixed methods of predetermined hypothesis verification, manipulation and control of variables, and generalizations.	Usually *qualitative* (before quantitative) evolving flexible methods of working hypotheses, emergent designs, transfer left to the reader and subject-negotiated.
Sampling choices	Ideally (but not typically) random.	Typically purposeful and nonrandom.
Trustworthiness	Internal validity, external validity, reliability, and objectivity.	Credibility, transferability, dependability, and confirmability.

causality. They contend that reality cannot be fully known and that reality must be either constructed or created. Naturalists believe in multiple realities, since an infinite number of realities can be constructed or created. They presuppose that these multiple realities are synergistic (so summing parts alone will not bring understanding of the whole), therefore reality comes from the arrangement of persons, objects, or events into meaningful patterns and reality doesn't exist until it is perceived as such.

Inquiry guided by the positivistic paradigm is characterized by predetermined hypothesis verification, manipulation of variables, objectivity, and generalizations. Positivistic inquiry results in *nomothetic* knowledge (universal statements and general laws or theories). Understanding of phenomena comes through rigorous fixed methods. Positivistic research and evaluation attempt to be unbiased and value free. Positivists pride themselves in being objective about their inquiry, so as not to influence the results or methods by societal, cultural or personal norms. Outcomes are removed from their context as much as possible. This permits results to be generalized from one situation to another (a main purpose of positivism) by the producer of the study.

Inquiry guided by the naturalistic paradigm includes creation of working hypotheses, emergent designs, subjectivity, and reader-responsible transfer of knowledge. Naturalistic inquiry generates *ideographic* knowledge (a collection of characteristics, events or elements that represent reality in context). Understanding of phenomena comes through evolving flexible methods with an initial general question rather than a specific testable hypothesis. Naturalistic research and evaluation admit to being bias laden and value bound. Naturalists pride themselves in being subjective about their inquiry and so acknowledge that all aspects of a study design have been impacted by their personal values. Outcomes are bound by the societal or cultural context of the study (so cannot be generalized). Instead, transfer to congruent contexts that share familiar elements with the original study is left up to the reader or consumer of the study.

Historically, positivism has been the most followed inquiry paradigm in the profession of adventure programming and its many related disciplines. Today, research and evaluation are still mostly conducted under the constraints of the scientific method: formulate, design, test, verify and generalize from a predetermined hypothesis. However, naturalism has gained a substantial following and acceptance in the literature in recent years. Since exercising control over social interactions is very difficult under the scientific method, this most common paradigm has some serious shortcomings. The positivistic constraints have failed to address the complex web of human relationships common to adventure programming. Naturalistic inquiry is more congruent with the humanistic and holistic contexts of adventure programming than positivistic inquiry.

Therefore, naturalism may prove to be increasingly useful in future research and evaluation.

Methods

Since choice of inquiry paradigm is based on personal philosophy, people with different orientations tend to ask different kinds of questions and seek answers by different methods. Some paradigms are predisposed, but not sworn, to particular methods. Positivists tend to ask questions that are fixed in theory and are answered by *quantitative* methods (involving statistical analysis of numerical amounts or proportions). Naturalists tend to ask questions that are flexible in nature and are answered by *qualitative* methods (involving a description of patterns in distinguishing characteristics or feelings). However, both methods may be used under either paradigm.

With quantitative methods, data are typically collected by a questionnaire or similar survey instrument. Subjects respond to it by answering questions, circling numbers, shading in boxes or marking continuous lines. Their responses are assigned numerical values and then subjected to statistical analyses (usually by computer). The test outcomes tell the inquirer whether or not the findings are significant (the certainty that results are due to causality and not by chance). The outcomes are presented in tabular form with stated limits of probability and generalization.

With qualitative methods, data are typically collected by the inquirer observing and/or interviewing the subjects. Detailed field notes on what is observed, heard or experienced, and comments on surveys or writings in journals, provide sources of qualitative data. The inquirer looks for patterns of similarities or differences in these data, and interprets the meaning of those patterns in relation to the context of the study by using his or her personal intellect and insight. The outcomes are presented in thick, rich descriptive language that vicariously puts readers in the heart of the actual situation and gives them the responsibility of interpretation and transferability.

Inquiry question determines the choice of methodology, rather than paradigm preference (Klint and Priest, 1987). Always associating quantitative methods with positivism and qualitative methods with naturalism is a clear mistake (although this pairing is much more common than the alternative arrangement). For example, a positivist believes in causality and so asks the inquiry question: "What causes the development of self-concept?" In an attempt to answer this question, the positivist controls instructor type, teaching style and other leadership variables; and manipulates the participation duration, adventure activities and other program variables. Then the positivist measures self-concept before and after the adventure program with a quantitative survey which serves to remove the objective positivist from impacting the study. If manipulation of program variables always leads to increased self-concept under controlled situations, then the positivist may conclude causality. The more rigorous the methods (random sampling and counterbalanced or time series designs), then the more generalizable the outcomes will be.

As an alternate example, a naturalist believes in multiple and simultaneous realities, making causality impossible to accept, and so asks the inquiry question: "What interacts with self-concept?" In an attempt to answer this question, the naturalist spends many long days observing individuals (as one of the group) in a month-long adventure program. The naturalist becomes the qualitative instrument of inquiry bound by the culture being studied. After the initial observation, the naturalist deliberately interviews a couple of people on the basis of their extremely varied shifts in self-concept (both positive and negative). If reoccurring patterns can be identified during data analysis, then the naturalist can identify the self-concept connections. The naturalist presents these outcomes in thick and rich detail which describes the study situation in a way that the reader can personally identify with and thus apply to his or her own situation. The more rigorous the methods (purposeful sampling and multiple methods), then the more transferable the outcomes will be.

In both cases, the assumptions underlying the questions determined the choice of methods for answering. Belief in causality led the positivist to ask about and measure cause. Choice of measurement was likely to be more quantitative than qualitative, since the precision and rigor of quantitative measures fit better with the causal design of a positivistic experiment. Belief in multiple realities led the naturalist to ask about and explore patterns of connection. Choice of measurement was destined to be more qualitative than quantitative, since the freedom and flexibility of qualitative measures fit better with the emerging design of a naturalistic study.

Trustworthiness

No inquiry can be perfect. All research and evaluation will have some flaws in substance. As inquiry has become more scholarly over the centuries, academics have developed quality control criteria (referred to here as *trustworthiness* measures). Four criteria exist for positivistic inquiry: internal validity, external validity, reliability, and objectivity (Borg and Gall, 1983). Generally, positivists must demonstrate that their study has satisfied these four trustworthiness criteria. *Internal validity* addresses the treatment, control or manipulation inside the study—were the results due to some other intervening, confounding or extraneous variables not accounted for by the inquiry design? *External validity* addresses the extent to which the outcomes gained through inquiry can be applied outside the study to other situations—how far can the results be generalized? *Reliability* addresses the stability, predictability, and dependability of the outcomes—if the study was repeated, would the results consistently be the same? *Objectivity* addresses whether personal biases influenced the outcomes—did the inquirer's values confound the results in any way? Techniques such as the use of control variables, random sampling, and calibrated instrumentation have helped to ensure that these threats to the integrity of the positivistic inquiry are minimized.

The trustworthiness situation for naturalistic inquiry is somewhat different. Many experts believe that naturalism should undergo the same criteria as positivism. Some think that naturalism is beyond such quality control issues (since it has inherent quality and should not be bound by a positivistic need to measure quality). Most think that naturalistic inquiry should have its own set of trustworthiness measures: credibility, transferability, dependability, and confirmability (Lincoln, and Guba, 1985). *Credibility,* the counterpart to internal validity, addresses whether the outcomes identified are interpretable—does the knowledge and understanding gained from this inquiry form plausible and consistent descriptions of reality? *Transferability,* the counterpart to external validity, addresses the extent to which an outcome may be transferred to other situations— is the context described well enough so as to allow readers to apply the outcomes to similar situations? *Dependability,* the counterpart to reliability, addresses the extent to which the inquirer can be depended upon to measure a phenomenon—is the inquirer astute in perception and interpretation of the data? *Confirmability,* the counterpart to objectivity, addresses the extent to which the inquiry was neutral—did the inquirer acknowledge or account for personal bias in the perception and interpretation of the outcomes?

A naturalistic inquirer can use several approaches to establish the trustworthiness of outcomes. The naturalist collects information from a variety of sources, over a long period of time, and for lengthy episodes. This depth permits the naturalist to test different perspectives, to contrast emerging ideas with initial impressions, and to recognize dominant and atypical patterns. The naturalist also triangulates (cross-checks or verifies) information with peers (who analyze the data in parallel), the subjects themselves (to reaffirm their contributions), and outside experts (who act as devil's advocates). This breadth allows the naturalist to gauge emerging patterns against the external opinions of others and to identify bias, which permits a reexamination of data in light of the bias. The naturalist also keeps a journal with reactions and personal reflections that aids in the recognition of bias. This journal and the naturalist's field notes permit others to audit the trail of information followed during the inquiry and, through comparison of their own perceptions, to establish the study's dependability.

Statistics

Statistics are a tool of the quantitative inquirer. They are a body of tests or procedures used in the understanding, analysis and interpretation of data. *Data* are a collection of numerical information arranged into variables. A *variable* is a characteristic of interest to the inquirer, and which is free to vary or hold different *values*. For example, age (36.5 years), race finish (fourth), and gender (female), are all examples of variables (with values in parentheses).

Variables may be formatted as *interval* (continuous numbers having equal intervals) such as 490 and 78.21; *ordinal* (placed in rank order) such as first, second, and third; or *nominal* (named categories) such as hair color (redhead, blonde or brunette); and religion (Catholic, Protestant, Jewish, agnostic, or atheist). This data format is the first important concept used to select the correct test or procedure for data analysis.

Statistics have two principle branches: inferential and descriptive. *Inferential* statistics are used to generalize or infer from a sample to a population. *Descriptive* statistics are used to depict the frequencies of values for a single variable and to describe the central tendency (mean, median or mode), variability (range, variance or standard deviation), or normality (skewness, kurtosis or homogeneity) of that variable's distribution. *Normality* is the second important concept for choosing between two families of inferential statistics: parametric or nonparametric.

A frequency distribution of values for a single variable is normal, if that distribution fits within the model of a normal or bell-shaped curve. Variables with abnormal distributions that are kurtotic (too flat or too peaked) or skewed (tailing off to one side or the other) demand *nonparametric* procedures (tests that are free of distribution parameters or requirements). Variables with reasonably normal distributions that are not kurtotic (nicely rounded) and not skewed (equally shaped on both sides) have met normality assumptions and so may be analyzed by *parametric* procedures (tests with distribution parameters or limits).

Patterns

Qualitative data are analyzed very differently from the statistics used on numerical quantities. No hard or fast rules and few guidelines exist to govern qualitative data analysis, because each and every study is unique. Inquirers are encouraged to do their best to fairly represent the data and to choose whatever approach makes the most sense (Patton, 1990). Choices may be based on the reasons for conducting the study (generalizable research or program evaluation), the audiences reading the study (practitioner or academic), and the report formats used to communicate the study (formal or informal). Data come in several varied forms such as written comments on a survey, answers to interview questions, thoughts written in a journal, or actions observed in a group. The analysis process may begin with context setting, may be followed by pattern identification, and may end with outcomes interpretation.

Context setting describes the people, places and other data of the study. A picture is painted with sufficient thick and rich detail so that the reader becomes wrapped in the context of the study. This context forms a foundation for the readers to understand the inquirer's interpretation of the outcomes. It also sets the stage for the inquirer to organize the raw data and search for patterns.

For example, an interview may ask the same standard questions of a variety of people, or may ask varied questions of the same type of people. While other combinations of people or questions might be possible, these two arrangements make the best sense. The former design permits descriptions to be structured by standard question and for answers to be examined across people. The latter design allows for descriptions to be organized by people and for answers to be analyzed according to question topics. Both arrangements lead into the identification of patterns or commonalties in the data.

Pattern identification can follow a combination of at least three forms: content analyses, case analyses, and inductive analyses (Patton, 1990). Content analysis examines the actual words that form the data content. The transcripts of the data (collected from survey comments, written journals, tape-recorded interviews, or observation field notes) are read through carefully and any ideas, patterns, or themes which are noted by the inquirer are labeled directly onto the transcript. These predetermined labels act as indexing anchors for the later retrieval and merging of these common contents. Case analysis is used to identify these predetermined labels across cases studied. The example of interviews with standard questions or similar people are cases organized by question and person. These case analyses are followed by cross-case analyses over person and question respectively. Case and cross-case analysis together provide a double check for patterns, ideas, themes, and their repetition across more than one variable. In inductive analysis, the ideas, pattern and themes are not predetermined, but arise either from within the data (the subject's use existing labels) or the inquirer's early analysis of these data (the inquirer creates the labels).

Once patterns have been identified by one of these three forms, ongoing data analysis does not just look to confirm the ideas, but more so to find evidence of contradictions. If the study is being conducted under a naturalistic paradigm, and if these patterns arise within an emergent design, then data continue to be collected with a view to their use for invalidation of any evolving hypotheses. Both these seemingly negative tactics are necessary to corroborate the strength of the patterns.

Outcome interpretation aims to present the data and its patterns in a manner which permits the reader to replicate the inquirer's analysis and interpretation processes to reach similar, but not necessarily precisely the same, outcomes. Giving the reader this amount of freedom demands that descriptions of the data and its patterns be thick and rich within the context of the study. The inquirer decides what is meaningful, what should be included in the outcomes, how it should be interpreted and how best to present it. Presentations can range from telling stories one case at a time, through sharing composites from several cases, to using metaphors as a way to communicate parallels, analogies, and patterns within the data. All choices rest with the inquirer, but the inquirer must clearly detail the rationale behind how choices were made, so that readers have sufficient background to repeat the analysis and interpretation or make reasonable meaning of the inquiry.

Research and Evaluation

Whether positivistic or naturalistic, *research* literally means to look (or search) and look again (re-search) for understanding and knowledge. It is a *systematic* inquiry or investigation of a topic in search of knowledge or understanding and it is a repetitive quest for truth which follows a scientific process aimed at answering specific questions. These questions follow a sequence of inquiry shown in Figure 41.1 (where IT is the phenomenon being studied). When inquirers first encounter a new phenomenon, they begin to build a base of knowledge and understanding about IT. They start by describing the new occurrence: what does IT appear to be? Next, they move to the differentiation stage by determining what IT is similar to and different from. Then, they consider relationships (things associated with IT) and influence (things IT effects or is affected by). Finally, they attempt to regressively predict (will IT happen?) and experimentally control (can IT be made *not* to happen?) for the particular phenomenon. The key point being that "new looking" takes place atop "old looking." In other words, future inquiry is based on present knowledge and understanding, which is determined from past inquiry results (Priest, Attarian, and Schubert, 1993).

Consider earthquakes as the phenomenon of study. The first thing early scientists did *not* do, was to attempt prevention, since they lacked a sufficient base of experience with earthquakes to know how to proceed. Instead the scientists described and recorded earth-

quakes as a violent shaking of the ground with occasional cracking of its surface (Stage 1: description). Initially, earthquakes were compared and contrasted with volcanic eruptions (Stage 2: differentiation). Later, they were found to be associated with fault lines (Stage 3: relationships) and impacted by the stress of tectonic plate systems (Stage 4: influence). Today, with their body of truth, scientists are attempting to correctly predict earthquake occurrences (Stage 5: discrimination and regression). In the future, once a predictive equation has been established, then (and only then) will scientists attempt to gain control over and thus prevent earthquakes (Stage 6: experimentation and causality).

Unfortunately, this pattern of a sequential inquiry process is not being followed to the extent it should be in adventure programming. A fair descriptive base exists as to what programs are like, what they contain, and what happens during them. Some differentiation has taken place with aspects of adventure programs being compared or contrasted with contemporary educational and recreational offerings. However, very little of the middle stage inquiry

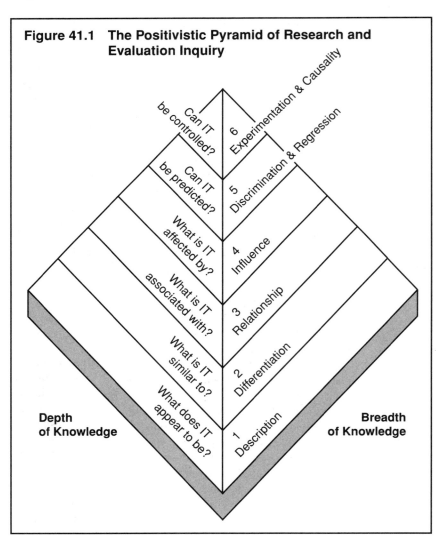

Figure 41.1   The Positivistic Pyramid of Research and Evaluation Inquiry

has been conducted on relationships and influences such as identifying precise parts of a program associated with specific human behaviors and vice versa. Instead, inquiry has jumped to the upper levels of predicting changes in human behavior and trying to "prove" the changes are the result of the adventure programming. These top efforts frequently crumble and fall down (due to poor design and lack of rigor) resulting from unsettled lower layers (a weak understanding and knowledge of previous inquiry on the very phenomenon being studied). Note that a naturalist would not necessarily follow this sequence for inquiry.

Several types of research exist (Isaac and Michael, 1983). Historical research reconstructs the past from primary (firsthand observations) and secondary (interpretations of the firsthand observations of others) data sources. Field research is a study conducted in a real situation (rather than a laboratory). Case research is a study of a single subject or group without comparisons or controls. Causal-comparative (or ex post facto) research is conducted after the fact in an attempt to determine the earlier cause of a past effect. Experimental research involves control groups which remain uninfluenced compared with experimental groups which are manipulated with varying treatments (Campbell and Stanley, 1966). Quasi-experimental refers to similar designs, but without the tight controls or careful manipulations of true experiments, since some circumstances are beyond the command of researchers such as nonrandom sampling (Cook and Campbell, 1979). Action research is aimed at solving problems where new solutions (obtained from the study) are put into action to change the problem during the study. Evaluative research is an assessment of usefulness and effectiveness (usually for making decisions about program maintenance).

Evaluation differs from research by its results not needing to be generalized beyond the program studied and not needing to be added to the professional body of knowledge. Therefore, evaluation does not require rigorous sampling, treatment, control, and measurement techniques as is common in other more stringent forms of research. Evaluation is concerned with documenting the worth of a program and improving its practice—finding a better way to provide a service to clients. As such, evaluation tends to focus on goals and objectives. The Association for Experiential Education's program accreditation process (measured against standard performance criteria) is an example of evaluation.

In summary, evaluation is an abbreviated form of *applied* rather than *basic* research. Applied research aims to solve a problem: its results are used to make modifications in a process. Basic research aims to discover new knowledge: its results are not necessarily useful (other than for its own sake). Evaluation aims to establish the merit of a program: its results are useful for making decisions rather than testing hypotheses. For example, a study on a corporate adventure program that examines the best way to de-

velop group trust would be applied research; a study on the nature of trust and how it develops in a group would be basic research; and a study on how well the program meets group needs for trust development would be evaluation.

Evaluation can be as easy as calculating participation frequencies (who was involved in a program and for how long), as moderate as surveying participant satisfaction (who had a good time and why did he or she enjoy himself or herself), or as complex as measuring participant achievement (who changed and what program components contributed to the alterations). The latter complexity is based on meeting the program goals and the client's objectives. The same quantitative and qualitative research techniques can be used in evaluations.

Future Directions

More inquiry is sorely needed to provide evidence that adventure programming is more than just fun and games, and to support it as the powerful form of change that practitioners tacitly know it to be. Specifically, several areas of study are necessary: examining the elements of adventure programming and the means by which these elements bring about change, transferring change to the client's real life and sustaining that change in the face of a contrary environment. In other words: what transfers, how much of it, for how long, and because of what program elements or barriers? Studies should examine these program elements: duration (one versus multiday programs), content (activity numbers, lengths, types, and debriefings), location (indoor or outdoor), setting (urban, rural or wilderness), follow-up (transfer strategies, reflection, and integration), clients (types, ideal numbers, and gender), and leadership (facilitation techniques, teaching styles, and genders).

With an understanding of the need and the methods of research and evaluation, outdoor leaders can contribute to its production and consumption. As *producers,* outdoor leaders can conduct projects or assist others with their studies. Learn how to be a researcher or an evaluator by taking a course in research or evaluation. Get help from university faculty and support the efforts of students doing studies in order to graduate. As *consumers,* outdoor leaders can read and critique existing published research and evaluation. When reading a study, check to see that the flow is logical and organized; that the intent of the study (purpose, questions or hypothesis) is connected to the outcomes (findings, discussion or conclusions); and that the study is easily understood (well-written, clear tables or reasonable recommendations). When critiquing a study ask two questions: does this make sense and could it apply to my program? The first question refers to validity and reliability—can the outcomes be explained by some other sensible option? The second question refers to generalizability—how are the outcomes and their context the same as, or different from, other adventure programs. Outdoor leaders don't have to be research and evaluation experts in order to examine and comment on such studies: common sense is often sufficient expertise.

Nevertheless, producers of research and evaluation are likely to encounter a few *difficulties* routine to inquiry into adventure programming. First, credible adventure programs operate under the ethic of *challenge-by-choice,* which means subjects will always be voluntary and sampling can never be truly random (people are ready to take risks). The consequential lack of skeptics and timid or fearful participants will limit the study's application to all people. Second, small groups of eight to twelve people, typical of adventure programming, means that distributions are more likely to be abnormal and require nonparametrics (distribution free tests). Nonparametric procedures are generally less well accepted than parametric statistics by scholars. Third, this sample size concern cannot be overcome by combining several groups with the exact same adventure, because truly effective programs customize the activities to best meet the clients needs. If the program gets modified to suit the study, then the program suffers; and if the reverse is done, then the study suffers. Fourth, obtaining clean control groups (those not engaged in a program) is extremely difficult, because the experimental groups (those involved with the adventure) can often "contaminate" the purity of the controls by sharing experiences outside the study. Since the best controls are selected from the same situation as the experimentals, one can expect them to interact at home, school, work, or play and thus change the way each other responds to instruments. Fifth, the phenomena studied in adventure programs are mostly human qualities and are not easily measured in a quantitative manner. Since few valid and reliable instruments exist, the use of qualitative methods to measure qualities appears most logical. Sixth, some adventure programs and their clients do not want to be studied, in case an inquirer discovers that they are ineffective in some way. Furthermore, research and evaluation can interfere with running a smooth program by interrupting processes or preventing people from concentrating. These six difficulties highlight the shortcomings of a positivistic approach and perhaps accent the advantages of a naturalist approach (Priest et al., 1993).

In addition, consumers of research and evaluation face an enormous gap between a producer's study and their comprehension of that study. One or two producers are unethical, a few are just ignorant and some are simply incompetent. The errors of a minority give a bad reputation to the majority. As a result, many consumers are reluctant to accept anything, although most consumers simply gobble up everything, unaware of the subtleties of inquiry, and eager for knowledge. This makes some credible inquirers reluctant to report outcomes from their study, for fear these will be exaggerated out of proportion. Education of producers

and consumers is the answer to bridging the gap and ethical inquiry is the place to begin.

Like outdoor leaders, researchers and evaluators have an *ethical code* to follow for inquiries. Ethical inquiry operates under challenge-by-choice just like adventure programming. In almost all cases (except those where deception or concealment are both justified and necessary), subjects must have the risks and responsibilities of the study explained to them verbally or in writing. Subjects should provide signed consent (verbal agreement to participate is acceptable in general public surveys, but not in experiments where subjects are assigned to treatment or control groups). Warning and informing prior to signature, ought to include the sponsoring institution, project title, inquirer's names and contacts, a description of the study, inherent risks, benefits expected and safeguards employed. Two rights of "only answering question subjects wish to" and "being able to withdraw from the study at any time without penalty" must be clearly communicated to all subjects. A copy of the results should be given to those subjects who request one. Guarantee of confidentiality must be made by stating that individual responses will not be named, but instead will be reported in aggregate or averaged forms. Real names will be changed to protect subjects and the names of organizations (clients or programs) will be withheld for reasons of anonymity.

Inquirers should resist the temptation to overgeneralize. Lack of random sampling techniques means that results cannot be generalized beyond the groups or individuals studied. Generalization is frequently delimited to a particular program or training treatment. The perfect study is rare, as most research or evaluation is limited and flawed to some extent. People who fail to acknowledge these flaws in their work are claiming credibility of research and evaluation which simply does not exist and may be willingly misrepresenting the authenticity of their studies.

The purpose of a peer review or refereeing process, prior to publication in scholarly or academic journals, is to draw attention to these possible flaws and to either improve marginal studies or prevent poor studies from getting published. Therefore, inquirers would be unwise to release research or evaluation in prepublication manuscript form to anyone other than producers of research and evaluation. The latter are assumed to have the abilities to discern flaws and limitations, while novice consumers of research and evaluation (such as practitioners or the media) may not have such competence.

These novice consumers can easily be lead astray by their hunger for data-based inquiry into adventure programming and by their lack of a theoretical inquiry background. They also run the risk of generalizing beyond the intent of the study. Treating the outcomes as gospel has the potential to harm the profession by incorrectly communicating results in the popular literature. To prevent this, inquirers have the ethical obligation to correctly interpret their work in order to make it understandable for the layperson. Last, if a study fails to find significant change, differences or relationships; this should never be interpreted as the fact that none ever existed! They simply were not detected in this instance.

References

Borg, W. R., and Gall, M. D. (1983). *Educational research: An introduction.* New York, NY: MacKay.

Campbell, D. T., and Stanley, J. C. (1966). *Experimental and quasi-experimental designs for research.* Chicago, IL: Rand McNally.

Cook, T. D., and Campbell, D. T. (1979). *Quasi-experimental design and analysis of issues for field setting.* Chicago, IL: Rand McNally.

Isaac, S., and Michael, W. B. (1983). *Handbook in research and evaluation.* San Diego, CA: EdITS.

Klint, K. A. (1988). *An analysis of the positivistic and naturalistic paradigms of inquiry.* Unpublished doctoral dissertation, University of Oregon, Eugene, Oregon.

Klint, K., and Priest, S. (1987). To thine own self be true: Points on naturalism and positivism (letter to the editor). *Journal of Experiential Education, 10*(3), 50–51.

Lincoln, Y. S., and Guba, E. G. (1985). *Naturalistic inquiry.* Beverly Hills, CA: Sage.

Patton, M. Q. (1990). *Qualitative evaluation methods.* Beverly Hills, CA: Sage.

Priest, S., Attarian, A., and Schubert, S. (1993). Conducting research in experience-based training and development programs: Pass keys to locked doors. *Journal of Experiential Education, 16*(2), 11–20.

Section 8

The Setting for Adventure Programming
Places for Risk Taking

Nature provided most of the settings for early attempts at adventure education. Kurt Hahn took his boys to sea. Outward Bound in America went to the mountains, lakes, deserts, and the seas. Adventure educators sought environments that contrasted to the normal settings of their clients. They sought places that would provide a break with the familiar, places that would add an ingredient of challenge and risk to the adventure. Adventure program participants came from a society dominated by a compelling passion for control of self, of others, and of nature. Control would bring comfort, safety and security. What places might offer less of these, might force the student to test and stretch his or her abilities and yield discoveries about self, society and nature?

One such place, as Miles points out, was and is wilderness. When wild places are accessible, adventure educators use them. After millennia of efforts to conquer nature and eliminate wilderness, people today seek its risks and uncertainties for the lessons to be learned there. Wild places are rare and fragile today. Miles suggests that educators must nurture, conserve, and even restore this resource of central value to them.

Contemporary society has such technological capability that many of the risks posed by nature in wilderness can be reduced or eliminated. Cellular phones, global positioning systems, and helicopters make rescue possible from the most remote locations. Wilderness areas are "managed" by bureaucrats who perceive one of their tasks to be the protection of visitors from themselves. How much protection, asks McAvoy, is too much? He offers a proposal for rescue-free wilderness areas. The very idea is anathema to land managers and many adventurers equipped with all of the latest technology, and is fraught with moral issues for adventure educators. The threat of overregulated, monitored, and policed wildlands, where achievement of challenges and self-reliance is difficult, is worthy of careful examination, and McAvoy's approach should stimulate careful consideration of the possibilities.

All adventure educators cannot, of course, transport their clients to natural wild areas. Most such places are in the rural American West, while most adventure education clients are in the urban East. Proudman argues that urban settings are good settings for developing programs for inner city youth. Curricula and learning models must and can be adapted to this setting. He contrasts the wilderness and urban settings and reviews the issues posed by efforts to use the latter. In this edition of this book, he adds a postscript to his essay after his Chicago program has ended. He remains a believer in the concept and does not retract his earlier advocacy, but he has "been there, done that" and has learned a few lessons in the process.

Adventure educators have sometimes also found it useful and necessary to create their own resources, including the settings for adventure activities. Attarian and Rohnke describe the principal directions this creation has taken. Climbing walls have been designed in various ways, pools and gyms have been used, and the ropes course (with less ropes and more cables than in a earlier time) has evolved into one of the most widely used "environments" for adventure programming. As adventure programs have proliferated and evolved, the ingenuity of practitioners has yielded new ideas for facilitating challenge, and Attarian and Rohnke offer an overview and perspective on the ever-growing constructed settings for adventure education.

Finally, Kiewa offers a reminder that ultimately the setting for all of this is the human body itself, and the body (or mind and body, for they are integrated) thrives on the kinesthetic experience that is involved in many adventure activities. These activities can remind people of the potential latent in their bodies and help them to "be at home" there. At a time when many are "alienated" from their bodies by advertising, lifestyle, and unrealistically idealized depictions of physical perfection, the kinesthetic awareness that can come from well-conceived adventure programming, argues Kiewa, has the potential to restore perspective on the physical self.

Chapter 42

Wilderness

John C. Miles
Western Washington University

Wilderness is a place where the processes of nature occur as they always have, where grizzly and wolf, golden eagle and great white shark stalk their prey, where such organisms live and die as they have since their creation. Trees grow there for a thousand years, and then fall over and rot, giving nutrients to the next generation. The sun rises and sets over land that changes, sometimes quickly, but usually slowly, constantly and according to the inexorable rhythms of nature. Rocks and boulders rattle and tumble off wilderness peaks. Winds pound and snows smother the uplands while heat shatters the rock of deserts, and flood undermines and fells the eagle tree. Individuals and species come and go and life triumphs in wild places. The river of time flows steadily, regularly, predictably.

Such is wilderness, a description of which is difficult without reference to human experience. In human terms, wilderness is "an area where the earth and its community of life are untrammeled by man, where man himself is a visitor who does not remain" (The Wilderness Act of 1964). Wilderness is an environment in which people can exercise less control than usual. When a storm descends on wilderness travelers, there is no climate-controlled retreat available. They must cope with the resources at hand. Predictability of experience is reduced by this lack of control—the wilderness traveler faces more unknowns than usual. Can these be handled? This element of uncertainty is always present in wilderness, and this ingredient prompted adventure educators to take their students there.

What qualifies a place to be considered a wilderness suitable for adventure? The pioneering ecologist and wilderness advocate Aldo Leopold once defined wilderness as a place where a person could take a two-week pack trip and not encounter the works of humans. That was in the early 1920s. By the late 1960s with roads in many places wild in Leopold's day, the U.S. government thought 5,000 acres a reasonable minimum size for an area to be included in the National Wilderness Preservation System. The size of the natural area is important only in terms of its effect on wilderness values like solitude, beauty and naturalness. An uninhabited island of 500 acres surrounded by hundreds of square miles of ocean could be as wild as a two-million acre tract in a remote part of Alaska.

Another set of qualifications for wilderness involve human experience of a place. Can the traveler find the physical and emotional challenge of the unknown there? In New Hampshire, two small boys pack their rucksacks and venture forth into woodlands in a place settled for over 300 years. They are small, the woods are big. They perceive their adventure as risky—wild animals out there in the dark, no parents to help them cope with fear, no McDonald's to tap for food supplies. They camp, in their minds, in a wilderness.

The point is that the wilderness used by adventure educators is both a physical and conceptual place. Wilderness is an idea, a state of mind. It is relative rather than an absolute conception and condition. People are arguing about whether grizzly bears should be reintroduced into the North Cascades of Washington state. "Do it," say some people. "The Pasayten will be really wild with them there." Others argue against the idea. "Grizzlies are too dangerous. The increased risk will reduce the recreational value of the place for me and for others. People will be frightened to go there." All the debaters like to travel to "wilderness." Some like more "wild" in their wilderness than others. Some, like adventure educators, desire an element of risk, of mystery and challenge in the places they go with their students. Other wilderness travelers seek a relatively safe environment where they can retreat from the cares of the world. This illustrates how people have come to variously define "wilderness."

Adventure educators take their students into the full range of wilderness places. They go where they can find the environments that challenge the students—onto rivers, into caves, over mountains, across deserts, through swamps and to lake and sea. They look for places that are physically difficult and demanding for travel, that present exacting but soluble problems, that give instantaneous reward for effort, that grant the opportunity for solitude, that allow immersion in the unfamiliar and the unknown with the anxiety that such produces. They seek places where the illusion of total human control of nature is banished, places that engage the whole person—mind, body and spirit—places that are pervaded by a sense of power, mystery and awe. They go where there is danger but where the danger can be assessed and managed. They help students convert danger, fear and anxiety into achievement and mastery through skill, cooperation and hard work. Many educators have found this combination of qualities and learning opportunities in wilderness.

Students go into wilderness and most come away changed. Their self-confidence is increased. Some who consider themselves failures come away with taste of personal success. New skills are learned and perspectives gained. Boundaries defining what is possible for them in various areas of their lives are moved, extending their visions of their personal potential. Most students in wilderness adventure education programs come away more physically challenged and fit than they have ever been before. Some have, for the first time, reflected on some of life's deeper issues. Has wilderness brought about these results? Not by itself. A combination of program and place have produced the results. The educator has designed the experience to take advantage of the qualities of the place that suit his or her purposes. No research has been done to determine how much the place contributes to the achievement of adventure education program objectives. There is no doubt, though, that certain learnings are made much more possible by the setting of wilderness.

Wilderness is a resource for adventure education and an increasingly scarce one. It is more scarce in some regions than others, and development is inexorably reduc-

ing the overall availability of this resource. As of 1998, the designated wilderness areas encompassed 104,571,334 acres or 4.52 percent of the land area in the United States. In the lower 48 contiguous states, wilderness occupies 2.39 percent of the land area (Landres and Meyer, 1999).

Many millions of wild acres in national forests, parks, wildlife refuges and rangelands are not officially part of the system. Struggles to assure preservation of more wilderness are under way, but every fight is difficult—the forces for development, road building, mining, logging, snowmobiling, off-road vehicle driving and tourism development are strong. The wilderness system in the United States may grow to 120 million acres. As this occurs, the total resource will shrink as development advances in unprotected areas.

On the surface the wilderness resource supply might look good—120 million acres is a lot of land. Unfortunately, wilderness is not evenly distributed. There is relatively little wilderness in the eastern United States. Many states have no designated wilderness (yet have most of the human population). Alaska has 56 million acres of official wilderness and California nearly six million. The majority of the National Wilderness Preservation System is too far from most people to be accessible to them. Thus, while four percent of the American land may become official wilderness with long-term protection from development, access and supply will become an increasing problem as population, recreational use, and adventure education programming grow.

The situation of wilderness worldwide is more difficult to adequately describe. Park and wilderness preservation began in the United States and progressed farthest here. Many nations around the world, even developing countries, have followed the United States' example by establishing national parks and preserves. Still, there is precious little wilderness, and what there is suffers the pressures of development and growing population. Biologist George Schaller traveled the Himalayan mountain range and found wildlife populations decimated everywhere by people desperate for food and cash. Even Antarctica, relatively inviolate until now, faces the juggernaut of oil and mineral exploration and development. There is, in short, little wilderness left on a planet inhabited by a rapidly growing population of more than five billion humans. The future promises continued shrinkage of the wilderness.

Adventure education is a relative latecomer in the widespread business of teaching and learning. Its emergence has, ironically, coincided with decline of the wilderness resource upon which it depends. This is not surprising since the reason people now program "adventure" is because it is no longer a normal part of life. Humans sought for millennia to subdue wilderness. That process was dangerous, uncomfortable, and often fatal. Now that wilderness seems to be conquered, humans miss the challenges the struggle provided. They recognize the values provided by that struggle, values not appreciated then and not now available in the normal course of life. So, in compensation, they venture forth in growing numbers in adventure sports and even program risk for their youth.

There can be no adventure education if there is no physical place for adventure. Thus it is incumbent upon educators who use wilderness to do all that they can to maintain and sustain this resource. Adventure educators must be advocates of wilderness. They must work for preservation of the tiny fraction of the world's surface that remains wild. Others are working to do this in political arenas. Enlightened self-interest requires adventure educators to join in that effort.

Secondly, adventure educators should program a proper wilderness use ethic into the experience of their students. Some programs currently do a better job of this than others. All programs must do this job well. Official wilderness has caretakers, but users cannot leave the wilderness maintenance job to official caretakers. There are too few of them to do the large job. Educational programs using wilderness must train all of their leaders in minimum-impact technique and teach them to effectively teach this technique. All programs must embrace an ethic of service which has them working to mitigate the inevitable impact they have when they use wildlands, no matter how hard they work to minimize their impact. Damage to wilderness, as to all environments, is incremental—a little here and there, which over time adds up to destruction of the values of beauty and solitude, naturalness and mystery that make such places useful to educators.

Valuable lessons useful in life's larger context are learned in adventure education. Some of these lessons can and should be about the human species' relationship to and its dependence upon, nature. Students, most of whom will come from urban backgrounds, can learn to see nature in new ways, to appreciate how complex, beautiful and organized it is. Awareness that they, as humans, are nature bound by ecological constraints, can grow. Humility in the face of grand space and time can give perspective on human enterprise. Human control of nature can perhaps be seen for what it is—an illusion. All of these lessons can help the students understand themselves as humans, as members of the biotic community. Perhaps they can even begin to grasp their

special responsibilities as human beings which derive from their understanding of how nature works. Humans are, as far as they know, the only organisms who are conscious of the process of evolution and can make decisions accordingly. They may come to see this gift of knowledge as a burden and an opportunity but will not be able to escape it. Thus, their wilderness education can be an introduction to planetary citizenship.

Some may respond that this is expecting a lot of an usually short educational experience confined by specific goals and learning processes, and it is. Yet a visit to wilderness is a rare gift and the most must be made of the opportunity the visit provides. Wilderness travel is to outdoor experience what a symphony is to music—the ultimate opportunity to encounter the depth and scope of the medium. Aldo Leopold, as a pioneering thinker on wilderness and ecology, thought integrity, stability and beauty were the ultimate values of the natural world. These qualities can be experienced and understood in wilderness settings.

When a person goes to wilderness often, as most adventure educators do, there is temptation to become complacent and blasé about the place, to take it for granted and think it commonplace. Wilderness is rare and valuable in the modern world. The educator who uses wilderness should treat it like he or she would an ancient and rare book—with great awe and care and affection. Much can be learned from the book, but only by those who study it carefully and patiently. And even as educators should treat a rare book, gently and cautiously with careful attention to its fragility and for its longevity, so must they treat wilderness. Only then will they assure that future generations of wilderness educators and students will be able to take lessons from the wilderness.

References

Landres, P., and Meyer, S. (1999). *A national wilderness preservation system database: Key attributes and trends, 1964–1998* [On-line]. Available: www.wilderness.net/nwps/

The Wilderness Act of 1964. (16 U.S.C. 1131 et seq.: 78 Stat. 890).

Chapter 43

Rescue-Free Wilderness Areas

Leo McAvoy
University of Minnesota

A challenge environment is often listed as one of the necessary experiential components in adventure education programs (McAvoy, 1987). Although challenging environments can be found in school and urban settings, many adventure programs have traditionally utilized the more remote, undeveloped outdoor recreation resources found in national parks, national forests, and in designated wilderness areas. These adventure programs use wilderness areas because of the opportunities there to have participants experience the beauty and grandeur of nature, and also because of the risk, challenge and opportunity for self-sufficiency that the wilderness provides. But some fear that opportunities to experience risk are diminishing in these times of heavy wilderness use and the tendency of wilderness managing agencies (e.g., National Park Service) to assume responsibility for user safety. Will there be opportunities in the future for adventure education programs to utilize wilderness for risk and challenge if current trends in wilderness management continue?

In a 1981 issue of the *Journal of Forestry,* a colleague and I introduced the idea of rescue-free wilderness areas in which recreationists would have an opportunity for complete self-sufficiency (McAvoy and Dustin, 1981). We proposed that rescue-free zones be established in some existing remote wilderness areas. In these zones the wilderness users would be completely responsible for their own safety. The government agencies managing these rescue-free zones would be absolved, indeed prohibited, from con-ducting or sponsoring any search and rescue operations for wilderness users in the area. The managing agency would be responsible for informing the users of the principle risks in the area and informing visitors that no governmental rescue services would be available for a recreationist there. Otherwise the rescue-free zone would be managed like most other wilderness areas; there would be a user quota system to keep the number of visitors low to protect the resource and the wilderness experience, no motorized vehicles would be allowed, and no signs or trails or bridges would be maintained. The visitors to these rescue-free areas could experience the self-growth that comes from the challenge of testing themselves and taking full responsibility for their actions (McAvoy and Dustin, 1983). The following is a rationale for rescue-free wilderness and how such areas relate to the goals and practices of adventure education.

Philosophical Basis for Rescue-Free Areas

Wilderness is usually regarded as a block of land. The Wilderness Act of 1964 legally defines certain blocks of land as being wilderness. There are now over 100 million acres of officially designated wilderness in the National Wilderness Preservation System (NWPS) in this country, with more being proposed.

Wilderness is also an experience, and it is the opportunity for that experience that attracts visitors to wilderness. If the experience opportunities were gone there would likely be no wilderness areas today. Our cultural perception of wilderness has many dimensions (Nash, 1982). It is a place to experience beauty, serenity, primeval forces of nature, undeveloped places, primitive and unconfined recreation, historical significance, and a place of scientific wonder. It is also a place to experience freedom, solitude, challenge, risk, and self-reliance. It is these last few experiences (challenge, risk, and self-reliance) that some believe we are in danger of losing.

Our cultural value of, and need for, wilderness was articulated in the mid 1800s by the transcendentalist philosopher and author Henry David Thoreau. In 1851 he ended a lecture by stating that in wildness is the preservation of the world (Nash, 1982). Those were radical words for a country that was trying to create a civilization out of a vast wilderness. Over the years since 1851, our society has held that there is more to the preservation of the world than wildness. Yet, we as a society have also decided that wildness is one of the aspects of this world we want to preserve. And, we have done so in our 100-million acres of designated wilderness areas. The question is, are we allowing that wildness to slip away?

Early visionaries of a national wilderness system argued that risk and self-reliance were vital parts of the wilderness experience and should be preserved. Bob Marshall, the founder of the Wilderness Society, wrote in the 1930s that wilderness should provide opportunities for complete self-sufficiency (Marshall, 1930). More recently, others interpreting the 1964 Wilderness Act have argued that wilderness is a place where users are responsible for their own safety, where a physical and mental challenge to survive exists, and self-reliance reigns (Nash, 1982, 1985). Part of the definition of wilderness in the Wilderness Act states that it is a place that is untrammeled, which means uncontrolled or unrestrained. Wilderness is the uncontrolled, the uncontrolled is unpredictable and therefore potentially dangerous. The uncontrolled and unrestrained are important aspects of what wilderness is, or at least what it was intended to be by the shapers of the Wilderness Act of 1964.

Need for Rescue-Free Areas

The need for rescue-free wilderness zones centers around three issues: wilderness management agencies assuming responsibility for visitor safety; the development of "high-tech" equipment for wilderness use and rescue; and, the growth of an insurance mentality. Over the past 30 years, there has been an increase in wilderness management by federal agencies. This has been mainly to protect the integrity of the natural resources from the damage of overuse. In some wilderness areas, regulations have had to be imposed limiting use numbers and use types. More recently, management intrusion on the visitors has increased as part of the process of collecting fees for wilderness use. This wilderness management has also resulted in governmental agencies such as the park service and forest service assuming a growing amount of responsibility for the safety of the wilderness user. This is appropriate in most developed outdoor recreation resources, but some question the need to extend this safety net mentality to all wilderness areas.

Wilderness management is somewhat of an oxymoron. *Wilderness* implies freedom, the uncontrolled, risk, and self-reliance, while *management* implies control, restraint and security. There are still some remote wilderness areas where people can go to experience a feeling of complete self-reliance either because of the remoteness of the area or the current lack of agency use monitoring. But will these opportunities continue in the light of federal agencies moving further into wilderness management?

The continuing development of high-technology equipment is making the wilderness less than wild. Wilderness visitors enjoy the benefits of development in fabrics for lightweight tents, packs, and clothing and high-tech synthetic insulation for sleeping bags. These developments make wilderness accessible to almost anyone. The somewhat negative developments (for self-reliance purists) are the high-altitude all-weather helicopter, cellular and satellite phones, locator beacons (EPIRBS), global positioning systems (GPS), and computerized altimeters. Most wilderness users know all too well that should they be declared overdue, ill or injured, most wilderness is accessible in a few moments time for a helicopter rescue to fly them to the wonders of the modern hospital emergency room (Markoff, 1995). The availability of high-technology rescue equipment causes some individuals and groups to enter wilderness areas ill prepared to be self-sufficient because they know the governmental managing agencies will coordinate a rescue operation if needed (Johnson, 1993; Krakauer, 1996; Warren, 1993). This not only costs all of us money, but it often places rescuers in dangerous situations (Krakauer, 1997). There have even been cases of hikers and climbers calling the park service on their cell phones asking for a helicopter rescue, only to later reveal that they were late for a business appointment and needed a quick ride out of the wilderness.

A third phenomenon creating a need for rescue-free areas is a general insurance mentality in American society. Many people want to be protected from all risk. They want the benefits of high-adventure activities (personal growth, stimulation, enhanced awareness, self-fulfillment) but they want the potential costs to be borne by others, usually borne by the government (Aharoni, 1981). Persons with this insurance mentality want illusions of challenge, risk, and self-reliance but they want a governmentally sponsored safety net (Meier, 1993; Sax, 1980). And, they tend to believe that everyone else should share this insurance mentality.

Governmental wilderness managing agencies feed into and support this insurance mentality by placing visitor protection as an overriding top priority. An illustration of this trend is the approximately $3 million spent each year by U.S. governmental agencies in rescue operations in national parks (Egan, 1993). Also, the number of search and rescue operations per million visitors in the national parks has been rising. There were 12 such operations per million visitors in 1987 and 19.4 in 1991 (Meier, 1993). More people are searching for the thrills of wilderness, but then expecting the government to come searching for them if things go wrong. Well-meaning governmental managers have often extended the visitor safety policies that are necessary in developed parks to the wilderness, where such policies run counter to the purpose of wilderness.

Public discussion of these rescue-at-all-cost issues seems to follow a pattern. After a series of highly publicized accounts of expensive rescue operations in 1993, a series of articles addressed the rescue issue in major national media outlets (Egan, 1993; Johnson, 1993; Meier, 1993; Warren, 1993). Wilderness management agencies then tried, in some cases, to address the issue by proposing user fees to cover potential rescues, or to propose requiring rescue insurance for those engaged in risky activities like climbing (Egan, 1993). These strategies seem to still keep the emphasis on the managing agency being responsible for the well-being (rescue) of wilderness visitors. Perhaps it is time to approach the issue differently and put the responsibility solely on the wilderness visitor.

Experiential Benefits of Rescue-Free Areas

Rescue-free areas would preserve that rare opportunity for self-growth that wilderness can provide. They would provide opportunities for challenge, choice, and the personal testing of oneself at the edge of life (Miles, 1978; Schreyer, White, and McCool, 1978). But one cannot really approach the edge if one knows the edge is fenced with a rescue policy.

Risk, challenge, self-reliance, and complete self-sufficiency are legitimate experiences to be preserved in the American wilderness. Freedom and choice are highly valued in American culture. Rescue-free areas would extend that realm of choice. Rescue-free areas would not be forced on anyone. They would be available for those visitors who desired that type of experience. They would expand the range of choices available for wilderness users. They would be a few remote sections of existing wilderness areas where the visitor could experience complete self-sufficiency without the ultimate protection of a governmental agency standing by to rescue.

There will certainly be some injuries in rescue-free wilderness zones, and there may be deaths. But they will be rare. Visitors entering such an area would be better prepared and more careful than the average wilderness users because they would know they were responsible for their own safety and for the safety of those in their group. Ninety-nine point nine percent of visitors to rescue-free areas would return home from their wilderness outing intact, and infused with a new sense of confidence in their ability to take charge of their lives. They would have tested themselves at the edge of life successfully, much the way that sky divers and blue water ocean sailors do.

Worst Case Scenario

The following is a worst case scenario for a rescue-free area if such an area was established as part of the wilderness system. Let's assume that four friends want to visit a rescue-free zone and experience complete self-sufficiency. They receive all necessary information from the wilderness managing agency. They are advised that no governmental rescue will be available to them. They decide they want to assume responsibility for themselves, and so they go into the area. After a long trek into a climbing area they set up a base camp in a valley and survey the climbing opportunities. Early the next morning they start up a challenging face in two rope teams. Two members fall and are seriously injured. Neither is able to get off the mountain without assistance. The rescue-free policy would work as follows. First, the managing agency would not come looking for the party if it was declared overdue. If the uninjured members of the party came out seeking a rescue, there would be no governmental agency rescue personnel, equipment, or service available for that zone. The agency would be prohibited from organizing or sponsoring a rescue operation in the zone. This includes park service, forest service, military, or local governmental sponsored rescue. The party is entirely responsible for the welfare of its members.

Let's say in this case the uninjured party members decided to go out of the area and get friends to help in the rescue. Private citizens could go into the area to attempt a rescue. But they would have to abide by use rationing or quota restrictions on use currently in effect for the area. They would have to assume responsibility for themselves, because if they become injured the rescue-free concept would apply to them as well. They would also have to comply with other wilderness use policies such as no motorized vehicles. In the case of this scenario, the party members alone would be responsible for themselves. They must rely on their own resources. Once they decide for complete self-sufficiency, and enter the area they are on their own completely.

Response to Common Criticisms of Rescue-Free Areas

Criticisms of the rescue-free proposal have been characterized by an undercurrent of negativism (Allen, 1981; Williamson, 1984). The emphasis of these criticisms has been on what could go wrong in a rescue-free area rather than the positive aspects of what could go right. The negative visions of broken bodies lying unattended at the foot of the cliff and desperate pleas for help going unheeded, serve to swing attention away from the positive personal and group benefits and growth that would accrue to the overwhelming majority of visitors to rescue-free wilderness. But practicality dictates that a response must be made to such criticisms, even though the potential benefits far outweigh the potential personal and societal costs (in my opinion).

Some wilderness managing agency staff argue that rescue-free wilderness areas are impossible because agency policy dictates that search and rescue services will be available to all visitors. A rescue-free advocate answers this by simply saying the policy can be changed so those services are not available for certain zones. Also, wilderness management agencies are authorized to provide rescue services, but are not mandated to do so. It may take legislative action, executive direction, or agency policy shifts, but agency policies can be changed if enough citizens exert appropriate political pressures.

Another common criticism heard from managing agencies and others is the fear of legal liability. If a managing agency like the National Park Service or the U.S. Forest Service did not provide rescue service, couldn't it be successfully sued by either the injured party or the party's family? Legal scholars have researched this rescue-free concept and have decided that a managing agency that chose to not provide rescue would not be successfully sued by either an injured party or his or her family. In undeveloped wilderness areas, the duty of the managing agency is only to inform the prospective visitor of principle dangers and to inform the visitor that no rescue services would be available while in that area (Frakt and Rankin, 1982). The managing agency does not have the responsibility to guarantee absolute protection of a person in a remote wilderness area (Rankin, 1984).

In a case in Grand Teton National Park (Johnson v. U.S. Department of Interior, 1991), the park service was sued because it did not provide a rescue service in what the plaintiff claimed was a timely manner. This case concerned the death of a climber in the park. The court held that in national parks, rescue services are considered a discretionary function. The park service is authorized, but not mandated, to assist visitors in emergencies. The park service can decide on a case-by-case basis if, when, or how to initiate a search and rescue effort. This decision should be based on the park service's judgment in maintaining the park according to the broad statutory directive that established the park service. There are virtually no cases of successful litigation against managing agencies concerning injuries that have occurred in undeveloped wilderness areas. From the adventure program perspective, it would seem that adventure education agencies that sponsor trips to such areas would not have to fear liability problems if they have qualified staff, adequate supervision, inform participants of risks through informed consent procedures, and have appropriate group responses to handle emergency situations (McAvoy, Dustin, Rankin, and Frakt, 1985).

The legal question aside, many would argue that it would be ethically inexcusable for a managing agency like the National Park Service or U.S. Forest Service to refuse a request for search and rescue. The rescue-free advocate would counter by pointing out that it is ethically inexcusable for governmental officials to deny people the opportunity for self-determination. If we are going to give people an opportunity to grow through challenge and experiencing self-reliance then we must provide that type of wilderness experience. Opportunities for risk, challenge and complete self-sufficiency should be provided in the American wilderness system. We should respect the choice of those who would want to have and visit such a rescue-free area. We are a democracy that prides itself on respecting the rights and desires of the minority. Informal research indicates a significant minority who want to see rescue-free areas become a reality in our wilderness system.

Conclusion

A proposal for rescue-free wilderness is not a macho, extremist, "man against the wilderness" attempt to make the wilderness more dangerous than it already is. It is not a proposal championed by insensitive people. Rather, it is an attempt to preserve a few places to experience what wilderness was intended to be, the untrammeled experience full of opportunities for self-reliance, risk, challenge and self-growth. It would preserve in the American wilderness system legitimate opportunities for testing and expanding one's capabilities. This proposal does not ask that all wilderness be rescue free, only selected zones in existing remote wilderness areas. No one would ever be forced to go to a rescue-free wilderness zone, but it would be an opportunity for those who chose to go.

It is still possible to get a *de facto* rescue-free experience in little used wilderness areas. But if wilderness use and wilderness management continue on current trends, all wilderness areas in the future may be as heavily regulated, policed and monitored as some national parks are now. Risk, challenge, and self-reliance may not be available in the American wilderness of the future unless steps are taken now to preserve these experiences. Discussion of rescue-free areas would encourage wilderness managers to develop policies that encourage wilderness users to assume responsibility for their own safety.

The goals of adventure education programs and activities include personal testing, challenge and risk (Ewert, 1989). Adventure programs assist participants in developing physical, intellectual and emotional skills which allow them to test themselves at increasingly higher levels of difficulty. To complement this progression of challenge, skills, and personal development, participants should be given increasing amounts of freedom and responsibility to exercise their competence and self-sufficiency (Dustin, McAvoy, and Beck, 1986). Rescue-free wilderness areas appear to be a logical extension of this competency and self-sufficiency component of adventure education. Rescue-free areas may not be the best answer, but adventure educators must consider the role of self-reliance and risk in wilderness and how that can be preserved. If not through rescue-free areas, how?

References

Aharoni, Y. (1981). *The no-risk society.* Chatham, NJ: Chatham House.

Allen, S. (1981). Comment: No-rescue wilderness— A risky proposition. *Journal of Forestry, 79*(3), 153–154.

Dustin, D., McAvoy, L., and Beck, L. (1986). Promoting recreationist self-sufficiency. *Journal of Park and Recreation Administration, 4*(4), 43–52.

Egan, T. (1993). Two parks to require rescue insurance for climbers. *The New York Times,* September 14, p. A18.

Ewert, A. (1989). *Outdoor adventure pursuits: Foundations, models, and theories.* Columbus, OH: Publishing Horizons.

Frakt, A., and Rankin, J. (1982). *The law of parks, recreation resources and leisure services.* Salt Lake City, UT: Brighton Publishing.

Johnson, W. O. (1993, March 8). Snow business. *Sports Illustrated, 18,* 19–22.

Krakauer, J. (1996). *Into the wild.* New York, NY: Villard Books.

Krakauer, J. (1997). *Into thin air.* New York, NY: Villard Books.

Markoff, J. (1995). If you need a helicopter rescue, press 1. *Minneapolis Star/Tribune,* February 27, p. 4.

Marshall, R. (1930). The problem of wilderness. *Science Monthly, 30,* 141–148.

McAvoy, L. (1987). The experiential components of a high-adventure program. In J. F. Meier, T. W. Morash, and G. E. Welton (Eds.), *High-adventure outdoor pursuits.* Columbus, OH: Publishing Horizons.

McAvoy, L., and Dustin, D. (1981). The right to risk in wilderness. *Journal of Forestry, 79*(3), 150–152.

McAvoy, L., and Dustin, D. (1983). In search of balance: A no-rescue wilderness proposal. *Western Wildlands, 9*(2), 2–5.

McAvoy, L., Dustin, D., Rankin, J., and Frakt, A. (1985). Wilderness and legal-liability: Guidelines for resource managers and program leaders. *Journal of Park and Recreation Administration, 3*(1), 41–49.

Meier, B. (1993). With rescue costs growing, U.S. considers billing the rescued. *The New York Times,* March 28, p. 12Y.

Miles, J. (1978). The value of high-adventure activities. *Journal of Physical Education and Recreation, 49*(4), 27–28.

Nash, R. (1982). *Wilderness and the American mind.* New Haven, CT: Yale University Press.

Nash, R. (1985). Proceed at your own risk. *National Parks, 59*(1–2), 18–19.

Rankin, J. (1984). Land features, locality and liability in park injury cases. *Trends, 21*(3), 9–12.

Sax, J. (1980). *Mountains without handrails.* Ann Arbor, MI: University of Michigan Press.

Schreyer, R., White, R., and McCool, S. (1978). Common attributes uncommonly exercised. *Journal of Physical Education and Recreation, 49*(4), 36–38.

Warren, J. (1993). What if we ignored the SOS? *The Los Angeles Times,* November 30, pp. A1, A28–A30.

Williamson, J. (1984). You can always say no to a rescuer. *Backpacker, 12*(5), 60–63, 68, 69, 88, 92.

Chapter 44

Urban Adventure in 1989 and Reflections 10 Years After

Steve Proudman
The Proudman Group

The aim here is to challenge thinking and basic assumptions about what constitutes adventure education. Analysis begins with an examination of the problems and realities facing urban youth in American society and the potentials for adventure education of an urban environment. It is assumed that society's future economic, political, and social functions depend on successful transition into adulthood of today's youth. The focus is on urban youth, though many observations also apply to adults in urban settings.

The first section of this chapter explains the rationales for urban adventure programming in 1989. The city of Chicago will provide an example of the condition of urban youth. The second section explores the potentials for developing programs for inner city youth. The contemporary curricula, experiential learning models, and network utilization of the late 1980s will be discussed. The third section will examine some issues such as professional (adventure education) lifestyle conflicts, safety concerns, and cultural barriers inherent when operating in urban settings which emerged in the late 1980s. Finally, the fourth section will look back at these issues from the perspective of 1999.

Passow (1982), writing on urban education's trends and issues for the 1980s states that:

> cities constitute rich environments for educating individuals of all ages. The urban environment contains cultural, educational, social, economic, physical, and natural resources that influence the development of its inhabitants. Urban education, when it consists only of that which takes place at that site called "school," is clearly too limited and limiting.

Adventure education is presented here as offering potential for expansion of learning beyond conventional approaches in urban settings.

Why Urban Adventure Programming?

Risk taking is a principal component of any adventure education curriculum. These risks are perceptual and highly controlled in the design and delivery processes. In urban environments, risks are part of a youth's daily existence.

The 1980 census reports that 503,086 youth, aged 10–19, lived in the city of Chicago. Sixty-seven percent of these were Black and Latino (U.S. Census Report, 1980). In July 1986 the late Mayor Harold Washington established the Mayor's Youth Development Coordinating Committee (YDCC). Their function was to examine both the successful passage to adulthood and the problems unique to adolescents. In their reports they estimated that in 1987:

1. 75,000 youth would be seeking work, but would remain unemployed;
2. 50,000 youth would leave school before graduating;
3. 45,000 youth would be arrested by Chicago police;
4. 60,000 youth would have substance abuse problems; and
5. 15,000 female adolescents would become pregnant. (YDCC, 1987)

Additional statistics revealed the gravity of the problems facing Chicago youth:

1. It is estimated that one in three children in Chicago live in families with incomes below the national poverty levels ($10,609 for a family of four). More than half of these children in poverty grow up in single-parent, female-headed households (Testa and Lawler, 1985).
2. The Gang Crime Unit of the Chicago Police Department estimates that there are 120 street gangs in Chicago, with over 15,000 members. There are, on average, one to four gangs present in each Chicago public school. There were 14,000 active gang members arrested in 1986. Gangs are constantly recruiting members, providing safety and a sense of belonging to troubled youth (YDCC, 1987).
3. In 1985, 18.5 percent of all live births in Chicago were to teenagers. That translates to 10,222 babies (YDCC, 1987).
4. An estimated 10,000 youth are living on the streets of Chicago, nearly 4,000 of them pregnant and/or parenting teens. Many of these youth are victims of family violence, abuse, and neglect (Chicago Coalition of the Homeless, 1985).
5. Chicago was the most residentially segregated city in the nation in 1980. The Chicago public schools have the greatest level of Black-White student segregation of any city school system in the United States (Chicago Urban League, 1987).

The YDCC reported that the number of "at-risk" Chicago youth is growing. A generation of young people are lacking opportunities for positive experiences that will contribute to their transition to productive and contributing citizens of Chicago.

This state of affairs facing many urban youth should be seen as an impelling motivator and challenge to the adventure education profession. How can we better serve the needs of urban adolescents who might otherwise never benefit from our processes of learning? The answer may be to bring the program closer to their world by implementing adventure education in and around the city.

Today's youth are the caretakers of tomorrow's society. The future economic, political, and social success of American society depend on youth to develop the capacities they need for a successful transition into adulthood. Greenberger and Steinberg (1986) state that "rapid changes and multiple choices that currently characterize American society require adolescents to develop capacities that give them the flexibility and competence to meet demands that may change several times during their adult lives."

The Center for Youth Development at the University of Minnesota has done extensive research on youth needs in the developmental process. They state the following:

> Development of a sense of self is the critical foundation for the transition into adulthood. Youth need to feel significant, important and unique; experience others being affected by their actions and decisions; interact positively with others; have a sense of belonging; love and be loved, trust and be trusted, respect and be respected. They need to experience a range of emotions, including success and failure, in a supporting context.
>
> Moreover, youth need to develop a sense of engagement: experiment without irrevocable commitment; have opportunities to make contributions to their world; experience a range of cultures, classes, languages; engage in adventurous activities; experiment with ideas and behaviors; and engage themselves physically.
>
> Finally, youth need to develop critical choice: reflect on and discuss needs and feelings; deal with uncertainties and be challenged and excited by change; have the opportunity to discuss conflicting values while formulating their own; gain experience in decision making; know who can help in developing effective management of their affairs; develop the capacity for sustained, intense involvement in activities. (YDCC, 1987)

Present "school" experiences aim to prepare adolescents to become productive members of our materialistic society. They do not need a materialistic experience, but rather a humanistic or spiritual one. Through adventure education commonly held societal values are taught: persistence, perseverance, compassion for others, critical thinking skills, a sense of individual strengths and community interdependence. Urban adventure programming can provide a necessary balance of humanistic needs required for the holistic development of adolescents, complementing the functional skill orientation of conventional schooling.

The National Commission on Youth (1980) concludes that young people respond positively when given opportunities for meaningful participation in society. The capacities that youth develop are dependent on the opportunities available to them. Opportunities that come as direct experience contribute to the formation of concepts of self, of responsibility, to modes of thinking about moral-social problems, of interpersonal relationships, and to the capacity for feeling joy and empathy (Gilligan, 1982). Adventure education can help build these capacities.

Costello (1980) also identified four capacities that adolescents acquire, and adults need—and will continue to need—to function in society. These capacities are physical vitality, resourcefulness, social connectedness, and the ability to sustain caring relationships. In a report by the Chapin Hall Center for Children at the University of Chicago (Wynn, Richmond, Rubenstein, and Littell, 1987) these capacities are now fully described as follows:

1. Physical vitality: optimal health, energy, stamina, resistance, and resilience.
2. Resourcefulness: ability to act effectively to achieve objectives for oneself and others. Components include the possession of practical knowledge and skills (beyond streetwise), the ability to seek and sift information (critical thinking), to learn new things, and to apply knowledge and skills in effective action.
3. Social connectedness: sense an individual has of affiliation with a social community that validates his or her identity, provides supports and services, and requires contribution in return.
4. Ability to sustain caring relationships: capacity to give and accept care in return. Capacity for self-worth.

Outward Bound, as a leading organization in the adventure education field, has shown ways to nurture such capacities in people of all ages, but especially among youth. The philosophical foundations upon which Kurt Hahn created the first Outward Bound learning model in Gourdonstoun, Scotland, are physical fitness, self-reliance, craftsmanship, and compassion. In comparing these four tenets with those identified by contemporary youth experts, some interesting parallels emerge. Outward Bound's organized group experiences offer the following opportunities:

1. To participate in adventure activities, which are at times designed to be physically demanding. Through these experiences, physi-

cal vitality is enhanced as physical fitness is discovered.
2. To learn new skills: cognitive, kinesthetic, and social. By solving problems, working on technical competency, and working with others in cooperative relationships, a sense of craftsmanship and self-reliance are developed and resourcefulness is increased.
3. To participate in a group context with peers, toward the pursuit of common interests. A community of bonding results as group members learn to resolve conflicts, express feelings, care for and listen to others. This develops a sense of compassion in relating to others and enhances caring relationships and a sense of social connectedness.
4. For students to learn knowledge and skills that are directly transferable to their more accustomed "familiar" environments. With help from a community of supports a student's experience with adventure education programs can be validated and can have a significant meaning in their lives.

As professionals, adventure educators have an obligation to continue to explore the ways their methods and tools can have greater impacts on the growing problems in American society, particularly those confronting urban youth. The second section will explore some examples and possibilities.

Shifting Paradigms— Creating Urban Programs

To broaden the population of youth served by adventure education, programs need to be adapted to the realities of inner city youth. To be maximally effective and preventative in impact, programs need to be offered to youth aged 10 to 15. Youth are most vulnerable at this age. The pressures for choice are real, yet often the choices and support systems are limited. The challenge to the adventure education profession is to design programs that address the needs of this age group and that are accessible and attractive to them.

Urban adventure programs' views of the city resemble other adventure programs' view of their more traditional outdoor environments. Each environment becomes a dynamic classroom. The city and its multiple physical, natural, and human resources are the classrooms through which curricula are developed. Urban waterways can serve as corridors for adventures for learning natural history, architectural history, principles of ecology, or as a means to access and explore new neighborhood environments. Through a well-designed urban experience, students can explore new parts of their "hometown" and themselves in a highly interactive process.

Urban exploration in the form of a group road rally curriculum (Woodward, 1988, personal correspondence) can be designed to focus on personal growth and group process objectives. The personal growth objectives can include increasing self-esteem, self-awareness and self-assertion through using map and compass skills, using knowledge of the city, and by interviewing strangers. The group process objectives can include intimacy, mutuality, cooperation, cohesiveness, problem solving, and conflict resolution. The activities involved can be traveling in small groups to new and unknown places, using consensus decision making, experiencing limited cash resources for a day, or doing a several day service project.

Service learning is a worthy endeavor in and of itself and provides another approach to adventure education in the city. In an adventure-based curriculum its inclusion can serve as the cornerstone of a powerful and relevant experience for students. Lyn Baird, a past director of the National Center for Service Learning believes that:

> Only reality can prepare students to cope sensitively and compassionately with the real world. The process of service learning involves mutual risk and involvement. Through this process the realization that we need each other hits home. Seemingly opposite concepts—giving and getting, acting and reflecting, serving and learning—begin to emerge. (Baird, 1985)

From community service experiences students are confronted with values different from their own. Through this exposure comes a deeper understanding of themselves and their roles in society. As they discover their own sense of worth they learn about self-confidence, courage to risk, and self-reliance. The opportunities for growth can assist a young person's transition from dependent adolescence to responsible adulthood. In urban settings service learning opportunities abound. They are an essential experience to be included in a program design.

More traditional adventure activities such as rock climbing and a ropes course can provide a high-impact experience in a curriculum. Ropes courses and team challenge courses may already exist in an urban area. Through contractual arrangements these resources may be accessible. Natural climbing sites may be secure to nonexistent near an urban area. *Buildering*, the use of building structures for climbing activities, may be an option. Other possibilities might include indoor climbing walls and artificial climbing towers. A solid network of adventure educators in an urban locale may prompt greater utilization of existing resources and expand program outreach. However the components of a program's curriculum are

decided, they need to be consistent with the objectives of a selected learning model, not haphazardly or unconsciously conducted for recreational purposes.

Adventure education is an applied method of experiential learning. Pfeiffer and Jones (1973) describe an experiential education model that includes five steps:

Step 1: experiencing—involvement in the activity;

Step 2: publishing—sharing the reactions and information;

Step 3: processing—emergent dynamics are explored and discussed with other participants;

Step 4: generalizing—extracting generalizations from the experience; and

Step 5: applying—plan applications of principles derived from the experience in other settings. When this new learning is used and tested it becomes a new experience, closing the loop.

Beyond these components of a workable program, Meier, Morash, and Welton (1980) add several ingredients that add to the desirable effectiveness:

1. a moderate amount of stress,
2. group living,
3. success for the individual and the group,
4. a new environment, and
5. an individual experience separate from the group, as time for reflection and assimilation.

Urban programs that currently exist in the United States typically use these model elements in fashioning a model suited to their situation. Course lengths can vary from one day, to single or consecutive weekends, to one week. A new environment for an inner city youth may simply be going to a different neighborhood from his or her own, or it may be exploring a city, county or state park system. Finding a "solo" site may prove to be more difficult (churches have been used). The experiences that become the final adventure program should never be underestimated for their potential educational impact.

The practitioners of adventure education are continually adapting their talents to impact on mainstream education. Adventure education alternatives exist in public and private school's physical education programs, special education courses, and faculty in-service days as part of adult development. Change comes slowly and with difficulty. Yet by adopting the risk-taking mind-set of a social entrepreneur and working within the mainstream educational system, a dedicated educator can address the personal and social needs of urban youth.

Futurist Robert Theobald describes our era of human development as one of interrelationships of the "compassionate era" (Theobald, 1986). Theobald's vision of this era's characteristics include the support of diversity and differences, the challenges of cooperation between these differences, the inevitability of uncertainty and change, and the values of honesty, responsibility, humility, faith, and love. Many of these compassionate virtues can be taught through adventure education.

Expanding networks and linkages between the public and private educational sectors, the business and social service sectors, and the multiple institutions and organizations in an urban center are necessary for implementing new programs. The complexities of these networks will lead to conflicts, but they can and must be resolved. Issues will arise as people attempt to work together in the urban setting.

Emergent Issues for Discussion

Three issues have been selected for discussion here. These are professional lifestyle conflicts between urban-based and wilderness-based adventure programs; safety considerations in planning and implementing programs; and the fundamental issue of cultural barriers in staff compositions and student to staff relations.

At the fifteenth annual Association for Experiential Education conference in Port Townsend, Washington, November 1987, a workshop on exploring metrophobic biases within the outdoor- and wilderness-based adventure professional community was conducted (Moriah and Proudman, 1987). A question was posed to 30 participants asking them to identify the positive attributes of working in an outdoor (wilderness-based) setting and in an urban setting. The attributes they listed were:

1. Wilderness-based:

   - multidimensional,
   - stimulating,
   - physically oriented,
   - aesthetically pleasing,
   - observing participants,
   - more freedom to participate,
   - being a "guru,"
   - direct consequences,
   - spirituality through contact with nature,
   - small group intimacy,
   - earth connection,
   - rediscovering heritage, and
   - no clocks or watches.

2. Urban-based:

   - modern comforts,
   - human cultural diversity,
   - news and information,
   - anonymity and privacy,
   - cultural events,
   - immediacy of human problems,
   - availability of resources,
   - continuing support systems,
   - raising families (social systems),
   - recreational opportunities (spectator sports),
   - access to human solutions,
   - transforming urban "jungle" into "jungle gym," and
   - new challenge.

According to the group, outdoor professional settings offered more benefits to an individual's spiritual and ecosophical attunements. Urban areas were places of greater access to human problems and solutions. Is the adventure education profession, by nature of its history and roots, biased in favor of outdoor and wilderness environments for teaching and learning?

Attracting excellent staff away from wilderness settings to work in large urban areas is not easily done. Conflicts in values and fears and prejudices concerning the urban environment may affect an individual's decision to bring his or her talents of working adventure education programs into urban areas. It could be argued that a tremendous amount of personal and professional growth can be achieved by existing in both worlds—urban and wilderness. Tom James (1987), writing on the development of an Outward Bound center in New York City, argues that it is in the urban centers where the best and most talented instructors are needed. By testing their skills in urban program areas, wilderness instructors would, in many ways, be entering directly into the same educational process that students experience coming from urban areas into wilderness programs sites. The benefits to the individual and the subsequent program could be enormously positively.

Ultimately, the decision to choose one's place of work and lifestyle is a personal one. As the level of professionalism increases, perhaps more practitioners will examine their values and will take some risks in expanding their talents and scope of their work.

Safety considerations need to be thoroughly evaluated in the program planning process. Once a curriculum is constructed, a reconnaissance trip is essential for gathering information. A network of supportive volunteers can provide assistance with this. The goals of a reconnaissance effort are to identify potential people to be interviewed; to explore the side canyons, that is the sites of interest along an itinerary path; to assess the important logistical elements of time and timing of sequential events; and to recognize safety hazards, problems and safe zones.

Urban safety maps can be useful for identifying where a route is planned and what areas are to be avoided. Criteria used for these purposes can be based on crime rates, known gang concentration centers, level of lighting at night, proximity to other people and the level of activity on the streets, to name a few. The evidence can come from police units, local residents, local merchants, neighborhood organizations, and precourse reconnaissance trips.

Communicating with all of the necessary players in an urban experience is important. Parental or guardian approval and support, administrative clearance and permission from authorities is important. Retaining a well-informed and briefed field staff helps prevent problems from developing. Good relations with all program contacts is necessary for a positive public image and to ensure program acceptance.

There is a saying in the urban adventure profession that "it is much easier to ask for forgiveness than it is to ask for permission." If the program plan calls for an activity that may need special permits or approval don't expect an immediate yes answer. Rappelling off of a public building may at first be prohibited. But with persistence, diplomacy, and education, permission may be granted. All of the contact that occurs in the field, be it personal or professional, has potential public relations impact. Running urban programs can attract a lot of attention and curiosity. Safety needs should never be sacrificed or compromised.

The process of thinking preventatively is the same in both wilderness and urban settings. Each place has its unique hazards. Neither should be considered more or less safe than the other. A sharper eye for safety develops over time through experience with running urban programs. Always early in the design process before students become involved ask the question, "What is unsafe about this activity?"

The final issue deals with cultural barriers. Adventure education staff and participants have largely been members of an upper middle-class Anglican culture in America. This will continue until more effort is made to transcend cultural barriers for recruiting students and staff.

The composition of staff in the field is in need of diversification for several reasons. At present, there are few available role models in the adventure education field for younger Black, Hispanic, Asian, and Native-American participants. What does this reflect about the values minorities have for the utility and relevance of adventure education? Or is the problem a lack of access to training opportunities? How might the profession begin to remedy this imbalance?

Another reason for lack of minority participation is the difference in cultural values. Are adventure programs willing to examine their premises and assumptions to broaden their inclusion of differing beliefs and values? Many current adventure programs conflict with the basic cultural values of inner city adolescents. The idea of "pushing one's limits" contradicts having been taught to accept one's own limitations.

The need to communicate across cultural divisions begins with sincere, honest, and compassionate efforts and expressing an openness to learn from each other. Finding commonalities among the differences could lead to greater levels of trust and collaboration. Recognizing, acknowledging and reinforcing differences is equally important.

Tomorrow's urban world will be more complex than today's and will demand higher levels of mutual cooperation and interdependence. The challenge for the adventure education community is to adapt its strengths to meet the greater needs of society. As the profession matures, this will be a natural and necessary evolutionary step as it merges with the more traditional and mainstream learning approaches from which we are all by-products. The question remains whether or not we are willing to meet the challenge.

Ten Years After—Reflections

In the time that has passed since I was working at the fledgling Chicago Outward Bound Center I have often reflected on the lesson I took from that experience. It was an interesting time in my professional development as a practitioner of experiential education and ultimately as an administrator. In my process of recollecting I spoke with several colleagues who worked in the urban adventure field to explore their experiences and incorporate their thoughts into this afterward. My thoughts are based on my experiences and are only one perspective to a complex and fascinating chapter in the evolution of experiential education in the United States.

In the late 1980s there was considerable effort to create urban Outward Bound centers in the United States. I was drawn to the work to challenge myself and to place myself in a new and exciting environment. My youthful idealism hadn't completely evaporated, so I committed myself to assisting in the development of the Chicago Outward Bound Center, hoping to bring the spirit of Outward Bound to Chicago's youth.

Chicago Outward Bound grew out of my role as a marketing representative for the Voyageur Outward Bound School (VOBS). I was working as a wilderness instructor for five months of the year and sought work to fill the "off season." I ended up making countless presentations in Chicago and networked with regional businesses, schools, youth organizations, social clubs, churches, healthcare institutions and most importantly the Outward Bound alumni network living in the Chicago area. I played this solo role for two years prior to the start-up of the center, eventually proposing the idea of launching a programming initiative.

Planting the seeds had been done through my many meetings with CEOs of Chicago-based corporations, the mayor's office, the archdiocese of Chicago, neighborhood leaders, professional athletes, executive directors of non-profit youth organizations, foundation directors, the superintendent of the Chicago public schools, media contacts, police chiefs, and numerous other people interested in the vision of having an Outward Bound operation serving the needs of Chicago's youth. Many people embraced the idea with enthusiasm and offered assistance in a variety of in-kind ways. This is the only way that such a center could have been started as we were long on ideas and short on capital.

The chapter I wrote for the first edition of this book (the first sections of this chapter) captured my enthusiasm and interest in urban sociology, institutional reform, change theory, systems thinking and community development. I was fresh out of the wilderness settings of Montana and Minnesota, up for the challenges that living in a city brings. The least amount of experience I had was twofold. Living in a city was new for me and administering the growth of a start-up operation. I was learning to create and read new maps for experiential learning to follow. My story here, added to the original words, is a glimpse into the world I was immersed in and eventually left.

I consider myself to be a suburban refugee and a fringe radical. My leaning was towards the small group of innovators in the Outward Bound system. I was attracted to the action taking place in Minneapolis, where David Moriah, a veteran Outward Bounder, had started the Voyageurs in the Parks (VIP) program. VIP was the first "urban" program venture within VOBS and one of the earliest of its kind in the national Outward Bound system. It broke all the rules about "course structure" and brought Kurt Hahn's educational philosophy to youth (10- to 14-year-olds) in the Twin Cities. The other group I connected with were those lively heretics at the New York City Outward Bound Center (NYCOBC). My experiences with the NYCOBC and VIP were the inspiration for the vision I helped to create for Chicago. The reality, at that time, was that there was no one else as foolish as I who was willing to give up a life in the wilderness world and move to a place as "concretized" as Chicago.

We began operations in 1988. We were shut down in 1991. The fall of the center was a result of difficult financial times for our parent organization VOBS and the unfortunate realities of organizational politics of which I had little experience and minimal mentoring. Conflicts arose around vision, philosophy, management style, and power and control. The lessons I learned through my brief tenure there inspired me to become an organization development consultant, which is what I do full time now. The details of this brief history are best left in the oral tradition. I'll share some of what I learned.

The urban expansion was an exciting time for our field. NYCOBC, the Atlanta Outward Bound Center, the Baltimore–Chesapeake Bay Outward Bound Center, and Thompson Island Outward Bound Center in Boston are the success stories of this era. Many other sites came and went for many reasons, mostly related to financial viability. The people involved in these efforts were all intrinsically driven to spread positive energy across the social fabric of our urbanized world.

As one colleague shared with me:

> The work in the programs was outstanding. We were doing real cutting edge work. Did it change anyone's life? Maybe not for many. Was it worth the effort and would I do it again? In a heartbeat. The saddest part of my experience was to see the inability of the administrative system to rise above the political and parochial attitude that limited opportunities for real success. It's ironic and sad to have had such a talented group of innovative people jamming away to create new adventure paradigms for Hahn's vision and have a management and governing structure that was stuck in old paradigms of thought. Maybe that's the creative tension that goes with any change process.

Another colleague shared this:

> The whole experience was mind-blowing. Better than drugs. These kids would light up with the newness that came from exploring unfamiliar neighborhoods, paddling on rivers they normally rode over and meeting new people, sometimes not more than a half-mile from their home neighborhood.

The service ethic was an area of the curricula that had unlimited learning potential in the urban settings. This was the most powerful part of Chicago's programming. The relationships which grew out of the connections that were made are what often led to initiatives beyond our work that we helped to kindle. Homelessness in America had become more visible and gathered media attention throughout the Reagan era and into the late 1980s. The intensity of the perceived risks in being with homeless people, in conversing with them, eating with them, experiencing the spirit of play with them and even sleeping along side them in shelters raised the veil of suspicion and fear in our students and staff. These experiences revealed a real sense of compassion and humanity that was at the core of the original philosophy of Hahn's vision. I believe he would have encouraged this work.

I still believe that the experiential education field can mature as its practitioners evolve their social understandings and comforts in moving their work and careers to places that stretch and challenge their sense of self. I learned that a challenge is far more than a difficult rock climb or a mosquito-infested solo site. A challenge can test our sense of values, commitment, beliefs, and ultimately faith. I have faith in the power of learning through experiences. Our lives are a collection of experiences. Not all of us have access to the same options of choice. My work in the inner city of Chicago reinforced this belief.

Wilderness may be a great tonic for our technological society. I still go there to feed my spirit. However, as a White male, I think the way American society is designed and interpreted reflects the dominance of a White-male bias. Outward Bound is the oldest adventure program organization that grew out of the British private school system. Its roots in the United States are connected to the independent school system. The historical demographics of the leadership of the movement are of well-intentioned White males. I offer this not as a criticism but as a fact that I and others struggled with in trying to cross racial and ethnic boundaries at all levels of our work in Chicago. As we tell our students, we did our best and learned together, though awkward at times.

If you are reading this and reflecting on how you want to deepen your experience base, my humble advice is to keep challenging yourself to grow. I'm not talking about climbing higher mountains or steeper cliffs or paddling more raging whitewater. I'm referring to the pursuit of discomfort on the social level that can lead to deeper insights toward spiritual growth and awareness. In my studies of adult education it was often stated that for adults to be learning at a deeper level there needs to be a certain degree of discomfort present. Not in the sense of physical pain, more along the lines of what happens when your value system and belief structures experience other value systems. Cross-cultural experiences are a good example. When adults are challenged to move out of their routines, to reprogram their thinking at the cellular level, that is when people start to struggle. Embracing the struggle is to embrace the joy of learning.

People live in cities or near them for many reasons. They aren't places to be feared or viewed in a negative light. Cities are amazing classrooms, full of the richness and diversity that reflect our society at any given time. I have always admired the creators of "Sesame Street" for inventing a hip and adventurous world for kids. Adventure is as much a state of mind as it is defined by a set of experiences. I would argue that the world of adventure education can take place as readily in a city as it can in a place as pristine as a wilderness environment. What we attempted in Chicago was immensely more difficult, in my experience, than what I did in wilderness settings.

I remember leading a visioning exercise many years ago for a life or career renewal course at VOBS, asking people to draw themselves in the present and how they view themselves in the future. I did the exercise with my students and recall wanting to be comfortable and effective professionally in both the wilderness and urban worlds. Twelve years later I feel I reached that vision. Now I am in the adventure of living in small-town America being a husband and father. Does anyone know of a guidebook I can follow?

Many of the people I met during my work with urban adventures have, like myself, moved on to new paths in life. The beauty is that the learning goes with us. The spirit of adventure never really leaves you even if you leave the setting that you have come to associate with those powerful experiences. The field of education is boundless. As William James said, "Experience is never limited and it is never complete." I hope you keep your spirit of inquiry and the adventures that it brings burning bright inside you, wherever your path may lead.

References

Baird, L. (1985). Fanning the flame. In D. Kraft and J. Kielsmeier (Eds.), *Experiential education and the schools*. Boulder, CO: The Association for Experiential Education.

Chicago Coalition for the Homeless (1985). *Youth homelessness in Chicago* [annual report]. Chicago, IL: Author.

Chicago Urban League (1987). *Basic facts: National statistic on Blacks—Research edition* [annual report]. Chicago, IL: Author.

Costello, J. (1980). *Criteria for evaluating and planning public policies for children*. Unpublished manuscript. Chapin Hall Center for Children at the University of Chicago, Chicago, Illinois.

Gilligan, C. (1982). *In a different voice: Psychological theory and women's development*. Cambridge, MA: Harvard University Press.

Greenberger, E., and Steinberg, L. (1986). *When teenagers work: The psychological and social cost of adolescent employment*. New York, NY: Basic Books.

James, T. (1987). *An urban strategy: Outward Bound in New York city*. Unpublished manuscript. Education Department, Brown University, Providence, Rhode Island.

Leroy, E. (1985). Adventure and education. In R. Kraft and M. Sakofs (Eds.), *The theory of experiential education*. Boulder, CO: The Association for Experiential Education.

Meier, J., Morash, T., and Welton, G. (1980). *High-adventure outdoor pursuits*. Salt Lake City, UT: Brighton Publishing Company.

Miles, J. C., and Priest, S. (1990). *Adventure education*. State College, PA: Venture Publishing, Inc.

Moriah, D., and Proudman, S. (1987). *Overcoming metrophobia: New perspectives on urban adventuring and outdoor lifestyles.* Workshop presented at the 16th Annual conference of the Association for Experiential Education, Port Townsend, Washington, November 15–18.

National Commission on Youth (1988). *The transition of youth to adulthood: A bridge too long.* Boulder, CO: Westview Press.

Passow, A. H. (1982, April). Urban education for the 1980s: Trends and issues. *Phi Delta Kappan,* pp. 519–522.

Pfeiffer, J. W., and Jones, J. (1973). *A handbook of structured experiences.* La Jolla, CA: University Associates.

Testa, M., and Lawler, E. (1985). *1985 state of the child in Illinois.* Chicago, IL: The Chapin Hall Center for Children at the University of Chicago.

Theobald, R. (1986). *The rapids of change.* Wickenburg, AZ: Action Linkage.

U.S. Census Report (1980). *Census 1980.* Washington, DC: Government Printing Office.

Wynn, J., Richmond, H., Rubenstein, R. A., and Littell, J. (1987). *Communities and adolescents: An exploration of reciprocal supports.* Chicago, IL: Chapin Hall Center for Children at the University of Chicago.

Youth Development Coordinating Committee. (1987). *A Chicago youth agenda: Meeting the needs of a generation at risk.* Chicago, IL: Mayor's Office.

Chapter 45

Artificial Climbing Environments

Aram Attarian
North Carolina State University

Introduction

A variety of climbing activities can be successfully introduced and conducted on artificial environments created or adapted specifically for the activity. Artificial environments are any human-made structure that can be used for teaching or participating in a climbing-related activity. Instruction takes place in a controlled environment. Missing are the objective hazards commonly associated with the activity. Climbing walls, gymnasiums, and other structures (stairwells, buildings, bleachers) have been successfully adapted for use as artificial climbing environments. This chapter will explore the use of these structures as environments for rock climbing.

Climbing Walls

Artificial climbing walls have become popular environments for introducing people to the sport of rock climbing. While climbing outdoors continues to be the principal type of climbing, indoor climbing is not far behind (Outdoor Recreation Coalition of America [ORCA], 1997a). As predicted, indoor climbing has become the "sport of the 1990s" (Attarian, 1995). This is supported by a *Climbing Magazine* survey that reported more than 71 percent of the magazine's 50,000 readers have climbed on an indoor climbing wall (ORCA, 1997a). An earlier *Rock & Ice Magazine* survey of climbing gyms found that one-

fourth of the gyms surveyed reported that 70 percent of their members never climb outdoors (Soles, 1993).

Many schools, colleges, fitness centers, and other leisure service organizations are including indoor climbing walls as part of their programs and facilities. In addition, a new industry has emerged that plans, designs, and constructs climbing walls and related components. Enterprise, a leading manufacturer of indoor climbing walls reported that their business has tripled every year since 1992 (Greenwald, Marchant, Perman, and Savaiano, 1996)!

History

According to one source, the first climbing wall was built in France during the early 1500s to train soldiers in castle storming techniques (Thomas, 1988). Four hundred years later, the first twentieth-century climbing wall was constructed in Milan, Italy, during the 1920s and utilized iron rungs for holds (Thomas, 1988). The earliest organization to build and use an artificial climbing wall in the United States was the William G. Long Camp near Seattle, Washington. Known as the "Schurman Rock," this structure was built by the Works Project Administration in 1939 and created of natural stone (Smutek, 1974).

Following World War II the French, encouraged by Maurice Hertzog and Gaston Rebuffat, both respected mountaineers, began to build adjustable wooden climbing walls. During the 1960s, the British made significant contributions to climbing wall technology. By 1970, more than

50 artificial climbing walls were operating in Britain, expanding to more than 300 by the early 1980s (British Mountaineering Council, 1988). A similar interest in climbing walls is currently booming in the United States. Early climbing walls in the United States were built primarily in colleges and universities, most notably at Hampshire College, Massachusetts, and the University of Washington in 1975 (Attarian, 1991). The first commercial climbing wall in the United States, the Vertical Club, was opened in Seattle, Washington, in 1987. Today, there are more than 300 climbing walls in use throughout the United States in a variety of settings (ORCA, 1997a).

Instructional Implications

Artificial climbing walls have many applications and uses in an adventure education program:

1. When constructed indoors, the climbing wall provides year-round programming options.
2. Climbing walls offer climbing opportunities when nearby climbing areas are nonexistent.
3. Adventure activities can be incorporated where none may have existed due to lack of suitable areas.
4. Programs can be developed for all age groups and ability levels.
5. They provide an opportunity to participate in an adventure activity to those living in urban areas.
6. Instruction takes place in a controlled, safe environment.
7. Prerequisite skills can be taught and perfected before climbing on natural rock.
8. Greater student participation occurs through regularly scheduled classes and workshops.
9. There is a reduction in environmental and social impacts at natural climbing sites.
10. The need to transport students, staff, and equipment to a climbing site that may be hours away is eliminated.
11. They give participants physical and mental challenges in a unique physical environment.
12. They allow participants opportunities to achieve beyond preconceived expectations, thus enhancing self-esteem.
13. There is a focus on issues of trust, commitment, and risk taking.

On the negative side, a climbing wall may be too expensive to build and maintain, functional wall space or an appropriate facility may be nonexistent, and the lack of administrative support and liability concerns may prohibit construction.

Climbing Wall Use

Climbing walls have many diverse uses and applications. Schools, colleges and universities, the military, private and commercial fitness centers, and climbing schools are all realizing the potential of climbing walls. Climbing walls are currently being used for instructional purposes, recreation, training and fitness, and competition.

Instructional uses. A variety of leisure service organizations are using climbing walls to supplement existing climbing programs or create new ones. The instruction of basic climbing skills is the main goal of these programs. Programs are also using climbing walls to introduce team-building activities to help develop self-confidence, leadership, risk taking and communication skills.

Recreation. Climbing walls can add an extra dimension to a school or community recreation program by providing opportunities for an adventure-based activity where none may have existed before. Indoor climbing gyms have become popular venues for introducing people to the sport of climbing. In addition, mobile climbing walls have been introduced that make it possible to rent or lease these structures. These portable climbing walls can be trailered or built on-site for special events or program purposes. Programs have been initiated for specific populations (families, physically challenged, and youth at risk) with the climbing wall as the central focus. The Climbing Gym Association (CGA) established in the early 1990s to promote responsible growth and professionalism within the indoor climbing industry had a membership of 89 climbing gyms in 1994. Today this number has grown to more than 200 (ORCA, 1997a).

Training and Fitness. Fitness centers, especially in areas with traditionally large climbing populations continue to add climbing walls and related equipment to their facilities. These centers allow climbers to train year-round to perfect techniques, strength, flexibility and balance. Focus on basic rock-climbing instruction is also possible through a well-equipped center.

Competition. The development of climbing walls has led to most climbing competitions. The American Sport Climbing Federation (ASCF) was established in the late 1980s as an organization of competitive climbers and a sanctioning body for competitions. The first sanctioned climbing competition on an artificial wall in the United States was held at Snowbird Lodge, Utah, during the summer of 1988 (Benge, 1988). Since then many other regional and international competitions have been conducted. Currently there are more than 300 members in the ASCF, with nearly half the membership under age 18 (ORCA, 1997d).

General Guidelines for Constructing a Climbing Wall

The Climbing Wall Industry Group (CWIG) was established in 1993 as a subgroup of the ORCA (1997b). One of its primary purposes is to promote climbing safety through public education, testing, research, and establishing standards for the climbing wall industry. The CWIG recommends that (1) a licensed engineer design the climbing structure (2) confirmation is obtained that the building can support the additional loads transferred to it by the climbing wall, and (3) work is done with an experienced climbing wall designer. According to the CWIG (ORCA, 1997b) the following steps should be followed when constructing an artificial climbing wall:

1. A reputable company should be considered to design your structure. Design should be compatible with anticipated clientele and the space available for building. Many projects are done as do-it-yourself projects. Care should be taken if this approach is used. Consultation with other climbing wall owners, structural engineers, risk managers, and climbers is recommended.
2. A contractor must be selected that will construct the structure.
3. The project's blueprints should be created according to current industry specifications and standards, local building codes, zoning ordinances and restrictions. Building permits must be obtained, inspections by local building inspectors conducted and occupancy permits issued.
4. The supporting frame is constructed.
5. The climbing surface is attached to the frame (plywood, panels, other surfaces).
6. Upper and lower anchor points are installed.
7. An impact absorbing surface is installed (mats, shredded rubber, pea gravel).

Risk Management of Climbing Wall Environments

Risk management plans for indoor climbing environments should be started to prevent damage or destruction of property, reduce potential injury or suffering to participants, implement loss-reducing and prevention programs, and transfer risk when control by other means is difficult (van der Smissen, 1990). Risk management plans should focus on developing and implementing policies, facility and climbing structure specifics, selecting and maintaining the appropriate equipment, consideration to the health, safety, and well-being of the participants, and hiring, training, and

retaining qualified staff (Attarian, 1995). While risk management plans cannot eliminate all lawsuits, they can show the organization's concern for the well-being of its participants while reducing unnecessary risk.

The Climbing Gym Association (CGA) has developed a set of accepted industry practices that should be adopted by climbing wall operators (Table 45.1, page 344) and has produced the *Accepted Industry Practices Handbook* (ORCA, 1997c) which outlines the important issues to consider in the operation of an indoor climbing facility.

Types of Climbing Walls

There are many different methods and techniques currently used to design and build climbing walls. Many of the early climbing walls were built as "do-it-yourself" projects. This approach kept costs down, involved volunteers to help with construction, and used the expertise of experienced climbers to help with design ideas. While this practice continues today, a new industry has emerged that makes the design and construction of climbing walls a relatively simple process. Many climbing wall manufacturing companies offer "turnkey" operations that include a number of services: planning, wall design, construction and setup, business plans, operations manuals, training and support (once the wall is built), and an ongoing maintenance program.

By far the simplest approach to constructing a climbing wall consists of using wooden, stone, or molded handholds screwed, bolted, or epoxied to flat or irregular surfaces. Brick, cinder block (which offers the best friction), or concrete is best suited for this type of application. Plywood (three-quarter inch) is a popular medium, since it is economically priced, readily available, and can be painted, shaped, and attached to other surfaces.

Besides plywood, other commercially made surfaces have been developed by the climbing wall industry. Some of these include fiber reinforced concrete (FRC) panels which look and feel like real rock; plywood laminated with resinous concrete with modular holds attached to its surface; fiberglass panels that feature sculpted surfaces, and ferrous concrete with permanently sculpted or moveable holds or a combination of the two. Interior or exterior stone walls can be modified for use as climbing walls with help from experienced stone masons (March and Toft, 1979).

The proper design, use, and installation of handholds can be an important safety consideration for any climbing facility. Most artificial handholds are made from casts consisting of a polyester resin with crushed rock or sand mixed in for texture (plastic). Wood, natural rock, and ceramic are also used in the manufacture of handholds. Many creative designs, shapes, sizes, and materials are available. When purchasing handholds consider comfort, cost, form and aesthetics, material, and maintenance (Raleigh, 1992/1993). Obtaining a variety of handholds from different manufactures will keep the climbing routes interesting.

Table 45.1   Climbing Gym Association Accepted Practices

Area Covered	Description
1. Duty to Notify	First visit climbers should be briefed about the risks inherent in indoor climbing and be qualified as to their climbing experience, knowledge of the sport, belaying experience, and notified of the climbing facility rules.
2. Age Restriction	It is recommended that climbers be 18 years of age or older to use the climbing facility without a parent or legal guardian's signature on the waiver. Notes from parents are not sufficient. It is also recommended that an age restriction be placed on unsupervised belaying.
3. Waiver Forms	All participants must read, understand, and sign a liability waiver release prior to climbing in the facility. These forms must comply with and be worded to appropriate state laws.

4. Belay Check	All participants must be "certified" prior to using belay systems. It is recommended that the following steps be taken to initiate the process:
	  a. Have the climber put on his or her harness and demonstrate its proper use and application.
	  b. Attach the climbing rope to the harness via a figure-of-eight-follow-through knot.
	  c. Have the climber demonstrate a proper belay setup. The belay device, carabiner, and rope are handed to the climber separately. Demonstrate proper signals and belay technique.
	  d. The climber should be advised that the belayer and climber are to double check one another for proper harness, rope, carabiner, belay device, and any other equipment setup before attempting a climb.
	  e. Notify the climber of specific rules and regulations related to climbing in the facility.

5. Supervision	Appropriate supervision by a qualified staff member is mandatory while the facility is operating. This will help ensure that policies and procedures are being followed.
6. Safety Records	All accidents, incidents, and near misses should be documented and kept on file.
7. First Aid	At least one staff person supervising the floor should be trained and certified in First Aid and CPR.
8. Staff Training	Staff should be trained on safety (including emergency response) and policy issues. This training should be documented.

SOURCE: ORCA, 1997d.

Design should be a primary consideration when purchasing handholds. Holds that are well-designed can prevent injury, reduce boredom, are useful in all orientations, come in a variety of sizes, and the bolt by which the hold is attached is compatible with other systems. Holds with round edges tend to be user friendly and should be considered for beginners, warming up or working on endurance.

Other Climbing Activities

The open space found in gymnasiums make them an inviting facility to conduct a variety of adventure activities. Walls are ideal for the construction of climbing structures and rappelling platforms. In some cases a climbing wall project can double the amount of usable square footage found in a typical gymnasium (Steffen and Stiehl, 1995). Ceiling rafters and beams can be used for the construction of indoor challenge courses. The climbing activities of rappelling and ascending can be taught effectively using constructed or adapted environments.

Rappelling

No aspect of rock climbing has excited the beginning climber more than rappelling. Beginners often seem quite eager to learn how to rappel, more so than climb (Lough-man, 1981). Rappelling is a skill that can be taught as part of a basic rock-climbing program or as an individual adventure activity. Basic rappelling techniques and general safety guidelines can be taught on artificial climbing walls, specially constructed rappelling platforms, buildings, stairwells, bleachers, or on other structures.

Ascending

Ascending is a mountaineering technique that allows the climber to ascend a fixed rope by using a prusick knot (or other friction knot) or mechanical ascending devices. This climbing procedure is commonly used by climbers in a variety of climbing situations, rescue, and by cavers as a basic skill requirement in single rope technique. Ascending can be a relatively easy activity to set up and monitor in an indoor setting. By using the traditional gymnasium climbing rope (usually a three-strand manila rope $1^1/_4$-inch in diameter and approximately 25 feet long) participants can learn the basics of ascending a fixed rope in the relative comfort and safety of a gymnasium. All climbers should be belayed in this activity. Standard climbing ropes (both dynamic and static) can also be used for this purpose. This activity provides an opportunity for the gymnasium climbing rope to be used in a creative way and allows students an opportunity to reach a "summit."

Litter Lowers

Stairwells, bleachers, and buildings can be used as effective litter lowering sites. Litter lowers teach the techniques and complexities of rigging a litter (a Stokes basket or similar litter) and provide opportunities for enhancing teamwork, leadership, and communication skills. This activity can also be used as a group initiative to reinforce previously learned rock-climbing skills (knots, appropriate equipment use, belaying, rappelling).

For more information on artificial climbing environments contact the Climbing Wall Industry Group or the Climbing Gym Association, both belonging to the Outdoor Recreation Coalition of America (see the Appendix for address information).

Warning: Those unfamiliar with the aforementioned activities should seek the appropriate training and instruction before attempting any of these activities.

References

Attarian, A. (1991). *An overview of artificial rock-climbing walls in the United States and Canada.* Paper presented at the American Alliance for Health, Physical Education, Recreation, and Dance Convention, Indianapolis, Indiana.

Attarian, A. (1995). *Safety and risk management of artificial climbing environments.* Paper presented at the American Alliance for Health, Physical Education, Recreation, and Dance Convention, Portland, Oregon.

Benge, M. (1988, August). Off the rock. *Climbing, 109,* 44–56.

British Mountaineering Council. (1988). *Development, design and management of climbing walls.* London, UK: Author.

Greenwald, J., Marchant, V., Perman, S., and Savaiano, J. (1996, August 26). Grabbing customers. *Time,* p. 34.

Loughman, M. (1981). *Learning to rock climb.* San Francisco, CA: Sierra Club Books.

March, W., and Toft, M. (1979). The conversion of exterior wall facings for climbing activities. *Journal of Physical Education, Recreation and Dance, 50*(1), 30–32.

Outdoor Recreation Coalition of America. (1997a). *1997 State of the industry report.* Boulder, CO: Author.

Outdoor Recreation Coalition of America. (1997b). *Climbing wall industry group: Specifications for artificial climbing walls.* Boulder, CO: Author.

Outdoor Recreation Coalition of America. (1997c). *Accepted industry practices handbook.* Boulder, CO: Author.

Outdoor Recreation Coalition of America. (1997d, Spring). Climbing Gym Association accepted industry practices. *Climbing Industry Update, 4*(2), 7.

Raleigh, D. (1992/1993, December/January). The modular squad. *Climbing, 135,* 119–123.

Smutek, R. (1974, October). Spire rock grows. *Off Belay, 17,* 39–41.

Soles, C. (1993, November/December). Survey of climbing gyms. *Rock and Ice, 45,* 119–123.

Steffen, J., and Stiehl, J. (1995). Does your gym have six walls? *Journal of Physical Education, Recreation and Dance, 66*(8), 43–47.

Thomas, R. (1988, November/December). Building your own climbing wall. *Rock and Ice,* 35–37.

van der Smissen, B. (1990). *Legal liability and risk management for public and private entities.* Cincinnati, OH: Anderson Publishing Company.

Chapter 46

Ropes Courses:
A Constructed Adventure Environment

Karl Rohnke
Project Adventure

A ropes course just ain't a ropes course anymore.

Twenty-five years ago the ropes appellation fit but now the ropes association is minimal as cable has become the connector of choice. From the standpoint of preventing vandalism, precluding unauthorized use and durability, cable makes a lot of sense; but it's just not rope. . . .

Because I've been involved with challenge ropes course design and construction since 1968, practitioners are convinced that I have the history of challenge courses well-defined and researched. I don't. Over the years I've always been more interested in design and implementation than where The Wall and Beam came from. Even writing this less-than-definitive essay on ropes courses doesn't tempt me to "go for the roots."

Nonetheless, here's what I've experienced, read, and heard about.

George Hébert, an officer in the French Navy during the late 1800s, as part of his military commission, became responsible for the physical training of all French Navy recruits. Hébert, somewhat of an original thinker and quite the physical person himself (performing as a professional acrobat at one point in his career), favored "natural" exercises: walking, crawling, climbing, and swinging for conditioning purposes rather than the traditional and often tedious exercises that were favored by exercise professionals during the latter part of that century.

Hébert must have been as persuasive as he was personally fit, because he developed a following of supporters who enthusiastically promoted his then offbeat notions about exercise with missionary-like zeal. There was no mention made at this time about growth of self-concept, increased communication, or developed cooperation—just exercise.

Hébert and his disciples developed and adapted "natural" exercises into something that can be compared to a rudimentary ropes course experience. I am of course referring to Project Adventure's established curriculum that utilizes ropes challenge courses as a tool for increased self-awareness, enhanced physical growth, group cohesiveness, cooperation, and communication.

An interesting account of Hébert's work is presented in the booklet *Hébertisme,* written by Claude Cousineau, a professor at the University of Ottawa in Canada. Cousineau writes:

> Hébert was opposed to analytical exercises and controlled movements which he considered artificial and purposeless. The exercises had to be functional, useful and in the open air. Everything was based on the fundamental movements of human kinetics: walking, running, crawling, climbing, jumping, balancing, throwing, lifting and carrying. Therefore, every indigenous physical obstacle became the essence of Hébertisme.

There seem to be still quite a few of these Hébertisme courses extant in Canada, used primarily by summer camps to pursue exactly what Hébert had in mind over 100 years earlier, fitness through natural exercise.

There have been other organizations in the past utilizing challenge courses as part of their initiative to increase physical fitness, the military being an obvious example. But a change was taking place, the ropes venue was being more frequently used as a site for building character and attempting group problem-solving tasks rather than strictly as a "grunt" challenge. Used by the military, the choice of participating or not participating was "do it fast, or do it slow, but *do it!*" In a disciplined military situation, people's lives depend upon immediate reaction to orders. The rugged individual doing his own thing and the myth of challenge-by-choice is a civilian extravagance.

I have visited two well-known military obstacles courses in the United States. (An obstacle course is a ropes course that you have to do.) Each challenge venue had elements that displayed design ingenuity and were well-put together. Each course also had high events (40-plus feet) that displayed no hint of a belay setup—none! I commented to one of the well-starched sergeants attending our civilian group, "I notice that there are no belay ropes on the high events. Have there been any injuries?" His terse and serious reply told me more than I wanted to know, "Yes sir!"

In contrast, students participating on high ropes course elements today are protected by high-tensile cable, massive drop forged bolts, double and sometimes triple belay systems, helmets, mechanical belay friction devices, full body harnesses, fail safe belay devices and a ton of standards. Can you be too safe? Truly a loaded question, but when a participant recognizes that all risk has been removed, the activity becomes less an adventure and more of a roller coaster ride; still fun, but. . . .

Considering the quasi-military setup of the initial Outward Bound (OB) schools in Europe and Kurt Hahn's rationale for initiating a "survival"-type of training for British merchant seaman during World War II, it's not surprising that most, if not all, of the 43 OB schools in the world use a ropes course as part of their self-confidence training. The implicit challenge at Outward Bound, as the result of training and confidence building exercises, is to perform beyond perceived capabilities. A ropes course makes up part of that challenge.

Project Adventure began in 1971 at the Hamilton-Wenham Junior-Senior High School in Hamilton, Massachusetts. The original Project Adventure staff were heavily imbued with this continent's interpretation of Kurt Hahn's Outward Bound philosophy. As new employees of a fledgling adventure organization we were ready to "serve, strive, and not yield" (I heard that one of the International Outward Bound Schools decided to drop the "and not to yield" from their motto; bummer.), but weren't quite sure how

that was going to fit into the flow of the public school's organizational format. Could we get permission to take students from class for a three-day solo, and where were we going to fit in a final expedition? Facetious perhaps, but the first few weeks of this new experiential program did have us scrambling for "civilized" ideas, and wondering if our wilderness orientation was going to do us any good in the "burbs." Specifically, how were we going to transfer the most usable and effective techniques available in a 26-day, residential, wilderness program into three, 50-minute class sessions per week: a formidable task.

The one tangible thing that we knew was transferable (other than the proven OB concepts) was the challenge ropes course, so it became a priority to get one built on school property. At the time, I had two ropes courses "under my belt" and remember feeling confident in my knowledge and expertise level. Even considering all we know now about improved construction techniques and safety systems, I'm still pleased in retrospect at how well the challenge elements went together in and among that beautiful stand of mature beech trees situated behind the track at the high school. (The original Hamilton-Wenham and Project Adventure ropes course, including that stand of trees, has been bulldozed to make way for a new middle school.) Since that time, over 26 years ago, Project Adventure (PA) has been directly responsible for the construction of thousands of indoor and outdoor rope challenge facilities and for having trained, directly or indirectly, the majority of current professional ropes course builders in this country and internationally.

The first few courses that I built for PA were patterned after what I learned at the Outward Bound Schools where I had worked, Hurricane Island in Maine and the North Carolina school specifically. As we continued to fit adventure into the public school's 50-minute time slot, it became obvious that the characteristic OB ropes course of connected high events was functionally giving way to individual challenge events spaced throughout a wooded area. Having only a comparatively short time span to work with the students in a school setting, it made more sense to install the events separate from one another so that at the end of D Block the instructors did not have half a dozen statically belayed students stranded at height on a series of connected events. Sequenced events make a lot of sense in a residential program where time is not a factor; we were adapting again to the needs of a daily (by the bells) school schedule.

Another major difference in the ropes course approach, that became obvious in the developmental stages of the program, involved the amount of time that the ropes facility was utilized with a group of students. As an OB instructor, I used the ropes course for about half a day during the 26-day cycle. At Project Adventure, the course was used throughout the year, and soon became symbolic of the adventure associated with the program.

When it became obvious that the ropes course was going to be used extensively as a training tool, there were initial doubts as to whether the students would maintain an interest over a year's period of time. As it turned out, the uniqueness of the program (new vocabulary, venue, emphasis on trying rather than performing, new games, upgraded system, and no uniforms) captured the interest of an age group that was disinterested and bored with the alternative. Facilitating the attractive content of this rapidly expanding outdoor curriculum was a breeze; compare teaching ancient history, calculus or statistics to instructing rock climbing, canoeing, or ropes course skills.

Ropes course participation, mud walks, winter camping trips, fun runs, parachute sailing, hang gliding, cross-continent bicycle trips, unidentifiable games, boat building, recycling, yurt construction, dory trips, salt marsh camping, Allagash canoe trips. . . . Project Adventure became the vehicle for exciting hands-on curriculum. The challenge-by-choice philosophy, though still in its nascent stages and not yet formally identified, became an integral part of the instructional matrix; no one was being coerced (persuasively cajoled) into doing something that they chose not to. Adventure and experiential education were becoming mainstream and being recognized as a dramatic and effective way to stimulate student interest in the life skills of effective communication, problem solving and learning to trust.

The point at which we (PA) began to separate from our OB roots and develop roots of our own was the realization that dramatic changes in student self-concept could be achieved on campus as well as in a wilderness setting, and even more significantly, a student's choice of what, where, and how he or she wanted to challenge himself or herself was more important than the quality of his or her performance. What a relief, for both teacher and student, to know that participation (trying) was more important than execution or "winning." Once a student recognized that the safety procedures were predictable and he or she did not have to perform on request or to someone else's expectation, his or her willingness to contemplate an "impossible task" became increasingly obvious.

At the beginning of a ropes course semester, we found it important to spend two to three weeks "on the field," i.e., preparation spent working together totally removed from the ropes course venue. During this time, various unique games, problem-solving initiative tasks, physical stunts and trust activities were presented in an attempt to bond the group in such a way that the high ropes course elements became more of an extension of their training and less of a cheap thrill.

There are currently three basic areas of ropes course participation; low and high events, and permanently installed initiative problems.

Low- and High-Challenge Course Events

The Triangular Tension Traverse

The triangular tension traverse is a low-challenge course element. The tension traverse is an event that emphasizes trust and personal challenge, i.e., competition with self.

Three lengths of high-tensile galvanized cable are tautly strung parallel to and about 24 inches above the ground between, and connected to, three well-spaced support trees—like a triangle. In addition, two lengths of rope are attached to one of the support trees at a height of about 20 feet. Participants attempt to "walk" each cable length, traversing around the triangle using one of the suspended ropes for tenuous support. Two to four spotters attend each participant (depending upon the wire walker's size) being alert to the possibility of a slip from the cable, which occurs predictably and frequently on this event.

The tension traverse is a particularly useful low element because it challenges the individual and provides a responsible and active role for the spotters. By this time in the program, the person walking the cable should be confident that his or her spotters have the ability to spot effectively.

Balancing around the cabled triangle is fun and infectiously appealing. It's unlikely after a slip from a cable that the detached funambulist will remain passive about his or her attempt. A frequently heard comment: "Lemme try again, I know I can do better next time." And, of course there is a next time, and another time . . . until the instructor, recognizing flagging enthusiasm or flat-out fatigue, calls an end to the attempts.

The Pamper Pole

The pamper pole is a high-challenge course element. This dramatic event consists of climbing to the top of a 30- to 70-foot vertical pole or log, standing on top of that pole unsupported (but on belay), and diving for a suspended trapeze that hangs a tempting six to seven feet from the precariously balanced climber.

Climbing the pole and standing on the ridiculously small platform is obviously challenging, but the real challenge is initially overcoming the often incapacitating fear associated with the attempt. A frequently heard comment from pole-sitting participants is, "The climb wasn't too bad, but standing up on that pole and thinking about diving for the trapeze was the hardest thing I've ever done." This poignantly honest evaluation of commitment and emotion, points out the largely mental aspect of this element in particular and ropes course events in general.

The dichotomy of physical and mental challenges on a ropes course offers an insight into the planning and rationale that must be considered before construction of the various elements begin. A builder must not only take into consideration performance potential and frustration levels for each individual or group (including age and maturity), but also try to arrange the elements in an aesthetic, environmentally unobtrusive, and functionally sequenced series. A hammer, saw, and drill do not a ropes course make.

A Challenge Course Initiative Problem—The Mohawk Walk

An initiative problem is a fabricated puzzle presented by the facilitator with no solution offered. The Mohawk Walk consists of a series of cables connected to chosen support trees in a zigzag sequence. The five to seven taut cables are installed parallel to and no more than 18 inches off the ground. The object (problem) is to move the entire group across these sequenced cables, from beginning to end, without making contact with the ground. No props are allowed to be used.

Tree to tree cable lengths vary from 10 to 30 feet. It's not overly difficult to scoot solo across a taut 10-foot-long cable, but not many funambulators have the balance control to navigate a 30-foot length of the same cable. As with most initiative problems, the crux becomes what an individual can or cannot accomplish as compared to what a group can achieve working together.

It doesn't take much brainstorming or trial-and-error (mostly error) to figure out that to move the entire group from start to finish, across the series of connected cables, each member of the group must help the others by providing hands-on balance aid and emotional support. (A typical postevent debriefing statement: "I could never have made those last few feet without the group's help and support.") Minutes into the problem everyone is fiercely and unselfconsciously holding onto some body part in order to balance themselves and one another on the cable.

It is the facilitator's role to be supportive, define the perimeters of the initiative problem, set safety standards, then step aside and let things happen. If the facilitator, through frustration or inexperience, steps in and offers supportive hints, the group's eventual solution will be diminished. Not teaching is one of the hardest things a new facilitator has to unlearn.

Ropes Course Rationale

There is undeniable carry-over from these adventure and play simulations to real-life situations, but parents will ask (and you better have an acceptable answer), "Why does my son (daughter) have to climb over a 12-foot high wooden wall when it's obvious all he has to do is take a few steps around its edge? What are you people teaching here, anyway?"

An answer to you: In today's push-button world there are not as many unequivocal physical challenges for young

people as there were 50 years ago. There are obvious social, moral, and intellectual challenges, but few of the type that result in working together on a demanding physical task that involves reasonable risk; for example, the high-risk-high-reward challenge situation (ropes course, canoeing, rock climbing) contrasted to a high-risk-low-reward scenario (drugs, illicit sex, crime). If a group is presented with a task that seems initially impossible, but as the result of a sustained group effort (cognitive and psychomotor) they overcome the challenge, the next "impossible" barrier won't appear so daunting.

An answer to the parent: Your son (daughter) doesn't have to climb or be boosted over the wall. All the activities associated with the program offer a challenge-by-choice alternative to the participants. If he would rather watch for awhile until he becomes more comfortable with the situation, that's acceptable. If he decides not to try today, there's plenty of time for him to change his mind, and lots of other challenges available later in the program. In addition, if your son (daughter) tried to climb the Wall by himself, he would find the task impossible, but with the help of his teammates the up-'n'-over traverse can be successfully and safely accomplished.

Recognize that the challenge isn't getting over the wall, the challenge is *the wall*. Walking around the obstacle ignores the challenge; life's not like that. Climbing over a fake facade might not look impressive on a college or job application, but the personal rewards of having achieved a difficult goal (perceived as initially impossible) results in carry-over confidence that far exceeds the in-your-face simplicity of the event itself.

Indoor Ropes Courses

Indoor ropes courses and climbing walls proliferate in geographic and demographic areas where the weather is unpredictable (usually bad) or where challenge course security is a problem (unauthorized use and vandalism).

Construction of both low and high elements inside a gymnasium can be accomplished without alienating the basketball or volleyball coach by hauling the events up and out of the way using pulley and rope systems or temporarily removing the gear by utilizing connecting turnbuckles. Almost all challenge elements that make up an outdoor ropes course have already been adapted to indoor facilities. Much of this adaptation, of course, depends upon the gym's construction: drop ceilings, I-beam placement, wainscoting, alarm conduits, championship banners. . . .

Fabricated climbing walls represent a combination of synthetic materials creatively designed to duplicate as closely as possible the vertical difficulties inherent in rock climbing. High-tech and expensive climbing walls have received considerable press lately, as world class climbers choose these synthetic vertical venues to display their unique brand of athleticism.

Evolution of Ropes Challenge Facilities

Hébert would be amazed. His simplistic approach to natural challenges and exercise, though still effective, pales in comparison to the grandiose, complex and often very expensive "ropes" challenge facilities currently available in many parts of the world. Have Hébert's basic physical challenges (balancing on a log over a stream versus walking across a log suspended high in the air) been changed for the better as much as the cost and complexity of the modern ropes course might indicate?

The course built at Hamilton-Wenham Junior-Senior High School in 1971 cost about $750. I have recently visited and been much impressed by modular courses in other parts of the world that cost in excess of $1 million; things have changed. And not only changed financially but also from an implementation and hardware standpoint:

- In the early 1970s the rope of choice for belaying was Goldline, a strong but very elastic synthetic rope.
- Goldline belay rope was connected to the climber with a single turn of rope around his or her waist, or if a fall was anticipated, perhaps two or three wraps.
- The belay technique at that time was probably the standing hip belay (hawser laid Goldline rope was too stiff to feed through a Stitcht plate and, as yet, there were no Tubers, Trangos, ATCs or Grigris).
- The belay protection rope was reeved up and through a single locking steel carabiner on the belay cable or perhaps two carabiners in tandem if you were trying to impress someone.
- There were no staples or pegs on the support trees to climb, so access to high events was limited to extension or rope ladders.
- Helmets were something you experienced in the military or observed on motorcycle racers.
- Liability releases were represented by a vague, small-print document you signed before jumping out of an airplane.
- Challenge-by-choice referred to when and how an instructor chose to challenge the group.
- Groups competed against one another to see which "team" could get over the wall the fastest, and hanging upside down on the wall to grab the final person was not only allowed but encouraged.

Ropes course construction is currently big business as evidenced by the proliferation of challenge courses and the companies that install them. In 1971 I'd speculate Project Adventure was the only organization that built ropes courses on a regular for-hire basis. In the late 1990s there are more companies building challenge facilities than actual ropes courses in existence in the late 1960s.

In 1993 builder and challenge course designer Mike Fischesser pulled together those individuals who were installing ropes courses independently and sponsored a conference for sharing information and liability concerns. That first meeting led to the eventual formation of the Association of Challenge Course Technology (ACCT), a respected national organization that establishes technical standards for ropes courses. The industry feeling was, "Let's regulate ourselves before someone ends up dictating what we do and how we do it."

One of the characteristic drawbacks of using a ropes challenge course is the bottleneck situation that develops as participants queue up for their individual try at whatever high challenge is currently being attempted. One or two people actually climbing leaves the remainder of the group impatiently waiting for their attempt.

During this time you hope the group pays attention to the climber, offering whatever verbal and emotional support they can, but it's a numbers game, and the 50-minute class block is not working in your favor. The bottleneck scenario has historically been the catalyst for deciding whether to put more people on the high course using static belays (decreasing the challenge and increasing the potential for rescues) or reduce the number of climbers by using a dynamic "slingshot" belay (increasing the wait for those still on the ground).

In keeping with this ongoing static-dynamic belay dialogue, more attention has been paid recently to creating and efficiently installing events that allow more people to participate simultaneously, helping one another overcome whatever the physical challenge happens to be. Russell Moy, overseas challenge course designer and builder, has created an innovative tower climb that encourages teams of five participants to operate together, independent of other teams of five, to a total of 20 people on the tower simultaneously. This type of creativity is essential toward meeting the needs of schools, corporate groups and other educational facilities that recognize the increased educational benefits of a team experience as contrasted to the classic individual challenge event.

Ropes courses are being used today by a wide range of organizations and for a variety of purposes. Looking through the brochures of leading vendors offers some indication of the variety offered: teachers, administrators, outdoor educators, camp staff, social service providers, counselors, hospital and treatment center clinicians, business executives, management development professionals, school children, interested parents, people. . . .

The use of a ropes course provides strong evidence to an individual that he or she can accomplish more than he or she expected of himself or herself, and have fun doing it. Although the feeling 25 years ago was that ropes course participation was primarily for young people who needed a symbolic rite of passage challenge, today's ropes courses offer a dramatic educational medium for anyone who is interested in stretching personal limits, working intensely as a team, and rediscovering the joy of playful participation.

Considering the number of challenge courses currently being installed each year around the world, there's no doubt that this unique challenge vehicle has established itself as a universally recognized and effective curriculum tool for learning.

Well, maybe it ain't called a ropes course anymore . . . but it is.

Chapter 47

Kinesthetic Awareness: At Home in Our Bodies

Jackie Kiewa
Griffiths University

To climb is to be intimate with the very stuff of our habitat, to smell its minerals (the struck-match odor of split rock or rock in a heat wave), to imitate the lie of it in the twisting and flexing of your muscles, to relish its most durable elements through the nerves of your finger ends. . . . (Craig, 1987, p. 6)

Introduction

The total absorption of oneself in wilderness creates a sense of well-being that seems to reach back to our biological roots. As Craig observes, the nature of climbing, which involves such close contact with the stuff of the earth, induces such absorption very quickly, and he suggests that the body yearns for such intimate contact. The hand sinks sideways into a dark crack, toes take the shape of the rock, nose smells moist fiber inches away as fingernails delve into earthy crevices, arms embrace a burnished yew trunk, eardrums vibrate to the hoarse hissing of jackdaw chicks three feet inside the rock. . . . I had a sense of myself cladding the rock as closely as the clay applied to a sculpture to make a mold (Craig, 1987, p. 74).

In marked contrast to the images invoked by Craig, Western society has a history of alienation both from our bodies and our natural surroundings, and a denigration of both that is characterized by an attitude of exploitation. This chapter focuses on our need to become at home in our own body.

The Technological Body

A continuing feature of our present society is what Brian Pronger (1995) has called the "technological body." In using this phrase, Pronger is emphasizing that technology is a *state of mind* that views everything as a potential resource: something that could be useful in the creation of something else. Thus the technological approach to rivers is not that rivers have any intrinsic worth in themselves, but that they could be dammed to produce hydroelectric power. The technological approach to the human body is that it is a resource which is of use to something or someone. Pronger suggests that it is quite commonplace to hear that "the nation's children constitute its greatest resource," and notes that personnel departments are now called departments of human resources. In other words, our bodies exist as economic resources which will contribute to our country's gross national product, through our function as workers or producers.

We also contribute to the economy through our function as consumers. In our avid consumption of food and drink, clothes, and cosmetics, we pamper and shape our bodies according to the dictates of society, and, at the same time, maintain a large number of huge multinational corporations. Thus we have a dual role: we must produce and we must also consume. Susan Bordo (1990) points out a difficult contradiction which is created by this dual role: in order to maintain the economy, we must be encouraged to consume, passionately, excessively; we must become "creatures who hunger for constant and immediate satisfaction," and advertisements endeavor to sustain this consumerist approach. On the other hand, also in order to maintain this economy, we must work in order to produce, and this means self-denial and -control. In our present culture, self-denial and -control have come to be characterized by a fit, well-muscled body.

This contradiction creates a good deal of anxiety. Generally overweight, we live in a society which adulates slimness. In sedentary jobs and always short of time, we are nevertheless pressured to turn our blob-like bodies into the lean hunting machines of our ancestors. Susan Bordo points out that this contradiction is also denied by much consumerist advertising which suggests that we "can have it all"—that if we simply use such and such a product, we will lose kilograms of fat quite effortlessly. The obsession with remaining slim in a generally fat society has reached the point where it had become the "central organizing principle" of the lives of up to 80 percent of nine-year-old girls in a study conducted in San Francisco (quoted in Bordo, 1989).

The fit body is more than a symbol of willpower and control; it also represents a more useful resource, less likely to succumb to ill health, and more likely to be able to put in longer hours at the job. It is also seen as more attractive generally, and thus more useful for public relations work: hence the corporate exercise programs which have been developed by a number of companies (Shephard, 1986, as cited in Pronger, 1995).

The perceived attractiveness of the slim and fit body is, of course, not just of economic use. In a society which has become obsessed with appearance, an attractive body is almost essential in the achievement of popularity and attention, particularly for young women. A woman needs to look good in order to achieve status in our society. The attractive body is made up of a number of parts, each of which should conform to some ideal. Thus hair should be shiny, and "full of body and bounce;" eyes should be large and fringed by long eyelashes; ears and nose should be small; mouth full (but not too full); breasts large but firm; waist small and tummy flat; legs long; and feet small. Skin should be satin-like and unblemished. These and other body parts have been described in such minute detail throughout the media that every woman knows how each part of her should look, and every woman knows that there are lots of bits of her which don't look as they should. Women are experts at dissecting their bodies, and are generally unhappy about what they discover (Franzoi, Kessenich, and Sugrue, 1989). This unhappiness is fed through a large number of businesses, via the media, which capitalize on the consequent need for women to consume creams and potions, makeup and make-overs, and diet and exercise regimes. Thus women are alienated from their bodies, and, to an ever-increasing extent in our appearance-oriented society, the same can be said for men.

Mind and Body Alienation

This technological approach to the human body has come about because we have been able to create a distinction between us and our bodies. "We" are some kind of disembodied spirit or mind, and somehow our bodies are separate from ourselves. The distinction between body and mind has been with us for thousands of years, certainly since the time of the Greek philosophers of the sixth century B.C., but it reached some kind of fulfillment in the work of Descartes, who viewed mind and body as two fundamentally different entities. Descartes aligned the body with nature, which was of a lower order than mind, being subject to decay and death. Mind, on the other hand, is transcendent, and not subject to death. Grouped with the body are emotions, passions, and sensuality; with the mind is pure, abstract, and rational thought. Within the Cartesian system, it is the task of the mind (or abstract reason) to control the material world, which includes the body and nature.

That this conceptualization of the world is particularly Western in nature has been noted by Yasuo Yuasa in 1987, in his book *The Body: Toward an Eastern Mind-Body Theory*. Yuasa does not suggest that the distinction between mind and body does not exist in Eastern philosophy, but he suggests that the distinguishing feature of Eastern systems of thought is that mind-body unity is seen as an accomplishment, achieved by exceptional people. In the West, systems of thought have investigated only the normal state of affairs, and have therefore assumed that mind-body unity must remain a theoretical possibility. Western intellectual history has avoided the discussion of the perfected human being, and, where the exceptional is examined, the focus tends to be more on the negative side, that of the abnormal or diseased (Kasulis, 1987).

Mind and Body Integration

One Western psychologist who has differed from this rule is Maslow, who carried out a study of exceptional people in the 1970s. Maslow came up with a number of indicators of what he called *self-actualization*. This is the first:

> Self-actualization means experiencing fully, vividly, selflessly, with full concentration and toil absorption. It means experiencing without the self-consciousness of the adolescent. At this moment of experiencing, the person is wholly and fully human. This is a self-actualizing moment. This is a moment when the self is actualizing itself. (Maslow, 1979, p. 44)

Total absorption in experience implies a sense of mind-body unity. The nature of the absorbing experience was further investigated by Csikszentmihalyi, who first coined the word *flow* in 1975. As detailed elsewhere in this book, the elements of the "flow experience" include:

- focused concentration: merging of action and awareness;
- centering of attention on limited stimulus field;
- loss of ego: transcendence of individuality;
- sense of control or competence: balance of challenge and skills;
- clear goals, and immediate, unambiguous feedback;
- autotelic nature: needs no goals or rewards external to itself; and
- distorted sense of time.

The elements of this experience, which Csikszentmihalyi has suggested is the key to a contented life, are quite opposed to the "normal" elements of technology or utilitarianism and dualism, particularly mind-body dualism.

Csikszentmihalyi's focus on rock climbers in his first study created a good deal of interest amongst outdoor recreators and educators, who found in his work a theoretical explanation of the "good feelings" engendered by the rock-climbing experience. This theoretical explanation has been supported by a research study (Kiewa, 1996) which examined the experiences of a group of women involved in outdoor recreation. These women claimed to achieve a high or very high sense of mind-body unity whilst involved in their outdoor activity. In commenting on this phenomena, many women noted that mind-body unity tended to occur in a context of a high level of challenge matched to a high level of competence. They commented that this integration of mind and body produced the state of total absorption which was necessary in order to perform at the level required to meet these challenges. Frequently, they mentioned the exhilaration and satisfaction which seems to inevitably follow such an experience, suggesting that it is the experience of mind-body unity which draws them to the activity again and again. Illustrative comments follow:

It is imperative when involved in potentially dangerous activities to have a two-way monitoring process going on between mind and body.

Best days in any outdoor activity are days where everything just flows. You dance up cliff, execute perfect carve on the face of a wave, or perfect 360s as you thermal to 5,000 feet. These are days you can do no wrong. Operate by feel. Mind and body are one. Utopia.

When the activity is not challenging or intense in some way full focus and unity drop to some degree.

If my mind wanders I make errors. There's no room for dreaming.

Some of my best and most beautiful climbing experiences have been when it just happened—no conscious mental effort at all.

Wonderful sensation—like children—complete absorption in the moment.

One of the great lasting joys of climbing mountains or rock—is the total focus of mind and body it brings—and a detachment from mundane daily business. I think that it is this that is addictive, not the adrenaline.

Kinesthetic Awareness

The exhilaration of movement over rock has been cited numerous times by climbers as one of the major rewards of climbing. In 1966 Chris Bonnington called it the "rhythm of climbing" and described it as "a drug more exhilarating than any purple heart or jab of cocaine and every bit as addictive in its aftereffects; once you've tasted this feeling you can't live without it" (Bonnington, 1966, p. 191). David Craig describes the sensation as "the brilliant minutes when that fusion of thought, sensation, and bodily movement happens yet again, as though a flare had exploded and shown you the features of your earth as you had never seen them before" and suggests that it is like swimming "as fluently as a dolphin in its halcyon element" (Craig, 1987, p. 3). Susan Edwards observed a distinct change in her climbing as she moved from an "aggressive, conquering" style, in which she tended to fight the rock, to a style which emphasized "kinesthetic awareness"; she notes that she:

felt more gentle, deliberate, delicate, relaxed, flexible and, at the same time, more powerful. These mental and physical changes held out the possibility for more consistent enjoyment in climbing and gave the whole experience of the sport more depth and meaning. (Edwards, 1992, p. 252)

The deep-rooted joy which seems to emanate from an immersion in kinesthetic awareness reflects the possibility suggested by John Gill: that such experiences create meaning in our lives:

In those moments when your mind becomes saturated with kinesthetic awareness, cosmic chaos assembles in a sharp and meaningful design, inseparably combining climber and rock in an interlude of destiny. (quoted in Edwards, 1992, p. 254)

It should not be thought that the benefits of the integration of mind and body within a process of kinesthetic awareness exist only in the act of climbing. Susan Edwards first began to experience the phenomenon through her practice of the Eastern tradition of Wu-chu. The women in the research study mentioned previously came from a variety of outdoor recreational experiences which included such activities as kayaking, sailing, bush walking and skiing. Nor should it be considered the privilege only of the highly trained and experienced: David Craig has the following description of his first day's climbing:

> Chris took me up the Slab and the cracked wall to its left, I didn't fall off, and a delicious sense of rubbery power began to steal into my tendons, through my forearms and shoulders. To feel upwards, to pull strongly, smoothly, to rise and keep on rising—here was one of the best states in the world! (Craig, 1987, p. 37)

The common elements seem to be a challenge which is enough to be absorbing, without becoming so stressful that one becomes paralyzed with fear (the flow model again), accompanied by an attitude of mind which is tuned to view our natural environment as simply that: the place where we belong, rather than an alien environment which is to be fought and subjugated. At home in our bodies, at home in the wilderness: it is an ideal which should be a major goal of any outdoor program.

References

Bonnington, C. (1966). *I chose to climb*. London, UK: Victor Gollancz, Ltd.

Bordo, S. (1989). The body and the reproduction of femininity: A feminist appropriation of Foucalt. In A. M. Jaggar and S. R. Bordo (Eds.), *Gender/ Body/Knowledge: Feminist reconstructions and being and knowing* (p. 26). New Brunswick, NJ: Rutgers University Press.

Bordo, S. (1990). Reading the slender body. In M. Jacobus, E. F. Keller, and S. Shuttleworth (Eds.), *Body politics: Women and the discourses of science* (p. 96). New York, NY: Routledge.

Craig, D. (1987). *Native stones: A book about climbing*. London, UK: Fontana Paperbacks.

Csikszentmihalyi, M. (1975). *Beyond boredom and anxiety*. San Francisco, CA: Jossey-Bass.

Edwards, S. (1992). It's the dance that counts. In R. da Silva (Ed.), *Leading out: Women climbers reaching for the top* (p. 252). Seattle, WA: Seal Press.

Franzoi, S. L., Kessenich, J. J., and Sugrue, P. A. (1989). Gender differences in the experience of body awareness: An experiential sampling study. *Sex Roles 21*(7/8), 499–515.

Kasulis, T. P. (1987). Introduction. In Y. Yuasa, *The body: Toward an eastern mind-body theory*. New York, NY: State University of New York Press.

Kiewa, J. (1996). *Outdoor recreation: More than just a pastime*. Keynote address presented at From Mystery to Mastery Conference, Outdoor Pursuits Centre, Turangi, New Zealand.

Maslow, A. (1979). *The farther reaches of human nature*. New York, NY: Penguin.

Pronger, B. (1995). Rendering the body: The implicit lessons of gross anatomy. *Quest 47*, pp. 427–446.

Yuasa, Y. (1987). *The body: Toward an eastern mind-body theory*. New York, NY: State University of New York Press.

Section 9

The Clients of Adventure Programming
Application of a Generic Model

The historical overview earlier in this volume revealed that the first clients of adventure education programming were well-to-do young men in an English public school. A quarter-century after Hahn, the clientele of Outward Bound in the United States was still projected to be young men. One of the primary characteristics of the adventure education movement in the past half-century has been a steady extension of adventure-based learning models to diverse clientele.

The eight contributors to this section reveal how ethnic minorities, women, the disabled, at-risk youth, university students, business executives, tourists and senior citizens have been served by adventure educators. The clientele has become diverse and will continue to be so but, as Roberts and Washington indicate, the potential for this diversity will only be achieved by educators committed to the goal of embracing diversity within culture and trained in the methods of contributing to its achievement. Practitioners of adventure programming are indeed embracing this goal, as these essays document. Women have become extensively, though still not adequately, served. People with disabilities have benefited from great program-

ming ingenuity, but there is much work to be done to make further progress. A major challenge grows as the portion of the senior population increases.

The extension of adventure education to diverse clients reflects, perhaps more than any other development in the field, changes in the social environment. The twentieth century has witnessed a progressive, if halting, movement toward equality and justice in America and elsewhere in the world. While adventure education is but a small piece of this movement, it has demonstrated its ability to play a significant role. The word *empowerment* has been so overused as to be rendered a cliché, but no word better describes the consequences for people participating in adventure education programs.

People gain strength from their adventure experiences, and can use this strength to tackle challenges and opportunities. Some groups face greater challenges than others and, by providing resources to these groups, educators of whatever ilk aid in the essential work of social progress. Adventure programmers can count themselves among these contributors to progress, as the writings in this section attest.

Chapter 48

Adventure Education for Teaching Cross-Cultural Perspectives

Sharon J. Washington
Springfield College

Nina S. Roberts
Student Conservation Association

Introduction

From our early relationships with siblings and family, to our relationships in our neighborhoods, schools, places of worship, workplaces, as well as in the broader world there is a need to function effectively in pluralistic environments. No longer can the majority of people in the United States and Canada live their entire lives in a monoculture environment. In fact, the United States has never been a monoculture. The indigenous people of the land were comprised of numerous Indian nations, each with its own set of mores, cultural practices and beliefs. Moreover, the early Spanish, British and French immigrants, the forced immigration of Africans and Chinese, and more recent immigrants have all brought unique cultural beliefs and practices with them. Some of the cultural norms became dominant in the United States through the assertion of power and the mythical phenomenon of the "melting pot" which rendered languages, cultural practices and beliefs invisible as the price to become an "American." Those who successfully "melted" were primarily Europeans, although not exclusively.

It is not our differences, but our attitudes about difference which is the problem. We learn very early in our lives that it is not okay to be different or talk about our differences with people who are different from ourselves. Children learn through both verbal statements and nonverbal actions what is considered appropriate behavior. For in-

stance, there are labels for the group of studious students in school, those who participated in sports (different names for boy/men and girl/women athletes), and those who wear baggy clothes. Nonetheless, the socialization starts well before formal schooling. Children are wonderfully curious and often want to know why something is the way that it is. Imagine a small child of three to four years of age with a parent in a crowded mall. The child sees a woman in a wheelchair and wants to know, "How come that lady's in that funny chair?" At this point the parent may respond in one of several ways: (1) try to silence the child; (2) pull the child away from the woman; or (3) ignore the child. Any of the three actions will accomplish the same end, especially when repeated in a variety of situations and the child will learn: (1) that it is not okay to talk about people who are different, especially in front of them; (2) that somehow their curiosity is bad and they need to keep it to themselves; and (3) to view differences as bad or ignore them and eventually the people who are different than themselves.

Adventure education claims to challenge individuals to go beyond perceived limitations, foster group cohesion, trust, and effective communication, to name a few. The attitudes we have about each other, especially those who are different than ourselves, can be addressed through the work in adventure education. The world needs individuals who can thrive in a pluralistic society and the role of adventure educators in meeting this need is the premise of this chapter.

Historical Perspective

Great Britain was the first nation to institute a formal training program for outdoor leaders and its evolution consisted of several distinct layers from certification to standards (Priest and Gass, 1997). Subsequently, any history of adventure education typically begins at the earliest stages with Kurt Hahn. A twentieth-century educator and founder of Outward Bound, Hahn believed that life-enhancing experience is obtained through the sea, the mountains, the wild lake country, and the desert (Miner, 1991). He sought to create an educational environment where "healthy passions—craving for adventure, joy of exploration, zest for building, devotion to a skill demanding patience and care, love of music, painting or writing—would flourish as guardian angels for adolescence" (Miner, 1991, p. 60).

Early Outward Bound, as well as other programs of similar structure, were designed for the acquisition of skills. Powers of resilience, coordination, and endurance were examples of the desired outcomes of participation (Priest and Gass, 1997). Traditionally, wilderness programs were aimed at conquering personal weaknesses, facing unfamiliar and sometimes scary tasks, and succeeding far beyond personal expectations. With the inclusion of women's voices in adventure education, program goals expanded to incorporate individual needs through challenges by choice and a valuing of "soft" skills. Over time, the desired outcomes of outdoor education included technical and interpersonal skills, risk management, expedition planning, and minimum impact, among others.

Understanding the Need

Many experiential educators understand the importance of treating all people with respect regardless of their differences. However, that does not mean that similarities should be highlighted while differences are downplayed. Recognizing differences among people based on dimensions of age, gender, religion, socioeconomic status, sexual orientation, disability, and racial and ethnic background is essential to ensure competent leadership is being provided and to facilitate the acquisition of awareness and cross-cultural skills in others.

Leadership training must stress the development of cross-cultural competencies. By increasing the scope of quality training and education, leaders can assist with developing and expanding the connection for diverse populations to wilderness or adventure-based experiential learning. Additionally, this will better prepare the predominantly White participants to be effective members of a pluralistic society. Important to note is that outdoor programs are part of the fabric with which we infuse our personal bias, prejudice, or stereotyping into our relationships and structures that also permeate most other aspects of our lives (Roberts and Gray, 1997).

Roberts and Gray (1997) indicate that leadership training must therefore also include concepts relating to "how dominant or privileged groups benefit (sometimes in unconscious ways) from the disempowerment of oppressed groups" (p. 47). Their conviction is that once White managers and leaders of outdoor programs acknowledge the benefits they gain from access to social power and privilege, not equally available to other individuals, programs are more likely to be enjoyed safely and successfully by those considered *other:*

> Because the appreciation of differences are inextricably linked to social justice, and the ways that power and privilege construct differences unequally in every aspect of society, both leaders and participants must be educated to how this pertains to safe program operations and group dynamics. (Roberts and Gray, 1997, p. 47)

Consequently, a culturally competent and responsive program is one that demonstrates sensitivity to, and understanding of, cultural differences in program design, implementation, and evaluation. The other issue that relates to this revolves around determining the outdoor leader's role in justifying a social prescription for change. Draguns (1989) expresses the reality of this quite clearly as it pertains to issues of justice. He explains that our legitimate role as agents of social change is limited by our level of knowledge on the one hand, and by the imperative of imposing one's convictions and beliefs upon a client on the other (p. 15).

Reflective Assessment of Leadership Issues on Diversity

Outdoor leaders indisputably bring a wealth of knowledge, skills and experiences to their work. Based on research and various theories developed, there are certain leadership skills and common characteristics that outdoor leaders should possess. The top competencies of outdoor leaders are reported as follows: judgment, problem solving, decision making, effective communication, awareness and empathy, group interaction and dynamics, safety and risk management, program planning, environmental ethics, outdoor skills and techniques, navigation, and philosophical foundations (Ewert, 1989; Ford and Blanchard, 1993; Priest and Gass, 1997). Greater importance is placed on those expectations and responsibilities in that they are directly related to the health and well-being of our clients. Because all clients and leaders are not the same in all dimensions of diversity (e.g., gender, race, ability, and sexual orientation), the issue of cross-cultural competencies is not separate from the previously stated competencies of outdoor leaders, but essentially infused throughout. This consideration has created the need for a significant emphasis on diversity education which facilitates awareness, knowledge, skills and connection to the competencies. If the skills and competencies identified are the blueprint for measuring an "effective" leader, how do we incorporate cross-cultural competencies?

Professional Development

Essential to the ability to learn cross-cultural competencies is a need to understand personal leadership qualities in relation to diversity issues. There are many authors who have written on leadership theory in management (Blanchard, Zigarimi, and Zigarimi, 1985; Burns, 1985), and several authors who have looked at the impact of diversity in leadership (Gardenswartz and Rowe, 1994; Loden and Rosener, 1991). The common thread throughout the writings on leadership is the need for leaders to assess their qualities and skills as a leader.

Leaders, instructors or program managers who want to facilitate cultural competency in participants to live and work effectively in a diverse world, will first need to understand their own attitudes towards diversity as well as comprehend the following specific elements (Adams, Bell, and Griffin, 1997; Lustig and Koestner, 1996):

- acknowledge culture as a predominant force in shaping behaviors, values, and institutions;
- acknowledge and accept that cultural differences exist and have an impact on program delivery;
- believe that diversity within cultures is as important as diversity between cultures;
- respect the unique, culturally defined needs of various client populations;
- recognize that concepts such as "family" and "community" are different for various cultures and even for subgroups within cultures;
- understand that people from different racial and ethnic groups and other cultural subgroups are usually best served by persons who are a part of or in tune with their culture; and
- recognize that incorporating the strengths of all cultures enhances the capacity of everyone.

Gardenswartz and Rowe (1994) in their book *Diverse Teams at Work: Capitalizing on the Power of Diversity* outline 10 qualities of effective leadership. Two of the qualities are highlighted here because of the way in which they illustrate how effective leadership is leadership that includes awareness of diversity:

> Effective leaders have self-esteem and confidence, which creates a nondefensive, open environment. This sense of wholeness and confidence is important in any environment. But it is more so in a pluralistic one because perceptions of unequal treatment and conflict take on extra volatility when the racial, ethnic, and gender mix of the group is complex. Without a solid foundation of self-confidence, it is difficult for the leader to remain nondefensive and maintain an even tone of voice in dealing with hot spots. The self-esteem and confidence a leader feels is broadcast and extended to others. It creates a feeling of security and stability on which the team can build group confidence.
>
> Effective leaders expand their knowledge and awareness of culture and its influence, as well as other diversity-related issues. Diversity, as we have been saying throughout this book, includes everyone. It's not a Black thing, a gay thing, or a woman's thing. A leader who wants to maximize output and help all people grow and contribute understands that diversity includes White men too, discusses cultural norms with team members, and stops perpetuating the myth that you have to be a person of color to have a culture. An effective leader doesn't advocate any particular group's position, but understands or is willing to explore issues and customs of members from all groups. (p. 218–219)

A Three-Dimensional Approach to Diversity Education

What we need to know in order to tap into the richness of a multicultural society can best be summarized in a three-dimensional approach: (1) diversity knowledge, (2) social justice awareness, and (3) cross-cultural skills (Figure 48.1, page 362). The absence of any of the three dimensions will prove inadequate when trying to create inclusive multicultural recreation environments (Washington, 1996). Creating educational experiences for each of the three dimensions is not difficult and can occur in many settings.

Diversity knowledge is the information about cultural groups which gives a broad picture of the cultural expressions of the group. Traditional ethnic foods, fashions, festivals and celebration of holidays, and the values that shape behavior can be helpful most often in terms of exposure to cultures that traditional education programs have historically ignored. "Ethnicity refers to affiliation with a social group due to heritage or nationality" (Aguilar and Washington, 1990, p. 150).

Social justice awareness refers to the understanding of present day and historical social inequities. How these

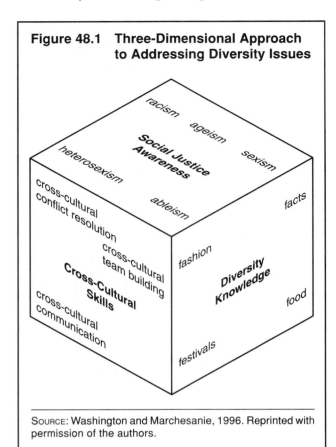

Figure 48.1 Three-Dimensional Approach to Addressing Diversity Issues

SOURCE: Washington and Marchesanie, 1996. Reprinted with permission of the authors.

inequities continue to influence the attitudes and behavior of everyone, due to the pervasiveness of oppression in society is acknowledged. Cross-cultural skills are those competencies which promote positive interactions between and within cultures. Cross-cultural communication, cross-cultural conflict resolution, and inclusive team building are essential skills to possess for effective leaders of any program.

Strategies for mastering the competencies can be accomplished through ongoing professional development which views issues of diversity as integral to all other competencies. Workshops, discussion groups, readings and interactions with others who are different than ourselves are all approaches to diversity education. Professional development strategies for diversity education (Table 48.1) is an adaptation from the work of Aguilar and Washington (1990), and outlines a variety of approaches which can be used to provide staff the skills necessary to facilitate and create adventure experiences which will both meet the needs of all participants while enhancing attainment of the goals of adventure education.

Making a Commitment

The primary goals of adventure learning as stated in Priest and Gass (1997) discuss the common "products" of adventure programs include acquiring facts about an activity and/

or the environment; technical skill development; and emotional and social development (Ford and Blanchard, 1993; Priest and Gass, 1997). The goals of adventure education are more effective for all participants, leaders and administrators when a commitment is made to infuse social justice awareness, diversity knowledge and cross-cultural skills into the competencies of outdoor leaders.

People with disabilities, women, people for whom English is not the first language, people of color, and others traditionally not represented, bring different and beneficial perspectives to our programs. The benefits which can be gained when a diverse group comes together to develop, implement, process and evaluate adventure programs will result in programs which nurture development in everyone and provide effective skills for working, learning and living in a pluralistic society. When allowed to, members of varying ethnic and cultural backgrounds can help programs grow and improve by challenging basic assumptions about the organization's operations, practices, and methods of teaching.

Conclusion

Transferring the concepts from intellectual knowledge to practice takes time. When a small child hears not to touch the stove because it is hot, it takes only the instant of touching a hot stove to learn that doing so will hurt. Diversity knowledge is not learned as quickly because people and situations are not all the same. Just because the stove is hot, does not mean the child then understands that campfires, matches, and light bulbs are also hot. Transferring knowledge about diversity into practice as leaders, directors, and managers of adventure education programs is a lifelong process. This is not just about making a commitment to "walk the talk," but rather a commitment to the process of "walking toward the talk." The process of diversity education is cyclical, filled with moments of brilliant clarity, confusion, fear and joy, and takes a commitment to stay on the path.

Suggested Resources

Cox, T. (1994). *Cultural diversity in organizations: Theory, research & practice.* San Francisco, CA: Berrett-Kochler.

Cushner, K., McClelland, A., and Safford, P. (1992). *Human diversity in education: An integrative approach.* New York, NY: McGraw-Hill.

Ewert, A. W., Chavez, D. J., and Magill, A. W. (Eds.). (1993). *Culture, conflict, and communication in the wildland-urban interface.* Boulder, CO: Westview Press.

Gardenswartz, L., and Rowe, A. (1994). *The managing diversity survival guide: A complete collection of check lists, activities, and tips.* Chicago, IL: Irwin Professional Publishing.

Table 48.1   Professional Development for Teaching Cross-Cultural Competencies

Format or Activity	Primary Goal(s)	Strengths	Limitations
Workshops	Increased awareness of need for addressing diversity skills	Topics tailored to organization	Breadth not depth; one-time workshops limited in impact
Structured discussion groups	Discuss experiences with diversity; examine personal barriers; awareness	Personal growth; establish support groups; connect to discipline	Fear of exposure; time commitment; requires leadership
Culturally diverse guest lectures and panel presentations	Appreciate cultural differences, knowledge, awareness	Direct exposure to diversity; message by authority	Passive participation; availability of speakers
Ongoing reading groups	Examine literature on diversity; application to experiences and discipline; knowledge	Active participation; depth; educational resource	Small groups only; time commitment; selected readings
Diversity education courses/Professional development series	Increased knowledge and understanding of cultural groups; skill building	Intense educational experience; longer time; classroom exchange	Time, financial and staff commitment
Consultants	Create organizational diversity education strategy; skills, knowledge, awareness	Exposure to current issues and state-of-the-art in diversity education	Resources needed; cooperation of critical mass of staff
Resource center	Collection of media and other educational materials; knowledge	Convenience of one location for resources; self-paced development	Need for coordinator; central location; commitment of funds
Community services and events	Exposure to programs serving culturally diverse groups; knowledge	Direct contact with diversity; increased knowledge of cultural groups	Limited by existing opportunities or settings; time commitment

SOURCE: Adapted from Aguilar and Washington, 1990, p. 52.

Katz, J. H. (1978). *White awareness: Handbook for antiracism training.* Stillwater, OK: University of Oklahoma Press.

Meier, K. S., and Stafford, J. S. (1995). *25 diversity exercises to bridge cultural barriers.* Jacksonville Beach, FL: Talico, Inc.

Myers, S., and Lambert, J. (1994). *Diversity icebreakers: A trainers guide.* Solana Beach, CA: Intercultural Development.

Nilson, C. (1993). *Team games for trainers.* New York, NY: McGraw-Hill.

Thomas, R. R. (1991). *Beyond race and gender: Unleashing the power of your total work force by managing diversity.* New York, NY: AMACOM.

Washington, S. J. (1992). Results and implication of the 1991 multicultural curricula survey of recreation and leisure studies. *Journal of Recreation and Leisure, 12*(1), 14–20.

References

Adams, M., Bell, L. A., and Griffin, P. (1997). *Teaching for diversity and social justice: A source book.* New York, NY: Routledge.

Aguilar, T. E., and Washington, S. J. (1990). Towards the inclusion of multicultural issues in leisure studies curricula. *Schole: A Journal of Leisure Studies and Recreation Education, 5,* 43–52.

Blanchard, K., Zigarimi, P., and Zigarimi, D. (1985). *Leadership and the one-minute manager: Increasing effectiveness through situational leadership.* New York, NY: William Morrow and Company.

Burns, J. M. (1985). *Leadership.* New York, NY: HarperCollins.

Draguns, J. (1989). Dilemmas and choices in cross-cultural counseling: The universal versus the culturally distinctive. In P. Pederson, J. Draguns, W. Lonner, and J. Trimble (Eds.), *Counseling across cultures* (pp. 3–21). Honolulu, HI: University of Hawaii Press.

Ewert, A. W. (1989). *Outdoor adventure pursuits: Foundations, models, and theories.* Worthington, OH: Publishing Horizons.

Ford, P., and Blanchard, J. (1993). *Leadership and administration of outdoor pursuits* (2nd ed.). State College, PA: Venture Publishing, Inc.

Gardenswartz, L., and Rowe, A. (1994). *Diverse teams at work: Capitalizing on the power of diversity.* Chicago, IL: Irwin Professional Publishing.

Loden, M., and Rosener, J. B. (1991). *Workforce America! Managing employee diversity as a vital resource.* Homewood, IL: Business One Irwin.

Lustig, M. W., and Koestner, J. (1996). *Intercultural competence: Interpersonal communication across cultures.* New York, NY: HarperCollins.

Miner, J. L. (1990). The creation of Outward Bound. In J. C. Miles and S. Priest (Eds.), *Adventure education* (pp. 55–66). State College, PA: Venture Publishing, Inc.

Priest, S., and Gass, M. A. (1997). *Effective leadership in adventure programming.* Champaign, IL: Human Kinetics.

Roberts, N. S., and Gray, S. (1997). The impact of diversity issues on risk management. *Conference Proceedings,* Wilderness Risk Managers Conference, October 12–14, 1997, Snowbird, Utah. Lander, WY: National Outdoor Leadership School.

Washington, S. J. (1996). Diversity education for professional practice. *Leisure Today, Journal of Physical Education, Recreation and Dance, 67*(2), 42–44.

Chapter 49

The Use of Adventure-Based Programs With At-Risk Youth

Jennifer Davis-Berman
The University of Dayton

Dene Berman
Lifespan Counseling Associates

Adventure-based programs are often utilized with adolescents, many of whom are labeled as "at risk." In this chapter, we will briefly discuss this population, focusing on teens at risk for both mental health and delinquency problems. Next, we will examine a few examples of adventure-based programs, and comment on their effectiveness. Finally, we will close this chapter by discussing the appropriateness of these programs for at-risk youth, and by discussing critical issues in the field.

Adolescence

Adolescence is often described as both an exciting and tumultuous time. The first psychological theory of adolescence was posited by G. Stanley Hall in 1916. He suggested that the dramatic physical changes that occur during this phase of life lead to related psychological stress and change. It was his belief that adolescents emerged from this stage morally stronger.

Others, like Erikson (1968), supported this *Sturm und Drang* (storm and stress) conceptualization of adolescence. He suggested that the conflicts of adolescence must be successfully resolved for healthy adult functioning to emerge. The primary adolescent crisis according to Erikson involves the resolution of the identity versus role confusion dilemma. During this period, adolescents try to make sense of physical changes and incorporate them into a coherent identity. They also experiment with a variety of different roles, often modeling the behaviors of significant others (Erikson, 1968).

The adolescent challenges of girls are explored in the bestseller, *Reviving Ophelia* (Pipher, 1994). In this book, a therapist recounts cases and analyzes the stress placed on teenage girls, and the symptoms and disorders that they express as a result. In particular, she discusses depression, substance use, and body image distortion in teen girls. In the end, Pipher (1994) characterizes early adolescence in girls as a hurricane that most survive, although it is difficult.

In a perfect world, we would hope that all teens would successfully weather the storms of adolescence, would optimally complete their developmental tasks, and come away with a solid sense of security and positive identity. Those who work with adolescents, however, know that this is often not the case. While some young people seem to sail through this life period, others really struggle. These are often the kids whom we end up seeing in adventure-based programs. Before one decides that they are simply bad or troubled or even at risk, it is important to quickly reflect on some of the stressors encountered by young people today.

At-Risk Youth

Simply put, life is hard, and it is especially hard for certain groups, including adolescents and children. Poverty is a devastating problem for children. From the late 1980s to the early 1990s, the number of children aged six and under in poverty grew by one million, representing the largest rate in 25 years. Sadly, 57 percent of these children live in families where one or both parents work full time (Knitzer and Aber, 1995).

Young people of color are even more likely to be poor, with 33 percent of poor children being Black, and 21 percent being non-White Hispanic (Connell, 1994). Needless to say, poverty causes family instability, and its effects are profound on the youth of this country. From this stressful beginning, we see kids move to the streets, to delinquency and to some often serious mental health problems. It is beyond the scope of this chapter to address the alarming poverty and present assault on the social welfare system. However, social workers and other human service professionals are struggling with how to do more with less. With recent changes in the welfare system, these efforts must intensify. Interested readers are referred to an issue of *Social Work* that focuses on this crisis (National Association of Social Workers, 1996).

Within this societal context, adolescents suffer from mental health problems, become delinquent and are often labeled as at risk. Although it is difficult to accurately determine the scope of the problem, it is considerable. Estimates suggest that about 15 percent of the adolescent population suffers from a diagnosable mental health disorder (Brandenburg, Friedman, and Silver, 1990), and that over the past 30 years, the suicide rate for this group has tripled, now representing the third leading cause of death (Berman and Jobes, 1991). Unfortunately, children and adolescents tend to be an underserved population in the mental health system. It has been estimated that less than one-third of children and adolescents needing services actually receive them. Additionally, when services are provided, they are often inappropriate (Children's Defense Fund, 1994). In fact, it has been suggested that there is a real lack of intermediate level mental health services for children and adolescents. As a result, there is an overreliance on the more restrictive, inpatient option (Collins and Collins, 1994).

Similar to the mental health impact on vulnerable adolescents, the interface of the court system with adolescents has rapidly increased over the past few years. In fact, studies have shown that the number of violent offenses committed by juveniles is on the rise, and that excluding rape and prostitution, 19 percent of the sex offenses in 1993 were committed by juveniles (U.S. Bureau of the Census, 1995). In response to these increases in violence, dollars were allocated under the Violent Crime Control and Law Enforcement Act of 1994 for the establishment of military-like boot camps for youthful offenders (U.S. Department of Justice, 1995). Many of these camps use strict discipline combined with outdoor experience to work with delinquent kids. Perhaps in these days of diminished federal responsibility and family instability, these "boot camp" approaches will gain popularity as alternatives to previously ineffective traditional approaches to rehabilitation and treatment.

These approaches, however, are not new. Rather, the use of the out-of-doors as treatment for at-risk adolescents dates back to the early 1900s, with Camp Ahmek. This program served adolescent boys, and had as one of its stated goals the socialization of the camper's behavior (Dimock and Hendry, 1939). Early writings (e.g., Harms, 1947) extolled the virtues of the use of the out-of-doors in a therapeutic fashion with youth. Numerous outdoor programs geared toward working with "at-risk" teens are described in the literature (see Davis-Berman and Berman, 1994), which clearly establish a historical precedent for the development and implementation of programs today.

Programs

During the process of writing a book on wilderness therapy, we had the opportunity to talk with representatives of hundreds of programs throughout the United States. The types of adolescents served in mental health programs varies widely. Some may be experiencing family problems, while others suffer from low self-esteem. Others are struggling with anger control issues, and some are diagnosed with depression. Often, adolescents who are experiencing delusions or hallucinations are excluded. The court-related programs, of course, serve adolescents that are in the criminal justice system. Other programs attempt to prevent delinquency in high-risk adolescents. The following section of this chapter reports on the findings of some of this research describing mental health and court-related programs (Davis-Berman and Berman, 1994; Davis-Berman, Berman, and Capone, 1994).

Mental Health Programs

We began our survey of adventure-based therapeutic programs by compiling a list of current programs. These programs ranged from intensive mental health programs to enrichment programs for those who were very high functioning. Sources for identifying programs included the professional literature, and the referrals of other program operators.

In order to more fully understand the operations of these adventure-based programs, telephone surveys were done with the program administrators. Through these interviews, the structure, funding and staffing patterns of the programs were described. Other issues like program evaluation, cost, and type of treatment were also discussed. The following represents some of the findings of this research.

Generally, mental health programs serving at-risk youth are usually outpatient, inpatient, or residential in design. Additionally, many programs that identify themselves as therapeutic are focused on the problem of youth substance abuse. Not surprisingly, many of the residential or inpatient programs are privately sponsored, with some for-profit and some nonprofit facilities. Most of the outpatient programs are also privately sponsored, again, with a mixture of for-profit and nonprofit sponsorship. The fee schedules for these programs vary widely, dependent on sponsorship type, program design, and type of client served. Based on these variables, fees ranged from zero to almost $10,000 for a 30-day experience.

The type of outdoor experience offered in the treatment programs also varies widely. Many of the inpatient programs offer a rather restricted experiential therapy component, with the most popular modality being ropes courses. Other programs do offer a more extensive outdoor component, including wilderness expeditions and wilderness base camp experiences. Outpatient programs generally offer more intensive, lengthier wilderness experiences, sometimes involving up to a month in wilderness settings.

In terms of therapy, the approaches reported are as diverse as the clients served and the program designs. Interestingly, the majority of programs examined failed to specifically describe their therapeutic modalities. Some mentioned group therapy, the use of metaphors, and cognitive approaches. However, more specific information was usually not given.

Finally, the majority of the programs appear to collect evaluation data in a very informal fashion. Questionnaires are sent to families and participants after the program for the impressions of the participants and families. Some programs, however, do administer quantitative evaluation materials before and after the outdoor experience.

An interesting outpatient program in the Midwest provides services at no cost to clients, as the Department of Human Services supports the program. While enrolled in this program, participants live at home and engage in outdoor activities throughout the year. During their time in the program, participants experience individual, group and family therapy. Thus, in this program, the outdoor activities serve as an adjunct to more traditional therapy services.

Another program example is a longstanding residential camp in Texas. Adolescents reside at this camp for a period of usually six to nine months. In this program, small groups are formed, and participants engage in backpacking and canoeing activities. Students must attend an onsite school and must participate in both group and family therapy while involved in the therapeutic experience (Davis-Berman and Berman, 1994; Davis-Berman, Berman, and Capone, 1994).

Court-Related Programs

Although a number of the mental health programs include clients with court-related issues, there are some wilderness programs devoted strictly to the treatment of delinquents. Interestingly, however, the number of court-related programs is far fewer than those devoted solely to mental health.

The severity of the difficulties experienced by the delinquent clients truly makes these court-related programs distinct from those solely focused on mental health. Adolescents sent to the court programs have often been in numerous outpatient and inpatient settings, and have failed to change in meaningful ways in these programs. Thus, adventure-based programs for delinquents sometimes serve as an alternative to traditional incarceration, or as an adjunct to some kind of residential care. Similar to the mental health offerings, there is a great diversity in the funding of court-related programs. However, some interesting public-private joint programs do exist. There is also a tremendous variety in the extensiveness of the adventure or wilderness experience between programs. Some programs offer limited experiences, such as low and high ropes. Others offer more in-depth backpacking and camping expeditions.

One of the more interesting court-related programs is based in the West, and has been operating for more than 20 years. This program is rather controversial, as it has been criticized for being very survivalist in its orientation. Utilizing a multistage format, this program includes base camp, counseling, and the choice of participating in a number of different outdoor activities.

A residentially oriented program in the East begins with participants embarking on a wilderness trip. At the conclusion of this trip, some are ready to leave the program. Others continue to live in the camp-oriented base camp, going to school and engaging in school, work, and service.

The court-related programs seem to have done a better job with program evaluation than some of the other types of programs. This might be due to the requirements of some of the federal and state funders more likely to be involved with the court-related programs (Davis-Berman and Berman, 1994).

A Look at Effectiveness

It is clearly beyond the scope of this chapter to comprehensively cover the relevant research that has been done to support the efficacy of the mental health and court-related programs. However, we will highlight some of the classic findings, and whenever possible, refer the reader to reference sources. Those interested in further evaluation research are referred to studies done on the Outward Bound program (e.g., Bacon, 1988; Shore, 1977) and to a more recent meta-analysis of data (Cason and Gillis, 1994).

Mental Health Programs

The mental health programs often try to document self-concept or self-esteem change as a result of program participation. As early as 1973, Krieger found significant increases in self-concept in campers as opposed to a control group. Similarly, Chenery (1981) found significant increases in self-concept after the adventure program, with a decrease in what were identified as negative behaviors.

As part of our work and interest in wilderness therapy, we reported on the results of four wilderness therapy trips. All participants in these groups were adolescents with family problems, depression, and/or anger and impulse control problems. At the conclusion of the treatment program, a significant increase in both self-efficacy and self-esteem were found. Participants also experienced a general decrease in symptomatology at posttest (Davis-Berman and Berman, 1989).

Cason and Gillis (1994) presented a meta-analysis looking at 43 adventure-oriented studies of programs serving adolescents. Basically, it was concluded that the adventure programs were associated with increased self-concept, attitudes and grades. Adolescents were also found to become more internal in their locus of control following treatment.

Continued discussion of the need for research on program effectiveness has occurred both informally and in the literature. In fact, this issue has taken such precedence that it was highlighted in an issue of the *Journal of Experiential Education* devoted solely to adventure therapy (Berman, 1995).

There are a few classic outcome studies done on delinquency programs that continue to be frequently cited, and even set the standard for future research. Kelly and Baer (1968) were pioneers with their evaluation of an Outward Bound program in Massachusetts. They found significant changes in characteristics such as asocial behavior, aggression, and social maladjustment. Additionally, the recidivism rate for the treatment group after nine months was 20 percent, as compared to a rate of 34 percent in the comparison group.

Similarly, Willman, and Chun (1973) evaluated an Outward Bound program geared toward delinquents. Fourteen months after the end of the program, the recidivism rate of the treatment group was 20.8 percent, as compared with a rate of 42.7 percent for the control group. For further discussion of the effectiveness of adventure-based programs for delinquents, the reader is referred to reviews by Wichmann (1983) and Roberts (1988).

It appears that adventure-based programs are most effective in promoting change in self-esteem levels in participants. It also seems that programs geared toward delinquents do seem to reduce the recidivism rates among this population. Obviously, more research needs to be done to evaluate the effectiveness of adventure-based programs. This is especially important in these days of managed care, if programs are to rely on insurance reimbursement.

Due to the innovative nature and design of adventure-based programs, they are difficult to evaluate. Often activities are taking place in wilderness or other outdoor environments. Other programs are so intense that evaluation would seem to detract from the treatment process. Some programs do not have well-developed treatment methods, thus, evaluation is difficult. Finally, small sample sizes and the difficulties in securing comparison groups add to the challenge of evaluating adventure-based programs (Davis-Berman and Berman, 1994).

Why Adventure-Based Programs Work

It is usually in the best interest of the child or adolescent to be treated in what is generally called *the least restrictive environment*. In other words, an effort is made to maintain as much personal freedom and control for clients as possible. Many times, adolescents can be treated outside of the hospital even for fairly serious disorders. Adventure-based programs provide an adjunct to treatment, which may intensify the experience, thus avoiding the need for more restrictive hospitalization. This was illustrated on a wilderness therapy trip with hospitalized adolescents. Interestingly, the majority of the participants did very well outside of the restricted hospital environment, with some experiencing faster change than would be expected during a typical hospitalization (Berman and Anton, 1988).

In addition to the restrictions of the traditional therapy setting, therapy requires that the adolescent be attentive, introspective and verbal. It also requires that the client trust and confide in the therapist fairly rapidly (Saffer and Naylor, 1988). This can be very difficult for many adolescents, and may be frustrating for those unable to be verbally expressive. Adolescents with attention deficit disorder (American Psychiatric Association, 1994) may not respond very well to traditional therapy. Finally, the traditional therapy notion of the "50-minute hour" may not fit well with the personality and experiences of the adolescent, and in fact, may become a deterrent to progress in therapy.

The use of adventure-based methods and outdoor environments opens the possibilities for change. Adolescents can be exposed to methods that are active rather than passive. Although there surely will be talk therapy in wilderness therapy programs, action-oriented methods will also abound. For some, these experiences serve as a catalyst to encourage further exploration and growth. For other adolescents, these experiences in and of themselves are all that they can handle at the time. Others may become quite sophisticated with the use of the metaphor in therapy (Gass, 1993).

It is beyond the scope of this chapter to detail the use of metaphors in adventure-oriented therapy. The interested reader is referred to Gass (1993). Others (e.g., Handley, 1992; Pinkard, 1995; Priest and Gass, 1993) have presented in-depth discussion of the use of metaphor in adventure therapy, and serve as resources in the field.

In addition to the use of metaphor as a more novel approach to therapy, placing adolescents in adventure-based programs puts them outside of their comfort zones. For some, this involves engaging in activities in which they are not familiar, and that threaten their security. For others, this means being in an unfamiliar wilderness environment—feeling the insecurity that comes with that experience. Nadler and Luckner (1992) among others have suggested that our greatest change and growth can occur when participants are at the edges of these comfort zones. Another element of adventure-oriented programs for adolescents that may facilitate change is the notion of perceived risk in programs. Although there has been debate in the literature regarding the appropriateness of the perception of risk (e.g., Mitten, 1996), it appears to be a common element. Many programs attempt to create a perception of risk, with the actual risk to the participants being quite low (Davis-Berman and Berman, 1994).

Finally, the characteristics of wilderness environments which are often used in adventure-based programs contribute to the efficacy of this approach with adolescents. First, the outdoor environment provides natural and direct consequences for the behaviors of adolescents. Thus, acting out or lack of cooperation need not be dealt with by staff as closely; rather, the natural consequences of these acts take over. As a result, adolescents sometimes begin to cooperate more easily, and may even relate to the leaders of the trip in a more healthy fashion. According to this model, trip leaders are positive role models, directing behavior and encouraging both cooperation and leadership in the participants (Davis-Berman and Berman, 1994).

Critical and Emerging Issues

Throughout this chapter, we have looked to the past and have discussed the present as related to adventure-oriented programs for at-risk youth. In closing, we turn an eye to the future and detail some of the issues that are being identified as critical to the development of this field.

The need for well-designed and analyzed research studies has been previously discussed for a number of years. However, this lack of research continues to plague the field. Recent authors continue to call for refined research on the effectiveness of adventure-oriented programs (e.g., Berman and Davis-Berman, 1995; Gillis, 1995). It has been suggested that this need for research is even more important due to the influence of managed care companies in the provision of mental health services. If adventure-oriented programs are to be accepted as legitimate therapy, outcome research must support this contention (Davis-Berman and Berman, 1994).

Of course, the transfer of learning and the permanence of change continues to be a critical issue in this field. It is important to question the ethics of providing adventure-oriented programs if the "high" that one might experience and the great insights gained are temporary. It might even be true that the elements of these programs that contribute so much to their effectiveness may, themselves, set adolescents up for a crisis (Berman, Davis-Berman, and Gillen, 1997). Practitioners in the field must continue to think about

developing methods to facilitate the transfer of learning and therapeutic progress (Gass, 1993; Nadler and Luckner, 1992).

The fairly recent public attention to tragedies in "wilderness therapy" programs (e.g., Carpenter, 1995; Griffin, 1995; Matthews, 1991) highlights the need for the continued development of program standards and regulations. The advent of accreditation by the Association for Experiential Education has been a big step in the right direction.

However, in addition to examining programs, it is important to think about the credentials of the staff working in the programs. Some have called for the development of standards or achieved competencies. Others have taken a more stringent approach and called for education and licensing requirements for program staff (Davis-Berman and Berman, 1994). This debate is far from over, and forms the basis for one of the most critical issues in the field.

The continued growth of the managed care industry makes this issue even more compelling and pressing, as most of these companies credential individual practitioners. We would also assert that this individual credentialing is critical because of the need for emotional safety. It is interesting that so much is written in the field of adventure therapy on physical safety and technical skill. Although certainly critical, we would assert that emotional safety and skill in counseling and therapy is as essential as the skills that are labeled as "hard" (Berman et al., 1997; Vincent, 1995). At the present time, the best and most consistent way of acquiring this skill is through the appropriate education and licensing processes.

Summing Up

This chapter has introduced the use of adventure-based approaches in therapeutic programs for at-risk youth. Unfortunately, this task has been made more difficult due to the lack of a well-conceived definition of adventure-based programs. There is also no clear agreement on the distinctions between therapy and therapeutic programs (Davis-Berman and Berman, 1994).

Despite these shortcomings, the application of adventure-oriented programs to adolescents in need continues to occur. In support of this contention, we described a few representative programs in the field, with existing research studies suggesting program effectiveness. Finally, we concluded by trying to identify elements of adventure-based programs that make them especially applicable to troubled adolescents. This chapter ended with a discussion of salient issues in the field.

The use of adventure-based programs for at-risk youth is exciting, creative, and efficacious. There is much more work to be done, and critical discussions still need to take place. Those of us who are committed to the continued care and treatment of children and young people look forward to these debates and to the further definition of the field.

References

American Psychiatric Association. (1994). *Diagnostic and statistical manual of mental disorders* (4th ed.). Washington, DC: Author.

Association for Experiential Education. (1995). *Journal of Experiential Education, 18*(2).

Bacon, S. (1988). *Paradox and double-binds in adventure-based education* (Eric Document Reproduction Service No. 296832). Greenwich, CT: Outward Bound.

Berman, D. (1995). Adventure therapy: Current status and future directions. *Journal of Experiential Education, 18*(2), 61–62.

Berman, D., and Anton, M. (1988). A wilderness therapy program as an alternative to adolescent psychiatric hospitalization. *Residential Treatment for Children and Youth, 5,* 39–52.

Berman, D., and Davis-Berman, J. (1989). Wilderness therapy: A therapeutic adventure for adolescents. *Journal of Independent Social Work, 3*(3), 65–77.

Berman, D., Davis-Berman, J., and Gillen, M. (1997). *Crisis management in adventure education.* Unpublished manuscript.

Berman, A., and Jobes, D. (1991). *Adolescent suicide: Assessment and intervention.* Washington, DC: American Psychological Association.

Brandenburg, N., Friedman, R., and Silver, R. (1990). The epidemiology of childhood psychiatric disorders: Prevalence findings from recent studies. *Journal of the American Academy of Child and Adolescent Psychiatry, 29,* 76–83.

Carpenter, B. (1995). Taking nature's cure. Do expensive wilderness therapy camps help or hurt troubled teens? *US News and World Report, 118*(25), 54–58.

Cason, D., and Gillis, H. L. (1994). A meta-analysis of outdoor adventure programming with adolescents. *Journal of Experiential Education, 17,* 40–47.

Chenery, M. (1981). Effects of summer camp on child development and contributions of counselors to those effects. *Journal of Leisure Research, 3,* 195–207.

Children's Defense Fund. (1994). *Mental illness in the family: Mental health statistics.* Rockville, MD: Center for Mental Health Services.

Collins, B. G., and Collins, T. M. (1994). Child and adolescent mental health: Building a system of care. *Journal of Counseling and Development, 72,* 239–243.

Connell, R. W. (1994). Poverty and education. *Harvard Educational Review, 64,* 125–149.

Davis-Berman, J., and Berman, D. (1989). The wilderness therapy program: An empirical study of its effects with adolescents in an outpatient setting. *Journal of Contemporary Psychotherapy, 19*(4), 271–281.

Davis-Berman, J., and Berman, D. (1994). *Wilderness therapy: Foundations, theory and research.* Dubuque, IA: Kendall/Hunt Publishing Co.

Davis-Berman, J., Berman, D., and Capone, L. (1994). Therapeutic wilderness programs: A national survey. *Journal of Experiential Education, 17*(2), 49–53.

Dimock, H., and Hendry, C. (1939). *Camping and character: A camp experiment in character education.* New York, NY: Association Press.

Erikson, E. H. (1968). *Identity: Youth crisis.* New York, NY: Norton.

Gass, M. H. (1993). *Adventure therapy: Therapeutic applications of adventure programming in mental health settings.* Boulder, CO: Association for Experiential Education.

Gillis, H. L. (1995). If I conduct outdoor pursuits with clinical populations, am I an adventure therapist? *Journal of Leisurability, 22*(2), 5–15.

Griffin, K. (1995). Dangerous discipline. *Health, 9*(3), 94–99.

Hall, G. S. (1916). *Adolescence.* New York, NY: Appleton.

Handley, R. (1992). *The wilderness within: Wilderness enhanced programs for behavior disordered adolescents—A cybernetic systemic model.* Paper presented at the 4th National Conference on Children with Emotional or Behavior Problems, Port Kembla, Australia.

Harms, E. (1947). Camps as mental health institutions. *The Nervous Child, 6,* 173–177.

Kelly, F. J., and Baer, D. J. (1968). *Outward Bound schools as an alternative to institutionalization for adolescent delinquent boys.* Boston, MA: Fandel Press.

Krieger, W. (1973). Study on self-concept change in campers. *Camping Magazine, 45*(4), 16–17.

Knitzer, J., and Aber, L. (1995). Young children in poverty: Facing the facts. *Opinion, 65,* 174–176.

Matthews, M. (1991). Wilderness programs offer promising alternatives for some youth: More regulation likely. *Youth Law News, 12*(6), 12–15.

Mitten, D. (1996). A philosophical basis for a women's outdoor adventure program. In K. Warren (Ed.), *Women's voices in experiential education.* Dubuque, IA: Kendall/Hunt Publishing Co.

Nadler, R., and Luckner, J. (1992). *Processing the adventure experience: Theory and practice.* Dubuque, IA: Kendall/Hunt Publishing Co.

National Association of Social Workers. (1996). *Social Work, 41*(5).

Pinkard, J. (1995). *Mapping out the territory: Beyond isomorphs and metaphors in adventure-based programs.* Paper presented at the 9th National outdoor Education Conference, Southport Australia.

Pipher, M. (1994). *Reviving Ophelia: Saving the selves of adolescent girls.* New York, NY: Ballantine Books.

Priest, S., and Gass, M. (1993). Five generations of facilitated learning from adolescent experiences. *The Journal of Adventure Education and Outdoor Leadership, 10*(3), 23–25.

Roberts, A. (1988). Wilderness program for juvenile offenders: A challenging alternative. *Juvenile and Family Court Journal*, 1–12.

Saffer, J. B., and Naylor, K. A. (1988). Difficulties encountered in the treatment of outpatient adolescents. *Adolescence, 22*, 143–147.

Shore, A. (1977). *Outward Bound: A reference volume*. Greenwich, CT: Outward Bound, Inc.

U.S. Bureau of the Census. (1995). *Statistical abstracts of the United States*. Washington, DC: U.S. Government Printing Office.

U.S. Department of Justice. (1995). *The nation's prison population grew almost nine percent last year*. Washington, DC: U.S. Government Printing Office.

Vincent, S. (1995). Emotional safety in adventure therapy programs: Can it be defined? *Journal of Experiential Education, 18*(2), 76–81.

Wichman, T. (1983). Evaluating Outward Bound for delinquent youth. *Journal of Experiential Education, 5*(3), 10–16.

Willman, H., and Chun, R. (1973). Homeward bound: An alternative to the institutionalization of adjudicated female offenders. *Federal Probation,* September, 52–58.

Chapter 50

Adventure Programs in Higher Education

Michael A. Gass
University of New Hampshire

Introduction

As adventure activities began to be adapted to meet the specific needs of certain populations, one of the first applications was for programs in higher education. In fact, in a meeting that led to the development of the Association of Experiential Education in 1974, a large number of conference participants were professionals from colleges and universities (Miner and Boldt, 1981). The intent and perspective of adventure programs in higher education are often extremely varied. From preparing sophomore high-school students for the rigors of college to offering programs for students graduating from undergraduate programs, a number of efforts have been made to implement adventure experiences into programs in higher education.

While the existence of such programs is not a recent development in the field of adventure education, the growth and utilization of such efforts has been comparatively small. Most existing programs have not developed through a general need perceived by higher education professionals, but usually by the self-designed efforts of one or two individuals at a particular institution. These individuals, usually after participating in or learning of the values of adventure experiences, devised adventure programs to meet the specific needs of their program and/or institution. While this type of "internal" development has led to a variety of applications, adventure programs in higher education have just begun to receive external professional acceptance.

Another factor that has limited the expansion of adventure programs in higher education is that programs tend to operate independently of one another. This independent growth has enabled creativity in development, but has also limited the potential expansion of such efforts.

The greatest development and application of adventure programs in higher education has been with incoming student orientation, continuing student development, and residential life training programs. Other applications have been utilized (e.g., potential college applicants, student teacher programs, physical education activity classes and curricula, and the use of adventure experiences to enhance curricula) and will briefly be discussed at the end of this chapter, but these programs have not received the same level of professional acceptance.

Incoming Student Orientation Programs

In order to ease the transition of incoming students into the educational and social experiences of university life, institutions of higher learning have implemented a variety of assistance programs, often falling under the label of "orientation programs." Since the inception of programs at Dartmouth College in 1935 and Prescott College in 1968, a number of schools have developed incoming orientation programs that incorporate adventure experiences. In a study done to examine the purposes of such programs, Gass (1984) identified 41 colleges and universities that utilize adventure experiences for incoming student orientation programs.

Most of these adventure programs focus on the same purposes as traditional orientation programs; to reduce the attrition of the undergraduate student and/or to ensure a more positive transition to college life. Other adventure programs exist that focus on other goals (e.g., providing a means of introduction to the school's outing club), but these instances occur less frequently.

Unfortunately, many early efforts in adventure programming for incoming students neglected to focus program goals on specific areas of student development. Failure to tailor these programs to the particular needs of these students inhibited many programs from reaching their full potential. Recognizing this problem, several individuals have advised program directors to focus the selection and utilization of adventure experiences to meet the needs of the incoming college student. In a paper addressing this concern, Parchem (1975) provided the following thoughts for professionals:

> In a program run at Denison University during the summer of 1974, we had incorporated a four-day and three-night solo experience. Within the traditional Outward Bound framework, the solo experience is considered to be an opportunity to reflect upon the recent challenging experience (such as a major climb), to test one's self-discipline by fasting (this differs from instructor to instructor), and to prepare oneself for the final expedition. These goals are well and good—for Outward Bound. But they did not adequately reflect what we believed college students should be getting out of a program run by an institution of higher education. In other words, we recognized that the use of the solo experience by us had different goals than such an experience has for Outward Bound. Consequently, we designed and conducted a series of value clarification exercises prior to putting people on solo. In addition, we told them in advance that part of their postsolo interview would be spent negotiating an informal contract as to what they were going to attempt to accomplish in the remainder of the course and what they wished to accomplish academically during the school year. (pp. 3–4)

Many existing programs have taken the direction of Parchem and others (e.g., Gass, Kerr, Garvey, 1986; Hansen, 1982; Stogner, 1978) and have focused program activities on developing certain areas pertinent to student adjustment. These developmental areas are crucial for all

incoming student orientation programs, whether they utilize adventure experiences or more "traditional" methods. Achievement in these critical areas generally leads to positive integration of students into the college environment. Failure to reach these areas often results in adjustment problems for students, which can lead to individuals dropping out or leaving school. These areas crucial to the development of incoming students include:

1. attachment to and isolation from peers,
2. faculty-student interaction and/or isolation,
3. focus on career development and major course of study,
4. academic interest or boredom,
5. inadequate preparation for college academics, and
6. dissonance and compatibility with college environment and student expectations.

Why Adventure Education for Incoming Students?

Given the positive effects of incoming student orientation programs using adventure experiences that focus on these six areas, what are the reasons for their success? How can placing incoming students into environments quite different than that of a university classroom (e.g., unfamiliar wilderness settings) have such a strong influence on a student's ability to adjust to school? Questions like these are often asked by administrators, parents, and incoming students. Clear and well-supported answers to such questions often mean the difference between maintaining an integrated, well-respected program or struggling with an isolated and often fragmented effort.

Several areas of explanation exist that substantiate the use of adventure experiences for incoming orientation programs. Most of these areas relate to the effectiveness of using an adventurous environment to reach the developmental areas described previously (Figure 50.1).

Developing Meaningful Peer Relationships

One goal critical to student adjustment is the development of meaningful and positive peer relationships. Attachment to a positive peer group is seen as an extremely valuable step for students making the transition to university life. This has been particularly true in areas of academic success and persistence (Astin, 1975; Tinto and Cullen, 1973), positive academic and social integration skills (Astin, 1975), and in developing greater levels of trust, independence, and individuality (Winston, Prince, and Miller, 1983). Others (e.g., Astin, 1975; Faugh et al., 1982; Tinto and Cullen, 1973) have found isolation from peers highly related to academic failure and attrition from school.

Figure 50.1   Areas That Lead to Student Development

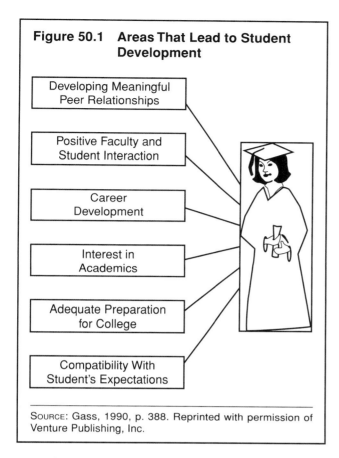

- Developing Meaningful Peer Relationships
- Positive Faculty and Student Interaction
- Career Development
- Interest in Academics
- Adequate Preparation for College
- Compatibility With Student's Expectations

SOURCE: Gass, 1990, p. 388. Reprinted with permission of Venture Publishing, Inc.

Adventure activities, especially those that are conducted in small groups, are extremely well-suited to nurturing the formation of positive peer group development with incoming students. The bonds and interdependence developed to overcome the difficulties of the wilderness are used to overcome similar difficulties experienced by students in their first year of school. These meaningful peer relationships continue to be reinforced as students utilize the behaviors learned and implemented from their adventure experience in their established peer reference groups as they enter college. Participants turn for help and to help fellow students at school, just as they gave and received assistance in the adventure experiences.

Faculty-Student Interaction

Interaction with faculty members has also proven to be extremely helpful in the transition of students to college life. Several researchers (e.g., Faugh et al., 1982; Ramist, 1981; Terenzini and Pascarella, 1980) have found it to be positively related to both student academic as well as interpersonal growth. Terenzini and Pascarella (1980) also reported that the lack of nonclassroom interaction with faculty, especially concerning intellectual or subject-related matters, is connected to student withdrawal.

Interaction with group members in adventure experiences requires support and reciprocity (Kerr and Gass,

1987; Walsh and Golins, 1976). Being placed in these types of situations with faculty members provides incoming students with a sense of personal validity and a feeling that the university is concerned about the student as an individual. It is also felt that by using adventure experiences as a base to begin such relationships, students and faculty will attain more accurate perceptions of one another. Students also develop a more comfortable feeling about approaching faculty and positive relationships are fostered through involvement in adventure experiences. Such contacts are extended into the school year and act as a base for students to achieve positive integration into the university community. It is often felt that this type of medium is much more appropriate to use as a student's first interaction with faculty, rather than in a room with 300 other incoming freshmen during the first day of classes!

Focus on Career Development and Major Course of Study

A number of individuals (e.g., Ramist, 1981; Tinto and Cullen, 1973) have illustrated the negative effects of students lacking direction toward career goals or major areas of study. In the same study, Ramist (1981) found that even if students are unclear about a choice of a career or major, direction toward even tentative study plans led to greater motivation to do coursework.

Much of the time spent by faculty advising incoming students during adventure experiences focuses on answering questions about being a student in a college setting and providing accurate information to plan appropriate goals for school and career. Faculty, staff, and upperclassmen are often utilized as instructors or facilitators in adventure experiences for incoming freshmen. When in this role, it is their intent to utilize adventure experiences as a means to generate discussions concerning career development and provide feedback to incoming students about the academic decisions they are contemplating.

One example of utilizing an adventure experience for career development can be seen in the planning of a hiking experience by the orientation group. Here the beneficial elements of planning the hiking experience are linked to the elements of planning a positive educational experience. In both situations, similar elements of providing appropriate resources, selecting appropriate goals based on personal and supporting resources, choosing a path that is challenging and enriching, and persisting to accomplish a long and difficult goal are required to complete both tasks. These tasks are metaphorically linked together so that learning the proper planning of the hiking experience facilitates the development of the students' decision-making process in preparing and planning for study areas and career considerations. This form of metaphoric transfer (Bacon, 1983) is critical in the utilization of adventure experiences for a variety of populations.

Academic Interest or Boredom

The amount of academic interest, and conversely, the lack of academic stimulation, have been found to play an important role in student transition and persistence in school. Several individuals (e.g., Astin, 1975; Ramist, 1981; Tinto and Cullen, 1973) have found that low academic stimulation and the inability of students to reach their potential in academic areas often leads to student withdrawal.

Metaphoric transfer from adventure experiences can also be used to provide incoming students with other perspectives of the academic world of higher education. The outdoors, like the world of academia, possesses a great deal of stimulating opportunities. There are other times, however, that an individual encounters activities in both environments that are not as exciting as others, yet necessary to achieve desired goals. Whether it be a student studying for a final examination, or the same person struggling over a mountain pass, each person must learn to search for personal relevance in their efforts and determine the means to motivate oneself. The ability to provide personal motivation in one situation (e.g., tedious hiking to achieve a desired goal) is metaphorically linked to the other.

Inadequate Preparation for College Academics

Given the reduction of many schools' academic standards for admission, the number of students leaving due to inadequate preparation for school has increased (Green, 1985). While many of the factors in this lack of preparation include inadequate cognitive abilities (e.g., intellectual skills; Ramist, 1981), other related factors also play an equally important role. These factors include an inadequate concept of the meaning of work and a lack of self-discipline (DeBoer, 1983), a lack of motivation (Robertson, 1978), and an inability to assume responsibility (Astin, 1975). In an interesting discussion of all of these factors, DeBoer (1983) found that students with this problem often overestimate their abilities, are too quick to discount the effects of greater effort, and are too eager to blame external factors for poor performance. He also found effort in academics to be equally as important as student ability.

While the ability of any incoming student orientation program to compensate for poor cognitive abilities is limited, there are several factors related to inadequate college preparation that adventure programs can positively influence. As stated previously, many of the difficulties students encounter in higher education can be resolved through more accurate self-perceptions, greater persistence and effort, and self-responsibility. When focused to address these issues, adventure experiences are well-suited to positively influence and motivate incoming students in these areas. This is particularly true when one considers the motivational characteristics inherent in such activities

and that these activities are accomplished with the assistance of positive peer and faculty support.

An example of this can be seen through the use of an activity such as rock climbing. Here students are presented with a novel learning situation that appears to be extremely demanding and one that will be difficult, if not impossible, to complete. Through taking personal responsibility for themselves and others, utilizing high levels of persistence, and receiving encouragement and support from peers and faculty, students succeed in accomplishing this difficult task. Students are encouraged to reflect on the processes they utilized to accomplish this task and acknowledge the factors that led to their success. The focus of this entire process is to integrate these factors (e.g., persistence, responsibility, not discounting the value of hard work) into the novel environment the student will be entering into as an incoming first-year student.

Dissonance and Compatibility With College Environment and Student Expectations

Noel (1977) identified one of the strongest indicators of student adjustment as the relationship between what the incoming student expected college to be like and what it actually was. He also found that the larger the gap between these two factors, the more difficult the transition for students and the greater their chance of dropping out.

As incoming students approach their undergraduate education, they often rely on a number of sources of information to ascertain what "college life" is truly like. Many of these sources often provide these students with an unrealistic viewpoint of what higher education can provide for each individual. The gap between the students' expectations of college life and what it actually is can create an unpleasant dissonance as students search for perspective in their first year of school. Placing incoming students in an adventurous environment that mirrors such incongruence (i.e., one that in reality is quite different than what the person initially expected) can provide a positive environment for incoming students to reduce this dissonance. This is particularly true when one considers that these activities are done with students and faculty that are knowledgeable of the resources and realities of the school.

While it is not possible in some programs to focus on all six of these goals, adventure programs focusing activities based on these needs have demonstrated a large degree of success. This success has been found to translate into greater levels of student retention (Gass, 1987), higher first-year grade point averages (Gass, 1987; Stogner, 1978), greater levels of student development (Gass, 1987; Hansen, 1982), and increased levels of self-esteem (Jernstedt, 1986; Wetzel, 1978).

Continuing Student Orientation Programs

As efforts to enhance the orientation process in higher education have developed, there has been an expanding sensitivity to view the orientation of students to school as a continuing process, not just one that exists for individuals during their first year of school. A variety of models have been utilized in targeting the needs of these individuals (e.g., Chickering, 1969), with a predominate focus being directed to the development of students' intellectual, moral, identity, and interpersonal abilities.

The focuses in these areas of development have also created the establishment of programs that utilize adventure experiences to help reach the goals of the upperclassman. While not as numerous as efforts with incoming orientation students, a number of programs exist that utilize adventure experiences to assist in the continuing orientation process of upperclassmen (Gass et al., 1986; Smith, 1984).

As with incoming student programs that use adventure experiences to enhance the orientation process, continuing programs have focused on using such activities to meet the needs and goals of students as they continue to grow in their university experience. Gass et al. (1986) describe one such model where the intellectual, identity, and interpersonal needs of upperclassmen are met through a continuing orientation program that uses adventure experiences. These needs are achieved through the following six goals (Figure 50.2):

1. *Provide a forum for students, faculty, and staff members to participate as colearners in a vigorous learning environment.* By bringing students together with faculty and staff members as colearners, students gain the opportunity to be involved in the "process" of problem solving. In most traditional teacher-student relationships, students are often denied the opportunity to witness how a faculty member arrived at an answer. Adventure activities place faculty and students in a novel environment where the entire group works together as partners making decisions, analyzing various options, and following a plan to its conclusion.

2. *Encourage the development of responsible behavior while working as a group member.* Adventure activities are designed so that par-

ticipants are required to exercise self-control, consideration of others, and good judgment related to understanding one's own strength and limitations. The success of the experience is often the result of the cooperative posture of group members. The focus of these activities is to transfer these qualities into the students' lives where responsible behavior is required, thereby contributing positively to the life and vitality of the campus.

3. *Offer a variety of "vigorous learning environments" to the university community.* Too often learning at universities becomes extremely theoretical and students experience very little mastery of the subject material. One of the goals of adventure experiences used in continuing orientation programs is to permit students to experience a wide range of learning environments that require the utilization and completion of tasks. The completion of such tasks broadens students' perspectives of how they learn and provides motivation to attempt new areas of learning and discovery.

4. *Use the wilderness as a natural setting for the study of female and male roles.* The wilderness provides an excellent setting for participants to gain an understanding of the limits inherent in traditional sex role stereotyping. Activities are structured so that participants are encouraged to transcend these

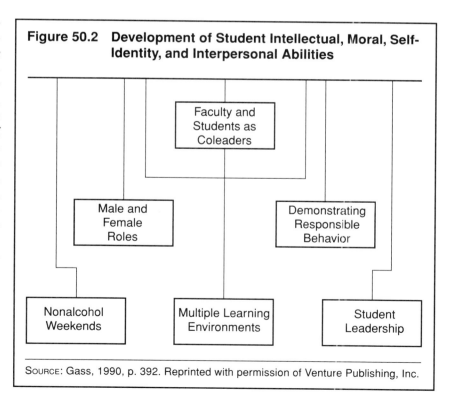

Figure 50.2   Development of Student Intellectual, Moral, Self-Identity, and Interpersonal Abilities

Faculty and Students as Coleaders

Male and Female Roles

Demonstrating Responsible Behavior

Nonalcohol Weekends

Multiple Learning Environments

Student Leadership

Source: Gass, 1990, p. 392. Reprinted with permission of Venture Publishing, Inc.

limitations and explore new perspectives relative to the role of men and women in other settings.

5. *Provide nonalcoholic programs on weekends for students.* Many institutions in higher learning are continually addressing the issue of alcohol and other drugs in campus life. By conducting nonalcoholic weekend experiences for students, programs ask students to focus on the role of alcohol in their lives (e.g., the need for alcohol to have a good time, the reasons why students use alcohol, the role of alcohol in relating to peers).

6. *Provide learning experiences in leadership positions for students.* Much of the learning in colleges precludes students from accepting responsibility and being placed in positions of leadership. The role of many continuing orientation programs that use adventure activities is to place students in positions of leadership and responsibility that require problem-solving skills, intellectual growth, and practical application. Active forms of learning replace passive ones as students attain responsible leadership experience with the guidance and support of faculty and other students.

Other models also exist that provide a basis for continuing orientation programs utilizing adventure experiences. One common model is based on the work of Chickering (1969) and Winston, Miller, and Prince (1983). Here the needs of the continuing student are identified through seven major "development vectors." These vectors include:

1. achieving competence,
2. managing emotions,
3. becoming autonomous,
4. establishing identity,
5. freeing interpersonal relationships,
6. clarifying purposes, and
7. developing integrity.

These vectors represent areas critical to the growth and development of the undergraduate. In both of the models presented here, adventure activities are selected based on their ability to reach the goals of the particular model. It is important to remember that such activities are not being utilized as recreational outlets for the college student, but to provide a viable means of meeting needs critical to the development of the undergraduate.

Adventure Programs for Resident Assistants

Another common application of adventure programming in higher education has been the use of adventure experiences to train resident assistants. The job of a resident assistant (RA) is extremely critical to university life, yet one that is demanding and difficult. In these positions, undergraduate students are asked to work in direct contact with peers in a supervisory role, balancing both personal needs with the needs of the institution. As stated by Cook (1980):

> RAs have responsibilities to individual students, to student groups, to other RAs within the hall they are located, to their supervisory staff, and to the university. A special kind of person is needed who can successfully handle the variety of responsibilities, while still maintaining a personally successful and rewarding university program of study. (p. 4)

Because of the complexity of the position and the vital role that RAs play in higher education systems, colleges and universities often implement training programs to enhance the skills necessary for RAs to be successful. While these models vary in application, most focus on one or all of the following four areas critical to the development of RAs:

1. student development—learning about students' personal and academic development and the residential context where this occurs;
2. self-awareness—learning about one's ability to interact with others;
3. interpersonal skill development—actual skills needed when working with and relating to others; and
4. leadership development—ability to accomplish tasks in leadership situations.

One popular model that integrates all four of these factors into a RA training program is one created by Upcraft (1982; see Figure 50.3). In this training model, the acquisition of skills needed for RAs are broken down into the four critical areas of development and training activities are implemented based on their ability to enhance this development.

Independent from understanding the implications and direction of such a model, adventure programs have proven to be effective in assisting in the development of some of these areas. Schroeder (1976) found that adventure activities increased the ability of new RAs to understand group modeling skills. Cook (1980) found that the RA adventure training program at Penn State developed group cohesion between RAs. In a program for Stetson University, Smith

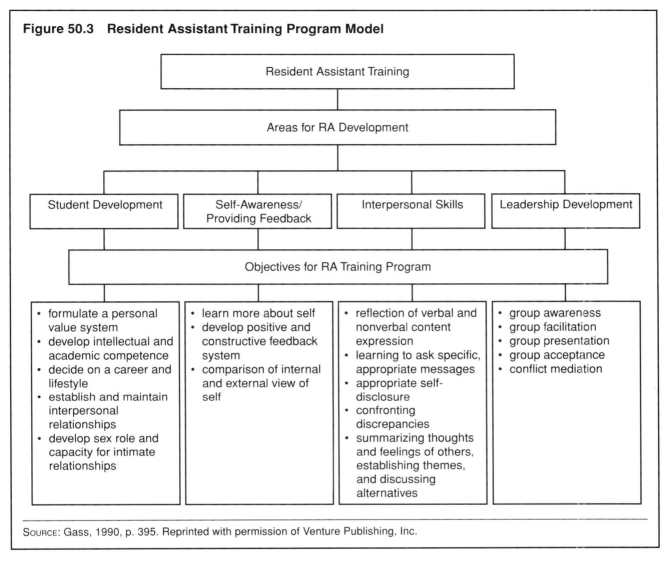

Figure 50.3 Resident Assistant Training Program Model

Resident Assistant Training

Areas for RA Development

| Student Development | Self-Awareness/ Providing Feedback | Interpersonal Skills | Leadership Development |

Objectives for RA Training Program

• formulate a personal value system • develop intellectual and academic competence • decide on a career and lifestyle • establish and maintain interpersonal relationships • develop sex role and capacity for intimate relationships	• learn more about self • develop positive and constructive feedback system • comparison of internal and external view of self	• reflection of verbal and nonverbal content expression • learning to ask specific, appropriate messages • appropriate self-disclosure • confronting discrepancies • summarizing thoughts and feelings of others, establishing themes, and discussing alternatives	• group awareness • group facilitation • group presentation • group acceptance • conflict mediation

SOURCE: Gass, 1990, p. 395. Reprinted with permission of Venture Publishing, Inc.

(1984) created an adventure program to develop leadership skills in RAs and increase their interpersonal skills and effectiveness. While the results of these programs illustrate some of the strengths that adventure programs hold for training RAs in requisite skills, they still fall short of the potential that these programs can reach.

Since these efforts, adventure programs have found that in order to reach their true potential in enhancing the training of RAs they must directly address the specific needs of RAs while still utilizing the strength of adventure activities. Peterman, Pilato, and Upcraft (1979) have demonstrated the ability of experience-based training programs to positively influence RAs personally and on their ability to meet the responsibilities of their job. Based on the steps in the model illustrated in Figure 50.3, the following illustrations are offered as examples of how adventure activities can develop to have a stronger effect on the training of RAs.

Student Development in the Residential Context

One concept vital to the development of RAs is learning how to accept individual differences and promote growth in people with different levels of cognitive, affective, and physical development. The primary step in acquiring these skills is each RA understanding how he or she perceives and stereotypes others and how this affects his or her interaction with people. Many of these perceptions are often observed in sex role stereotypes and projections from past interactions with other individuals that "appear to be similar." Using the novelty of adventure environments as a microcosm of resident halls and campus, training programs lead individuals to look at each person's true competencies and transcend sex role, racial, and other types of inappropriate stereotyping.

Examples of this can be seen in a variety of contexts of adventure experiences: a female being an assertive leader for her male peers in a particularly demanding exercise, a male showing compassion to another individual as he or she struggles to complete a task, or an individual performing a skill in a manner that isn't expected based on the group's first impression of that individual. Each of these scenarios is complemented and enhanced by the straightforward and stimulating medium present in adventure activities. This learning is generalized from the RA adventure experience to use in their interactions with others in their resident halls on campus.

Self-Awareness and Providing Appropriate Feedback

Two related concepts that are critical to the training of RAs are developing an awareness of how one is perceived by others and the ability to provide appropriate feedback. Any time people interact with other individuals, they are at some level of personal risk. This type of risk can have negative consequences (e.g., rejection, humiliation, loss of respect) or positive ones (e.g., greater trust, insight, better relations with others). Taking such self-exposing risks and learning under what conditions such risks are appropriate and which will provide positive, and not negative, outcomes is extremely important for each person. Using the risks presented in adventure experiences as a basis for directly and realistically focusing on these issues can provide RAs with valuable information for them to utilize in their residential setting on campus.

Also related to these principles is the ability of the RA to give and receive feedback to others. Upcraft (1982) defines feedback "as the exchange of verbal and nonverbal responses among groups members based on commonly observed behavior" (p. 80). Appropriate feedback, based on this definition, has the following seven characteristics (Upcraft, 1982, pp. 81–83):

1. It must be descriptive rather than evaluative.
2. It must be specific rather that general.
3. It must be well-intended.
4. It must be directed toward a behavior that the person can do something about.
5. It must be well-timed.
6. It must be checked out with the sender.
7. It must be checked out with the group.

Adventure activities create a valuable, safe, and non-threatening environment for RAs to experience these concepts as a recipient and a provider of feedback. While in a training session using adventure activities, RAs are placed in realistic, consequential activities where giving and receiving appropriate feedback is crucial to the success of the group. From these feedback processes, RAs are provided with actual opportunities to practice appropriate methods of feedback for use on campus.

Interpersonal Skills

Related to how an individual is perceived by others is his or her ability to interact and work with others in periods of both agreement and conflict. These interpersonal relationship skills serve as the basis for RAs to effectively perform the functions of their position. In the model shown in Figure 50.3 (page 379), interpersonal skills are viewed as effective when the RA possesses the following three skills (Upcraft, 1982):

1. responding—a respectful and nonevaluative understanding of what a person is thinking and feeling achieved through appropriate listening skills;
2. self-disclosing—the ability to share one's thoughts and feelings openly and honestly; and
3. initiating skills—confronting or summarizing ideas from interpersonal interaction to bring about change.

Adventure activities can provide an effective medium to develop and achieve strong areas of competence with these three areas of interpersonal skills. Adventure experiences are conducted in small groups where success is highly dependent upon sharing the thoughts and opinions of each group member and resolving interpersonal conflict when it arises. Processing techniques also accompany adventure activities to further enhance the future utilization of these interpersonal skills. An example of one such technique is the "full value" or "no-discount" contract (Gass, 1985; Schoel, Prouty, and Radcliffe, 1988). This contract asks each individual to:

a. fully value their own feelings, thoughts, and opinions as they participate in the group and
b. fully value the feelings, thoughts, and opinions of all other individuals that are also participating in the adventure experience.

Using such a policy requires each person to openly and honestly confront and address personal and group issues and work toward resolving such issues. Developing the interpersonal skills to accomplish a positive resolution to the problems encountered in the adventure experience provides an invaluable training medium for the RA.

Leadership Development

A final area necessary for training RAs is the development and application of leadership skills. Without strong capabilities to lead and work with groups, the ability of the RA to carry out the function of his or her job is severely diminished. Upcraft (1982) identifies these necessary capabilities as including:

a. a strong awareness of group dynamics;
b. the ability to facilitate groups in accomplishing tasks;
c. active and effective participation by the leader in group activities;
d. the ability to present material to group members so it can be used and/or implemented; and
e. participation by the leader that is accepted and respected by group members.

Adventure activities provide a real and consequential medium to learn, enhance, and/or practice these qualities. Group dynamics become actual leadership issues, as individual as well as group decisions must be made in order to accomplish difficult tasks. As leaders of such tasks, RAs find they must take an active role to ensure that each member contributes and has his or her needs met. Leaders also find it necessary to take on different roles to accommodate the needs of different group members and mediate conflict as the group finds itself in stressful situations. A healthy respect for the meaning of leadership and its uses and abuses is also obtained with a personal and group knowledge of leadership strengths and weaknesses.

Other Adventure Programs in Higher Education

While the three models presented in this chapter represent the most common areas of use in applying adventure programs in higher education, they are by no means the limits to applications in the 1990s. As the adaptation, integration, and strength of adventure programs/models in higher education continues to develop, more applications will be created. The applications that will briefly be discussed here include precollege preparation programs, student teacher preparation programs, developments in college and university physical education departments, and curriculum enhancement programs.

Precollege Preparation Programs

One such application in higher education that is receiving attention is the use of adventure activities with high-school students preparing for college. Some of the programs involved in preparing these students have found adventure components to be extremely valuable in reaching certain specific objectives of their programs. One example of a successful application has been with Upward Bound programs. Upward Bound is a federally funded program designed to assist high-ability disadvantaged youth to enter and complete programs in higher education. One of the goals of this program is "to develop the motivation, self-confidence, attitude, and self-concepts necessary for high-school graduation and matriculation in postsecondary edu-

cation programs" (Steel and Shubert, 1983). Upward Bound programs have applied the strengths of adventure education programs to assist them in successfully reaching this goal for their students. In a study done at Johnson State College, the Upward Bound program found that its outdoor experience program developed more positive attitudes, higher levels of self-concept, and greater levels of motivation in schoolwork (Anderson, 1984).

Teacher Preparation Programs

Another use of adventure activities has been with teacher training programs. Here adventure programs have been used as means to provide student teachers with insights into how students learn, what school is like for children that have difficulty learning, and how placing students in stressful situations affects their learning. Such programs have also focused on having student teachers assume responsibility for learning so they become more self-reliant and cooperative as teachers and highlighting the need for teachers to individualize learning for students based on their emotional as well as intellectual abilities. As stated by Eder (1976):

> What do the (adventure) experiences say about teaching? For the group, the rockface has become a metaphor for learning; the ropes have come to represent the different ways to learn. The meaning behind the symbols also became sharper. Since human diversity is a fact of school life, then they—as teachers—must be able to provide students with learning alternatives and an encouraging environment, just as the climbing instructors were doing for each of them. (p. 5)

Adventure programs have also been used with several applications for veteran teachers. Goals with these programs have included providing a means for enhancing current teaching effectiveness by providing teachers with safe yet novel environments to experiment with different curricula, instructional strategies, and staffing patterns (Eder, 1976).

Physical Education Programs

As illustrated in earlier chapters, physical education activity programs have commonly been a vehicle for adventure activity in higher education. Uhlendorf and Gass (1992) identified 200 colleges and university physical education departments that possess some type of activity class in outdoor leisure and adventure pursuits. The focus of such programs are often educational and/or recreational in purpose and usually serve the general university population as well as physical education majors.

Two major concerns are presently being confronted by physical education departments in higher education pertaining to the offering of adventure activity classes. The first is the training and certification of physical education majors to become teachers. In the most recent publishing of the National Council for Accreditation of Teacher Education (NCATE) Guidelines (1987) for physical education preparation programs, it is required that all potential physical education teachers must demonstrate skill and knowledge regarding outdoor leisure pursuits "so they can plan, implement, and evaluate" (p. 53) such offerings in physical education programs. In her study analyzing such practices, Uhlendorf (1988) found that even though half of the physical education programs in the United States have some form of outdoor leisure pursuit classes, most physical education teacher preparation programs are deficient in their ability to train students in these activities.

The other concern is the ongoing philosophical debate of physical educators on whether the use of physical activity primarily for affective development, and not psychomotor development, should be part of physical education curricula. Both of these concerns are important for physical education programs in higher education to address and the urgency of answering both will be strong professional focuses in the next few years.

Adventure Education to Enhance Higher Education Curricula

Physical education departments are not the only academic programs that have incorporated adventure activities into higher education. While suffering from the same problems as other efforts in higher education addressed earlier (e.g., isolation of programs, programs revolving around one individual), there have been several successful efforts to utilize adventure education to enhance curricula in higher education.

Much of the success of these programs is due to the fact that the learning in adventure education is experienced based and incorporates both action and reflection to attain educational objectives. As stated by Medrick (1973):

> The student is placed in a situation where he (she) learns through direct experience and where what he (she) learns is immediately tested and, if workable, reinforced through his (her) achievements and successes. (p. 1)

The success of most curricula have been their abilities to integrate the learning from the adventure experiences into the particular academic needs of the college coursework, whether it be philosophy, areas of science, languages, education, or literature. Illustrated in a series of articles, Beidler (1980, 1985, 1987) has demonstrated the ability to use adventure experiences to enhance the

learning of college students. These activities place the students in novel situations where direct experience, personal and group interaction, individualized learning, and the benefits of problem solving work to empower the learning processes.

Conclusion

As stated throughout the chapter, the applications of adventure experiences in higher education are extremely varied. Whether it is due to this variation, the novelty of this type of learning, and/or the isolation of existing programs, such experiences are far from reaching the potential influence they can have on institutions of higher learning. To reach this zenith, interested professionals must work to validate as well as demonstrate the true abilities of their programs and focus on the transfer of learning from adventure experiences to colleges and universities. Past accomplishments have provided an incomplete outline of what can be attained with such programs. The much more difficult tasks of improving and integrating adventure learning in higher education hold the merits of what can truly be achieved in the future.

References

Anderson, J. (1984). *Results from the outdoor education component of the Johnson State Upward Bound program.* Johnson, VT: Johnson State College, Upward Bound Project.

Astin, A. W. (1975). *Preventing students from dropping out.* San Francisco, CA: Jossey-Bass.

Bacon, S. (1983). *The conscious use of metaphor in the Outward Bound experience.* Denver, CO: Colorado Outward Bound School.

Beidler, P. G. (1980). A turn down the harbor. *Journal of Experiential Education, 3*(2), 24–32.

Beidler, P. G. (1985). English in the tree tops. *Journal of Experiential Education, 8*(3), 34–41.

Beidler, P. G. (1987). Bee weekend. *Journal of Experiential Education, 10*(3), 23–27.

Chickering, A. W. (1969). *Education and identity.* San Francisco, CA: Jossey-Bass.

Cook, K. V. (1980). *The effectiveness of an outdoor adventure program as a training method for resident assistants* (ERIC Document Reproduction Service No. 210 142). Unpublished master's thesis, Pennsylvania State University, University Park, Pennsylvania.

DeBoer, G. E. (1983). The importance of freshmen students' perception of the factors responsible for first-term academic performance. *Journal of College Student Personnel, 24*(4), 22–29.

Eder, S. (1976). Learning on the rocks. *American Education, 12*(1), 24–29.

Faugh, S., et al. (1982). *Significant others: A new look at attrition.* Paper presented at the Annual Meeting of the American Counseling and Personnel Association, Detroit, Michigan. (ERIC Document Reproduction Service No. 225 446)

Gass, M. A. (1984). *The value of wilderness orientation programs at colleges and universities in the United States* (ERIC Document Reproduction Service No. 242 471). Durham, NH: University of New Hampshire, Outdoor Education Program.

Gass, M. A. (1985). Programming the transfer of learning in adventure education. Journal of *Experiential Education, 8*(3), 18–24.

Gass, M. A. (1987). The effects of a wilderness orientation program on college students. *Journal of Experiential Education, 10*(2), pp. 30–33.

Gass, M. A. (1990). Adventure programs in higher education. In J. C. Miles and S. Priest (Eds.), *Adventure education* (pp. 385–401). State College, PA: Venture Publishing, Inc.

Gass, M. A., Kerr, P. J., and Garvey, D. (1986). Student orientation in wilderness settings. In R. J. Kraft and M. Sakofs (Eds.), *Experiential education in the schools* (pp. 320–330). Boulder, CO: Association for Experiential Education.

Green, D. (1985, February 6). Student retention programs of colleges should be more than self-serving scams. *The Chronicle of Higher Education,* p. 96.

Hansen, R. N. (1982). QUEST: Career exploration in the wilderness. *Journal of College Student Personnel, 23*(4), 344–345.

Jernstadt, G. C. (1986). *Procedures, materials, notes for the Outward Bound impact study.* Hanover, NH: Dartmouth College.

Kerr, P. J., and Gass, M. A. (1987). Group development in adventure education. *Journal of Experiential Education, 10*(3), 39–46.

Medrick, F. W. (1973). *Outward Bound and higher education: A rationale and outline for college development.* Denver, CO: Colorado Outward Bound School.

Miner, J., and Boldt, J. (1981). *Outward Bound USA: Learning through experience in adventure-based education.* New York, NY: William Morrow.

Parchem, A. (1975). *Notes on the evaluation of outdoor experience programs.* Paper presented at the Annual Conference on Outdoor and Experiential Education, Mankato, Minnesota.

Peterson, D., Pilato, G., and Upcraft, M. (1979). A description and evaluation of an academic course to increase interpersonal effectiveness of resident assistants. *Journal of College Student Personnel, 20,* 348–352.

Ramist, L. (1981). *College student attrition and retention college board report No. 81-1* (ERIC Document Reproduction Service No. 229 075.). New York, NY: College Entrance Examination Board.

Robertson, T. (1978). *Title III proposal: Linfield out-of-doors.* An unpublished manuscript. Linfield College, McMinnville, Oregon.

Schoel, J., Prouty, D., and Radcliffe, P. (1988). *Islands of healing: A guide to adventure-based counseling.* Hamilton, MA: Project Adventure.

Schroeder, C. G. (1976). Adventure training for resident assistants. *Journal of College Student Personnel, 17*(1).

Smith, K. D. (1984). *Beyond wilderness skills: Education for the individual and group development* (ERIC Document Reproduction Service No. 252 368). A paper presented at the American College Personnel Association Conference in Baltimore, Maryland.

Steel, L., and Shubert, J. G. (1983, April). *The effectiveness of Upward Bound in preparing disadvantaged youth for postsecondary education* (ERIC Document Reproduction Service No. 235 262). Paper presented at the annual meeting of the American Educational Research Association, Montreal, Canada.

Stogner, J. D. (1978). *The effects of a wilderness experience on self-concept and academic performance.* Dissertation Abstracts International.

Terenzini, P. T., and Pascarella, E. T. (1980). Student/faculty relationships and freshmen year educational outcomes: A further investigation. *Journal of College Student Personnel, 21*(6), 521–528.

Tinto, V., and Cullen, J. (1973). *Dropout in higher education: A review and theoretical synthesis of recent literature.* Washington, DC: Office of State Planning, Budget, and Evaluation, U.S. Dept. of Education.

Uhlendorf, K, and Gass, M. A. (1992). The preparation of physical education majors in adventure activities. *Physical Educator, 49*(1), 33–38.

Upcraft, M. L. (1982). *Learning to be a resident assistant.* San Francisco, CA: Jossey-Bass.

Walsh, L., and Golins, G. (1976). *The exploration of the Outward Bound process.* Denver, CO: Colorado Outward Bound School.

Wetzel, M. A. (1978). *Self-concept change in participants of a wilderness learning experience.* Unpublished master's thesis, Minnesota State University, Mankato, Minnesota.

Winston, R. B., Miller, T. K., and Prince, J. S. (1983). *Assessing student development.* Athens, GA: Student Development Associates.

Chapter 51

Programming Adventure for Older Adults

Deborah Sugerman
University of New Hampshire

Several factors have produced an increasingly large number of older adults who have the time, health, and finances to pursue leisure activities and interests. People are living longer and are increasingly active at an older age. Females and males born in 1989 have a life expectancy of 78.8 and 71.9 years respectively, compared to a life expectancy of 47 years of an infant born at the beginning of the twentieth century (Hooyman and Kiyak, 1993). According to Backman and Backman (1993, cited in Krauss, 1997) the age at which people retire has decreased between four and five years from the 1950s, extending the number of years that people are in retirement.

Advances in medicine and medical technology and knowledge of the importance of nutrition and exercise to health have made it possible for individuals to avoid many acute illnesses and diseases and to live relatively healthy lives. Many older adults have the discretionary income to be able to participate in leisure activities. According to the U.S. Senate Special Committee on Aging (1990) 88 percent of older people live above the poverty level as compared to 65 percent in the 1950s. Although Social Security remains the major source of income for older Americans, there is a trend in the rising importance of income from assets and private pensions (Moody, 1994).

Concurrently, a growing national interest in the outdoors has opened doors to older adults. According to the President's Commission on Americans Outdoors, the demand for outdoor recreation is steadily increasing, with 90 percent of Americans seeking enjoyment from mountains, seashores, lakes, pathways and playgrounds. The Commission also found that the average age of outdoor enthusiasts is steadily climbing (Alexander, 1987). With the increasing number of older people taking part in leisure activities, it is important for adventure educators to understand the biological, sociological, and psychological aspects of aging. This knowledge will aid in providing meaningful and satisfying programs for older adults.

Biological Aspects of Aging

Biological aging refers to the normal process of changes in the body that occur over time. The changes caused by aging are a natural process and vary greatly from person to person depending on heredity and lifestyle. In general, the changes include a reduction in the efficiency of the organ and circulatory systems (Hooyman and Kiyak, 1993). Biological aging may cause a person to require a longer adjustment period after activity to resume normal respiration and pulse rate. Changes occur in sensory function which may affect visual acuity, depth perception, and kinesthetics. The process of biological aging may also change a person's sleep patterns and tolerance for temperature extremes. Changes in muscle mass and tissue elasticity occur, which may affect speed, strength, endurance, coordination and flexibility. Taking into account biological changes that occur in older people, the following considerations may be helpful:

1. make sure there is plenty of light and give people time to adjust to changing light conditions;
2. when speaking, make sure everyone can see you and try to eliminate background noise that may mask what is being said;
3. allow time to warm up before doing activities to increase range of motion and flexibility;
4. gradually build up physical capacity based on ability levels of participants;
5. allow for longer rest times after strenuous activity based on the needs of participants; and
6. be aware of the diminished response to temperature changes.

Sociological Aspects of Aging

Sociological aging refers to an individual's changing roles and relationships in the social structures of family, friends, work and religious, social and political organizations (Hooyman and Kiyak, 1993). Havighurst (1972) described the sociocultural tasks of later life as the following:

1. adjustment to retirement: this significant change provides the opportunity for increased leisure time, while it reduces economic resources;
2. adjustment to the death of a spouse: this task is faced by more women than men and involves social, personal, and economic adjustments;
3. establishing an explicit affiliation with one's age group: this is important in order for older people to develop social networks; and
4. meeting social and civic obligations: older adults have more time to become involved in creating social responsibilities to future generations and to society at large.

Adventure education programs can provide an opportunity for the older adult to successfully deal with these tasks and to begin to develop new roles. Group-centered activities increase mutual support and trust in participants and begin to develop social networks that can be continued after the course is finished. Through successful completion of activities, participants can be recognized by the group as a person of worth and can recognize in themselves new roles with which they may feel comfortable.

Psychological Aspects of Aging

Psychological aging refers to the behavioral capacity of individuals to adapt to changing environmental demands (Austin and Crawford, 1996). As a result of the increase in

life expectancy people are becoming more interested in the concept of "successful aging," which involves the continuation of optimum functioning in later life (Moody, 1994). Leviton and Santoro Carnpanelli (1980) described the foremost predictors of successful aging or life satisfaction to be socioeconomic status, personality, perceived health, activity, and intimate friendships above and beyond one's family. According to Siegenthaler (1996), research in recreation and older individuals strongly supports the relationship between activity and life satisfaction. Based on the research, it appears that activity provides a means for individuals to fulfill personal needs and to age successfully. The important implication of these studies is that not all activities are equal in helping older people adjust to aging or in helping them to reach the goal of successful aging. It is not the frequency of the activity that is important, but the quality of the activity (Hull, 1990).

Although adventure challenge programs have little to do with socioeconomic status, they do have a direct influence on the remaining predictors of life satisfaction: personality, perceived health, activity, and intimate friendships above and beyond one's family. The goals of adventure challenge programs relate directly to life satisfaction. As a result of the successful completion of challenging activities, the development of personality is seen through an increase in self-confidence and self-esteem, self-discovery, leadership development, creativity, and decision making. People become aware of the importance of good physical and mental health. Many new skills are learned and developed on adventure courses, skills that participants can continue to use in their personal lives after the course is finished. Close bonds develop between group members as a result of intimate friendships, which continue long after the course is over (Miles, 1980).

Planning Adventure Programs

Planning adventure programs for older adults, like planning programs for any specific population, involves a series of steps. The first step is to define the goals of the program. What do you want to accomplish? What are the needs of the group? How can you mesh the group's needs with your goals? The program planner should be familiar with the biological, sociological, and psychological aspects of aging. With knowledge of the aging process and the importance of activity to life satisfaction, the planner can design goals that will fit the needs of older people. The goals should evolve from a holistic view of adventure education and include the social, emotional, and physical realms.

The next step involves designing the specific schedule of activities. When planning the schedule it is important to consider specific information concerning physical aspects (i.e., longer adjustment period after activity; possible decline in strength, endurance, and coordination; and decrease in efficiency of senses), sociological aspects (i.e., importance of role development) and psychological aspects of aging (i.e., predictors of life satisfaction). Criteria for selecting the activities should include such considerations as the appropriateness of the activities to the clientele, suitability for the intended group, effectiveness of the activities in reaching the goals and objectives, and the pacing and variety of activities (Szczypkowski, 1980). In researching the meaning of the camping experience for older adults, Chenery (1987) found the importance of having:

1. a range of levels and kinds of activities;
2. success-oriented activities;
3. opportunities for varying levels of physical demand and social interaction;
4. the ability to choose among activities; and
5. socialization.

The next planning step involves resources. What will you need in order to run the program in terms of equipment, staff, environment, and information? What adaptations of the resources will be necessary to fit the physical and emotional needs of the participants? Hiring and training a good staff is key to any effective program. Staff should be mature and personable, be knowledgeable in the content areas of adventure education, have skill in teaching and be able to facilitate the participants' abilities to pursue their own goals. Effective instructors are able to gain insight into students' historical experiences, their beliefs and values, and their present situations. Throughout the course, as instructors develop a warm, caring climate with mutual respect between themselves and the participants, they foster the belief that both leaders and participants have roles in the teaching and learning process and that both can respect the knowledge and experience of the other. Training staff in the specifics of working with older adults and understanding health issues, the concept of successful aging, developmental aspects, how to provide an intense yet enjoyable experience and techniques for helping participants overcome stereotypes of themselves is important.

Medical information is specifically important in planning adventure education programs for older adults. The administrator needs to develop a medical form to be given to participants that will give complete medical information pertinent to the program. Specific questions pertaining to biological aging need to be included such as current condition of heart, lungs, joints, gastrointestinal and urinary systems, the senses, blood pressure, current medications, and current level of physical activities. The form may include a physical examination, copies of a recent electrocardiogram, and/or a signed statement from the participant's physician. Foret and Clemons (1996) offer resources for screening forms in their article on physical activity for older persons. This specific information can help the administrator plan the program to more closely

fit the physical abilities of the participants, and can help the instructors know what kinds of issues they may run into in the field.

The next planning step is to develop an information packet to be sent to participants before the course begins. Just like anyone else, older adults may feel inadequate when thinking about participating in an adventure experience. "Will I be able to do it? Am I too old? Will I hold the group back?" The administrator needs to be aware of these concerns and take steps to deal with people's feelings. The participants should be given enough information concerning the goals of the course, the schedule, and the medical aspects before the course so that they can make a decision whether or not to participate. Expectations should be thoroughly explained so that participants know specifically what will be happening in the program and what they will be expected to do.

The last step in the planning process is to design evaluation procedures. How will the course be evaluated along the way and when it is completed? Evaluation can be done cooperatively between participants and instructors. Ideally the instructors have provided regular opportunities throughout the course for feedback from the group so the program can be adapted to more closely fit their needs and goals. Participants can provide useful feedback for future programs.

Running the Program

The development and learning techniques of older adults are different from any other age group. The instructor needs to tailor his or her teaching and leading styles to fit the unique characteristics of this particular group. Adults are increasingly self-directed and are problem-centered in their learning. They have a rich background of experience that can play a vital role in their learning new skills as they learn new knowledge by relating it to what is previously known. Adults are more motivated by internal incentives than by extrinsic rewards.

At the beginning of the course it is important for the instructors to learn participants' expectations of themselves and the leaders. The instructor, knowing the needs and goals of the group, will be able to direct the course to meet them. This will result in greater motivation and learning for participants. Garvey and Garvey (1997) suggest developing activities early on in the program to allow participants to share personal accomplishments to help increase commitment.

If possible, participants should be involved in planning the content of the course. This will help make them feel more at ease, reduce anxiety, and result in more commitment to the course. By providing an atmosphere of support and group cooperation, the instructor can help participants verbalize their feelings and learnings. Individuals should be encouraged throughout the course to share their knowledge, ideas and skills. They have a wealth of information, and sharing helps develop new roles within the group that can be carried into their lives at home.

Instructors should continually encourage the development of group cohesiveness and strive for a supportive, interactive group. In their article concerning facilitating learning with older adults, Garvey and Garvey (1997) discuss the technique of framing activities so that participants understand the purpose behind the activities and are better able to internalize learnings. They also suggest providing opportunities for the participants to make metaphoric connections between the adventure experience and life experiences which aids in the transfer of learning.

At the end of the course it is important for instructors to process the experience with the participants, and to talk about how to link the adventure experiences with everyday life. These links can provide more meaning to the experience. Participants need to be able to bring closure to the experience and to process what it has meant to them. They should be helped and encouraged to develop ways to keep the social networks continuing after the course is over. Instructors and participants may discuss the concept that the course is a means, not an end.

Conclusion

Older adults are a growing segment of our population whose leisure needs must be met. They are a challenging population, and rewarding to work with. Several authors (Ewert, 1983; Garvey and Garvey, 1997; Hupp, 1987; Jensen, 1995; Kennison, 1985; Rillo, 1980) feel that this population has been seriously neglected and that there is a need to develop programs for them that revive former skills and interests and teach new ones.

Adventure education programs can challenge, revitalize, and provide new directions for older persons. It is important for everyone who desires an adventure experience, no matter what his or her age or ability level, to be able to share the joys and satisfactions of living with a group in the wilderness. One participant on an adventure education course said it best: "Thank you for letting me do this course. So many people think that old people can't do these things, and won't even let us try. I appreciate your giving us this opportunity."

References

Alexander, L. (Chairman). (1987). *President's commission on Americans outdoors.* Washington, DC: U.S. Government Printing Office.

Austin, D. R., and Crawford, M. E. (1996). *Therapeutic recreation.* Needham Heights, MA: Allyn and Bacon.

Chenery, M. F. (1987). Research in action: Camping and senior adults. *Camping Magazine, 59*(5), 50–51.

Ewert, A. (1983). Adventure programming for the older adult. *Journal of Physical Education, Recreation, and Dance, 54*(3), 64–66.

Foret, C. M., and Clemons, J. M. (1996). The elderly's need for physical activity. *Journal of Physical Education, Recreation and Dance, 67*(4), 57–61.

Garvey, D., and Garvey, D. (1997). Facilitating learning with older adults. *Journal of Experiential Education, 20*(2), 86–93.

Havighurst, R. J. (1972). *Developmental tasks and education.* New York, NY: David McKay.

Hooyman, N. R., and Kiyak, H. A. (1993). *Social gerontology.* Needham Heights, MA: Allyn and Bacon.

Hull, K. V. (1990). *Special problems of the elderly.* ERIC # 327758.

Hupp, S. (1987). Camping in the third age. *Camping Magazine, 59*(3), 20–22.

Jensen, C. R. (1995). *Outdoor recreation in America.* Champaign, IL: Human Kinetics.

Kennison, J. A. (1985). Outdoor education and recreation must not neglect the 60-plus crowd. *Nature Study, 38*(2/3), 5–6.

Kraus, R. (1997). *Recreation and leisure in modern society.* Reading, MA: Addison-Wesley Educational Publishers, Inc.

Leviton, D., and Santoro Carnpanelli, L. (Eds.). (1980). *Health, physical education, recreation, and dance for the older adult: A modular approach.* Reston, VA: American Alliance for Health, Physical Education, Recreation and Dance.

Miles, J. C. (1980). The value of high-adventure activities. In J. Meier, T. Morash, and G. Welton (Eds.), *High-adventure outdoor pursuits organization and leadership.* Salt Lake City, UT: Brighton Publishing Co.

Moody, H. R. (1994). *Aging: Concepts and controversies.* Thousand Oaks, CA: Pine Forge Press.

Rillo, T. J. (1980). *Outdoor education—The past is a prologue to the future.* ERIC #212 392.

Siegenthaler, K. L. (1996). Leisure and the elderly. *Journal of Parks and Recreation, 31*(1), 18, 20–21, 23–24.

Saczypkowkski, R. (1980). Objectives and activities. In A. B. Knox and Associates (Eds.), *Developing, administering and evaluating adult education.* San Francisco, CA: Jossey-Bass.

U.S. Senate Special Committee on Aging. (1990). *Developments in aging: 1989. Vol. 1.* Washington, DC: U.S. Government Printing Office.

Chapter 52

Women's Outdoor Adventures

Karen Warren
Hampshire College

The North American Outward Bound schools opened their doors to women in the 1960s, instigating a significant development in serving women in adventure programming. Women-only outdoor programs soon followed with the advent of women's adventure businesses starting in the mid 1970s (Hardin, 1979). By creating courses that included women, adventure organizations took great preliminary strides in validating women's outdoor experiences. Adventure leaders must recognize that a woman's experience in the wilderness is unique, and that programming should correspond to this different perspective. To simply sign up a group of women for a standardized course and enlist the services of available women instructors ignores the specific needs of women in the outdoors.

In looking at adventure programming from a feminist perspective, relevant questions emerge. Is traditional outdoor experiential education practice an effective methodology for women's growth? How can existing wilderness course models be adapted to respond to women's needs? How is the outdoor experience of this clientele unique and what implications does that have for programming? To answer these questions it is useful to explore several myths which underlie our conceptions of women's adventure experience. These myths, which cause adventure programs to be unresponsive to women through ignorance rather than intention, also serve as stoppers for women at various stages in their pursuit of meaningful outdoor challenges. After defusing the myths by recognizing their existence and reconciling their impact, adventure programs can respond to the needs of women in the wilderness.

The Myth of Accessibility

The myth of accessibility is based on the misconception that outdoor experiences are widely available to women. As more women participate through organized coed programs as well as emerging women's tripping businesses, the appearance of equal access is fostered. However, women's reality doesn't support this notion as social and economic factors serve to limit women's participation. Women's economic inequity, well-documented in their statistically lower earning power, is the first deterrent to involvement in adventure programs. A woman struggling with the grocery bills may not be able to consider a backpacking trip. Furthermore, while a man has a sense of the value of adventure experiences based on previous exposures, a woman with no prior background may not be willing to assume the financial risk for an unknown commodity. She is unsure if adventure-based education makes economic sense.

Women's adventure organizations have consistently given attention to equitable accessibility. Woodswomen, Inc. and Women Outdoors, Inc. are among the women's programs offering scholarships. Other women-only programs use a sliding scale course fee structure based on participant income.

The primary factor that advances the myth of accessibility is a woman's social conditioning. When deciding between the needs of her loved ones and her own desire for adventure, an outdoor trip seems frivolous and trivial compared to a child who night need her. Making the choice to take for herself when she is trained to always give to others creates an internal conflict. Messages of guilt at pursuing her own needs are a powerful deterrent from seeking adventure opportunities.

In addition, social conditioning inundates a woman with the insistent directive that the woods is no place for her. Not only must she reconcile her own doubts on a personal level (i.e., guilt at leaving the family alone, economic stress), a woman faces substantial societal risks in pursuing adventure experiences. Historically a masculine domain, the wilderness trip is painted by the message bearers of the media and tradition as a scary, uncomfortable, and intimidating event. The moment she steps into the woods her femininity is in question. Faced with these odds, it is a great social risk for women to be involved in outdoor programs. By not being a part of the male network that validates outdoor challenges, a woman misses the external prompting and support to seek the offerings of adventure programs.

For women of color interested in an outdoor adventure experience issues of accessibility are particularly troublesome. Racism and classism in outdoor experiential education combine to create a strong deterrent to participation by women of color who may not have been socialized to view outdoor adventure as a plausible opportunity (Roberts, 1996).

Outdoor programs with a mandate for equal access will work along avenues women trust to minimize factors that prevent women's full participation in wilderness activities. Forming networks of women who have found value in the outdoors, promoting adventure options through women's educational, social and cultural organizations, and offering short courses which allow women to sample the wilderness without making a huge time or financial commitment are all possibilities for adventure institutions to pursue to avert inaccessibility.

The Myth of Egalitarianism

This myth is predicated on the notion that the wilderness is an ideal place to revise prevailing social conditioning. As outdoor experiential educators, we are imbued with the power of the mountains to enact changes in people's lives. We therefore believe a viable corollary to the wilderness as social healer axiom is that the outdoors is the perfect place to eradicate any inequalities based on gender. We can encourage women to light stoves while the men do the cooking and in the process redefine acquired sex roles. The fallacy of this aspiration lies in the fact that the wilderness is not a natural place to break stereotypes. When it's pouring rain, the group has been hiking all day and it's

growing dark, the most expedient way to set up camp is for people to do tasks that are comfortable and familiar. In spite of our noble intentions of egalitarianism, when efficiency is important in a trying situation, women often do end up cooking.

The coed wilderness trip also serves as a constant, insidious reminder to women that their intrinsic worth on the course is in doubt. Weight distribution on a backpacking course illustrates this point. Since women have lower weight-carrying capabilities than men, when it comes time to divide up group responsibilities, the message which subtly prevails is that the woman is not carrying her weight. Someone else is doing it for her. What the woman makes up for in load transporting by her nurturing, endurance, and facilitation is often not given comparable acclaim because her contribution to the trip is more intangible.

It is important for adventure course leaders to understand how wilderness experiences that subtly emphasize physical prowess perpetuate the myth of egalitarianism and undermine a woman's experience outdoors. Since research has demonstrated that women have proportionately less absolute strength than men (Maughan, 1983), wilderness course components that favor strength discriminate against women. Yet this discrimination is rarely blatant; therein lies its tyranny. My favorite example to show this elusive dynamic is about learning to single carry a canoe while I was portaging in the Boundary Waters of northern Minnesota. As I repeatedly struggled unsuccessfully to raise a 77-pound Grumman to my shoulders, my male counterparts who also had not yet mastered the technique could still succeed by muscling the canoe up. My friends constantly reminded me that upper body strength was unimportant if I had perfect technique. These encouraging exhortations made it no less obvious that I was a failure because my technique was unrefined while my equally inexperienced male friends were shuffling down the portage trail with the canoe on their backs. This example shows that while both male and female participants may be similarly skilled in a particular course component, if the task is better suited to the male body type, the woman faces initial failure and feelings of inadequacy. Instead of changing the emphasis of the task, women are expected to be perfect and therefore may be discouraged from seeking additional adventure situations.

The myth of egalitarianism offers an excellent rationale for women-only programs. Since all the available roles on women's courses, including the traditionally male held roles, must be filled by women, equality is promoted. Women have the opportunity to try out outdoor activities in a supportive atmosphere without immediate comparison to men's adventure experience.

Adventure program leaders sensitive to the issues of egalitarianism have altered course components that unconsciously discriminate against women. Obviously it is not suggested that adventure programs simply make courses easier for women; that idea has been put to rest by those who realize that merely advocating an easier version of a standard course is condescending to women and not a useful methodology for their growth. What emerges is a different approach for women engaged in adventure education. For example, egalitarianism at the climb site means concentrating on climbs that emphasize less upper body strength and more grace. It means selecting ropes course events that will extend realistic challenges based on women's skills and abilities in endurance, flexibility and balance and avert the predetermined failure intrinsic to elements which invalidate women's strengths. It also means elevating perceived risk while deemphasizing intensive physical strength in challenging situations. By extending the feminist philosophy of comparable worth to the outdoor adventure field, the myth of egalitarianism could be unequivocally denied.

The Myth of Square One

The myth of square one is apparent at the start of most beginning level wilderness education courses. Outdoor instructors often assume that beginners arrive with the same lack of skills and similar disadvantages; in other words, all participants start at square one. This unfortunate assumption can be detrimental to women, especially if it affects the type of instruction they receive because of it. Lacking the same precursory experiences which men have acquired through their conditioning, women embark upon a wilderness adventure at a disadvantage. I have identified three major precursory experiences which directly influence the quality of women's outdoor undertakings. Because women lack technical conditioning, role models, and an internalized assumption of success they are thwarted in maximizing wilderness learning situations.

The first precursory experience denied women, technical conditioning, affects her aptitude to easily and enjoyably learn wilderness skills. Mechanical unfamiliarity may hinder her ability to grasp stove use and repair, while math anxiety prevents her from learning map and compass skills as quickly as her male counterparts. Rock climbing, an activity which usually creates some anxiety in participants regardless of gender, becomes more problematic for a woman because she has not had the same opportunity to handle ropes and tie knots as her Boy Scout–trained cohorts. Therefore, it is paramount that enlightened adventure programs take women's shortage of technical training into account when planning instruction. When instructors do not recognize that they must first peel back the layers of technical apprehension that trouble most women, they promulgate the myth of square one.

The invisibility of acceptable role models also prevents women outdoors from starting at square one. I remember very distinctly my first day instructing at the Outward Bound School in Minnesota when I found out the student patrol groups were named MacKenzie, Pond, Radisson, and Hennepin after the explorers and traders of the north woods. Where were the women? It's not that no role models exist; women have been active in the outdoors throughout history yet their story is hidden, unspoken, trivialized or ignored. It's time to reclaim the Isabella Birds, the Fanny Workmans and the Mina Hubbards from their historical burial grounds and restore them as role models to young and old adventurous women. It's time to put aside our campfire tales by London and Service and share the women's outdoor stories in such books as *Rivers Running Free* (Niemi and Wieser, 1987), *Daughters of Copper Woman* (Cameron, 1981), or *Solo: On Her Own Adventure* (Rogers, 1996).

The final precursor deficient in a women's outdoor experience is an internalized assumption of success. A woman who constantly encounters surprise that "she got as far as she did in the wilderness" will soon internalize the message that she is expected to flounder. So not only is the woman's presence in the wilderness questioned, her ability to cope once there has been traditionally discredited. Realizing this social prejudice, it is understandable that when a woman is faced with a challenging situation in the outdoors, the little voice of anticipated failure comes back to color her response. She is no longer simply figuring out how to fix a broken tent pole or taking a compass bearing, the woman is first forced to wrestle with her fear of defeat; her fear frequently becoming a self-fulfilling prophecy.

The uniqueness of how women learn intervenes as well. While men have been urged to learn experientially women are often left to learn by observation. Wilderness skills, which are usually task-oriented, allow a man to step forward buoyed up by the supposition that he will succeed. So inspired, he masters the task. On the other hand, the woman who watches the demonstration of an outdoor skill has the weight of a double doubt bearing down on her. Her confidence is undermined by both the absence of an internalized expectation of accomplishment as well as her inexperience in learning by doing. Adventure educators must be prepared to advocate for different styles of learning and to critically examine how their own attitudes may unconsciously contribute to women's inner predictions of failure.

The Myth of the Superwoman

While the effects of this myth eventually filter down to all outdoorswomen, the myth of the superwoman most acutely maligns women outdoor leaders. In order to achieve an advanced rank in the outdoor field, women leaders acquire exemplary competence in all outdoor skills. In this common scenario, she can carry the heaviest pack with a smile on her face. She demonstrates complete command of her camp stove, compass and canoe. She is comfortable in the mountains and woods, confident in her unequaled proficiency. Yet the Catch-22 is exactly that competence which women leaders have worked years to gain and refine. For with superior abilities, she becomes the superwoman, a woman unlike the rest of the population. Her students no longer have to view her competence for what it is—the ongoing struggle to gain parity in a male-dominated profession.

The effect of the superwoman on wilderness course participants is unintentionally detrimental. Participants, both men and women, struggle with the dissonance created by the conflict between their indoctrination that implies a woman doesn't belong in the wilderness and the reality of the woman outdoor leader guiding them. The existence of the superwoman gives them a way out of this nagging conflict. Due to her exemplary outdoor achievements the superwoman is the exception to other women. She's extraordinary, unique, not normal. As an anomaly the superwoman instructor can be cast aside and made invisible in the minds of her students. When she is perceived as being unrepresentative of ordinary women, participants are no longer forced to deal with their sexist conditioning; they need not reappraise their world-view of women. They merely write off this one superwoman as incongruous and leave the course with the same cultural baggage they had when they arrived.

The implications for women participants are notably profound. While the woman instructor might serve as a wonderful role model to other women, her superwoman status disallows this. Women, especially beginners in the outdoor field, may feel great admiration for the superwoman but are intimidated by this woman who, in addition to her superlative technical skills, may display no apparent fears or doubts. The "I can never be like her" statement that rings in the minds of her female students robs the competent outdoor leader of her opportunity to be a role model.

Adventure program leaders and administrators can counter the myth of the superwoman by being conscientious of the style of leadership they value. Sharing leadership by consensus decision making, demystifying competency and revealing vulnerabilities may be one method of confronting the myth. With attention to the tenets of a feminist vision of outdoor leadership, the superwoman has no impetus to be born.

The Myth of the Heroic Quest

The final myth to be explored centers on women's spiritual identity in a wilderness adventure situation. A metaphor employed by adventure programs is a model of the heroic quest prevalent in classical and contemporary literature (Bacon, 1983). The participant undergoes a real-life experience in the wilderness that parallels the mythical quest of the hero. The student hears a call to adventure, leaves home, encounters dragons on the way and slays them, reflects on the conquest, and returns home as a hero with a clearer understanding of self.

Upon closer examination, the heroic quest is a metaphor that has little meaning to women (Christ, 1980). Each stage of a woman's journey in the wilderness is a direct contradiction of the popular quest model. A woman rarely hears a call to adventure; in fact, she is more often dissuaded by the factors discussed in the myth of accessibility from leaving home to engage in adventurous pursuits. The dragons looming in a woman's path on a wilderness course are equally ambiguous. Are these metaphoric limitations a personal block or are they societally imposed? It's impossible for her to sort out. Which dragons should she slay? Needing a point of reference to discern the difference, a woman finds confusion at this stage of the model. Furthermore, a woman's experience often is not compatible with viewing challenges in the wilderness in a militaristic framework; she is more likely to ally with the metaphoric dragons than to conquer them. Returning home is also problematic for women if the myth of the heroic quest is given credence. While a man's mythical journey in the wilderness parallels his everyday situation, a woman's does not. Encouraged to be bold and assertive in the woods, this style transfers readily for a man upon return. The woman who has learned to be strong, assertive and independent on a wilderness course encounters intense cognitive dissonance back home because these traits are not presently valued for her in society. Transfer of her newly acquired understanding of her strengths to her real world life is jeopardized. Finally, as argued in the section on the superwoman, the generic model of heroism, because it necessitates the emergence of a hero or superperson, incites a tradition that is a disservice to women.

The answer, therefore, is not to engage women in the heroic quest cycle, but to inspire a new heroic for adventure programming (Galland, 1980). A heroic based on bonding with the natural world rather than conquering it may be the foundation of a new metaphor for men and women alike. Adopting women's emphasis on merging with nature and the attention to spiritual completeness and process valued by many women outdoors, wilderness programs may increase the transfer potential and eventually the social significance of their course offerings.

Implications and Recent Trends

Outdoor adventure programs running all-woman trips have made significant strides in developing a cogent philosophy of working with women in the outdoors. The development of a feminist model for outdoor adventure education has been the result of this work (Warren, 1996). It is important to remember that outdoor adventure education has traditionally been a White, male-dominated field with programs evolving from and emulating these roots. Therefore, in order to be sensitive to the needs of women, programming that is distinct from established adventure education philosophy has to be articulated and implemented. Specifically, leadership, decision making, co-leading, diversity and teaching styles are some areas of divergence from conventional wilderness education theory.

Leadership in a feminist model of adventure education is based on the premise that a group needs leadership rather than omniscient leaders (Kokopeli and Lakey, 1979). The role of the guide then is to facilitate rather than to control, to distribute leadership functions rather than to seek to fill them all, and to utilize the resources of the group rather than relying primarily on self. The result is that participants themselves have opportunities to experiment with different leadership styles. It also prevents the dynamic of the leader as superwoman.

Decision making in traditional courses tends to be reserved to the judgment of the leader or, at best, democratic. In women-only programming, there has been a trend toward consensus decision making where the needs of each group member are heard and considered in the cooperative development of a decision.

This avoids the up to 49 percent dissatisfaction possible in majority rule decision making. It also frees the leader from interpreting and determining the needs of the individuals in a group as each member has the responsibility of voicing his or her own needs (Warren and Tippett, 1988).

All-woman programs typically have eschewed a hierarchical style of leadership where there is a head instructor supported by assistant leaders. Coleading, true shared leadership, is based on the supposition that all leaders bring valuable skills and experiences to a trip. While there are always power differentials based on experience, specific technical or communication skill proficiency, age or gender, the goal of true coleading is to recognize and minimize these differences. The work done by coleaders to downplay power inequalities impacts the group as the message portrayed is that differences are appreciated and beneficial.

Women's programs have been on the cutting edge of advocating for diversity. Making outdoor trips accessible to women of different backgrounds has been important enough to such organizations as Women Outdoors, Inc. that its brochure includes a diversity statement. In addition, Women in the Wilderness and Outdoor Vacations for Women Over 40 are among women's businesses offering trips geared specifically for older women. New Routes, Inc. has expanded into outdoor programs for survivors of domestic violence and incest. There has been a genuine emphasis in women's programs to encourage all women to participate.

Teaching styles used in all-woman courses often shun dichotomous thinking; emphasizing that there are not right and wrong ways of performing skills. Teaching tends to acknowledge different learning styles and accentuate connections with other participants and the earth. It is built on relationship rather than rules.

Conclusion

The goal of this discussion has been to point out that women bring to adventure experiences not only distinct needs that programs must acknowledge but also a unique perspective that would be beneficial if incorporated in all facets of outdoor experiential education. By labeling myths that impede our realization of gender differences, we take the first step in insuring that outdoor adventure will be a positive, holistic experience for women. The demise of the myths frees adventure leaders to conceive and restructure programs that will be on the cutting edge of growth for men and women alike.

References

Bacon, S. (1983). *The conscious use of metaphor in Outward Bound*. Denver, CO: Colorado Outward Bound School.

Cameron, A. (1981). *Daughters of copper women*. Vancouver, BC: Press Gang Publishers.

Christ, C. P. (1980). *Diving deep and surfacing*. Boston, MA: Beacon Press.

Galland, C. (1980). *Women in the wilderness*. New York, NY: Harper & Row.

Hardin, J. A. (1979). *Outdoor/wilderness approaches to psychological education for women: A descriptive study*. Unpublished doctoral dissertation, University of Massachusetts, Amherst, Massachusetts.

Kokopeli, B., and Lakey, G. (1979). *Leadership for change: Toward a feminist model*. Philadelphia, PA: New Society.

Maughan, J. J. (1983). *The outdoor woman's guide to sports, fitness and nutrition*. Harrisburg, PA: Stackpole Books.

Niemi, J., and Wieser, B. (Eds.). (1987). *Rivers running free: Canoeing stories by adventurous women* (2nd ed.). Seattle, WA: Seal Press.

Roberts, N. S. (1996). Women of color in experiential education: Crossing cultural boundaries. In K. Warren (Ed.), *Women's Voices in Experiential Education* (pp. 226–240). Dubuque, IA: Kendall/Hunt Publishing Co.

Rogers, S. F. (Ed.). (1996). *Solo: On her own adventure*. Seattle, WA: Seal Press.

Warren, K. (Ed.). (1996). *Women's voices in experiential education*. Dubuque, IA: Kendall/Hunt Publishing Co.

Warren, K., and Tippett, S. (1988). Teaching consensus decision making. *Journal of Experiential Education, 11*(3), 38–39.

Chapter 53

Adventure in the Workplace

Todd Miner
Cornell University

Yolanda Jones and Tim Buckner clasp hands, balanced on a wooden plank and metal milk carton. Their perch is on a lawn, in front of a nondescript office building, and they appear to be trying to join a small group less than 20 feet away. A parking lot is in the near distance and cars can be heard whizzing by on the street behind that. Their small nearby group consults their watches, shouts directions, and jumps up and down in excitement urging them on. Several people stand alone, objectively jotting down observations. On the opposite side of the large lawn, several hundred feet away, another small group talks, sitting in a circle on the ground. Like their comrades, Yolanda and Tim are dressed as if it were "casual Friday" at the office.

What is going on? How does this suburban scene relate to adventure education? Where is the wilderness? The ropes? The risk?

Experienced-Based Training and Development as Adventure

The scene described here is a typical example of an experience-based training and development (EBTD) program. EBTD goes by many names (corporate adventure training,

outdoor management development, outdoor training), but whatever it is called, it is without question a form of adventure education; in fact, it is one of the newest and most vibrant forms of adventure education being practiced. Using Priest's (1990) definition, EBTD is a form of adventure because it involves a situation in which the outcome is unknown (will Yolanda and Tim be able to join their compadres in the allotted time), the participants have a role in the outcome (through cooperation, problem solving, balance, and persistence, among other skills), and there is risk (in this case mostly psychological, social, and self-risk).

EBTD is a different kind of adventure education because its principal focus is on improving workplace performance, rather than on an individual's personal growth. The setting for EBTD—for example, offices, corporate "campuses," retreat, or conference centers—is often different than most adventure education programs. And the clientele—intact work groups and mostly healthy (if out-of-shape) adults—is a far cry from the stereotypical Outward Bound, outdoor school group, or college outing program. However, despite these differences, EBTD remains a form of adventure education.

Definition

There is no commonly accepted definition of EBTD. The issue is important enough that developing a definition is one of three main mandates of a 1997 EBTD task force set up by the Association for Experiential Education (Bill

Proudman, personal communication, September 26, 1997). For the purposes of this chapter EBTD is defined as a process which uses challenge, adventure, or risk (perceived or actual, physical or psychological) combined with participant processing, usually in an outdoor or wild setting, to improve employees' workplace performance (Miner, 1991a).

Roots

Like adventure education in general, the work of Dewey and Hahn has been the principal foundation for EBTD. However as a distinctive form of adventure education, the roots of EBTD come more from the organization development, adult education, and training and development literature. Kolb's experiential learning cycle has had particular impact (Miner, 1991b).

The case has been made that Outward Bound was founded in the early 1940s as an EBTD organization in as much as the client of the first Outward Bound program was a private shipping company that wished to enhance the performance of commercial sailors in emergency situations (Miner, 1993). A little later the work of Lewin in the United States and Bion in Britain influenced a growing trend which became known as experiential training. Experiential training emphasized the self-examination of group process. It had a short period of popularity in the 1950s and early 1960s before a concern over lack of documented results, transfer to the workplace, and psychological safety, led to its demise. In the meantime Outward Bound, and a number of imitators grew and prospered, particularly in Great Britain and to a lesser extent in North America.

Project Adventure, founded in the early 1970s as a way to bring the Outward Bound concept into suburban schools, was another source for the EBTD field. Project Adventure pioneered the concept of keeping the adventure, challenge, and risk alive while adapting small group multiweek wilderness expeditions to very short-term (one hour to several days) time frames in suburban and even urban settings to large numbers of individuals, often intact groups. The field also adopted Project Adventure's terminology as expressed in "challenge-by-choice" and the "full value contract."

In Britain EBTD (more often called *outdoor management development*) emerged mainly from Outward Bound, the development training movement, and the military (Bank, 1985). The first explicitly EBTD programs were run there in the late 1940s. In North America EBTD's roots were primarily from Outward Bound, Project Adventure, and the experiential training field. The first programs in North America began in the early 1970s, with rapid growth in the late 1980s and early 1990s. However it was not until the early 1990s that EBTD had grown enough that providers came together to try to organize their efforts and share ideas. The Association for Experience-Based Training and Development was a short-lived attempt at a stand-alone organization. It ultimately foundered as members returned to their traditional professional organizations, either the American Society for Training and Development or the Association for Experiential Education (AEE). Within AEE a professional group (EBTD) was formed and it continues to be one of the organization's largest and strongest professional groups.

Goals

The overarching goal of EBTD is to improve workplace performance. But what factors does the field try to influence to do so? In surveying North American providers of EBTD, Miner (1991b) found that over half the programming was used to build teamwork. Approximately 25 percent was directed at enhancing leadership with less than 20 percent of programming aimed at general personal development. Wagner, Baldwin, and Roland (1991) surveyed corporate trainers (generally the consumer of EBTD programs) in North America. They divided EBTD programs into those who primarily used wilderness and those who used the outdoors but in more controlled settings (conference centers, lawns, challenge courses). They found that wilderness programs tended to stress leadership while the outdoor-centered programs overwhelmingly stressed team building. A survey of consumers done in Britain in the mid 1980s found that personal development was the primary benefit derived (Bank, 1985). Given the rapidly changing field, it would be interesting to see if these results are holding steady, more than five and ten years later.

Whatever the goal of a specific program, the field of training and development is increasingly going beyond mere "smile sheets" (participants' reviews of how they liked a training program) to focus on transfer of learning to the workplace. EBTD as a subset of the training and development field, is likewise emphasizing the connection to the workplace and the application of learning on the job.

Methodology

Myths of the Three Rs

The media is fond of portraying the "sexy" part of EBTD, the high-adventure activities which Miner (1991b) has called the "myth of the three Rs"—rafting, rock climbing, ropes courses. However, the reality is that the methods of EBTD have more in common with experiential training than they do with high adventure. These methods include assessment and program design, before ever delivering learning interventions, and then framing, activities, and debriefing with the clients, followed by evaluation and follow-up.

Assessment and Program Design

One of the unique factors of EBTD as a form of adventure education is the emphasis on the organization as the subject or client. Each organization is unique; no longer does "one size fit all." As Gass, Goldman, and Priest (1992) point out, "failing to design the context of the activity to mirror the workplace creates programs that produce 'hit or miss' strategies" (p. 36). To determine the need for an intervention, as well as its design (to determine what will be mirrored), a needs assessment is done.

As Seibert (1995) has pointed out, EBTD programs are most effective when designed in conjunction with a needs assessment. A needs assessment helps determine training content, collect case material (to customize the program), and to begin to develop a relationship with the organization and its employees (Silberman, 1990). The needs assessment is often done in conjunction with an EBTD professional and the head of a organization or a subunit or one of its internal trainers. If the organization has not already done a needs assessment then the EBTD professional will do one. The needs assessment normally involves a review of written materials, a site visit, and interviews with a few selected employees. It may also include more in-depth interviews with a wider base of employees, surveys, and repeat site visits. Based on the needs assessment and logistical realities such as time and fiscal resources available, a number of outcome goals are established.

A program design is then developed based on the outcomes desired. The program design includes what specific activities will be done, the sequencing of events, a safety plan, and a schedule. As Gass (1991) has written, one of the critical aspects of a superior program design is the development of isomorphic metaphors (see Facilitation). The program design will also include an evaluation phase and, depending on resources and need, a follow-up.

Activities

EBTD activities include initiatives, challenge course elements, and wilderness or high-adventure programming. Initiatives include portable games and challenge activities which generally are used for deinhibitizing, trust building, problem solving, and other team-building purposes. Karl Rohnke (1984, 1989) and the Project Adventure staff have written extensively about these activities. Challenge (or ropes) courses activities are artificial "obstacle courses" constructed of cable, wood, and ropes in trees, rafters, or telephone poles. They can be low, in which case a participant is no more than a few feet off the ground, or high, in which case the participant is belayed and can be scores of feet off the ground. Low-challenge course activities are generally used for team building while high activities or elements are used for self-assessment, risk taking, and leadership development. Rohnke, as well as Webster (1989),

has written commonly cited sources for the use of challenge courses. Wilderness or high-adventure activities used by EBTD include rock climbing, mountaineering, sailing, canoeing, whitewater rafting, backpacking and other outdoor pursuits.

If EBTD uses the same activities as other forms of adventure programming, how does it differ? While the media continues to be infatuated with the "sexier" rocks, ropes, and rafting, Miner (1991b) found that the reality as reported by EBTD providers is considerably different. EBTD providers report that only 20 percent of programming time is spent in backcountry environments, doing rock climbing, rafting, or other pursuits traditionally associated with adventure. Almost half of activity time is spent on initiatives—problem solving and team challenge events in which collaboration, cognitive ability, and persistence play a much bigger role than strength, bravery, or outdoor skills. About a third of activity time is spent on challenge (or rope) courses. For every hour of activity, almost a half-hour is spent on discussion, either framing or debriefing.

EBTD programming in the early 1990s was reported to last an average of 2.7 days or 30 hours (Miner, 1991b). This is probably shrinking, but no figures are available to support this statement. Less than a quarter of programming is done in the wilderness with about a third being done at an EBTD provider's site and nearly another third done at a resort, retreat, or training center. Almost 15 percent is done at the client organization's place of work (Miner, 1991b).

One of the confounding aspects of EBTD activities is that they range considerably in length and they are often part of more traditional training and development programs. They are an hour here, or a morning there; part of a multiday program involving didactic lecture, simulations, and technical training. This makes research and even communication about EBTD programming a sometimes challenging proposition.

Facilitation

Facilitation is the key element which separates EBTD from the company picnic or softball game. It takes place both before activity (front-loading, framing, briefing) and after (reflection, debriefing, processing). In EBTD programs, as opposed to recreation or general outdoor education, facilitation is fourth or fifth generation, emphasizing front-loading and framing (Priest and Gass, 1996). The facilitation is generally both micro, focused on the immediate activity being conducted, and macro, focused on the overall program and cumulative activities. As in adventure therapy, EBTD facilitation can be viewed as part of an "adventure wave," in which a group is briefed, the activity takes place, and then the activity is processed or discussed (Schoel, Stratton, and Radcliffe, 1988).

Facilitation helps link the activity to the workplace and assists in the learning being transferred and applied back on the job. Because EBTD participants are normally intact work groups, an EBTD professional (facilitator) can customize the activities and particularly the facilitation to ensure that the program is directly relevant to the workplace issues with which an organization is dealing and to the outcome goals developed in the assessment. The ability to customize and connect the learning to the workplace is the defining aspect of a high-quality EBTD program.

The customizing begins with developing isomorphic metaphors (Gass, 1991) between the EBTD activities and the workplace. Isomorphs are two separate entities or concepts which, because of analogous elements, can serve as a bridge for learning. Their shared similarities can help EBTD participants see how coping with "toxic waste" (to use the generic name for a common initiative) has relevance and meaning to the issues they deal with back at work. To truly make an initiative isomorphic with the workplace the name of the initiative is changed, the rules are modified, the consequences are adapted, and even the desired outcome is customized.

Front-loading, or "punctuating the key learning points in advance of the adventure experience" (Priest and Gass, 1996, p. 8), is another facilitation technique that enhances EBTD learning. Front-loading, particularly front-loading of isomorphic metaphors, enhances learning *during* the activity, as opposed to it principally occurring afterwards during processing (Gass, 1991). It provides a framework for the participants to organize their learning during the hectic activities.

Generic facilitation or processing of EBTD initiatives is no longer sufficient. If the learning is to be transferred back to the workplace, isomorphic program design and facilitation, enhanced by front-loading, are necessary. Learning which occurs in EBTD programs is not a product like a widget or a car, constructed in an assembly line approach in which the same various parts (or activities) are installed. Rather each activity is custom designed and delivered to ensure a tight connection and continuity from the training to the workplace.

The EBTD Industry

The scope and nature of the EBTD field was examined in the early 1990s by Miner (1991b) and by Wagner et al. (1991). Based on results of two surveys sent out to EBTD providers in the early 1990s, Miner estimated that 200,000 clients were annually served in North America. Randomly surveying Fortune 500 companies, Wagner et al. found that almost one in six U.S. corporations used some form of EBTD. Miner estimated that in the early 1990s the North American EBTD industry generated between $100 and $200 million in annual sales.

Participants and Client Organizations

EBTD is done for the for-profit, not-for-profit, and governmental sectors. Employees from all levels of organizations participate in EBTD programs. As providers are finding that working with intact work groups (as opposed to open entry–type programs) is more effective (Wagner and Roland, 1992), intact groups are becoming more the norm, particularly in the non-wilderness-type programs. Executives more often are involved with wilderness programs (Wagner et al., 1991), presumably because they are more expensive.

One of the challenges faced by the EBTD field is that the organizations that seek its help have generally come from the extremes of performance. They tended to be the organizations that were either very high performing (and so had the resources and/or insight to afford the expenditure) or they had problems—often serious—and so sought the intervention of training or organization development professionals. It is only more recently, as EBTD programs have become more common, that EBTD practitioners regularly see a "normal" organization.

EBTD professionals come from two rather separate backgrounds. A majority come from an experiential or adventure background, with a minority from a training and development or organization development background (Miner, 1991b). As facilitator skill is one of the key factors in EBTD effectiveness (Wagner and Roland, 1992) more research on what makes for an effective facilitator is needed. Well over 100 North American providers were reported in the early 1990s (Miner, 1991b).

Several in-depth reviews of the EBTD field were done in the early 1990s. Unfortunately, little has surfaced since. A contemporary and thorough review of the field would be useful both for painting a more current picture of the field, but also to demonstrate what changes have occurred in the last five-plus years.

Challenges

A number of challenges face the field of EBTD. These include perceived saturation, being defined by the margins (Bill Proudman, personal communication, Sept. 30, 1997), safety, ethics, proven efficacy, diversity, research, and competition from other experiential training and development techniques. If these challenges can be faced and dealt with, the field will grow beyond "fad" status to become a standard tool of the training and development and organization development field.

Perceived Saturation

The EBTD field is caught in a paradox. On one hand the adventure techniques continue to be seen as faddish and extreme. On the other hand, as adventure in the form of challenge courses, initiatives, and artificial climbing walls becomes more common—not just in the workplace, but in schools and recreation programs as well—the techniques are increasingly viewed by participants as "ho-hum." EBTD providers report hearing participants or potential participants say "We did that stuff last year" or "I've done a ropes course before," as if the training was no more than the activity, rather than the facilitated learning. Part of this challenge has been brought about by the EBTD providers themselves as they have touted the newness and excitement of the learning environment. And as EBTD and other adventure programs grow, this challenge will only mushroom. There is no easy solution to this dilemma, but certainly part of the answer is for EBTD providers to stay away from the easy marketing of adventure's "sexiness," and instead focus on promoting the unique power of well-facilitated and isomorphic adventure programs.

Defined by Margins

EBTD has always been defined by its margins. It is the margins—fire walking, bungee jumping, survival exercises, and the like—which make exciting media stories and catch the public's attention. Good facilitation is hard to capture on videotape and doesn't come across well on a 30-second news "bite!" While these margins make up a very small percentage of programming, they will continue to define the field until a more proactive professional organization develops standards, codes of ethics, best practices, accreditation or similar benchmarks.

Safety

Because EBTD programs deal with an adult and largely sedentary population participating in adventurous activities, safety is a constant concern. At least half a dozen fatalities have occurred on high ropes courses over the last decade (Cryer, 1994; Miner, 1991a), presumably mostly in EBTD programs. Injuries, particularly to joints, muscles, and backs, are also of concern. Such injuries can be caused by reinjury of old problems and the by the generally less flexible, resilient, and fit bodies of an older population.

In addition to physical safety, psychological safety also has to be taken into consideration. Because EBTD programs work with intact groups, participants may be more subject to stress transferred from the workplace and to psychological risk. Many criticisms from outside the field (Falvey, 1988; McNeil/Lehrer Newshour, 1989) and cautions from inside the field (Ringer and Gillis, 1995; Smolowe, 1990) have been voiced about this issue.

Answers to safety challenges include patient risk assessment or screening (Hubbell, 1995), careful sequencing, modifying of elements or individual participation, use of challenge-by-choice ethics, facilitator training, and management of psychological depth (Ringer and Gillis,

1995). It also includes reporting both safety incidents and near misses and a professional group ready to collect, disseminate, and learn from the incidents.

Ethics

In a field that is largely profit driven, where relatively large amounts of money can be made, and where little or no standards exist, ethics are going to be an issue. Ethical controversies over safety issues, pirating of clients, and plagiarizing of methods, among others, have cropped up and will continue to occur. Can challenge-by-choice really exist when employees are pressured or coerced into attending programs? Ethical questions between providers and clients, providers and each other, and providers and their employees can and have appeared. Answers to ethical issues can be at least partly dealt with through accreditation or establishment of standards. Collaboration and open communication among providers will help, as will ongoing education and training.

Competition

Probably a bigger cause for concern for the field than internal competition is the competition from other innovative training and development techniques. Will computer simulations, CD-ROM "games," interactive video, action learning, on-the-job learning, or other experiential technique prove to be more effective, more efficient, or just "sexier"? A 1993 issue of *Training and Development* (October, 1993) included five articles on "learning by doing" or experiential training; not one word was written about "traditional" EBTD programming. Are EBTD techniques so commonplace now that they are taken for granted? Is this good or is this the end of one fad and the beginning of another?

This challenge must be dealt with by EBTD practitioners constantly "sharpening their saw" and by developing new tools as well. It probably means integrating EBTD techniques into traditional training and development and into the new techniques as they develop. It means that practitioners must be ready to demonstrate the efficacy of EBTD methods.

Diversity

The U.S. training and development field faces pressure to acknowledge cultural diversity and to ensure that programs are sensitive to, and effectively reaching, a diverse audience. This pressure to adapt to a more diverse clientele is both because the country as a whole is becoming more diverse and because of the globalization of the economy.

This pressure is especially strong for adventure-based training and development as minorities have traditionally underparticipated in outdoor activities (Carr and Williams, 1993). Likewise, the outdoors has traditionally been seen as primarily a male domain (Henderson, Winn, and Roberts, 1996). As a result minorities and women may find the outdoor setting of most EBTD programs to be more unfamiliar and more intimidating than those from the dominant culture. In international situations it is critical for facilitators to be sensitive to language and cultural issues from around the world (Campbell et al., 1995).

Research

Much of the research on EBTD has been very positive and has lent support to this method's effectiveness (Priest, Attarian, and Schubert, 1993; Roland, 1981). However, more highly visible research (Stoltz, 1992), and media reports of research (Deutsch, 1991), discussing EBTD failures may create challenges. Beyond refuting negative results, it is the field's responsibility to conduct and publicize solid research which documents EBTD efficacy. The fact remains that few providers or clients conduct research and the need for additional research has been repeatedly made (Kirkpatrick, 1995; Priest et al., 1993; Wagner et al., 1991). In addition to conducting the research, it is critical that the EBTD field communicate the findings to its clients, the media, and ultimately, to the public.

One Final Thought

EBTD is important because it can help make for a more productive workplace and it can enliven employees' lives. It is also important to the adventure education field and to adventure educators (Garvey, 1989). EBTD offers a career track with far more professional opportunities than is the norm in the adventure field. This includes higher salaries and more advancement opportunities. There are also lateral career moves which open up, such as into more traditional training and development, management, or organization development. Adventure educators can work a normal work schedule and have the opportunity to work with functional, adult populations, if they so choose.

EBTD offers the adventure education field a chance to impact mainstream adults as well as high-level executives, something which is almost impossible for other forms of adventure education. It is a chance for decision makers at all levels of companies, nonprofits, and governments to be exposed to the benefits of adventure techniques, and thus to become supporters of the methodology in its other forms and environments—schools, hospitals, social service agencies, and recreation programs.

Conclusion

Is "adventure in the workplace" an oxymoron or is it an absolute business necessity? Business and leadership experts (Kouzes and Posner, 1987; Peters, 1988, 1994) consistently answer with the latter: a sense of adventure in the workplace is very much a necessity. If organizations are going to "thrive on chaos," they are going to have to rely on their people to find and nurture that sense of adventure. EBTD offers an excellent way to do so.

With the powerful learning of experience-based training and development Yolanda and Tim, as well as their colleagues, will gain much. More importantly, they will know how to transfer the learning back to the workplace and they will be motivated to do so. Yolanda and Tim, and their team, will have learned to achieve extraordinary things in their organization.

References

Bank, J. (1985). *Outdoor development for managers.* Aldershot, UK: Gower.

Campbell, J., Wagner, R. J., Brown, H., Kolblinger, M., Lim, T. K., and Main, M. (1995). International and multicultural perspectives. In C. C. Roland, R. J. Wagner, and R. Weigand (Eds.), *Do it and understand: The bottom line on corporate experiential learning* (pp. 139–159). Dubuque, IA: Kendall/Hunt Publishing Co.

Carr, D. S., and Williams, D. R. (1993). Understanding the role of ethnicity in outdoor recreation experiences. *Journal of Leisure Research, 25*(1), 22–38.

Cryer, J. (1994). Reducing the risks of heart attacks on high ropes courses. *Association for Experiential Education EBTD Professional Group Newsletter,* Spring, p. 4.

Deutsch, C. H. (1991). Back from the great outdoors: Corporate leaders are finally challenging the value of outdoor training programs. *New York Times,* May 19, p. 1.

Falvey, J. (1988). Before spending $3 million on leadership, read this. *Wall Street Journal,* October 3, p. 16.

Garvey, D. (1989). The corporate connection: From bowlines to bow ties. *Journal of Experiential Education, 12*(1), 13–15.

Gass, M. A. (1991). Enhancing metaphoric transfer of learning in adventure education. *Journal of Experiential Education, 14*(2), 6–13.

Gass, M. A., Goldman, K., and Priest, S. (1992). Constructing effective corporate adventure training programs. *Journal of Experiential Education, 15*(1), 35–42.

Henderson, K. A., Winn, S., and Roberts, N. S. (1996). *King of in the middle: The meaning of the outdoors for women students.* Paper presented at the Coalition for Education in the Outdoors Research Symposium, Bradford Woods, Indiana.

Hubbell, F. R. (1995). Adventure and cardiac risk. *Zip Lines* (27), 27–29.

Kirkpatrick, D. L. (1995). How is training evaluated? In C. C. Roland, R. J. Wagner, and R. Weigand (Eds.), *Do it and understand: The bottom line on corporate experiential learning* (pp. 118–131). Dubuque, IA: Kendall/Hunt Publishing Co.

Kouzes, J. M., and Posner, B. Z. (1987). *The leadership challenge: How to get extraordinary things done in organizations.* San Francisco, CA: Jossey-Bass.

MacNeil/Lehrer Newshour. (1989). *Focus—Upward Bound (Motivational training for employees).* Show #3551, Monday, September 4, 1989. New York, NY: WNET. (Transcript by Strictly Business, P. O. Box 12361, Overland Park, KS 66212.)

Miner, T. A. (1991a). Safety issues for experience-based training and development. *Journal of Experiential Education, 14*(2), 20–25.

Miner, T. A. (1991b). A descriptive analysis of the experienced-based training and development field. In C. Birmingham (Ed.), *Association for Experiential Education: 1991 conference proceedings and workshop summaries book* (pp. 59–66). Boulder, CO: Association for Experiential Education.

Miner, T. (1993). *A comparison of isomorphic and generic processing approaches for team building through experience-based training and development: A quantitative and qualitative analysis.* Unpublished doctoral dissertation, Boston University, Boston, Massachusetts.

Peters, T. (1988). *Thriving on chaos.* New York, NY: Knopf.

Peters, T. (1994). *The pursuit of wow.* New York, NY: Random House.

Priest, S. (1990). The semantics of adventure education. In J. Miles and S. Priest (Eds.), *Adventure education* (pp. 113–117). State College, PA: Venture Publishing, Inc.

Priest, S., and Gass, M. (1996). Front-loading with paradox and double blinds in adventure education facilitation. *Journal of Adventure Education and Outdoor Leadership, 11*(1), 8–10.

Priest, S., Attarian, A., and Schubert, S. (1993). Conducting research in experience-based training and development programs: Pass keys to locked doors. *Journal of Experiential Education, 16*(2), 11–20.

Ringer, M., and Gillis, H. L. (1995). Managing psychological depth in adventure programming. *Journal of Experiential Education, 18*(1), 41–51.

Rohnke, K. (1984). *Silver bullets.* Dubuque, IA: Kendall/Hunt Publishing Co.

Rohnke, K. (1989). *Cowstails and cobras II.* Dubuque, IA: Kendall/Hunt Publishing Co.

Roland, C. C. (1981). *The transfer of an outdoor managerial training program to the workplace.* Unpublished doctoral dissertation, Boston University, Boston, Massachusetts.

Schoel, J., Stratton, J., and Radcliffe, P. (1988). *Adventure-based counseling.* Hamilton, MA: Project Adventure.

Seibert, P. S. (1995). The importance of a thorough needs assessment. In C. C. Roland, R. J. Wagner, and R. Weigand (Eds.), *Do it and understand: The bottom line on corporate experiential learning* (pp. 59–64). Dubuque, IA: Kendall/Hunt Publishing Co.

Silberman, M. (1990). *Active training: A handbook of techniques, designs, case examples, and tips.* New York, NY: Lexington Books.

Smolowe, A. (1990). Challenge-by-choice in adventure-based management trainings. *Zip Lines* (Spring), pp. 8–9.

Stoltz, P. G. (1992). An examination of leadership development in the great outdoors. *Human Resource Development Quarterly, 3*(4), 357–372.

Wagner, R. J., Baldwin, T. T., and Roland, C. C. (1991). Outdoor training: Revolution or fad? *Training & Development Journal, 45*(3), 50–51, 53–57.

Wagner, R. J., and Roland, C. C. (1992). How effective is outdoor training? *Training and Development Journal, 46*(7), 61–66.

Webster, S. E. (1989). *Ropes course safety manual.* Dubuque, IA: Kendall/Hunt Publishing Co.

Chapter 54

Programs That Include Persons With Disabilities

Leo McAvoy
University of Minnesota

Greg Lais
Wilderness Inquiry, Inc.

Introduction

Persons with disabilities are a major and growing market segment for those involved in providing adventure education services and facilities. The passage of the Americans With Disabilities Act (ADA) has focused attention on persons with disabilities and on the public and private services available to them. According to the ADA, there are over 43 million people in the United States who are considered to have a disability. Although the leisure preferences of persons who have disabilities are as diverse as the rest of the population, a significant number of these persons are participating and seeking to participate in outdoor recreation and adventure activities (Leitman, Cooner, and Risher, 1994). Persons with disabilities are going to public and private areas and facilities to experience the benefits of participation in these activities. They are going to camps, ropes courses, parks, wilderness areas, whitewater rivers, the ocean, the mountains, and winter environments. They are canoeing, boating, rafting, sailing, camping, hang gliding, snorkeling, hunting, fishing, rock climbing, kayaking, dogsledding, and all of the other recreation and adventure activities that are so popular with the population at large.

Adventure education agencies and businesses are paying increased attention to offering quality services to a wider range of clients, including persons with disabilities. The movement toward universal access, where persons of all abilities are welcome and accommodated, will result in more persons with disabilities participating in adventure programs. Technology is aiding the development of new equipment to make access more possible and effective. Adventure education agencies and businesses are also developing new management technologies to enhance adventure opportunities for persons with disabilities as well as for the population as a whole. This chapter will discuss a rationale for integrated adventure education programming and present a number of management technologies that can make these integrated programs a reality. We will also address a number of myths regarding disabilities and programs. Myths like "handicapped programs are enough, we don't have to make our other programs accessible," "those folks are 'handicapped,' but i am not," or "we can't make our programs accessible because it is too dangerous and we don't have either the staff or the equipment."

The passage of the ADA has mandated that facilities available to the public must be accessible to persons with disabilities. The ADA also indicated that access to these facilities and services be provided in the most integrated setting possible. The most integrated setting is one which enables interaction between persons with and without disabilities. Persons with disabilities have become aware of the potentials for access in recreation, education, and adventure settings; are aware of the law; and are becoming more assertive in making more public and market-driven demands for accessible facilities and services. It is now time for the managers of adventure education programs and facilities to provide universal access to these programs in as integrated a way as possible.

The Americans With Disabilities Act states that an individual with a disability is one who has a mental or physical impairment which substantially affects one or more of the major life activities or has a record of such an impairment or is regarded as having such an impairment. The major physical life activities are those an individual does in the course of a typical day, such as walking, hearing, seeing, speaking, dressing, eating, manipulating objects, and driving. The cognitive activities include understanding, problem solving, and remembering. When one sees the word *disability* or the word *disabled* the usual image created in one's mind is that of a person with a mobility impairment in a wheelchair or a person with a visual impairment using a guide dog or white cane. But the ADA has a much broader definition of disability. Other conditions covered by the definition in the ADA include persons with mental illness, emotional illness, mental retardation or developmental disabilities, and chemical dependency.

In this chapter, we are not talking about the "handicapped adventure program." The days are gone where an adventure education manager could offer only segregated programs; programs where those with disabilities participate in one program or facility specifically designed for them, and all others participate in the "regular" or "normal" programs and facilities. A major philosophy and intent of the ADA and other legislation is that services, programs and activities be provided in the most integrated setting possible. The most integrated setting is one which enables interaction between people with and without disabilities. Integration includes both physical and social integration. Social integration seeks to develop acceptance for mutually beneficial relationships between individuals with and without disabilities (Lais, 1987). The goal of social integration is to ensure that persons with disabilities are accepted as full members of the community, permitted to participate in the activities of life enjoyed by others, and able to participate alongside their peers who do not have disabilities. Adventure education programs are now often being utilized as vehicles for integration (Schleien, McAvoy, Lais, and Rynders, 1993). Our emphasis throughout this chapter will be on the benefits of, and the management of, integrated adventure programs which include persons with and without disabilities.

Benefits of Adventure Education for Persons With Disabilities

We often hear that persons with disabilities receive unique benefits from adventure programs. Others, including many with disabilities, would say that persons with disabilities do not receive unique benefits. Rather, they receive the same benefits as everyone else. Persons with disabilities are accessing adventure education areas and will continue to do so as they become increasingly aware of the benefits of adventure. What is unique is the place from which persons with disabilities start. Their day-to-day reality is different from those who do not have a disability. The realities of a disability, and the societal attitudes that place limits on those with disabilities, make adventure just that much more precious. We believe that persons with disabilities do not find unique benefits in adventure programs, it is just that they often thought they would not be able or be allowed to receive those benefits. Maybe that is why these benefits seem a bit more precious to those with disabilities.

The literature documenting the effects of adventure programs on persons with disabilities centers on the psychological, social and mental health benefits (McAvoy, Schatz, Stutz, Schleien, and Lais, 1989; McAvoy and Schleien, 1988; Robb and Ewert, 1987; Schleien et al., 1993) These benefits include enhanced self-concept, self-esteem, and self-fulfillment; personal growth; increased leisure skills; increased social adjustment and cooperation; enhanced body image; and positive behavior change.

Research on integrated adventure experiences where persons with and without disabilities participate together has indicated positive attitude and lifestyle changes (recreation patterns, interpersonal relationships, social patterns); increased willingness to take risks; higher feelings of self-efficacy; and a number of spiritual benefits (McAvoy et al., 1989; Stringer and McAvoy, 1992). This same research has documented the benefits that accrue to persons without disabilities on these integrated programs, including increased understanding of the capabilities of persons with disabilities, more positive attitudes about persons with disabilities, and increased tolerance of differences among people.

A recent longitudinal study of the benefits of integrated wilderness adventure experiences confirmed many of the previously mentioned results and also found that participants reported improved sensitivity to the needs of others, an increased sense of priorities, and an increased respect for nature (Anderson, Schleien, McAvoy, Lais, and Seligman, 1997). These integrated adventure programs produced mutual benefits to all participants, including the capacity for persons without disabilities to better understand the capabilities as well as realistic limitations of persons with disabilities.

The study by Anderson and her colleagues found that attitudes towards persons with disabilities remained highly positive over time (the 36 months of the study). Friendships were made as a result of participating together in this adventure program. These friendships extended beyond the adventure experience. One result of the integrated adventure experience was that persons without disabilities were making choices to include persons with disabilities into their lives as friends. The participants in this study who had disabilities reported that the wilderness environment appeared to intensify and focus individual efforts producing a dramatic impact on group development and enhanced social integration of group members. The wilderness setting appeared to be crucial in helping groups form and perform together. The theme of "the wilderness" seemed to permeate the journal entries and interview transcripts that were analyzed for this study.

Persons with disabilities have had limited opportunity to experience adventure programs in the past because of the stereotypic attitudes of service providers that limited opportunities, overprotectiveness of well-meaning family and caregivers, lack of role models, and a lack of appropriate equipment. Adventure education program managers often did not think persons with disabilities would want or be able to do things like hike, camp, canoe, kayak, rock climb, or participate in ropes courses. The typical adventure environment was deemed to be too dangerous and inaccessible to persons with disabilities. One result of this pattern of exclusion is that many persons with disabilities have never had the opportunity to develop the skills necessary to participate in many lifelong leisure activities like camping, canoeing, horseback riding, kayaking, sailing, or skiing.

Adventure education programs can provide the exposure and the skill-building opportunities for persons with disabilities to develop skills in these adventure and leisure activities. Anderson et al. (1997) in their study offered skill training for persons with disabilities in canoeing and camping, and then used task analysis procedures to measure changes in skill level after intervention (training and practice) over time. They found a significant increase in targeted adventure and leisure skills over time, in this case canoeing and camping skills. Outdoor adventure activities appear to be an opportunity for people to gain and use lifelong leisure skills because of the complexity and functionality of the recreation setting.

Persons with developmental and cognitive disabilities are often left out in typical consideration of persons with disabilities. Persons with developmental disabilities are included in the definition of disabled in the Americans With Disabilities Act, and persons with developmental and cognitive disabilities are capable of realizing all of the benefits of adventure programs that are gained by other population groups (McAvoy and Schleien, 1988). Research on integrated outdoor and adventure programs has indicated a number of benefits that accrue to the participants who have developmental disabilities, including cognitive gains in environmental concepts, increased levels of social interaction between persons with and without disabilities, increased peer acceptance, a decrease in socially inappropriate behaviors, and an increase in learning lifelong outdoor leisure skills (Schleien et al., 1993).

Therapeutic outdoor and wilderness adventure programs utilize adventure as the setting for treatment of psychological and social illnesses. Camping and other adventure-based activities including rock climbing, canoeing, rafting, and skiing, are utilized as a therapeutic modality. As part of the mental healthcare system, these programs are often sponsored by institutional or outpatient organizations. The clientele are several mental health populations including psychiatric patients, persons with mental illness, the chemically dependent, persons with autism, or the emotionally disturbed. Research has suggested a number of benefits from therapeutic adventure programs, including reduced symptomatology and enhanced ability to function in the community (Driver, Peterson, and Easley, 1990; Gillis and Thomsen, 1996; Witman, 1993). Researchers and authors have stressed that these therapeutic adventure programs have not been studied with the necessary rigor to prove direct benefits from the adventure program (Gillis, 1992; Kelley, 1993). These programs cannot be expected to provide major cures for psychological and social illnesses, but they can add a piece to the overall therapeutic goals of helping a person reach mental health.

Administrative Issues

When the managers of an adventure education agency or business consider initiating integrated programs that will include persons with and without disabilities, a number of administrative issues come immediately to mind. These issues often include cost, staffing, physical accessibility of facilities, and safety and legal liability. These are legitimate issues to consider, but they need not be barriers to offering integrated adventure education programs. If an adventure agency or business identifies integrated programs as one of the priority program areas, these issues and potential costs can be managed just like any other of the myriad issues handled by managers every day.

There will be some additional costs initially in starting integrated adventure programs. These relate mainly to another of the previously mentioned issues, staffing. Staff will have to be trained in how to effectively plan and lead integrated programs. There may have to be some facility improvements to provide greater levels of access for persons with disabilities. Some adapted equipment may have to be obtained, although the staff can often come up with appropriate adaptations of existing equipment through innovative thinking. The major cost in running integrated programs is the increased level of staffing needed, depending on the level of functioning of the participants. This increased staffing level can often be managed through cooperative programming with other agencies who have staff trained in working with persons with disabilities, such as occupational or rehabilitation therapists, therapeutic recreation specialists, and special education teachers. Another source of staffing support can come from trained volunteers, interns, and former participants (with and without disabilities) who can work part time on an as needed basis.

Adventure education facilities are often not very accessible to persons with disabilities. Adventure program staff must inventory their facilities to determine the levels of access of all parts of their sites and the sites typically used by the program. All buildings and their associated elements (parking lots, walkways, entrances, informational signs, educational displays) must be accessible according to the standards in the Americans With Disabilities Act (Architectural Transportation Barriers Compliance Board, 1991). Managers should also move to install telecommunications devices for the deaf (TDDs) in adventure facility offices. Outdoor facilities must also be inventoried. Guidelines are available to assist managers in this process of inventorying outdoor facilities (USDA Forest Service and PLAE, Inc., 1993), and standards are being developed that will make these guidelines more formal and mandatory. A good resource for up-to-date information on accessibility guidelines and standards for outdoor and camp facilities is the National Center for Accessibility (address in resource list at end of this chapter). A good resource for ideas on how to make ropes and challenge courses more accessible is the Mark Havens text *Bridges to Accessibility* (1992).

The ADA recognizes that the process of making a program or facility accessible should not substantially alter the nature of the activity. Accommodations expected are such that they would not fundamentally alter the nature of the services provided by the program. When an accommodation would result in a substantial economic or administrative burden, or would result in a fundamental alteration of the nature of the service, a manager may refuse to make accommodation. Examples of reasonable accommodations would include auxiliary services like sign language interpreters, assistive listening devices, large print materials; removing architectural barriers like curbs, steps, inaccessible rest rooms; and providing accessible transportation if transportation is part of the activity.

After inventorying their adventure education facilities, managers should initiate a plan to begin making their facilities accessible according to the available standards and guidelines, and to start the process of bringing their facilities up to standards. These facility improvements should have as a priority making the primary program facilities accessible. A key element in this facility accessibility issue is to have information readily available that indicates the level of access available at your site. This information should be communicated to all prospective participants so they can make informed decisions about whether to utilize your site and program or not. Adventure programs often occur off-site in parks and other outdoor recreation areas. Staff need to do a general site analysis of these areas to become aware of the levels of access found there, and especially to identify areas that may be particularly challenging. The expected level of access for these outdoor facilities should also be communicated to prospective participants.

Adventure program managers unfamiliar with integrated programs often think that safety and legal liability are major impediments to offering these types of programs. They are not. Actually, the issues of safety and liability are no greater for integrated programs than for the more traditional adventure programs we are all used to seeing. The key elements in managing a safe program, one that has few dangers of major liability problems, are the same for integrated programs as they are for other programs. The key elements are have trained staff in appropriate numbers; use appropriate and safe equipment; have staff make appropriate leadership decisions; and be sure participants are placed in situations that are appropriate for their abilities and skills. Recommended guidelines for these elements of safety are available in Schleien et al. (1993) and from existing organizations that offer integrated programs. Established integrated programs have found that liability insurance costs do not depend on if the program includes persons with disabilities or not. The insurance costs are more typically based on the record of the organization regarding safety, the credentials of the program leaders, and certain organizational safety policies (e.g., requiring all participants to wear personal flotation devices when in watercraft, wearing safe footgear when walking in water, wearing helmets when climbing or on ropes courses).

Staff Training and Factors in Participation

Of all the factors to be considered when making programs accessible to everyone, none is as important as properly trained staff. It is staff that create the inviting atmosphere, figure out how to overcome obstacles, and learn to adapt to each individual's needs. Good staff training on certain key issues is essential!

Wilderness Inquiry, Inc. of Minneapolis is a nonprofit organization which offers outdoor recreation programs that are socially integrated to provide opportunities for persons of all abilities. Wilderness Inquiry has developed and refined a comprehensive staff training curriculum over the past 20 years. The key features of this curriculum include:

- disability awareness,
- social integration,
- risk management,
- group processing,
- specific disability information,
- technical disability skills such as transferring and dispensing medications, and
- adapted equipment.

Training in all of these areas is considered in the context of the Universal Program Participation Model (UPPM), a system for developing integrated programs that encourage full participation by everyone. UPPM is essentially a process of matching people's needs with the service capacity of the provider, the demands of the environment, and the needs of other participants in order to provide high-quality, socially integrated activities. It is a process of seeking the right "fit" between participant needs and quality experiences, allowing service providers to analyze the factors that go into successful programming.

Careful planning can minimize the problem of inappropriately placing people in programs that do not meet their needs. Thus, in placing potential participants, the following factors must be taken into account:

- environment,
- activity,
- participants, and
- resources (agency capacity).

These factors are interactive. Together, they determine the parameters of what is possible in socially integrated outdoor adventure programming. In considering the four factors separately, we must never forget their interactive nature.

The Environment

The environmental setting of an adventure is one of the factors that determines the success of participation of persons with varying needs. In determining whether a specific environment is appropriate, it is important to keep in mind the type of challenge desired by both the individual and the collective group.

Basic Accessibility

Getting to the terrain where an activity will occur is obviously important, especially for persons with mobility impairments. Long-distance travel through steep or rocky terrain may effectively limit the ability of most wheelchair users to participate.

Remoteness and/or Proximity to Help

In remote areas the potential for delayed evacuation must be taken into account. Some persons may have disabilities that periodically require medical attention (e.g., kidney dialysis). If the attention cannot be provided on the trail, such persons may have to be excluded from activities into remote areas.

Natural Hazards

The potential effects of various environmental hazards must be taken into consideration when people with disabilities are integrated into high-adventure programs. Such hazards include poisonous snakes, extreme cold, and biting insects. For example, persons with poor circulation and/or those who lack mobility are at a distinct disadvantage in cold weather. Persons who have reduced use of their arms are at a disadvantage when it comes to fending off mosquitoes and biting flies. In most cases natural hazards need not specifically exclude persons with disabilities, but they must be considered and adjustments may need to be made.

The Activities

Different kinds of physical and cognitive skills are required in different outdoor activities. These activities also interact with the environment. A distinction must be made between skills required to safely participate in an activity and those required to master the activity. Mastery is not needed to safely participate if the chosen environment does not demand it. For example, kayak touring on a small lake requires less skill than kayak touring on the ocean.

Cognitive Ability Required for Activity

Complex activities that require good memory and the integration of many facts may not be appropriate for persons with cognitive impairments. The less capable a participant is to assimilate information, the more supervision is required.

Physical Ability Required for Activity

To participate in some activities persons must be able to perform basic physical requirements. It is important to know what the essential physical activities are in order to integrate people with disabilities.

Cooperation or Teamwork

Some activities are solo in nature whereas others involve teamwork. If participants are to learn a particular activity that requires teamwork, it is important that they be included with people who have similar background skills or with those who are willing to tolerate diversity in physical or cognitive ability.

Time Required

Different activities require different lengths of time. A 700-mile Alaskan canoe trip, for example requires a minimum of 25 days. A 5-mile jaunt on a local river, on the other hand, may be accomplished in an afternoon. Longer activities in remote places require a much greater level of knowledge about participants than do short local trips.

The Participants

Attitudes, abilities, and interests of participants are the key determinants of successfully integrated programs. The more staff knows about the participants, and participants about the experience they are applying for, the greater the chances for success. Participant factors should be considered on both an individual and a collective group basis. Not only is it important that each persons' needs are met, but also that they fit into the group without conflict or undue burden to other group participants.

Functional Limitations

In considering the right "mix" of participants, the interactions of people with different limitations must be considered. For example, if someone who is blind is paired with someone who is deaf in a canoe their relative limitations (difficulty in communication) are exacerbated. In other situations, however, a person's limitations can be combined to overcome obstacles. For example, a person who is blind may team up with a person using a wheelchair to make their way across a trail. The wheelchair user provides visual support, and the person who is blind can help the wheelchair user over rough spots on the trail. In determining how a person will fit into an experience it is often helpful to develop some characterizations as suggested here:

1. physically strong—adds to physical capacity of group,
2. physically able—neither adds nor detracts from physical capacity,
3. physically semidependent—needs assistance that *may* slow group, and
4. physically dependent—needs assistance that *will* slow group.

In developing these characterizations it is very important to remember that each person is unique—he or she often does not fit into one category or another. The ability to determine where group members fit in these four categories allows the staff to evaluate the overall strength of the group.

Degree of Self-Knowledge

While there is no replacement for staff awareness of participant health concerns, some participants come better equipped to take care of themselves than others. For example, a doctor with diabetes is more likely to successfully provide self-care than is an individual who is profoundly mentally retarded. In the case of traumatic injuries, it often takes time for an individual to learn how his or her body responds to different situations. Therefore, a person who acquired a disability years ago is more likely to know his or her body than someone who was discharged from the hospital just last month. The degree of self-knowledge is an important factor in determining the level of support necessary for an individual to safely participate in a high-adventure activity.

Levels of Special Support Required by Participants

Persons with hearing impairments may require a sign language interpreter and persons who are unable to attend to their personal hygiene needs may require a personal care attendant. Other "regular" participants should never be expected to provide such significant levels of special support since this is likely to detract from their own adventure experience and build resentment toward the person with a disability. In most cases, people who provide this support are either paid or participate in the activity at no or reduced cost.

Abilities of Other Participants

To be successful, any group must *collectively* possess a minimum level of skill to safely enjoy the experience. A primary consideration in screening participants, therefore, is the overall level of skill and ability in the group. Each individual's abilities must be considered in the context of the larger group. In this sense, integrated groups are often "assembled" with different criteria than nonintegrated groups. Many traditional programs use a "first-come, first-served" basis for confirming people on activities. Integrated groups must have a minimum number of participants who are capable of safely accomplishing the activities. Therefore, the program must use the collective group ability as the primary criteria for assembling groups.

Motives of Participants

As important as participants' abilities are their motives for participating in an integrated activity. Some nondisabled participants become involved because of misguided altruism: to "help the handicapped." This attitude can often come across as condescending. Condescension is most frequently found among people who do not have a disability, but it can also be found among those who are disabled but view themselves as "more fortunate" than someone with what they view as a "worse" disability. In any event, condescension is a barrier to integration because it divides people rather than connects them. Some participants may seek participation in a high-adventure activity because they want to become expert in an activity or to otherwise challenge themselves. These participants can be demanding when it comes to having their needs fulfilled. Indeed, they pose potential problems for staff of mixed ability adventures where the needs of the many must be balanced with the demands of the few.

Finally, staff may be surprised to find that not everyone favors social integration, especially if the individual thinks that he or she will lose out somehow in the process. For example, some people with spinal cord injuries may resent being integrated with persons who are mentally retarded or blind. Many people believe that everyone with a disability has an open and accepting attitude toward others with disabilities. Unfortunately, this is not always the case. People with disabilities are, above all else, human. Although not acknowledged by many people, a "pecking order" is sometimes found among persons with disabilities. In general, people with cognitive disabilities or disabilities that affect speech or communication are at the low end of the order.

The Resources (Agency Capacity)

Success in any program is often determined by the capacity of the agency or organization conducting the program. Capacity, in this context, means human and material resources. It includes issues such as collective knowledge (e.g., experience in conducting an event, degree of organization). The better prepared an agency is, the higher quality programming it will be able to provide.

Training and Skill of Staff Members

Staff members must fully understand what social integration is, its value, and the various means to achieve it—especially as they relate to the adventure in question. Thorough training of staff members in disability issues allows a greater safety margin in integrated activities because they will be able to compensate for screening errors and the unexpected. Another consideration is the physical capabilities of the staff conducting the event. Physically strong staff have greater capacity to take persons with mobility impairments to remote areas.

Until agency staff become more familiar with integrated programming, they may want to consider ranking integrated activities from easy to more difficult. Different levels of screening should be set for each rank. For example, when applicants for two-hour activities are screened, issues of personal hygiene are not as important as they are for multiday adventures. In the same way, screening for events that take place in accessible areas may not require as much detail regarding an individual's capacity to ambulate independently.

Marketing Capacity of Agency

Most organizations specialize in a specific type of clientele. Successfully integrated organizations depend on the ability to attract and hold people from a variety of backgrounds and ability levels. Insufficient enrollment for activities usually forces the agency to accept anyone who comes along, regardless of other factors. This procedure can be dangerous and shortsighted. Another consideration is the amount of appropriate information provided to participants. Imagine being the only nondisabled person on a kayak trip with people who are quadriplegic. Or, if you are quadriplegic, imagine going on the same trip with a group of kayak experts who view you as a nuisance. The ability to market to a diverse population in order to create successful combinations of people is essential.

Possession of Required Equipment

By possessing properly adapted equipment, organizations increase their capacity to serve a variety of people. Special seats for canoeing and kayaking, adapted paddles and pulk sleds are examples of equipment that can facilitate the participation of people with disabilities. The degree to which an agency can provide this dictates to some extent the degree to which it will have success with integrated groups.

Level of Support Staff Provided by Agency

One of the issues agency staff will need to address is whether they will accept participants who need a personal care attendant (PCA). Generally, attendants are required when the participant cannot take care of his or her bowel or bladder needs independently or when he or she requires significant help in personal hygiene. Occasional help dressing, transferring, or with other clean and easy tasks usually does not require an attendant. Another issue is whether an agency will provide sign language interpreters for people with hearing impairments. The ability to respond to these issues also impacts the agency's capacity to deal with a wide range of abilities.

As a final note on staffing and programming, staff must recognize that the Universal Program Participation Model is a tool to review the factors that go into developing and implementing successful programs. It is not an exact forecast of success or failure. Realistically, it is often difficult to predict in advance whether any program will meet the expectations and needs of every person who enrolls. The Universal Program Participation Model allows staff to examine the different facets that make up a program experience and evaluate the strengths and weaknesses of its program in light of the model.

Guidelines for Program Adaptations

An overarching goal of integrated adventure education programming is that people should participate in programs in as normal a manner as possible. There may be some instances when programs need to be adapted to make them accessible to as wide a range of abilities as possible. If a program is adapted, the following are some guidelines for successful and appropriate adaptations (Schleien et al., 1993):

- Adapt only when necessary. Do not underestimate the ability level of participants. A simplified version of an activity may not be required.
- View adaptations as temporary and transitional. Sometimes adaptations are a poor substitute for the real thing. As an example, an outdoor team-building initiative course may not be able to provide access to persons with mobility impairments because of unstable surfaces (sand) and elements that are too high or too steep. A short-term lack of funding may preclude the immediate building of a new, more accessible course. Instead, a temporary indoor initiative course is provided that is more accessible. As soon as funding can be obtained the outdoor initiative course should be rebuilt to allow access to the course for everyone.
- Adapt on an individual basis. Treat all persons as individuals and make special arrangements on an individual basis.
- Adapt for normalization. If an individual requires a modification, keep it as close to the standard version as possible. Promote social integration by making people aware of similarities rather than differences.
- Adapt for availability. Try to have the adaptation be as close to the real thing as possible and as close to the conditions the person with disabilities will encounter at other sites and programs.

Adaptive Equipment

The major assistive device one thinks of regarding persons with disabilities is the wheelchair. But the standard wheelchair does not provide easy access to many outdoor adventure sites for many persons with disabilities. The narrow wheels, small front tires, weight, and other features make the traditional wheelchair difficult to maneuver in areas that have soft surfaces, steep slopes, cross slopes, and uneven surfaces. New wheelchair designs, often generated by interest in sports participation by persons with disabilities, feature lightweight materials and other features (such as knobby tires) that make them much more effective as a mobility devise in a wider variety of surfaces and situations.

Quickie Designs of Fresno, California, has been a leader in designing mobility devices that can be used in outdoor recreation areas. Its sport chair designs incorporate lightweight materials, traction tires, larger front wheels, and increased mobility. Quickie has also designed an adaptation of the bicycle which is a three-wheeled device where the rider provides the power through a hand pedal system. Using modern bicycle gear and frame technology, this hand-operated bike provides the same level of speed and maneuverability of a street bicycle. Several devices have been developed to expand the design of the typical wheelchair to allow access to the more difficult terrain found in outdoor recreation areas. An example is the Cobra, sold by Up and Over Engineering, which is an off-road wheelchair designed for mountain trails. As more persons with disabilities discover the benefits of outdoor recreation and adventure, and as technology continues to improve, we expect a lot more high-tech devices will make access to outdoor environments much more possible and prevalent.

Canoeing is one of Wilderness Inquiry's primary activities. The staff and other cooperators have developed equipment adaptations and new designs to make canoeing available and enjoyable for persons with a range of abilities. With the goal of providing access to water related recreation, the Wilderness Inquiry staff brainstormed with consumers who have disabilities, outdoor recreation consultants, and designers. Two equipment developments through Wilderness Inquiry include the paddler's seat and the portage frame/rowing system. The paddler's seat helps solve the problem a number of persons have with stability on a typical canoe seat. It helps stabilize the lower torso of the paddler by providing a firm backrest and side panels that provide lateral stability. The paddler's seat is made of hard plastic with an adjustable cushioning material, connects to a regular canoe seat, and is easily removed for transport. It will accommodate personal wheelchair cushions and is adjustable for individual size. The portage frame/rowing system clamps onto a regular canoe. It offers the participant with balance and coordination impairments the stability needed to row instead of paddle a canoe. The frame can then be used to assist in carrying a person across a trail between lakes, if that is necessary and appropriate for that person. Wilderness Inquiry has also developed a wheelchair portage assist device which is a harness system with traces attached to a wheelchair allowing an able bodied person to assist a person's motion or braking power in a wheelchair.

Two assistive devices for snow provide opportunities for persons with disabilities to access outdoor recreation areas in the winter. The sit ski developed by Ski for Light of Minneapolis is a cross-country sled on skis that provides independent cross-country-skiing-type use for those with good upper body strength, and provides a stable base for those with more severe disabilities to be pulled by companions or dogs. Pulk sleds developed by Beneficial Designs and by Ski-Boggan, both of California, are fiberglass shells with harness systems that allow a person to be pulled by a skier or by dogs. Additional recommendations for program adaptations for a range of disability types can be found in Schleien et al. (1993) and in Havens (1992).

General Guidelines for Integration

Many persons with disabilities have been told for years that they cannot do certain things. And, many adventure education program managers and staff assume the same set of limitations. Instead of concentrating on a person's abilities, society often places too much emphasis on limitations. In setting the tone for integration in adventure programs, staff members must essentially mold the group norms to identify potentials instead of limitations. This reframing requires an open-minded approach to problem solving and a basic recognition that everyone can and needs to make some contribution to the group. A key element in integrated adventure programs is the emphasis on the group rather than on the individual. Some individuals in any group may have difficulty during an adventure activity. But the group working together can often overcome some individual difficulties. The group together can work out a way for the group to reach its goals; and, therefore the individual members to reach the goals of the adventure program.

The suggestions and techniques discussed in this section can be summarized into three categories: (1) establishing ground rules for how people treat each other; (2) facilitating participant efforts to reexamine preconceived limitations and their own value system for measuring accomplishments; and (3) initiating methods and approaches that enhance participation in satisfying common group goals and needs.

Seek Input From Persons With Disabilities

This may come in the form of advisory committees, surveys or focus groups, from contacting representatives of various advocacy groups for persons with disabilities in the community, and from individual program participants who have disabilities. Beware of getting information from a limited number of self-proclaimed experts who say they speak "for the disabled community." There are a number of professional organizations that work with persons with disabilities in outdoor programs that can be of help, as well as national advocacy groups with local chapters that can help in this consultation (see Schleien et al., 1993, for a list of resource organizations). Adventure program managers should tap the resources within their communities that can help in understanding the needs and the capabilities of persons with disabilities. Many communities have Centers for Independent Living, local advocacy groups, rehabilitation facilities, and others that can provide information.

Respect Each Person's Dignity

This is the key to successful integration. Once group members know they are accepted and respected for who they are, they will participate more readily in attaining the group goals and objectives. In mixed ability groups, the process of developing mutual respect is complicated by the unfamiliarity of different participant needs and expectations. It is easy to make wrong assumptions about what a person actually needs in a given situation. Respecting dignity begins with avoiding condescending attitudes. Too many well-meaning but unthinking people develop a patronizing or condescending attitude toward those who they consider to be "less fortunate" than themselves. This attitude often manifests itself in offers to "help." A helpful guide in identifying condescending attitudes is to think of the differences in behavior appropriate for interaction with a child as opposed to what might be appropriate for adult interaction.

In arranging adaptations, staff should consider as many options as safely possible to avoid compromising a person's dignity. Some situations may demand unglamorous solutions, but these are relatively few. Often in the rush to get things done expediently, there is a great temptation to implement the quickest, physically easiest solution, such as lifting a person with a disability out of a wheelchair and carrying him or her over a rocky trail. This may give the person with a disability the feeling that he or she is being treated like a sack of potatoes, a load for the group. Addressing the issue of adaptations openly and in advance with the person involved will help give that person input and will gain acceptance for the solution. Don't make assumptions. Ask people what they recommend to solve the problem.

Maintain Open Lines of Communication

When integrating people with diverse backgrounds and abilities, it is essential to have clear communication, for group members to feel comfortable talking about their needs, desires, and expectations of the experience. One of the first objectives in any integrated adventure program should be to encourage frank and honest discussion about needs and expectations. An informal group discussion early in the program about what each person needs to have a successful adventure experience can help to get this communication going for all group members. Staff can make it easier for participants to share their physical and emotional needs by modeling such disclosure at the start of the discussion. During the adventure program staff should frequently ask for the opinions of participants. Participants often have excellent suggestions on ways which they can become more involved.

Establish Patterns for Integrated Decision Making

Decision-making styles have an influence on a group. The degree to which each person is involved in decision making is often interpreted as a sign of his or her status within the group. Staff can effectively elevate a participant's status by bringing him or her in on making decisions. Too many decisions are made *for* people, instead of *with* them, especially when persons with speech or communication difficulties are involved. In addition to cutting off potentially valuable information and opinions, the repeated habit of making decisions for people discredits their intelligence, insight, and judgment. In effect, it compromises their dignity. Unfortunately, some persons with disabilities are so accustomed to being left out of decision-making processes that they have become used to it. In the rush of making dozens of quick decisions, staff are susceptible to making autonomous decisions that really should have the input and active involvement of those affected. Although faster, autonomous decision making does not inspire the affected individuals to accept decisions as their own. By actively soliciting the opinions of all participants when making decisions, staff can facilitate the process of integration. When participants perceive that they have equal say in decisions, it enhances the concept of equal peer status.

Emphasize Contributions of All Types

In an adventure program setting like a ropes course or a wilderness trip, many people have a tendency to measure their worth according to their ability to perform physical tasks and activities. One of the biggest challenges faced by staff of integrated adventure programs is to counter this myth. This is complicated by the fact that adventure settings are generally less accessible for people with physical disabilities. Mobility or sensory impaired persons are often less able to make tangible physical contributions at an adventure site than they may be at home. In one of the first group discussions in a program, staff should suggest that the group place a higher value on effort than actual physical accomplishments. Participants should know that if they make an effort to utilize fully the abilities they have, they will be fulfilling their expected role. This is not to suggest that physical accomplishments are unimportant; without them the group will go nowhere. However, physical accomplishments must take their place alongside other, equally important accomplishments. It is also important to stress the value of a positive attitude. In many cases, a good joke or a smile under adverse physical conditions does more to boost group morale than sheer muscle power. Individual attitudes, whether negative or positive, can be very contagious in group settings. Staff should emphasize that a person's attitude is perhaps the most important con-

tribution he or she can make to the group. Everyone has limitations; we must each live with them. However, most people—not just people with disabilities—underutilize their personal resources and are afraid to test their limits. Once participants start thinking differently about physical accomplishments and challenges, they are less likely to measure their worth to the group along traditional, physically oriented benchmarks. By emphasizing the value of effort, positive attitudes, and making better use of existing abilities, staff of mixed ability groups can enhance the process of integration by establishing a more equal set of standards by which participants can measure their efforts.

Focus on Group Challenges and Activities

Fostering positive group dynamics is one of the primary goals of integrated adventures. In many respects, an adventure program group is the ultimate team. Group members must live, work, and play together in an unfamiliar, often remote environment. An adventure program setting is naturally conducive to team building, and staff can facilitate this process. Some adventure programs emphasize individual challenges and activities, but in mixed ability groups, the goal of integration is better served if programs give higher priority to group functions. This helps to value everyone's participation, thereby avoiding the tendency for some to sit on the "sidelines" during certain activities.

Staff can help to build a sense of community and teamwork by stressing the importance of group functions and accomplishments. In this particular context, an individual's abilities are not as important as what the group collectively can accomplish.

Delineate and Delegate Tasks

It is often easier to talk about deemphasizing the value of physical contributions or group decision-making processes in the abstract than it is actually to implement these ideas. Staff members must know how to break down any task into steps that can be attained, and, at least initially, be prepared to delegate these steps to the appropriate people. Delegation of tasks is another way staff members can elevate a person's status within the group. In delineating and delegating, tokenism is to be avoided at all times. If a staff member delegates a task or authority, the task must be a legitimate function; otherwise, the individuals involved will easily see through it. It may be difficult to give some people physical tasks, but staff can delegate other legitimate functions. For example, a person with a disability could be asked by staff to lead a discussion, plot the route, decide what to eat and how to cook it. Many programs stress the rotation of certain tasks among group members, with each participant being expected to take part in a given activity an equal number of times. This system works well when all members of a group are capable of doing the same tasks, when people are physically unable to perform similar tasks. However, the rotation system can skew the work load toward the more physically capable, which discourages contributions from less physically capable people. Therefore, in a mixed ability group, if everyone wants to contribute equal effort and energy to the benefit of the group, it may be necessary to have certain people perform the same tasks on a repeated basis. In the end, this system may better serve the goal of integration.

Someone who can only participate in limited areas should be allowed the freedom of choice to participate in those areas as often as he or she feels the need. For some, this may mean cutting wood, carrots, or bread. Others may be able to help with recording the group's progress, or observing the group as a whole and leading the discussion or debriefing of the group's activities and processes. The important issue is that most tasks can be broken down into components that can be "fit" to a person's ability. This may involve two or three people teaming up to get a job done, but with each tangible contribution to the process, the goal of integration is more fully achieved.

Develop Symbiotic Relationships Among Participants

Within each integrated adventure program group, there is great potential to team people with differing abilities to accomplish group tasks. Some examples of this pairing include the following:

- Persons with visual or balance problems can be teamed with persons who use wheelchairs to traverse trails. Those who can walk can push the chairs when needed, while the person in the chair can provide them with stability and/or serve as the "eyes" for the person who is blind. *Note:* Staff should be sure to assess the safety of the trail first!
- Persons who are unable to carry packs may be able to help steady someone with poor balance or may serve as the eyes for someone who is blind. This technique can be used on trails or in camp.
- Persons who experience seizures or who are cognitively disabled may serve as guides for blind persons.
- Older or younger participants can be used as guides or as stabilizers for those who have trouble walking.
- Persons in wheelchairs can help others who are hemiplegic and need help dressing and tying their shoes.

- Persons who are unable to carry heavy loads may be able to help someone else eat or get dressed.

In promoting and arranging symbiotic relationships, it is important to recognize that every participant needs to make some contribution to the group's welfare in order to achieve the status of an equal team member. In pairing individuals, staff should always check with both parties to ensure that the help offered is both needed and desired. Arranging mutually beneficial task relationships is a skill that requires a constant search for the right fit of abilities and tasks.

Conclusion

Some adventure education organizations may tend to view the ADA and the mandates or pressures to make facilities and services accessible as a legal- and compliance-based issue. We urge adventure agencies and businesses to view it more as a market and customer quality service-based issue. Times are changing and so are population demographics. The number of persons who can benefit from accessible adventure education programs and services are increasing. The development of new assistive equipment, new management technologies, enhanced transportation accessibility, and the overall improvement of the quality of life for persons with disabilities will continue. Persons with disabilities and their families and friends are a largely untapped market for adventure education services. Agencies and businesses need to accommodate and encourage the use of adventure education programs by persons with disabilities and their families. These same adventure education businesses and agencies need to utilize the new management technologies presented here to position themselves to serve this developing market for adventure education services.

Sources for Information

Beneficial Designs, Inc.
  5858 Empire Grade
  Santa Cruz, CA 95060-9603
  408-429-8447

National Center on Accessibility
  5020 State Road 67 North
  Martinsville, IN 46151
  www.indiana.edu/~nca
  800-424-1877

Quickie Designs, Inc.
  2842 Business Park Avenue
  Fresno, CA 93727-1328
  209-292-2171

Ski-Boggan Company
 6341 Ridgeway Drive
 Pollock Pines, CA 95726
 916-644-3400

Up and Over Engineering
 John Castellano
 1509 Liberty Street
 El Cerrita, CA 94340
 510-233-1328

Wilderness Inquiry, Inc.
 1313 Fifth Street SE, Box 84
 Minneapolis, MN 55414
 www.wildernessinquiry.org
 612-379-3858

References

Anderson, L., Schleien, S., McAvoy, L., Lais, G., and Seligman, D. (1997). Creating positive change through an integrated outdoor adventure program. *Therapeutic Recreation Journal, 31*(4), 214–229.

Architectural Transportation Barriers Compliance Board. (1991). *Americans with disabilities act: Accessibility guidelines for buildings and facilities.* Washington, DC: Author.

Driver, B. L., Peterson, G. L., and Easley, A. T. (1990). *Benefits perceived by past participants in the NOLS Wind River Wilderness course: A methodological inquiry. The use of wilderness for personal growth, therapy, and education* (General Technical Report RM-193, 52–62). Fort Collins, CO: USDA Forest Service Rocky Mountain Forest and Range Experiment Station.

Gillis, H. L. (1992). Therapeutic uses of adventure-challenge-outdoor-wilderness: Theory and research. In K. A. Henderson (Ed.), *Coalition for education in the outdoors research symposium proceedings* (pp. 35–47). Cortland, NY: Coalition for Education in the Outdoors, State University of New York at Cortland.

Gillis, H. L., and Thomsen, D. (1996). A research update of adventure therapy (1992–1995): Challenge activities and ropes courses, wilderness expeditions, and residential camping programs. In L. H. McAvoy, L. A. Stringer, M. D. Bialeschki, and A. B. Young (Eds.), *Coalition for education in the outdoors research symposium proceedings* (pp. 77–90). Cortland, NY: Coalition for Education in the Outdoors, State University of New York College at Cortland.

Havens, M. D. (1992). *Bridges to accessibility.* Dubuque, IA: Kendall/Hunt Publishing Co.

Kelley, M. P. (1993). The therapeutic potential of outdoor adventure: A review with a focus on adults with mental illness. *Therapeutic Recreation Journal, 27*(2), 110–125.

Lais, G. J. (1987). *Toward fullest participation: Suggested leadership techniques for integrated adventure programming* (Bradford Papers Annual). Bloomington, IN: Department of Recreation and Parks, Indiana University.

Leitman, R., Cooner, E., and Risher, R. (1994). *NOD/Harris survey of Americans with disabilities.* New York, NY: Louis Harris and Associates, Inc.

McAvoy, L. H., Schatz, E. C., Stutz, M. E., Schleien, S. J., and Lais, G. J. (1989). Integrated wilderness adventure: Effects on personal and lifestyle traits of persons with and without disabilities. *Therapeutic Recreation Journal, 23*(3), 51–64.

McAvoy, L. H., and Schleien, S. J. (1988). Effects of integrated interpretive programs on persons with and without disabilities. In L. A. Beck (Ed.), *Research in interpretation: Proceedings of the 1988 national association of interpretation research symposium* (pp. 13–26). San Diego, CA: Institute for Leisure Behavior, San Diego State University.

Robb, G. M., and Ewert, A. (1987). Risk recreation and persons with disabilities. *Therapeutic Recreation Journal, 21*(1), 58–69.

Schleien, S. J., McAvoy, L. H., Lais, G. J., and Rynders, J. E. (1993). *Integrated outdoor education and adventure programs.* Champaign, IL: Sagamore Publishing.

Stringer, L. A., and McAvoy, L. H. (1992). The need for something different: Spirituality and wilderness adventure. *Journal of Experiential Education, 15*(1), 13–20.

USDA Forest Service and PLAE, Inc. (1993). *Universal access to outdoor recreation: A design guide.* Berkeley, CA: PLAE, Inc.

Witman, J. (1993). Characteristics of adventure programs valued by adolescents in treatment. *Therapeutic Recreation Journal, 27*(1), 44–50.

Chapter 55

Adventure Travel and Ecotourism

Graeme Addison
South African Rivers Association

Introduction

A person standing at any airport on earth is no more than 48 hours from Timbuktu, on the edge of the Sahara, once considered the most remote city on earth. Nowadays, tourists crowd the post office to send cards stamped *Timbuktu* to friends back home. So writes adventure author Tim Cahill in the twentieth-anniversary issue of *Outside* magazine (1997, p. 79), one of many outdoor-oriented media that have contributed significantly towards shrinking the planet in the minds of the current generation. Popular exploration almost anywhere in the world is accessible today thanks to travel literature, world tourism infrastructure, and mass marketing by the travel industry. At the same time, the growth of ecoadventure challenges like the Raid Gauloises, nine-years-old in 1998, has carried competition sports into the distant outdoors, accompanied once again by the media.

In the same commemorative issue of *Outside,* journalist Bob Shacochis describes the centuries-old Nepalese village of Kathmandu as the spiritual center of world adventure tourism—and with that, he says, it has become traffic clogged and filthy. The Annapurna trail hosts 50,000 trekkers a year and the local culture is eroding now that the Coca-Cola genie is out of the bottle. How much of this is for the better and how much for the worse, asks Shacochis. Yet he points out that such concerns may be expressing a patronizing attitude towards people who really do want to share the fruits of Western culture and technology (Shacochis, 1997, pp. 146–150).

For good or ill, adventure travel is at the cutting edge of world tourism. The value of adventure to those who take part in it is undoubted, since travel has always been a great teacher. Still, tourism's impact on the environment and other cultures is growing, and this is particularly true of adventure travel which penetrates the last untouched areas of the planet and reaches people who have previously had little contact with the outside world. Tourists may get to visit the Himalayas and hike around the flanks of Annapurna or land in Zimbabwe to go whitewater rafting on the Zambezi River in the morning and big game viewing in the afternoon or pick a trip to the icecap of Antarctica, the Amazon basin, the Siberian tundra, the jungles of Borneo or the deserts of Australia. Nor does one need to go to the ends of the earth to experience the novelty of what has been called the "activity holiday." Domestic adventure travel takes Americans rafting on the Grand Canyon of the Colorado River, while Europeans climb the Alps in their own backyard and Australians scuba-dive along the Barrier Reef. Every destination is coming under pressure.

With all this, adventure travel is very diverse. It includes nature-based and cultural tourism which together are often referred to as *ecotourism*. Travel inevitably raises questions about the relationships between guides and clients, men and women, the able-bodied and the less so, the rich and the poor, the state and the citizen. This chapter touches on all these relationships and outlines the complexity of adventure travel today, set in the context of the global economy, since travel is a global business. Beyond the statistics lies the terrain of discovery, where countless generations of humankind have trod before us. The history of adventure travel has shaped our perceptions of what is possible and what is left undone. As the developing world makes its bid for a larger share in tourism, new relationships are being forged and Westerners need to revise their attitudes and practices. Accepting an ethical approach towards all travel relationships is an urgent priority for those who are active in this field.

Travel and Work

Adventure travel offers exchange opportunities for students, longer term jobs in the outdoors, and business openings for those wanting a career in tourism management (Collins, 1995; *Working Holidays,* 1995). Jobs in tourism are many, and terminologies may be confusing so a travel industry dictionary may come in handy (Medlik, 1993). The person who accompanies and couriers or leads a group of paying customers or clients is known as a tour guide, and the business that employs the guide is run by an operator or outfitter. Conducting tours is not easy and requires training (Mancini, 1990), while the management of visitor attractions is a highly skilled craft (Swarbrooke, 1997). In many countries, guides and operators must be registered with a central authority or voluntary industry body before being allowed to work, and a work permit or business license is needed. For temporary workers like students, work permits may not be necessary or could be overlooked; but immigration bureaucracies are far stickier when it comes to allowing one to settle down to earn one's living in a foreign country as this is usually reserved for citizens. Having a contract with a local employer or travel wholesaler is usually essential, and paperwork needs to be completed well ahead, motivated on the basis of unique skills. The adventure guide has natural advantages because skilled outdoor leaders are hard to come by in many countries.

It is vital for outdoor guides to have a first-aid certificate and driver's license, and important to study the history, wildlife, habitats, languages and cultures of the region one works in so as to provide interpretative insights along the trail. A background in biological sciences, forestry, farming, marine studies or environmental science is useful; many also enter the field with recreational and sports qualifications, or simply as graduates in the humanities (Shenk, 1992). The adventure sports disciplines of hiking, climbing, rafting, skiing, horseback riding, mountain biking, fishing and diving represent some of the standard fare of adventure tour operators. The intending guide should be trained and confident before entering the field, or be prepared to learn as a lowly apprentice at nominal (if any) pay.

A tour operator assembles the components of a tour and manages the sales and administration of tour bookings. Destination managers sit in the office, while field operations managers take care of the actual running of the tour on the ground. Field operations require knowledge of transportation logistics, catering, public relations, bookkeeping and computer skills if one is to support the guides well with a professional outfit and backup. Fortunately or unfortunately this combination of skills is in rare supply as the pay is seldom good; mostly, the lifestyle has to suffice. Many an outfit hires on sight, and its clients bear the chaotic consequences. Travel publicity also has many jobs, some very well-paid. Later the role of travel wholesalers, agents, publicists and journalists in the marketing chain is discussed (Rubin, 1986).

Travel as Education

The threefold combination of activity, nature, and culture marks adventure travel as an all-round challenge. It is a uniquely educative opportunity to learn one's own capabilities and get to know the world and its peoples. Though geographers have charted the globe, subjective knowledge comes only through direct contact. Travel induces self-discovery and should promote respect for the outlook of others. Add to this the heightened awareness stemming from physical exercise, and adventure travel would seem to be the complete recipe for intellectual and moral improvement. The development of a respectable self-concept may take place when the individual reflects on what he or she has seen and done, and one way to achieve this is to keep a daily journal. Travelers, after all, have produced an entire literature including great works of adventure (see the *Picador Travel Classics* series, for instance).

What the individual gains from adventure travel may be very much a product of prior learning and attitudes. Rejuvenation does not always follow from immersion in the lifestyles of foreign countries, whose diet, norms of behavior and taboos may annoy the traveler and provoke a prejudiced response that strikes local people as rude, even immoral. Travel writer Paul Theroux warns:

> Extensive travel induces a feeling of encapsulation, and travel, so broadening at first, contracts the mind. (Cohen and Cohen, 1980, p. 327)

Four centuries ago, the essayist Francis Bacon remarked that for youth, travel was "a part of education" while for older people it was simply "a part of experience" (Cohen and Cohen, 1962, p. 18). Many young people take a year or two to travel before embarking on their careers. For their parents, travel may remain a lifelong learning project; the baby boomer generation of the 1950s is still sending middle-aged kayakers and climbers out into the world. Some travel programs are devised with specific educative goals in view. To take one commercial example: in South Africa a number of adventure operators run team-building rafting tours in order to promote joint tasking and reconciliation between corporate staff members of different races (Bloch, 1997). In general, the lessons of adventure travel are complex and hard to formulate in a program. Nevertheless, the lessons are there, as a popular guide to the "savvy traveler" puts it:

> There is not much to compare with travel—it will give you more than you can possibly take from it. It will take you out of the comfort and complacency of all that is familiar; it will feed your senses and your intellect; it will heighten your understanding and compassion; and it will bestow upon you good friends and memories. Even the unfortunate travel experiences are not without their value—you are usually wiser for having gone through them! (Burns and Clarkson, 1987, p. 6)

All travel involves relationships between the traveler and many others, in multifaceted, mutually responsive roles in which people learn from each other. Companionship is one of the greatest benefits to be found in adventure travel, and is also severely tested under stress. British mountaineer Roger Chapman once remarked:

> Compatibility is the most important requisite of all. The reason I say this is, I think of all the times that we've been chucked together, either in a tent halfway down some icefall, or underneath the stars out in the desert, or under an upturned riverboat propped on the side of a river when it's pissing down with rain, just passing a little snicker of warm drink to each other, compatibility is vital. (Gifford, 1983, p. 35)

Sexual tensions can ruin a trip, as can the egotistical behavior of some guides, and the exploitation of local people by uncaring travelers, provoking a hostile reaction, is one of the least pleasant features of modern tourism. This chapter argues for greater sensitivity in order to enrich the travel experience for all concerned. Writing on the "human perspective" in tourism, Richard Voase has suggested that the motive for travel is:

> the attractiveness of "abnormality," usually defined by the anthropologists as "otherness," in the tourist experience. The abnormality [has] meaning both in the sense of the pursuit of the bizarre, such as a ride on a roller coaster, and in terms of difference from routine. (Voase, 1995, p. 45)

Excursioning of all kinds involves this pursuit of otherness, and hence the connection between adventure travel and the hunger to learn is a close one. Much of the meaning of the travel experience is probably to be found in how its unexpected happenings and rewarding relationships add to one's awareness of the world at large and the value of life itself.

History

Adventure travel has only recently become a pastime for holiday makers. The origins of the word *adventure* lie with the Latin *advent,* to begin (*Merriam-Webster,* 1991, pp. 96–98), while the word *travel* derives from *travail* or suffering (*Merriam-Webster,* 1991, p. 473). Adventure travel thus implies launching into the unknown with the expectation that it could turn out to be an ordeal. In the past, adventure was a by-product of exploration. The Spanish conquistadors plundered South America for its gold and, in passing, unveiled the magnificent kingdoms of the Aztecs and the Incas and ascended the Andes. Dr. Livingstone, who went to Africa to combat slavery and spread Christianity, was the first European to see the Victoria Falls, which he named after his Queen.

Over the ages, travel has been largely a privilege of the upper classes as well as the soldiers and sailors who served in their religious and military quests. Princes like Richard the Lion-Hearted crusaded to protect the Holy Land. Shakespeare's fellow playwright, Christopher Marlowe, was a spy who toured through France sending back secret reports. In the Victorian era it became a hobby for daring gentlemen like Sir Richard Burton to pass themselves off as natives amongst strange tribes, as he did in Arabia. Then it was the turn of scientists like Darwin, who crossed the horizon on the good ship *Beagle* searching for the origin of species. All of these adventurers were on their own missions, and were not tourists.

Mass tourism really began in Britain during the Victorian age when beach holidays at Blackpool became popular (see Argyle, 1996, pp. 1–32, for a succinct "history of leisure"). This was hardly adventurous, and true adventure continued to be privileged and individualistic. The novelist Robert Louis Stevenson became a precursor of the modern adventure traveler when he paddled his canoe along the canals of Europe (1878) and plodded over the Cervennes mountains in France with a donkey (1879). Stevenson adventured in order to write books, prefiguring a whole industry of travelogue writing. Although he did not require financial backing, the name of his canoe foreshadowed a controversial issue in sponsorship: it was called *Cigarette.*

By the late nineteenth century, Alpine mountaineering had become well-established amongst the fit and well-to-do of Europe. Meanwhile in 1869 in the United States, Union army Major John Wesley Powell led a party of 10 men down the Grand Canyon in wooden boats or dories of a type which are still in use on the river to this day (Bangs, 1985, p. 141). Powell justified this life-and-death escapade as a survey, for which the Smithsonian Institute gave its backing, but he was indulging his spirit of adventure all the same, and several of his men perished as a result. In 1845 another strand of adventure travel was spun when Henry David Thoreau retreated to the woods at Walden Pond to live out his philosophy of individualism. He rejoiced in nature, eschewed luxuries and comforts, abhorred government (he was an anarchist), and bothered no one as he wrote up his great journal of 1854. By the turn of the century, adventure travel was becoming a common option for the common man. One slightly uncommon traveler was Theodore Roosevelt, former President of the United States, who ventured into Africa to hunt specimens of big game and into the Brazilian wilderness on a horrendous trip to map the Rio da Divuda; the resulting malaria and dysentery cost him his health.

The brave example of Powell, the iconoclastic personal musings of Thoreau, and the swashbuckling of Teddy Roosevelt, along with many other inspirational influences over the years, have permeated the ethos of modern adventure travel. Equally important has been the institutional growth of travel agencies, the first of which was started by Thomas Cook in England in 1841. Cook originated the Grand Tour of Europe, the first of a multitude of modern tour packages charging a single price for the full integrated service of booking a tour. Cook's agency supplied the traveler with monetary warrants ("traveler's checks" today) that were honored all over the Continent. So vast were Cook's resources and contacts that he was able to transport an entire army up the Nile to attempt to lift the siege on General Gordon of Khartoum in 1884; but in a violent world, even the best agencies sometimes fail. Gordon met his end at the hands of the Mahdi's forces (Swinglehurst, 1974).

Guiding formed part of the Thomas Cook package and tours were mounted all over the world with experts leading them. Today's commercial relationship between the adventure guide and the client has developed from this. Previously, local guides who knew the terrain and the languages were employed by the likes of Dr. Livingstone, but not as expedition leaders. Explorers were not holiday makers looking for excitement; guides were servants and were not expected to provide a good time, ensure safety, and make important decisions. Guides now do carry these responsibilities, and clients are correspondingly more dependent on them. Adventure used to be seen as an ordeal that called forth qualities of self-sufficiency and endurance in the exceptional individual. It is less so today, except where self-directed travelers choose to go it alone.

Tourism has become big business, though the example set by Cook's professionalism has not been uniformly followed by the travel industry, which has had its share of fraudulent dealings and collapses during the twentieth century. Regulation of the travel industry by the State and voluntary industry bodies is a common feature in most countries today. Control of standards of service, the proper handling of tour bookings, honest advertising and the registration of trained and competent tour guides are amongst the matters regulated (Foster, 1985, and Stabler, 1990, pp. 97–126, both review leisure management). The level of professionalism in developed countries ensures that standards are generally upheld and public expectations met. For the less developed countries, unfortunately, history has left stumbling blocks. Colonialism and racism prevented many local people from entering tourism as guides or entrepreneurs, so that when the colonists left there were few indigenous skills to build on. In a general introduction to the problems, John Lea notes the "relatively minor" participation of local sources in Third World tourism, as business flows to enclaves of privilege owned and managed by expatriates (Lea, 1988, pp. 30-31).

The great age of exploration may be over, but adventure travel today still has its star performers whose triumphs and tribulations get extensive media coverage. Since most of the world has been mapped and studied, true adventure has become more deliberate, specialized and technically demanding, as well as being somewhat arbitrary in its selection of targets for conquest. There is little geographical need to "discover" places on earth (satellites can do the job), so what remains is the pure brutality of the elements and the interest of the "inner journey" made by the explorer. This is not to forget that feats of valor generate very useful exposure for sponsors. Extremism, reflection and promotion characterize the achievements of the man often called "the world's most famous living explorer," Sir Ranulph Fiennes. He has executed polar icecap crossings on foot for the sake of charities for the disabled. In 1992 he and Dr. Mike Stroud, having dragged their heavily laden sleds to the South Pole, continued across the second half of the continent without taking advantage of the warmth and food of the Antarctic ice base. To do so would have meant receiving outside assistance and so possibly losing their claim to be the first to cross the continent under their own power (Fiennes, 1993; Stroud, 1993).

Defining Adventure Travel: A Typology

Adventure travel may be defined as any activity trip close to nature that is undertaken by someone who departs from known surroundings to encounter unfamiliar places and people, with the purpose of exploration, study, business, communication, recreation, sport, or sightseeing and tourism. Tourists are people who visit out of their own neighborhood for leisure or other purposes connected with travel. Our concepts of adventure travel should not be limited to tourism only, which would imply that all adventure travel is a form of leisure. Historically it has covered a far wider ambit. A coherent typology of adventure travel will help to draw distinctions between, say, adventure tourism, adventure competition, recreational adventure and journeys of exploration. A good typology forms the basis for theory building, and though we are not close to having a social theory to account for the role of adventure travel in human affairs we can begin by inspecting our terminology. Ultimately it may be possible to model the role of adventure travel, as an innovative form of experience, in personal and social development. Over the centuries, travelers have brought people and ideas into contact with each other, opened up trade, changed our lifestyles and modified our values. With so much exchange going on between cultures, and with near space tourism a distinct option for adventurers in the new millennium, the cycle of discovery and social rebirth may be about to repeat itself.

In Figure 55.1, adventure is divided into quadrants corresponding to high and low levels of adventure, and high and low levels of independence. The *level of adventure* is determined by the danger element and technical skill needed, while the *level of independence* reflects the degree to which those taking part are reliant on others to organize the experience for them or do it themselves. Each axis is a continuum from low to high; the quadrants are merely groupings of conventional activities that we can easily recognize—for example, the stark contrast between leisure and high adventure. Plunging down a whitewater chute in Disneyland only superficially resembles the real experience of exploring an unknown river canyon by raft for the first time. Comparing these activities, there is hardly anything to connect them except that participants get wet. The interplay of adventure and independence determines how we shall describe an activity.

Adventure, on the left side of the scale, is an activity whose control is external to the participant. It rises from fully laid-on amusements through guided tours to organized adventure sports. On the right, the activity is fully controlled by the participant but goes from easy recreation through the self-development of an education program to the higher levels of exploration. Although participants on the left side of the picture may be said to have their activity arranged for them it is nevertheless the case that they do need to make an input, especially as the level of intensity of the adventure gets higher.

Commitment and involvement are mandatory because the activity is inner directed rather than following an imposed plan. Recreationists are people who refresh their bodies and spirits by playing sports or indulging in activity holidays such as weekends away hiking in the mountains. The "weekend warrior" who is deskbound from Monday to Friday may decide to attend a training course to upgrade his or her adventure capabilities, but would be foolhardy to attempt anything too ambitious on Saturday morning. Education through adventure travel may be designed by an outdoor center, which takes its students on wilderness trips abroad in order to facilitate the self-discovery process; this differs from being merely guided in the outdoors. The exploration of hidden corners of the planet is often referred to as high adventure because anything could happen, or more to the point, go wrong. Diving for sunken wrecks involves serious risk from sharks, currents, and sharp bits of ironmongery scattered on the ocean floor: experts are required. The more independent you are, the more you need a range of skills and inner reserves.

Differing types of adventure vary in their impacts on the environment and traditional societies. The typology here can be used to guide public policy. While all manner of adventurers may enter fragile areas, mass leisure activities are mass based and should be kept to threshold areas rather than allowed into the undisturbed heartlands. Ecochallenges can draw hundreds of entrants along with TV crews, helicopters and brigades of support vehicles. Recreationists and explorers may leave few footprints but their own, but there is always the possibility that the masses will follow after them, and therefore the rights of access should limit group size and frequency. In lesser known parts of the planet controls may not be necessary for the moment but eventually the pressure of numbers will tell. A revised international convention regulating tourist access to Antarctica would be the correct response in that region. In 1997 it was reported that Air Antarctica—"the ultimate bush pilots"—handled a dozen round trips to the South Pole in a season and that more than 8,000 sightseers visited the coast by cruise ships (*Men's Journal,* August 1997).

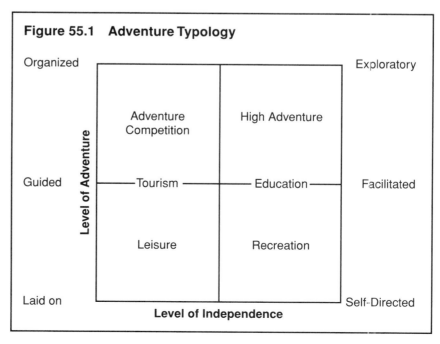

Figure 55.1   Adventure Typology

Comfort and Challenge

Adventure travelers, then, are greatly differentiated in terms of their motives, expectations, abilities and impacts. It is misleading to speak about "adventure" in general without recognizing that the "industry" has diversified greatly to appeal to different segments of humanity. Many tour clients expect to be catered to and that is what they think they are paying for when they go with a guided group. Others, however, embrace the idea that true adventure only happens when you are stretched well beyond daily normality and must fall back on your own resources. The World Tourism Organization (WTO) in its Vision 2020 outlook for the turn of the millennium, has noted a "polarization of tourist tastes: the comfort-based and the adventure-orientated" (1997a, p. 28). This is taking place in a shrinking world where tourism is drawing certain travelers into fashionable and theme-based entertainment, while others want to rough it.

In Figure 55.2, the distinction between comfort seekers and those who look for challenges is shown to apply even within the field of adventure travel. There are clearly forms of activity which do not extend the participants very much. Easy trail hiking is comfortable, but whitewater rafting tends to put most people out of their comfort zones. Adventure competition is well beyond comfort: it is exhausting and mentally taxing, requiring a combination of advanced skills like orienteering and rappelling. At the limits of daring, extreme adventure is fueled by a glory-or-die attitude. The danger is accentuated by being far from rescuers. Its adherents often aim to be the first to achieve some feat like climbing a peak without ropes or kayaking over a high waterfall, their evident intention being to win immortality in the *Guinness Book of Records*.

A major element of discomfort, and thus challenge, is uncertainty. Programmed activities that are run according to a tour itinerary contain little that is unpredictable or that demands a quick response in the face of the unexpected. The timid tourist who would like to walk in the Himalayas but is afraid of sleeping out in case there are bandits in the vicinity has his uncertainty reduced by getting a full itinerary including secure hostels for overnighting. Ecochallenge teams, on the other hand, facing a test to see who can reach the end first, may suddenly have to make up their minds which route to follow in order to reach a distant point in the shortest time: the river valley or the spine of the mountains. Although every detail is mapped, a choice has to be made, and a wrong decision could cost a team the race.

It has been mentioned before that self-development is an important goal of education through adventure travel. Figure 55.2 suggests that development and discovery form part of a continuum as the one shades off into the other. Quite possibly, one cannot develop through adventure without first discovering things in the challenge zone and any outdoors instructor will tell you that sometimes the most extreme challenges which happen unexpectedly (like an avalanche burying members of the group) bring out the best in people as they discover their inner strengths. This can be as true of "unstructured" and "informal" adventure travel experiences as it is of formal programs designed to bring out those qualities. The difference is that the traveler may make no attempt to bring the incident to full awareness and spell out the lessons to himself or herself.

Managed Risk

For any form of tourism to be commercially viable it must attract numbers of clients and assure them of a reasonable degree of safety and enjoyment. Although both "discovery" and "teamwork" take place in the course of commercial adventures, the dominant motive is pleasure and fun within a framework of managed risk supervised by the tour operator. Some would say that any activity done for money and carried out according to an itinerary with prepared background information, cannot be an adventure because it does not break new ground. The mythology of adventure travel inflates the client's notions of what is being accomplished, but the reality is that the guide is doing most of the thinking and much of the work. The client trusts to what sociologists call an *expert system*. In modern society, experts

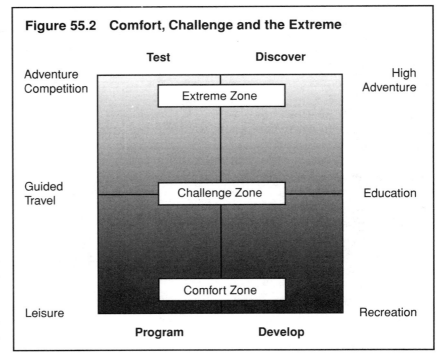

Figure 55.2 Comfort, Challenge and the Extreme

embody the abstract qualities that we call professionalism, to which we give our largely unquestioning assent (Giddens, 1990, pp. 84–92). In relation to a guide, the adventure tour client is in the same relation as any lay person to an expert who professes to know what he or she is doing. Trust in the expert comes to replace trust in oneself or, to put it another way, the tourist surrenders a large degree of independence and self-reliance to the operator and guides in charge of the adventure tour.

This relationship is fraught with difficulties because adventure is inherently risky and uncertain. Experts cannot always cope, no matter how good their systems. Tricky practical, legal and moral issues were dramatically highlighted in a disaster on Mount Everest on 10 May 1996. Although an experienced climber himself, Jon Krakauer joined a guided party to climb the peak and witnessed the full horror of multiple deaths when the guiding system broke down under the stress of a storm. In all, eight died, including three guides, partly because one of the unwritten rules of Everest was broken: they reached the top of the mountain too late in the afternoon. Somebody should have ordered them back—and that somebody would have had to be a person with the authority of a guide. Krakauer's book, *Into Thin Air,* is a description of what happened in the course of which he meditated in some depth on the mutual dependence of—and tensions between—clients and guides. He quotes one as saying that guides think they are there to look after their client's safety, but in reality clients paying as much as $65,000 a head just want to get to the top (Krakauer, 1997, p. 225). In pursuit of the dream, clients pushed themselves, or allowed guides to push and drag them, well beyond their levels of skill.

> No episode in the history of Everest has generated more controversy than the May Massacre. No episode in the history of tour guiding raises more unanswered, perhaps unanswerable, questions. Should a commercial operation stretch the limits of safety because the customer must be satisfied and the customer is always right? (Addison, 1997a, p. 62)

Deaths happen on self-guided trips too, but the Everest calamity pointed to the need for a strict code of practice to curb dangerous enthusiasm on commercial expeditions. A guide performs correctly when placing professional judgment and self-discipline ahead of gratification. The reciprocal relationship in which guides and clients egg each other on has the effect of reducing the authority of the guide. There are limits

to treating inexpert clients as full partners in adventure. River rescue expert Charles Walbridge expresses the view that experience comes from "bad judgment," which causes accidents (Walbridge, 1994). He may be right, but that is a painful way to learn.

Most types of adventure, even at the lower levels, seem to be driven by a craving for direct sensory experience. Why else would throngs of willing victims line up for the looping roller coaster or engage in mule trekking through the heat of Arizona, unless they wanted to find out how it feels and talk about it afterwards? People go for adventure with a fairly conscious aim of self-actualization, to apply Maslow's term for meeting the personality's meta-needs after basic physiological and psychosocial needs have been satisfied. Self-actualization is a marketable tourism product, and the dynamics that drive it can be summarized as the "three Es." The WTO Vision 2020 study quoted previously argues that the market for tourism will develop around entertainment, education and excitement (1997, p. 28).

Figure 55.3 suggests that all three are present in the guided adventure experience. The client's enjoyment of a trip is enhanced by receiving interpretative trail information ("education") about the peoples and places seen; by experiencing the thrill of adventure without being too exposed to its dangers ("excitement"); and by allowing the client to relax and seek diversion ("entertainment"). Guides are therefore not simply conveying people from point A to point B but can add value by making the trip meaningful and challenging (but not too uncomfortable), and laying on amusements to pass the time. If the client also happens to learn some adventure sport techniques ("paddling your own canoe") that is all to the good.

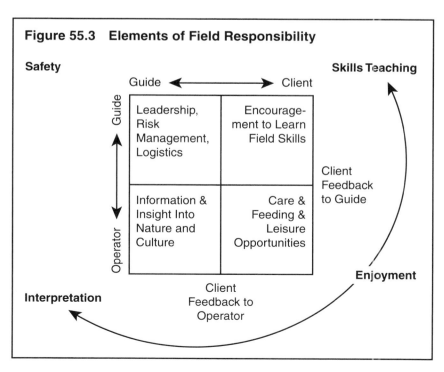

Figure 55.3   Elements of Field Responsibility

Guides and their clients may live cheek-by-jowl for days or weeks on a major trek, and inevitably an interactive relationship develops. Because they give feedback, clients are never purely recipients of preplanned leisure itineraries, much as they may have started out thinking that they were. Their behavior and suggestions will contribute to the running of the trip and the eventual quality of the outcomes. Both the organization of a trip (in terms of transportation, catering and accommodation) and its guiding (safety, teaching and interpretation) will evoke reactions and perhaps comment from clients. This, of course, is widely understood and has the greatest relevance to the guide's employer, the operator. Customer satisfaction is the joint responsibility of operations managers and guides.

Guides have a direct personal responsibility for the safety of those in their charge. Operators bear a more general responsibility to devise a policy and procedures for risk management so that no one is exposed to needless danger or left to fend for himself or herself when expert leadership is supposed to be on hand. The legal principle covering guide-operator responsibility is known as the *duty of care* (or standard of care). This is a duty owed by any person who holds himself or herself out to be capable of leading others in situations where the latter are not experts. Clients have a right to expect to be cared for, and the failure to exercise this duty is called negligence (Addison, 1997b, p. 15).

Adventure businesses usually require each client to sign an indemnity or waiver declaring that he or she is undertaking the trip at his or her "own risk" and will not hold the organizers responsible for inconvenience, loss, injury, illness or death (Addison, 1997b). Indemnities have limited application and may fall away if the guide is grossly negligent or if the trip is not conducted according to what was advertised. In any case, a client signing such a waiver may not sign away the rights of family dependents or business associates who could claim against both the operator and the guide for loss of income. The same legal sanctions may be held to apply to clubs and the organizers of competitions because they too have a duty of care; but private trippers may bear little or no legal responsibility for what happens to their companions.

Clients signing the indemnity should be urged to read the print that warns of the nature of the risk they are undertaking. Adventure travel is more unpredictable than sitting on a hotel porch for the holidays, but some people do not realize this until they have it pointed out to them. Operators try to reduce risk and uncertainty by planning ahead, using checklists and standard operating procedures. This allows the field staff to routinize their work. It is largely this service for which payment is made because it is expensive to assemble, equip, provide meals for, and lead a trip off the beaten track. In the forefront of the client's perceptions, however, is the guide, and a guide who communicates well, acts responsibly and shows concern for clients is far less likely to be blamed for mishaps than someone who is withdrawn, egotistical, and reckless. Clients are rarely expected to perform at a high level of technical competence in any skill, but the moment may come when they face real danger and have to be truly guided or helped through it. Nowadays the challenges of Himalayan climbing and Grade 5 river rafting reflect that clients are becoming more expert and can meet higher standards, by completing easier trips first.

The Market

Despite its evident growth, adventure travel is the Cinderella of tourism, at least as regards statistical analysis. Regional and global tourism figures collected by WTO and the World Travel and Tourism Council (WTTC) have not dealt with adventure tourism as a category, and so reveal no trends. But there are a few useful indicators. The world's top-five general tourism destinations in 1996 were (in this order) China, the United States, France, Spain and Hong Kong. The top outbound countries sending tourists into the world were Germany, Japan, the United States, China and the United Kingdom, in that order (WTO, 1997a). I estimate conservatively that at least 10 percent of these are adventure travelers, and the figure is growing. This would imply that of the total 709 million international tourists in 1996 (WTO, 1997a), nearly 71 million were nature bound. A study of travel trends by the Travel Industry Association of America (TIA), provides rare statistics on travel tastes in adventure. Adventure travel is far higher than was thought, with nearly half of U.S. adults, or 98 million people, having taken an adventure trip in the past five years (TIA, 1997). The TIA study made a distinction between "soft" and "hard" adventure. Soft activities were those with lower risk thresholds (such as camping, easy hiking, horseback riding, flatwater canoeing, and snow skiing), while hard activities were tougher with higher risk (such as rugged backpacking, caving, rock climbing, bungee jumping, and hang gliding). About a third of adventure travellers engaged in hard activities like whitewater rafting, scuba diving, and mountain biking. There was a fivefold increase in the numbers of U.S. adventure travellers in a decade from the mid 1980s (TIA, 1997). The authoritative California-based *Adventure Journal* has said that in Nepal, the number of trekkers from 1980 to 1991 increased 225 percent (1998).

Since the Second World War, the challenge of adventure has attracted tens of thousands of travelers from the developed world who have happily taken advantage of cheaper airfares to go abroad, either on package tours or independently. I counted 32 different categories of outdoor adventure, from abseiling (rappelling) and ballooning to trail running and whale watching, in a brief survey of magazines. Who goes in for adventure travel? Pearce (Argyle, 1996, p. 152) researched a list of 20 types of tourism and came to the conclusion that "environmental travel" was educative rather than exploitative, merely pleasurable, or distinctly spiritual. He grouped anthropologists, conservationists and explorers together in the same cluster, distinguishing them from other types like businessmen, holiday makers and missionaries whose motivations for travel were rather different. Various commentators have that men predominate and that adventure attracts well-informed, upper income people (Argyle, 1996, p. 30; Torkildson, 1986, p. 96). Adventure has come of age as a recreational option lying outside the standard hotel and beach holidays of the past. A major market is the New Age tourist (Turnbull, 1996, pp. 47–62) who is looking for added value for money without conforming to stereotypes of how to take a vacation. These travelers are prepared to make a bit of extra effort to reach the so-called "pleasure-periphery" of unspoiled natural areas. For many New Agers, outdoor adventure is a continuation of their home and gymnasium fitness programs, and constitutes a search for heightened excitement, at prices they are willing to pay.

The travel marketing chain extends from operators, who get busy developing the product; through wholesalers, who package the tour operations for domestic and international markets; to travel agencies, who sell tours on commission; and finally back to the operators who run the tours on the ground. There are many more links, including the service providers such as airlines and car-hire companies, hotel groups and ecotourism lodges; professional associations representing the travel industry and guides; and national tourism or governmental marketing arms, all of which contribute to the frenetic business of selling travel (Foster, 1985, pp. 49–78). Information technology is making deep inroads into traditional sales methods as the Internet "disintermediates" (removes the intermediaries in) the process of delivering the product to the customers. From New York you can book directly with Big Five game tour operators in Zululand via an on-screen form. The Travel Industry Association predicted that in 1998 there would be over 75 million Americans going on-line to get information and make travel bookings (NUA Internet Surveys, 1997). Smaller operators in adventure travel and tourism may benefit from this trend of cheap and direct sales.

Niche marketing is having an influence on the shape of adventure today. Special adventure tours appeal to sports players like golfers, and to the disabled, ethnic minorities, and the elderly. A booming sector of tourism caters specifically to women. Niche marketing individualizes products and is a feature of what has been called the "demassification" of culture and marketing (Toffler, 1991, pp. 335–6). In postindustrial societies, market research becomes more and more powerful and detailed through the use of information technology. Producers are able to target the specific needs and interests of particular groups of consumers, moving production away from a mass basis towards tailored packages for particular kinds of tourists (Ryan, 1995, p. 8). It follows that as more travelers dictate their preference for adventure, more adventure options become available.

There is a growing market amongst independent women who see activity holidays as a way of improving their self-image. According to a survey reported in the *Melbourne Age* (August 14, 1997), as women enter the twenty-first century, they are more pragmatic than the militants of the 1970s and many reject the concept of the superwoman, but they are concerned about relaxation, a balanced diet and getting some exercise while minimizing risks. In terms of our typology, these women are not so much "independent" at a high level, as likely to take part in self-directed recreation or organized tours. However, adventure is no longer the preserve of privileged males, but has spread to all who have the freedom and the money to try it.

Women in Adventure Travel

No discussion of contemporary adventure travel would be adequate without paying specific attention to the recent upsurge of women adventurers and writers. Many fit the tradition of high adventure and have been exceedingly self-reliant. Women bring a different perspective to exploration, inspiring other women by example, and their many books and articles stand as an important contribution to the corpus of world adventure literature. Since modern feminism became a mass movement in the 1960s, women's exploits have raised awareness of gender issues in the outdoors and highlighted questions of identity and achievement associated with voyages of discovery (Meyer, 1994; Thomas, 1997). Race and gender have also been of concern, with travel by Black women being seen as a spiritual quest and an opportunity for growth (Lee, 1997).

Long before the 1960s, women adventurers were active in many fields. Perhaps this section should have been included with the history of exploration, but the fact is that the story of women in adventure needs to be told separately, and anyway much of it represents newly assembled material. The British explorer Mary Henrietta Kingsley was the first European to visit parts of Central and West Africa and in 1895 climbed the highest peak in the region, the 14,435 foot Mount Cameroon (Frank, 1986). In the early days of motoring when it was still truly an adventure, the American novelist Edith Wharton took a ride through the "enchanting motor-grounds" of France (1908/1995). In aviation, Amelia Earhart was the first woman to fly solo across the Atlantic. In 1937 Earhart and copilot Frederick Noonan disappeared somewhere near New Guinea while attempting to fly around the world (Janney, 1997), a feat that was recently completed in Earhart's honor by the solo pilot Linda Finch using a similar plane (Finch, 1997).

The motives of women are, arguably, quite different from those of men undertaking similar challenges and require evaluation in their own right. The issue was highlighted in a magazine polemic involving the women's world extreme skiing champion, Wendy Fisher of the United

States, appearing in *Gravity* (1997). Fisher, a free-skier and cliff-jumper, responded to the sentiments of a "macho man" who had written that "participating in extreme sports takes balls, and women go for the guy with the biggest balls." Not disputing that impressing the opposite sex could be a basic male impulse, Fisher challenged the genetic argument that men were more risk-orientated than women. Only women could set the standards of what they should or should not be capable of, and what she sought as a daredevil, Fisher said, was respect and a bigger audience.

> We are different [from men] because my motive is the joy of shocking people; showing the audience that women can take risks. A few women perform like I do, and I hope to create a chain reaction in other women believing they can too. (Fisher, 1997)

Ego is a factor here, although this view is not representative of all women adventurers. Other women adventurers have chosen to go it alone, with minimum technology, in order to find fulfillment through direct experience rather than in relation to audiences, and certainly not for the sake of impressing men. A fairly common notion in recent women's travel writing is that men are alienated from the environment and cannot be trusted to give a sympathetic picture of nature because their contact with the outdoors is so often mediated by the power of technology; for example, by using 4x4 vehicles. Women have challenged the notion of conquest over the environment, linking it to the psychology of male dominance (Gomes and Kanner, 1995, pp. 113–16).

In the 1970s, Robyn Davidson, as a rank beginner, trained a pack of camels herself and walked across the Australian outback with them, 1,700 miles of desert from Alice Springs to the west coast. Alone most of the time, she went slightly crazy, but got help from hospitable Aborigines. A convoy of tourists that she encountered struck her as boorish and insensitive, "daring the great aloneness together like they were in some B-grade Western" (1982, p. 178). Back in the frightening glass canyons of civilization, she concluded that she had learned essentially simple lessons:

> The trip was easy. It was no more dangerous than crossing the street or driving to the beach or eating peanuts. The two important things that I did learn were that you are as powerful and as strong as you allow yourself to be, and that the most difficult part of any endeavor is taking the first step. (p. 247)

If education continues throughout life, no one embodies this better than the 60-year-old Irish adventurer, Dervla Murphy. Amongst her feats, she crossed Ethiopia on a mule and cycled 1,800 miles from Kenya to Zimbabwe along the feared "AIDS route," the *Ukimwi Road,* where the disease is now the chief cause of death in several regions (1993, p. 149). Murphy's status as an elderly woman protected her most of the time, but it amused officials, attracted cheats, and did not prevent a beating by paramilitaries.

The first woman to lay claim to walking around the world, Ffyona Campbell, later admitted that she took to drugs and contemplated suicide after concealing the fact that she had skipped 1,000 miles in her 11-year odyssey (*London Sunday Times,* November 1, 1996). Campbell started her walk in 1983 at age 16, soon after the death of the British climber, Alison Hargreaves, on Everest. At 18, while crossing the United States from Los Angeles to New York, she rode in the support van from Indianapolis to Fort Sumner because she had become pregnant and weak after an affair with the driver of the vehicle. Having had an abortion after four months, she resumed the walk which eventually took her across Australia, Asia and Africa to complete some 18,600 miles on foot (Campbell, 1997). Her achievement, recorded in the *1997 Guinness Book of Records,* was to be erased from the 1998 edition following her admission of cheating (*London Sunday Times,* November 7, 1996).

Numerous women today work as adventure guides in commercial operations. Training centers for guides such as the Nantahala Outdoor Center (NOC) in Tennessee report a marked increase over the past decade in the number of women learning professional guiding skills (G. N. Addison, personal communication, 1997). South African oarboater Jane Dicey, who since 1981 has worked the Tugela River in Zululand, the Zambezi and California's American River, believes that:

> women guides have a definite role to play in the adventure industry. They have more finesse in dealing with clients, because they show sympathy and understanding for the real fears of people. It's true that we generally don't have the strength that men have. But we make up for it more in relying on technical skills, so we can become as good as—if not better than—male guides especially because we try harder to communicate. (J. Dicey, personal communication, 1997)

Few of the writers or field professionals quoted here directly advocate the rights of women, but instead demonstrate their self-confidence by confronting the world head on. Most have had to deal with incidents of sexism and threats to their safety, as well as incomprehension from men who did not understand why they wanted to go adventuring in the first place. If women adventure travelers have proved anything universal, it is that, irrespective of gender, self-reliance is essential to survival.

Ecotourism Origins

The impact of tourism on marginal areas of the world and ancient societies is becoming a matter of grave concern (Harrison, 1992; Lea, 1988). Ecotourism, which combines nature-based with cultural tourism, aims to sustain habitats and heritage in cooperation with local communities. It is inseparable from the idea that the possibilities for adventure travel will steadily decline and ultimately disappear unless those who do it agree to explore but not exploit. The origins of the term *ecotourism* can be traced back at least to 1983, when it was used by the Mexican architect and environmentalist Hector Ceballos-Lascurain (Van der Merwe, 1997, p. 41) in making recommendations for the conservation of a wetland in Yucatan. He began to apply the word broadly to nature-based tourism in which host communities had an economic stake. Because communities stood to benefit from protecting their natural and cultural heritage, argued Ceballos-Lascurain, local people would foster conservation and use their resources sustainably far into the future. By the same token, visitors, and especially tour operators, should ensure that their activities made a tangible contribution to the local economy. Ceballos-Lascurain emphasized that ecotourism had to be economically sustainable, which meant that it should not destroy its own resource base.

As a philosophy, ecotourism forms part of the broader green movement concerned with saving Planet Earth. Logically, the argument is that all life shares a common support system, the biosphere, and therefore human cooperation and harmony with the environment are essential. In terms of this, any economic growth, including that of tourism, must be sustainable. Sustainability was defined in the World Conservation Strategy as "development that meets the needs of the present without compromising the ability of future generations to meet them" (Simpson, 1990, p. 14; see also Elliott, 1994, and Gupta, 1988). The campaign for sustainable growth passed an important milestone when it was included in the influential 1987 Brundtland Report, *Our Common Future,* devoted to Third World development within the limits posed by the environment (Simpson, 1990, p. 104). The 1992 Earth Summit held in Rio de Janeiro strongly endorsed sustainability and included it in the Agenda 21 global action plan for the coming century. At the summit, convened by the United Nations, more than 100 heads of state and 20,000 nongovernmental representatives agreed to forge a global partnership, which included ecotourism-related conservation projects. It was by now widely understood that people living in or near wildlife parks should be integrated into parks management and allowed to benefit from the income generated by ecotourism (Simpson, 1990, p. 149).

The ideas of Ceballos-Lascurain and his followers caught on rapidly. They had special appeal in places like southern Africa, where human population pressures threaten the environment and the poaching of protected game is rife. As a practical program, ecotourism offers a rationale for community-based conservation efforts and at the same time justifies the opening up of marginal areas to visitors, with a corresponding increase in the infrastructure of roads, communications and accommodation facilities. One fruit of this thinking has been the international Peace Parks Movement, which, after the ending of the Cold War, seeks to turn border war zones into protected transfrontier conservation areas (TFCAs) in hopes of attracting tourism investment and producing income for impoverished villagers (Addison, 1998a).

Critique

Looking back over 13 years of ecotourism in a 1996 review for the World Conservation Union (IUCN), Ceballos-Lascurain drew attention to the many complex issues that had arisen from his original idea. He expressed qualified approval of the achievements so far (Ceballos-Lascurain, 1996). In the first flush of enthusiasm for ecotourism, its proponents had said that tourists would be encouraged to move away from concentrated areas, where their impact was heavy, to visit underpopulated wilderness regions. This displacement meant, in effect, that ecotourism would *increase* the pressure on the environment in areas which could perhaps least afford it, but the contradiction was overlooked at the time. Later, as the impacts of ecotourism began to register, countries began to look for ways to retain the goal of sustainability without ditching tourism. In 1995 the first World Conference on Sustainable Tourism, meeting in Spain, adopted the Lanzarote Charter aimed at preventing the overdevelopment of tourist destinations. The conference recognized that "well-managed tourism is a good friend of the environment," and because tourism needed a high-quality environment it would promote environmental awareness (WTO, 1995).

Others were not so hopeful. At the 1997 Earth Summit 2, a conference reviewing what had transpired since Rio, governments were criticized for not implementing Agenda 21 (Greenpeace, 1997). Ecotourism was criticized there and elsewhere for not delivering on its promises (Addison, 1997a). The jobs it creates tend to be menial and seasonal, the traditional culture is turned inside out by salesmanship, and few new businesses get off the ground successfully because they lack capital and managerial skills.

Despite criticism, ecotourism does offer one way to develop communities, not forgetting that there are other ways like farming and manufacturing which need not impinge on conserved areas. In 1996 the World Bank carried out a review of the problems, and decided to continue its support for ecotourism as one of a range of developmental strategies (Brandon, 1996). Ecotourism operators can and do make a difference because they experience the realities firsthand. It is at this micro level, says the Worldwatch Institute, that continuing global decline can be arrested, by means of:

literally millions of small actions and decisions in villages, farms, businesses, and cities around the world. (French, 1995, p. 188)

Figure 55.4, the "ecotourism diamond," shows the four-way dynamics set in motion by a self-conscious program to promote growth by means of ecotourism. The resource base of "nature" (the environment and wildlife) and "culture" (the heritage of tradition with all that implies) is to be protected. Ecotourism makes it worthwhile for people to recover their all-but-lost expressive arts, such as music and woodcarving, marketed through village craft and entertainment centers. Threatened natural areas may be protected from mining and construction, as well as from excessive tourism, if strategies to this end are worked out by all parties to land ownership. Awareness building forms a very important part of the process. In negotiating the setting aside of protected areas and wildlife, the local community needs to "buy in" to ecotourism and strike a pact with conservationists and private landowners. In this process of negotiation, established operators are likely to be very influential because they can provide jobs and bring in customers, build tourism lodges, enter partnerships with local people, and lobby the government authorities for better transport and communications infrastructure.

Tour operators and guides should also promote awareness amongst their clients by providing information and discussing the issues. Ecotourism has a significant educational dimension. Literature on how to deal with the impacts of ecotourism is becoming widely available (Malek-Zadeh, 1996; Whelan, 1991). Ecotourism education is a *process* of rather than the delivery of a packaged message, since much of what occurs is innovative and everyone is on a learning curve. Ecotourism educates because it bridges

distances, such as that between urbanites and rural surroundings (Van Rensburg and Shongwe, 1996):

> For many tourists, a visit to an ecodestination [overcomes] that sense of distance from the biophysical world, "nature" if you wish, which so many city dwellers experience. Environmentalists hope . . . the experience [will] instill a sense of responsibility towards the environment in the visitor. . . . (p. 1)

Apart from educating the clients, there are other gaps to bridge. The network of interests which ecotourism brings together in functional relationships is depicted in Figure 55.5. Linked around the circle are the stakeholders in ecotourism. The relationships are often confused and riven by politics. Some are relatively distant from each other—marketers abroad may have little contact with community-based organizations in a Third World country, but some are very close—conservation bodies, which may be engaged by international aid agencies, deal with remote village communities quite frequently. Everywhere, the public and private sectors overlap as government and private enterprise become jointly involved. Connecting the players are networks of communication, the local, national and global channels of informal influence, lobbying, formal decision making and the public media and communications system. Tour operators and their guides often act as intermediaries because they work in the field and make contact with community-based organizations, but also have ongoing contacts with landowners, conservationists, government regulators, investors, marketers and the media. Tourism professionals are well-placed to interpret situations and influence outcomes.

Ethics and Media

Ethical codes set out guidelines for minimum impact on the environment and maximum respect for cultural heritage and differences. Before sustainability became a central tenet of green awareness, many codes focused solely on safeguarding the wilderness. Ethics today are more broadly concerned with relationships between the adventurer and the surrounding natural as well as social environment, with attention to job creation. The United Nations Environmental Program (UNEP) has produced a summary of various codes (UNEP, 1995). A further example is the Code of Practice of the Ecotourism Association of Australia (WTTC, 1997), which is directed at tour operators. It mentions the standard rules of best practice, safety and obeying the law but adds that operators should:

- strengthen the conservation effort;
- respect the sensitivities of other cultures;
- keep waste to a minimum and recycle wherever possible;

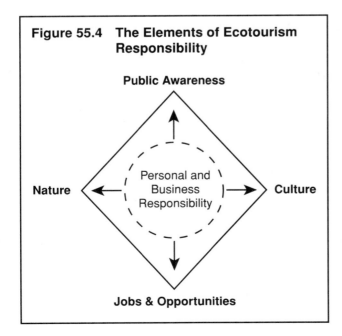

Figure 55.4   The Elements of Ecotourism Responsibility

Public Awareness

Nature

Personal and Business Responsibility

Culture

Jobs & Opportunities

- raise environmental, historical and social awareness in clients, and network with stakeholders who apply the code; and
- use locally produced goods but not from endangered species.

Voluntary control is one thing, but consumers can bring pressure to bear by insisting that tour operators conform to best practices. McLaren (1997a) says tourists should not be misled by the "greening" of American businesses, and should carefully select their tour operators based on their past record, commitment to low impact, pattern of ownership and employment, education provided for tourists, and revenue directed towards local communities. Flexibility in the application of codes is necessary because situations differ, so good judgment is called for, based on a public culture of ethical practices.

The Australian code quoted previously calls for "truth in advertising." The mass media have promoted adventure travel and therefore carry some of the responsibility for shaping its future development. New publishing titles, broadcast programs, and now Internet pages have kept pace with the growth of adventure itself. Those who interface with journalists by providing information and prompting opinions now need to draw attention to the problems of tourism and to suggest ways of improving the traveler's interactions with the countries and people visited.

Less Developed Countries

In truth, adventure travelers continue to be a privileged minority who can afford to travel for pleasure. Even by the year 2020, the number of tourists crossing international boundaries will still only constitute seven percent of the world's population, which makes tourism an infant industry with large room for expansion (WTO, 1997a, p. 3). The bulk of tourists will continue to be from the developed nations while those in the less developed countries (LDCs), will increasingly serve the holiday makers rather than taking breaks for their own amusement. Adventure travelers, with their high-technology toys like 4x4 vehicles, hang gliders, and kayaks constitute a readily identifiable privileged group whose very visibility could make them a target for resentment. Against that, tourists bring jobs, dollars and opportunities into the LDCs.

Tourism is now perceived as both an opportunity and a threat by the LDCs. Tourism is the world's biggest business and revenue generator, so the temptation to sacrifice nature and culture for the sake of dollars is immense. According to the WTO (1997a), by the year 2020 global tour-

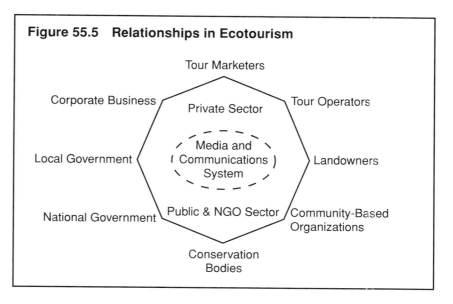

Figure 55.5   Relationships in Ecotourism

ism as a whole will see some 1.6 billion people crossing international borders, three times the number of 595 million recorded in 1996. They will be spending more than $5 billion a day or more than five times the $425 billion spent throughout 1996 (WTO, 1997a). Especially as regards the less developed countries (LDCs), the appeal of tourism is overwhelming: it brings in much-needed foreign exchange and can attract investment from international hotel groups and the like.

Take the case of Africa's leading tourist destination, South Africa, which in 1996 attracted 4 million tourists, or under one percent of international travelers (WTO, 1997a). South Africa is a middling country by per capita income standards, not a poor one. After years of social conflict it is hoping to build its national reconstruction and development program partly on tourism by doubling the number of jobs to a million by the turn of the century: one-seventh of the total labor force. To do this, it needs every tourist it can get. Some 40 percent of foreign visitors come to participate in ecotourism, which includes game viewing, cultural tours, and outdoor adventures (Addison, 1997c). One urgent need is to provide low-cost training for a new generation of Black adventure guides and give opportunities to Black tour operators who were previously excluded under the apartheid regime (Addison, 1997b).

Different, and yet the same: Sri Lankan "street guides" are being drawn into the formal system in order to legalize their way of life and reduce complaints from visitors (Harrison, p. 138). Experience has shown that tourism is extremely vulnerable to fluctuations in international trade as well as to political upheavals and wars. Tourism businesses in the relatively stable developed world have an advantage here. By contrast, the killing of scores of tourists at Luxor in Egypt by Muslim fundamentalists during 1997 immediately knocked the bottom out of the country's tourism trade, and it may be many years before it recovers. Travelers can pick and choose their destinations at whim, bypassing troubled areas and opting for those that offer the best combination of price, excitement and accessibility. To stabilize tourism arrivals and promote new tourism by gaining a reputation for good food, fun and service is the aim of many national development plans.

But not all travelers want comfort, and a little ruggedness goes a long way when effectively marketed. The difficulty is that it also has impacts. The explicit ecotourism aim of drawing people into rural areas has succeeded, insofar as destinations like Annapurna and Machu Picchu now contend with package tourism on a large scale. Many governments set quotas for tourist numbers or simply push up the price of permits as another way of controlling numbers. A gathering of tourism leaders from 64 nations in Manila during 1997, under the auspices of the WTO, committed itself to fair, equal and ethical standards. Philippine President Fidel Ramos referred to himself as "the number one tourist" in his own country, but warned that the tourism sector must become more equitable and socially responsible. He went on:

> Our idea of tourism cannot simply be that of setting up a world-class resort for affluent tourists with thousands of unemployed and hungry people milling outside the gates. Rather we must engage the skills and energies of the many, especially those of the surrounding community, knowing that they can be amongst our strongest attractions. (WTO, 1997b)

Ecotourists are most likely to confront the social ills that tourism brings because they move outside the gates and in amongst the people. The challenge is to translate insights into action. The rethinking of tourism and ecotravel is gathering pace (McLaren, 1997b). There is evidence of growing consumer consciousness of the need for sustainable tourism and fair trade practices (WTO, 1997a). As McLaren puts it, the responsible tourism movement is turning ecotourists into activists.

Conclusion

This chapter has attempted to spell out a general ethos for adventure travel. The history of exploration suggests that travel brings innovation to human civilization, through new encounters in the realm of the hitherto unknown. Encounters with cultural otherness and the wilderness change our view of human life and of the universe we live in—that is, if we make the effort to become aware of what we are confronting. The realm of the hitherto unknown includes the undiscovered self and its unstated values, which is why the discoveries of women, with their conscious challenge to male values, add a new dimension to the meaning of adventure. Any attempt to spell out an ethos for adventure

travel raises the question whether those who travel do make the effort to interpret the experience and relate it to their inner lives and outer lifestyles. There is no obligation to do this, especially if one is a paying client, but ultimately everyone has a responsibility to do so: it comes with the territory. It helps to keep a journal and to vocalize one's findings and doubts. No one can be shepherded through every situation that may arise on a trip. The relationship between guide and client, which is supposed to shield the latter from discomfort and danger, is one of service; yet there is also a two-way exchange between them. At the lowest end of the adventure scale, leisure poses few physical, moral or spiritual challenges. At the extreme top of the scale, dealing with the unknown is the whole purpose of the trip. In between are all the permutations of adventure from guided tours to educational tours that enhance individual initiative and encourage group understanding. In one way or another, adventure teaches participants to become more self-reliant and also to examine relationships that would otherwise be taken for granted. Ecotourism does this too, within the context of nature and culture, confronting the individual with deep social questions.

As was said at the outset, adventure is very diverse, and the issues it raises no less so. The common thread that this chapter has traced is that of accepting responsibility. In an essay criticizing the notion that the wilderness is a kind of museum of raw nature where civilized beings do not belong, environmental historian William Cronon writes that:

> wilderness can teach profound feelings of humility and respect as we confront our fellow beings and the earth itself. Feelings like these argue for the importance of self-awareness and self-criticism as we exercise our ability to transform the world around us, helping us to set responsible limits to human mastery. . . . (1996, p. 105)

The wilderness and travel to foreign societies may temporarily distance us from ourselves. Eventually we return to home base to reconsider who and what we are. Adventure travel should be an educative experience, and ecotourism should assist emergent countries to develop economically and save their heritage. Adventure and ecotravel are more than just exciting and colorful ways of spending a holiday: they are also a test of wilderness ethics, gender and race relations, social sensitivity, and good sense. Those participating in the growth of this world industry owe it to themselves and to humankind to ensure that they put in more than they take out.

References

Addison, G. N. (1997a). The great ecotourism debate. *Out There, 20*, 48–52.

Addison, G. N. (1997b). Go ahead, kill me. *Out There, 22*, 62–69.

Addison, G. N. (1998a). Peace parks. *Leadership, 16*(4), 64–74.

Addison, G. N. (1998b). Satour. *Marketing Mix,* January/February.

Adventure Journal. (1998, August 19). *Adventure Journal fact sheet.* San Francisco, CA: Travel Publishing Group.

Argyle, M. (1996). *The social psychology of leisure.* London, UK: Penguin.

Bloch, L. (1997). Adventure training. *Out There* Adventure Annual.

Brandon, K. (1996). *Ecotourism and conservation: A review of key issues.* New York, NY: World Bank.

Burns, D., and Clarkson, S. M. (1987). *Tips for the savvy traveler.* Pownall, VT: Storey Communications.

Cahill, T. (1997, October). Forbidden. *Outside,* twentieth-anniversary issue, pp. 70–73.

Campbell, F. (1997). *The whole story: A walk around the world.* London, UK: Orion.

Ceballos-Lascurain, H. (1996). *Tourism, ecotourism and protected areas: The state of nature-based tourism around the world and guidelines for its development.* Geneva, Switzerland: IUCN Publishers.

Cohen J. M., and Cohen, M. J. (1962). *Penguin dictionary of quotations.* London, UK: Jonathan Cape.

Cohen J. M., and Cohen, M. J. (1980). *Dictionary of modern quotations* (2nd ed.). London, UK: Penguin Reference.

Collins, V. R. (1995). *Working in tourism: The UK, Europe and beyond.* Oxford, UK: Vacation Work.

Cronon, W. (1996). The trouble with wilderness. In R. Atwan (Ed.), *The best American essays, 1996.* Boston, MA: Houghton Mifflin.

Davidson, R. (1982). *Tracks.* London, UK: Paladin.

Ecotourism Association of Australia. (1997). *Code of practice* [On-line]. Available: http://www.wttc.org.

Elliott, J. A. (1994). *An introduction to sustainable development.* London, UK: Routledge.

Fiennes, R. (1993). *Mind over matter.* New York, NY: Delacorte Press.

Finch, L. (1997). *World flight* [On-line]. Available: http://worldflight.org/

Fisher, W. (1997). Wendy Fisher takes on the macho man. *Gravity,* Winter.

Foster, D. (1985). *Travel and tourism management.* London, UK: Macmillan.

Frank, K. (1986). *A voyager out: The life of Mary Kingsley.* Boston, MA: Houghton Mifflin.

French, H. F. (1995). Forging a new global partnership. In L. R. Brown (Ed.), *State of the world 1995.* New York, NY: Norton/Worldwatch Books.

Giddens, A. (1990). *The consequences of modernity.* Stanford, CA: Stanford University Press.

Gifford, N. (1983). *Expeditions and exploration.* London, UK: Macmillan.

Gomes, M. E., and Kanner, A. D. (1995). The rape of the well maidens: Feminist psychology and 10 environmental crises. In T. Roszak (Ed.), *Ecopsychology.* San Francisco, CA: Sierra Club Books.

Greenpeace. (1997). Available: http://www.greenpeace.org/~climate and http://www.greenpeace.org/search.shtml

Gupta, A. (1988). *Ecology and development in the third world.* London, UK: Routledge.

Harrison, D. (Ed.). (1992). *Tourism & less developed countries.* London, UK: John Wiley & Sons.

Janney, R. P. (1997). *Search for Amelia Earhart.* Sisters, OR: Multinomah Publishers.

Krakauer, J. (1997). *Into thin air.* London, UK: Macmillan.

Lea, J. (1988). *Tourism development in the third world.* London, UK: Routledge.

Lee, E. (Ed). (1997). *Go girl: The Black woman's guide to travel and adventure.* Portland, OR: Eighth Mountain Press.

Malek-Zadeh, E. (1996). *The ecotourism equation: Measuring the impacts.* Hartford, CT: Yale University Press.

Mancini, M. (1990). *Conducting tours: A practical guide.* Cincinnati, OH: South-Western Publishing Co.

McLaren, D. (1997a). *Evaluating ecotourism operators and agents.* In El Planeta Platica [On-line]. Available: http://www.txinfinet.com/mader/planeta/

McLaren, D. (1997b). *Rethinking tourism and ecotravel: The paving of paradise and how you can stop it.* West Hartford, CT: Kumarian Press.

Medlik, S. (1993). *Dictionary of travel, tourism and hospitality.* Oxford, UK: Butterworth/Heinemann.

Merriam-Webster (1991). *New book of word histories.* Springfield, MA: Author.

Meyer, K. (1994). *How to shit in the woods: An environmentally sound approach to a lost art.* Berkeley, CA: Ten Speed Press.

Mill, R. C. (1995). *Tourism: The international business.* Englewood Cliffs, NJ: Prentice-Hall.

Murphy, D. (1993). *The Ukimwi Road.* London, UK: Flamingo.

NUA Internet Surveys. (1997). *USA today: Travelers are turning to the Internet* [On-line]. Available: http://www.nua.ie/surveys/index.cgi

Rubin, K. (1986). *Flying high in travel: A complete guide to careers in the travel industry.* New York, NY: John Wiley & Sons.

Ryab, C. (1995). *Researching tourist satisfaction.* London, UK: Routledge.

Shacochis, B. (1997, October). Roof of the World, Center of the Universe. *Outside,* twentieth-anniversary issue, pp. 144–152.

Shenk, E. (1992). *Outdoor careers: Exploring occupations in outdoor fields.* Harrisburg, PA: Stackpole Books.

Simpson, S. (1990). *The Times guide to the environment*. London, UK: Times Books.

Stabler, M. (1990). Financial management and leisure provision. In I. P. Henry (Ed.), *Management and planning in the leisure industries*. London, UK: Macmillan.

Stroud, M. (1993). *Shadows on the wasteland*. London, UK: Jonathan Cape.

Swarbrooke, J. (1997). *The development and management of visitor attractions*. Oxford, UK: Butterworth/Heinemann.

Swinglehurst E. (1974). *The romantic journey: The story of Thomas Cook and Victorian travel*. London, UK: Pica Editions.

Thomas, C. (1997). *Becoming an outdoors woman: My outdoor adventure*. Helena, MT: Falcon.

Travel Industry Association of America. (1997). *The adventure travel report, 1997* [On-line]. Available to TIA members: http://www.tia.org/tiadev/press/022098adven.stm. Summary facts available: http://www.tia.org/press/fastfacts8.stm.

Toffler A. (1991). *Powershift*. New York, NY: Bantam Books.

Torkildson, G. (1986). *Leisure and recreation management*. London, UK: Chapman and Hall.

Turnbull, N. (1996). *The millennium edge*. St. Leonards, Australia: Allen & Unwin.

United Nations Environmental Program. (1995). *Environmental codes of conduct for tourism*. Paris, France: Author.

Van der Merwe, C. (1997). Some definitions. *Out There, 20,* 52.

Van Rensburg, E. J., and Shongwe, D. (1996). *Of journeys, packages and distances*. Paper presented at EcoWorld Media Day Symposium, Rhodes University, Grahamstown, South Africa.

Voase, R. (1995). *Tourism: The human perspective*. London, UK: Hodder & Stoughton.

Walbridge, C. (1994). *Heads up! River rescue for river runners* [video]. Springfield, VA: American Canoe Association.

Wharton, E. (1995). *A motor-flight through France*. London, UK: Macmillan/Picador. (Original work published 1908)

Whelan, T. (1991). *Nature tourism: Managing for the environment*. Washington, DC: Island Press.

Working Holidays. (1995). *The complete guide to seasonal jobs, 1995*. London, UK: Central Bureau for Educational Visits and Exchanges.

World Tourism Organization. (1995). *Sustainable tourism charter adopted at Lanzarote* [Press release].

World Tourism Organization. (1997a). *Tourism 2020 vision: Executive summary*. Madrid, Spain: Author.

World Tourism Organization. (1997b). *Tourism sector unites over social problems* [Press release].

WTO web page press releases. http://www.world-tourism.org/calen.htm

World Travel and Tourism Council. (1997). *The WTTC Website* [On-line]. Available: http://www.wttc.org.

Section 10

Extensions of Adventure Programming
Environmental Trends and Issues

What will be the future of adventure education and programming? The prospect seems to be for a continued broadening of goals, refinement of technique, deeper understanding of process, and extension of contribution to society's educational and social aspirations. This revised edition of the original 1990 collection suggests these trends, and that they will continue. The field is building, maturing, engaging in critical reflection, evaluation, and research. The introduction to this last section in the previous edition suggested that there was promise of a bright future for adventure education and programming, and after nearly a decade of development, that promise is being achieved.

Everything exists in an environment, including adventure education, and adventure programmers should be, and to some degree are, paying close attention to their environment. They work in a social and cultural environment where people strive to satisfy their needs, yearn and work for safety, security and fulfillment. "Culture wars" rage in which people struggle to define the "good" life and the core values that will guide them. Too often the values of nature upon which the human community builds its prosperity, are overlooked or ignored. The goal of environmental sustainability is not examined.

Adventure education has the potential, as authors in this section suggest, to immerse people in the natural world and awaken them to the need to consider the part of their identity that involves the community around them. Ecologist Aldo Leopold once wrote that the land ethic "simply enlarges the boundaries of the community to include soils, waters, plants, and animals, or collectively: the land." He went on to observe that this ethic "changes the role of *Homo sapiens* from conqueror of the land-community to plain member and citizen of it. It implies respect for his fellow-members, and also respect for the community as such" (1949, p. 204). Adventure programs conventionally emphasize the importance of respecting others in the social community and working with them to achieve individual and community goals which, it often turns out, are the same. So it may be with the enlarged community that Leopold describes, and the immersion in the natural world that is part of many adventure education programs has great potential to contribute to the environmental education of participants. They may, as the authors here point out, learn of their biological and spiritual connections to the natural world, to the enlarged community, which is the foundation upon which all human society and culture is constructed.

Reference

Leopold, A. (1949). *A sand county almanac*. New York, NY: Oxford University Press.

Chapter 56

A Synthesis of Environmental and Adventure Education Concepts: A Professional Responsibility

Camille J. Bunting and J. T. Townley
Texas A&M University

In the *Journal of Environmental Education,* Priest (1986) uses a tree to represent the concepts of outdoor education. The outdoor education tree has two primary branches, one representing environmental education and the second branch representing adventure education. Theoretically, the two types of education are both based on relationships. For environmental education, the relationship focus is ecology and ekistics, whereas adventure education's focus is on intrapersonal and interpersonal relationship development. In this chapter, we would like to take a closer look at the concept of relationships, and present the idea that not only do environmental and adventure education share a general relationship focus, but that they also share the same concepts. One of the components of scholarship, defined by Boyer (1990) in *Scholarship Reconsidered,* is analyzing and then synthesizing information to allow for fresh understanding and application. This chapter is an attempt to synthesize a few general concepts and demonstrate their application to the ecology of the environment as well as the ecology of adventure education.

In years past, learning about the environment meant memorizing names of trees, flowers, insects, and species, a method quite dissimilar from experiential learning. However, in the early 1970s, Steve Van Matre spawned the acclimatization idea for environmental education. The objective of acclimatization or earth education is to teach others how to learn about the environment experientially and to become "one" with the environment through sensory awareness. Through such adventures, an individual becomes naturally inquisitive about the environment and motivation for learning is greatly increased. About the same time that Van Matre published his book *Acclimatization,* other similar projects developed outdoor activities for teaching environmental concepts. All of these attempted to capitalize on the motivational impact of adventure or experiential learning. Some examples include educational projects such as *Outdoor Biology Instruction Strategies, The Green Box, Project Wild, Project Learning Tree,* and other environmental activity books. Environmental education adopted experiential or adventure-based educational methodology.

Outdoor adventure has been defined as activities that involve humans grappling with problems that are naturally present in a particular environment (Miles, 1978). It is the process of learning through physical involvement that engages the psychomotor, affective, and cognitive learning domains in a natural outdoor environment. Whenever physical activity is dependent upon some type of interaction with the natural environment, challenge is present. The adventure lies not in overcoming the natural challenge, but in communicating or negotiating with it. Such communication requires appropriate skills, respect, and adequate knowledge of the particular environment. Ideally, over time and through a series of experiences leading to appropriate change and adaptation, interdependency develops between participants as well as between the environment and the participants. Although there is a general understanding and acceptance of inter-dependency in nature, there is little sub-stantive discussion of its meaning in adventure education.

In *Sunship Earth,* Steve Van Matre (1979) presents environmental defini-tions for the general concepts of energy, cycles, diversity, interrelationships, community, change, and adaptation. Af-ter thinking about these concepts in as-sociation with both branches of outdoor education, it becomes apparent that they are important in the context of adven-ture education as well as environmental education. Expanding our perspective of these concepts can assist in developing a clearer understanding of adventure education. The concepts are listed in Table 56.1 with a brief explanation of each as it relates to both environmental and adventure education.

Energy

Outdoor adventure is synonymous with challenge, and it is this challenge, stress, exhilaration, or creative tension that cre-ates the energy. This flow of energy is transferred from a situation to the par-ticipants, as well as between participants. While the tension created as a result of the interaction of group members in ad-venture activities may not always be euphoric in nature, it can prove to be both invigorating and energizing if dealt with properly.

Cycles

The experiential nature of adventure education has proven to be unique with potentially insightful characteristics. When experiential learning is most ef-fective, it is cyclical. One means of ex-pressing such a cycle is with a model developed to illustrate appropriate se-quencing of experiential activities (Fig-ure 56.1). As the application of learning takes place, further experiences are needed that are sequentially more com-plex and consequential (Bunting, 1985).

Table 56.1 Environmental and Adventure Education Concepts

Environmental Education	Concepts	Adventure Education
Sunlight energy is transferred from plants to animals to food decomposers	Energy Flow	Challenge and creative tension is transferred to and from situations and individuals
Nutrient cycles in the earth's reservoirs of air, soil, and water allow life to continue	Cycles	Experiential learning goes in a cycle, from experience to observation to processing to learning and back to experience
Different nutrient and sunlight requirements permit diverse plants and animals to share the earth	Diversity	Individual diversities increase the potential for learning and growth
Plants and animals coexist where essential nutrients best meet their individual needs	Community	Mutual support is developed in situations that require individual needs to be met by other group members
Constant interaction with each other and surroundings as plants and animals meet one another's needs	Relationships	Constant interaction with each other and surroundings as individuals meet one another's needs and they meet the environment's needs while the environment meets their needs
Resulting from all of the above, all plants and animals are in the process of becoming something else	Change	The sum of our experience, if learning results, allows us to remain "becomers"
Some plants and animals improve as a result of the ever-changing conditions of where they live	Adaptation	The result of energy, cycles, diversity, community, inter-relationships, and change for those desiring growth

SOURCE: Environmental concepts adapted from Matre, 1979.

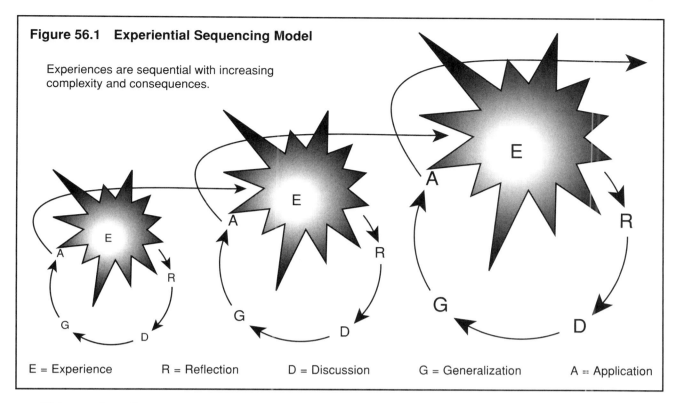

Figure 56.1 Experiential Sequencing Model

Experiences are sequential with increasing complexity and consequences.

E = Experience   R = Reflection   D = Discussion   G = Generalization   A = Application

Diversity, Interrelationships, and Community

The concepts of diversity, interrelationships, and community are very closely intertwined in the realms of both ecology and outdoor adventure. In the realm of adventure education, these concepts are directed primarily toward the complexities of interpersonal relationships, rather than the ekistic and ecosystemic relationships examined through environmental education. In his article "Landscapes of Change: Toward a New Paradigm for Education," Sam Crowell (1995) discusses the importance of recognizing connections between and within educational disciplines:

> In education, as in the rest of the culture, our practice is driven by assumptions about our world. . . . If we think that our world is divided into objects that are basically unconnected, then we will tend to divide our curriculum into subjects, topics and unrelated categories. Moreover, we will project sensitivities that reflect separateness. . . . If, on the other hand, we view content as events, if we perceive our world as connected in fundamental ways, if we view action as self-generated within a particular context, then our curricular and instructional decisions may be very different. (p. 12)

This sense of "connectedness" within educational contexts in general is paramount to understanding the interdependency between environmental and adventure education. Furthermore, Crowell's notions concerning the significance of establishing connections in education can be applied specifically to the concepts of diversity, community, and interrelationships. Our individual differences offer unlimited growth potential through learning and playing together; effectively dealing with such diversity provides the element of challenge which creates energy flow. As relationships are developed through interactions with diverse others, a connectedness is formed which can often be identified as community. "The experience of true community is a unique way of communicating, of sharing our deepest thoughts and feelings without fear or guilt" (Peck, 1987). Creating such a sense of community and interdependency, not only between individuals, but also between the branches of outdoor education, proves to be one of the most crucial objectives for adventure education.

Change and Adaptation

As the concepts of diversity, community, and relationships are intertwined, so are the concepts of change and adaptation. Through the process of experiential learning, the most fundamental aspect of adventure education, experiences should continue to change and challenges increase as we grow and develop. If the process is successful, then adaptation (growth) will result: adaptation to ourselves, to others, and to our environments. Although such adaptations may occur in response to a variety of stimuli, adventure education provides an environment uniquely suited for personal and interpersonal growth.

Professional Significance

Professionals who use adventure as an educational tool are generally familiar with Kolb's (1984) experiential learning cycle. It provided the basis for the sequencing model presented in Figure 56.1 (page 435). The experiential learning cycle illustrates the idea that true learning involves reflecting upon an experience, discussing the experience and reflections, making generalizations to a larger frame of reference, and then applying those "learnings" in another experience or context. Continuing the synthesis of environmental and adventure education concepts to elucidate the adventure learning process, an expanded or holistic learning model is offered (Figure 56.2). We can see that the experiential learning cycle is at the heart of the image. However, with a broader perspective, the synthesis of environmental and adventure concepts can be depicted.

The methodology and process of adventure education extends beyond the activity itself. There should be purposeful planning of the activity or experience to make it appropriate for a particular group of diverse people. In the planning process, the professional is mindful that a long-term goal is change (growth) and adaptation. Intermediate steps toward that goal are the development of respect for the significance of cycles and interrelationships, with an understanding of community and what is required to achieve it. The catalyst for progressing through these steps toward change and adaptation is the spiraling cycle of experience, reflection, discussion, generalization, and application to another experience. But as the expanded learning model implies, the goal is not just the application of what has been learned, it is personal and interpersonal change and adaptation to the ongoing adventure of life.

It is incumbent upon professional adventure educators to understand and convey the holistic nature of our methodology. Without the ability to do so, we yield to the lure of compartmentalization and loose sight of our own connectedness, as well as the ability to inspire our students with the significance of interdependency.

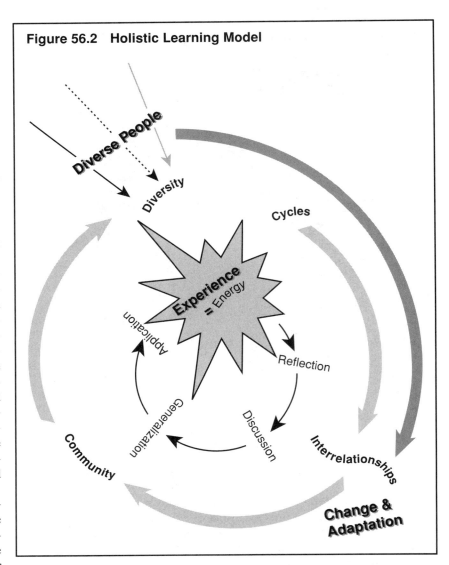

Figure 56.2   Holistic Learning Model

Many adventurers often fail to be sedulously prudent with the resources so necessary for their activities. Such individuals may have been introduced to adventure pursuits by someone who lacked an understanding of interdependency's holistic concepts. Therefore, recreational activity skills were all that were taught. This cycle of misconception and negligence must be recognized and reversed. Without a commitment to the value of an interdependent ecology in both environmental and adventure education and an understanding of the expanded view of experiential learning, outdoor adventure opportunities may not be available to future generations.

References

Boyer, E. (1990). *Scholarship reconsidered.* Princeton, NJ: Carnegie Foundation for the Advancement of Teaching.

Bunting, C. J. (1985). *Venture dynamics*. College Station, TX: Texas A&M University Outdoor Education Institute.

Crowell, S. (1995). Landscapes of change toward a new paradigm for education. In B. G. Blair and R. N. Caine (Eds.), *Integrative learning as the pathway to teaching holism, complexity and interconnectedness.* Lewiston, NY: The Edwin Mellen Press.

Kolb, D. A. (1984). *Experiential learning: Experience as the source of learning and development.* Englewood Cliffs, NJ: Prentice-Hall, Inc.

Miles, J. C. (1978, April). The value of high-adventure activities. *The Journal of Physical Education, Recreation and Dance—Leisure Today,* 3–4.

Peck, M. S. (1987). *The different drum.* New York, NY: Simon and Schuster, Inc.

Priest, S. (1986). Redefining outdoor education: A matter of many relationships. *Journal of Environmental Education, 60,* 13–15.

Van Matre, S. (1972). *Acclimatization.* Martinsville, IN: The American Camping Association.

Van Matre, S. (1979). *Sunship earth.* Martinsville, IN: The American Camping Association.

Chapter 57

The Place of Deep Ecology and Ecopsychology in Adventure Education

Robert Henderson
McMaster University

Have you ever taught canoeing at an indoor swimming pool? I have, and while people learned necessary physical skills, I was left thinking I hadn't really taught canoeing, per se. The place within me that understands the adventure in adventure education from an ecopsychology stance, a place that is supportive of the deep ecology movement, could not accept the swimming pool teaching and learning as canoeing. Real canoeing demands a relationship with the earth, with wind on your face, and the life force ever outward with one's paddle stroke into the lake, river, watershed. Real canoeing involves a feeling of resonance with the earth. To compare the pool to the lake (the indoorness of lights, walls and reverb sound to the out-of-doors of wind, sun and open vista) proves to be a haunting illustration of a decline in quality; though this is a quality we have come to accept as the norm, with our shift from out-of-doors to indoors.

It would be the same for the indoor climbing wall as compared to the mountain experience or viewing the CD-ROM nature series as compared to the misty morning "nature" walk. The former, in all cases, might even provide more concrete "skill" development, but the latter, the experience of self within the more-than-human realm of nature, involves potential for a deep emotive relationship, an extending of the cognitive physical process. And this quality is certainly a lofty skill to learn as well. Admittedly, *deep* is a vague term here. The hope is that the "deep" of deep ecology for the adventure educator will find some personalized apprehension with this writing.

To be a supporter of the deep ecology movement (to be called a *deep ecologist* is to miss the point that given our cultural context, the deep of this ecology is more a quest than a checklist), and to think of your work as "cultural work" in ecopsychology (some people consider ecopsychology an applied deep ecology) is to be concerned for a particular quality of adventure education. That quality concerns our relationship to the earth: how we dwell on the earth, the care of our soul—our inner psyche—with the earth, our healing as tied to our ways of being and knowing with the earth. We may call it *earth bonding* or the spiritual dimensions of adventure education. We may think of it as a cultural adventure: the adventure of regaining our intuitive impulse and allurement with the earth. For this, we only need to shed our culturally determined skin, an armor which leads us towards a primarily objective, consumptive, competitive "nature." As we peel away layers, we are drawn towards a manner of being and knowing that is more connected, more communal and strangely "already familiar" (Pivnick, 1997). We wouldn't only see more, we would see differently. No small task this, but one that is at the heart of our cultural attentions to change our path of environmental degradation and to change our self-attention toward our personal healing within our open spaces, wood lots, wilderness, and cities.

This place of practice is linked directly to much of our modern ills and alienations, our general lack of wholeness and knowledge within ourselves and our local bioregions. While the adventure educator is comfortable working towards intrapersonal and interpersonal objectives with others, the ecopsychology place of practice would add the relationship *of* self to *place* to the common focus of self to self and self to other. Furthermore, in ecopsychology, the self to place to universe is integral to the healthy intrapersonal relationship. You do not teach a person the joy of viewing a moose while on a morning paddle or the joy of the fragrance of the misty pine forest. One is born with this understanding and love. Educator Janet Pivnick (1977), quoting Jack Kerouac, reminds us that nature is within us, "like an old dream, like a piece of forgotten song drifting across the water." As embodied knowing we should not think of learning how to acquire, to instill, to produce, a relationship with nature. (Pivnick cleverly exposes this convention language in leading environmental education sources.) Rather we need the liminal space or time out of our daily realities to *remember.*

Adventure educators should have no trouble understanding the basic foundational thought of ecopsychology. For the adventure educator, adventure as an idea is innate, part of essential humanness, a fulfillment of the best we can be, a yearning, an impulse. Adventure, when missing from our lives, can be thought of as a lost impulse, a displaced vital need, a loss of our essential humanness. The adventure educator strives to bring adventure back into people's lives because it is a part of our basic ancestral sensibilities. If we lead adventure-rich lives then there would be no need for such a label as *adventure education.* And, presumably there would be less neurosis, less apathy, less mediocrity. Conversely, there would be more generic character skill development and change born in social and personal attention to our vital needs and aspirations. The title, an adventure educator would be . . . well . . . silly.

In the same way, an ecopsychology inquiry shares this notion of the drawing out of an inner yearning. Let me repeat much of the above from the less familiar context of ecopsychology. Ecopsychology is an inquiry that acknowledges our deeply rooted ancestral sensibility, the bonds of our inner psyche with the earth. How did William Blake put it, close to two centuries ago:

> Every wolf's and lion's howl
> Raises from Hell a Human soul.
> The wild deer, wandering here and there,
> Keeps the Human soul from care. . . . (1997,
> p. 71)

In short, and to be purposefully repetitive, for the ecopsychologist, our psychic relationship with the earth is innate, part of essential humanness, a yearning. Theodore Roszak first calls this "our lost religious impulse" (1972, p. xv). Without this connection, we are sensory undernourished. We become alienated from a part of our true being.

Neurosis and modern day ailments, physical and mental, follow. The ecopsychologist strives to bring the adventure of earthly relationship back into people's lives. In a healthy society, fully conscious of our organic reality celebrating the earth as primary, the ecopsychology label would be not just a redundant type of label, but a tautology. We don't need to be told and study the fact that we are of the earth, that ecology and psychology are linked. How silly. My goodness. This is a given. Like the adventure educator, a tautology; repeated elements of meaning.

In the same way, the adventure educator can understand conceptual similarities to a supporter of the deep ecology movement. Both attempt to ask deeper questions of the human condition in relationship. Both attempt to entice a learner to reflect on his or her condition with the purposes of reaching his or her full potential. This will mean exploring self-misunderstandings and consciously and intentionally seeking a more self-determined, less societally determined self. With both adventure education and deep ecology the learner must choose to participate. It is a challenge-by-choice learning scenario. For both, one must acknowledge some sense of personal angst and crisis, both deeply personal, and deeply cultural. Personal and environmental crisis cannot be easily separated out (though we try to delude ourselves this way more often than not). You cannot have healthy people on a sick planet. Irish playwright Samuel Beckett in *Endgame* put it this way, "you're on the earth, there is no cure for that." For a more positive and educational spin, Roszak (1978) has said, "the needs of the person are the needs of the planet." The wellness movement cannot be removed from the environmental movement. An adventure of the spirit is central to both. Each shares a desire for change.

The question remains for each, wellness, environment and adventure educations: how "deep" is that change to be? What is the nature of the personal and/or sociocultural transformation that follows one's personal and purposeful desire for change? Let's look at ecopsychology and deep ecology more closely.

Deep ecology, also called *radical environmentalism ecology,* is a grass roots movement that emerges from a swell of consciousness acknowledging our flawed cultural and self-assumptions in relation to the earth. Our environmental crisis, evident in unsustainable practices, is more accurately framed as a culture crisis. Ecocatastrophe is no longer a shocking idea. We live with it now. Our self-apathy and/or self-deception is to be marveled at. Our problems on the earth are no longer able to be thought of as management issues. We must come to explore our problems as ones of fundamental design (Cayley, 1991). Accepting environmental crisis as cultural crisis is one's starting point. Without some state of crisis there is no need for change. When one culturally comes to understand that the way we dwell in Western societies is ultimately untenable, then one can either abdicate all responsibility and bear the burden of this unviable stance, or one is compelled to question more deeply towards a change of cultural assumptions and practice. This disorienting thinking, like putting on a new set of eyeglasses, is not easy, but strangely comforting, for at least a genuine inquiry is at play.

The following platform principles of deep ecology have received a general acceptance as a way of describing the movement as a social and political consciousness. They offer a personal rationale for holistic identity, a foundation towards cultivating an ecological consciousness and importantly they culminate in responsibility for action to achieve a new inclusive society (Chamberlin, 1997, p. 82). They help define a vision and aspiration to living:

1. The well-being and flourishing of human and nonhuman life on Earth have value in themselves (synonyms: intrinsic value, inherent value). These values are independent of the usefulness of the nonhuman world for human purposes.

2. Richness and diversity of life forms contribute to the realization of these values and are also values in themselves.

3. Humans have no right to reduce this richness and diversity except to satisfy vital needs.

4. The flourishing of human life and cultures is compatible with a substantial decrease of the human population. The flourishing of nonhuman life requires such a decrease.

5. Present human interference with the nonhuman world is excessive, and the situation is rapidly worsening.

6. Policies must therefore be changed. These policies affect basic economic, technological, and ideological structures. The resulting state of affairs will be deeply different from the present.

7. The ideological change is mainly that of appreciating life quality (dwelling in situations of inherent value) rather than adhering to an increasingly higher standard of living. There will be a profound awareness of the difference between big and great.

8. Those who subscribe to the foregoing points have an obligation directly or indirectly to try to implement the necessary changes. (McLaughlin, 1993, p. 70)

Most critical to this list is the eighth principle which demands some form of transformative action. Transformative action can take place at two main domains. First, at the level of the self, one may come to attend to the need to work on the self. One of the ultimate norms of deep ecology is self-realization, which stems from the conscious attention towards developing a personal philosophy, an ecosophy, which by definition will be counter to the current cultural principles of conduct. Self-realization involves the extension of one's personal identity to expand one's personal capacity to act in harmony, to care, and understand. Expressed in a different way within religious traditions, as *the* central quest to wisdom, this broadening of personal identification is what Aldous Huxley referred to as the perennial philosophy. This spiritual adventure is thus commonplace to the human spirit and not needing to be instilled, but rather distilled or revealed within. Philosopher Alfred North Whitehead put it this way: "The many become one and are increased by one" (1972, p. 162). Comedian Woody Allen captures the antithetical modern Western human dilemma of an erroneous dualistic spirit with the epigram, "I am two with nature." One can also work at the institutional level and thus be concerned for restructuring economic and political systems. This is a sociopolitical stance found in environmental, social justice–related activism.

The environmental thought framed by the term *deep ecology* exists in early philosophical writing; Spinoza, in feminist writing, i.e., ecofeminism, with primal peoples where primal means closer to the fundamentals of the earth, and with eastern philosophy. The ideas find their contemporary origins with a 1973 article by Norwegian philosopher, Arne Naess, who wished to make a clear distinction between a deep ecology which explores the roots of environmental crisis and a shallow ecology (reform environmentalism) concerned with alleviating immediate environmental hazards (1973). The 1985 reader, *Deep Ecology: Living as if Nature Mattered,* by Bill Devall and George Sessions, helped broaden the audience. Since then the movement has found its voice in a variety of mediums and publications including adventure-based learning settings and journals.

Ecopsychology is concerned with man's homelessness. Chellis Glendinning, in her explicitly titled book *My Name is Chellis and I'm in Recovery From Western Civilization,* puts it simply, "we want to go home" (1994, p. 122). To be a detached, exotic species, a displaced self without a cosmic grounding and purpose on the earth is to not be well. And, while therapy of the conventional habit seeks to heal our ills between the self and self, family, and society, ecopsychology is concerned with healing of our alienation between the self and the natural environment. This particular alienation is not part of standard therapy because we have not made it a focus of study, for example, compared to mother-child relations. This is not true of other cultures where a rite of passage (i.e., a vision quest, adds to the maturation of the child through stages that lead to an ecological maturity). Paul Shepard believes we are left in limbo at adolescence, devoid of a broad-based, culturally sanctioned process that boosts us into a relational identity with our broader earthly surroundings (1982). Can our earth-focused adventure travel and adventure initiative programs be consciously or even unintentionally serving this function?

To foster ecological consciousness or a participatory consciousness, in Morris Berman's words (1981), one can turn to many sources. Ecopsychology may draw on the traditional healing techniques of primary peoples, sensory awareness activities, nature mysticism as expressed in religion and art, and the experience of wilderness. In all, there can be the healing effort to disorient oneself from the culture comfort zone for the resurfacing of latent qualities within. The strength of one's embodied knowing of the earth, one's receptivity and allurement for the earth are shockingly powerful, "healing" awakenings and not the stuff of conventional psychology. Ecopsychology brings ecological thought (ecophilosophy) and psychology together. This is an old idea being revisited anew. One ecopsychologist Robert Greenway has written: "Something happens to people who leave the overt reinforcements of the culture [i.e., in wilderness travel], but it is too simplistic to say that the culture falls away and 'nature comes in and heals'" (1995, p. 184). The cultural, embedded and reinforced, valorization of dualities such as nature and culture, men and women, mind and body, and art and science create an orientation we have come to accept and, in fact, cling to. This peeling away of our culture skin for an adventure of emerging ecological ego is a slowly evolving transformative presence within our daily affairs.

Ecopsychology is a primal instinct and ancient inquiry of humanity throughout time. *Ecopsychology,* a word coined in Theodore Roszak's 1992 book *The Voice of the Earth: An Exploration of Ecopsychology,* conveys a modern expression for this concern for our psyche. Some practitioners may have once thought of themselves as educators, but given their place of practice, now think of themselves as therapists. An "applied" deep ecology can lead one to a ecopsychology label.

Am I an ecopsychologist? Are you? Certainly I am a supporter of the deep ecology thinking vis-à-vis the cultural realities of environmental degradation as a cultural crisis, but the label is, at first thought, an awkward one for an adventure-based travel guide. Or is it? As a travel guide, I lead trips with the intention of therapy by bringing people closer to the earth. Simply being there, in the wilds, is a significant first step but not a guarantee towards healing. It should be added at the outset that people heal and learn from their own will and needs. The guide and educator creates an ambience for possible outcomes. A curriculum however involves objectives and a planned sequencing of activities towards achieving these objectives. So, there is an intended effort towards cultivating ecological consciousness. However, it is a lofty aspiration that must follow or compliment the social and physical skill development within the adventure. The adventure educator works within the lived experience of this adventure of spirit with the group, involved in the same aspirations.

Fellow travel guides, Duenkel and Scott have referred to the "wilderness reality":

> On wilderness travel excursions the "here and now" is no longer the reality of everyday life, but a unique firsthand experience of the natural world. The immediacy of this novel world and the physical distance of the everyday life world allows the wilderness reality to become predominant. (1994, p. 42)

If one is excited in the ensuing disorientation from one's day-to-day reality, and discovering a pleasing, liberating surfacing of selflessness detached—more connected, less guarded, more open—then the transition to the wilderness reality is relevant, even absorbing. We, as adventure educators, have become involved in a cultural adventure taking people to a place (a way of being, knowing and valuing) where their day-to-day culture is not. This new sense of possibility, within an altered liminal cultural space is emancipatory. It is real and it is, at the time, a healing force.

As a travel guide, I do what I can to advance this disorientation turned emancipatory surfacing. I do this only because people respond so favorably. On our first night of travel, for example, I try to put a pause into the overwhelming enthusiasm for the social "getting to know you" space. With lantern and tea we conduct a silent tea ceremony shrouded by the woods and north sky. People stop and look and many notice—deeply—where they are. Similarly as we approach our first night's campsite, I consciously try to change the conventions for a closer linking to one's immediate surroundings. As we approach our campsite, that distance point down the lake, I pull out the guitar and play on the water in my canoe. While all are bent on arriving, this can have a dramatic effect. Sometimes we drift, sometimes we lily dip. People might be a bit annoyed at first. Nothing is said, but the subtle push to relax and look around and enjoy the stillness can do more than simply stall our campsite arrival. It can change the perspective concerning travel itself. People might realize they have already arrived. This moment might just be their personal entry to the way home "within" nature and "of" nature, not simply "in" nature or "against" nature. Pulling out the guitar at that critical, "let's get there moment" is an effort to disorient people. The first time I did this it was a practitioner impulse on my part. Once I read in people's trip journals that for many, this had been a way to approach the whole trip, I discovered I'd found a future curricular (a plan based on an objective) strategy. It is a moment for the place of ecopsychology in adventure education.

These curricular moments (the adventure will have hundreds of such moments) are intended to draw people towards the wilderness reality. The choice is theirs. The setting is provided. I have been amazed at how many people choose to go there (to that place where their conventional day-to-day is not). In fact, I did not have ecopsychology as a framing theory early on. I did not think of my role as therapy. I was, at first, a travel guide, one who was competent at leading a trip full of physical and social adventures. Adventures of the spirit were possibilities, but out of my main concern. So theory did not precede practice. Rather, I discovered the theory much later by asking questions that emerged from my practice of adventure guiding. Such questions include, why are so many people saying this has been the best experience of their lives? There is more to this adventure experience than superficially conceived. Why are these moments of intensity with the wilds so predominant within their journal writing? Why does stillness and space (space to be reflective and simply "to be") prove to be most valued? And are we not *remembering* a resonance within us, more so than connecting, acquiring, this resonance to nature? What I am trying to draw out seems already familiar even if the quality of resonance is felt in fleeting moments. Years of reading trip field notes (writing on the trip) and journals (writing following the trip) helped me come to the theory of ecopsychology and my role, reluctant at first, as "therapist" as much as educator. I was engaged in a form of wilderness reality therapy whether I wanted to or not, by the attention I had placed on meeting students' apparent vital needs.

From my experience with adventure education in wild settings I can comfortably concur with Duenkel and Scott; the leader can guide, and perhaps morally should guide, towards:

- dispelling the myth of dualism and encouraging the feeling that humans are part of, and not apart from the natural world;
- developing a sense of humility and grasping humans' insignificance in the greater scheme of things;
- awakening the perception of how our everyday constructed reality has removed people from the natural world, as well as from the nature within;
- moving towards a deeper understanding . . . of the underpinnings of environmental problems; and
- realizing that it is not a matter of putting an end to concepts such as "growth," "progress," and "success," but rather redefining them. From a deep ecological perspective "progress" would be redefined along the lines of achieving a means of coexistence with the natural world (1994, p. 43).

The adventure travel experience can, and I believe often does, become for people an opportunity to experience the adventure of these cultural possibilities. The trip then becomes exemplary of an engaging "withinness," counter-

ing dualities, an uplifting humility, an awakening critique, a deeper knowing and a renegotiating of life's meanings. Helping people draw out of themselves qualities that are within proves to be quite different than trying to offer to people something that they did not already have. Surfacing is an apt metaphor here. And once surfaced, the presence must be reckoned with and its surfacing becomes even more possible. The ecopsychology guiding mind-set works in subtle ways in the adventure education context to draw out the ancestral sensibilities within. Those early morning paddles become silent paddles. The evening campfire and star gaze become more important than tomorrow's agenda. The time to admire the raging rapids is valued along with decisions as to whether it is runnable. The cool, hard, ancient granite is celebrated at the top of the long hill climb.

How we dwell on the earth has emerged as central. Our work becomes cultural work and the place of practice in which we reside as adventure educators includes assumptions and practice of deep ecology and ecopsychology. In this place of practice, the earth is foundational but this assumes the necessary concurrent work with self and group. I discovered I was working in the domain of ecopsychology. The question remains: are you? Well, as an adventure educator, while the labels of ecopsychology and deep ecology may be new to you, the thinking and practice may not be new. If you believe our personal and cultural adventure must bring us closer toward our organic reality of living on this earth and we must reinterpret the dualistic cognitive process that creates detachments from self, other and place, then your general inquiry can bring you to ecopsychology and deep ecology. If you create learning objectives and curriculum activities that aspire to this, then you are practicing a "cultural work" for change. What you call yourself is less important.

I will finish with a passage from philosopher Alfred North Whitehead, who referred to adventure—the idea—as one of humanity's civilized virtues. Here *adventure* is a most general term. Adventure is a big idea, an idea that is well-suited to deep ecology and ecopsychology:

> Sometimes adventure is acting within limits. It can then calculate its ends, and reach it. Such adventures are the ripples of change within one type of civilization, by which an epoch of given type preserves its freshness.
>
> But given the vigor of adventure, sooner or later, the leap of imagination reaches beyond the safe limits of the epoch, and beyond the safe limits of learned rules of taste. It then produces the dislocation and confusions marking the advent of new ideals for civilized effort. . . .
>
> A race preserves its vigor so long as it harbors a real contrast between what has been

and what may be; and so long as it is nerved by the vigor to adventure beyond the safeties of the past.

Without adventure, civilization is in full decay. (Whitehead, 1947, p. 360)

The adventure of ecopsychology, an applied deep ecology, does mark the advent of new ideals for civilized effort: a big adventure for adventure education indeed. The first step isn't as simple as it sounds: Get outside!

References

Berman, M. (1981). *The reenchantment of the world.* Ithaca, NY: Cornell University Press.

Blake, W. (1997). Auguries of innocence. In D. Wall (Ed.), *Green history: A reader in environmental literature, philosophy, and politics.* London, UK: Routledge.

Cayley, D. (1991). *The age of ecology: The environment on CBC radio's ideas.* Toronto, Ontario: James Lorimer.

Chamberlin, C. (1997). The practice of citizenship as support for deep ecology. *The Trumpeter: Journal of Ecosophy, 14*(2), 82–85.

Devall, B., and Sessions, G. (1985). *Deep ecology: Living as if nature mattered.* Salt Lake City, UT: Gibbs Smith.

Duenkel, N., and Scott, M. (1994, October). Ecotourism's hidden potential: Altering perceptions of reality. *Journal of Physical Education, Recreation, and Dance,* pp. 40–44.

Glendinning, C. (1994). *My name is Chellis and I'm in recovery from Western civilization.* Boston, MA: Shambhala.

Greenway, R. (1995). Healing by the wilderness experience. In D. Rothenberg (Ed.), *Wild ideas.* Minneapolis, MN: University of Minnesota Press.

McLaughlin, A. (1993). *Regarding nature: Industrialism and deep ecology.* Albany, NY: State University of New York Press.

Naess, A. (1973). The shallow and the deep, long-range ecology movement. *Inquiry, 16,* 95–100.

Pivnick, J. (1997). A piece of forgotten song: Recalling environmental connections. *Holistic Education Review, 10*(4), 58–63.

Roszak, T. (1972). *Where the wasteland ends: Politics and transcendence in post industrial society.* New York, NY: Anchor Press/Doubleday.

Roszak, T. (1978). *Person/planet: The creative disintegration of industrial society.* Garden City, NY: Anchor Press/Doubleday.

Roszak, T. (1992). *The voice of the earth: An exploration of ecopsychology.* New York, NY: Simon and Schuster.

Shepard, P. (1982). *Nature and madness.* San Francisco, CA: Sierra Club.

Whitehead, A. N. (1947). *Adventures of ideas.* Cambridge, UK: Cambridge University Press.

Whitehead, A. N. (1972). In C. Hartshorne (Ed.), *Whitehead's philosophy: Selected essays 1935–1970.* Lincoln, NE: University of Nebraska Press.

Chapter 58

Navigating the Terrain:
Helping Care for the Earth

Randolph Haluza-Delay
Lakehead University

The true role of a teacher is not to take you anywhere, but to help you pay attention to where you already are.

—Beverly DeAngelo

I remember strolling Jasper's Skyline Trail high above timberline. A summer storm was blowing in fast. I moved speedily—shelter was a long way down the ridge. Huge raindrops pelted the dust of the path, the adjacent heather and me. I exulted, realizing the vitality that life knows when it is pressed by more elemental forces. "It is good to be alive!" I shouted dozens of times, emphasizing different words, bellowing it to the winds. Only when the hailstones reached a painful size did I seek shelter to watch dark clouds pass overhead and recede beyond the eastern ranges.

»«

At one time it was my morning habit to roll out of bed, pull on clothes and shoes, and take a morning walk. Up the neighborhood streets and down the alleyways I strolled as the seasons rolled through town. I watched the chickadees welcome back finches, sparrows and waxwings. When the trees budded, the sun began rising earlier than I did. Gentle summer breezes brought odors of garbage along with dogwood blossom. In winter the sometimes bitter chill kept the wood smoke settled thickly into the valley in which the city snuggled. My feet splashed throughout the year in rain puddles, new snow, blown newspapers and the varied hues of fallen leaves. I startled at barking dogs and lumbering garbage trucks. It was a prayerful, meditative time. And even here amidst the concrete and asphalt, there was natural space.

The stories presented here begin to describe what I mean by nature and environment. Although at first impression, "nature" is often associated with wild, undisturbed land, we should be keenly aware that no places are removed from the effects of human activity. Air pollution from coastal cities weakens trees in the high mountains and PCBs float into the Arctic from sources that are thousands of miles away.

The natural world seems to speak to me with a loud tongue. In going to natural settings such as the Skyline Trail, I am reminding myself that I too am a part of what is nature, recognizing anew the connection of myself with the rest of creation. But then I return home to live in a way that tries to reflect this "creaturely perspective." As an adventure educator, I hope that participants will develop a similar sense, and take home from the program a desire to care for the environment.

This chapter comes from my experience as a leader and administrator of adventure programs, from reflection of other practitioners and instructors, and from ethnographic research on a 12-day teen wilderness program (DeLay, 1996a). I speak from nearly 15 years leading adventure programs and teaching in the outdoors. I knew early in my career that I did not enjoy being merely an outdoor recreation leader. I wanted to teach *for* the natural environment instead of merely in it.

There is promise that adventure programs can reach this goal but there are barriers. I will first consider some of the barriers to the transfer of a sense of environmental care. Then some possible solutions to the obstacles will be addressed, with the ultimate aim of helping adventure program participants develop a meaningful and compassionate sense of place, linking care for the self, others and the environment. A beginning assumption of this chapter is that most adventure education is done outdoors, much of it in relatively natural or wilderness settings. The way individuals experience and think about the natural world is the critical landscape for environmental education on adventure programs.

The Promise of Wilderness Programs

A generally assumed benefit of outdoor adventure programs is that participants will develop a sense of environmental concern. For example, the mission statement of one adventure education program states that participants will learn "self-reliance, self-esteem, concern for others and care for the environment."[1] Another program emphasized development of "the three cares . . . care for self, care for others, and care for the earth."[2] This is an often unexamined assumption. Little research actually focuses on the role of adventure programs in promoting environmental action (Hanna, 1995).

Twenty years ago William Unsoeld, mountaineer and Outward Bound instructor, described one role of wilderness experience as promoting a type of "cosmic humility":

> A sense of ultimate dependence on forces outside our own . . . [that] straightens you up to look at the world with new eyes. The chance is of a truly compassionate existence . . . [and] an ultimate sense of joy at having a part in this complex world of ours. (Unsoeld, 1975)

There is eloquence in the argument of those who advocate the potential of wilderness programs to educate for the environment:

---

[1]Pacific Crest Outward Bound School, Portland, Oregon.

[2]Strathcona Wilderness Centre, Sherwood Park, Alberta.

Program participants witness their dependence upon the natural elements, and discover their natural kinship with, for example, squirrels and hawks. This is not some mystical pantheism but simply an opportunity for participants to see clearly the part of themselves that is a creature of the earth and to experience in all its simplicity and cruelty the natural struggle for survival. (Zook, 1986, p. 56)

Unfortunately, I doubt many programs approach such lofty goals. Sometimes I fear our wilderness leadership may do more to harm the cause of environmental care than to help it. Perhaps a final anecdote from a trip I helped lead a few years ago may help illustrate this fear:

> *The eight teens and two leaders had faced an August snowstorm, saw sun that streamed in rivers through rain clouds, shared lunch accidentally with a marmot, relished Rocky Mountain splendor, talked about wilderness and nature and even "belonging" to it, watched toads along the trail and shared 12 good days together. On the last day as we paddled toward the final destination, the teens argued about picking up group litter, discussed feeding Drano to sea gulls to watch them explode, and amused themselves with a dragonfly no longer able to fly well enough to escape their torments. And when they came home, the participants assumed nature was "out there," so there was no hope or need for care for the home environment.*

Barriers in the Terrain

There are barriers, both programmatic and societal, that hinder participants from transferring a sense of care for the wilderness environment to the very different environment at home. It cannot be assumed that participants are taking some sort of ethic of care for the environment home simply because they have spent time in an adventure program taking place outdoors. This broad list of barriers and the discussion that follows is not meant to be exhaustive. Furthermore, I have not meant to suggest that the entire field is guilty of some of the caricatures I have painted. Still, these are common elements of many adventure education programs that can serve as obstacles to the promotion of environmental care.

Leaders Trained in Technical Skills, Not Education

Most wilderness programs make claims about what participants will learn. Therefore, wilderness leaders must understand and implement appropriate educational principles. A body of knowledge and research about the educational effectiveness of experiential programs exists (Knapp, 1992; Riggins, 1986). From my experience, many practitioners do not have this knowledge. Leaders are often hired on the basis of technical skills needed to run an adventure program. These skills are learned through personal practice, or in recreation programs at postsecondary institutions where pedagogical principles are not taught. Although dedicated and capable in many ways, leaders may have only a rudimentary level of knowledge in the theory and practice of experiential and adventure education.

The program of a wilderness trip could be considered a curriculum (and is explicitly referred to as such by some organizations). The role of a leader in experiential programs is to provide opportunities for the participant to construct new knowledge. Curriculum theorists discuss the difference between the planned and the "lived curriculum." While leaders and teachers may have great hopes and a well-designed plan for what will be taught, this designed curriculum will not be what happens on the trip. As the program goes forward, leaders and participants create the real learning circumstances—"the lived curriculum." New experiences, old knowledge, and unintended messages are combined by the learners and participants to form new knowledge. Many of the barriers discussed later arise in this process of cocreating the lived curriculum.

Finally, understanding how people learn is helpful to teaching or leading wilderness experience. Experiential education is founded upon a process wherein the participant is responsible for his or her learning (Knapp, 1992). New knowledge is "constructed" by the participant through the experience, not because the trip leader taught it (DeLay, 1996b). This helps to explain how two participants can have very different outcomes from what is presumably the same experience. For example, if I have been convinced that the natural world is "dirty," I will have a different learning experience in the outdoors than someone excited to see bears. Still, leaders have an influence on this construction process by the way they set up and lead the program. Therefore, we have an obligation to help participants openly consider the world through which they travel. Finally, one of the knowledge sets adventure educators could develop is basic understanding of ecological processes.

Program Subculture Forms Counterproductive Norms

Adventure educators are facilitating experiences that are often powerful, involving small groups, and intense shared experiences. Each program can be called a mini-society, developing its own culture and having a powerful, but subtle effect on participants. The program or trip culture—of course, influenced by the bigger society—has its own ways of thinking about such things as the natural world, the group, lifestyle choices and values.

Since the aim of most adventure education programs is to provide a powerful experience, the influence of the developing group culture and its norms will be heightened. Program leaders must be aware of this influence and, keeping programmatic goals in mind, have a responsibility to guide the experience so that counterproductive group norms do not develop. Many of the barriers discussed later are examples of cultural norms that often form. For example, a focus on the group during a program could lead to an insistence that participants stick close together while hiking. This will mean the trail is more of a social experience than a chance to walk in the wilderness in quiet.

Emphasis on Activity

Adventure programs are usually oriented around outdoor pursuits. Whether these pursuits are hiking, climbing, whitewater rafting, ropes courses or some other activity, the underlying philosophy is similar. The outdoor environment is usually the setting for the activities—the "unique, unfamiliar physical setting" into which participants are placed and where they are off-balance enough to be challenged and learn (Walsh and Golins, 1976). To this way of thinking, the outdoor, natural setting is not valued for itself; it is a glorified playland. The natural world is objectified, used, the focus is on its utility for human purposes.

If the activity becomes the focus, the opportunity for attention to the natural setting is limited. I have led trips where we were so destination-focused, there was little time to watch the scenery, much less ponder the natural history of the toads that hopped along the trail, or our place in this environment. On other trips, the distances were so long and we were so tired at the end of the day that our eyes closed before we could watch the stars spin through the sky. I know we all missed something on such programs.

Secondly, wilderness programs are often focused on travel, which may weaken the connection with the place. Ethnographic researchers report locals sitting on the riverbank shaking their heads at the recreationists, so intent on their journey they barely notice the land around them (Raffan, 1992; Heine, 1995). Movement on the land becomes the tool through which the program provides experiences for the participants to learn from. For example, one of the founders of Outward Bound in North America stated "We teach *in* the mountains, not *for* them" (Miner, 1964). There are still elements of this view in the way many adventure programs are structured. This lack of opportunity to pay attention to the natural world through which the program moves sends a strong hidden message that the natural world is secondary and irrelevant.

Finally, because of the activities which we choose to utilize, adventure programs often use outdoor locations. But is this setting *necessary* for the outcomes desired in participants to be achieved? Are the unique qualities of the outdoors or natural world really being utilized or is it just a place for the important stuff—the activity? Could participants in an adventure therapy program get the same benefit from indoor climbing walls as from climbing on actual rock? To some extent, these are philosophical questions. But in a world where wilderness areas are declining, and are facing increased pressure from recreational use, we need to ask whether we really *need* to add to the use (and abuse) these places are experiencing. And if adventure programs are there, I would argue they do have a moral obligation to teach *for* the mountains (and rivers and forests), as well as *in* them.

Challenge May Turn the Natural World Into the Adversary

The challenge in an adventure program is one of the fundamental elements of the adventure education process. Since most often the challenge is mediated by the natural world—cold, rain, insects, uphills, dirt, whitewater, lack of showers, the dark, scary animals, uncomfortable ground to sleep on, and so on—the natural world could become the opponent, against which participants struggle. This is a strong criticism of adventure programs. Discomfort, adversity, and difficulty may turn people off, influencing participants' perceptions and relationships to the natural world.

A "conquer the mountains and find yourself" ethic is still heard in some program literature. Rather than work around it, some climbers are willing to yank out an in-the-way bush clinging to a rocky cleft. While employed at one program that worked primarily with troubled and incarcerated youth, a senior leader told me, "you take them out and hike the *hell* out of 'em." This philosophy is certainly not likely to encourage a positive environmental concern in participants.

Emphasis on the Group

Most adventure education programs are structured to focus on the interpersonal interactions of members of the program group. Hiking together, encouraging each other, daily evening circles, group decisions, and many other program elements make the social group an important part of the program experience. Maybe even the *most* important part of the experience. One instructor explained that he always used a candle for evening circles so that no one would be distracted by anything outside the group, including the stars! One of the cultural norms in the adventure program group I studied was that deliberate attention to nature was odd; participants were subtly encouraged to pay attention to the social interaction (DeLay, 1996a). As the program progressed and group members become more important to each other there is less wandering off, less spontaneous observations of their surroundings, more conversation. My experience is that wilderness trip participants pay more attention to the natural world when alone, or in small groups of pairs or trios. This may also explain why solitude experiences can be such a powerful program tool.

The interactions of participants with each other influence the experience of other elements of the program, including the natural world. When the social experience predominates the program, the natural world again becomes merely the backdrop for the human drama. The hidden curriculum or unintended message, again could be that the natural world is irrelevant. As we shall discuss later, this mirrors the predominant messages in our society.

Care for the Environment Is Limited to Practice of Minimum-Impact Camping Techniques

The inclusion of minimum-impact camping practices (sometimes known as *no-trace camping*) as a barrier to effective transfer of a sense of environmental care should surprise many outdoor educators. It is included here for two reasons. First, minimum-impact camping can be a method of distancing humans from the rest of the natural world during the wilderness experience. Secondly, the practice of minimum-impact camping is as far as many programs go to discuss environmental care, and may hinder a sense of care for the home environment.

Most outdoor adventure programs practice some form of minimum-impact camping. The intent is to minimize the human effect on the wilderness environment by staying on trails, using backpacker stoves rather than gathering firewood, burying fecal matter carefully, sleeping on foam mats and in synthetic sleeping bags rather than cut pine boughs. Some programs go to heroic measures to eliminate human trace in the backcountry. One effect is to move the impact elsewhere, i.e., the gas refineries and factories that turn petroleum into nylon and plastic. Another effect is to suggest that humans and their activity have no place in the wilderness. We are visitors, who do not remain, and who (almost) should not be here. This probably reinforces the notion that humans are not part of nature, as we shall discuss later. It certainly means we encounter the natural world on our terms and do not rely on it for any of our needs. Wilderness travelers mediate their relationship with the natural environment through food from the supermarket, warmth from a sleeping bag, shelter from a colorful waterproof nylon covering.

Minimum-impact camping may be as far as some wilderness programs go in considering environmental concerns. However, wilderness areas are affected by human actions that transcend wilderness boundaries. These include air pollution, noise pollution, light pollution, aircraft overflight, wildlife displacement, and damagingly heavy recreational use. In addition, wilderness users driving long distances from their home to the recreational site use large amounts of fossil fuels. These are issues of environmental ethics and practice. Furthermore, most outdoor adventure pursuit participation is a privilege reserved for those who have the economic resources or time to develop the skills, get the gear and get out there.

Helping participants make sense of how to care for the environment at their homeplace is a step that many adventure programs miss. We rarely talk about "minimum-impact lifestyles," for example. Research in environmental education shows that even individuals motivated to protect the environment must understand the action steps they could take (Hines, Hungerford, and Tomera, 1986). Simpson (1993) describes how wilderness programs that imply minimum-impact camping as following certain rules actually could inhibit participants from developing their own environmentally ethical behavior.

No-trace camping heroics reinforce a certain notion of nature as a place "out there" away from home. This barrier will be discussed in detail later. However, by expecting a more stringent ethic in the backcountry than in the places where we live, adventure programs may unwittingly teach participants that environmental care at home is not possible. In a queerly anthropocentric fashion, minimum-impact camping makes humans and every human trace the bad boys on the wilderness block—we don't belong, and our presence is the environmental problem. If this ethic was transferred directly back to the nonwilderness environment a logical extension would be fatalistic—that the earth's environment will not improve until humanity is gone.

The Notion That Nature Is "Out There"

I started this chapter with my own tales of connecting with the natural world, consciously suggesting that nature is not just to be found in the spectacular and pristine—majestic peaks, raging rivers, towering old growth forests. However, wilderness programs may help participants form or reinforce the more prevalent image. Talking with the teen participants of a 12-day program in the weeks and months following their experience, it was clear that their perception was that nature is "out there," not here at home. Nature was in the unfamiliar environments where there are no people, it is undisturbed and lacks human development, where a sense of peace and freedom reigns (DeLay, 1996a). Conversely, the implication for these participants was that there is little or no nature where they live, and that their home environment was too damaged for care of the environment to make a meaningful impact. As one participant said to me, "I recycle here, but to me it's a lost cause. Picking up garbage will make it look nice, but it can't help the plants to grow." In this construction of nature and the environment, the individuals mirror the dominant views of nature and civilization that our society tends to hold.

Another strong criticism of adventure programs is whether any awareness developed through a wilderness trip in another environment will transfer to the participant's home setting (Raffan, 1990). If participants form such extreme either-or constructions of their home environment and the wilderness as described here, this criticism would seem valid for a great many programs. On the other hand, it is intuitively possible that people who have a positive experience in one natural environment might begin to develop an emotive bond with nature as a whole, and therefore with their home environment.

The Nature-Civilization Duality of Our Society

Many commentators have described the world-view, or way of thinking, that dominates our society and influences each of us. This world-view is dualistic, separating categories into careful boxes, and segregating humans, civilization and human culture from nature and wilderness. According to most cultural observers, we in the Western world of Europe and North America hold as a fundamental belief that humans are not part of the natural world, and that the natural world is something to be controlled (Merchant, 1980; Nash, 1967). Some of the other barriers listed previously are small-scale reflections of this larger, societal attitude.

Wilson (1991) offers a comprehensive look at the North American attitude towards nature, land, wilderness and the environment. Since the end of World War II, he writes, there have been two primary forms of land use: either total preservation or total development. The construction of nature described in the last section as developed by teen participants on an adventure program reflects this dichotomy. Nature and civilization were mutually exclusive realities that adventure programs do not blur. The contrast between the two worlds may be even more potent for participants who have had more outdoor, wilderness experience. I have certainly heard this language of "nature" and "civilization" used on many trips by both participants and leaders. This is a deep-seated barrier that penetrates further than the adventure education field. The problem for leaders in helping participants develop a meaningful environmental ethic and lifestyle is that a change of mind-set is needed to overcome this barrier, not just increasing comfort in outdoor settings.

Directions for Navigation

An adventure education program, taking participants to unfamiliar physical and social environments, is ideally suited to help participants (re)consider their place in the world. By this I mean both their personal role(s) as well as physical location. Adventure program participants occasionally describe sense of connection to the natural world on the program. This implies that the personal growth of the person was pulled into some relationship with this thing called nature. An individual's awareness and moral vision may widen through the reflection that follows a powerful experience. This is the compassionate sense of place, a mindful sense of the connectedness between self, others and the broader world.

Leading an adventure program to enhance the growth and development of participants is a difficult task. Given the many objectives that adventure programs attempt to cover, helping participants transfer a sense of care for the environment home from the wilderness is even more difficult. This is challenging terrain since the way individuals experience and think about the natural world can vary so greatly even within a presumably similar experience. Commitment to successfully navigate this terrain will involve several components.

Addressing the Program

Leaders need to consider carefully how the program structure and their leadership sends messages to participants. Although participants are ultimately responsible for their learning, leaders will have a large influence on the group norm formation, especially in the initial stages. Careful consideration must be given to the programmatic goals. Reviewing the program elements and leadership to ensure alignment with these goals is helpful. Due to their experience and role, leaders have a responsibility to help form or constrain the possible constructions that participants may be developing. For example, leaders do not act passive in the face of a poorly functioning team; neither should they be inactive in helping participants form an appropriate relationship with the environment through which the program travels.

Leaders can watch that counterproductive norms, for example the generalization that the natural world is the adversary or enemy of the individuals on the program, do not form. They should beware of an overemphasis on the activities of the program. Leaders could act to ensure that the time together is not just a social or group experience, to the exclusion of other benefits, by planning opportunities for interaction with the natural world as carefully as they plan opportunities for group sharing, challenging activities or other program elements. Adventure educators should also scrutinize their marketing efforts to ensure that what is being promised is accurate and does not contribute to inappropriate participant expectations. Marketing materials are another opportunity to educate participants.

There are excellent examples of program design in adventure programs that enhance the relationship with the natural world and the transfer of environmental care. LaChapelle (1991) describes her program's emphasis on working with the natural environment, discovering concordance and growth through harmony rather than a "conquer the mountain" mentality. Brown (1989) described a

transformational process, elements of which I have used on adventure programs, to help participants move beyond themselves in self-awareness and relationship with the natural world. Other ideas include:

- Allow and encourage participants to leave the campsite or group and explore apart from the other participants. Provide opportunities to be alone.
- Deemphasize the group experience with specific planning to counteract the tendency to stay in the group.
- Plan the program to include less activity, or shorter distances. Ensure that the amount of time spent on program elements corresponds to the objectives of the program.
- Empower individuals to act on their own. This is an important personal characteristic for participants in order to take action for environmental care when they return home.
- Focus end of program debriefings forward into the journey home, rather than backwards in review of the program. This will aid the participant in making a connection between learning on the program and applying the knowledge at home. Help participants see what they can do to care for the home environment.

Training of adventure educators must also include basic knowledge of ecological principles and activities that will help participants connect to the natural world. Staff training that focuses on technical skills, safety, reflection and facilitation without equal time given to the teaching of environmental awareness sends a message to staff, which gets passed on to participants, that sensitivity to the natural world is not particularly important.

Developing Sensitivity to the Natural World, Wherever It May Be Found

The importance of regular exposure to the natural world from an early age to the development of environmental concern has been shown by many studies (Tanner, 1980). Since the natural world tends to be relegated to a taken-for-granted backdrop for human activity rather than a player in the drama, sensitivity to the natural world must be developed in participants. Youth without a social scheme that supports attention to nature on the trip or environmental concern at home are not likely to go against social standards that see these interests as irrelevant. It cannot be assumed that deliberate attention to the natural world will occur in the ordinary course of events during an adventure program. Therefore, leaders should specifically plan program time within the activity framework to promote the connection of the participant and the natural world.

The natural world can be fascinating, unfamiliar and mysterious—a place to explore! And since the natural world is so taken-for-granted, participants will probably have to be encouraged and even taught how to observe. Exploration of the small wonders as well as the spectacular is a strategy that helps break stereotypes of nature, especially since this will be more similar to the natural world participants would likely find at their homeplace. Magnifying glasses can make insects, leaves and the inner workings of flowers become alive with detail. Observe children when you can. Their fascination with the tiny wonders of their world is an example for us. While adults are focusing on far off mountains and magnificent scenery, children are playing with pinecones and looking for neat pebbles (Nabhan and Trimble, 1995). Other ideas include:

1. Provide opportunity for solitude experiences, self-reflection and observation of the natural world. Options in a "bag of tricks" include solitude time, nature walks, scavenger hunts, 100-centimeter hikes (micro hikes), nature identification, or activities from Project Wild or other environmental education resources. Cornell (1979) is an excellent resource that I have found useful for all populations.
2. Participation on adventure programs can be challenging or uncomfortable. Help participants manage their psychological discomfort. Assist them in investigating the source of their discomfort. Is it the natural setting or a part of themselves?
3. Discuss with participants how they might explore the environment at home. Awaken participants to the possibility that they may see things at home in a new light.
4. Discuss the feelings that nature produces. Especially if the feelings are positive, encourage consideration of how individuals could recapture these feelings at home. As one example of a questioning strategy, the sequence below led to one of the most intense discussions I have witnessed on this subject among teens:

   • What are the feelings you have in nature?
   • What do you mean by relaxed, at peace?
   • Why is it different than the feeling you have at home?
   • How could you recapture these feelings at home?
   • Why is home so different in feeling?
   • Where do you have nature at home?
   • Why isn't there nature there? (Sic)

• What can you do to make home more like here then?

(This discussion does beg a broader philosophical question: why do we have a tendency to associate a sense of peace and relaxation with natural environments?)

In my own outdoor program leadership, I try to help people connect broadly to nature in general, rather than the specific location. We do learn some of the natural history of the area, but I take the view that a person appreciates the symphony better when he or she understands something about classical music. Even on recreationally oriented adventure programs leaders may find that after breaking through initial barriers, participants will find paying deliberate attention to the natural world enjoyable. It becomes a change in pace to the often frenetic level of activity on wilderness programs, and a respite from the social experience.

Addressing the Nature-Civilization Dichotomy

The nature-civilization dichotomy is counterproductive to developing an ethic of care for the environment where humans live. If the dichotomy is maintained, it seems participants will have little motivation to take care of the environment at home. On the other hand, for many trip participants, this dichotomy accurately describes the world in which they live. In addressing the nature-civilization dichotomy, the emphasis must be on blurring rigid boundaries and modifying the notion that there is no nature at home.

Simpson (1993) suggests that minimum-impact camping practices could be a vehicle for teaching broader environmental ethics. His process moves from following specific rules, to understanding reasons for specific practices, to participants making their own choices in varying ecological conditions, including a nonbackcountry setting. Leaders may still face participant opinions that the wilderness is a far different reality with a set of norms that do not have any application to their home reality. Other ideas include:

• Discuss the notion of a minimum-impact lifestyle at home. Why does it seem a tougher code of environmental care is expected (and followed!) in the backcountry than in the places we live?
• Review with the participants the connections between this outdoor place, especially wilderness areas, and human habitations. Air pollution and wind patterns, disturbance in animal migration, land use on the edge of

wilderness boundaries, economic growth and consumerism driving resource extraction are possible topics to show participants that this place and home are not so disconnected.

- Address the apparent dichotomy straight on with participants. "Are you part of nature? How do you care for something of which you are a part?"
- Be careful about reinforcing the dichotomy. Reconsider what language or thought patterns are more a part of the dominant, familiar society than of the outdoor setting. Examples would include talk of conquering or overuse of clock time rather than diurnal rhythms.

Leaders need to help the group members balance their needs for comfort and familiarity without letting the more familiar become primary. It seems possible that the more participants maintain of the old routines, the less they would attune to the rhythms and patterns of living in this new reality of the wilderness. Finally, program advertising could also be scrutinized as to whether it tends to objectify the natural world or use it as a means to an end. Ultimately, far deeper societal change needs to happen then adventure education programs will be able to effect, but outdoor experiential programs can be an effective starting place.

Developing Programs Appropriate to the Home Context

The field of outdoor education could reorient and be more effective in helping individuals connect to their homeplace. More adventure programs that do not take people to pristine wilderness could be encouraged. Obviously, part of the appeal of many adventure programs is the opportunity to experience this type of environment, but program developers could include a section in other environments, even in heavily human-impacted areas. People can be helped to look for wild nature at home, not as just "out there" in the spectacular and wilderness places.

The true ecological hero is not the raging activist or back-to-nature "granola." Instead, this hero is the one who, in a thousand different ways on a daily basis, quietly lives out his or her values, taking the extra attention to acting in an ecologically aware way. Not many will notice these actions or give credit, nor does this hero expect it. This is personal character, something that adventure programs are very good at emphasizing. Individual action is a start to overcoming societal structures that encourage waste, consumerism, overuse of resources and environmental degradation; personal character can begin to make a difference. Helping individuals feel they can do something in their own life circumstances is vital. Other ideas include:

- Address nature at home. It is the foundation for all life. Even city dwellers breathe oxygen that has just been recirculated by green plants, share carbon molecules with other organic creatures, and drink water that had to come from somewhere. Explore these connections.
- Encourage close exploration of the small items rather than just the spectacular. Remystify the city. Look for beauty and mystery in blades of grass poking through sidewalk cracks, sparrows, and frost on window panes. The challenge is to make the familiar sufficiently unfamiliar to invoke the sense of curiosity that we all had as children.
- Participants often have a sense that "nature" has a sense of peace that "civilization" does not. Develop "urban solos" and other programs to help participants explore their inner world and recover this feeling as part of a holistic connection to place and a genuine sense of self.

Part of the challenge is to break through the feeling of futility that many people have when it comes to social change or environmental protection. Adventure programs can overcome this hurdle through their traditional emphasis on participants' rising to the challenges they face. By using effective experiential techniques leaders help individuals construct knowledge relevant to their lives.

Charting the Inner Landscape —A Compassionate Sense of Place

Adventure programs need to critically address dominant social constructions of nature, environment and the human "place." The two anecdotes with which this chapter began are an attempt to address for myself the questions of what is nature and how do I relate to this world. How people understand the land is the study of geography. Within that discipline the human geographers use the term *sense of place* to describe the notion of attachment to the land or place. Raffan (1992) characterizes sense of place as "meaning a quality of space that lives in the minds and emotions of people who live there" (p. 21). Sense of place is part of the inner landscape of the individual.

Humans are part of the earth's ecological community; therefore, it seems reasonable to suggest that we have a need for close relations with the natural world. Bob Henderson's chapter on ecopsychology and deep ecology earlier in this book addresses this topic at more length. Caring for self, others and the earth are inextricably bound together in the personal growth and sense of being that adventure educators hope to encourage in participants.

Personal growth must have a direction, otherwise, it is just change. Compassion gives a direction. Sense of place also needs direction. Wilderness programs can be a powerful experience. They are good at providing an experiential identification with what participants have encountered. The next step is to move to an identification with the whole and, thus, appreciation of each part. As Doug Aberley (1993, p. 53) wrote:

> My need *now* is for my own "sense of place" which depends not simply on discovering my own neighborhood, community or local region, but upon seeing the relationship of my own local places to every other place on the planet. I need a sense of my whole planet, of my continent, and the major subparts of my continent in order to see how my local places are parts of these wider regions of natural life and human living.

Raffan's criticism of adventure programs, especially those in wilderness, is that a sense of place, as specific to a particular location, may not transfer to the participants' homeplace. The wider connection exemplified by Aberley may be the route by which outdoor education needs to go. Outdoor programs that take people from their home environs into a wilderness setting may need to concentrate on broader constructs of "nature" in order to help participants transfer any attachment that begins to form during the program. The topic of sense of place has been less studied among nonresidents of a place, but I would argue that even nonresidents or travelers can have an attachment to the land (Cuthbertson, Heine, and Whitson, 1996). Outdoor instructors, many of whom are dedicated to care for the environment, are among the most itinerant groups in our population.

Conscious effort is needed to help participants connect with their home milieu. By helping participants find wild nature close to home, instead of just in the spectacular and wild places, adventure educators help them maintain the reflective awareness and sense of wholeness that is at the root of a compassionate sense of place which consciously links care of self, others and the earth.[3]

Beringer (1990) suggests that youth (and others) need to establish a sense of being, based in a sense of place that encompasses both their location in the social scheme of things as well as a connection with particular places. Other environmental educators have also mentioned the close relationship between knowing one's self and bonding with the natural world. In Horwood's (1991, p. 25) words, a sense of one's identity is an "antidote for alienation." Knowing oneself increases bonds of identification with the

world, he writes, summarizing the deep ecological formulation of self-realization. Alienation involves distorted relations with self, others and place.

I have assumed that the caring for the earth involves a sense of one's place in it. A popular artist earlier in the decade sang, "Hear me asking, where do I belong . . . [I'm] looking . . . for my place in the world, my place in the world" (Smith, 1993). The connotation is that knowing where we belong in relation with other things around us is part of knowing who we are.

A compassionate sense of place links the person and his or her surroundings. From it flows a desire to make relationships more full and genuine, including relationships with the whole earth, linking ecological sensitivity in a web of concerns. Care for others logically includes care for the air we all breathe, or providing healthy, unpoisoned food and water for others to consume. A compassionate sense of place goes even further to extend moral consideration to the planet upon which we depend. Although there are potential barriers, adventure programs would seem to be ideally situated to help participants develop a compassionate sense of place, since such programs often promote care for self and others.

Conclusion

Alberta's Matterhorn-like Mt. Assiniboine towered above the lake and reflected in it. Clouds whipped around the summit and billowed over the ridge. The teens wandered around the lake high in the mountains. JJ, usually gregarious, chose to ramble alone along a creek tumbling across the rocks. He came back unusually contemplative and philosophical. Weeks later he told me he had thought about "how it came to be" and that he felt connected to nature at that time. "It was like you were supposed to be there your whole life," he mused.

The outdoors provides a chance for me to think and breathe deeply while my body gets worked. I return from the wilderness refreshed and re-created, and with a greater motivation to care for the earth and people. I also seek these opportunities in the built environments where I, like most people, have spent most of my life. I realize anew that we are part of the environment—that web of interrelationships between all biotic and abiotic elements.

Ecologically sensitive lifestyles include understanding our place on the earth and living in the land and according to the guidance of ecological integrity. Even in the built environments of city and suburb we still feel wind, breathe air, drink water that flows through the hydrological cycle. Wilson (1991, p. 87) concludes that the environmental movement must "directly engage the social debate

---

[3]The term *compassionate sense of place* was coined by Brent Cuthbertson, dissertation in progress, University of Alberta.

for the culture of nature—the ways we think, teach, talk about and construct the natural world—is as important a terrain for struggle as the land itself." Nature is not just a backdrop upon which humans act out the dramas of *our* history. The natural world is something that entwines through our very existence as human beings.

While there may be barriers within an adventure program that need to be overcome in order to help participants take a sense of care for the earth home from the outdoor or wilderness environment, these are also opportunities to more effectively care for self, others and the earth. If adventure educators are to lead programs in the forests, mountains, oceans, rivers, and other natural environments, they have a moral obligation to also teach for their protection and help participants care for the earth after they come home from the wilderness.

References

Aberley, D. (Ed.). (1993). *Boundaries of home: Mapping for local empowerment.* Gabriola Island, British Columbia: The New Catalyst Bioregional Series, New Society Publishers.

Beringer, A. (1990). Understanding moral development and environmental values through experience. *Journal of Experiential Education, 13*(3), 29–34.

Brown, M. B. (1989). Transpersonal psychology: Facilitating transformation in outdoor experiential education. *Journal of Experiential Education, 12*(3), 47–56.

Cornell, J. B. (1979). *Sharing nature with children.* Nevada City, CA: Amanda Publications.

Cuthbertson, B., Heine, M., and Whitson, D. (1996). *Producing meaning through movement: An alternative view of sense of place.* Presentation at The Learneds Societies, Montreal, Quebec.

DeLay, R. B. (1996a). *Constructing the uninhabited home: Participants' experience of nature during and following a wilderness trip.* Unpublished master's thesis, University of Alberta, Edmonton, Alberta.

DeLay, R. B. (1996b). Forming knowledge: Constructivist theory and experiential learning. *Journal of Experiential Education 19*(2), 76–81.

Hanna, G. (1995). Wilderness-related environmental outcomes of adventure and ecology education programming. *Journal of Environmental Education, 27*(1), 21–32.

Hines, J. M., Hungerford, H. R., and Tomera, A. N. (1986). Analysis and synthesis of research on responsible environmental behavior: A meta-analysis. *Journal of Environmental Education, 18*(2), 1–8.

Horwood, B. (1991). Tasting the berries: Deep ecology and experiential education. *Journal of Experiential Education, 14*(3), 21–26.

Knapp, C. E. (1992). *Lasting lessons: A teacher's guide to reflecting on experience.* Charleston, WV: ERIC.

LaChapelle, D. (1991). Educating for deep ecology. *Journal of Experiential Education, 14*(3), 18–22.

Merchant, C. (1980). *The death of nature.* New York, NY: Harper and Row.

Miner, J. L. (1964). Is our youth going soft? *Princeton Alumni Weekly, XLIV,* 14.

Nabhan, G. P., and Trimble, S. (1995). *The geography of childhood: Why children need wild places.* Boston, MA: Beacon Press.

Nash, R. (1967). *Wilderness and the American mind* (2nd ed.). New Haven, CT: Yale University Press.

Raffan, J. (1990). The failed curriculum. *Journal of Experiential Education, 13*(3), 47–49.

Raffan, J. (1992). *Frontier, homeland and sacred space: A collaborative investigation into cross-cultural perceptions of place in the Thelon Game Sanctuary, Northwest Territories.* Unpublished doctoral dissertation, Queen's University, Kingston, Ontario (ERIC microfilm ED-356 937).

Riggins, R. D. (1986). Effective learning in adventure-based education: Setting directions for future research. *Journal of Environmental Education, 18*(1), 1–6.

Simpson, S. (1993). The intrinsic value of minimum impact. *Journal of Experiential Education, 16*(2), 34–37.

Smith, M. W. (1993). Place in the world. On *First decade* [CD]. New York, NY: BMG Records.

Unsoeld, W. (1975). *Keynote address* [personal audiotape]. American Association of Physical Education Recreation and Dance conference, St. Paul, Minnesota.

Tanner, T. (1980). Significant life experiences: A new research area for environmental education. *Journal of Environmental Education, 11*(4), 20–24.

Walsh, V., and Golins, G. (1976). *The exploration of the Outward Bound process.* Denver, CO: Colorado Outward Bound School.

Wilson, A. (1991). *The culture of nature.* Toronto, Ontario: Between the Lines.

Zook, L. (1986). Outdoor adventure builds character five ways. *Parks and Recreation, 21*(1), 54–57.

Chapter 59

Enhancing Spiritual Experience
in Adventure Programs

Rebecca Fox
Griffith University

[F]ew of us know how to gently approach the mysteries and wonder of nature, to find real simplicity in the wilds, to set the stage for an experience of the eternal, the infinite, the ineffable. With few exceptions, organizations that lead people into wild country simply hope that such special experiences will occur, for these are the moments we remember and cherish most. We know we are moved by our experiences in nature, but few of us can really articulate how or why. (Brown, 1988, p. 5)

It is believed that experiential and adventure education provides many opportunities for personal development through social, physical and mental challenges. However, very little is known about the effects of adventure and wilderness experiences on spiritual development. This chapter will discuss the importance of spiritual health and wellness, introduce past research in wilderness spiritual experience, and recommend program strategies to enhance spiritual opportunities in wilderness and adventure education.

Key Terms and Their Definitions

Some key terms that require definition are *spirituality, spiritual experience* and *spiritual growth*. The definition of spirituality has been attempted by many writers, and is often associated with religion. However, spirituality is not necessarily synonymous with religious experience (McDonald and Schreyer, 1991). For the purpose of this chapter, *spirituality* is defined as an altered state of consciousness where an individual may experience a higher sense of self, inner feelings, inner knowledge, awareness and attainment to the world and one's place in it, knowledge of personal relations and the relationship to the environment, or a belief in a power greater than imaginable.

Spiritual experience is associated with moments of transcendence and spiritual enchantment. Feelings of enrapture characterize these transcendent episodes and include experiences of sudden awakenings, something inexplicable, or something of natural beauty. Recent research (Fox, 1996; Stringer and McAvoy, 1992) suggests that *spiritual experiences* are triggered through events which are enhanced by nature, self-awareness and group interaction.

Spiritual growth is defined as delayed awareness arising from spiritual experience. As McDonald (et al., 1988, cited in McDonald and Schreyer, 1991, p. 189) suggest, spiritual growth:

> occurs over a period of time, but may include sudden experiences of insight and understanding. . . . This awareness impacts individuals to the degree that their view of their life-world is changed, reflecting the new awareness we labeled "spiritual growth."

Spiritual growth, by definition, requires a change (in awareness), which is rarely planned or calculated.

Spiritual Health and Wellness

There is an increasing awareness for the need of adventure programs to address the spiritual health and wellness of clientele. Many authors suggest that spirituality and one's spirit are generally ignored in programs (Bretenstein and Ewert, 1990; Sabo and Davis, 1990). Often there is a preference for the physical challenges, social skills, interpersonal communications and pursuit competence. Outdoor and experiential practitioners are focusing less on the spiritual side of participants, and are therefore dismissing the holistic approach of adventure education, focusing on the integration of the mind, body and spirit.

Chandler, Holden, and Kolander (1992) suggest that health is divided into six interrelating and functional properties: spiritual, emotional, social, intellectual, occupational and physical health. In their Holistic Wellness Model, shown in Figure 59.1, spiritual health is not separated from the five other dimensions of wellness. The spiritual component is strongly interrelated, and a central dimension for the overall wellness of an individual. It is suggested that "without attention to spiritual health in each dimen-sion, the individual remains incomplete" (Chandler et al., 1992, p. 171).

Practitioners within the fields of psychology, sociology and education are including spiritual health in their programs as a means of healing self and encouraging optimal health and well-being for their clientele (Prest and Keller, 1993; Szilagyi, 1996).

Characteristics of Spirituality in Wilderness and Adventure Education

Experiences defined as spiritual may occur in a number of settings, both natural and human-constructed, but natural environments have been utilized in the past and the present day to escape everyday life and routine, retreat to a place of solitude, and to gain spiritual insight.

Spirituality, or the notion of spiritual, outside of the theological context, has been regarded as hard-to-define, or in many cases seems vague. However, most *anecdotal* accounts discuss the following characteristic qualities of spirituality:

1. *Spirituality as a fundamental aspect of human nature.* Maslow (1971) introduced spirituality as a concept relating to human beings and contended that spirituality is part of every person. Chandler et al. (1992) further suggest that spirituality is innate to all human beings, and is the part of human beings that needs attention and fostering as much as the mind and the body.

2. *Spirituality as a sense of mystery.* Spirituality has a power or essence greater than oneself. Spirituality involves a sense of mystery about the world and the things that exceed our analysis or understanding, and a belief in a power greater than oneself (Henderson, 1993). Spiritual experience is latent in everyone and under certain conditions is awakened within us, or "triggered" as Maslow (1971) suggests. This can be interpreted as self-actualization. These sudden awakenings are also described as mystical or mystic visions.

3. *Spirituality as the sense of awe or wonderment.* Wilderness settings contribute to a sense of wonder, humility, and connectedness to nature. Awe and wonder are often the first emotions individuals develop when they encounter something new. After wonder, people move to other emotions such as love, joy, elatedness or sadness as more is discovered about the object of attention.

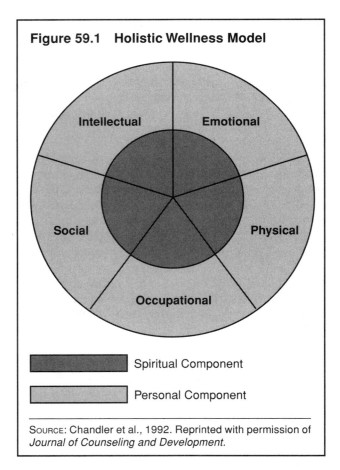

Figure 59.1   Holistic Wellness Model

- Intellectual
- Emotional
- Social
- Physical
- Occupational

■ Spiritual Component

□ Personal Component

Source: Chandler et al., 1992. Reprinted with permission of *Journal of Counseling and Development*.

4. *Spirituality as the belief in the connectedness or sense of oneness toward people, self, and all things.* The common denominators of a sense of spirituality include a sense of purpose in life, and a belief in a connectedness to people and all earthly things. Wilderness has a potentially extraordinary rich source of milieus—experiences which tend to promote health and well-being. Milieus include a sense of unity with nature, and a sense of oneness with earth.

In nature, one may become immersed in the elements, and listen to inner thoughts, become reflective and contemplative and may feel a union with nature, impressed with its complexity and scale. Through inner journeys and time alone one may experience a sense of revitalization and connection to self, life's priorities, and sense of self-importance and self-enlightenment (Henderson, Bialeschki, Shaw, and Freysinger, 1989).

5. *Spirituality as aesthetic beauty.* Wilderness areas provide natural beauty, space, expansive views, color, and different formations and shapes that contribute to the visual opportunities for aesthetic delight. These beauties of nature often promote transcendence, or peak experiences, where people may experience, through the beauty and aesthetic values of nature, the simplicity, peacefulness and timelessness of wilderness.

6. *Spirituality as transcendent.* Phillip Phenix (1974, p. 8) interprets the sense of connectedness with nature as the "transcendent;" referring to the experience as limitless, going beyond any given state or realization of being. Transcendence can be unlimited, giving ultimate meaning, or go beyond natural realms and the essential being.

7. *Spirituality as peak experience.* Spirituality and its transient moments are compared to Maslow's (1968) theory of peak experience. Transient moments induce self-actualization, in which long-lasting cognitive changes may take place. Peak experiences are also experiences that are meaningful, unimaginable, infinite, awakening, and give one an insight into revelation, to the sacred, and sense of the overwhelming. Other terms that categorize particular aspects of peak or spiritual experience are amazement, humility, uniqueness, loss of fear, and great moments of truth.

8. *Spirituality as creating a sense of inner peace, oneness and strength.* Common themes expressed about spirituality include the inner feelings of peace, oneness, strength, sublime, reverence, hope, joy, calm, exaltation and happiness.

9. *Wilderness as a spiritual attraction.* Spiritual needs attract people toward wilderness experiences. Spiritual needs are identified as escape from routine and stress; need to relax; need for the stimulation of beauty, adventure and wonder; or need to be renewed and get back in touch with nature. Wilderness gives the chance to overcome problems, to get in touch with self and nature. Being in wilderness enhances immediacy of thought and observation, and time in wilderness may lead to spiritual experience.

Research Into Wilderness Spiritual Experience

If spiritual experiences are to be a purposeful element of adventure programs, then there is a need to know more about spirituality in general, and specifically about spiritual experiences in the context of wilderness adventure activities. (Stringer and McAvoy, 1992, p. 13)

Experiential and adventure educators are often concerned about the education of the whole person: mind, body and spirit. While there is solid research on spirituality and its related fields of theology and religion, there has been little research done on the spiritual experiences induced by wilderness exposure, even though spiritual experiences are desired or assumed to occur in adventure education programs.

Recently, in a welcome review of nature-spirituality links Driver and Ajzen (1996, pp. 431–439) highlighted the essential research needs to better understand spiritual experience in nature-based settings. They also recognized the difficulty associated with researching "hard-to-define" human experiences, and stressed the importance of qualitative measures for identifying and defining specific dimensions of spiritual experience. Significant recent qualitative studies include research conducted by Stringer (Stringer, 1990; Stringer and McAvoy, 1992) and Fox (1996, 1997). Their findings are discussed, with a view to better understanding wilderness spiritual experience: its characteristic processes and benefits.

Stringer (Stringer, 1990; Stringer and McAvoy, 1992) designed a study to explore wilderness spiritual experience through in-depth interviews with 26 adventure education participants comprising a combination of people with disabilities and able persons. The key research questions were associated with defining spiritual experience and exploring the nature of such experiences and factors that may have contributed to them.

Stringer's results suggested that spiritual experience was defined differently by each individual, but encompassed the following common attributes:

- the shared or common spirit between and among people,
- a power or authority greater than self,
- clarity of inner (or self) knowledge,
- inner feelings (especially of peace, oneness, and strength),
- awareness of and attainment to the world and one's place in it,
- the way in which one relates to fellow humans and to the environment, and
- intangibility. (Stringer and McAvoy, 1992, p. 16)

Attributes of spirituality and associated emotions and feelings of spiritual experience that emerged from the research are highlighted in Figure 59.2.

They also found that the nature of spiritual experiences was mostly associated with the development of group closeness and strong interconnections with individuals in the group. Exposure to the natural environment and its unique beauty also triggered spiritual experience. Contributing factors that enhanced or inhibited spiritual experience were numerous (as shown in Figure 59.3) but mainly centered around the group's level of cohesiveness, prior personal experience, time constraints, and being in the natural environment.

Research by Fox (1996) endeavored to further comprehend spirituality and spiritual experience induced from wilderness exposure, and also aimed to develop a better understanding of the process and outcomes of wilderness

---

Figure 59.2 Attributes, Emotions and Feelings Associated with Spiritual Experience

Attributes or characteristics of spirituality:

- awareness,
- human interconnectedness,
- attunement,
- inner feelings,
- connection or relation to a greater power and/or deity,
- inner self-knowledge,
- faith or beliefs,
- inner strength,
- sense of wholeness or oneness,
- sense of peace and tranquility,
- values,
- intangibility, and
- shared or common spirit.

Emotions and feelings associated with spirituality:

- accomplishment,
- optimism,
- exuberance,
- calmness,
- quietness,
- gentleness,
- clarity,
- security,
- hope,
- curiosity,
- tranquility,
- joy,
- equilibrium,
- warmth,
- oneness,
- exhilaration,
- awe,
- peace,
- fear,
- centeredness,
- reverence,
- happiness,
- contentment,
- serenity,
- humbleness,
- empowerment,
- trust,
- majesty,
- excitement, and
- wonder.

SOURCE: Stringer and McAvoy, 1992, p. 16. Reprinted with permission of the authors.

Figure 59.3 Factors Contributing to or Inhibiting Spiritual Experiences

Contributing factors:

- prior awareness of one's own spirituality;
- camaraderie or the unusually close bonds between people;
- needing to confront and deal with personal questions;
- physical activity;
- predisposition toward spiritual reflection and/or experiences;
- previous spiritual experiences;
- prompting by other participants, leaders, or the researcher;
- The natural environment or being in a wilderness environment;
- the people on the trip (sharing; the variety of thoughts, opinions, backgrounds, and experiences);
- time off (from activities or from the group); and
- structure, organization, and components of the trips:

  - changing paddling and tent partners,
  - opportunity to teach a prepared lesson to group,
  - food,
  - lack of responsibility for planning and leading trip (i.e., being a participant instead of a leader),
  - physical challenges and demands,
  - relaxed atmosphere,
  - weather, and
  - leadership styles.

Inhibiting factors:

- not enough time to feel, see, and/or process experiences;
- not having time or enough time off or alone;
- not looking for spiritual experiences; and
- too large a group.

SOURCE: Stringer and McAvoy, 1992, p. 18. Reprinted with permission of the authors.

spiritual experience. The study explored wilderness spiritual experience through the analysis of personal journals, in-depth interviews and focus group interviews with six women on a wilderness expedition incorporating a solitude component.

The results supported the findings from Stringer and McAvoy's (1992) study, and also uncovered new information, with reference to the barriers, stages and dimensions of spiritual experience. The findings suggested that spiritual experiences are strongly associated with wilderness exposure and solitude, have a complex process, and a powerful transference into participant's lives.

Spiritual experiences occurred when the participants felt safe in their environment, relaxed and open to new situations. However, to reach this comfort zone where spiritual experiences could occur, fears and anxiety had to be overcome, and an environment in which the participants felt safe and protected had to be found. Hence fear, anxiety, and establishing a sense of place were barriers toward spiritual experience.

Once these barriers were confronted and rationalized, the participants opened opportunities to explore and become familiar with their surroundings. Through this, fears became less prevalent, anxiety was reduced, and the feelings of relaxation, appreciation and exploration were triggered. Through time in nature to explore or watch, listen and absorb, the participants developed a strong connection feeling with nature and the surrounds, and began to appreciate the beauty and mastery of nature.

The research findings identified four main stages of spiritual experience. First, there were the individual- or group-focused events that triggered spiritual experience, such as deep reflection, something of natural beauty, sudden awakenings, something of surprise, something inexplicable, the ancient and historic, or a sudden encounter. This may happen in a group setting or individually. Second, the spiritual events were followed by associated feelings and emotions best described as awe, wonderment, timelessness and absorption. Third, were the delayed responses such as feelings of tranquillity, calmness, elation and peacefulness. Finally, the fourth stage of spiritual experience encompassed spiritual growth.

The benefits of spiritual experience were the strong feelings of transcendence which contributed to an intense continuum of spiritual growth. Spiritual growth was reflected in Fox's (1997) work as encompassing feelings and emotions of empowerment, inner strength, inner peace, clarity, contentment, accomplishment, awareness and connection (to self, womanhood, nature, spirits and other people). Spiritual growth seemed to enhance positive transference into everyday activities and influenced behavioral change. The participants in the study described returning home in terms of feelings of elation, inner happiness, inner strength, inner peace, clarity, pride in self, and an enhanced connection to spirituality, nature and self. Changes in behavior

and values were instigated from the positive feelings that transcended from spiritual growth. The participants carried their inner strength and feelings of self-control (from the feelings of empowerment, clarity, inner peace) into their workplaces, their families (as positive role models), and their lives (feeling more in control and stronger towards personal goals, roles in life and other relationships).

The spiritual experience process funnel (SEPF—as shown in Figure 59.4, page 460) suggests a useful grounded theory framework for interpreting the process of spiritual experience. The SEPF displays not only a process for achieving spiritual experience and its outcomes, but also identifies six emergent grounded themes from the research results which filter the experience. The six themes are as follows:

- People carry "baggage" into wilderness adventure experiences which influences perceptions and may generate fears toward nature.
- Acceptance or rationalizing fears helps feelings of self-control. In turn, this feeling of control aids relaxation, and familiarity with nature and reduces stress and anxiety caused by fear.
- When relaxed and in control, people open opportunities for spiritual experience.
- Spiritual experience encompasses intense emotions and feelings which contribute toward feelings of connectedness to nature, to spirits, to the inner self, to life perspectives, to one's sexuality, and toward a connection with other people.
- Spiritual experiences are transcendental, and over time contribute to spiritual growth.
- Spiritual experiences enhance positive transference and spiritual growth into participant's lives. Outcomes contribute toward significant changes in attitude and adoption of new behaviors.

Programming to Enhance Spiritual Opportunities

Brown (1989) proposes the need for wilderness and experiential programs to focus on techniques for awakening deep levels of awareness and exploring higher states of consciousness in order to facilitate greater transformation and personal growth. He incorporates the theory of transpersonal psychology, involving a process of transformation of the human psyche, into his programs and recommends a similar approach for encouraging the awakening of spirit. Activities such as meditation and yoga, and strategies that may enhance altered states of consciousness, trance, profound grief, and other deviations from normal awareness are all techniques for opening an individual's psyche through inner work and rediscovering spirituality. The use of wilderness experience and transpersonal psychological techniques may deepen awareness and increase the transformative power of spirituality within adventure programs.

Within a more traditional approach, adventure practitioners may consider the following 32 program recommendations to encourage spiritual opportunities:

- allow time for relaxation;
- time for solitude: personal reflection time;
- time to explore and interrelate with nature alone;
- developing a theme of open-mindedness toward spirituality and spiritual experience;
- increase a nurturing approach and respect for all living and nonliving things;
- encourage voluntary simplicity;
- permit flexible schedules to allow for alterations and time in reflection;
- time to think, reflect and share amongst other group members on a personal level;
- develop a special place for retreat;
- celebrate group and individual events and achieving goals;
- share spiritual experiences verbally;
- time to write and draw through a reflective journal;
- allow a sense of newness into a program: schedule, goals and environment;
- foster emotional involvement and extend emotional limits;
- involve participants in interpretations of history and ecology of place;
- allow personal spiritual journeys;
- adapt an indigenous (Native American or Australian Aboriginal) approach to environment and culture of program (e.g., adapt a theme surrounding a Vision Quest, rite of passage, initiation);
- encourage creativity and drawing;
- exposure to nature's beauty (e.g., utilize sunsets, night skyline and sunrise as special times to connect to natures beauty);
- meditation and yoga;

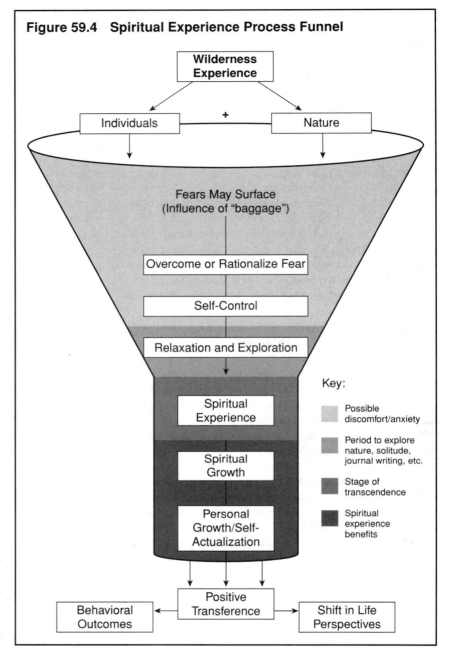

Figure 59.4   Spiritual Experience Process Funnel

- share inspirational readings;
- deviate away from normal routine;
- encourage group bonding and openness and trust;
- encourage single-gender groups;
- encourage talking about fears and rationalizing fears;
- reduce power and competition between group members;
- encourage people into nature's pace and time (remove watches);
- encourage small groups (group of 6–10 people is ideal);

- reduce stereotypical role playing; allow people to be themselves and/or reverse role plays;
- encourage fasting;
- allow nudity where appropriate; and
- encourage extended solitude: expeditioning or base camping (2-plus days).

Conclusion

Through research, practitioners are discovering the depth, characteristics and rewards of opportunities for "hard-to-define" (Driver and Ajzen, 1996) spiritual experiences in wilderness settings. Adventure educators are beginning to gain a better understanding and appreciation of spiritual experience and are also discovering the enormous benefits of spiritual opportunities and the need to enhance spiritual health.

This chapter highlighted that practitioners have the potential to tap into enormous personal development opportunities through the facilitation of spiritual experiences. Spiritual experience transfers powerful feelings into people's lives, such as empowerment, self-clarity, inner strength, self-control, and an enhanced connection to self, sexuality, nature and other people. In turn, spiritual growth influences perceptions and behavior change. Evidence supports that spiritual growth enhances positive transference into everyday activities and influences positive behavioral change toward self, family, society and life (Fox, 1996).

Wilderness exposure can enhance transcendent and peak experiences through spiritual opportunities, and research findings have now revealed how such opportunities can be created. Spiritual growth, like other aspects of programming, requires the implementation of spiritual enhancement approaches. Some examples of program strategies that may promote spiritual opportunities include the introduction of more solitude time, reflection time, celebration and exposure to nature's beauty.

Overall, spirituality is a fundamental aspect of human nature and needs to be nurtured in a holistic program approach to achieve positive health and wellness. Introducing self-focused activities such as solitude, meditation, relaxation, and reflection in adventure programs can enhance spiritual experience and refocus attention on the trilogy of mind, body and spirit.

References

Breitenstein, D., and Ewert, A. (1990). Health benefits of outdoor recreation: Implications for health education. *Health Education,* January/February, 16–20.

Brown, M. H. (1989). Transpersonal psychology: Facilitating transformation in outdoor experiential education. *The Journal of Experiential Education, 12*(3), 47–56.

Chandler, C. K., Holden, J. M., and Kolander, C. A. (1992). Counseling for spiritual wellness: Theory and practice. *Journal of Counseling and Development, 71,* 168–175.

Driver, B. L., and Ajzen, I. (1996). Research needed on hard-to-define nature-based human experiences. In B. L. Driver, D. Dustin, T. Baltic, G. Elsner, and G. Peterson (Eds.), *Nature and the human spirit: Toward an expanded land management ethic* (pp. 431–439). State College, PA: Venture Publishing, Inc.

Fox, R. J. (1996). *Women, nature and spirituality: An exploration into women's wilderness experience.* Unpublished masters dissertation, Griffith University, Brisbane, Australia.

Fox, R. J. (1997). Women, nature and spirituality: A qualitative study exploring women's wilderness experience. In *Proceedings from the 3rd Conference of the Australian and New Zealand Association for Leisure Studies—Leisure, People, Places and Spaces* (pp. 59–64). The University of Newcastle, New South Wales, Australia.

Henderson, K., Bialeschki, M. D., Shaw, S. M., and Freysinger, V. J. (1989). *A leisure of one's own: A feminist perspective on women's leisure.* State College, PA: Venture Publishing, Inc.

Henderson, K. A. (1993). Rediscovering spirituality. *Camping Magazine,* March/April, 23–27.

Maslow, A. H. (1968). *Towards a psychology of being.* New York, NY: Van Nostrand Reinhold.

Maslow, A. H. (1971). *The farther reaches of human nature.* New York, NY: Viking.

McDonald, B. L., and Schreyer, R. (1991) Spiritual benefits of leisure participation and leisure settings. In B. L. Driver, P. J. Brown, and G. L. Peterson (Eds.), *Benefits of leisure* (pp. 179–194). State College, PA: Venture Publishing, Inc.

Phenix, P. (1974). Transcendence and the curriculum. In Misner et al. (Eds.), *Conflicting connections of curriculum.* Berkeley, CA: McCutchan Publishing.

Prest, L. A., and Keller, J. F. (1993). Spirituality and family therapy: Spiritual beliefs, myths, and metaphors. *Journal of Marital and Family Therapy, 19*(2), 137–148.

Sabo, F., and Davis, B. (1990). Health as a sacred journey. In *Integrating Experiential Education: AEE 18th National Conference—Proceedings Manual* (pp. 105–106).

Stringer, L. A. (1990). Spirituality and experiential education: Research results and program implications. *Integrating Experiential Education: AEE 18th National Conference—Proceedings Manual* (pp. 113–117).

Stringer, L. A., and McAvoy, L. H. (1992). The need for something different: Spirituality and wilderness adventure. *The Journal of Experiential Education, 15*(1), 13–21.

Szilagyi, B. (1996). Spiritual health. In *Active Connections: The 20th Biennial National/International ACHPER Conference Proceedings, Australia* (pp. 241–243).

Chapter 60

Critical Outdoor Education and Nature as a Friend

Peter Martin
La Trobe University

Introduction

The Marshall Islands consists of 29 atolls and 1,225 islets scattered over three-quarters of a million square miles of the Pacific Ocean. In response to research that shows global warming due to greenhouse gases will raise sea levels and inundate many of the islands, the Marshall Islands has developed a total population evacuation plan. As a member of the Association of Small Island States (AOSIS) they have been lobbying industrialized nations to support a worldwide reduction of 20 percent in greenhouse gas emissions (compared to 1990 levels). The United States is aiming for stabilization at 1990 levels by 2010, and Japan a 5 percent reduction by the year 2010 (Nuttall, 1997, p. 4).

Australia, an island less threatened by sea level rises, claims the best it can achieve by the year 2010, is an 18 percent *increase* from 1990 levels. While the Australian Government has developed strategies to reduce greenhouse gas emissions, it seems that there exists a deep reluctance to curtail or modify activity that contributes to economic growth, albeit at an environmental cost. Australia is not ignorant of environmental imperatives, rather "countries like Australia have a cultural momentum and economic interdependence with other countries that make impediments to economic growth unthinkable" (Beder, 1993, p. xi). "The Lucky Country" has enormous natural resources,

including fossil fuel deposits, which can only contribute to the gross domestic product if they are exploited.

Despite the Australian government's stance on greenhouse emissions, Australians do have a concern for environmental issues. A 1994 survey canvassed opinions concerning environmental problems; results indicated the two most commonly cited concerns were air and ocean pollution (34 percent and 26 percent of the population respectively). The greenhouse effect was an issue for only 9 percent of the population (Australian Bureau of Statistics, 1994, p. 7). In Australia 85.3 percent of the population live in urban settings, most commonly on the coastal fringe (Australian Bureau of Statistics, 1996). Air and ocean pollution have an immediate connection to the life quality of Australians in a way similar to the links between greenhouse warming and the residents of the Marshall Islands. The direct connection between lived experience and environmental concern is to be expected; important implications for education outdoors are also evident.

What Role for Outdoor Education?

The significant contribution of outdoor education to education is something I have pondered for some time (Martin, 1993a). As a beginning teacher, I can clearly remember justifying outdoor activities in terms of individual growth outcomes for students. Outdoor activities offered

Thanks to Mary Faith Chenery for her helpful critique and editorial comments on drafts of this chapter.

students an opportunity to experience success at physical endeavors and broaden their recreation or leisure options. Often kids less suited to competitive team sports would do well at outdoor activities: skills around the camp, with a compass, paddle, or feel for the bush, didn't fall all with the gifted school athlete. Personal development outcomes are still considered a major rationale for outdoor education's place in schooling, its popularity with students, and application to fields as diverse as corporate management and at-risk youth.

Although none of the personal development benefits of outdoor education have changed, in the light of mounting evidence that environmental problems of global dimensions have developed and that human economically driven activity is a primary cause, I would argue that outdoor education should have a primary role in educating for environmentally sustainable living. The pollution Australians care about now is the visible pollution that impacts upon their lives. Australians could also care more about natural settings if experiences in the outdoors became more a part of their personal life experiences.

Since 1992 outdoor education has been a part of the formal education on offer in schools in the southern Australian state of Victoria. A higher secondary school certificate subject, outdoor education has a "human development" focus:

> The primary focus of Outdoor Education is on understanding people's relationships with the outdoors. In developing an understanding of this relationship some matters will be learned through direct experience outdoors, while some will be learned in the classroom. . . . The activities selected should enable the students to develop a sympathetic understanding of nature and should specifically exclude the use of weapons (archery, target shooting) or mechanical devices which replace human effort (trail bikes, water skiing, jet skis). (Board of Studies, 1994, p. 5)
> [A human development approach seeks to help students understand their own participation in outdoor activities] in its broader cultural and historical context and assists students to reflect on the complex range of influences which structure everyday life. (Victorian Curriculum and Assessment Board, 1992, p. 10)

It is in this broader cultural and historical context that outdoor education content which I consider unique and defensible can evolve. It is an education well-suited to the coming millennium:

> Problems associated with ethnic, gender, and class inequities are indeed daunting, and deserve immediate attention . . . the current debate over what constitutes appropriate education . . . for the accelerating rate of technological innovation indeed involves important issues. But if the thinking that guides educational reform does not take into account how the cultural beliefs and practices passed on through schooling relate to the deepening ecological crisis, then these efforts may actually strengthen the cultural orientation that is undermining the sustaining capacities of natural systems upon which all life depends. (Bowers, 1993, p. 1)

Any education that takes place in, or concerns the use of, the natural environment must surely embrace Bower's comments to the greatest possible extent. Learning from outdoor adventure, outdoor recreation and outdoor education needs to go beyond consideration of the superficial aspects of minimizing impact. What I like to call *critical* outdoor education can contribute distinctively to education for the planet, by focusing on the cultural beliefs and practices that may be contributing to the ecological crisis. (Outdoor education may also assist in addressing educational dilemmas associated with ethnic, gender and class inequities, but these are not the focus of this essay.)

One readily identifiable aspect of school-based outdoor education is that it has traditionally sought to leave the confines of the school, for several days at a time, and has had students engaged in adventure activities in a natural setting. Students have liked it for that. Time in the bush can let students begin to understand themselves, others and nature in a different way. It can help students to develop a different, often critical, perspective on society. I am careful here to say "can help," because outdoor activities can as easily reinforce exploitive patriarchal values as they can help develop a critical perspective.

Critical Theory in Outdoor Education

One of the academic bases which can be of assistance here in helping outdoor education to offer a different perspective on outdoor recreation activity is critical theory. Critical theory is concerned with social justice issues. It is a perspective which argues that all action is either maintaining or resisting the dominant social order (Giroux, 1983). Critical outdoor education is aimed at examining outdoor recreation and environmental issues in light of their relationship to the dominant social order.

For critical outdoor education, the central issue is humanity's relationship with the outdoors (or nature). Critical outdoor education would accept that there exist both local and global environmental crises, and that social and environmental injustice are both a cause and consequence of these crises. Critical outdoor education would examine outdoor recreation beliefs and practices in terms of whether they maintain or resist the dominant historical human-nature relationship: one of exploitation.

The dominant western social order, of which we are a part, is built on excessive faith in scientific rationalism; has human rather than nature-centered priorities; holds individualistic rather than community goals; and has an unswerving belief in progress typified by technological innovation (Chenery, 1994). Feminist critiques also tie the western mind-set to a patriarchal system of beliefs and attitudes (Plumwood, 1993). In such a world, women, nature, and knowledge other than the scientific are subordinate or hold less value.

So Why Outdoor Education and Critical Theory?

> The conceptual basis of industrial society has been based on assumptions that, if we continue to live by them, will further accelerate the rate of environmental damage. . . . In effect, the evidence of environmental disruption and system breakdown is a clear message that our most basic cultural assumptions are going to have to be reexamined and, in many instances, reconstituted in ways that take into account the interdependence of culture and natural environment. (Bowers and Flinders, 1990, p. 249)

Reexamining and in some instances reconstituting basic cultural assumptions will never be an easy task. The task becomes even more difficult when a critique is conducted while fully immersed in the culture under scrutiny. Critical outdoor education can construct an alternate reality or community so that some of the taken for granted assumptions of everyday living become slightly more visible. What is important on a long bush walk, a climbing trip, or a downriver journey is seldom the same set of imperatives as those that demand attention in everyday living. Critical outdoor education can enable students to understand that central aspects of our lives which we take for granted, are actually social constructions of our own doing; many of the things we regard as important are dependant on contexts, time and space. As the critical theorist Giroux (1983, p. 8) explains:

> Money, consumption, distribution and production . . . do not represent objective facts or things, but (are) historically contingent contexts mediated by relationships of domination and subordination.

What critical outdoor education tries to do is raise students' awareness of understandings about their society which have previously gone unacknowledged. Critical outdoor education goes to the bush, not just to recreate and have fun, but to look back with a critical perspective at the contexts left behind, particularly to those sets of beliefs which help shape human-nature relationships.

Human-Nature Relationships

The argument for outdoor education to concern itself fundamentally with human-nature relationships is compelling. The global and local environmental crises we currently face are those born of a culture that has lost its sense of connectedness with nature. As a culture, we have taken the words of Genesis to have "dominion over the earth" to "subdue . . . and multiply" too literally. In decision making at all levels of government, economic "imperatives" hold sway over environmental concerns. One distinctive and worthy path is for critical outdoor education to concern itself primarily with establishing or perhaps reestablishing, a sense of personal relatedness to nature.

Wendel Berry (1992) comments on the importance of this relatedness:

> A culture capable of preserving land and people can be made only within a relatively stable and enduring relationship between local people and place. (Berry, 1992, p. 171)

(As an aside: the need for relatedness raises serious questions for any education interested in promoting environmental understanding and activism. How can students act on environmental problems or issues for which they have no connectedness or personal experience? Basically I don't think they can. Failure to act on environmental issues due to a lack of relatedness is recognized by the advocates of bioregionalism who argue that direct immediate connections and relationships to place are fundamental to "right" behavior [Sale, 1991, p. 53].)

To help in developing a direct personal relationship with nature my teaching outdoors is guided by the metaphor "to know nature as a friend." It is one of the models my students consider in the classroom as well as the bush. Deep ecology, Judeo-Christian images, early European beliefs, and media portrayals, offer other human-nature models which are useful in developing the realization that how we relate to nature is problematic and a social construction. Power relationships between people and place differ in these models. Although to consider "nature as a friend" still places humans separate from nature, it does treat nature as a subject, not an object, and is a model I find students can more easily understand. It also has interesting implications for the way outdoor education is practiced.

Nature as a Friend

The dominant behavior I have in the relationship with my friends is underscored by respect and caring; the source of knowledge about respect and caring is mostly intuitive, receptive, and based on experience. The philosopher Nel Noddings, in her work on ethical caring between people, suggests that caring, empathy and relatedness underlies much of women's ways of knowing:

> Women . . . define themselves in terms of caring and work their way through moral problems from the position of one caring. (Noddings, 1984, p. 8)

Noddings' position of "one caring" is typified by a person who is motivated to act in the interests of another. I believe human-nature interactions can share qualitative similarities with the interactions between humans as described by Noddings. In so doing, adopting the "position of one caring" when concerned with the moral problems associated with the environment (as opposed to an economic rationalist position) would represent a major shift in thinking: a shift consistent with the concept of regarding specific environments more personally as a close friend. However, we need to move beyond philosophy into practice, a point argued by Simpson. "The problem now lies not in the lack of the philosophical discussion about the environment, but in a failure to translate such philosophy into useful action" (1996, p. 14).

The practical implications of critical outdoor education which approaches nature as a friend are many—implications in terms of the knowledge held to be important, the content selected to be taught, the teaching processes employed, the venues identified as appropriate, the learning outcomes emphasized. Implied in this summarizing list is the central role of the teacher in shaping learning experiences. While I am certain that students construct their own learning outcomes, I am equally convinced of the need for teachers to acknowledge the important moral responsibility and influence they accept in the selection of teaching strategies and program content. Part of that responsibility is recognizing that a "nature as a friend" metaphor can be extended and developed as an image of human-nature relationships to pervade an entire program, indeed a whole way of living.

The remainder of this chapter will discuss the practical implications of teaching outdoors guided by the metaphor of "nature as a friend."

The Knowledge Held to Be Important

Consciously and subconsciously as teachers and leaders we give credibility to particular types of knowledge. For the last 400 years rational objectivity has been the dominant way of thinking that has been valued by Western culture. Rational objectivity underscores much of today's technological advancement, much of which is of great benefit to humans. Emotion and sentiment are not part of rational objectivity. Traditional schooling holds rational objectivity to be most valued. I grew up being reminded by both parents and teachers to "think rationally, . . . leave your emotions out of it, . . . don't cloud your thinking with emotion. Be objective!" In contrast, to treat or conceive of nature as a friend demands that emotions be recognized and nurtured. If Western culture is to redress the environmental harm induced by technological, rational thinking, then educators need to accept and foster more balanced ways of understanding the world.

In the outdoors it is easy to recognize and reify a diversity of ways of knowing. Getting to know nature as a friend challenges the dominance of rational objectivity, and encourages students to acknowledge the importance of experiential, tacit, or emotional responses to the outdoors.

Experiential knowing becomes important in the outdoors, it's the core around which outdoors people build competence and skill mastery. Experiential knowledge can also be a meaningful way to know outdoor environments. The knowledge of the Mt. Arapiles cliffs because I have climbed there is very different from the geological knowledge I can derive from reading a text or studying the rock strata. I have argued previously that rock climbing itself can be a powerful and personally significant way to know (Martin, 1993b). The feel of rock, the way it's shaped, cracked, and formed is something every climber recognizes as particular to specific places and climbs. To give another example, Polynesian navigators can accurately discern landmass and direction by interpreting detailed knowledge of star patterns or through interpretation of wave sequences felt while lying in the bottom of boats floating on the open ocean. Described by Howard Gardner as typical of "spatial intelligence," the navigator's experiential knowledge is almost untenable to the rational mind (Gardner, Kornhaber, and Wake, 1996). Significantly for critical outdoor education, experiential knowledge builds relatedness, and it is relatedness that is of prime importance in determining the degree of compassion and action in caring (Noddings, 1984).

Contained within the wisdom of experience is tacit knowing as described by Polanyi (1966). Polanyi recognizes that "we can know far more than we can tell" (1966, p. 4). This knowledge that comes from experience may not be able to be articulated, but it is certainly real. Tacit knowing also reminds me that written reflections or posttrip discussions can never consolidate all that is learned. Being satisfied as a teacher that sometimes the experience itself is significant learning, without the need for deconstruction or reinterpretation, is worth remembering.

Intuitive knowledge is also something most outdoor educators acknowledge. Numerous accounts exist of mountaineers sensing and responding to intuitive hunches or "feelings" prior to incidents such as avalanches or rockfalls. Intuition may have its roots in tacit knowing also. Again recognizing the importance and validity of intuitive knowledge is something outdoor leaders can acknowledge during teaching. In leading groups outdoors I often get a sense of aspects such as weather changes, imminent hazards or group dynamic issues. Often I attempt to make that intuition more public by thinking aloud to students.

Students easily grasp the significance of more personal responses in nature as valid ways to know; to many it comes as a relief (perhaps similar in a way to the mountaineers of the late 1800s who eventually worked up the courage to climb mountains for other than scientific rationales). However, acknowledging experiential, tacit, and intuitive knowledge is not just an easy escape route from rigorous thought. Rational thought is not discarded, but rather becomes another mode of consciousness to which students refer. This blending of both rational and emotive thought is what Belenky (Belenky, Clinchy, Goldberger, and Tarule, 1986), in a study of women's ways of knowing, describes as indicative of the most intelligent thinkers, whom she called "constructed knowers" (p. 131). Similarly, Fritjof Capra in discussing the distinction between science and philosophy considers a synthesizing central ground between the rational thinking and sensory perception of science and the intuitive, spiritual and inner experience of philosophy as the most valued of ways of thinking. *Idealistic* is the term he coins for the coming together of these ways of knowing (Simpson, 1996, p. 15).

Experiential knowledge, tacit knowing, and intuitive knowledge are all valid additional sources of evidence in decision making. That students understand the ideas associated with different ways of knowing is vital to critical outdoor education that seeks to establish validity in the power of place and personal relatedness with nature. Students need to know that it is perfectly acceptable to describe a personal relationship with place that is a blend of both rational objective knowledge, and personal, tacit or experiential knowledge. (The knowledge and love of my partner and children is no less real or valued a form of knowledge for not always being rational and objective.)

In the larger scheme of things, a culture that recognized the inherent value of human-nature relationships in other than rational objective (economic) terms would certainly be moving toward adopting the environmental ethic that Leopold sought so many years ago:

> No important change in ethics was ever accomplished without an internal change in intellectual emphasis, loyalties, affections and convictions. (Leopold, 1949, p. 246)

I have emphasized this blending of rationality and emotion because I consider it pivotal to the development of a relationship with nature that moves beyond the instrumental distanced relationship of the objective scientist, yet remains more grounded than the blind romantic. The importance of this constructed way of knowing is also evident in consideration of teaching content and processes.

The Content Selected to Be Taught

Teaching and leading will always be a moral endeavor. What I determine to be important enough to teach is a decision I do not take lightly, especially when student safety, environmental well-being, and scarce resources are at risk. As an ethical nonconsequentialist (Hunt, 1993, p. 19), the content I select for critical outdoor education guided by getting to know nature as a friend must support the ends of environmental connectedness and empathy.

Friendships develop over time as people gain personal knowledge and mutual experience. In the human-nature relationship there seems little difference. Essential content needs to include the skills to enable students to remain at ease and comfortable in the outdoors. Bush-living skills and specific outdoor activity skills become a means to enable a familiarity and friendship to flourish, rather than a collective of potential leisure options. In getting to know nature, the emphasis of activity skills becomes one of functional mobility and acquaintance, rather than technical improvement and the beating of challenges. For example, rock-climbing skills still need to be learned safely, but a multipitch climb up a long, exposed, but easy ridge is more appropriate to meeting a cliff as a friend, than is a short technically difficult problem. Similarly, cross-country ski touring needs to enable students to explore comfortably the winter high country; it doesn't matter if they can't ski as fast or as efficiently as those wearing Lycra suits closer to the ski resort.

Some outdoor activities invite students to return to the one place, repeatedly; others are built upon novelty and exploration. My teaching outdoors favors the return to familiar places. As a climber, I have been climbing at the same cliff for hundreds of days over the past 20 years, I feel I have come to know that cliff intimately as a result. I think that content which captures student's interest by relying primarily on novelty, is not helping them understand the importance of their relationship with place.

I also consider the history of the places students visit to be important content. What has the mountain seen and known before we met? What other inhabitants share the bushland with the students and what is some of their history and relationships? To climb at Mt. Arapiles and know nothing of the indigenous inhabitants' relationships, beliefs and knowledge, the early European settlers, the skinks and stumpy tail lizards, the early landform and remnant coastal vegetation, is akin to trying to get to know a friend without inquiring about his or her family or other life history. The history of a place then, is essential content of critical outdoor education. The twist that critical outdoor education adds to this content is that the experiences and influences related to Mt. Arapiles are understood in terms of how they shaped and molded the Arapiles I know today. Further, what in this history has served Arapiles well and what has altered it significantly? Importantly from a critical outdoor education perspective, how do I determine what is good and bad in this history, and by what criteria?

It is clear that much of the content of teaching human-nature relationships must be the experiences in the outdoors themselves. Experiential knowledge is fundamental to the development of human-human relationships. The extent to which people are motivated to *act* in caring is primarily determined by the degree of relatedness (Noddings, 1984). That is to say, we are more likely to act to help a person if we are connected or associated with them in some way. There is no reason to think otherwise for human-nature relationships. Students build associations and connections to place and therefore a motivation to act and care, through specific experience.

There is also content in the personal responses to place that students feel. Different places, and variations in weather at the same place, seem to create different moods. It is important to recognize and consider these responses as part of the building of friendship with place.

The Teaching Processes Employed

Teaching guided by a nature as a friend model also has implications for how programs are conducted. The way teachers and leaders structure and conduct outdoor experiences is infinitely varied and itself the subject of full university courses. Like the choice of content, the choice of teaching processes is also an ethical issue. For example, the initial introduction, the choice of equipment, sequencing of activity, and construction of differing contexts all have profound influence on student learning outcomes. Space is limited here to a few brief examples of the ways in which teaching processes can be guided by the nature as a friend metaphor.

Introductions to the outdoors need to parallel what we have learned through the experience of our own human friendships. Friendships build slowly, over time, without fear and discordant responses. For critical outdoor education this implies careful introduction, where getting to know the place takes priority over getting the campsite established, the equipment handed out or the "real" activity program underway. Often when I take students to climbing sites, I first encourage them to explore the area, to get a feel for the place and its personality. Students can also begin to relax, get to know this newness at their own pace, not that dictated by their imminent turn down the first abseil, their mounting fear and the instructor's initial focus on how dangerous the cliff may be. The initial slow

introduction also helps students place their later experience in a broader geographical context. Adventure activities demand attention, especially for novices. A slow introduction to the area (and deliberate time out during an activity) enables students to look around and begin to acclimatize to the broader environment in which they are immersed.

Equipment has a massive impact on what students learn about the outdoors. As an example, my own introduction to cross-country skiing was on waxed skis. The equipment demanded that I understand and observe snow conditions, likely changes in snow with terrain and aspect, future weather changes and past snowfall. Waxes provided a means by which I could comprehend the subtlety of snow metamorphosis. When students use patterned-base skis, they lose far more than the frustration and inconvenience of applying the wrong wax. The "progress" of waxless skis is an interesting example of the way in which technology has distanced the outdoor recreator from a need to understand nature. Other examples in outdoor recreation are easy to find: in climbing, camming devices are more easily placed, but demand less skill and understanding of rock formation than do chocks or nuts. The global positioning system (GPS) promises you will never be lost in the bush again. Plastic whitewater craft don't demand the same level of river-reading skills to successfully complete a whitewater trip compared to their fiberglass predecessors. Modern tentage allows the weary traveler to camp virtually anywhere, mindless of aspect, weather and topography. The detailed knowledge and skills concerning what wood will burn and to what temperature has been all but eclipsed by the lightweight stove and a sometimes superficial interpretation of minimum impact.

Experimenting with the type and extent of equipment can enable students to begin to understand how technology has profoundly influenced human-nature relationships. A watch, a water bottle, a Frisbee and a football, all bring with them particular ways of behaving, specific language, expectations and assumptions about humans and the environment. Critical outdoor education is attuned to making those expectations and assumptions more accessible for reflective discussion and informed action.

Sequencing activities also impact on the relationship students can develop with nature. As an example, the skills and feelings of competence and ease that students gain in the environment in one activity are frequently not transferred to the next. To be at ease in a canoe doesn't seem to help students' fear of heights! To develop deeper personal relationships with environments takes time and familiarity, so I prefer students to engage with nature, at least initially, in one activity area. A gamut of necessarily shallow encounters which I think inevitably result from briefly introducing students to a range of activities and/or environments, also helps reinforce exploitive human-nature relationships—relationships where students see the outdoors as a grand gymnasium or circus ground.

I consider it important for students to be able to repeat activities and experiences. A repeat experience helps students internalize learning, but it also allows them the freedom to relax their focus from the activity itself to the environment in which they are operating. Reclimbing the same climb, repaddling the same stretch of water, rewalking the same route build familiarity and confidence in the students' relationship and knowledge of place.

Contexts for learning in the outdoors can be altered enormously when compared to those imposed by the constraints of more conventional schooling. Living outdoors gives students the opportunity to begin to know the environment more intimately, to share with the bush a range of memorable experiences. Students need to be encouraged to meet the bush in as many different circumstances as possible. From each encounter, a little more is learned.

Each differing circumstance will naturally lend itself to different learning outcomes. Sleeping on a ledge or at the base of the cliff, feeling the heat radiate out of the rock, and gazing at the stars never fails to stimulate metaphysical thoughts and discussions. A small group sharing the intensity of a multipitch climb, sitting side-by-side, staring out on the vastness of the surrounding country, thinks and learns differently compared to the group top-roped climbing, en masse, near the campsite.

Critical outdoor education is mindful of the way in which the teaching-learning context carries assumptions about what is to be learned and valued. For example, on a bush walk, a mechanical time frame with predetermined campsites and daily walk schedules potentially signals human dominance over natural cycles and mastery of terrain. A different set of learning would inevitably result from a walk that was conducted more in tune with natural rhythms, interesting diversions, reading and responding to the land and weather, rather than to the map and route plan. Establishing a campsite and sleeping in tents is often unnecessary; tents may signify a need for protection from the imagined evils of the bush at night and also serve to isolate students from the full cycles of the day and the learning that promotes.

In rock climbing, the use of a ground belay system for top-roped climbing increases safety and is more easily supervised, but is less suited to environmental outcomes and conveys impressions of climbing in a gymnasium. A ground belayed top rope increases physical impact when students gather at the base of the cliff; the dynamic is that of a larger group (usually more competitive, less personal, louder, more frivolous, less reflective); and the focus is primarily on technical climbing because all students face the cliff and have a somewhat restricted field of vision. The satisfaction of completing the climb and sitting next to the belayer, which comes from belaying on top of the cliff, is absent. Instead, the ground belay demands that the climber is immediately lowered back into the cluster of people he or she just left; there is no journey, physical or symbolic.

A context driven by the nature as a friend metaphor would not see the lizards, bird life, or animal tracks noticed during the safety briefing as an interruption or distraction. Rather, human-nature interaction is the very reason for the student's presence in the bush, the activity itself is secondary.

The Venues Identified as Appropriate

Venues appropriate for critical outdoor education are not necessarily the same as those sought by outdoor recreation. The aim of getting to know nature as a friend dictates that places are specific, individual and personal. There are no generic "cliffs" as there are no generic "people." Each cliff is different, with its own characteristics, idiosyncrasies, moods, and tolerances. Mt. Arapiles seems to tolerate more climbers; Bundaleer is brooding and solemn. One of the questions that becomes essential to ask in critical outdoor education is, why go to this place, or as a reminder, how central to the program is this specific place.

Specific relationships with place create the realization that it is not possible to know and care for all places, all environments. Limiting the scale or extent to which caring occurs is also a point pursued by Noddings, who when speaking of human-human relationships, contends that it is not possible to truly care, for example, for all the starving children of the world (1984, p. 86). To do so would necessitate abandoning the caring already undertaken; a matter of limited resources and capacities:

> [It is] painful to acknowledge that an ethic
> of caring limits our obligation to those so far
> removed from us that completion is impossible . . . but this seems intuitively right.
> (Noddings, 1984, p. 153)

For environments, this too makes sense. I have little affinity for the ocean. I grew up far from the sea and, while I have fond memories of playing in the waves on holiday, I do not have a sense of relatedness to the ocean. I care and act on environmental issues at Mt. Arapiles because I do have a relatedness to that environment, built up over time.

One of the dangers of adventure-based outdoor education is that it potentially teaches students to appreciate only places which afford positive adventure outcomes. Critical outdoor education needs to be aware of this risk. For critical outdoor education, language which describes cliffs as worthless, rivers as boring, or bush as monotonous and uninviting, needs to be interpreted and understood in terms of the human-nature assumptions that it carries. Critical outdoor education would also seek to encourage students through revisits and attention to place characteristics and "personality" to develop relationships with more common land. Bioregional concepts, such as local watershed or food sources, have as much influence upon the choices a critical outdoor educator makes about a venue as might the recreational opportunity the venue affords.

The Learning Outcomes Emphasized

If developing an understanding of human-nature relationships is the primary goal, then the activity needs to be conceptualized as such. This understanding then takes precedence over all other aspects; it must pervade the entire program, from activity and equipment choices through to the place you select to sit and eat lunch. Outdoor education happens 24 hours a day and free from the imposed contexts and agendas of conventional schooling. Letting the learning goals influence total choices is both challenging and enjoyable. Orford describes the need for pervasiveness in this way:

> Making the most of learning opportunities can be done by understanding that *everything* during the outdoor education experience is program. This includes preplanning, the bus trip, arrival, setting up, outdoor activities, community living (meals, free time, bed time, cooking, dishes) evening programs, packing up, the trip home, and follow up afterwards. Whatever time is available should contribute to the purpose. . . . (Orford, 1993, p. 31)

LaChapelle describes a similar focusing of learning experiences when describing her program called Breaking Through. LaChapelle relates the importance of a total mindset which has students recognizing that "nature affords experiences" rather than people enacting them (1991, p. 20). In this sense students are encouraged to see their actions in the environment as a result of nature cooperating with them, rather than being an inert playing field for their desires.

Concluding Thoughts

A primary rationale behind advocating approaching nature as a friend and the development of critical outdoor education which focuses on understanding human-nature relationships, is to promote ethical action towards the natural environment both in the outdoors and in everyday living. Caring for nature is a primary goal of the nature as a friend model. For this caring to be sustained students need to perceive an improved relationship, a reciprocation or response with nature and place (see Noddings, 1984). If students perceive their efforts at getting to know nature are fruitless, then their efforts will diminish. Fortunately, this is rarely a practical problem. The enthusiasm with which students open up and perceive responsiveness and positive growth from personal human-nature relationships is always a pleasure to watch and share. It is my greatest satisfaction as a teacher.

Improving human-nature relationship through personal outdoor experiences is not only possible, it's profoundly rewarding.

References

Australian Bureau of Statistics. (1994). *Environmental issues: People's views and practices.* Canberra, Australia: Author.

Australian Bureau of Statistics. (1996). *Australians and the environment.* Canberra, Australia: Author.

Beder, S. (1993). *The nature of sustainable development.* Newham, Australia: Scribe Publications

Belenky, M., Clinchy, B., Goldberger, N., and Tarule, J. (1986). *Women's ways of knowing.* New York, NY: Basic Books.

Berry, W. (1992). *Sex, economy, freedom and community.* New York, NY: Pantheon Books.

Board of Studies. (1994). *VCE outdoor education study design.* Melbourne, Australia: Author.

Bowers, C. A. (1993). *Education, cultural myths and the ecological crisis: Towards deep changes.* Albany, NY: State University of New York Press.

Bowers, C. A., and Flinders, D. J. (1990). *Responsive teaching: An ecological approach to classroom patterns of language, culture, and thought.* New York, NY: Teachers College Press.

Chenery, M. F. (1994). *Looking back from the Bush: A view of ecoethical thinking from the perspective of Australian outdoor education.* Paper presented to the ART Seminar on Ecoethical Thinking in Cross-Cultural Perspectives, University of the Saarland, Saarbrücken, Germany, July 28–August 3.

Gardner, H., Kornhaber, M., and Wake, W. (1996). *Intelligence: Multiple perspectives.* Fort Worth, TX: Harcourt Brace College.

Giroux, H. (1983). *Critical theory and educational practice.* Melbourne, Australia: Deakin University Press.

Hunt J. (1993). *Ethical issues in experiential education.* Boulder, CO: The Association for Experiential Education.

LaChapelle, D. (1991). Educating for deep ecology. *Journal of Experiential Education, 14*(3), 18–22.

Leopold, A. (1949). *A sand county almanac.* New York, NY: Oxford University Press.

Martin, P. (1993a). Future directions for outdoor education—Are they worth the costs? *Adventure Education, 10*(3), 16–19.

Martin, P. (1993b). Outdoor education: practical implications of a deep ecology philosophy. *The Outdoor Educator, 12*(3), 10–16.

Noddings, N. (1984). *Caring: A feminine approach to ethics and moral education.* Berkeley, CA: University of California Press.

Nuttall, N. (1997). Pacific nations prepare to evacuate disappearing islands. *The Australian,* December 1, pp. 4.

Orford, G. (1993). Everything is program: Maximizing the message. *The Outdoor Educator, 12*(2), 30–31

Polanyi, M. (1966). *The tacit dimension.* London, UK: Routledge & Kegan Paul Ltd.

Plumwood, V. (1993). *Feminism and the masters of nature.* London, UK: Routledge.

Simpson, S. (1996). A Leopold for the nineties: The ecological age and outdoor recreation. *Journal of Experiential Education, 19*(1), 14–21.

Sale, K. (1991). *Dwellers in the land: The bioregional vision.* Philadelphia, PA: New Society Publishers.

Victorian Curriculum and Assessment Board. (1992). *Outdoor education: Course development support material.* Melbourne, Australia: Author.

Chapter 61

Future Trends and Issues in Adventure Programming

Simon Priest
eXperientia

Michael A. Gass
University of New Hampshire

The future can only be predicted if you carefully looked at the present and the past, connected the interdependent patterns, and then risked being incorrect. And herein lies the danger of predicting the future: we are wrong more often than we are right! Consider this tidbit:

> Around the turn of the last century, not one of the futurists predicting our prospective lives, mentioned anything remotely connected with the computer.
> —John Scully, Apple Computer

We begin by examining what is going on with the world. We will look at what this means for our profession. And we may learn from the mistakes of those who have walked in history before us (Priest and Gass, 1997).

What Is Going on With the World?—Global Trends

Ewert (1989) and Miles (1990) identified several societal trends and changes in global and local issues that are relevant to the future of adventure programming. These can be summarized as:

1. shift from industrial toward information and service;

2. rapid technological advances will continue;
3. decreased earning, morality, and compassion will ensue;
4. increased crime, consumption, and debt will result;
5. more people will seek experiences outdoors;
6. more environments will get damaged; and
7. litigation will still drive decision-making processes.

Shift From Industrial Toward Information and Service

With current gains in medicine and healthcare people will live longer. The average age of the populous will continue to increase. Relaxed attitudes toward birth control and reproduction will further accelerate the population explosion. With over five billion inhabitants, we have far surpassed our planet's carrying capacity by a factor of a thousand and the situation will get far worse before it gets better. In our time on earth, humans have evolved from hunters and gatherers through an agricultural society to the industrial revolution. Now we are well into the information age with a service orientation.

Rapid Technological Advances Will Continue

Scientific progress has made the information age possible. Breakthroughs in data management abound and these newly developing methods of communication and transportation will effectively continue to shrink the world. From a laptop computer, powered by a solar panel and connected to a cellular phone, one can dial up and *slip* into a personal access account. From there, one can search the World Wide Web for information on everything from the newest outdoor gear to wilderness area access. Then one can send an e-mail message instantly ordering the equipment or requesting permits. These still arrive many days later by snail-mail, but that will all change some day, too!

Decreased Earning, Morality, and Compassion Will Ensue

The instantaneous ability to store, retrieve, access, and deliver such a rapidly expanding information base, will mean that the dominant global culture moves in the direction of being more empirical, rational, utilitarian, and manipulative. As a result, global markets for goods, services, or ideas will become easy to access, yet heavy with competition for customers and resources. The developing nations will catch up to the developed nations in economic production. This will result in a split of Western classes around time and money. White-collar workers will get richer and work fewer hours, thus giving them more unobligated time and disposable income for leisure. Blue-collar workers will work longer hours for less money and will have a greater need for leisure time, but have less of it.

Increased Crime, Consumption, and Debt Will Result

People will increase their levels of debt and mortgage their futures in order to sustain their present affluence at their past levels. More people will switch careers several times within their working lifetimes in an effort to stay ahead. The appearance of more double income families (as both parents work to maintain their standard of living) and more single parent families (as the one must work to survive debt free) will translate into increasing numbers of children becoming alienated from their families. Growing intellectual, cultural, and ethical anomie among young people will result in more drug abuse, crime, and suicide. Society will become more consumptive, dominant and manipulative and less moral, conservative, and compassionate. The need for leisure and adventure will be greater than ever.

More People Will Seek Experiences Outdoors

With more and more humans on the face of the planet, it stands to reason that more people will choose to go outdoors for their recreation. As more people have greater leisure time, they will spend longer periods in the outdoors. This trend will also be driven and accelerated by the large number of university graduates who cannot find a job in the limited recreation field and so must begin their own company, thus enticing more people outdoors.

More Environments Will Get Damaged

The increasing numbers of people going outdoors, and for longer periods of time, will place the natural environment under increasing stress, and will result in greater nonrecoverable damage to the resource base. In short, more people will love the outdoors to death more often! Resource managers will compensate by adding greater restrictions.

Litigation Will Still Drive Decision-Making Processes

Among all of this, litigious attitudes will prevail in Western cultures and lawyers will play an even more influential role in determining what people can and cannot do in the outdoors. America has more lawyers per capita than any other nation in the world. They too, make their own jobs as they go.

What Does This Mean for Adventure Programming?— Local Trends

These global growth areas will generate several trends for adventure programming:

1. adventure programs will continue to grow in popularity;
2. the size and number of organizations will increase;
3. program operations will be more regulated and complex;
4. artificial adventure environments will dominate;
5. the profession will expand and diversify;
6. programs will be brought to the learner; and
7. the profession will mature through self-examination.

Adventure Programs Will Continue to Grow in Popularity

Some increases will be due to the need for greater leisure opportunities and others will also be necessary to address society's problems. This trend is already obvious from the increasing participants and revenues in outdoor recreation.

Programs Will Be Brought to the Learner, Rather Than Vice Versa

With the interaction of issues of "shrinking" wilderness, accessibility, fiscal restraints, and efforts to make concepts more applicable to clients' real lives, a number of professionals have called for adventure programs to center efforts more around the learner and the "adventures" in their environment. One example of this is the growth of urban adventure programming (Proudman, 1990). Urban adventure has several potential advantages over more "wilderness-based" programming, which may include greater accessibility to a larger number of clients, clients who directly benefit from adventure, environments with cultural diversity, immediacy of human problems and solutions, availability of differing resources, continuing support systems, greater transferability to clients' future, and a wider range of learning environments and programming options.

Program Operations Will Be More Regulated and Complex

Less governmental funding, more human accidents, and environmental damage, all bring increasing regulation from resource managers. Concerned with their liability and visitor safety, these managers will set further policies and procedures to moderate resource use. Resource management agencies have introduced guidelines governing permit use, program licensing, and access fees. On some public lands, adventure programs must obtain permission via a lottery, be accredited by the Association for Experiential Education (AEE) or American Mountain Guides Association (AMGA), and pay a fee for the use of those lands. These measures have been implemented, in part, to cover shrinking bureaucratic support and increased problematic use of the natural resources.

Artificial Adventure Environments Will Dominate

To some extent this is already the case. In North America, group initiative tasks and ropes or challenge courses have all but replaced the classic outdoor pursuits with corporate clientele. A proliferation of course builders has created the Association for Challenge Course Technology (ACCT) to standardize construction and safety for thousands of American courses in use today. These numbers are expected to grow exponentially in the future, with similar patterns of growth and standardization now being seen in Australia, Canada, Britain and the rest of Europe. The shrinking natural outdoor settings, coupled with the cost and danger of transporting clients (the most dangerous part of most programs) will necessitate that alternatives be found. Some alternatives might include the already popular climbing walls, ski slopes, kayak roll tanks, and whitewater canoe chutes. Others have yet to be invented.

The Size and Number of Organizations Will Increase

Since the origins of the first AEE conference in 1974, with only 130 individuals preregistered (Garvey, 1990), this leading organization for adventure programming had over 2,000 members in 20 countries, a mere two decades later. AEE has spun off several other organizations with unique foci, and its unique approach and intent have been copied in several nations around the world. Other outdoor organizations proliferate in North America and specialized adventure organizations are also becoming more common in other countries.

The Profession Will Expand and Diversify

For example, the latest version of the AEE's *Directory of Experiential Therapy and Adventure-Based Counseling Programs* (Gerstein, 1992) lists over 257 organizations that utilize adventure experiences with therapeutic intent. Within this listing, programs are identified as having applications for clients who are "youth at risk," adult corrections, families, psychiatric inpatient, addictions, terminally ill patients, juvenile corrections, sexual victims, sexual perpetrators, and developmentally disabled. We can expect this same type of prescriptive diversification for other client groups such as corporations and schools.

The Profession Will Mature Through Self-Examination

By formulating ways to investigate and theorize about the processes of adventure programming, the profession will grow to be more professional. One important step toward this professionalism is the development of a unique body of knowledge. This has already been accomplished by publishing professional safety guidelines (Priest and Dixon, 1990) and program accreditation standards (Williamson and Gass, 1995). These "evolutionary benchmarks" highlight the profession's ability to identify, document, and refine the expression of practices to practitioners and customers alike.

What Does This Mean for Adventure Programming?— Local Issues

In addition to these trends, several key issues will continue to prevail:

1. the environment will become even more regulated;
2. technology will become a concern for all of us;
3. staff will continue to be "burned out" by work;
4. professionalism will suffer and become legislated;
5. certification will be replaced with accreditation;
6. university preparation of leaders will fluctuate; and
7. research will become a necessary "evil" of ours.

The Environment Will Become Even More Regulated

As already stated, the outdoors is reeling from the actions of many untrained visitors. Their increasing numbers have directly led to degradation of natural areas, so much so that access is being restricted by resource managers. Their carelessness has led to constraints (permits and fees) on the very freedom they seek to enjoy. In 1995 the administration agencies for Joshua Tree National Park, California, and Red Rock Canyon Conservation Area, Nevada, decided that only adventure programs accredited by the AMGA or the AEE will be permitted to conduct rock-climbing programs in these areas. Many others areas can be expected to follow suit with regard to climbing. If this same attitude infects other outdoor pursuits, this could severely influence the manner in which adventure programs conduct their services.

Technology Will Become a Concern for All of Us

As mentioned earlier, technology is changing quicker than people can get keep up. Note the advances in climbing protection and belaying devices. Are these driven by safety concerns, efficiency, litigation, or other forces? The advent of global positioning systems (GPS) and the availability of cellular phones might mean a lawsuit could result from the lack of their use in adventure programming. GPS is a locating device that scans for the location of at least 3 of 24 satellites in orbit around the planet and uses their locations to triangulate its location pinpointed by six digit grid refer-

ence accurate to within a few meters or yards. Cellular phones can be used on the edge of some wilderness areas to pick up radio coverage from conspicuously located antennae. What would be the result if a group was lost or someone injured without either piece of technology present? If brought on a wilderness trip, what would be their impact on naturalness, solitude, and self-sufficiency?

Staff Will Continue to Be "Burned Out" by Work

Leading outdoor experiences can be a very enriching experience, but at the same time can be extremely draining. Gass (1993) has pointed out that the very features which often attract individuals to becoming outdoor leaders also lead to professional burn-out when not properly addressed. Outdoor leaders are particularly susceptible to experiencing professional burn-out because of their high commitment, independence, lifestyle, experience base, and hopes and dreams. To reverse some of these negative contributions to professional burn-out, outdoor leaders should consider the four interconnected qualities of security, success, appropriate financial support, and balance (Gass, 1993).

Professionalism Will Suffer and Become Legislated

Three fatalities in the North Star, Challenger, and Summit Quest programs have brought further criticism to bear on adventure programs in America. Although these three Utah programs for at-risk teenagers called themselves adventure therapy, they had a history of conducting operations in a manner that most practitioners would consider outside the realm of adventure programming. Withholding food and water in order to manipulate children's behavior, operating coercively, and failing to have safety and first-aid systems in place, scream out to governments to regulate the adventure programming profession.

A profession represents the interests and membership of its field or discipline. It may organize those interests and members around groups and has a few elements that define its professionalism. A profession establishes and utilizes a unique theoretical body of knowledge. A profession follows an ethical code of conduct that cares for client welfare. A profession requires skills that come from extensive training. A profession fulfils an indispensable social need (Ewert, 1989). Can we call adventure programming a profession like medicine or engineering?

Our growing list of publications describes a unique theoretical body of knowledge borrowed from several other "professions." We operate according to an ethical code of conduct that cares for client welfare such as challenge-by-choice and AEE's ethics. Being an outdoor leader takes skills that come from extensive training beyond simply doing the activities. The intent and outcomes of adventure programming are clearly directed toward addressing social concerns. Adventure programming may be a profession by definition, but is it professional?

Consider the recent and rapid growth of corporate adventure programs. Some operators, perhaps eager to recognize the financial benefits common to working with this clientele, simply provide the same program they would give a school group without modification, and are surprised when the corporation isn't a return customer. Not only does this affect the survivability of the adventure operator, but it adversely tarnishes our collective profession's image. When transferable benefits aren't realized, a company remarks, "All this adventure stuff doesn't work!" Repeating this to other companies means that the entire profession gets a negative reputation, as evidenced by recent columns in the popular press that suggest adventure programming is a waste of training money.

All of us are at risk of repeating this situation, unless we are clear about the level of programming we can supply and consumers are clear about their needs (Table 61.1). This also requires that we are clear about the level to which we can capably facilitate and the techniques we can effectively use. Until we are all open and honest about our strengths and weaknesses, this credibility crisis will continue. If our profession cannot manage itself, others and governments will gladly do it for us.

Certification Will Be Replaced With Accreditation

Certification of outdoor leaders was never an effective answer to the problems of adventure programming for a number of reasons. It tended to examine only the so-called "hard" skills: those technical pieces that were easy to train and assess such as the tangible activity, safety and environmental skills. Most certification avoided dealing with the so-called "soft" and "meta" skills: those people-oriented pieces that were much more difficult to train and assess such as the intangible instruction, facilitation, and communication skills of leadership. In this way the certificate that only measured technique couldn't be called a certificate of leadership without including all the other missing pieces like judgment.

The idea that certification ensured client safety or environmental protection was critically flawed. Consider a most capable outdoor leader with excellent judgment who is working in a program with old equipment, outdated educational philosophies, unethical client treatment, and a large group travelling through a dangerous and very fragile area. Whether this leader is certified won't make any difference

in avoiding accidents or preventing damage to nature for this substandard program.

Leadership is just one small element of overall program quality. The accreditation of programs takes into account all the elements of program quality (one of which is instructor qualifications and competence). AEE has chosen voluntary program accreditation over leadership certification in an effort to examine the bigger picture. In Britain, and in some parts of other Commonwealth and European nations, program accreditation is also being tested as a viable alternative to certification.

Accreditation implies that a program or institution has met certain predetermined standards of operation. Reduced insurance premiums, marketing advantages, and reduced program costs for accredited programs are often cited as some immediate benefits beyond the expected improvements in educational quality, accident safety, environmental impact, and ethical staff behaviors. In the accreditation process, the program is evaluated as a whole in meeting specific operation standards. In this way, program accreditation retains the strengths of leadership certification without being bound by some of its weaknesses. Accreditation provides adventure programs with the ability to meet standards without losing the flexibility of determining how these standards are met. It allows leaders to deviate from those standards when doing so is clearly in the best interest of a client's safety, growth, or psychological well-being. Accreditation takes a systemic view of the process of adventure programming, unlike leadership certification that divides it into individualized skills.

University Preparation of Leaders Will Fluctuate

Although certification may not be the answer, and despite the shift toward accreditation, the preparation of leaders will always be critical and necessary to reduce accidents, decrease environmental impact, and enhance interpersonal and intrapersonal change for people. In some countries, university and college programs connected with adventure programming are closing down and in others they are just starting up.

The university and some community colleges have become the training grounds of outdoor leaders. In a four-year baccalaureate degree, candidates ought to get a good

Table 61.1	Programming Types and Benefits	
Type	**Purpose**	**Outcomes**
Recreation	to change feelings	fun, enjoyment, reenergized
Education	to change thinking	ideas, new concepts, awareness
Developmental	to change behavior	increase functional action
Therapeutic	to change *mal*behavior	decrease *dys*functional action

blend of *foundation theory* (history, philosophy, and social psychology), *hands-on experience* (internships in adventure programs as apprentice leaders), *hard* skills (activity, safety, and environmental), *soft* skills (organizational, instructional, and facilitational), and *meta* skills (ethics, communication, flexible leadership style, problem solving, decision making, and experience-based judgment).

Unfortunately, universities tend to be much too theoretical and not practical enough for the critical demands of outdoor leadership preparation. Many courses tend to focus only on the academic and theoretical content, preferring to stay in the classroom (where supposed real learning takes place). Others spend a lot of time becoming competent at doing the activities in a safe and environmentally sensitive manner, but without students understanding how or why to use adventure as a catalyst for human change. A few manage to blend theory and practice, avoiding the information-rich and experience-poor imbalance that is all too common in ivory towers, but still don't provide the time needed to examine the depth of soft skills and meta skills necessary to bring about change. These concerns, coupled with growing financial cutbacks and course reductions in the tertiary education sector, may mean that the preparation of outdoor leaders is short lived in universities and colleges.

Research Will Become a Necessary "Evil" of Ours

Like university programs, increasing numbers of adventure programs in the United Kingdom are being terminated due to decreasing subsidized funding. A lack of research often leaves these programs "on the fringe" and unable to claim their effectiveness when seriously challenged. More research and evaluation would help to further establish their credibility and demonstrate their effectiveness; just as more evaluation would assist in enhancing their current practices and methodologies. Research "proves" how and why adventure works; while evaluation improves the way programming works.

More research and evaluation are needed to provide evidence that adventure programming is more than just fun and games, and to support it as the powerful form of change that practitioners tacitly know it to be. Several areas of study are necessary: examining the key elements of adventure programming and the means by which these elements bring about change, transfer change to the client's real life and sustain that change in the face of a contrary

environment. In other words, what transfers, how much of it, for how long, and because of what program elements or barriers? Studies should examine these program elements: duration (one versus multiday programs), content (activity numbers, lengths, types, and debriefings), location (indoor or outdoor), setting (urban, rural or wilderness), follow-up (transfer strategies, reflection, and integration), clients (types, ideal numbers, and gender), and leadership (facilitation techniques and teaching styles).

Our entire profession will cease to exist, as have many of our composite programs, unless we are prepared to scientifically examine our practice; therefore research has become our necessary "evil." This does not mean we must all rush out and learn to be researchers. This simply means we have to support research to ensure it gets done. Outdoor leaders don't have to be experts in order to ensure that research and evaluation are done, they just have to support others in their attempts.

References

Ewert, A. (1989). *Outdoor adventure pursuits*. Columbus, OH: Publishing Horizons, Inc.

Garvey, D. (1990). A history of AEE. In J. C. Miles and S. Priest (Eds.), *Adventure education* (pp. 75–82). State College, PA: Venture Publishing, Inc.

Gass, M. A. (1993). Enhancing career development in adventure programming. In M. A. Gass (Ed.), *Adventure therapy: Therapeutic application of adventure programming in mental health settings*. Dubuque, IA: Kendall/Hunt Publishing Co.

Gerstein, J. (1992). *Directory of experiential therapy and adventure-based counseling programs*. Boulder, CO: Association for Experiential Education.

Miles, J. (1990). The future of adventure education. In J. C. Miles and S. Priest (Eds.), *Adventure education* (pp. 467–471). State College, PA: Venture Publishing, Inc.

Priest, S., and Dixon, T. (1990). *Safety practices in adventure programming*. Boulder, CO: Association for Experiential Education.

Priest, S., and Gass, M. A. (1997). *Effective leadership in adventure programming*. Champaign, IL: Human Kinetics.

Proudman, S. (1990). Urban adventure. In J. C. Miles and S. Priest (Eds.), *Adventure education* (pp. 335–343). State College, PA: Venture Publishing, Inc.

Williamson, J., and Gass, M. A. (1995). *Manual of accreditation standards for adventure programs* (2nd edition). Boulder, CO: Association for Experiential Education.

Appendix

Resources for Adventure Programming

Jim Cain
Teamplay

Finding critically needed information can be an adventure in itself. In the search for knowledge in the field of adventure education, the following resources have proven useful.

Organizations

The Access Fund
    P.O. Box 17010, Boulder, CO 80308
    Phone: 303-545-6772, Internet:
        AccessFund@aol.com
    A nonprofit organization dedicated to preserving the interests of climbers and wilderness participants.

Adventure Education
    12 St. Andrews Churchyard, Penrith, Cumbria
        CA11 7LS United Kingdom
    Phone: 01768 891065, Fax: 01768 891914, E-mail: enquiries@adventure-ed.edi.co.uk
    Information, journals, training, maps, and more on British outdoor education issues.

Alliance for Environmental Education
    9309 Center Street, No. 101, Manassas, VA
        22110-5599
    Phone: 703-330-5667, Fax: 703-253-5811
    Environmental concerns, information, and education.

American Alliance for Health, Physical Education, Recreation, and Dance (AAHPERD)
    1900 Association Drive, Reston, VA 22091-9989
    Phone: 703-476-3400, Fax: 703-476-9527
    Resource information on health, physical education, recreation, and dance activities.

The American Alpine Club (AAC)
    710 Tenth Street, Suite 100, Golden, CO 80401
    Phone: 303-384-0110, Fax: 303-384-0111, Internet: amalpine@ix.netcom.com
    More than 90 years of advocation for mountaineers and climbers, publications, and expedition insurance.

American Camping Association, Inc.
    5000 State Road 67 North, Martinsville, IN
        46151-7902
    Phone: 800-428-2267 or 765-342-8456, Fax: 765-342-2065, E-mail: aca@aca-camps.org
    Books, educational materials, and seminars for all types of camping and outdoor activities.

American Mountain Guides Association
    710 Tenth Street, Suite 101, Golden, CO 80401
    Phone: 800-RU4-AMGA or 303-271-0984

American Park and Recreation Society
> 2775 South Quincy Street, Suite 300, Arlington, VA 22206
> Phone: 703-578-5558, Fax: 703-820-2617

American Society for Training and Development (ASTD)
> 1640 King Street, P.O. Box 1443, Alexandria, VA 22313
> Phone: 800-628-2783 or 703-683-8100, Fax: 703-683-8103
> Books, seminars, conferences, and journals.

Association for Adventure Sports (AFAS)
> House of Sport, Longmile Road, Dublin 12, Ireland
> Courses on outdoor education, recreation, and environmental activities.

Association for Business Simulations and Experiential Learning (ABSEL)
> Wayne State University Department of Marketing, 5201 Cass Avenue, Suite 300, Detroit, MI 48202
> Phone: 313-577-4551, Fax: 313-577-5486

Association for Challenge Course Technology (ACCT)
> 468 Salmon Creek Road, Brockport, NY 14420
> Phone/Fax: 716-637-5277, E-mail: acct@acctinfo.org, Internet: www.acctinfo.org
> The trade organization for challenge course professionals, specializing in building standards, technical specifications and professional networking.

Association for Experiential Education (AEE)
> 2305 Canyon Boulevard, Suite #100, Boulder CO 80303-5651
> Phone: 303-440-8844, Fax: 303-440-9581, Internet: info@aee.org
> Memberships are available for individuals and corporations. Information on experiential education for corporate, educational, institutional, and small groups.

Australian Outdoor Education Council
> GPO Box 1896R, Melbourne 3001, Victoria, Australia
> Phone: 61 3 9428 9920, Fax: 61 3 9428 0313, E-mail: voea@netspace.net.au

Bradford Woods
> 5040 State Road 67 North, Martinsville, IN 46151
> Phone: 765-342-2915, Fax: 765-349-1086
> The Outdoor Education Center for Indiana University, also has the National Center on Accessibility and the American Camping Association on site.

Breckenridge Outdoor Education Center (BOEC)
> P. O. Box 697, Breckenridge, CO 80424
> Phone: 303-453-6422, Fax: 303-453-4676
> Provides high-adventure activities for persons of all abilities.

Canadian Association for Health, Physical Education, Recreation & Dance (CAHPERD)
> 1600 James Naismith Drive, Suite 809, Gloucester, Ontario, Canada K1B 5N4
> Phone: 613-748-5622, Fax: 613-748-5737, Internet: CAHPERD@activeliving.ca

Christian Camping International
> P.O. Box 62189, Colorado Springs, CO 80962-2189
> Phone: 800-922-4872 or 719-260-9400, Fax: 719-260-6398, E-mail: cciusa@cciusa.org, Internet: www.cciusa.org

Coalition for Education in the Outdoors
> Department of Recreation and Leisure Studies, State University of New York at Cortland, P.O. Box 2000, Park Center, Cortland, NY 13045
> Phone: 607-753-4971, Fax: 607-753-5999

Cooperative Wilderness Handicapped Outdoor Group (C. W. HOG)
> Idaho State University, Student Union Box 8118, Pocatello, ID 83209
> A challenge and adventure organization for persons of all abilities in outdoor pursuits.

Council for Adult and Experiential Learning (CAEL)
> 243 South Wabash Avenue, Suite 800, Chicago, IL 60604
> Phone: 312-922-5909, Fax: 312-922-1769, Internet: cael@interaccess.com

Council for Environmental Education (CEE)
> School of Education, University of Reading, London Road, Reading, Berkshire, RG1 5AQ United Kingdom
> Phone: 1734 756061, Fax: 1734 756264

Council of Outdoor Educators of Ontario (COEO)
> 1220 Sheppard Avenue East, Willowdale, Ontario, Canada M2K 2X1
> Phone: 416-495-4264, Fax: 416-495-4310
> Promotes outdoor education in Ontario, Canada. Conferences, journal, and information.

Cumbria Association of Residential Providers (CARP)
12 St. Andrews Churchyard, Penrith, Cumbria, CA11 7YE United Kingdom
Phone: 01768 891065, Fax: 01768 891914
Workshops and training for outdoor educators and program providers in a variety of subjects, from risk management to outdoor education and adventure programming.

Earth Watch
680 Mount Auburn Street, P.O. Box 403, Waterton, MA 02272-9104
Phone: 800-776-0188 or 617-926-8200, Fax: 617-926-8532, Internet: info@earthwatch.org
A nonprofit organization that sponsors cultural and environmental research and studies.

ERIC Clearinghouse on Rural Education & Small Schools—ERIC/CRESS
P.O. Box 1348, Charleston, WV 25325
Phone: 800-624-9120, Internet: lanhamb@ael.org
An excellent information center supported by the U.S. government, which includes experiential and outdoor education topics.

ERIC Clearinghouse on Teaching and Teacher Education
American Association of Colleges for Teacher Education, One Dupont Circle NW, Suite 610, Washington, DC 20036-2412
Phone: 800-822-9229 or 202-293-2450

ERIC Document Reproduction Service (EDRS)
7420 Fullerton Road, Suite 110, Springfield, VA 22153-2852
Phone: 800-443-3742, Internet: edrs@gwuvm.gwu.edu
Resource information on paper, microfiche, and microfilms may be purchased through this organization.

Elderhostel
75 Federal Street Boston, MA 02110-1941
Phone: 617-426-8056, TTD 617-426-5437
Provides a listing of courses, classes, and events nationwide.

Institute for Earth Education (IEE)
Cedar Cove, Greenville, WV 24925
Phone: 304-832-6404, Fax: 304-832-6077
Formerly the Acclimatization Experiences Institute.

International Consortium for Experiential Learning (ICEL)
Argentine Craig, 309 East Cold Spring Lane, Baltimore, MD 21212
Phone: 410-433-6408, Fax: 410-433-0162
Global experiential learning opportunities.

The National Association for Outdoor Education (NAOE)
12 St. Andrews Churchyard, Penrith, Cumbria, CA11 7YE United Kingdom
Phone: 01768 65113, Fax: 01768 891914
Supporting the development of outdoor education for all.

National Outdoor Leadership School (NOLS)
288 West Main Street, Lander, WY 82520-3128
Phone: 307-332-6973, Fax: 307-332-1220
A variety of outdoor adventures, featuring extended sessions on land and water.

National Society for Internships and Experiential Education (NSEE)
3509 Haworth Drive, Suite 207, Raleigh, NC 27609-7229
Phone: 919-787-3263, Fax: 919-787-3381
Promotes experience methods in learning.

New Zealand Outdoor Instructors Association
P.O. Box 2551, Wellington, New Zealand
Phone: 04 728 058

Outdoor Recreation Coalition of America (ORCA)
P.O. Box 1319 Boulder, CO 80306
Phone: 303-444-3353
Publishes the ORCA *Programmers Resource Guide*.

Outward Bound
National Headquarters, Route 9D, R 2, Box 280, Garrison, NY 10524-9757
Phone: 800-243-8520 or 914-424-4000, Fax: 914-424-4280
A nonprofit educational organization offering a variety of programs for individuals, corporations, teachers, youth, and couples in wilderness and urban settings throughout North America and around the world.

Play for Peace
P.O. Box 6205, Buffalo Grove, IL 60089
Phone: 847-520-1444, Fax: 847-520-6391
An initiative of the Association for Experiential Education, where children of conflicting cultures come to know each other through play.

Sir Edmund Hillary Outdoor Pursuits Centre (OPC)
Private Bag, Turangi, New Zealand
Phone: 07 386 5511, Fax: 07 386 0204
Some programs (Hamilton Skills Group) incorporate Maori Tanga culture and language.

Victorian Outdoor Education Association
217 Church Street, Richmond, Victoria 3121, Australia
Phone: 03 9428 9920, Fax: 03 9428 0313

Wilderness Education Association (WEA)
Department of Natural Resource Recreation and Tourism, Colorado State University, Fort Collins, CO 80523
Phone/Fax 970-223-6252, Internet: wea@lamar.colostate.edu
Information, training, and certification for wilderness emergencies.

The Worldwide Outfitter and Guide Association (WOGA)
P.O. Box 520400, Salt Lake City, UT 84152-0400
Phone: 801-942-3000, Fax: 801-942-8095

Conferences, Seminars, and Workshops

ACA National Conference
5000 State Road 67, North Martinsville, IN 46151-7902
Phone: 800-428-2267 or 765-342-8456, Fax: 765-342-2065, E-mail: aca@aca-camps.org

Association for Challenge Course Technology (ACCT)
468 Salmon Creek Road, Brockport, NY 14420
Phone/Fax: 716-637-5277, E-mail: acct@acctinfo.org, Internet: www.acctinfo.org
Sponsors an international symposium on challenge course topics in January and/or February.

Association for Experiential Education (AEE)
2305 Canyon Boulevard, Suite #100, Boulder, CO 80303-5651
Phone: 303-440-8844, Fax: 303-440-9581, Internet: info@aee.org
Sponsors an international conference in the fall and regional conferences in the spring.

National Challenge Course Practitioners Symposium (NCCPS)
Leahy & Associates, 1052 Artemis Circle, Lafayette, CO 80026-2840
Phone: 303-673-9832
An annual conference held in the spring. A catalyst for the safe, ethical, and effective use of challenge courses

Teachers of Experiential and Adventure Education (TEAM) Conference
Northeastern Illinois University, 5500 North St. Louis Avenue, Chicago, IL 60625-4699
Phone: 312-794-2982
An annual conference held in February featuring two days of classes, events, and opportunities for learning and participating in experiential and adventure activities. Held at Northeastern Illinois University.

Wilderness Education Association National Outdoor Leadership Conference
Department of Natural Resource Recreation and Tourism, Colorado State University, Fort Collins, CO 80523
Phone/Fax 970-223-6252, Internet: wea@lamar.colostate.edu

Wilderness Risk Managers Conference
John Gookin, National Outdoor Leadership School, 288 West Main Street, Lander, WY 82520-3128
Phone: 307-332-8800 or 307-332-6973, Fax: 307-332-1220
or Lewis Glenn, Outward Bound USA, Route 9D R 2, Box 280, Garrison, NY 10524-9757
Phone: 800-243-8520 or 914-424-4000, Fax: 914-424-4280
An annual event sponsored by the Wilderness Risk Managers Committee with such organizational members as NOLS and Outward Bound.

Periodicals, Journals, Magazines, and Newsletters

Journal of Adventure Education and Outdoor Leadership
Outdoor Source Book
12 St. Andrews Churchyard, Penrith, Cumbria CA11 7LS United Kingdom
Phone: 01768 891065, Fax: 01768 891914, E-mail: enquiries@adventure-ed.edi.co.uk
Information, journals, training, maps, and more on British outdoor education issues.

AEE Horizon
AEE Jobs Clearinghouse
Journal of Experiential Education
2305 Canyon Boulevard, Suite #100, Boulder, CO 80303-5651
Phone: 303-440-8844, Fax: 303-440-9581, Internet: info@aee.org
Journal, newsletter, and jobs listing of the AEE.

Australian Journal of Outdoor Education
> c/o Margaret Nikolajuk, Administrator, Australian Outdoor Education Council
> GPO Box 1896R, Melbourne 3001, Victoria, Australia
> Phone: 61 3 9428 9920, Fax: 61 3 9428 0313, E-mail: voea@netspace.net.au

Camping Magazine
> 5000 State Road 67 North, Martinsville, IN 46151-7902
> Phone: 800-428-2267, Fax: 765-342-2065

Disabled Outdoors
> 5223 South Lorel Avenue Chicago, IL 60638
> Phone: 312-284-2206
> Articles and news items on living in the out-of-doors with special needs individuals.

The Outdoor Network Newsletter
> P.O. Box 4129, Boulder, CO 80306-4129
> Phone: 800-688-6837 or 303-444-7117, Fax: 303-442-7425

Parallel Lines—The Newsletter of ACCT
> 468 Salmon Creek Road, Brockport, NY 14420
> Phone/Fax: 716-637-5277, E-mail: acct@acctinfo.org, Internet: www.acctinfo.org

Pathways—The Ontario Journal of Outdoor Education
> 1185 Eglinton Avenue East, North York, Ontario, Canada M3C 3C6
> Phone: 416-495-4264, Fax: 416-495-4310
> Published six times a year by the Council of Outdoor Educators of Ontario

Taproot
> Department of Recreation & Leisure Studies, SUNY at Cortland, P.O. Box 2000, Park Center, Cortland, NY 13045
> Phone: 607-753-4971, Fax: 607-753-5999
> Dedicated to communication for the enhancement of education in the outdoors.

Zip Lines—The Project Adventure Newsletter
> P. O. Box 100, Hamilton, MA 01936
> Phone: 508-468-7981

Sources for Books, References, and Other Information

Adventure Education
> 12 Saint Andrews Churchyard Penrith, Cumbria England CA11 7YE
> Phone: 01768 891065, Fax: 01768 891914, Internet: www.adventure-ed.co.uk
> An international source for a variety of texts on outdoor programs and activities

American Camping Association Bookstore
> 5000 State Road 67 North. Martinsville, IN 46151-7902
> Phone: 800-428-CAMP, 800-428-2267 or 765-342-8456, Fax: 765-342-2065, E-mail: aca@aca-camps.org

Association for Experiential Education (AEE)
> 2305 Canyon Boulevard, Suite #100, Boulder, CO 80303-5651
> Phone: 303-440-8844, Fax: 303-440-9581, Internet: info@aee.org
> A variety of scholarly books on the use and application of experiential education.

Educational Resources Information Center—Clearinghouse on Rural Education and Small Schools (ERIC/CRESS)
> Appalachia Educational Laboratory, P.O. Box 1348, Charleston, WV 25325
> Phone: 800-624-9120, Fax: 304-347-0487, Internet: lanhamb@ael.org
> The U.S. Department of Education Center filled with microfiche articles, periodicals, and information about education, including adventure education.

The Contributors

GRAEME ADDISON has been a journalist in South Africa, a college teacher, and a professional river guide (South Africa's first). He pioneered major South African river routes, and today is a freelance writer and part-time college professor. Still an active river-runner, he is writing a book on world whitewater rafting.

ARAM ATTARIAN, Ph.D., is an associate professor in the Department of Parks, Recreation and Tourism Management at North Carolina State University. His academic interests focus on outdoor leadership and adventure recreation. He is also a senior instructor and course director with the North Carolina Outward Bound School.

DELMAR W. BACHERT, Ed.D., is an assistant professor in the Department of Health, Leisure and Exercise Science at Appalachian State University in Boone, North Carolina.

JOSEPH BAILEY is an organizational consultant, training specialist, and department chair of the Training and Business Development Center at Linn Benton Community College. He has spent 20 years working in the field of outdoor training and education and has traveled internationally for 35 years. His master's degree is in whole systems design from Antioch University, Seattle, and he holds a bachelor's degree in environmental studies from Huxley College, Western Washington University.

DENE BERMAN, Ph.D., is clinical professor of Professional Psychology and associate clinical professor of Medicine, Wright State University. He is the chair of the Therapeutic Adventure Professional Group of the Association for Experiential Education, and teaches a wilderness therapy practicum for the Wilderness Education Association. His e-mail is dene.berman@wright.edu.

CHRISTIAN BISSON, Ed.D., received his master's degree in outdoor teacher education at Northern Illinois University and his doctoral degree in pedagogy from the University of Northern Colorado. Acting as cochair of the Outdoor Education Department at Northland College, he teaches courses in adventure education. He has worked seasonally for National Outdoor Leadership School since 1990, and in 1997 received the Association for Experiential Education Outstanding Experiential Teacher of the Year award.

TERRY J. BROWN has been involved with outdoor recreation management and adventure, working in both Canada and Australia, for 20 years. He currently teaches in the School of Leisure Studies at Griffith University in Brisbane where he coordinates the Master of Arts in Outdoor Education Program. He currently is chair of the Fraser Island World Heritage Scientific Advisory Committee, sits as the recreation representative, and is risk management training consultant for the Duke of Edinburgh's Award Scheme in Australia.

CAMILLE J. BUNTING is the director of the Outdoor Education Institute, and associate professor in the Department of Health and Kinesiology, Texas A&M University. She has been an active professional in the field of outdoor experiential education for the past 20 years.

JIM CAIN is the author of the adventure-based, team-building book *Teamwork and Teamplay,* the executive director of the Association for Challenge Course Technology (ACCT), and the corporate programs manager for the Cornell University Team-Building Program. In addition to his adventure-based work, he also plays guitar, calls square dances, throws a mean boomerang, and generally has more toys than many developing nations. He is an active member of the Association for Experiential Education, ACCT, and the American Camping Association.

ISABELLA CSIKSZENTMIHALYI is a writer and editor in Chicago who shares her partner's passion for the study of flow.

MIHALY CSIKSZENTMIHALYI is professor and former chair of psychology at the University of Chicago. He has been researching and writing about flow for the past 30 years.

JENNIFER DAVIS-BERMAN, Ph.D., is an associate professor in the Department of Sociology, Anthropology and Social Work at the University of Dayton and associate clinical professor of Medicine, Wright State University. She is the author of *Wilderness Therapy: Foundations, Theory and Research* (1994) and is widely published in the field of adventure therapy. Her e-mail is berman@udayton.edu.

L-JAY FINE, Ph.D., oversees the E.D.G.E Adventure Challenge Program and the Adventure-Based Programming Certificate at California State University, Fresno. He currently serves as the interim coordinator of the Recreation and Administration and Leisure Studies Program and Gerontology Program, and teaches in the Interprofessional Collaboration Graduate Certificate Program.

REBECCA FOX has worked in the outdoor education field for 12 years. She received her Bachelor of Arts in outdoor education at La Trobe University, and earned her graduate diploma and master's degree in outdoor education from Griffith University. Rebecca has worked predominantly with disadvantaged youth, and has experience teaching at the secondary and tertiary levels. Currently, she is the manager of the Kindilan Outdoor Education and Conference Centre for Guides, Queensland.

DANIEL GARVEY is a faculty member in the Outdoor Education Program at the University of New Hampshire. He has served as executive director of the Association for Experiential Education in Boulder, Colorado, and as vice president of the American Youth Foundation, St. Louis, Missouri. He has been active in experiential education for 25 years.

MICHAEL A. GASS is a professor in the Department of Kinesiology in the School of Health and Human Services at the University of New Hampshire. He is the creator and Principal of the Browne Center at the University of New Hampshire, a program development and research center on adventure programming that serves over 8,000 clients each year with educational, therapeutic, and corporate objectives. Dr. Gass has written over 100 publications and presented over 125 professional lectures in the area of adventure programming. He has received several awards for his work, most recently the 1998 Outstanding Experiential Teacher of the Year from the Association for Experiential Education.

H. L. "LEE" GILLIS, JR., Ph.D., is a professor of psychology at Georgia College and State University in Milledgeville, Georgia. He has taught, counseled, evaluated, researched, and supervised participants and college students in therapeutic adventure and adventure settings since 1977. Since 1991 he has also been connected with the therapeutic work of Project Adventure, Inc.

CHARLES "REB" GREGG is an attorney in Houston, Texas, whose practice includes representation and consulting regarding legal issues in adventure programs. He has served for years as general counsel to the National Outdoor Leadership School, and his clients include a variety of recreational and educational outdoor programs throughout the country. Reb serves on the Wilderness Risk Manager's Committee, the Accreditation Council of the Association for Experiential Education, and the editorial board of the Outdoor Network. He lectures and writes frequently on legal issues pertinent to the outdoor industry.

RANDOLPH HALUZA-DELAY is an itinerant outdoor educator, now on the faculty of the School of Outdoor Recreation, Parks and Tourism at Lakehead University in Thunder Bay, Ontario. He has instructed for the National Wildlife Federation and Pacific Crest Outward Bound School and served as executive director of a nonprofit outdoor centre in Alberta. His favorite role is as the father of two kids whose favorite bedtime stories are from field guides to local birds.

DONALD R. HAMMERMAN, Ed.D., is retired after a long career in outdoor education, much of it at Northern Illinois University. He held many posts during his long career, among them chair of the Department of Outdoor Teacher Education and director of the Lorado Taft Field Campus at Northern Illinois University.

ROBERT HENDERSON teaches outdoor courses as a professor in the Department of Physical Education at McMaster University in Hamilton, Ontario, Canada. Henderson enjoys wilderness travel, canoe tripping, and retracing the journeys of early explorers.

JUDE HIRSCH, Ed.D, is an assistant professor and coordinator of academic programs for the Masters of Education in outdoor education administration and the Bachelor of Science in outdoor education program at Georgia College and State University. Active as teacher and consultant, she is an associate trainer with Project Adventure, Inc. and actively involved with the Accreditation Program for the Association for Experiential Education. Author of many publications, Jude recently coedited with Lee Gillis a workbook titled *Food for Thought: A Workbook & Video for Developing Metaphorical Introductions to Group Activities.*

BERT HORWOOD is a veteran of high-school and university teaching. In the course of some 40 years of professional work he has been a researcher, writer, supervisor, evaluator, administrator, workshop leader and just plain teacher. He thinks there is no greater adventure than being part of a learning community.

JASPER S. HUNT, JR. is professor of leadership studies and experiential education in the College of Education at Mankato State University and Director of University Adventure Education Programs there. Author of *Ethical Issues In Experiential Education* and many other publications, Hunt has wide experience in and diverse service to the field of adventure education in his 25 years of involvement in it.

JACKIE KIEWA lectures and researches in outdoor education and outdoor recreation in the School of Leisure Studies at Griffith University in Queensland, Australia. She has also been climbing and paddling for almost 20 years in many countries, including the United States, Uzbekistan, Kyghistan, Indonesia, and New Zealand.

KIMBERLEY ANN KLINT was a researcher in social psychology. Her doctoral dissertation won an award for its landmark comparison of research paradigms and methodologies. She has taught physical education, health studies, and qualitative research methods at several colleges and universities in Australia, Canada, and the United States. Dr. Klint is now a patient satisfaction and evaluation consultant to healthcare corporations.

CLIFFORD E. KNAPP is a professor of outdoor teacher education in the Department of Teacher Education at Northern Illinois University. For many years he has had deep interests in nature and human nature and recently has come to a better understanding of how these ideas are interconnected. His dedication to experiential ways of learning has guided his career choices for almost 40 years.

RICHARD J. KRAFT is currently the director of the Chancellor's Leadership Residential Academic and Certificate Program at the University of Colorado–Boulder. He has directed the Experiential Education Program in the School of Education for the past 25 years and continues to work as an educational consultant throughout the world. His current research and writing are primarily in the areas of service-learning and international education.

GREG LAIS is the executive director of Wilderness Inquiry, Inc., a national nonprofit organization which offers a variety of wilderness programs that include persons with and without disabilities. He has many years of experience in adventure program leadership and management, as well as partnership experience working with federal and state land management agencies on educational programs. He holds an Master of Business Administration in strategic management and organization from the University of Minnesota.

CHRIS LOYNES has been an outdoor educator for over 25 years working in schools, youth agencies, and corporations. He is a keen mountaineer and sailor. For 15 years he was editor of the UK magazine for Field Horizons. Loynes currently consults on program design and evaluation and staff development for experiential programs internationally.

FRANK LUPTON retired in 1993 after teaching and chairing the Department of Recreation, Park and Tourism Administration at Western Illinois University. In 1976 he created the semester-long Environmental Conservation Outdoor Education Expedition (ECOEE) which led him and Paul Petzoldt, Bob Christie and Chuck Gregory to the creation of the Wilderness Education Association (WEA). He has served as president, secretary, and trustee of WEA, and in 1999 he received the Paul Petzoldt Award, the WEA's most prestigious recognition for "excellence in wilderness education." He and his wife of 45 years have three daughters and six grandchildren.

PETER MARTIN is head of the Department of Outdoor Education and Nature Tourism at La Trobe University, Bendigo, Australia. He has taught at La Trobe since 1985. He currently serves as chair of the Australian Outdoor Education Council, a post he will hold through 2001. His research interests lie in the development of critical outdoor education pedagogy, particularly for enhancement of the relationship of humans and nature. He has a passionate interest in climbing, cliff environments, and family enjoyment of the outdoors.

LEO MCAVOY is a professor of Recreation, Park and Leisure Studies at the University of Minnesota. He teaches and researches in outdoor education, adventure programming, and in programming for persons with disabilities. He has many years of experience with wilderness program leadership, and includes wilderness trips in his teaching whenever possible. He holds a doctoral degree in education from the University of Minnesota.

JOHN C. MILES is professor of environmental studies and director of the Center for Geography and Environmental Social Sciences, Huxley College of Environmental Studies, Western Washington University. His teaching embraces environmental education, environmental history and ethics, and the literature of nature and place. He has written extensively about wilderness and national parks and about wild lands as learning places. Dr. Miles is an executive editor of the *Journal of Environmental Education,* and when not working is usually playing in his garden or in the North Cascades mountains. His e-mail is jcmiles@ cc.wwu.edu.

JOSHUA L. MINER was founder of Outward Bound USA and a director of the Colorado Outward Bound School. He is a veteran teacher who taught at Andover Academy and has been a leader of outdoor education in the United States for nearly 40 years.

TODD MINER is the executive director of Cornell Outdoor Education. Prior to joining Cornell University, he served as assistant dean for experiential education at Keuka College (New York), and as head of Alaska Wilderness Studies at the University of Alaska, Anchorage. Miner has facilitated experience-based training and development (EBTD) programs for organizations in the financial, natural resource, service, and governmental sectors. His dissertation at Boston University focused on team building using EBTD.

DENISE MITTEN is a consultant in gender issues, and the group dynamics of and ethics in adventure programming. She has worked in adventure travel, adventure therapy, and adventure for 25 years, doing pioneering work with groups of women, women offenders, women and children, and men working with women.

MARTY O'KEEFE is a professor at Warren Wilson College, Asheville, North Carolina. Dr. O'Keefe is an outdoor educator with experience working with a variety of groups in wilderness and classroom settings. She has worked with youth, educators, executives, people with disabilities, and college students. Her background, interests, and expertise include diversity issues, challenge course training, leadership development, and feminist pedagogy.

SIMON PRIEST is a leading researcher, writer and consultant on corporate experiential training and development and outdoor education leadership. Dr. Priest consults for a handful of progressive corporations interested in staying ahead of their global competition by focusing on the development and maintenance of human resource relationships. His consulting expertise lies in leadership, executive development and creating internal corporate universities. He taught at the University of Oregon, Texas A&M University, and Brock University before his retirement in 1997. He has held visiting and guest professorships at 20 universities, written a dozen books and over 150 refereed articles on adventure programming.

STEVE PROUDMAN is president of the Proudman Group, Inc., a "cirtual" organizational development consulting firm. His expertise is in designing and delivering experiential learning programs for teams and organizations. His consulting work combines the disciplines of interpersonal and group dynamics, leadership, and human impacts of organizational change in an intuitive adult education format. Proudman work for Outward Bound for seven years, instructed life-career renewal courses for the Voyageur Outward Bound School, and created and served as the director of the Chicago Outward Bound Center which aimed to serve inner city youth with urban-based adventure programs.

DICK PROUTY joined Project Adventure in 1980 and is its president and executive director. He was a social studies teacher for 11 years in Massachusetts before joining Project Adventure. He has extensive experience in innovative program development utilizing experiential learning techniques in a broad variety of settings to promote the development of positive learning, living and working environments. He is coauthor of *Islands of Healing*, a leading text on adventure-based counseling for schools and therapeutic agencies.

WILLIAM QUINN is an associate professor at Northeastern Illinois University in Chicago. Dr. Quinn teaches adventure education courses within the College of Education. He is also a partner in his own challenge course building company called Cliff & Cables.

EDWARD RAIOLA is chair of the Outdoor Leadership Studies Department at Warren Wilson College in Asheville, North Carolina. Dr. Raiola is also a member of the environmental studies faculty.

KARL RHONKE has been "playing around" in the field of adventure education for over 35 years, including four years as an outdoor education teacher in California, three years with Outward Bound, and almost 30 years working with Project Adventure. He currently lives with his wife Gloree in Vermont, works part time for Project Adventure, consults with many, and plays with all.

ANTHONY RICHARDS recently retired after 27 years of teaching at Dalhousie University, Nova Scotia, Canada. Dr. Richards came from the United Kingdom in 1971 and completed his doctorate at the University of Colorado-Boulder. He is currently a consultant in the field of service learning and developing human potential through service.

T. MARTIN RINGER is a socio-systemic management consultant in Perth, Western Australia. He has extensive experience in various aspects of adventure therapy and now provides training for leaders and facilitators of experiential groups.

NINA S. ROBERTS is a research associate with the Student Conservation Association and is pursuing a doctoral degree at Colorado State University in the Department of Natural Resource Recreation and Tourism. She is a former board member of the Association for Experiential Education and chair of the Publications Advisory Committee. As a biracial woman, Nina's research has guided her to write about people of diverse ethnic and cultural backgrounds, and to explore their connection to adventure activities in the outdoors. She is an outdoor leader, educator, consultant, and has presented her work at conferences regionally and nationally as well as in Southeast Asia.

DEBORAH SUGERMAN came to the University of New Hampshire in the fall of 1997 after teaching at Unity College for 16 years. She received her Doctorate of Philosophy in forest resources from the University of Maine in 1990. Her teaching includes courses in outdoor leadership and the theory of adventure education as well as backpacking and whitewater canoeing. Dr. Sugerman's areas of interest lie in working with older people and people with disabilities, group facilitation, and sea kayaking. She is director of the Undergraduate Outdoor Education Option at the University of New Hampshire.

CHERYL E. TEETERS is currently an associate professor of outdoor recreation leadership and management at Northern Michigan University. She holds a Bachelor of Science in education from Southeast Missouri State University, a Master of Science in recreation and park administration from Western Illinois University, and a Doctorate of Philosophy in environmental science from Oklahoma State University. She has been a member of Wilderness Education Association since 1980 and has served as the affiliate representative, president, past president and secretary on the WEA Board of Trustees.

J. T. TOWNLEY took degrees in outdoor education, English, and French from Texas A&M University. After graduat-

ing, he spent a year in France on a Fulbright scholarship, where he studied French language, culture, and literature. He has traveled extensively in Europe, North Africa, and North America. Currently he is backpacking and biking the Pacific Northwest and teaching French and rock climbing at the Portland French School.

BETTY VAN DER SMISSEN holds a law degree and is a member of the bar. She has given many presentations and workshops and is coauthoring a publication on risk management in adventure education programs. Dr. van der Smissen is author of a three-volume reference work on legal liability and risk management. At Michigan State University she teaches both an upper division and graduate level course on legal aspects of this field.

ALAN WARNER, Ph.D., teaches part time in the School of Education at Acadia University, Wolfville, Nova Scotia, Canada (earthns@istar.ca). He is a past editor of the *Journal of Experiential Education* and now designs, directs, and evaluates a wide range of environmental education programs. He also provides team-building, group work, and organizational development training for human service agencies.

KAREN WARREN is an instructor in the Outdoors Program and Recreational Athletics at Hampshire College in Amherst, Massachusetts.

SHARON J. WASHINGTON, Ph.D., is an associate professor and the coordinator of the education graduate programs at Springfield College, Springfield, Massachusetts. Her professional interests are in diversity, recruiting and preparing teachers for urban schools, and adventure education. Sharon worked six years full time in the field of adventure education before moving out of the elements and into full benefits.

RON WATTERS is the former director of the Idaho State University Outdoor Program and the author of seven books on outdoor topics. He was active in the formation of the Association of Outdoor Recreation and Education, and is the founder and chairman of the National Outdoor Book Awards. Currently he divides his time between teaching outdoor education classes as an adjunct faculty member with the university's Physical Education Department and runs a small publishing company which specializes in regional outdoor titles.

DAVID J WEBB has operated Brigham Young University's outdoor program, BYU Outdoors Unlimited, since its beginning in 1982. He has served the outdoor recreation profession nationally and internationally in many ways, and is the author of the *Outdoor Recreation Program Directory & Data/Resource Guide, 3ʳᵈ Edition* (1999). Webb has instructor certification in and has taught and guided rock climbing, winter mountaineering, rafting, windsurfing, cross-country skiing, and other outdoor recreation activities.

SCOTT D. WURDINGER is an associate professor in the Department of Leisure Studies and Wellness and coordinator of the Experiential Team-Building Program at Ferris State University in Big Rapids, Michigan. Dr. Wurdinger is the author of *Philosophical Issues in Adventure Education* and coauthor of *Controversial Issues in Adventure Education: A Critical Examination*. He lives in Big Rapids, Michigan, with his wife Annette and daughters Madeline and Lauren.

Index

Other Books From Venture Publishing, Inc.

File o' Fun: A Recreation Planner for Games & Activities—Third Edition
by Jane Harris Ericson and Diane Ruth Albright

The Game Finder—A Leader's Guide to Great Activities
by Annette C. Moore

Getting People Involved in Life and Activities: Effective Motivating Techniques
by Jeanne Adams

Great Special Events and Activities
by Annie Morton, Angie Prosser, and Sue Spangler

Inclusive Leisure Services: Responding to the Rights of People With Disabilities
by John Dattilo

Internships in Recreation and Leisure Services: A Practical Guide for Students (Second Edition)
by Edward E. Seagle, Jr., Ralph W. Smith, and Lola M. Dalton

Interpretation of Cultural and Natural Resources
by Douglas M. Knudson, Ted T. Cable, and Larry Beck

Intervention Activities for At-Risk Youth
by Norma J. Stumbo

Introduction to Leisure Services—7th Edition
by H. Douglas Sessoms and Karla A. Henderson

Introduction to Writing Goals and Objectives: A Manual for Recreation Therapy Students and Entry-Level Professionals
By Suzanne Melcher

Leadership and Administration of Outdoor Pursuits, Second Edition
by Phyllis Ford and James Blanchard

Leadership in Leisure Services: Making a Difference
by Debra J. Jordan

Leisure and Leisure Services in the 21st Century
by Geoffrey Godbey

The Leisure Diagnostic Battery: Users Manual and Sample Forms
by Peter A. Witt and Gary Ellis

Leisure Education: A Manual of Activities and Resources
by Norma J. Stumbo and Steven R. Thompson

Leisure Education II: More Activities and Resources
by Norma J. Stumbo

Leisure Education III: More Goal-Oriented Activities
by Norma J. Stumbo

Leisure Education IV: Activities for Individuals With Substance Addictions
by Norma J. Stumbo

Leisure Education Program Planning: A Systematic Approach—Second Edition
by John Dattilo

Leisure in Your Life: An Exploration—Fifth Edition
by Geoffrey Godbey

Leisure Services in Canada: An Introduction
by Mark S. Searle and Russell E. Brayley

Leisure Studies: Prospects for the Twenty-First Century
edited by Edgar L. Jackson and Thomas L. Burton

The Lifestory Re-Play Circle: A Manual of Activities and Techniques
by Rosilyn Wilder

Marketing for Parks, Recreation, and Leisure
by Ellen L. O'Sullivan

Models of Change in Municipal Parks and Recreation: A Book of Innovative Case Studies
edited by Mark E. Havitz

More Than a Game: A New Focus on Senior Activity Services
by Brenda Corbett

Nature and the Human Spirit: Toward an Expanded Land Management Ethic
edited by B. L. Driver, Daniel Dustin, Tony Baltic, Gary Elsner, and George Peterson

Outdoor Recreation Management: Theory and Application, Third Edition
by Alan Jubenville and Ben Twight

Planning Parks for People, Second Edition
by John Hultsman, Richard L. Cottrell, and Wendy Z. Hultsman

The Process of Recreation Programming Theory and Technique, Third Edition
by Patricia Farrell and Herberta M. Lundegren

Programming for Parks, Recreation, and Leisure Services: A Servant Leadership Approach
by Donald G. DeGraaf, Debra J. Jordan, and Kathy H. DeGraaf

Protocols for Recreation Therapy Programs
edited by Jill Kelland, along with the Recreation Therapy Staff at Alberta Hospital Edmonton

Quality Management: Applications for Therapeutic Recreation
edited by Bob Riley

A Recovery Workbook: The Road Back From Substance Abuse
by April K. Neal and Michael J. Taleff

Recreation and Leisure: Issues in an Era of Change, Third Edition
edited by Thomas Goodale and Peter A. Witt

Recreation Economic Decisions: Comparing Benefits and Costs (Second Edition)
by John B. Loomis and Richard G. Walsh

Recreation for Older Adults: Individual and Group Activities
by Judith A. Elliott and Jerold E. Elliott

Recreation Programming and Activities for Older Adults
by Jerold E. Elliott and Judith A. Sorg-Elliott

Recreation Programs That Work for At-Risk Youth: The Challenge of Shaping the Future
by Peter A. Witt and John L. Crompton

Reference Manual for Writing Rehabilitation Therapy Treatment Plans
    by Penny Hogberg and Mary Johnson
Research in Therapeutic Recreation: Concepts and Methods
    edited by Marjorie J. Malkin and Christine Z. Howe
Simple Expressions: Creative and Therapeutic Arts for the Elderly in Long-Term Care Facilities
    by Vicki Parsons
A Social History of Leisure Since 1600
    by Gary Cross
A Social Psychology of Leisure
    by Roger C. Mannell and Douglas A. Kleiber

Steps to Successful Programming: A Student Handbook to Accompany Programming for Parks, Recreation, and Leisure Services
    by Donald G. DeGraaf, Debra J. Jordan, and Kathy H. DeGraaf
Therapeutic Activity Intervention With the Elderly: Foundations & Practices
    by Barbara A. Hawkins, Marti E. May, and Nancy Brattain Rogers
Therapeutic Recreation: Cases and Exercises
    by Barbara C. Wilhite and M. Jean Keller
Therapeutic Recreation in the Nursing Home
    by Linda Buettner and Shelley L. Martin
Therapeutic Recreation Protocol for Treatment of Substance Addictions
    by Rozanne W. Faulkner
A Training Manual for Americans With Disabilities Act Compliance in Parks and Recreation Settings
    by Carol Stensrud

 Venture Publishing, Inc.
1999 Cato Avenue
State College, PA 16801

Phone: (814) 234-4561; Fax: (814) 234-1651